C0-AVM-385

THE ARCHAEOLOGY OF ANCIENT CHINA

THE ARCHAEOLOGY OF ANCIENT CHINA

REVISED
AND ENLARGED
EDITION

by Kwang-chih Chang

Yale University Press, New Haven and London

Second printing, 1971.

Designed by Elizabeth Ann Hacker,
set in Baskerville type,
and printed in the United States of America by
the Carl Purington Rollins Printing-Office
of the Yale University Press, New Haven, Conn.

Distributed in Great Britain, Europe, and Africa by
Yale University Press, Ltd., London; in Canada by
McGill-Queen's University Press, Montreal; in Mexico
by Centro Interamericano de Libros Académicos,
Mexico City; in Central and South America by Kaiman
& Polon, Inc., New York City; in Australasia by
Australia and New Zealand Book Co., Pty., Ltd.,
Artarmon, New South Wales; in India by UBS Publishers'
Distributors Pvt., Ltd., Delhi; in Japan by
John Weatherhill, Inc., Tokyo.

Library of Congress catalog card number: 68–24780
ISBN: 0–300–0357–9 (cloth), 0–300–01458–9 (paper)

PREFACE TO THE REVISED EDITION

Among the many profound and trivial consequences of the Great Proletarian Cultural Revolution in China, officially launched in June 1966, is that in that month all archaeological periodicals and monographs either ceased publication or ceased being circulated abroad. Eventually no doubt their publication and circulation will resume, but at this writing I can say that the archaeological writings on ancient China that have appeared in print up to May 1966 constitute *all* the archaeological literature and *all* the raw materials for study that are available to most scholars outside mainland China. Since there is nothing one can do about it, this hiatus can perhaps be best made use of by reassessing the issues and hypotheses in the field of Chinese archaeology on the basis of all the available facts.

Four years have elapsed since the publication of the first edition of *The Archaeology of Ancient China* in 1963, and more than five years since its actual writing. During these years a vast amount of new material has become known and should now be incorporated into the work to bring it up to date. The new data are so abundant and important that minor revisions would not suffice. A completely rewritten book is called for simply to accommodate the new materials, and this is a good year to do it for the reason given above.

But the incorporation of new data is only one reason for revising the book. Other reasons are more compelling. When the book was prepared five years ago, for much of the chronological and theoretical structure I had to start from scratch. Many issues were clouded, such as the Neolithic developmental sequence of North China and the relationship of the Neolithic cultures in Central and South China with that of the North; and other issues were defined for the first time, such as culture prehistories of many peripheral regions and their relationship with the nuclear areas. In these instances I had to present much detailed evidence in the arguments and demonstrations, and to engage too often in controversy for a book of this kind. Now that many of the ideas are no longer new and we are in a position to view these issues in a somewhat calmer frame of mind, arguments can often be replaced by statements. New data in many regions have enabled a more detailed reconstruction of local cultures and chronologies than were hitherto possible. Moreover, even though the book was not badly received, many colleagues and students have offered constructive criticisms, and I wished to rewrite portions of the book accordingly. I myself have undertaken continued research into various aspects of the subject matter, and I would now like to present results and second thoughts. In addition, I have had time to polish the book with respect to its illustrations and style. In short, I have attempted to present, in this new edition, an improved as well as a newer book.

The overall organization of the volume remains largely as it was except for minor rearrangements within the individual chapters. The environmental portions of the original Chapter 1, however, have been enlarged by absorbing the descriptions of postglacial climatic changes in the old second chapter, and a vastly expanded section on the Palaeolithic archaeology of China has been combined in the second chapter with the Mesolithic part. These changes are necessitated by the increased information in Pleistocene geology and palaeobiology made available in the last five years and by the many new discoveries of Early Man fossils and Palaeolithic industries throughout China. Chapters 3 and 4 were almost completely rewritten to be consistent with the recent thinking on the subject, but Chapter 5 remains largely unchanged. Chapter 6 on the Shang has been expanded to include the newly discovered data on the early phases of this civilization, and much of Chapter 7 was completely rewritten and expanded. Chapter 8 again remains largely as it was, but extensive revision will be noticed in the last chapter on southern Chinese civilizations. The book now is probably as up to date as any such book can be at this time, but of course it cannot have complete and exhaustive coverage. The chapter on the Lung-shan cultures, for instance, could easily be doubled in size by adding more detailed descriptions of the local phases, and archaeological data on Chou warfare and currency are adequate for an additional section on each. The book is intended to present only a basic structure that gives the reader some assistance in further reading and research.

The preparation of the manuscript of this edition has been made possible by an Asian Studies grant awarded in 1967 by the American

Council of Learned Societies and the Social Science Research Council, and by a Faculty Research Fellowship of the Concilium on International and Area Studies of Yale University for the summer of 1967. To both I am greatly indebted. Miss Ward Whittington and Mrs. Susan Weeks, both of Yale University, are responsible for the new illustrations, and Miss Catherine Buckley assisted me with the photographic work. Mrs. Anne F. Wilde, editor at the Yale University Press, has helped heroically in editing the manuscript. Assembling the source materials has been greatly facilitated through the generous efforts of Mr. Wan Wei-ying, Curator of East Asian Collections at the Sterling Memorial Library, Yale University.

It would be impossible to thank everyone by name who has helped in this rewriting by providing advice, encouragement, and criticism of the previous edition of the book, and I shall not try to do so. I cannot promise that this revision will satisfy all critics, but I hope it will be found that every point raised has been appreciated and fully considered.

KWANG-CHIH CHANG

September 1, 1967
New Haven, Connecticut

FOREWORD TO THE FIRST EDITION

I first came to know Dr. Kwang-chih Chang in the fall of 1950, when he enrolled as a freshman in the Department of Archaeology and Anthropology, National Taiwan University. Four years later I saw him graduate, having just completed a bachelor's thesis on the Lungshan Culture, written under my direction. He impressed me then as a most promising young scholar of remarkable industriousness, gifted with a quick mind and abundant natural curiosity which, if duly disciplined, might lead him to scientific achievements of a very high order. And, indeed, it must have taken a considerable amount of mental acuity and applied effort to complete the thesis presented in this book.

The fact that this book contains many hypotheses which are yet to be substantiated perhaps deserves some explanation. There are practical reasons why a book on Chinese prehistoric and protohistoric archaeology, compiled at the present stage of research conditions in this field, has to go beyond the narrow limit of actual data, and be amply interpolated with some hypothetical interpretation. Of these reasons I shall mention only two.

Chang is trained as a specialist in Chinese archaeology. It is in China itself that he should carry on his scientific work in order to contribute his share to the understanding of China's past and test the hypotheses of other scholars as well as his own. This normal course, however, cannot be followed under the present political circumstances. Like many other specialists in Chinese archaeology on this side of the Iron Curtain, Chang is a victim of this tragic state of affairs. His industriousness and imaginative power can be applied only in the study of documentary data supplied to him by others. Fortunately, he has had the opportunity to study in the United States, where he has obtained the best possible training in anthropology at one of America's finest institutions of higher learning, an institution whose standard of discipline makes almost no allowance for the foreign student. In the United States he has been able to read the archaeological literature published in Communist China and, as a specialist with his particular training, to interpret the published material according to a well-planned perspective. As far as I can judge, he has made a good case on the basis of available data. He is naturally handicapped by the inherent weakness of the source materials, over which he has absolutely no control. His interpretations, wherever they are drastically new, must therefore remain hypothetical until they can be tested in the field.

There is certainly a need for new interpretation of Chinese prehistory and early historical archaeology. In the late twenties and early thirties, when my colleagues and I began to undertake scientific excavations in China, the country enjoyed little peace, and field work was frequently carried out in the midst of military campaigns; then followed the Sino-Japanese War and finally the Communist rebellion. I can recall all our difficulties in these years while we were engaged in archaeological investigations. Scientific data were only beginning to be accumulated, and systematic interpretations had scarcely been attempted, when the important archaeological collections, following their custodians, had to be evacuated from the continent.

During the thirteen years since 1949, under a totalitarian regime which has manpower to spare and uses archaeology as an effective political instrument, essentially the same group of trained field workers has been able to accumulate, at an accelerated rate, new archaeological materials, the amount of which has certainly outgrown the interpretative framework conceived before the war years by some of the pioneer workers. The time seems to have arrived when a number of possible new interpretations may be tried. The one chosen in this book is not necessarily the only one, but it provides something that can serve as a basis for further discussion as well as for the planning of future excavations by trained archaeologists like the author himself.

When the Yale University Press agreed to publish his *Archaeology of Ancient China,* the author asked me to write a foreword for this, his first book. I have consented to do it not without some hesitation. But I confess that I was very flattered. So, in concluding this short note, I cannot resist the temptation to quote M. C. Burkitt's Preface, written thirty years ago, for J. G. D. Clark's book, *The Meso-*

lithic Age in Britain, wherein Burkitt said: "It is true that I have had the privilege of giving him some part of his training in his prehistoric studies. But it is always refreshing when the new generation thinks it worthwhile to make such a request."

Li Chi

Academia Sinica
Nankang, Taiwan, China
November, 1962

PREFACE TO THE FIRST EDITION

Archaeology in the college curriculum rightfully belongs to both the humanities and the social sciences. In practice, however, Chinese archaeology as it is described and discussed in current scholarly literature too often associates itself unilaterally with technology or the fine arts. Museums exhibit beautifully painted pottery from Pan-shan and masterpieces of the Shang and Chou bronzesmiths; albums record and illustrate ceremonial vessels and jade carvings; textbooks describe the prehistoric and early historic peoples of China as they are characterized by the colors and decoration of potsherds and represented by the names of their rulers and their dynasties. But Chinese archaeologists have yet to describe and interpret the culture and the society of the early Chinese peoples for the edification of anthropologists, or the classification, relationships, and development of ancient cultural groups in China for the knowledge of prehistorians and historians.

Moreover, in the currently written ancient history of China, attention is often focused solely upon the civilizational development of the Yellow River valley, whereas the various local cultures in the rest of ancient China are often lightly dismissed as being either unimportant or archaeologically unknown. It is very true that the North China civilization played a leading role throughout the history of China. It was not, however, the only culture that mattered in the early segments of Chinese history, and the less glamorous cultures in the peripheral regions are often of greater concern to students of Far Eastern prehistory because these cultures extended beyond modern China.

To provide a balanced view of the early history of China according to the archaeological evidence is the immediate aim of the present book. It is intended to be balanced in that, first, it will describe a *history* of cultural development as well as provide a catalogue of archaeological discoveries and, second, it will cover all the areas of China where archaeological remains have been found sufficient for such an undertaking. I have designed this book with two considerations in mind. First, a cultural historical framework is indispensable, not only for understanding and interpreting Chinese prehistory and early history but also for a proper description of data properly placed in time and space. Second, Chinese history is only one part of the world history of man, and in order to compare the patterns of Chinese cultural growth with cultural growth throughout the world, Chinese archaeology must have a general historical framework to serve as a basis for comparison.

For forty years scientific archaeologists have been active in China, and a remarkable amount of data has been accumulated. Insofar as this discipline is a relative newcomer to China, we must certainly expect that working hypotheses are to be constantly offered and the general framework modified, improved upon, and retouched. I intend no more than to offer an up-to-date version of this general framework, grounded upon currently available data; but anyone familiar with the field will realize the difficulty of producing a new conceptual model when the old one has been outdated for some twenty years, while the same twenty years have witnessed a phenomenal increase of new materials needing interpretation. For this reason, as well as the fact that new data are constantly being made available, the results of the present undertaking must be regarded as highly tentative.

I have attempted to offer several things in this volume: to my fellow archaeologists specializing in China, a documented interpretation of the most relevant data now available in the field; to my fellow prehistorians, a cultural historical framework of a major world civilizational center, which might be susceptible to analytical and historical comparisons; to historians and sinologues, information and a structure on the basis of which Chinese history as it is now written might be enriched by archaeological materials; and, finally, to university students, an up-to-date, documented, interpretative textbook on Chinese archaeology. At this juncture, I would like to request the comment and criticism of my readers, since a book of this sort can benefit greatly from the response of its audience.

The field of Chinese archaeology is immense, and the knowledge required for writing the present volume manifold; without the help of many teachers and colleagues, it could not have been written. My thanks are due especially to Professors Li Chi, Tung Tso-pin, Ling Shun-sheng, Shih Chang-ju, Ruey Yih-fu, and Kao Ch'ü-hsün, of the Academia Sinica and National Taiwan University, for their guidance during my college years when I first became interested in the field of

Chinese archaeology; to the late Lauriston Ward, the late Professor Clyde Kluckhohn, and Professors Hallam L. Movius Jr., Gordon R. Willey, and Yang Lien-sheng, of Harvard University, for suggestions and advice on the early drafts of the various chapters in this volume; to Dr. Cheng Te-k'un, of Cambridge University, for continuous encouragement through the recent years; to Professor Irving Rouse, of Yale University, and Dr. Kenneth Starr, of the Chicago Natural History Museum, for invaluable suggestions which have been incorporated into the final version; to Professor Cornelius Osgood, of Yale University, for encouragement; to the Concilium on International Studies, Yale University, and Professor Arthur F. Wright, for encouragement and for a grant to cover the expenses of the preparation of the manuscript; to the Harvard–Yenching Institute, Cambridge, Massachusetts, for continuous financial support from 1955–61, the period during which most of the studies in this book were initiated; to Dr. K'ai-ming Ch'iu, Librarian of the Harvard–Yenching Institute, and Warren Tsuneishi, Curator of Far Eastern Collections of the Sterling Memorial Library, Yale University, for assistance in the use of the excellent collections of publications in Chinese archaeology; and, last but not least, to Hwei, my wife, whose assistance in more ways than one cannot be enumerated.

Portions of this book in an earlier form were included in a dissertation presented to the Department of Anthropology, Harvard University, in April 1960, in partial fulfillment of the requirements for the Ph.D. degree. Some of the original hypotheses in Chapters 1 through 4 of this book have been previously published in a number of professional journals (such as *Asian Perspectives, Harvard Journal of Asiatic Studies, Bulletin of the Institute of History and Philology, Academia Sinica,* and *Bulletin of the Institute of Ethnology, Academia Sinica*), but these are for the most part rewritten and greatly expanded in the present context. Christopher F. Carroll, Mrs. Charles Drake, and Mrs. Henry R. Swift have kindly and patiently helped to render the manuscript into readable English. The wise and experienced guidance of Jane V. Olson at the Yale University Press has proved indispensable for transforming the manuscript into a book.

K.C.C.

February 1962
New Haven, Connecticut

CONTENTS

ILLUSTRATIONS

TABLES

ABBREVIATIONS

AP *Asian Perspectives* (Bulletin of the Far Eastern Prehistory Association), Hong Kong

BIE *Bulletin of the Institute of Ethnology,* Academia Sinica, Taipei

BIHP *Bulletin of the Institute of History and Philology,* Academia Sinica, Nanking, Lichuang, and Taipei

BMFEA *Bulletin of the Museum of Far Eastern Antiquities,* Stockholm

GSoC *Geological Society of China,* Peking and Peiping

GSuC *Geological Survey of China,* Peking and Peiping

JZ *Jenruigaku Zasshi,* Tokyo

KK *K'ao-ku* (1959–), Peking

KKHP *K'ao-ku Hsüeh Pao,* Peking

KKTH *K'ao-ku T'ung-hsün* (title changed to *KK* after 1958), Peking

PFEPC *Proceedings of the Far Eastern Prehistoric Congress* (title changed to *AP* after 1957)

PS *Palaeontologia Sinica,* Peking and Peiping

QS *Quaternaria Sinica,* Peking

TYKKPK *T'ien-yieh K'ao-ku Pao-kao* (no. 1 of *KKHP*), Nanking

VP *Vertebrata Palasiatica,* Peking

WW *Wen-wu* (1959–), Peking

WWTKTL *Wen-wu Ts'an-k'ao Tzu-liao* (title changed to *WW* after 1958), Peking

INTRODUCTION

The following chapters outline a cultural historical framework into which the formative stages of Chinese civilization can be placed, and present the necessary data for its documentation. Much of the structure and practically all of the data come from the results of other scholars' studies, which span several centuries, but some parts are original with this volume. In order to provide a historical background against which the present interpretation appears, and to introduce to beginning students in Chinese archaeology the essential traditions and idiosyncracies of this field of learning, I shall begin with a brief summary of the development of prehistoric and early historic archaeology in China. An adequate treatment of this subject would require another book-length volume; therefore only a brief outline of the major trends of archaeology will be attempted.

Historical studies, as is well known, had an early start in China, and the study of bygone cultures and civilizations by means of their artifactual remains has also been a part of the historical method. Even in the Eastern Chou (ca. 770–221 B.C.) and Han (206 B.C.–A.D. 220) dynasties, when what to us is ancient history was contemporary event, and what to us are archaeological specimens of bronze, iron, and stone were still objects of daily use, and when prehistoric cultures remained faintly in the memory of the people in the form of legendary traditions, and their ruins and remains were still exposed on the ground or buried shallowly under the earth, there was already an archaeology of sorts. Han Fei Tzu says in *Shih Kuo:*

> When Yao governed the world, people ate in clay vessels and drank in clay mugs;
> Yü made ritual vessels, painting the interior in black and the exterior in red;
> The Yin people . . . engraved their utensils for meals and incised their utensils for drinking wine.

Wei Chü-hsien[1] thinks that Han Fei Tzu, a philosopher of the Warring States (ca. 450–221 B.C.) period, must have seen some excavated prehistoric ceramic remains and Yin bronzes and identified them with traditional ancient heroes, in order to have given such vivid descriptions of ancient artifacts. Ssu-ma Ch'ien of Western Han visited many ancient ruins and relics attributed to various preceding periods before he put the information that he considered verified and thus reliable into his great *Shih Chi, Historical Memoirs.* An even more interesting "archaeological" approach to history is seen in Yüan K'ang's *Yüeh Chüeh Shu.* In the chapter on Swords, Feng Hu Tzu, an Eastern Chou philosopher, is quoted by Yüan K'ang as saying to a king of Yüeh:

> In the Age of Hsüan Yüan, Shen Nung, and Ho Hsü, weapons were made of stones for cutting trees and building houses, and were buried with the dead . . . ;
> In the Age of Huang Ti, weapons were made of jade, for cutting trees, building houses, and digging the ground . . . and were buried with the dead;
> In the Age of Yü, weapons were made of bronze, for building canals . . . and houses . . .
> At the present time, weapons are made of iron.

In devising the Three Age system, Yüan K'ang's account of Feng Hu Tzu seems to have anticipated C. J. Thomsen of Denmark by more than a thousand years, and Yüan K'ang may thus rightfully rank with Lucretius as one of the world's first archaeologists to propose such a classification.[2]

But whatever credits one can give to these early scholars for utilizing material remains of ancient cultures to make historical studies, this archaeological fetus soon became undernourished during and after the Han Dynasty when the scheme of the ancient Golden Age

1. *Chung-kuo k'ao-ku-hsüeh shih,* Shanghai, Commercial Press, 1937, pp. 50–51.
2. Ibid., p. 58. George G. MacCurdy, *Human Origins,* New York, Appleton-Century, 1933, *1,* 9: "In his poem *De Rerum Natura* Lucretius (about 98–55 B.C.) says: 'The earliest weapons were the hands, nails, and teeth; then came stone and clubs. These were followed by iron and bronze, but bronze came first, the use of iron not being known until later.' "

of Three Dynasties and their Sage predecessors, systematized by the Confucian political philosophers and blessed by the royal governments, became the orthodox interpretation of ancient Chinese history. Studies of relics, largely confined to bronze vessels and stone tablets—hence the name *chin shih hsüeh,* or the "studies of bronzes and stones,"—continued throughout the Chinese historical periods, but a different attitude prevailed. Bronzes were collected as curios and heirlooms for their intrinsic value, artistic or fetish, and whatever studies were made of them were largely confined to their inscriptions which provided information confirming the Golden Age interpretation of ancient history or of paleographic interest. In addition, bronze weapons, mirrors, chariot and horse fittings, porcelains and ceramics, tiles and eave tiles, jade, seals, and so forth were also studied and, since 1899, oracle bone inscriptions of the Yin Dynasty have been added to this list.

In general, these studies of ancient artifacts, which have appeared throughout the historic period, either concentrated on the inscriptions as supplementary data for literary history or focused upon ancient institutions recorded in existing literary documents, which these artifacts confirm or refute. Little attention had ever been given to the historical information the artifacts themselves could provide, or which their cultural contexts, often unknown or neglected anyway, could suggest. In the famous *K'ao-ku T'u* compiled probably in the Northern Sung Dynasty, Lü Ta-lin recorded 211 bronzes in the palace and private collections and 13 jade objects, giving illustrations, place of origin if known, and dimensions and weight. This is one of the few archaeological books China produced before the modern period that comes close to the modern archaeological method, and the contributions of these rare books were never fully taken advantage of by historians. In short, China has had an indigenous tradition of archaeology, but this tradition had never gone much beyond the scope and spirit of antiquarianism before her contacts with the West. The reasons are clear to anyone who is familiar with the development of archaeology in the West and with the cultural and social history of China.

Modern scientific archaeology was born in China in the early twentieth century under the impact of Western civilization and scholarship. The roots of the new inspiration are multiple, and a sheer enumeration of them is necessarily arbitrary. But the following sources are clear.

First, of course, there was the tradition of antiquarianism and history in China, which represented both a deep-rooted scholarship of past institutions and historical events and an unfailing interest in things ancient, including early inscriptions. For a long period in the early decades of this century this tradition was under heavy fire from the new school of historians and archaeologists, but it nevertheless provided a historic background upon which new methodologies had to be shaped. When all things against it have been said, new archaeologists still cannot disregard the centuries-long experience of the antiquarians in dealing with objects of the historical period.

Second, with the Nationalist revolution of 1911 and the May Fourth Movement of 1919, the Golden Age interpretation of ancient China fell apart and a critical school of historical interpretation came into being, symbolized by the publication in 1926 of *Ku Shih Pien,* or *Critical Reviews of Ancient History,* edited by Ku Chieh-kang.[3] Li Chi states,

> Their slogan, "Show your proof," though destructive in nature, did bring about a more critical spirit in the study of ancient China. Thus, if one wants to pay excessive tribute to the Golden Age of Yao and Shun, well, Show your proof; if one wishes to talk about the engineering miracles of the Great Yü of the third millennium B.C., proofs must also be given. What must be remembered in this connection is that written records alone were no longer accepted as valid proofs.[4]

Ku Chieh-kang[5] proposed three new approaches to the study of ancient history, now that the traditional doctrines were being rejected and new substitutes needed: archaeology, critical reviews of false histories and pseudo-histories, and folklore.

In this atmosphere proofs were sought by the new historians to

3. Vol. 1, Peking, P'u-she, 1926.

4. Li Chi, *The Beginnings of Chinese Civilization,* Seattle, Univ. Washington Press, 1957, p. 4.

5. Ku Chieh-kang, ed., *Ku shih pien, 1,* 57–77.

substantiate the literary records of ancient history, and proofs were at the same time being produced by an assortment of scholars representing Western civilization and the Western methodology of historical study, who *excavated* data from the ground in various parts of China, dated not only to the historical periods but to the prehistoric periods as well. To such data and new techniques the new historians of enlightened China naturally turned for proof and for inspiration.

Western scholars came to China, a land of ancient civilization which they had admired in books, soon after the Manchu Dynasty bowed to Western gunboats. To Chinese Turkestan came the Grum-Grzimailo brothers from Russia in 1889, M. Grenard and D. de Rhine from France in 1892, and Sven Hedin from Sweden in 1896. To southern Manchuria from Japan came Torii Ryūzō in 1895. But these places were distant from North China, and what these visitors produced were either historical documents or studies of apparently insignificant relics from border countries which used to be occupied by "barbarians," and thus were of little importance to the historians of China. With J. Gunnar Andersson, a mining consultant hired by the Peiyang government of Peking in the early years of the Republic, things took a different turn.

In the early decades of the present century, study of the ancient history of China was indeed chaotic. Although Charles Darwin in his *Descent of Man* says that "there is indirect evidence of [flint tools'] former use by the Chinese and ancient Jews,"[6] this indirect evidence had never been substantiated, and such Western writers as Jacques de Morgan[7] and sinologists like Berthold Laufer[8] insisted that Chinese civilization had no prehistory. In China the critical school of historical studies found no confidence even in the Three Dynasties. But in 1920 Andersson discovered in Mien-ch'ih Hsien, western Honan, in the heart of Chinese civilization, a Stone Age site near Yang-shao-ts'un, which was to be followed by his discovery of another Painted Pottery site at the cave of Sha-kuo-t'un in Liaoning in 1922 and many other Painted Pottery Culture sites in Kansu in 1923–24.

In the meantime, in 1920 two Jesuit missionaries, Emile Licent

6. New York, Crowell, 1874, p. 224.
7. *Prehistoric Man,* New York, Knopf, 1925, p. 293.
8. *Jade: A Study in Chinese Archaeology and Religion,* Field Museum of Natural History Publication 154, Anthropol. ser. 10 (1912), pp. 29, 54–55.

and Pierre Teilhard de Chardin, found the first Palaeolithic implements at Ch'ing-yang, Kansu, and in the same year Andersson located fossiliferous sites in the Chou-k'ou-tien limestone hills near Peking. Bronze Age tombs were opened by farmers in 1923 at Hsin-cheng, in Honan, and at Li-yü-ts'un, in Shansi, which were soon investigated by antiquarians. Thus, within the short period of four years (1920–23), the existence of early man in China during both prehistoric and early historic periods could no longer be doubted. At that time the authenticity of the oracle bone inscriptions was also generally accepted as genuine Shang Dynasty writing. This sudden appearance of proofs needed by historians for the study of ancient Chinese history deeply impressed Chinese scholars, who thus found in field investigations a new source of historic data.

After the early 1920s when the field method was introduced to China by Western scholars, a new awareness of China's past, which was even more ancient than the Golden Age traditionally held it to be, and a new historical school came into being in which the new and the traditional were combined to the benefit of both. This new school of thought was symbolized by the founding of the Institute of History and Philology, Academia Sinica, in 1928, but was certainly not confined to this institution. Such scholars as P'ei Wen-chung, of the Geological Survey, Hsü Ping-ch'ang, of the National Research Institute of Peiping, and Kuo Pao-chün, of the Research Institute of Honan Antiquities, worked in the same field with Li Chi, Liang Ssu-yüng, and Tung Tso-pin, of the Institute of History and Philology, at one in spirit and principle, if not always in sentiment.

Chinese archaeology made considerable strides during the decade from the mid-twenties through the mid-thirties, when the outbreak of the Sino-Japanese War halted its further growth. The Palaeolithic sites at Chou-k'ou-tien were excavated by the Geological Survey, and the human remains and artifacts were ably studied by such geologists and palaeontologists as Pierre Teilhard de Chardin, Davidson Black, Franz Weidenreich, Young Chung-chien, and P'ei Wen-chung. Although Palaeolithic remains were known only from a few sites at Chou-k'ou-tien (mainly localities 13, 1, and 15, and the Upper Cave) and in the Ordos area, both Middle and Upper Pleistocene occupations of men were now substantiated, and a comparison of their physical types and cultures with other known Palaeolithic men in East Asia, such as *Pithecanthropus* in Java, threw much light on human origin in this part of the world. Elsewhere in China, J. H. Edgar collected a few Palaeolithic-looking implements from the Yangtze terraces in Szechwan, Russian and Japanese scholars collected Mesolithic implements at Djalai-nor and Ku-hsiang-t'un in Manchuria, the Geological Survey found some Mesolithic industries in limestone caves of Kwangsi, and G. H. R. von Koenigswald found in Hong Kong drugstores the giant anthropoid teeth which Weidenreich believed were from ancestors of *Pithecanthropus* and modern man. These Palaeolithic and Mesolithic data of varying importance, reliability, and quantity were sufficient to give scientists some substantial ideas about man and his culture in China during and immediately after the Pleistocene period. Toward the end of this decade, Helmut de Terra, Hallam L. Movius, Jr., and Pierre Teilhard de Chardin managed to pull together all the bits of information then known to construct a total picture of Chinese Palaeolithic and Mesolithic cultures, and to tie this in with the Himalayan Glacial sequence and with the history of early man in most of the Old World.[9]

In Neolithic archaeology, Li Chi, a Harvard-trained anthropologist, found and excavated another "Painted Pottery" site in southern Shansi in 1926. By this time the existence of a Painted Pottery Culture before the dawn of Chinese history in North China had been generally accepted, and the hypothesis had been advanced to identify this culture with that of the legendary Hsia Dynasty. The hypothesis was based on two assumptions: the first, which was beginning to be substantiated archaeologically at that time, was that the Painted Pottery Culture came before the Shang, and thus was apparently the Hsia which had preceded the Shang according to legends; the second was that the geographical distribution of the Painted Pottery Culture apparently coincided with the area of activities of the Hsia in the legendary accounts. Moreover, many scholars, particularly those who were aware of the Painted Pottery cultures in Western Asia, had

9. Helmut de Terra, *Pleistocene Formation and Stone Age Man in China,* Peking, Institut de Géo-Biologie, 1941. P. Teilhard de Chardin, *Early Man in China,* Institut de Géo-Biologie, 1941. Hallam L. Movius, Jr., *Early Man and Pleistocene Stratigraphy in Southern and Eastern Asia,* Papers of the Peabody Museum, *19,* Harvard University (1944).

noted a few similar decorative motifs in the painted ware of North China and that of western Asia, and it was considered without question by these scholars that the Yang-shao culture was an eastern offshoot of the Neolithic cultures of the West.

Against this historical background the importance attached to and the interpretations given to the so-called Lung-shan or Black Pottery Culture, identified in 1928 with the discovery of its type site, Ch'eng-tzu-yai, near Lung-shan Chen, Li-ch'eng Hsien, Shantung, can be understood. At this site, a different, wheel-thrown ware prevailed, characterized by its black color, thin wall, and lustrous surface. Together with this ware were found the *hang-t'u* structure and scapulimancy which were characteristic of the Yin–Shang culture and apparently quite different from the Yang-shao culture of that time. The two cultures were known to have different spheres of distribution. Thus the Two Culture theory gradually became generally accepted; if the Yang-shao culture was to be identified with the Hsia, then why should not the Lung-shan culture be identified with the Eastern Yi, known in historical literatures to have been in the lower Huangho and along the Pacific seaboard? If the Yang-shao culture was derived from western Asia, then the Lung-shan culture, in which many Yin–Shang elements were found, could be indigenously Chinese. In 1931, the Hou-kang stratigraphy afforded the first real key to the formative cultural sequence of North China (see p. 125). However, because the Two Culture theory fit what was then the understanding of ancient Chinese culture too well to be discarded, and because remains of both cultures were reported from western Honan by Andersson to be from the same stratigraphical position, the real significance of the Hou-kang stratigraphy was not fully realized until many years later. What Andersson said about this in 1943 may well sum up the majority opinion during the thirties:

> Owing to the Hou Kang section it has been held probable that Yang Shao is the older and Lung Shan the younger of the two. But the occurrence of black pottery with the painted ware at Yang Shao Ts'un, at Hsi Yin, at Sha Kuo T'un and some other sites, even in Kansu, raises the question whether it is not possible that the two are mainly synchronous in that painted and black ceramics occur together in the interior but the black pottery

> alone rules in the coastal provinces (Shantung and Chekiang?) and has there been given the name Lung Shan.[10]

Further discussion in the present volume will, I believe, make clear the specific reasons that lie behind the insistence that Yang-shao and Lung-shan were two contemporary cultures of the Neolithic period in North China.

Elsewhere in China, Neolithic and Neolithic-like cultures were found and identified in Manchuria, Mongolia, Sinkiang, and South China. In the first two areas, Lin-hsi (1922), Pi-tzu-wo (1927), Ang-ang-hsi (1928–30), Yang-t'ou-wa (1933), and Ch'ih-feng (1935) were among the most important sites excavated during the period. A Microlithic Culture was identified and formulated, and evidence was brought to light of both Yang-shao and Lung-shan influences. Their exact relationship was not yet clearly understood, however. From 1927 to 1934, Folke Bergman of the Sino-Swedish Expedition located a series of prehistoric sites in Sinkiang, among which the Microlithic and the Painted Pottery Culture sites drew most of the attention. In South China, the first stone implements were collected *in situ* from the lower Yangtze in 1930, and subsequently a Geometric Pottery Culture was identified from many sites in the southeastern part of China. Stone implements and pottery remains were collected extensively in the Red basin by J. H. Edgar, D. S. Dye, D. C. Graham, and N. C. Nelson from the twenties onward, although the existence of prehistoric remains in this area had been known since 1886 when an Englishman, C. E. Baber, purchased two polished stone implements near Chungking. In the Hong Kong area and on the coasts of Kwangtung, Neolithic stone implements and pottery were extensively collected during this period by C. M. Heanley, D. J. Finn, R. Maglioni, and W. Schofield. These investigations established the human occupation of South China from prehistoric times, but the time–space framework of prehistoric cultures and their relationships with North China and other adjacent regions in Southeast Asia were not at all clear.

Archaeology of the early historical civilizations of China probably made its most significant contribution during this period with the

10. Andersson, *BMFEA, 15* (1943), 292–93.

excavations of the Shang Dynasty site near An-yang, from 1928 through 1937, under the auspices of the Archaeological Section of the Institute of History and Philology, Academia Sinica, and the able direction of Li Chi. Aside from the significance of the An-yang excavations for the study of early Chinese civilization, they were also important in the history of archaeology in that during the ten years of excavations many young archaeologists received their field training at this site, participating in one of the most complicated diggings ever undertaken in China. Most, if not all, Chinese archaeologists now in their fifties, such as Yin Ta, Director of the Institute of Archaeology of the Communist Chinese Academy of Sciences, Hsia Nai, Deputy Director of the same Institute, Yin Huan-chang, of the Nanking Museum, and Shih Chang-ju and Kao Ch'ü-hsün, of the Academia Sinica in Taipei, received their training in the field at An-yang. So did Wu Chin-ting (discoverer of the Ch'eng-tzu-yai site), Ch'i Yen-p'ei, and Li Ching-tan, who passed away during or after the war, but who made important contributions to Chinese archaeology during their lifetimes. Some of these people, for example Hsia Nai and Wu Chin-ting, subsequently broadened their background in foreign institutions, but it is clear that their An-yang experience shaped their professional careers.

Aside from An-yang, Hsiao-t'un-like remains were reported from Shantung and Anhwei, but otherwise no well-established Shang Dynasty sites were known. Chou Dynasty sites were excavated here and there, such as the Hsia-tu of Yen (1929), the Warring States burials in Chün Hsien (1932), Chi Hsien (1935), and Hui Hsien (1935) in Honan, the Ch'u tombs in Shou Hsien (1934), Anhwei, and Ch'ang-sha, Hunan, and the Kwang-han find of jade artifacts (1934) in Szechwan. Stray finds of bronzes were reported from Yunnan and Szechwan, but no cultural contexts were identified.

What I have described so far are some of the most important discoveries of prehistoric and early historic period remains in China from the mid-twenties to the mid-thirties. Archaeological materials obtained during this period indicate a Palaeolithic and Mesolithic occupation of scattered areas, two Neolithic cultures in North China, a third along the northern borders (the Microlithic), and still another in the southeast (the Geometric), and Bronze Age civilizations in North China and scattered regions elsewhere, which tend to confirm and enrich the literary records of the Shang and the Chou dynasties. The theoretical trends during this period can be characterized as follows: first, an establishment of a scientific discipline of field archaeology; second, a tentative grouping of cultures for the whole of China and for the various periods in her cultural history, and a tentative alignment of the relationships among these different cultural groups in space and in time. Archaeological stratigraphy became a generally established principle of chronology, and typological comparison was the basic tool for the reconstruction of cultural sequences.

Looking back, we could criticize the archaeologists working during this period for their overindulgence in single tool and vessel types and their typological classifications. At this time, however, archaeological materials had just begun to accumulate, and cultural groups were being classified only tentatively. Moreover, Chinese and Western archaeologists were only repeating in China the basic fallacies in methodology then being followed in the West. The ultimate aim of archaeology in reconstructing prehistoric culture and society was not entirely unrecognized in theory,[11] and in practice, topical studies were not lacking. Many were particularly valuable, such as Kuo Mo-jo's studies of ancient Chinese society according to oracle bone and bronze inscriptions, Bernhard Karlgren's treatises on the stylistic development of Yin and Chou bronzes, and some others. But these scholars, original and brilliant as their works show them to be, utilized for the most part inscriptions and decorative designs on archaeological specimens, the provenance of which was often unknown, and frequently based their work upon preconceived ideas drawn from disciplines other than archaeology. Full advantage was seldom if ever taken of the underground context of ancient cultures excavated by the archaeologists' spades.

During and immediately after World War II, very little fieldwork was done in China. The enforced pause, together with the extremely difficult working conditions for archaeologists—several of whom died or became disabled as a consequence—provided opportunity for a synthesis of past accomplishments and for the formation of programs for the future. Many comprehensive volumes on Chinese prehistory

11. Li Chi et al., *Ch'eng-tzu-yai,* Kenneth Starr, trans., Yale University Publications in Anthropology, *52* (1956), p. 19. Li Chi, *Bull. College of Arts, Natl. Taiwan Univ., 1* (1950), 63–79.

and early historic archaeology appeared, and at the Institute of History and Philology a complete report of the An-yang excavations and several other monographs on relatively minor diggings were completed or underway.

Fieldwork was resumed soon after the establishment of the communist regime in 1949, and during the following eighteen years archaeology in all its phases of operation flourished in China as never before. With a few notable exceptions—Chou-k'ou-tien and An-yang, among others—the bulk of the most important archaeological material for the ancient period has been uncovered during this interval, as must be clear from a scrutiny of the footnotes of this book.[12] The Great Leap Forward of Chinese archaeology may be accounted for by several factors. Above all, the past eighteen years have witnessed a political stability in the country unparalleled since the Opium War of 1840–42, and her industrialization has been unprecedented. "During the past ten years," said Hsia Nai in 1959,[13] "in the course of economic construction . . . there have been discovered at many places ancient dwelling sites and burials, where many important artifacts were found. Archaeological advances have been brought about as a consequence." A notable example of archaeological discovery in the process of industrial construction is the large series of highly important Neolithic and Chou sites found in and near the Sanmen Gorge region of the Huangho in southwestern Shansi and northwestern Honan, the area of the much-heralded Sanmen Gorge dam project. In a country where archaeology as well as the economy is subject to neatly centralized planning, and where human resources and funds are not spared for causes deemed worthy by the regime, it should not be surprising that large teams of trained archaeologists are able to carry out salvage archaeological operations and to analyze and publish the results with speed and competence.

Ideology, too, plays a significant part in the archaeological upsurge in Communist China. As Gustorm Gjessing has pointed out, archaeology is often used in communist countries as a weapon for promot-

12. A summary of the archaeological work during 1950–60, with a useful bibliography, appears in *Hsin Chung-kuo ti K'ao-ku Shou-huo,* Peking, Wenwu Press, 1962. For a brief account of new findings afterward, see Hsia Nai, *KK* (1964/10), 485–97.

13. *KK,* (1959/10), 505.

ing solidarity of their peoples.[14] When a communist regime is also nationalistic, in a country whose people are fondly proud of their ancient heritage, history-conscious, and possessed of an antiquarian tradition, archaeology cannot help but boom. Many important sites have been found by farmers, who, instead of appropriating the finds and making a personal profit on the antiquities market (which of course no longer exists), are known to be in the habit of promptly reporting the finds to the proper authorities. A team of experts is soon dispatched, sometimes from a great distance, to investigate. The experts are organized in a nationwide hierarchy. At Peking, under the Chinese Academy of Sciences (Chung-kuo K'o-hsüeh Yüan), two national research institutes have been established for archaeological study—the Institute of Archaeology (K'ao-ku Yen-chiu Suo) and the Institute of Vertebrate Palaeontology and Palaeoanthropology (Ku Chi-chui T'ung-wu yü Ku Jen-lei Yen-chiu Suo). Also concerned with archaeology is the Ministry of Culture. The division of labor between the Academia Sinica and the Ministry of Culture is not clear to the outsider, but apparently the former emphasizes research and the latter handles administrative procedures. In many parts of the country and in each province and major city there is a Commission for the Preservation of Cultural Objects (Wen Wu Kuan-li Wei-yüan-hui), a Bureau of Culture (Wen-hua Chü), and/or a museum. All these local organizations appear to be administered by the Ministry of Culture. Many of these institutions have field personnel, often organized into teams or task forces to tackle chance discoveries or to engage in planned excavations. The two institutes also have a number of branches in the provinces. Many major local institutions have their own publications, but most of the important reports are published in Peking. Short reports are published in four major journals: *K'ao-ku Hsüeh Pao* (irregular), *K'ao-ku* (monthly), *Wen-wu* (monthly), and *Vertebrata Palasiatica* (quarterly), and long monographs are published in separate volumes (often in numbered series) by the Science Press and the Wenwu (Cultural Objects) Press in Peking.

As these publications show, Chinese archaeology in the past eighteen years has undergone considerable progress in planning of fieldwork and in technical and theoretical sophistication, and two stages

14. *Memoirs,* American Anthropological Association, no. 94 (1963), pp. 261–67.

of development can be distinguished. During the 1950s, most of the field operations undertaken were salvage projects, and planned excavations were a rarity. In method and theory there had been considerable confusion: a Marxist master scheme of interpretation of human history was imposed upon the archaeological data, but the technical equipment for the excavation was obsolete and interpretation of the actual data often naive and inconsistent. One notices a substantial change, an improvement, in the quality of the archaeological work undertaken during the 1960s. In an important article, "Retrospect and Prospect in Neolithic Archaeology," written in 1963 by Yin Ta, Director of the Institute of Archaeology, the "scientific" requirements of archaeology are greatly emphasized. In order to effectively advance Neolithic research, Yin Ta states, the archaeologist must carry out his work in three separate and successive stages:

> Scientific archaeological excavation and the preparation and publication of the excavation report are the most elemental task and the first important link of the whole process. The primary function of this step is to scientifically describe, in a total and systematic manner, the phenomena at single sites. Comparative and synthetic studies are a further step in depth on the basis of the scientifically excavated data, another indispensable step of archaeological research. At this stage one analyzes the complex phenomena reflected by the archaeological data from a theoretical level, and seeks to solve scholarly and theoretical problems. For both of these stages of work, an archaeological terminology is employed. The third stage can be reached only after the basic solutions have been obtained to problems that exist in archaeology, a stage of the study of the clan institutions on the scientific basis laid down in the two previous stages. At this point one must do everything possible to translate the archaeological terminology into a language customary for the historical social life, providing an atmosphere of humanity, life, and society, and to reconstruct material for whole and lively social histories from the fragmentary remains and relics.[15]

15. Yin Ta, *KK* (1963/11), 582.

The first two steps are, according to Yin Ta, the basis of archaeological work; in this article he also discusses several important topics in scientific archaeological excavation and synthesis, stressing problems in the use of relative and absolute chronological methods, the reconstruction of whole societies and cultures, care in the use of archaeological terms, and the interdisciplinary approach. This is by no means an archaeological manifesto of method and theory, but it does indicate a recent awareness of theory and methodological sophistication. This is further and more concretely shown by the publication in recent years of a number of major excavation reports, such as those of the sites in Pan-p'o-ts'un, Sian,[16] and on the west bank of the River Feng near Sian;[17] and the proceedings of the scientific papers delivered at a 1964 interdisciplinary conference on Cenozoic geology and palaeobiology and Palaeolithic archaeology in the area of Lan-t'ien.[18] There is no question that these publications, and the field and laboratory work they represent, qualify by any international standard for scholarly excellence.

Outside of mainland China, a wide diversity of work, synthesizing the archaeology of ancient China, has appeared. In Taiwan, scholars of the Academia Sinica and other institutions, under the leadership of the venerable Li Chi, have embarked upon an ambitious project to compile a history of ancient China, using archaeological as well as literary data, and individual chapters of the book have begun to appear in draft form.[19] Many books on Chinese prehistoric and early historical archaeology have also appeared in the English language.[20] One might have assumed that, since these are for the most part written by impartial observers, these syntheses would be quite objective and their conclusions would essentially converge; but comparison of these works, and their differences from my own and from one another will show that nothing could be farther from the truth.

This divergence of views, however, is no reason for sorrow, because competitive theories are a prerequisite for the eventual fruition

16. *Hsi-an Pan-p'o,* Peking, Wenwu Press, 1963.

17. *Feng Hsi Fa-chüeh Pao-kao,* Peking, Wenwu Press, 1962.

18. *Shensi Lan-t'ien Hsin-sheng-chieh Hsien-ch'ang Hui-yi lun-wen chi,* Peking, Science Press, 1966.

19. E.g. *Bull. College of Arts, Natl. Taiwan Univ., 14* (1965), 15–59.

20. See Recommendations for Further Reading.

of the archaeological synthesis of ancient China and also, more significantly, because the different points of view are the results of a number of necessarily different approaches to the same subject matter and the same corpus of data. Some of these recent works aim at summarizing the data without ambitious attempts at interpretation, thus providing invaluable material for study. Others stress the basic unity of human history as a whole and the pool of knowledge shared by the early segments of Chinese and Western culture histories. Still others describe artifacts and their significance to the history of Chinese art and technology.

What has convinced me that a volume like the present one is worth writing, even in this recently prolific field of ancient Chinese archaeology, is the fact that still another approach, one that has proved capable of bringing about fruitful results elsewhere in the world, has yet to be applied to the Chinese data. By this I mean the method of developmental classification which has been used with considerable success by V. Gordon Childe and Robert J. Braidwood for the Near East, and also by Gordon R. Willey and Philip Phillips for the New World.[21] This volume does not intend to adopt a monolithic point of view in methodology, and the historical framework it tries to set up is intended to be a balanced one. The reader, however, will not fail to notice that the developmental approach is emphasized somewhat at the expense of all others. I do this with deliberation, believing that in the field of Chinese archaeology there have been sufficient hypotheses on the problems of art and origins, and enough descriptive analyses of artifacts, whereas the process of cultural and social growth remains to be discussed in a general theoretical fashion.

In the following chapters the archaeological data of ancient China will be interpreted, processed, and arranged with such a perspective in view. Chronological sequences and cultural groups will be formulated for the total area of China and its various regions, and questions will be asked, and answers sought, as to how such sequences and

21. V. Gordon Childe, *What Happened in History,* New York, Penguin Books, 1942; *New Light on the Most Ancient East,* New York, Praeger, 1953. Robert J. and Linda Braidwood, *Cahiers d'histoire mondiale, 1* (1953), 278–310. R. J. Braidwood and Charles A. Reed, *Cold Spring Harbor Symposia on Quantitative Biology, 22* (1957), 19–31. Gordon R. Willey and Philip Phillips, *Method and Theory in American Archeology,* Univ. Chicago Press, 1958. Julian H. Steward, *Theory of Culture Change,* Urbana, Univ. Illinois Press, 1955.

groupings came about, and why such distinctive historical developments occurred in this part of the world. To put this another way: How did civilization arise in China, and what course of development did it take? To describe is inevitably to interpret, and an interpretation complete in all aspects of this development is not intended. If, for instance, I seem to have treated the Palaeolithic period in an unceremonious and summary manner, it is because I believe this period is irrelevant to the particular direction and process of Chinese civilizational development except for providing a general foundation of basic cultures and populations. If I seem to have underplayed at times the role of external influences in shaping the events and the courses of cultural development in ancient China, it is because such influences have been more than adequately dealt with by previous authors. I wish, instead, to stress the growth process of civilization itself and its formative antecedents which, above all, must be accounted for by what took place *in situ*.

In this respect, I find myself in complete agreement with Cheng Te-k'un that "as long as plain archaeological facts are not properly established in their native contexts, any comparison with distant parallels tends to be farfetched,"[22] and with Li Chi that "before we accept this [that the birth of all great civilizations is due to cultural contact] as true of any particular civilization, no effort should be spared to collect all available data in order to examine in detail the process of actual growth."[23] It is precisely around this process of actual growth of the Chinese civilization in its native contexts that the present study is centered.

22. *Prehistoric China (Archaeology in China, 1)*, Cambridge, Heffer, 1959, p. xix.

23. *The Beginnings of Chinese Civilization*, p. 13.

CHAPTER ONE

THE ENVIRONMENTAL SETTING AND TIME SCALE

GEOGRAPHIC SUBDIVISIONS OF CHINA

In discussing the early history of man in China, we must constantly bear in mind that the area known as China is continental in dimensions (ca. 3,700,000 square miles, as against Europe's 3,825,000 and the United States' 3,675,000). This area contains a great variety of topography, climate, and vegetation, ranging from tropical jungles in the southwest through subarctic taiga in Manchuria; from the vast Tibetan plateaus through river-dissected hills of the southeast; and from the deserts and steppes of Chinese Turkestan through the temperate alluvial plains of the lower Huangho Valley. In most of these widely differing geographical regions man's progress has been traced in some detail, indicating invariably that human life in each area adapted to its peculiar ecological circumstances.

Largely speaking, the subdivision of China into a northern part and a southern part has been a significant demarcation throughout the whole period of man's occupation. Further, in view of the special importance of the Huangho Valley in the early cultural history of China, North China can itself be divided in two. Thus, for the purposes of this volume, three ecological zones of the first magnitude are distinguished: the Huangho Valley, the southern deciduous zone, and the northern forests and steppes.

The landscape of China is dominated by mountains and hills which, in prehistoric times, were presumably covered with thick woods and jungles.[1] The activities of the prehistoric inhabitants, therefore, were largely restricted to the large and small river valleys. Furthermore, most of the great rivers lie horizontally in a west–east

1. George B. Cressey, *China's Geographic Foundations,* 2d ed., New York, McGraw-Hill, 1934, p. 37.

axis and flow into the Pacific Ocean. This results in a happy coincidence in that the great river valleys of concern to us seldom run through different major climatic and vegetational zones and hence can serve as a basis for a cultural as well as a geographical subdivision of China (Fig. 1).

The Huangho Valley. This region includes the drainage of the Huangho (Yellow River) and its tributaries, together with the upper courses of a few tributaries of the Yangtze River and several small independent drainage systems in the Hopei plain. The topography of the Huangho Valley is further divisible into three more or less distinct regions: the loess highlands in the west, the alluvial plans in the east, and the Shantung Peninsula along the seacoast. Generally these are all in the temperate climatic zone, with warm summers and cold winters and with moderate (400–800 mm) rainfall. The vegetational cover of the entire area can be characterized as mixed deciduous–coniferous forests, though part of the area is now entirely deforested and part of it has become semiarid.[2]

The southern deciduous zone. The boundary between the Huangho Valley and the southern deciduous zone lies midway between the Yangtze and the Huangho, near the thirty-third parallel. In the west, the line corresponds with the crest of the Tsinling Mountains; farther east it follows the Huai River.[3] This division between the north and the south is clearly marked by climate, natural vegetation, soil, and crops, as shown in Table 1.[4]

South China has a network of large and small river systems. These include the Yangtze, the Huai, the Pearl, and several smaller but independent drainages in the southwest and along the southeastern coast. Topographically, South China is divisible into three major regions: the hills, which cover most of the area and are drained by all the river systems mentioned above except the Huai; the Red basin of Szechwan, drained by the upper Yangtze and its several tributaries; and the Yangtze–Huai plain, drained by the lower Yangtze and the

2. James Thorp, *Geography of the Soils of China,* Nanking, National Geological Survey, 1936. George B. Cressey, *Asia's Lands and Peoples,* New York, McGraw-Hill, 1951.
3. Cressey, *Asia's Lands and Peoples,* p. 99.
4. Simplified after Cressey, *China's Geographic Foundations,* p. 15.

1. The geographic regions and landforms of China, divisible into three broad ecological zones. (1) The Huangho Valley: L (loessland), YP (Yellow plain), and SP (Shantung Peninsula). (2) The northern forests and steppes: MP (Manchurian plain), KM (Khingan Mountains), JM (Jehol Mountains), EMU (Eastern Manchurian Uplands), M (Mongolia), and S (Sinkiang). (3) the Southern deciduous zone: YP (Yangtze plain), SB (Szechwan basin), CMB (central mountain belt), SYH (south Yangtze hills), SC (southeast coast), CH (Canton hinterland), and SU (southwest uplands). (Base map by Erwin Raisz, courtesy Harvard-Yenching Institute. Adapted by Rowland Illick in George Cressey's *Asia's Lands and Peoples,* 2d ed., New York, McGraw-Hill, 1951.)

TABLE 1.

Geographic Contrasts between North and South China

North	*South*
Limited, uncertain rainfall, 400–800 mm	Abundant rainfall, 800–1,600 mm
Cold winters, hot summers, a little snow	Cold winters, hot, moist summers; snow and ice uncommon
Semiarid climate	Subtropical climate, summer monsoon rains, and typhoons
Unleached calcareous soils	Leached noncalcareous soils
Kaoliang, millet, wheat, beans	Rice the dominant crop
4 to 6 months growing season, one or two crops	Nine months to a year growing season; two or three crops
Mixed deciduous forests and grasslands	Subtropical and tropical forests
Brown and dustblown during the winter	Green landscape at all seasons

Huai. There are two principal lacustrine areas in South China, one among the hills in the middle Yangtze consisting of the remnants of the ancient Lake Yün-meng, and including such major lakes as Tung-t'ing (Hupei) and Po-yang (Kiangsi); and another situated on the lower Yangtze–Huai plain, which includes such major lakes as Hung-tze and T'ai.

The northern forests and steppes. The area immediately north of the Huangho Valley consists of the modern regions of Inner Mongolia and Manchuria. Topographically this area may be compared to a horseshoe, opening to the south. The space at the center is the erosion plain of Manchuria, drained by the lower courses of the Liao River and by the Sungari, and originally covered with mixed deciduous–coniferous forests. The eastern branch of the horseshoe is formed by the eastern Manchurian Uplands, and is drained by the T'umen and Yalu rivers and the lower Amur. The western branch is formed by the Khingan and the Jehol Mountains, and is drained by the upper courses of the Amur, the tributaries of the Sungari, and the upper Liao. These mountainous areas are covered with coniferous forests or parklands in the east and north, and steppes in the west. The latter extend westward into Mongolia and Sinkiang. Climatically, this entire area is extremely seasonal and continental, with long, severe winters and short, warm summers.

CHINA OF THE PLEISTOCENE PERIOD

The geographic features of China as we see them today characterize only the geological present; some of them have been around for many million years, but most are transitory. During the past million years or so, the period geologically and palaeontologically known as the Pleistocene or Quaternary, when the human animal lived here and left the remains of his activities, China's landscape, vegetation, and climate have undergone demonstrable changes—minor or drastic—some cyclical and repetitive, others unique and passing. The study of such changes is properly the job of natural scientists, but students of early China must acquaint themselves with the results. To understand the life of the early Chinese inhabitants we must have at least a general idea about their environmental surroundings, which to varying extents and in various aspects differed from one epoch to the next. Moreover, macroenvironmental changes provide a convenient and practical time scale for the relative placement of the archaeological data: what came before or after, and what was contemporaneous with what else. The chronological sequences and contemporaneity thus arrived at are in most cases only approximate unless absolute dates like carbon-14 determinations are available, but these rough estimates are largely adequate for much of human history because for the most part it has changed but slowly and in broadly defined steps.

The Pleistocene period, the last and the shortest of the geological epochs since the formation of our planet, and the interval characterized by the emergence and development of modern man and his nearest ancestors, is known to be a period in which a large series of interrelated upheavals in nature took place—tectonic movements, cyclical alternations of vastly contrasting climatic conditions, changes in the state and amount of water on land with resultant erosion and sedimentation cycles, and the movements and evolution of animal and plant groups adapting to shifting climatic settings, to mention only the most prominent. Evidence for such changes and movements makes it possible to characterize the Pleistocene events of various regions and to tie them together. The sequence that results can then serve as a time scale for generalizing the history of the period and dating assemblages of remains found at various localities.

In China such evidence is extensive. The most direct consists of glacial and periglacial sediments and deposits. J. S. Lee[5] was the first to recognize such remains at Lu-shan, in Kiangsi, and to distinguish three glaciations: Poyang, Taku, and Lushan. Another later glaciation—Tali—was recognized by H. von Wissmann[6] in Yunnan. During the last thirty years similar remains have been identified throughout the country (Fig. 2), and the four glacial and three interglacial periods are widely accepted. The four glaciations may possibly be correlated with the four glaciations of the Himalayas[7] and the Alps sequence from Günz to Würm.

Closely related to the glacial and interglacial intervals are the sedimentary and erosional cycles recognizable in the Pleistocene formations throughout China in river terraces and cave-fissure deposits (Fig. 3). Animal and plant (especially pollen) fossils from these formations are particularly useful for chronological purposes, for, adaptive to climatic conditions, animal and plant life often underwent appreciable change in severe cold conditions and is thus indicative of broad levels of time to which the formations belonged. According to the most recent studies[8] of this evidence, the Chinese Pleistocene is subdivided as follows.

Early Pleistocene

Early Pleistocene formations lie directly above the late Pliocene Pao-teh (Pontian) beds in marked disconformity—indicating a tec-

5. "Quaternary glaciation in the Yangtze Valley," *GSoC Bull., 13* (1933), 2–15; *Lu Shan During the Ice Age,* Institute of Geology, Academia Sinica, Monographs, ser. B, *2* (1937).

6. "The Pleistocene glaciation in China," *GSoC Bull., 17* (1937), 145–68; "Die quartäre Vergletscherung in China," *Ztschr. Gesell. Erd. Berlin* (1937), 241–62.

7. H. de Terra and T. T. Paterson, *Studies on the Ice Age in India and Associated Human Cultures,* Carnegie Institution of Washington Publication 493 (1939).

8. *Ti Ssu Chi Ti-chih Went-'i* (*Quaternary Geology Problems*), ed. by the Institute of Geology, Academia Sinica (Peking), 1964. *Shensi Lan-t'ien Hsin-sheng-chieh* (*Cenozoic in Lan-t'ien, Shensi*), ed. by the Institute of Vertebrate Palaeontology and Palaeoanthropology, Academia Sinica (Peking), 1966. P. Teilhard de Chardin, *Early Man in China,* Peking, Institut de Géo-Biologie, Publication 7 (1941). Hallam L. Movius, Jr., *Early Man and Pleistocene Stratigraphy in Southern and Eastern Asia,* Papers of the Peabody Museum, Harvard University, *19* (1944).

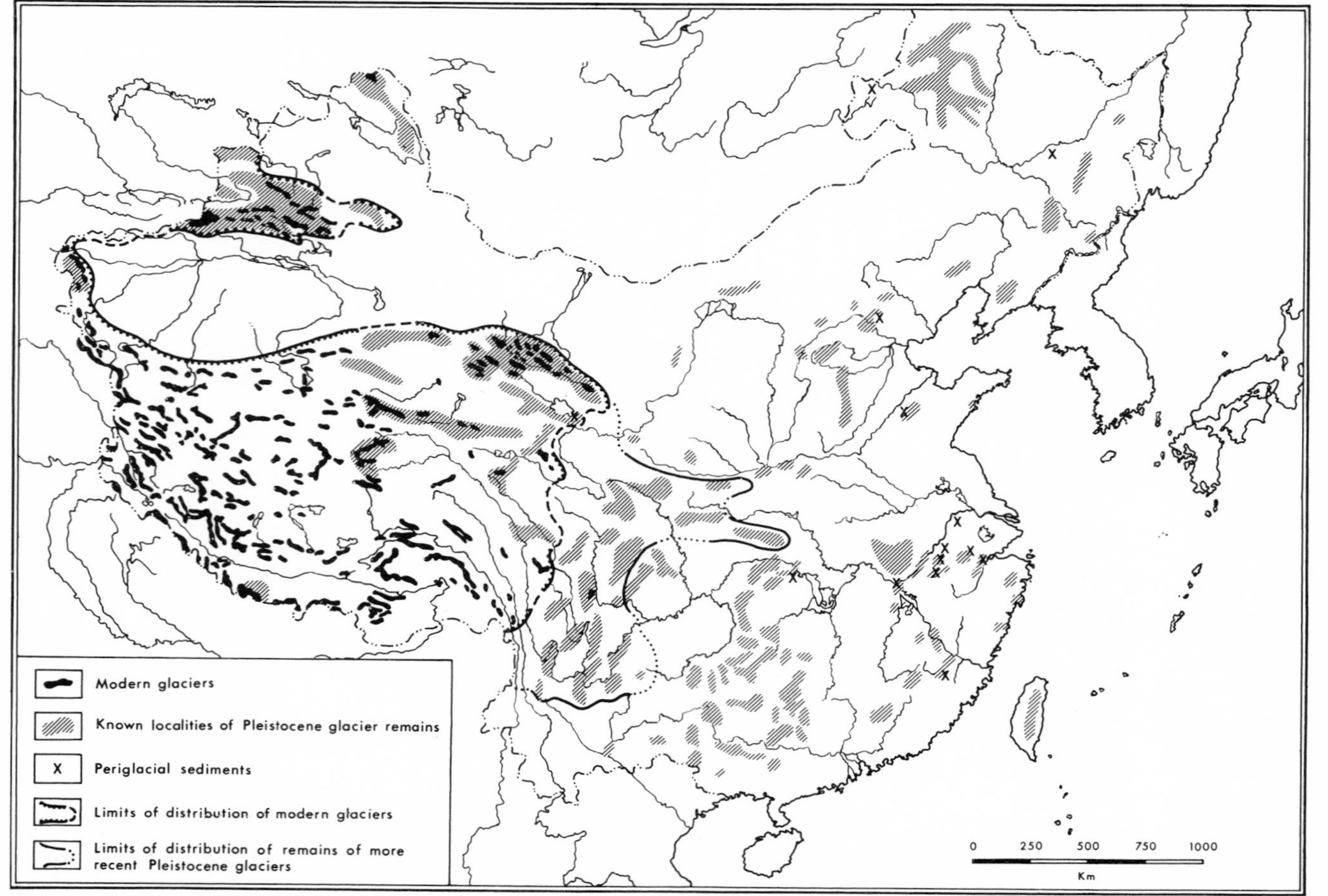

2. Glacial and periglacial remains in China. (After *Ti Ssu Chi Ti-chih Wen-t'i*, Peking, Science Press, 1964, Fig. 10.)

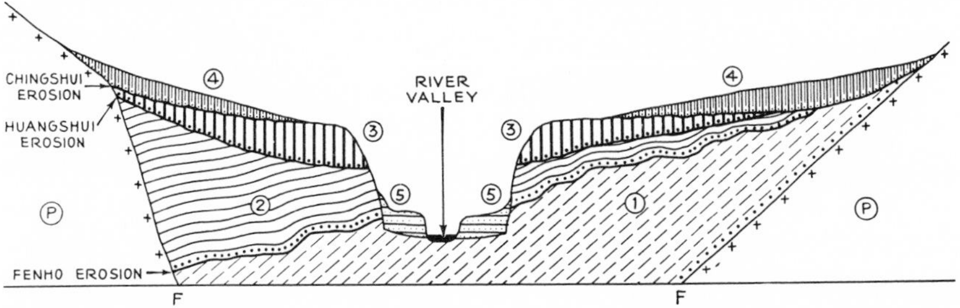

3. The structure of a late Cenozoic basin in North China. F, Fault; P, Palaeozoic rocks. (1) Pliocene deposits; (2) Lower Sanmenian Beds, Lower Pleistocene. (3) Choukoutien Red Loam and Basal Gravel, Middle Pleistocene. (4) Malan Loess and associated deposits, Upper Pleistocene. (5) Panchiao Alluvium. (From H. L. Movius, Jr., *Trans. Amer. Phil. Soc.*, n.s. *38*, 1949, p. 344.)

tonic uprising movement known as the Fenho Erosion. Such formations are represented by the Nihowan or Lower Sanmenian riverine–lacustrine sediments found throughout North China, the red and gray-greenish calcareous clays in scattered areas of North China, the Wucheng Loess of the middle Huangho, and isolated occurrences of gravels and conglomerates in both North and South China. Associated with these sediments are mammalian fossils of the Nihowan fauna of the north (*Bison, Equus sanmeniensis, Archidiskodon planifrons, Paracamelus, Proboscihipparion,* and *Postschizotherium*) and the Liucheng fauna of the south (*Trilophodon serridenstoides, Stegodon praeorientalis, Equus yunnanensis, Bubalus, Elephas* cf. *namadicus,* and *Gigantopithecus blacki*).

The early Pleistocene stage can be subdivided into two substages according to climatic changes marked in its sediments. An early substage is characterized by the lowered temperature and the advances of glaciers and ice sheets in the highlands and plateaus, and this corresponds to the Poyang Glacial advance of J. S. Lee. Fossil pollens of poplar (*Populus bifolia, P. euphratica*) have been identified from sediments of this level in Shansi and Sinkiang. In areas not covered by ice, moist pluvial conditions apparently prevailed, resulting in the riverine–lacustrine and conglomerate formations mentioned above. Corresponding retreats of seawater produced land bridges between continental Asia and Japan, and between Taiwan and many South Sea islands.

A late substage of the early Pleistocene is marked by interglacial and interpluvial conditions, an increase in temperature, and general aridity. The warming trend is well indicated by lateritization of the Red Clay sediments, the deposition of warm-type coral limestone and foraminiferous fossils, and occurrence of warm-temperature and subtropical fossil pollen species in Central and North China. In terms of the Lushan Glacial sequence, this warm interval corresponds to the Poyang–Taku Interglacial.

Middle Pleistocene

The most violent tectonic upheaval of the Quatenary in China took place at the end of the early Pleistocene; the Huangshui Erosion produced a major disconformity between the early Pleistocene and younger beds. A major (Choukoutien) sedimentary cycle, resulting from the uprising of the earth crust and growing aridity, came about in the form of clay and gravel deposits—gravels in the mountainous areas of the northwest, lateritized gravels in the Yangtze Valley, the Lishih Loess of the middle Huangho, and the reddish clay deposits in limestone caves and fissures. In association with these reddish clay, loessic, and gravelly sediments are the Choukoutien fauna of North China (*Hyaena sinensis, Machairodus inexpectatus, M. ultima, Dicerorhinus mercki, Equus sanmeniensis, Eurycerus pachyosteus,* and *Pithecanthropus pekinensis*) and the Wan Hsien fauna of South China (*Ailuropoda, Megatapirus, Stegodon orientalis, Pongo*).

Again two substages can be distinguished within the middle Pleistocene according to climatic data. The first is characterized by the most extensive glaciation known in the Chinese Pleistocene—Taku Glacial. Outside the highlands a pluvial interval is indicated by sediments of a cold and moist climate. This was followed by an extended stage of interglacial and interpluvial climatic conditions during which lateritic reddish clay was deposited in areas as far north as 43° latitude. Pollen analysis of the sediments from which early forms of man were found (at Chou-k'ou-tien and Ch'en-chia-wo) shows a prevalence of warm, dry climatic elements suited to the Taku–Lushan Interglacial interval.

Late Pleistocene

Toward the end of the long Choukoutienian sedimentation cycle, represented by Locality 15 and the upper strata of Locality 1 of Chou-k'ou-tien, the warm, dry interval apparently came to a gradual end, and glacial and pluvial conditions once again prevailed. Pollen analysis of a Locality 1 sediment sample yielded results indicating a cold, moist climate,[9] and animal fossils began to include Upper Pleistocene varieties. This period probably corresponds to J. S. Lee's Lushan Glacial.[10] At the end of this sedimentary cycle a series of new tectonic movements cut into the flat surfaces of the Lishih Loess and resulted in the disconformity between the Lishih Loess below and the Malan Loess above. This is the interval of Chingshui Erosion, during which formed the 20- to 50-meter river terraces of North China. Pollen profiles at two localities in the Lan-t'ien area of central-eastern Shensi in sediments of late-Pleistocene date indicate a cold, moist climate near the bottom and a warming, drying trend toward the top, very likely coinciding with the change from the uppermost reddish clay deposits to the Chingshui Erosion interval and suggesting an interglacial–interpluvial climate befitting the Lushan-Tali Interglacial.

The rest of the late Pleistocene stage witnessed the extensive deposition of aeolian loess on top of the Chingshui Erosion beds, resulting in the Malan Loess of the Middle Huangho. Contemporary with the Malan Loess are the sediments deposited at the same time but under different glacial and pluvial conditions, such as the riverine–lacustrine sediments of the Ordos region. In association with these sediments are the Sjara-osso fauna of North China (*Crocuta crocuta, Coelodonta antiquitatis, Megaloceros ordosianus, Spirocerus*), and the Tzuyang fauna of South China (*Ailuropoda, Homo sapiens, Mammuthus*). Both the woolly rhinoceros of the north and the mammoth of the south indicate a cold, moist climate, and pollen analysis of a number of Malan Loess localities shows conclusively that a cold vege-

9. B. Kurtén, *VP, 3* (1959), 173–75.

10. In a most recent synthesis of Pleistocene geology of China (*Ti Ssu Chi Ti-chih Wen-t'i,* 1964) Middle Pleistocene is considered to end with the termination of the Choukoutien sedimentation, and the Chingshui Erosion is made to correspond to the Lushan Glacial. This view is not adopted here, and I continue to use the older system of subdivision.

tation prevailed, reflecting an annual temperature probably 8° C lower than it is at present, a conclusion confirmed by the palynological analysis of a core of sediments taken from Lake Jih-yüeh-t'an of Taiwan[11] (Fig. 4).

Concluding the descriptions given above we can say that from geological and palaeontological evidence it is clear that the Chinese Pleistocene is marked by a series of climatic oscillations accompanied by changes in landform and animal and plant life; that four major cold-moist intervals are shown, probably correlatable with the four glacial advances of the highland areas; and that these oscillations and changes provide a practical time scale for dating human fossils and the Palaeolithic industries found in Pleistocene sediments. Table 2 gives a convenient summary of the time scale.

CLIMATE IN THE EARLY POSTGLACIAL PERIOD

With the retreat of the ice sheets and glaciers in the Himalayas and on other highlands at the end of the stage of the Malan Loess, the Recent (Holocene) geological period came to eastern Asia. Many of the Pleistocene faunal forms became extinct, such as the mammoth and the woolly rhinoceros, while the modern faunal group, which began to appear during the Upper Pleistocene period, came to dominate. There was probably a general rise in temperature and precipitation, together with an increase of vegetational cover, a gradual elevation of land, and a stage of erosion. These concurrent geological and palaeontological changes may have occurred in the different regions of eastern Asia with varying intensity and in different ways, but information from North and South China indicates that in these regions they were sufficiently intense to bring about widespread changes both in landscape and in the human cultures adapting to it.

The terminal Pleistocene period in North China, which was also the final phase of the Malan Loess stage, was characterized by a generally cool climate. With the beginning of the postglacial stage there was probably a general uplift in the mean annual temperature of

11. Matsuo Tsukada, "Late Pleistocene vegetation and climate in Taiwan (Formosa)," *Proc. Nat. Acad. Sci., 55* (1966), 543–48. "Vegetation in Subtropical Formosa during the Pleistocene Glaciations and the Holocene," *Palaeogeography, Palaeoclimatology, Palaeoecology, 3* (1967), 49–64.

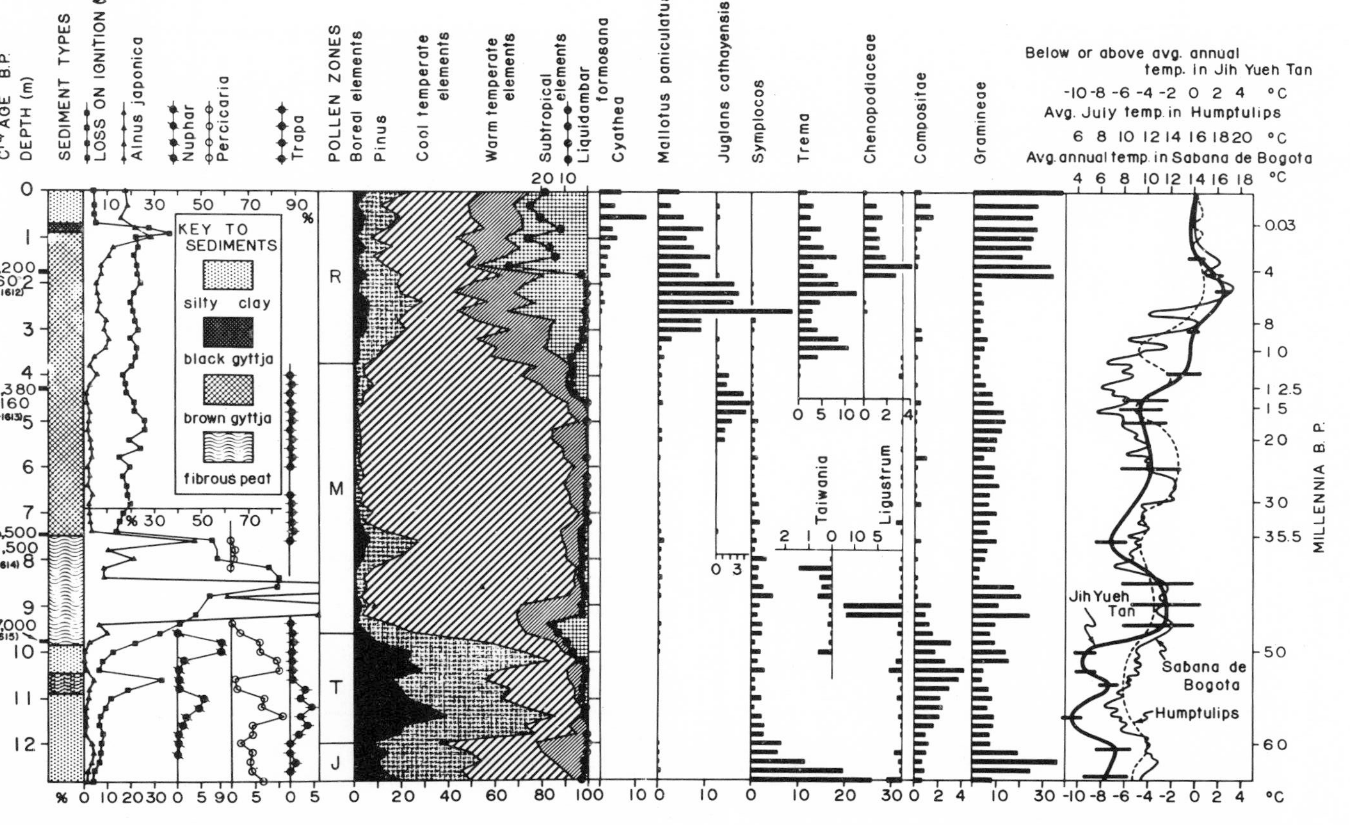

4. Pollen diagram for a 12.79-m core from Jih T'an (745.5 m), central Taiwan, showing sediment types in relation to loss on ignition, and pollen curves of *Alnus,* water plants, climatically grouped elements, and other selected species. At right, temperature curves from the present site, from Sabana de Bogota, Colombia, and from Humptulips, Washington, with a uniform scale for time as well as temperature, as far as the data permit. (From Matsuo Tsukada, *Proc. Natl. Acad. Sci., 55,* 1966, p. 544.) In the column "Pollen Zones," read T_1, T_2, and T_3 for J, T, and M.

TABLE 2.

Subdivisions of the Chinese Pleistocene

Stages	Glaciated Areas	Unglaciated Areas	Tectonic and Sedimentary Cycles	Pollen	Fauna
Late	Tali Glacial	Pluvial	Malan Loess / Riverine–Lacustrine Deposits	Cold	Sjara–osso Tzuyang
	Lushan–Tali Interglacial	Interpluvial	Chingshui Erosion	Warm	
	Lushan Glacial	Pluvial	Lishih Loess Reddish Clay Choukoutien Sedimentation	Cold	
Middle	Taku–Lushan Interglacial	Interpluvial		Warm	Choukoutien Wan Hsien
	Taku Glacial	Pluvial		Cold	
			Huangshui Erosion		
Early	Poyang–Taku Interglacial	Interpluvial	Wuch'eng Loess Red Clay	Warm	Nihowan Liuch'eng
	Poyang Glacial	Pluvial	Nihowan Beds	Cold	
			Fenho Erosion		

China, as indicated by the extinction of such "cool" fauna as the mammoth, the woolly rhinoceros, and *Bos primigenius;* the appearance of many southern species of modern fauna; the apparent thickening of vegetation and the increase of subtropical and warm-temperate species in a number of pollen profiles; and the erosion of landscape and the apparent abundance of water. During this warm, moist period Mesolithic and Neolithic cultures began and flourished throughout China. The relatively mild and moist climatic condition, however, began to deteriorate after the initial periods of the historic stage, until in the north the climate became cool and the landscape nearly barren, probably as a result of intensive and unrestricted deforestation and the gradual lowering of temperature.

With regard to erosion and the abundance of water during the early phases of the postglacial period, it is believed that beginning with the Holocene a new sedimentary cycle was initiated by the Panchiao Erosion stage. According to Pierre Teilhard de Chardin:

> That a positive movement of the land is today still in process is confirmed by the fact that, since the deposition of the Malan loess, the last remnants of the Pliocene lakes have been largely desiccated in the interior: Sjara-osso-gol depression, Lower Fenho and Taiyüan basins, Sungari Basin, Djalai Nor (and a number of other nors in Mongolia).[12]
>
> During the Late Pleistocene, the distribution and local facies of the modern deserts are fully recognizable. Yet their depressions are abundantly filled with temporary lakes, not so temporary however that they could not feed at places a rich population of Mollusks. Heaps of *Lymnaea* and *Planorbis* occur in the high terraces along the "nors" of East Mongolia . . . The continuation of this regime, or even a somewhat moister period, is necessary for explaining the distribution of human industry during Neolithic times. Since the Neolithic, an increasing aridity is positively indicated by a general extension of the sand dunes, a general reduction of the "nors," and a general deflation of the Late Pleistocene silts. The influence of human agency . . . seems to be, on the whole, insufficient for explaining the main phenomenon.[13]

12. Teilhard de Chardin, *GSoC Bull., 16* (1936/37), 199–200.
13. Ibid., p. 219.

These "nors" in Mongolia are now largely desiccated, but the windblown cultural remains in this region "occurred with such regularity in the various basins and hollows, large and small," as to suggest that their formation took place under climatic conditions decidedly different from those of the present day and when these basins were filled with water.[14] Similar climatic peaks during the early post-Pleistocene period are also indicated by peats at San-ho and Chi in Hopei in the plains area,[15] and by the high water levels near prehistoric sites in Honan,[16] as well as by the literary records of the existence of nors in Honan, Shansi, and Shensi in the western loesslands.[17]

Along with the moist climatic conditions in North China went a thick vegetational cover in areas that are now barren and semiarid, as indicated by a Black Earth horizon at some localities in the north. At Lin-hsi in Jehol, Sha-kang in Hsin-min Hsien, Liaoning, and Ang-ang-hsi in Heilungchiang, cultural deposits were found in a black earth layer which lies beneath a yellowish, sandy layer of Recent formation and above the loess deposits of Pleistocene origin.[18] This black earth layer, marking the transition from the semiarid loess stage of the terminal Pleistocene to the semiarid condition of the present day, probably represents an ancient forest cover.[19] The existence of a thick forest in North China and on the Manchurian plains is further indicated by such cultural remains from prehistoric sites as the abundance of charcoal and woodworking implements (ax, adz, chisel, etc.), and by the frequency of bones of wild game.[20] Some of these bones are definitely from forest-dwelling animals such as tigers and deer.

Of even greater importance is the fact that in the woods of that time were certain faunal and floral forms indicating a climate warmer than that of present-day North China. At the Upper Cave of Chou-

14. Nels C. Nelson, *Natural History, 26* (1926), 250. John Maringer, *Contribution to the Prehistory of Mongolia,* Stockholm, 1950, pp. 207–08.

15. J. G. Andersson, *Essays on the Cenozoic of Northern China,* GSuC, Mem., ser. A, *3,* 1923.

16. Andersson, *BMFEA, 19* (1947), 20–21.

17. Andersson, *BMFEA, 15* (1943), 40–41. Meng Wen-t'ung, *Yü-kung, 1* (Peiping, 1934), 14–15. Hu Hou-hsüan, *Chia-ku-hsüeh Shang-shih lun ts'ung,* 2 vols., Chinan, Chi-lu University, 1944/45.

18. Liang Ssu-yüng, *BIHP, 4* (1932), 5; *TYKKPK, 1* (1936), 9. Teilhard, *Mém. Soc. Géol. France,* n.s. *3* (1926), fasc. 3, 24. Wang Tseng-hsin, *KKTH* (1958/1), 1.

19. Teilhard, *Early Man in China,* pp. 38–39.

20. Andersson, *BMFEA, 15* (1943), 34.

k'ou-tien, which dates from the latest Pleistocene or the earliest Holocene, there appeared such warm-climate species as *Cynailurus* cf. *jubatus* and *Paguma larvata*.[21] According to the reports of some early postglacial geological deposits and Neolithic and Early Bronze Age archaeological sites,[22] there is evidence of the following "warm" species:

Bamboo rat (*Rhizomys sinensis; R. troglodytes?*): Yang-shao stage sites, An-yang
Elephant (*Elephas indicus*): An-yang
Rhinoceros: Ma-chia-yao
Bison (*Bos namadicus*): Ma-chia-yao
Tapir (*Tapirus* cf. *indicus*): An-yang
Water buffalo (*Bubalus mephistopheles; B. indicus*): San-ho
Water deer (*Hydropotes inermis*): Pan-p'o, An-yang, San-ho
Père David's deer (*Elaphurus davidianus*): San-ho
Menzies' deer (*Elaphurus menziesianus*): An-yang
Porcupine: Peking
Squirrel (*Tamiops*): Peking
Warmth-loving mollusks (*Lamprotula tientsiniensis; L. rochechouarti; L. leai*): Tientsin muds, Ch'eng-tzu-yai
Rice (*Oryza sativa*): Yang-shao-ts'un, Liu-tzu-chen(?)
Bamboo: inferred from the form of pottery and mentioned in early literary records

The existence of rice, bamboo, and elephants is corroborated by the written records,[23] while the presence of elephants and rhinoceri is further confirmed by sculptures and some zoomorphic bronzes from the archaeological site at An-yang.

21. P'ei Wen-chung, *PS*, ser. C, *10* (1940).

22. Andersson, *BMFEA, 15* (1943), 35–40. Carl W. Bishop, *Antiquity, 28* (1933), 389–404. Arthur de Carle Sowerby, *Jour. North-China Branch, Royal Asiatic Soc., 53* (1922), 1–20. Gad Rausing, *Bull. Soc. Lettres Lund, 3* (1956), 191–203. Li Chi et al., *Ch'eng-tzu-yai*, Academia Sinica (Nanking), 1934. Teilhard and C. C. Young, *PS*, ser. C, *12* (1936). Teilhard and P'ei Wen-chung, *Le Néolithique de la Chine*, Peking, Institut de Géo-Biologie, 1944. F. S. Drake, *PFEPC*, 4th, *1* (1956), fasc. 1, 133–49. *Hsi-an Pan-p'o*, Peking, Wenwu Press, 1963.

23. Ch'en Meng-chia, *Yen-ching Hsüeh Pao, 20* (1936), 485–576. Hu Hou-hsüan, *Chia-ku-hsüeh Shang-shih lun ts'ung, 2,* 1945. Meng Wen-t'ung, *Yü-kung, 1* (1934).

Finally, palynological study—commonly regarded as the most reliable means of determining ancient vegetations and thus the history of ancient climates which supported the various plant species—has recently been brought to bear on the problem of postglacial environment in China, with significant results. The pollen analysis of lake sediments collected in Taiwan by Matsuo Tsukada, of Yale University, shows a postglacial "climatic optimum" (postglacial hypsithermal interval) carbon-dated to the period between approximately 8,000 and 4,000 years B.P., during which the annual temperature in subtropical Taiwan was probably two or three degrees centigrade higher than the present level[24] (Fig. 4). Similar work has been undertaken with peat deposits near Peking[25] and with the Manchurian "black earth" sediments in Liaotung Peninsula,[26] with identical results. The northern palynological work did not have the benefit of carbon-14 dates, but for the southern part of the Soviet Far East, M. I. Neishtadt,[27] from data based on the pollen content of five peats in the Amur-Ussuri region, has divided the postglacial period of that area into four stages: *Archaic,* 12,000–9,800 B.P.; *Early,* 9,800–7,700 B.P.; *Middle,* 7,700–2,500 B.P.; *Late,* 2,500–0 B.P. The peak of broad-leaved forest lies in the *Middle* stage, whereas from 2,500 B.P. on, the Korea pine (*Pinus koraiensis*) begins to dominate the local vegetation, indicating a postglacial hypsithermal and a subsequent climatic deterioration similar in trend and in age to the Taiwan sequence. Since the interval 8,000 to 2,000 B.P. covers much of the late prehistoric period, the importance of such studies for students of early China cannot be overemphasized.[28]

24. Tsukada, *Proc. Nat. Acad. Sci., 55* (1966), 543–48.
25. Liu et al., *QS, 4* (1965), no. 1. Chou, *QS, 4* (1965), no. 1.
26. Ch'en et al., *QS, 4* (1965), no. 2.
27. M. I. Neishtadt, *Istoriia Lesov i Paleogeografiia SSSR v. Golotsene,* Moscow, Isd. AN SSSR, 1957.
28. It should be noted that the interpretation of pollen profiles from sediments deposited after the beginning of agriculture must take into serious account the part played by human and cultural factors in the local histories of vegetation. On the basis of analysis of pollen grains taken from the Neolithic habitation site of Pan-p'o-ts'un, near Sian, Shensi, for instance, Chou K'un-shu (*KK,* 1963/9) concludes that, since the pollen grains were predominantly from grassy species, the climate of the environs was "cool and dry" like the present—a conclusion at considerable odds with other evidence, notably zoological. It is possible that local variations existed in ancient climate as in culture, but Chou's interpretation failed to take into consideration the factor of deforestation of agriculturalists.

These bits of evidence together prove beyond doubt that the beginning of the postglacial stage in China was marked by a gradual rise of the mean annual temperature, accompanied by an increasing vegetational cover and corresponding faunal and floral assemblages. This conclusion is broad, but any finer conclusions will have to depend upon future investigations.

It is perfectly clear, however, that the climatic amelioration in China during the early postglacial period must have had considerable influence upon the human industries previously adapted to the cool semiarid loessic conditions. The inhabitants were now confronted with a changed environment and a widened range for development. Moreover, the higher temperature must have had different effects in different regions. We may infer that in prehistoric times most of North China, for example, which now constitutes the eastern low plains, was wet and marshy (Shantung Peninsula was probably an island surrounded by marshes and lakes if not by seawater),[29] while the western high loesslands were clad with forests and dissected by watercourses. If this is true—and the scanty evidence at our disposal leads us to think it is—it unquestionably had great bearing on the emergence and distribution of human cultures in postglacial times.

A NOTE ON POSTGLACIAL AND HISTORICAL CHRONOLOGIES

For an area as large and as complex in cultural variations through time as China, prehistoric events can hardly be pieced together in any coherent manner without a tight and accurate chronological control. None of the recently devised scientific methods for the determination of the absolute age of ancient sediments and artifacts has been employed in Chinese archaeology, with the exception of a uranium-thorium date for Peking Man (see p. 50) and a small number of carbon-14 dates from the southeastern coast. The only chronological methods that one can use for China as a whole, prior to the beginning of historic dates, are relative chronological methods such as stratigraphy, synchronism, and typological sequences and comparisons. In addition, absolute chronologies known from other areas of the world,

29. William S. Ting, *BIE, 20* (1965), 155–62. Li Shih-yü, *KK* (1962/12), 652–57.

where available and pertinent, could provide ranges of time for comparable events in the area of China.

As mentioned above, the progress of Palaeolithic man and his work was extremely slow and can be measured in geological terms. The Pleistocene subdivision described above certainly lacks refinement, compared with such well-studied regions as Western and Central Europe, but for our purpose here, dealing with a small amount of data for all of China, it is not entirely inadequate for seriating and synchronizing major events of the Chinese Pleistocene into an intelligible picture for the time being.

For the postglacial period, however, the situation drastically changes. Human progress in cultural achievements can no longer be measured in geological terms. The entire postglacial period, up to the present, is only about ten thousand years, but human accomplishment during it consists of a series of quantum and accelerated jumps, and a difference of a millennium, a century, or even a decade, might give rise to drastically different pictures in which various events through time and over space were structured into different, delicate balances.

Fortunately, precisely because of the rapid rate of cultural change, it is now possible to formulate microchronological segments according to minute cultural shifts and changes—a decorative motif on a pottery vessel may undergo appreciable transformations in a generation, as against a minute improvement in the preparation of a striking platform of a flint core that took millions of experiments and a quarter of a million years to perfect during the early part of the Pleistocene. It is therefore possible for later prehistoric periods to reconstruct cultural groups and sequences, even without any absolute age data, by means of very careful manipulation of the principles of stratigraphy, synchronism, and typology. Such archaeological concepts as culture, phase, regional chronology, horizon, and tradition may and will be fruitful if they are applied with care and caution. Most of these concepts have yet to be employed on the Chinese data, which have often been handled with an assortment of idiosyncratic systems of method and terminology that are difficult to evaluate and use for comparative purposes. I shall have to compromise in many situations, with the result perhaps in archaeological time that units are often too broad and too loosely structured to be satisfactory.

This is not to say at all that Chinese archaeology has no real need

TABLE 3.

Chronology of the Shang and Chou Periods

Dynasty	*Subdivisions*	*Events*	*Absolute Dates (B.C.)*
		Founding of dynasty by T'ang	? 1514–1722+
Shang		P'an Keng moves capital to An-yang	? 1291–1397
		Wu Wang conquest	? 1018–1122
	Western Chou	First year of the Kung Ho Era	841
Chou		P'ing Wang moves capital to Lo-yang	770
	Eastern Chou		
		Ch'in unification	221
Ch'in			

for scientific techniques, chronological or otherwise. The handful of carbon-14 dates from Taiwan has already given us a solid basis for dating entire horizons that could have a spatial span as broad as China itself. A wide use of such dates in the future may very likely revolutionize the entire prehistory of the land. Recent archaeological work at half a dozen localities scattered through China has demonstrated the usefulness of the pollen analytic method in chronology as well as in characterizing ancient environments. However, we have to leave these methods to the next decades, but meanwhile we must do what we can as carefully as possible with what we have.

The latest four thousand years or so are a different story again. The emergence of the Shang civilization means the dawn of written records. From about 1750 B.C. onward, textual materials are available so that historical events can be pieced together in calendrical language, and a useful chronological subdivision is possible for both the Shang and the Chou (Table 3).[30] For reasons to be given later this volume will arbitrarily end at 221 B.C. when the first unifier of China, Ch'in Shih

30. See the discussion in K. C. Chang, in *Chronologies in Old World Archaeology,* Robert Ehrich ed., Univ. Chicago Press, 1965.

Huang Ti, subjugated the last opposing state. For this millennium and a half, chronological segments as fine as necessary become available within the domain of civilized China. Even outside it, in areas peripheral to or even distant from the Chinese civilization, the historical chronology—the earliest available historical chronology in all of Asia east of the Urals—serves as a frame of reference for events that took place within the period. In these areas, however, where many things of relevance to Chinese civilization happened somewhat slower and later and persisted long after they had ended in North China, a clean break at 221 B.C. is more often than not impossible to make, and these events will be followed through to their ends, often into the Han Dynasty (second century B.C. to second century of the present era). As far as possible, however, this volume describes the history of cultures in China down to the beginning of the Ch'in and Han empires—the cutoff point that in historiographic tradition concludes China's ancient period.

CHAPTER TWO

PALAEOLITHIC AND MESOLITHIC FOUNDATIONS

Following general Old World archaeological usage we refer to human culture during the Pleistocene period as Palaeolithic, and to that from the beginning of the postglacial stage up to the advent of agriculture as Mesolithic. A "Chinese" culture tradition as we now know it did not become manifest in the archaeological record until after the emergence of farming villages, but its foundation was laid, and the stage set for its occurrence, during the Pleistocene; and the populations and cultures during that period in China were part of significant worldwide events.

The so-called Palaeolithic culture of the Pleistocene in the area of China is a new concept that did not emerge until this century. According to the legends upon which traditional Chinese history was based, the universe was made by P'an Ku, and mankind was created by Nü Wa. Then the world was ruled by a long series of sage kings, grouped into San Huang, the Three Sovereigns, and Wu Ti, the Five Emperors. These were followed by initial historical periods, the last two millennia B.C., which comprised the reign of the Three Dynasties—the Hsia, Shang, and Chou. A cumulative chronology of the reigns of the ancient sages would place the legendary beginning of Chinese ancient history well within the Pleistocene period, and, in fact, even now there are historians trying to reconcile the new and the old and attempting to identify remains of fossil man with legendary sages.[1] In scientific Palaeolithic archaeology, however, human and cultural *remains* must be recovered from Pleistocene deposits to be counted, and ancient artifacts themselves were not known in China from demonstrably Pleistocene contexts until 1920.[2]

During the half century since their first discovery, Palaeolithic sites and relics have been brought to light throughout China and from

1. Hsü Liang-chih, *Chung-kuo Shih-ch'ien-shih Hua,* Hong Kong, Asia Press, 1954.

2. P. Teilhard de Chardin, *Anthropologie, 33* (1924), 630–31. Teilhard and E. Licent, *GSoC Bull., 3* (1924), 45–50.

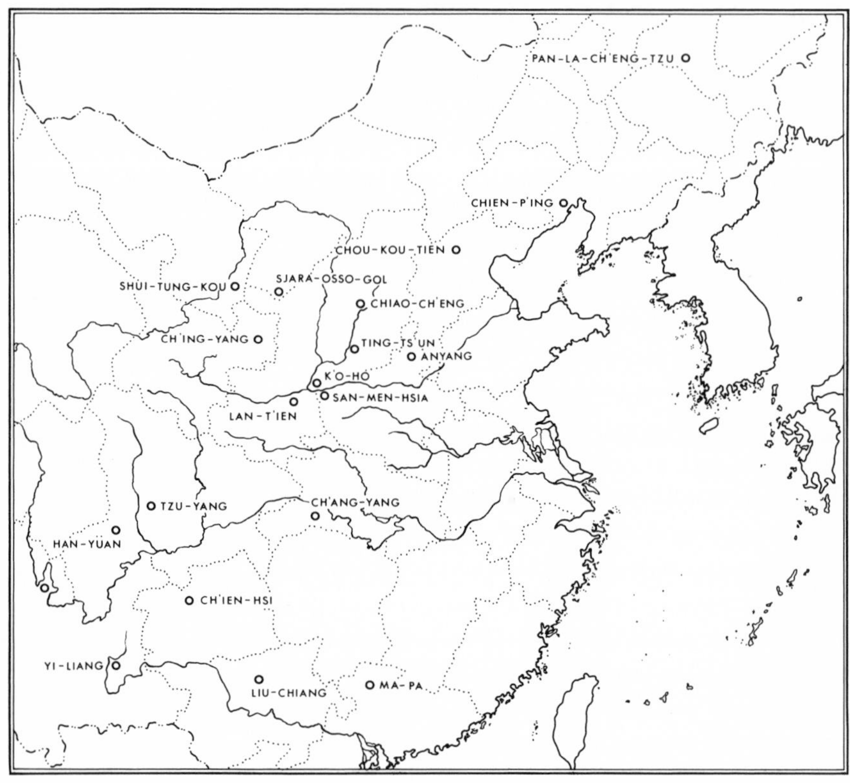

5. Major sites of Palaeolithic cultures and fossil man remains in China.

many different periods, including findings of great world significance (Fig. 5). The Pleistocene period is over a million years long, and the sites, although numbered in the hundreds, are few and far between. Because of the slowness of change during this ancient period, however, a brief sketch of the human and cultural developmental history in China is possible, and in places the story is even filled with significant and interesting details.

MAN OF THE EARLY PLEISTOCENE STAGE

Archaeologists and human palaeontologists now still hold to the view that during the Villafranchian stage China was not occupied by man.[3] There is some evidence to the contrary, however, and archaeological excavations in the near future may yet alter drastically the current picture of the emergence of man in this part of the world. Some forty years ago in the Nihowan beds (generally thought to be Villafranchian) of the Sangkan River valley of Hopei in North China, Emile Licent and Pierre Teilhard de Chardin discovered a so-called faceted stone and some bone fragments. The Abbé Breuil believed that this stone and some of the bone fragments were modified by human hands, but his view is generally rejected.[4] A new Palaeolithic site was discovered in 1959, and excavated in 1960 and 1961, on the back of a small hill northeast of Hsi-hou-tu village, approximately 3 kilometers east of the Yellow River, in Jui-ch'eng County, southern Shansi, where stone implements ("bilaterally retouched giant flakes, small scrapers, cores with a small number of flaking scars, and irregularly retouched flakes") of quartzite pebbles were reportedly uncovered from a sandy-gravel layer underneath the Reddish Clay stratum, in direct association with a typical Nihowan fauna. Apparently dating from the Poyang–Taku Interglacial period of Lower Pleistocene, this Palaeolithic assemblage may prove to be the earliest evidence of human occupation in China. The publication of a full description of the site, eagerly awaited, must be seen before we accept unreservedly the artificiality of its stone "implements."[5] Furthermore, there were some anthropoids in China during the Villafranchian stage, including the owner of the so-called *Hemanthropus peii* teeth, and the giant creature *Gigantopithecus blacki.* The teeth of the anthropoid were found by G. H. R. von Koenigswald in Hong Kong drugstores; Koenigswald believes that they were originally derived from South China Pleistocene deposits, and has compared them morphologically with the *Paranthropus* of South Africa.[6] *Gigantopithecus blacki* was first identified shortly before World War II by Koenigswald on the basis of three gigantic teeth which were also obtained from Chinese drugstores in Hong Kong, where they were used—as were many other palaeontologi-

3. F. Clark Howell, *Science, 130* (1959), 833.

4. Teilhard, *Anthropologie, 45* (1935), 736. Henri Breuil, *Anthropologie, 45* (1935), 746. Movius, *Trans. Amer. Phil. Soc., 38* (1948), 345.

5. For a preliminary report, see Chia Lan-p'o, *WW* (1962/4/5), 25–26.

6. G. H. R. von Koenigswald, *Koninkl. Nederl. Akad. Weternschap., Amsterdam, Proceedings,* ser. B, *60* (1957), 153–59.

cal specimens throughout China, as well as the *Hemanthropus peii* teeth—as an ingredient in drug-making.[7] Weidenreich thought that the *Gigantopithecus* might have been in the direct lines of descent which led to the *Pithecanthropus* groups and, finally, to modern man.[8] Weidenreich's hypothesis has been rendered obsolete by advances in the study of the African australopithecines, and the recent discoveries of three mandibles and over a thousand isolated teeth of this species *in situ* in southwest China have led P'ei Wen-chung and Woo Ju-k'ang to cast further doubts on it, although *Gigantopithecus* is still sometimes regarded as the anthropoid ape morphologically closest to the hominids of any yet discovered.[9]

LOWER PALAEOLITHIC CULTURE OF CHOU-K'OU-TIEN

The Chinese Palaeolithic can be broken down into lower, middle, and upper stages. The Lower Palaeolithic—the longest in time, spanning the entire Middle Pleistocene and at least the earlier third of the Upper—was a stage of crude beginnings of a stone industry characterized by painfully slow development of generalized, all-purpose implements. It is represented in China by three major archaeological sites: Chou-k'ou-tien, Lan-t'ien, and K'o-ho, all in North China in or near the Yellow River valley. Human pithecanthropoid fossils have been found at the first two sites.

Chou-k'ou-tien site, the first found of the three and still the best known, is near a small village 42 kilometers southwest of Peking at the foot of the West Hills (Fig. 6). The limestone caves and fissures west of Chou-k'ou-tien have been known archaeologically since 1918, and no fewer than twenty-two fossiliferous localities have been identified. At four of these, localities 1, 4, 13, and 15, Palaeolithic implements were excavated from 1921 to 1937 and again from 1959 to

7. Koenigswald, *Gigantopithecus blacki von Koenigswald, A Giant Fossil Hominoid from the Pleistocene of Southern China,* Anthropological Papers, American Museum of Natural History, *43* (1952), 301–9.

8. Franz Weidenreich, *Giant Early Man from Java and South China,* Anthropological Papers, American Museum of Natural History, *40* (1945), Pt. I; *Apes, Giants, and Man,* Univ. Chicago Press, 1946.

9. P'ei Wen-chung, *VP, 1* (1957), 2, 65–70; *Amer. Anthropologist, 59* (1957), 834–38. P'ei Wen-chung and Woo Ju-k'ang, *Acta Palaeontol. Sinica, 4* (1956), 477–89. P'ei Wen-chung and Li Yu-heng, *VP, 2* (1958), 193–97. Woo Ju-k'ang, *Chü-yüan hsia-eh-ku ho ya-ch'ih hua-shih,* Peking, Science Press, 1962. P. C. Tung, *VP, 6* (1962), 375–83.

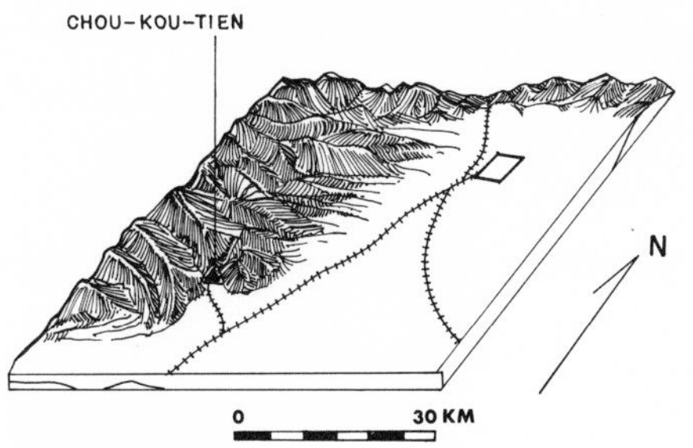

6. The caves of Chou-k'ou-tien in relation to the city of Peking and the West Hills. (After J. G. Andersson, *BMFEA, 15,* 1943, p. 21.)

date.[10] Locality 1, the Ko-tzu-t'ang Cave (Chamber of the Pigeons), is the most important, for from it have come not only the largest number and the longest series of stone artifacts but also a large number of human fossils.

The cave opened to the northeast at the time of its occupation and was about 175 meters long and 50 wide, filled with occupational debris and éboulis more than 40 meters deep, accumulated during a very long time (Fig. 7). Altogether thirteen natural strata are distinguished, numbered 1 to 13 from top to bottom. Three cycles of deposition are manifest: *Basal Gravel,* consisting of strata 11–13, a zone of red clay in which are embedded sands and gravels; *Lower and Middle Breccia,* strata 8–10, containing the fossil remains of *Hyaena sinensis;* and *Upper Breccia,* strata 1–7, with remains of *H. ultima.* There have been lengthy discussions about the respective ages of the three depositional cycles of Locality 1,[11] but a recent palynological profile taken from the sediments in the cave from 9.3 to 40 m, cutting through all

7. Ko-tzu-t'ang Cave, Locality 1 of Chou-k'ou-tien. (From J. G. Andersson, *BMFEA, 15,* 1943, p. 21.)

10. For a bibliography of the Chou-k'ou-tien excavations se K. C. Chang, *Arctic Anthropol., 1* (1963), 2, 31.

11. D. Black et al., *Fossil Man in China,* Peiping, 1933. H. L. Movius, Jr., *Trans. Amer. Phil. Soc., 38* (1948). L. P. Chia, *VP, 3* (1959), 41–45. T. K. Chao and Y. H. Li, *VP, 5* (1961), 374–78. H. D. Kahlke and P. H. Chou, *VP, 5* (1961), 212–40.

three divisions, is most revealing. Three pollen zones are distinguished, corresponding to the three depositional cycles:[12]

> The first stage (I), ranging from 40 m to 36 m, is represented by the basal gravel . . . The pollen of herbs is far above that of woody plants in number, . . . It is represented only by Chenopodiaceae, *Artemisia,* and other members of Compositae. Spores of *Selaginella* and Bryophyta are abundant. The presence of spores of *Botrychium lunaria* is rather significant. At present . . . in North China [it] grows only in high altitudes above 2,500 m, often associated with lichens, mosses, and grasses. So the climate then must have been much cooler than that of the present.
>
> The second stage (II), ranging from 36 m to 20.5 m, is mainly represented by the second cycle of deposition. The relative dominance of NAP [nonarboreal pollen] is rather characteristic. . . . At the beginning of this stage, trees of cold temperate zone like *Abies* and *Betula* existed. Afterward there was a rapid immigration of warm temperate elements, such as *Pinus, Quercus, Alnus, Salix, Celtis, Pistacea, Ulmus,* and *Fraxinus,* indicating that at that time a mixed forest [was] flourishing in the hills. At the end of this stage, there was a gradual decrease in the number of pollen grains of *Betula,* as well as that of the shrubs and the herbs, and a sudden appearance of the thermophile *Symplocos.* This indicates a tendency of rise in temperature.
>
> The third stage (III), ranging from 20.5 m to 9.3 m, is represented by the third cycle of deposition. It is characterized by the presence of some warmer temperate elements such as *Carpinus, Carylus, Ostrya.* At the same time *Symplocos* still existed. At present, *Symplocos* generally lives in regions almost 5 degrees south of Peking. . . . This indicates that at the beginning of this stage the climate would be warmer than that of the present, and probably represents the "climatic optimum" of the *Sinanthropus* [Peking Man] period. . . . At the latter part of this stage, *Betula* reached its maximum. That was the time of declining warmth.

From another sample, probably collected at less depth than 9.3 m, was obtained a palynological spectrum that led B. Kurtén[13] to con-

12. J. Hsü, *Scientia Sinica, 15* (1966), 412.
13. *VP, 3* (1959), 173–75.

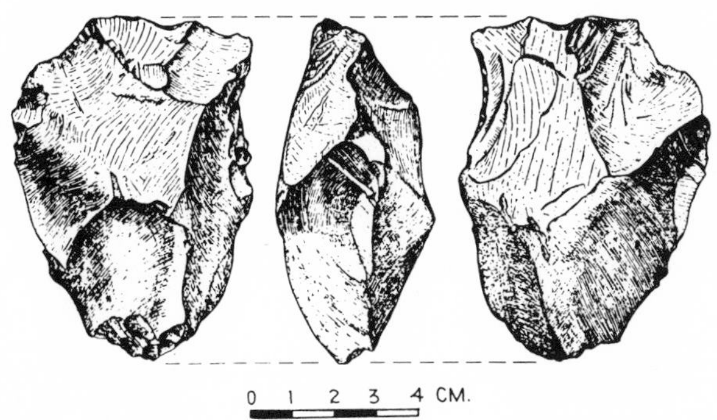

8. Chopping tool from Locality 13, Chou-k'ou-tien. (From H. L. Movius, Jr., *Trans. Amer. Phil. Soc.,* n.s. *38,* 1949, p. 391.)

clude that at the time of the sample the climate of Chou-k'ou-tien was cooler than that of today. Thus, the entire Choukoutien sedimentation cycle began and ended in climatic phases colder than now, through a middle phase warmer than the present. This is in complete accord with the geological placement in Chapter 1 of the Choukoutien sedimentation within the period represented by Taku Glacial, Taku–Lushan Interglacial, and Lushan Glacial. In other words, the Basal Gravel was probably deposited toward the end of the Taku Glacial; the Lower and Middle Breccia during the Taku–Lushan Interglacial; and the upper part of the Upper Breccia probably was laid down in the beginning of the Lushan Glacial. Locality 13[14] of Chou-k'ou-tien can be synchronized with the Basal Gravel of Locality 1 on zoological grounds, and localities 4[15] and 15[16] with the latest Upper Breccia or later. The bulk of Palaeolithic stone materials was excavated from the Breccia strata of Locality 1 and from Locality 15, thus dating from the Taku–Lushan Interglacial and the Lushan Glacial, and the entire collection of human fossils from the Breccia zones of Locality 1. One piece of stone implement was known from Locality 13 (Fig. 8),[17] and two pieces of stone of debatable artificiality were collected from the Basal Gravel strata of Locality 1.[18] Thus, early man at

14. W. C. P'ei, *GSoC Bull., 13* (1934), 359–67.
15. Ibid., *19* (1939), 207–34.
16. Ibid., *19* (1939), 147–87.
17. See n. 14.
18. L. P. Chia, *VP, 3* (1959), 41–45. T. K. Chao and Y. H. Li, *VP, 5* (1961), 374–78; but see S. S. Chang, *VP, 6* (1962), 278–79.

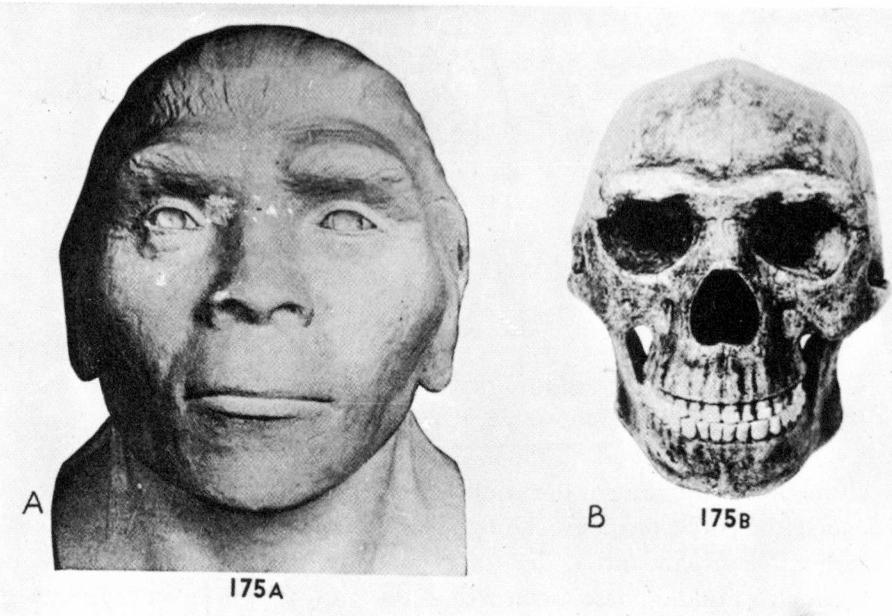

9. Reconstruction of the head of a *Pithecanthropus pekinensis* woman, and the skull on which the reconstruction was based. (From Franz Weidenreich, *PS,* n.s. D, no. 10, 1943, Pl. XLVIII.)

Chou-k'ou-tien began his occupation toward the end of the Taku Glacial, reached his maximal development during the Taku–Lushan Interglacial, and persisted into the Lushan Glacial.

Human fossils found at Locality 1 consist of bone fragments—including fourteen skulls, over a hundred teeth, and isolated postcranial bones—that belonged to over forty individuals.[19] Commonly known as Peking Man, they have been variously latinized as *Sinanthropus pekinensis, Pithecanthropus pekinensis,* and *Homo erectus pekinensis.* Whatever the appellation, they were possessed of hominid features: erect posture, considerable cranial capacity (average 1,075 cc), and the capability of making and using tools and implements (Fig. 9). On the other hand, other physical features distinguish them from *Homo sapiens:* the low skull vault, the great thickness of the skull wall,

19. D. Black, *PS,* ser. D, *7* (1927), 1–28. F. Weidenreich, ibid., *12* (1936), 4; ibid., *7* (1936), 3; ibid., n.s. D, *1* (1937); ibid., n.s. D, *10* (1943). J. K. Woo and T. K. Chao, *VP, 3* (1959), 169–72.

the bony crests around the skull's horizontal circumference, the receding chin, and other minute but important characters of dentition and tooth eruption. These place Peking Man in the same league as *Pithecanthropus* of Java, to whom all physical anthropologists agree he is related. From the length of a femur Weidenreich speculated that the stature of an adult male Peking Man was only about 156 centimeters, and that the female was probably 144 centimeters tall. The life span of the Peking Man population was brief by modern standards: 40 per cent died before the age of 14, and less than 3 per cent achieved the sixth decade of life.[20] Weidenreich believed that many of these people were cut down early in life by injuries.

> For the most part, only the skulls of Sinanthropus seem to have been brought into the caves at Choukoutien and, with the exception of the few fragmentary postcranial parts . . . there are simply no long bones, vertebrae, etc. in the deposits. It appears that these skulls were trophies of head hunters, and, furthermore, that said hunters usually bashed in the bases of the skull when fresh, presumably to eat the brains therein contained. Many crania also show that their owners met their deaths as a result of skull fractures induced by heavy blows.[21]

Apparently some portion of Peking Man's diet consisted of the flesh, brain, and marrow of their own kind. Their principal food, however, was meat of wild animals, 70 per cent being deer with very heavy horns (*Sinomegaceros pachyosteus*), to judge from the bony fossils found in the cave; the rest included leopard, cave bear, sabertoothed tiger, hyena, elephant, rhinoceros, camel, water buffalo, boar, and horse.[22] The many bits of charcoal in the cave, burned bony fragments, and hearths suggest that Peking Man was capable of making fire and cooked his meat.[23] Trees in the hills were cut for fuel, and timber was used. Some nuts found in the cave, such as those from *Celtis*, probably came from branches and twigs cut for fuel, but Pe-

20. F. Weidenreich, *Chinese Med. Jour., 55* (1939).
21. E. A. Hooton, *Up from the Ape,* New York, MacMillan, 1949, p. 304.
22. W. C. P'ei, *PS,* ser. C, *8* (1934), fasc. 1 and 3.
23. D. Black, *GSoC Bull., 11* (1931), 107–08. H. Breuil, *GSoC Bull., 11* (1931), 147–54; *Anthropologie, 42* (1932), 1–17; *Anthropos, 27* (1932), 1–10.

king Man quite likely also collected wild fruits and nuts to supplement his diet.[24] Primarily, however, he was a hunter of game, large and small, presumably using a variety of implements ranging from wooden throwing spears to traps and snares.

Other than pieces of bone that bear possible signs of incisions for use,[25] the artifacts of Peking Man consisted mainly of some hundred thousand stone implements, which provide the essential body of data for any study of their culture.[26] According to a recent analysis of 5,897 specimens by Chang Shen-shui,[27] of the Institute of Vertebrate Palaeontology and Palaeoanthropology (IVPP), the Peking Man stone industry has the following characteristics (Fig. 10):

1. The stone implements were mainly made of flakes.
2. They were made principally by means of unilateral percussion and retouched by the hammer technique. The principal raw material was vein quartz.
3. Many flakes were unretouched but had signs of use.
4. The implements and flakes do not have conventional forms.
5. There is great flexibility of technique and variation in the levels of skill throughout the layers of deposition.
6. The retouched edges are in most cases curved, showing marked scars left by retouching blows, indicating a very primitive level of stone technology.
7. Types of artifacts are not sharply demarcated. The principal categories are scrapers, choppers, points, and awls; there are some end scrapers, engravers, balls, hammers, and chipped pebbles. Many artifacts, however, can be classified in more than one category, and there are many multiple-purpose implements.

The conclusion of S. S. Chang is that such a stone industry is characteristic of the Lower Palaeolithic level and is more like the

24. R. W. Chaney, *Carnegie Inst. Wash. Bull.*, n.s. *3* (1935), 25, 199–202; *GSoC Bull.*, *14* (1935), 99–113. Chaney and Daugherty, *GSoC Bull.*, *12* (1933), 323–28.

25. H. Breuil, *GSoC Bull.*, *11* (1931), 147–54; *Anthropologie*, *42* (1932), 1–17; *PS*, ser. D, no. 6 (1939), 7–41. W. C. P'ei, *GSoC Bull.*, *12* (1932), 105–08; *KKHP* (1960/2), 1–9. L. P. Chia, *KKHP* (1959/3), 1–4.

26. W. C. P'ei, *GSoC Bull.*, *11* (1931), 109–39. Teilhard de Chardin and W. C. P'ei, *GSoC Bull.*, *11* (1932), 315–58. D. Black, et al., *Fossil Man in China*, 1933. H. L. Movius, Jr., *Early Man and Pleistocene Stratigraphy in Southern and Eastern Asia*, Papers of the Peabody Museum, Harvard University, *19* (1944); *Trans. Amer. Phil. Soc.*, *38* (1948).

27. *VP*, *6* (1962), 271–79.

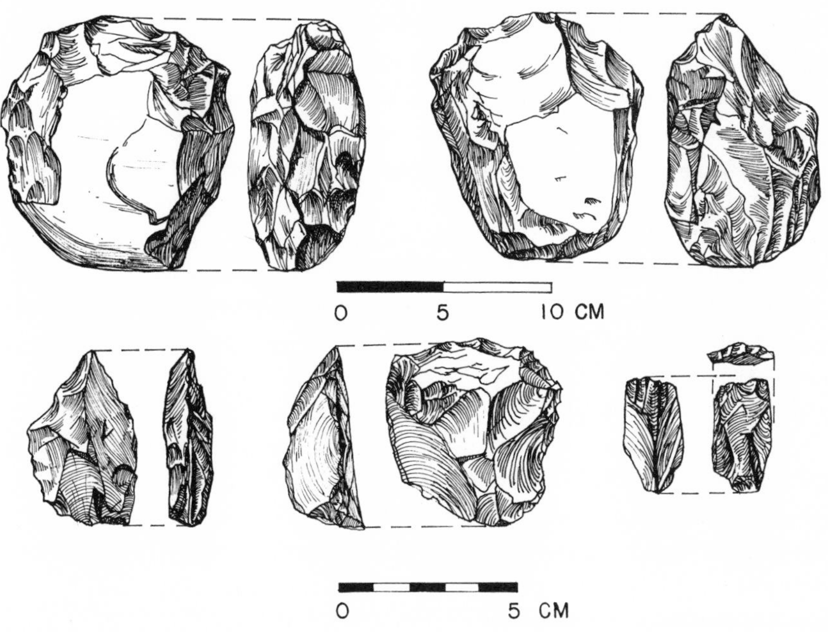

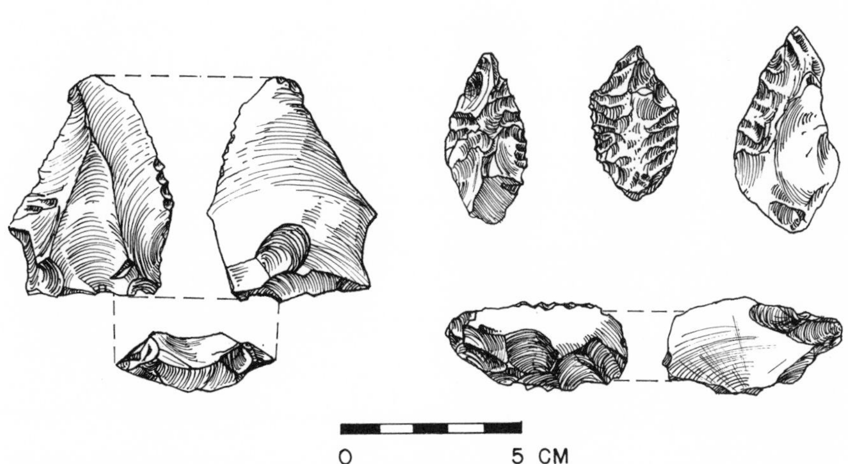

10. Lower Palaeolithic implements from Chou-k'ou-tien, Locality 1 (*upper group*) and Locality 15 (*lower group*). (After H. L. Movius, Jr., *Trans. Amer. Phil. Soc.*, n.s. *38*, 1949, Figs. 35, 37–39.)

Lower Palaeolithic assemblages of southern and eastern Asia than those of Europe and Africa. As early as 1944 Movius[28] pointed out that Lower Palaeolithic industries of southern and eastern Asia, i.e. the Soan of western Pakistan, the Anyathian of Upper Burma, the Patjitanian of Java, and the Choukoutienian of Peking, formed a so-called chopper–chopping tool complex and that, in contrast to the European and African Abbevillian and Acheulian industries with hand-axes and flakes struck from preworked cores with prepared striking platforms, the Asian industries were distinguished by implements struck from pebbles with only a few scars and generally simple forms. There is little question that the contrast between the east and the west existed as early as the Lower Palaeolithic, although whether or not this east and west were ancestral to what we now know as the East and West is a question unanswerable at present. On the basis of twelve morphological features of Peking Man—primarily the shovel-shaped incisors, the sagittal crest, and the mandibular torus—Weidenreich believed that some of the genes of Peking Man were transmitted into the modern Mongoloid populations who inhabit the same area of the world,[29] but this view is far from being generally accepted.[30]

LOWER PALAEOLITHIC CULTURES AT LAN-T'IEN, K'O-HO, AND OTHER SITES

The Peking Man fossils—bony remains of a small population including five nearly complete crania, excavated under close scientific supervision from well-documented depositional contexts in association with a Middle Pleistocene fauna and a Lower Palaeolithic stone industry—were China's contribution to world scholarship, palaeoanthropology's greatest catch. Safely buried underground, untouched by the great physical upheavals of the subsequent half million years,[31] these fossils were lost barely a decade and a half after their discovery. Although Peiping fell to Japanese invaders in 1937, scientists at the Cenozoic Laboratory of the Geological Survey of China were able to

28. Movius, *Early Man.*

29. F. Weidenreich, *PS,* n.s. D, *10* (1943), 253–54.

30. E.g. Woo Ju-k'ang and N. N. Cheboksarov, *Sovietskaia Etnografiia* (1959/4), 3–24.

31. V. V. Cherdyntsev, *Voprocy Geologii Antropogena,* Moscow, Isd. AN. USSR, 1961, gives a uranium–thorium date of 210,000–500,000+ for Peking Man.

continue study at Chou-k'ou-tien until 1939. Then, in 1941, decision was reached between the Chungking and American authorities to transport these fossils to the United States for safekeeping, and they were crated and moved to a warehouse in Ch'in-huang-tao, a small port city northeast of Peking, into the custody of the U.S. Marines. Just at this time Pearl Harbor was attacked. In the resultant confusion the fossils disappeared either from the warehouse or together with a sunken ship and have never been heard of since. A few teeth, a mandible, and a few long bones of Peking Man have been found since 1950 at Locality 1, but these are small recompense for the immeasurable loss.

The discovery of Lower Palaeolithic human remains in China has fortunately only just begun. In 1963, scientists of the Cenozoic Laboratory of the IVPP, Academia Sinica (Peking), discovered a pithecanthropoid mandible near the village of Ch'en-chia-wo, some 10 kilometers northwest of Lan-t'ien, in eastern-central Shensi, almost 1,000 kilometers southwest of Chou-k'ou-tien.[32] In 1964 a human skull of the same age was found at Kung-wang-ling, in the northern foothills of the Tsinling Mountains, more than 10 kilometers east of Lan-t'ien.[33] Both the mandible and the skull were probably from females. Their morphological features indicate close affinity with Peking Man, but they exhibit characteristics more "primitive" than their Peking counterparts—e.g. a more pronounced supraorbital torus, a thicker skull wall, a smaller cranial capacity (ca. 780 cc, as against australopithecine's 435–700 cc, Java Man's 775–900 cc, Peking Man's 850–1,300 cc, and modern man's 1,350 cc), and several other significant attributes (Fig. 11). Woo believes that Lan-t'ien Man was more primitive than either Peking Man or Java's *Pithecanthropus erectus,* and most comparable with Java's *Pithecanthropus robustus.* It may be interesting to note that the Lan-t'ien mandible lacked the third molar, the first known occurrence of agenesis in fossil man specimens. According to Garn,[34] the highest occurrence of agenesis in modern populations is among some American Indians, the Eskimos, and many Asians.

32. J. K. Woo, *VP, 8* (1964), 1–12.
33. Ibid., *10* (1966), 1–16.
34. S. M. Garn, *Human Races,* rev. 2d printing, Springfield, Ill., Thomas, 1962, p. 29.

11. The Lan-t'ien skull, frontal view. (From *VP, 10,* 1966, no. 1.)

Geologically the Lan-t'ien fossils occurred in strata broadly comparable with the Choukoutien sedimentation. Both the mandible and the skull were found in sediments on the banks of the River Pa, a tributary flowing out of the Tsinling Mountains into the Weishui near Sian (Fig. 12). At Ch'en-chia-wo the mandible occurred in a reddish clay stratum, separated by a line of disconformity from Lower Pleistocene deposits, in association with fossil remains of *Cuon alpinus, Felis tigris,* elephant, *Pseudaxis grayi, Sus* cf. *lydekkeri,* and *Mospalax fontanieri,* elements that recall the Choukoutien fauna.[35] Palynological data from these sediments indicate prevalence of grassy species and broadleaf trees of an interpluvial environment.[36] The Kung-wang-ling skull was found from Lishih Loess deposits, again above a line of disconformity that separates it from Lower Pleistocene deposits below, in association with a mixed Choukoutien–Wan Hsien fauna, including *Ursus thibetanus kokeni, Hyaena sinensis, Equus sanmeniensis, Ailuropoda melanoleuca* cf. *fovealis, Cynailurus pleistocaenicus, Nestoritherium* cf. *sinensis, Leptobos, Macacus, Megantereon, Stegodon, Tapirus,* and *Sinomegaceros.*[37] The occurrence of many South China faunal species here north of the Tsinling must in-

35. *Shensi Lan-t'ien Hsin-sheng-chieh,* ed. by IVPP, Academia Sinica (Peking), 1966, p. 17.
36. Ibid., p. 172.
37. Ibid., pp. 17, 287.

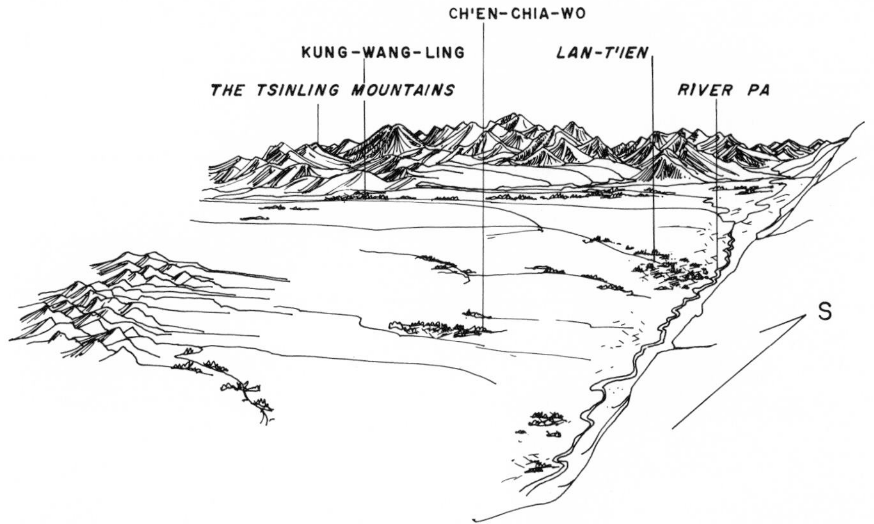

12. The Lan-t'ien Palaeolithic sites. (After *Shensi Lan-t'ien Hsin-sheng-chieh,* Peking, Science Press, 1966, p. 122.)

dicate immigration during a warm interval, and both localities were probably datable to the Taku–Lushan Interglacial, contemporaneous with Peking Man of Chou-k'ou-tien, though it is possible that there is minor temporal difference between Lan-t'ien and Chou-k'ou-tien, and between Kung-wang-ling and Ch'en-chia-wo. New excavations at Kung-wang-ling in 1965 produced mammalian fossils that suggest greater similarity with Locality 13 than Locality 1 of Chou-k'ou-tien.[38]

Habitation sites of Lan-t'ien Man have yet to be located. Fewer than twenty quartz and quartzite artifacts have been collected from the Lan-t'ien area from geological strata correlatable with the horizon of human fossils; these include cores, flakes, choppers, and chopping tools (Fig. 13). Some of the choppers and chopping tools are relatively large and roughly prismatic in cross section, and are described as "heavy pointed implements."[39] A small blade with a horizontal truncation appears to be much more advanced than the rest of the Lan-t'ien finds and than the Choukoutienian, but it was found con-

38. H. C. Wu et al., *VP, 10* (1966), 23–29.

39. E. C. Tai and H. H. Chi, *VP, 8* (1964), 155. E. C. Tai, *VP, 10* (1966), 30–32; *Shensi Lan-t'ien Hsin-sheng-chieh,* 151–52.

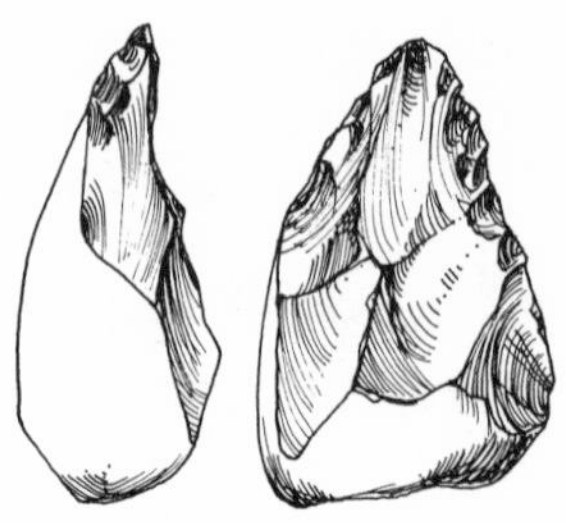

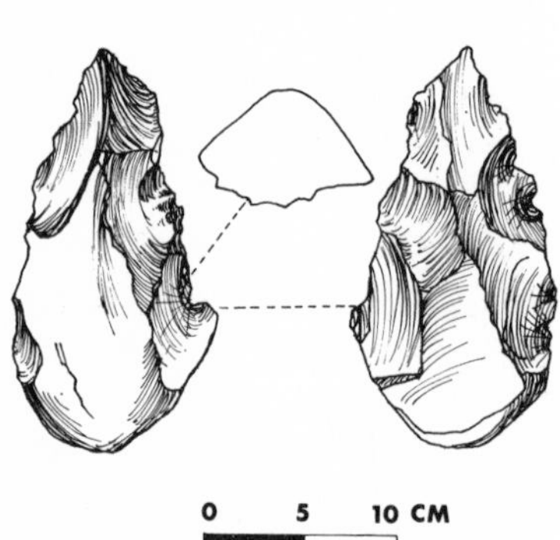

13. Two chopping tools from Middle Pleistocene deposits in the Lan-t'ien area. (*Upper,* from *VP, 8,* 1964, p. 155; *lower,* from *VP, 10,* 1966, p. 31.)

siderably above the human fossil horizon and its age is uncertain.[40] The use of quartz and the prevalence of flake and pebble implements recall Choukoutienian characteristics, but the small quantity of Lan-t'ien stone finds prevents a definitive comparison.

Stone assemblages of large numbers of implements of comparable age, however, are known from no fewer than eleven localities near the village of K'o-ho, in Jui-ch'eng Hsien, southwestern Shansi, approximately 150 kilometers east of Lan-t'ien.[41] At all these localities, Palaeolithic implements were excavated in 1960, by scientists from the IVPP, from a layer of slightly consolidated gravels lying below a thick bed of reddish clay and above an erosion surface of a layer of marly clay. The associated fauna were *Coelodonta* sp., *Equus* sp., *Sus* sp., *Sinomegaceros pachyosteus, S. flabellatus, Pseudaxis* sp., *Bubalus* sp., *Bison* sp., *Stegodon zdansky, S.* cf. *orientalis,* and *Palaeoloxodon* cf.

40. E. C. Tai, *VP, 10* (1966), 30.

41. L. P. Chia et al., *K'o-ho: Shansi hsi-nan-pu chiu-shih-ch'i ch'u-ch'i wen-hua yi-chih,* Peking, Science Press, 1962.

namadicus. The fauna more than the stratigraphy places the K'o-ho assemblage within the Middle Pleistocene, but the assemblage was probably deposited earlier than the main phases of Chou-k'ou-tien Locality 1, perhaps broadly contemporaneous with Locality 13.[42]

Except for rare vein quartz pieces, the K'o-ho stone industry was based on quartzite pebbles. Many of them retain the pebble cortex. Cores (53) and 66 flakes were collected from all localities, a few of them exhibiting signs of use and retouch. In addition, there are 19 definitely retouched artifacts, divided into five types: chopping tools and choppers of cores and flakes (7), scrapers (7), a heavy triangular point, a small pointed implement, and stone balls (3). Like the Choukoutienian, the stone-making technique was extremely primitive, characterized by flaking, large scars, and the lack of core preparation. Typologically, both the Choukoutienian and the K'o-ho industry contained principally pebble and flake implements—characteristic of Movius's chopper–chopping tool complex—and both are at a Lower Palaeolithic level of development. The Choukoutienian, however, appears to be slightly more sophisticated technologically: use of a flaking edge rather than the pebble cortex surface for a striking platform and greater refinement in retouching and in type control. On the other hand, the prismatic point implements, found both at Lan-t'ien and K'o-ho, were absent in Peking. It is possible that even for the Lower Palaeolithic there were already in North China regional stone-making traditions, but the recognizable differences among them are minor.

Lower Palaeolithic implements very similar to the K'o-ho industry (including flakes, choppers, chopping tools, heavy prismatic points, and stone balls) were unearthed at the sites of Shui-mo-kou and Hui-hsing-kou, in San-men-hsia, northwestern Honan, from geological strata identical with the K'o-ho beds, reinforcing the impression of a Huangho Big Bend center of Lower Palaeolithic cultures broadly similar to but specifically distinguishable from the Choukoutienian.[43]

Besides the above four regions of Lower Palaeolithic occurrence, evidence of human occupation during the same Reddish Clay period

42. For chronological controversies of the K'o-ho site, see ibid.; C. L. Ch'iu, *VP, 6* (1962), 291–94; L. P. Chia, *VP, 6* (1962), 295–98.
43. W. W. Huang, *VP, 8* (1964), 162–77.

is also known from Szechwan[44] and Kwangsi[45] of South China, but there are no excavated assemblages. The tooth that Koenigswald found in a Hong Kong drugstore in the late 1930s, from a hominid which he has termed *Sinanthropus officinalis,* he believes to have come originally from a reddish clay stratum somewhere in South China.[46]

MIDDLE PALAEOLITHIC

The Lower Palaeolithic human and cultural beginnings spanned in time the entire Choukoutien sedimentation cycle that climatically encompassed the Taku Glacial, the Taku–Lushan Interglacial, and the Lushan Glacial intervals. The Choukoutienian sequence, which was almost as long as the entire period in question, shows quite clearly that cultural development was slow and relatively unaccented from beginning to end. The human fossils found in association with Lower Palaeolithic industries were invariably pithecanthropoid in type.

In the remaining geological stages of the Pleistocene, the pace of human and cultural development was very much quickened. The last Glacial–Tali stage witnessed the emergence in China of *Homo sapiens* and blade industries throughout the country, and the change began to be appreciable during the Lushan–Tali Interglacial interval. In this sense, the Palaeolithic cultures during this transitional interval—the Chingshui Erosion—were Middle Palaeolithic. Human fossils attributable to this stage are generally described as neanderthaloid.

From deposits of Chingshui Erosion stage, Palaeolithic implements have been discovered in the Ordos area (from the so-called Basal Gravels strata at the base of the Malan Loess) and in the Fenho Valley in Shansi.[47] Three human teeth also came to light in 1954 at Locality

44. D. A. Hooijer, *Southwestern Jour. Anthropol., 7* (1951), 77–81. D. C. Graham, *Jour. W. China Border Res. Soc., 7* (1935), 47–56. H. de Terra, *Pleistocene Formations and Stone Age Man in China,* Peking, Institut de Géo-Biologie 1941, pp. 36–37.

45. P. Teilhard et al., *GSoC Bull., 14* (1935), 179–205.

46. *Anthropological Papers,* American Museum of Natural History, New York, *43* (1952), 308.

47. Teilhard, *Early Man in China,* Peking, Institut de Géo-Biologie, Publication 7 (1941), p. 68. W. C. P'ei et al., *Shansi Hsiang-fen Hsien Ting-ts'un chiu-shih-ch'i shih-tai yi-chih fa-chüeh pao-kao,* Peking, Science Press, 1958. L. P. Chia et al., *Shansi Chiu-shih-ch'i,* Peking, Science Press, 1961. T. Y. Wang, *VP, 9* (1965), 399–402. M. C. Chou et al., *VP, 9* (1965), 262–63. L. P. Chia and T. Y. Wang, *KKTH* (1957/5), 12–18.

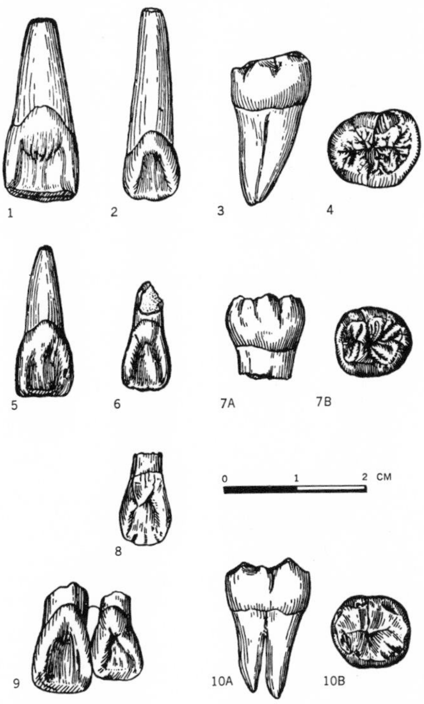

14. Teeth of ancient and modern North China inhabitants, showing the persistent occurrence of shovel-shaped incisors. 1–4: *Pithecanthropus* (1, left upper median incisor; 2, right upper lateral incisor; 3, right lower second molar; 4, left lower second molar). 5–7: Ting-ts'un Man (5, left upper median incisor; 6, left upper lateral incisor; 7A and 7B, right lower second molar). 8: Ordos Man, left upper lateral incisor. 9–10: Modern northern Chinese (9, right upper incisors; 10A and 10B, right lower second molar). (From Kuo Mo-jo et al., *Chung-kuo jen-lei hua-shih ti fa-hsien yü yen-chiu,* Peking, Science Press, 1955, p. 44.)

100 of Ting-ts'un, in Hsiang-fen Hsien, southern Shansi. The teeth, all probably from the same child, are said to exhibit neanderthaloid characteristics but also are similar to the dentition of Peking Man—two of the three are upper incisors which have pronounced shovel-shaped lingual depressions (Fig. 14).

The stone industries from these deposits indicate a considerable advance over those of the Lower Palaeolithic. While the predominant

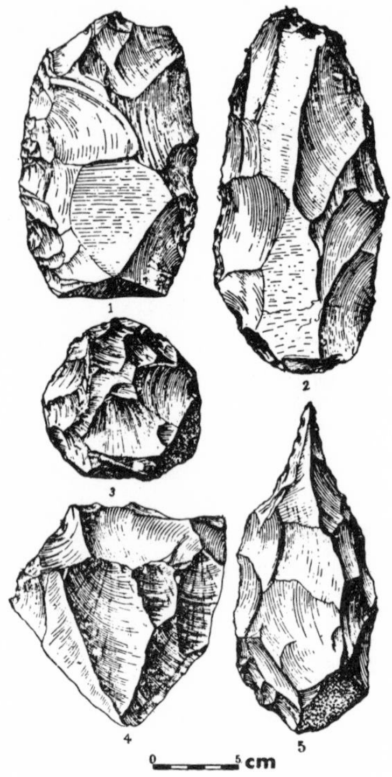

15. Ting-ts'un Palaeolithic implements. (From *Hsin Chung-kuo ti K'ao-ku Shou-huo,* Peking, Wenwu Press, 1962, p. 5.)

technological traditions continue to be characterized by flakes and choppers and chopping tools, the skills of stone-making (in particular in Ting-ts'un with hornfels, a difficult rock to work) were markedly more refined, and the various types of implements included heavy triangular points, polygonal scrapers, and stone balls, as well as points, scrapers, choppers and chopping tools (Fig. 15). Bifacially flaked core implements increased in number, the striking platforms and the core surfaces were quite often prepared before striking, and, most important, there were some finely made parallel-sided flakes which were probably the forerunners of the blades of the next geological stage. The heavy prismatic points and the stone balls in the Ting-ts'un assemblages are particularly noteworthy; apparently they carry on the same typological tradition of the Big Bend Lower Palaeolithic cultures.

Beside Ordos and the Fenho Valley, middle Palaeolithic industries are not significantly known from geologically established strata elsewhere in China, but human fossils described as neanderthaloid have been found in limestone cave deposits in China. These include a left maxilla and a premolar from Ch'ang-yang, in Hupei, Central China,[48] and a skullcap from Ma-pa, in Kwangtung on the southern coast.[49] It is apparent that by the Lushan–Tali Interglacial, early man throughout China had begun to step onto the modern stage. Whether the transitional features of a Middle Palaeolithic were confined to the north or occurred universally, remains to be shown by additional data from South China.

UPPER PALAEOLITHIC CULTURES OF NORTH CHINA

The last geological interval of the Pleistocene, during which the Tali Glacial occurred on highlands of the southwest and on Taiwan, was the period of culmination of the Chinese Palaeolithic development. In contrast to the slowly developing and relatively homogeneous industries of the Lower Palaeolithic, the Upper Palaeolithic cultures found in the Malan Loess and related deposits of the Tali Glacial stage were characterized by a gradual but sure emergence of regional phases of culture in which finely made blade implements of a variety of well-defined types occurred. The owners and makers of these implements were completely modern in physical characteristics—they were, in fact, *Homo sapiens*. The known sites of this stage form three clusters: loessic and sand–gravel deposits in the Ordos and in limestone caves on the lower Huangho and in the southwest.

"Ordos" is the Mongolian name of the northern grasslands of the middle Huangho where it flows northward, turns east, and returns toward the south; it includes the modern administrative units of eastern Ninghsia, southwestern Inner Mongolia, northern Shensi, and northwestern Shansi. Palaeolithic sites have been uncovered throughout the area, but particularly in the Huangho and the Sjara-osso-gol valleys since the 1920s, and are collectively known as the Ordosian culture. Associated human fossil remains, known as Ordos Man, include an incisor (Fig. 14), a parietal, a piece of facial skeleton, and a femur.[50] Be-

48. L. P. Chia, *VP, 1* (1957), 247–57

49. *WW* (1959/1), 47; *VP, 3* (1959), 104. J. K. Woo and J. T. P'eng, *VP, 3* (1959), 175–82.

50. E. Licent et al., *GSoC Bull., 5* (1926), 285–90. Y. P. Wang, *WWTKTL* (1957/4), 22–25; *VP, 7* (1963). J. K. Woo, *VP, 2* (1958), 208–12.

sides some "primitive" features in the parietal, the morphology of Ordos Man is insufficiently represented for any definitive study, but it must be noted that the shovel-shaped depression again occurs on the incisor.

Much is known, on the other hand, of Ordos stone industries. Although some seven or eight clusters of sites have been investigated and reported,[51] the best-known assemblages are those uncovered at Hsiao-ch'iao-pan in the Sjara-osso-gol Valley in southern Inner Mongolia[52] and at Shui-tung-kou in eastern Ninghsia east of the Huangho.[53] According to the various studies of these assemblages,[54] the main features of the Ordos industries may be summarized as follows (Fig. 16).

1. The two basic technological components of the Lower Palaeolithic, i.e. the use of flakes and pebbles for tool fashioning, remained in the Ordosian.

2. Significant technological advances, however, are observed in the new industry. Choppers and chopping tools are so rare as to be insignificant. More important, flakes were struck from elaborately prepared cores. This is indicated by prepared cores (discoidal, tortoiseshell, and prismatic), the faceted striking platform, and the uniformity of flake shapes.

3. Two kinds of flakes are most common: triangular flakes struck from discoidal and tortoiseshell cores, and parallel-sided flakes (blades) struck from prismatic cores. The significant concurrence of pebble tools, triangular ("Mousterian") flakes, and blades is an Eastern feature similar to the Upper Palaeolithic of Siberia.

4. In the total stone assemblages, artifacts with secondary retouch formed a very small percentage, but several "types" had become definitely established. These include the triangular flakes retouched along one or both long edges—probably scrapers; points of triangular flakes

51. K. C. Chang, *Arctic Anthropology, 1* (1963,) 2, 32–33.

52. Teilhard, *Anthropologie, 33* (1924), 630–31; *Natural History, 26* (1926), 239–42. Teilhard and Licent, *GSoC Bull., 3* (1924), 46–48. Licent and Teilhard, *Anthropologie, 35* (1925), 220–28. M. Boule et al., *Le Paléolithique de la Chine,* Paris, Institut de Paléontologie Humaine, Mém. *4* (1928).

53. Teilhard and Licent, *GSoC Bull., 3* (1924), 45–46. Licent and Teilhard, *Anthropologie, 35* (1925), 206–19. Teilhard, *Natural History, 26* (1926), 239. Y. P. Wang, *KK* (1962/11), 588–89. L. P. Chia et al., *VP, 8* (1964), 75–83.

54. Including the author's own study in 1959 of the Sjara-osso-gol and Shui-tung-kou collections at the Institut de Paléontologie Humaine at Paris, whose courtesy is gratefully acknowledged.

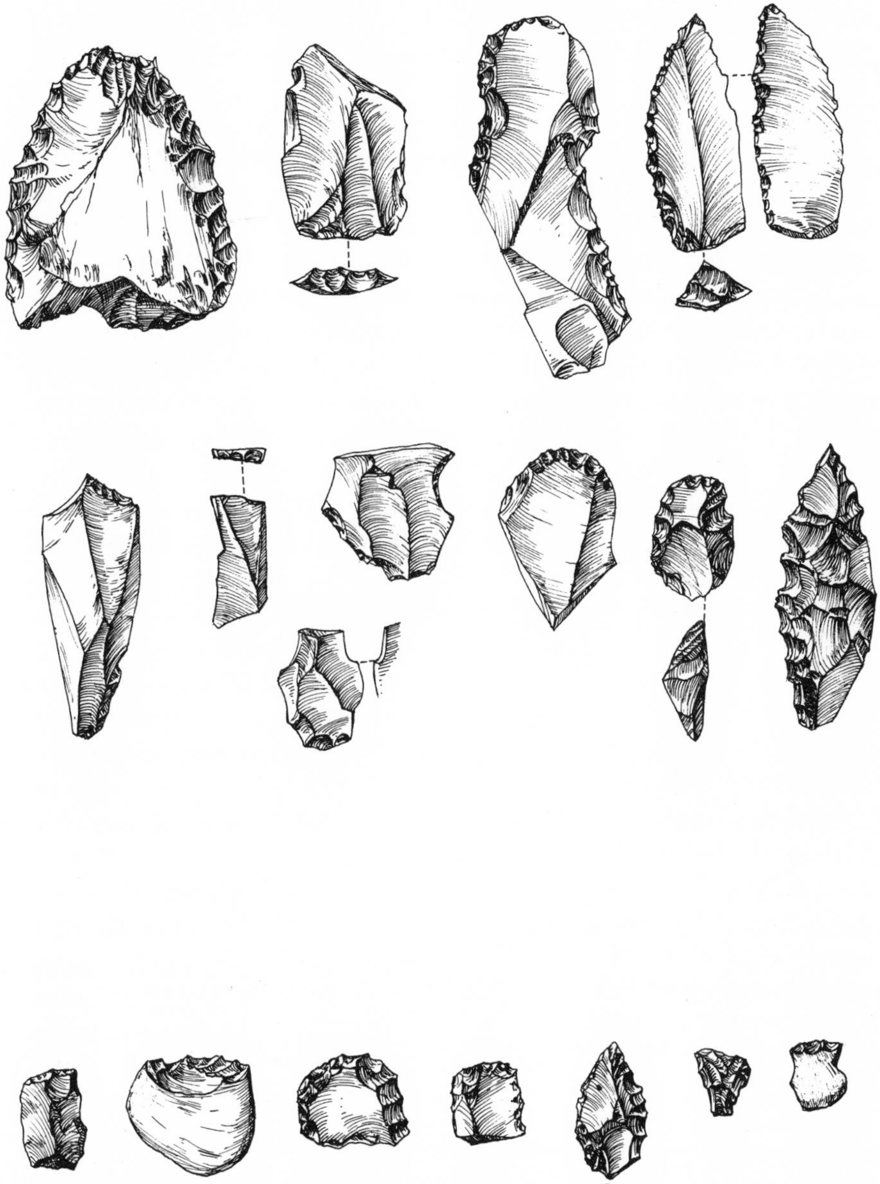

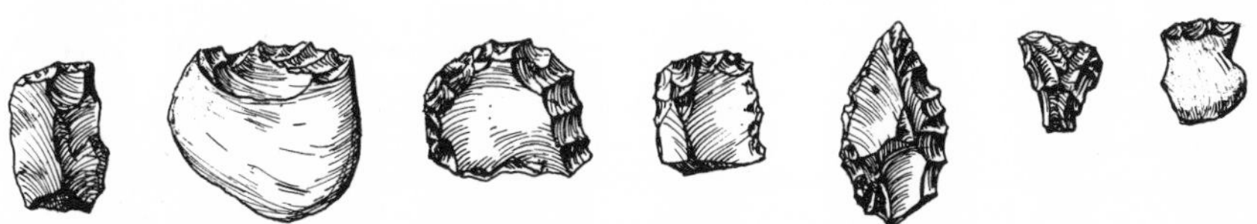

16. Upper Palaeolithic implements from the sites at Shui-tung-kou (*upper group*) and Sjara-osso-gol (*lower group*). (From M. Boule et al., *Le Paléolithique de la Chine,* Paris, 1928, Figs. 30–48 passim.)

retouched along both edges near the point; secondarily retouched blades; scrapers on ends of blades; and burins on ends of blades (of several varieties).

On the whole the blade artifacts of the Ordosian are identical with many Périgordian and Aurignacian types of Western Europe, but the rarity here of backed blades is conspicuous. Its comparative significance aside, the Ordosian stone industry exhibits a clear tendency to specialize: artifact types were no longer generalized, all-purpose implements, but each served a limited number of purposes. More specialized implements were obviously more effective, but each set of such tools must have had a more restricted range of uses and were adapted to certain kinds of environments and ecological situations. With these points in mind we cannot fail to recognize the potential significance of a very detailed study of the geological period in question—its regional facies and minute chronological divisions—and, in the meantime, the absence of such study in the current stage of our discipline in China. In comparing the Sjara-osso-gol and the Shui-tung-kou assemblages, W. C. P'ei and Y. H. Li have lately observed,[55]

> The Quaternary deposits in Sjara-osso-gol and Shui-tung-kou were formed at the same time in the same basin under identical conditions, and can be regarded as of the same geological stratum. Certain differences, however, existed between the two sites in animal fossils and stone artifacts, indicating that their geographic environments differed during the late Pleistocene stage. Specifically, a larger number of mammals lived in the Sjara-osso-gol region, which indicates that the area was more moist and more thickly vegetated, providing a larger number of game animals for man. But rock materials for stone manufacture were scarce here, and its inhabitants had to manufacture small stone tools. Living mammals, on the other hand, were fewer in the Shui-tung-kou region, which means the area was more arid and barren, and man's living resources were scanty. Rock materials here were more abundant, and a larger number of stone tools was produced.

P'ei and Li's inference here appears to be reasonable, but it may have given the human and cultural factors too passive a role. The differ-

55. *VP, 8* (1964), 114.

ences between the Shui-tung-kou and Sjara-osso-gol assemblages may very well be the result of active adaptation. Microlithic implements became highly popular during early postglacial times when the land was covered with heavy vegetation and game was abundant—favorable conditions for the development of composite implements made of bone shafts and microlithic blades. Quite possibly a microlithic complex was already coming into being as early as the final Pleistocene stage in relatively moist and vegetated areas like the Sjara-osso-gol. A cultural tendency to regionally different stone assemblages seems to be well on the way within the Ordosian itself.

Broadly contemporaneous with the Ordosian is yet another regional development in North China of the Upper Palaeolithic cultures in the lower Huangho Valley below the Big Bend. In a limestone cave in the hill region of Hsiao-nan-hai, 30 kilometers southwest of An-yang in northern Honan, ancient habitation remains were brought to light in 1960 in association with a typical Sjara-osso-gol fauna.[56] More than seven thousand pieces of stone were excavated, about 90 per cent chert, but only about a hundred were secondarily retouched artifacts. Again there is a combination of implements of pebble, flake, and blade, similar to the Ordosian, but a microlithic tendency is even more pronounced than at Sjara-osso-gol. A few types—especially a variety of heavy scrapers on sides of flakes—are distinctive here, but burins are poorly developed (Fig. 17). To emphasize its distinctiveness, An Chih-min proposes that it be called the Hsiao-nan-hai culture. Farther down the Yellow River another limestone cave site was discovered in Shantung in 1965. Heavy scrapers on sides of flakes are again distinctive of the stone assemblage here.[57]

UPPER PALAEOLITHIC CULTURES OF THE SOUTHWEST

Aside from scattered small finds of uncertain age in the upper Yangtze,[58] all Upper Palaeolithic discoveries in this region have been made

56. C. M. An, *KKHP* (1965/1), 1–27.

57. E. C. Tai and Y. C. Pai, *VP, 10* (1966), 82–83. For some reason the cave is referred to only as "a certain cave in Shantung," and no location is given. Since Shantung is a province of considerable size, this is an irresponsible reporting of archaeological finds.

58. Teilhard and C. C. Young, *GSoC Bull., 14* (1935), 176; J. H. Edgar, *Jour. W. China Border Res. Soc., 6* (1933/34), 56–61; *7* (1935), 47–56. G. T. Bowles, *GSoC Bull., 13* (1933), 119–41. Y. H. Li, *VP, 5* (1961), 143–49.

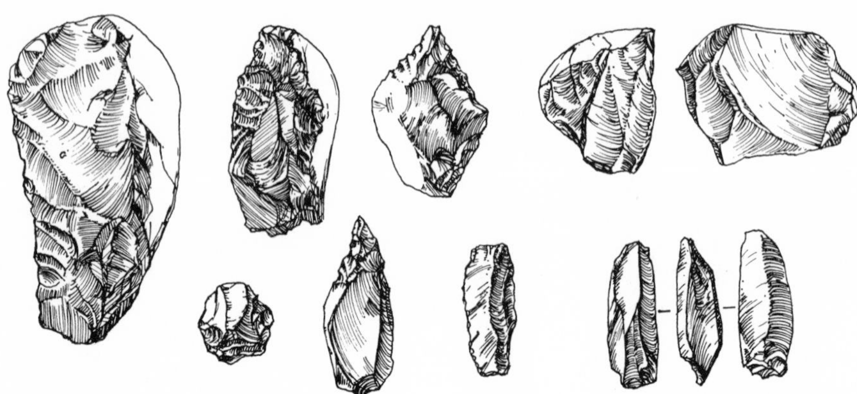

17. Upper Palaeolithic implements from Hsiao-nan-hai Cave near Anyang, Honan. (After *KKHP,* 1965/1, pp. 7, 10, 12, 14, 16.)

in recent years. They include fossil remains of two human skulls found at Tzu-yang in Szechwan[59] and Liu-chiang in Kwangsi[60] and stone assemblages in Ch'ien-hsi Hsien in central Kweichow,[61] Yi-liang Hsien in eastern Yunnan,[62] and Han-yüan Hsien in western Szechwan (formerly eastern Sikang).[63]

The Tzu-yang and Liu-chiang skulls were from deposits that are dated to the Upper Pleistocene by the mammalian faunas found with them. Both undoubtedly belonged to *Homo sapiens* but exhibit certain features which recall both Peking Man and the neanderthaloid types. Moreover, the Liu-chiang skull has some morphological attributes that are comparable with Oceanic Negroid characteristics, and both the Tzu-yang and the Liu-chiang skulls show similarities to features of modern Mongoloid populations. On the basis of the two skulls one might be tempted to suggest that the population in South China during the Tali Glacial stage represents an early form of *Homo sapiens* which later differentiated into some of the principal constituent elements of the modern Mongoloid and Oceanic Negroid populations. In this connection one may recall the persistence of certain morpho-

59. W. C. P'ei and J. K. Woo, *Tzu-yang Jen,* Peking, Science Press, 1957.
60. J. K. Woo, *VP, 3* (1959), 109–10.
61. W. C. P'ei et al., *VP, 9* (1965), 270–79.
62. W. C. P'ei and M. C. Chou, *VP, 5* (1961), 139–42. Y. H. Li and W. W. Huang, *VP, 6* (1962), 182–89.
63. L. Yang, *VP, 9* (1961), 353.

logical features throughout the fossil record of man in this part of Asia and into its modern inhabitants (such as the shovel-shaped incisors, the sagittal crest, and the congenital absence of the third molar). Coon's recent attempt to trace some modern Mongoloid elements back to Peking Man[64] may not have proved that mankind crossed the *Homo sapiens* threshold independently in the area of East Asia, but it has certainly brought serious attention to the need for further research into a highly important problem.

Each of the three Upper Palaeolithic sites in the southwest has its own peculiarities, which is understandable for this stage of cultural specialization and differentiation (Fig. 18). The Ch'ien-hsi finds consist of large and irregular flakes retouched on the edges by series of vertical blows. The Han-yüan assemblage is one of microcores and microblades, closely similar to the Sjara-osso-gol component of the Ordosian. The stone artifacts of Yi-liang, on the other hand, are flakes struck from pebbles (retaining much of the cortex) and retouched by unilateral and bilateral blows in the chopper–chopping tool fashion. These finds are devoid of a general pattern, and their datings are largely uncertain; one can only observe that in southwest China the archaic pebble and flake stone traditions persisted into the Upper Pleistocene and, also, that a blade–microblade industry occurred. It is impossible to say which of these diverse industrial elements was associated with the Tzu-yang and the Liu-chiang skulls.

MESOLITHIC CULTURES OF NORTH CHINA

It was mentioned above that the final Pleistocene cultural traditions in North China can be grouped into two major regional facies: the blade-and-flake tradition of the typical loessic landscape and the microblade tradition of the riverine–lacustrine subcycle. The former may have begun slightly earlier, but the latter grew in importance with time. The climate and landscape of the early postglacial period, as described in Chapter 1, may properly be regarded as an intensification and spatial expansion of the riverine–lacustrine facies to cover the entire area of North China. To a considerable extent, corresponding to this physiographical change, the early postglacial human industries underwent adaptive changes also. In other words, if the Recent period

64. C. S. Coon, *The Origin of Races,* New York, Knopf, 1963.

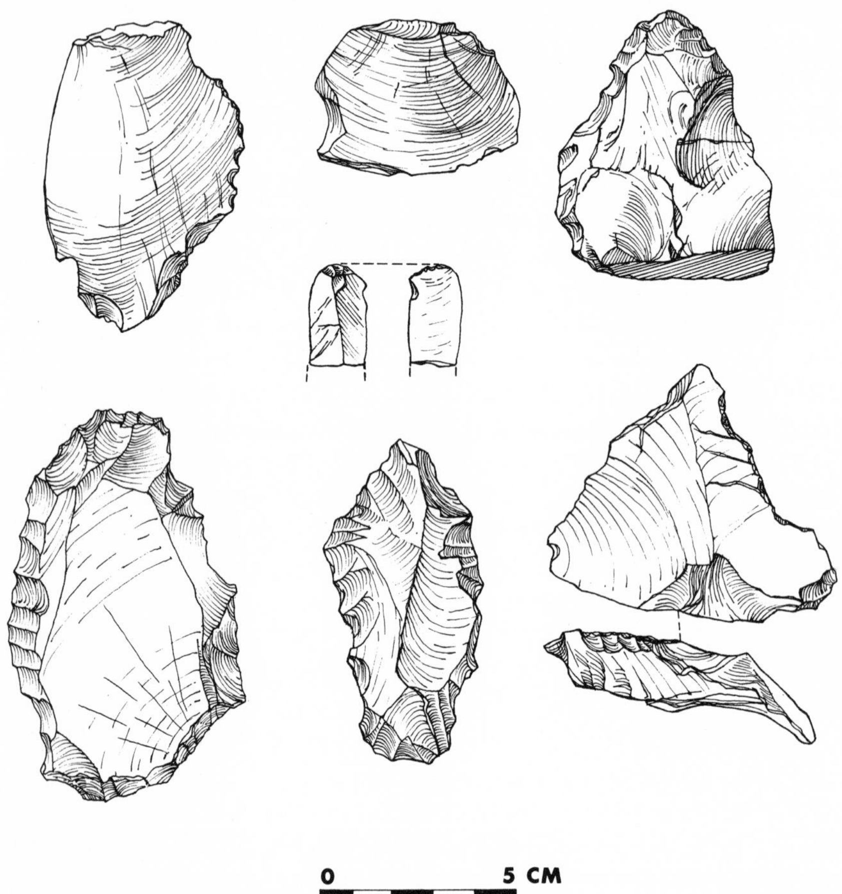

18. Upper Palaeolithic implements from Ch'ien-hsi (Kweichow) and Yi-liang (Yunnan). (*Lower half,* Ch'ien-hsi, from *VP, 9,* 1965, 277–99; *upper half,* Yi-liang, from *VP, 6,* 1962, pp. 184–87.)

brought the riverine–lacustrine landscape to North China and intensified it by a climatic amelioration, then the Recent period also brought the riverine–lacustrine facies of human industries to North China and, so to speak, intensified them as well. In the cultural history of North China we thus find a typological as well as a chronological Mesolithic stage, which is characterized by the predominance of the microblade tradition and the use of composite tools; the use of the pressure-flaking

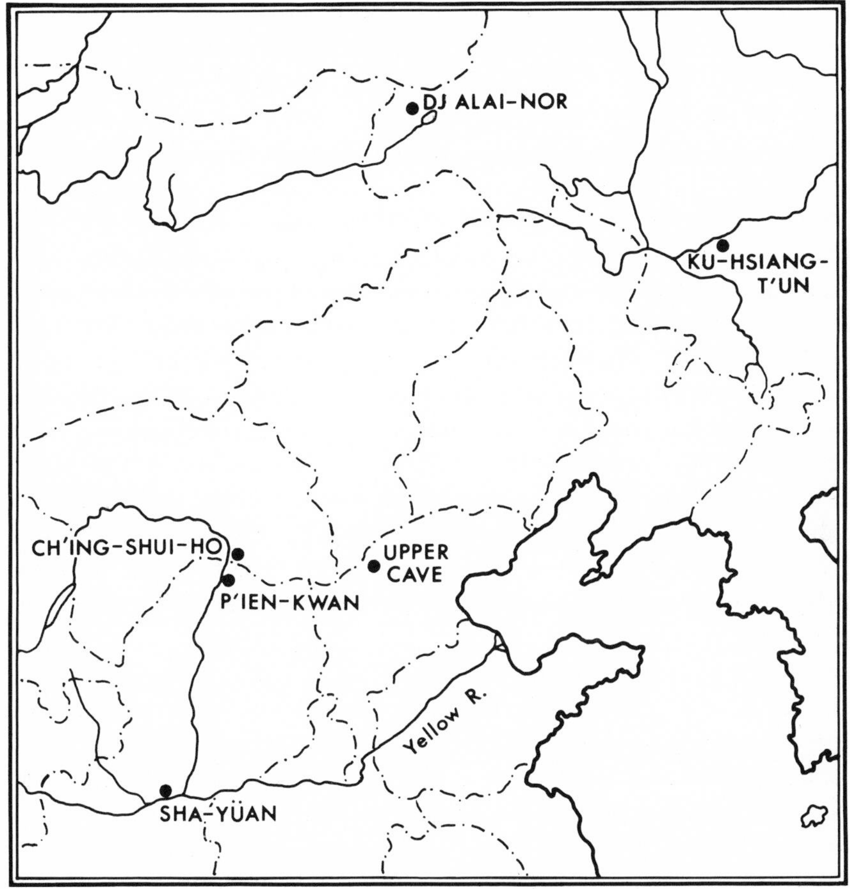

19. Mesolithic sites in North China.

technique; and the growing popularity of projectile points and bone implements. To date, only four (probably) Mesolithic sites have been excavated in North China and Manchuria: Djalai-nor and Ku-hsiang-t'un in Manchuria, the Upper Cave of Chou-k'ou-tien in Hopei, and the Sha-yüan region in Shensi (Fig. 19). In addition, a few isolated aceramic microlithic assemblages have been known in Inner Mongolia. It is significant that these Mesolithic sites have so far been found only on relatively high ground in the north and west, but not on the vast, flat plains in the eastern part of North China—a fact probably accounted for by the physiographical features of North China during that period.

During prehistoric times the Mongolian steppes formed a great oasis belt, and the early Recent inhabitants of this area manufactured microcores, microflakes, and microblades. Apparently they engaged in fishing and hunting near the now-dry shallow depressions which were then partially filled with water. Their main quarry seems to have been the ostrich, as shown by many ostrich-eggshell rings found at these and later cultural stations. From these sites very few arrowheads have been found, however, which indicates that hunting was probably of secondary importance. This inference is also supported by the scarcity of bone and antler remains and implements in the Mongolian sites, although this can partly be accounted for by the perishability of these remains and the unfavorable conditions for preservation.[65] The Mongolian Mesolithic tradition persisted in this region for a considerable time, even when areas to the south had become farmlands and when Neolithic techniques were introduced and gave the Mongolian Mesolithic a sub-Neolithic appearance. This will be discussed in a later chapter.

More is known about the forest dwellers of North China and Manchuria, who were clearly the direct descendants of the Upper Palaeolithic occupants of the area. One of the earliest Mesolithic assemblages in this region was found in the Upper Cave of Chou-k'ou-tien. Its fauna, still yielding remains of such persisting Pleistocene forms as *Hyaena ultima, Ursus spelaeus, Elephas* sp., and *Paradoxurus,* definitely testifies to the introduction of completely modern forms: *Homo sapiens, Cervus elaphus, Siphneus armandi,* and *Struthio,* as well as some southern warm species: *Cynailurus jubatus* and *Paguma.*[66] The site was probably a burial place and gives no indication of intensive occupation. The industrial assemblage includes some stone tools (scrapers, flakes, and chopper-chopping tools), and abundant bone and antler artifacts (worked bone, bone needles, worked antler, perforated teeth of badgers, foxes, deer, wildcats, polecats, and tigers), together with mollusk shells and fishbones (Fig. 20). According to W. C. P'ei,[67]

65. N. C. Nelson, *Amer. Anthropologist, 28* (1926), 307. John Maringer, *Prehistory of Mongolia,* Stockholm, pp. 90, 92, 140–43, 151–54, 201, 206.

66. P'ei Wen-chung, *PS,* ser. D, *10* (1940); P'ei Wen-chung, *VP, 1* (1957), 9–24.

67. *Chung-kuo shih-ch'ien shih-ch'i chih yen-chiu,* Shanghai, Commercial Press, 1948, pp. 72–73.

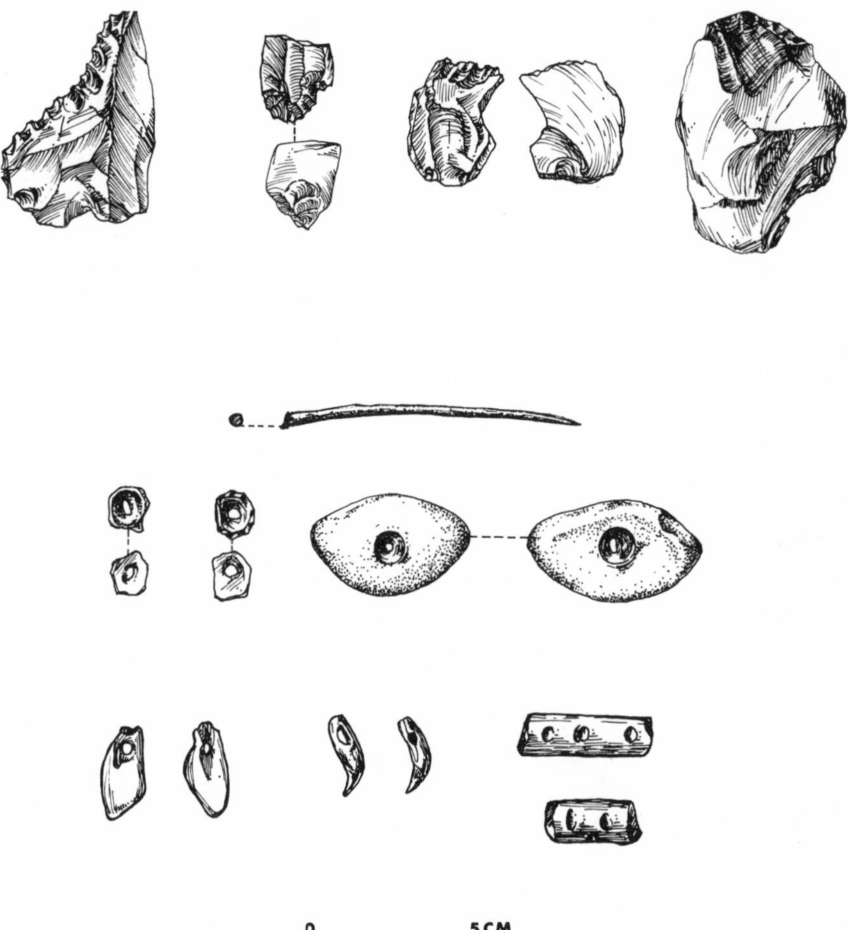

20. Artifacts of the Upper Cave, Chou-k'ou-tien. (After W. C. P'ei, *PS,* ser. D, *9,* 1939.)

The Upper Cave Man lived in calcareous caves. Nearby there were woods in which tigers, leopards, bears, and wolves dwelt; there were steppes on which the Chinese deer, the red deer, and gazelle roamed about; and plains and lakes in which gigantic fish swam. The man hunted in the woods and fished by the lakes, and made abundant bone and shell artifacts.

The marine shells in this site indicate also either extensive trade connections or long-distance seasonal migrations. In the cave were found skeletal remains of man, apparently seven individuals. Since skulls or skull fragments and lower jaws are preserved, Weidenreich has been able to determine that this population was composed of an adult male over sixty, a relatively young male adult, two young adult females, one adolescent, and two children. It is interesting to note that all of the remaining skullcaps show depressions, fractures, or holes which, according to Weidenreich, "apparently have been caused by heavy blows with sharp and blunt implements delivered at a time when the scalp still covered the bones." Weidenreich thus infers that these were the remains of a single family who, being "victims of a sudden attack and dismembered, were thrown into the cave."[68] This suggestion is certainly plausible, but other explanations cannot be ruled out. The earth which surrounded the skeletons was partly covered with hematite, indicating that funeral rites probably took place. The damage to the skulls, as W. C. P'ei has suggested, could have been caused later by rockfalls from the cave ceiling. It is therefore entirely possible that the family, if it was one, fell victim to a local epidemic and was buried in the cave by kinsfolk or companions.

Another intriguing aspect of the Upper Cave skulls concerns their racial characteristics. The morphological analysis of the three best-preserved adult skulls by Weidenreich has convinced him that "they typify three different racial elements, best to be classified as primitive Mongoloid, Melanesoid, and Eskimoid types."[69] This conclusion has led the late Ernest A. Hooton to discuss the Upper Cave population in his *Up From the Ape* under the heading "The Old Man of China who Married an Eskimo and a Melanesian."[70] Recent findings about Upper Palaeolithic man in South China as mentioned above has shed much new light on this problem. If Wu Hsin-chih is right in identifying the Upper Cave specimens as altogether Mongoloid, according to recent studies of casts,[71] it then seems that by the beginning of the Recent period the population in North China and that in the southwest and in Indochina had become sufficiently differentiated to be

68. Franz Weidenreich, *Bull. Natural Hist. Soc. Peiping, 13* (1938/39), 163.
69. Ibid., p. 170.
70. P. 401.
71. Wu Hsin-chih, *VP, 5* (1961), 181–203.

designated as Mongoloid and Oceanic Negroid races respectively, even though both of them may have evolved out of a common Upper Pleistocene substratum as represented by the Tzu-yang and the Liu-chiang skulls.

It is quite possible that Manchuria in the initial postglacial period was covered by woods, and its climate was probably cooler. Here also several surviving Pleistocene faunal forms are found in association with Mesolithic industries. From the Mesolithic sites at Ku-hsiang-t'un (and possibly Ta-kou), near Harbin, stone (scrapers, willow-leaves, microliths), bone (knives, spearheads, and barbed points), and antler implements were found, indicating that the Mesolithic inhabitants of this region lived in woods and hunted game.[72] Farther north, at Djalai-nor, implements of stone, bone, and antler, and willow basketwork have been found in direct association with remains of woolly rhinoceros, bison, and mammoth, indicating a similar ecology and culture.[73]

The Sha-yüan assemblage of Shensi is of uncertain age, but it is believed to date from early postglacial times. Cultural remains from fifteen localities were collected during 1955 and 1956 in the area of Chao-yi Hsien and Ta-li Hsien in the central part of eastern Shensi, an area in the western portion of a sand-dune region (referred to as Sha-yüan by the local inhabitants) of considerable dimensions.[74] Many of the flakes, stone implements, and bone fragments that were collected are badly rolled, and no habitation layers have been recognized, indicating that the original cultural deposits have been destroyed by strong sand-bearing winds blowing through centuries. The frequent movements of the sand dunes may also have disturbed the original distribution. The fifteen localities, therefore, are really nothing more than fifteen spots where cultural remains happen to have been concentrated.

Surface specimens, 519 in all, were singled out as representative by the investigators of the Institute of Archaeology, Academia Sinica.

72. Tokunaga Shigeyasu and Naora Nabus, *JZ, 48* (1933), 12; *Manshuteiko Kitsurinshō Ku-hsiang-t'un kaiikkai hakkutsu butsu kenkyu hobun,* Tokyo, Waseda University, 1934.

73. V. J. Tolmatchov, *Eurasia Septentrionalis Antiqua, 4* (1929), 1–9. Teilhard, *Early Man in China,* p. 78.

74. An Chih-min and Wu Ju-tso, *KKHP* (1957/3), 1–12. Chang Shen-shui, *VP, 3* (1959), 47–56.

Most of these consist of chipped flakes and implements, of which only a few were secondarily retouched. The rest include two polished stone arrowheads—presumably later intrusions—a bone bead, a mollusk shell ornament, and a fragment of a stone ornament. The chipped stones fall into two major categories. The microliths consist of small flakes and blades made of flint, quartzite-silicate sandstone, agate, opal, jade, and light-colored siliceous pebble by means of indirect percussion and pressure flaking. Retouching, when it occurs, is in most cases limited to a single surface. In typology, these microliths include cores, leaf-shaped points, microblades, points, arrowheads, and scrapers. The other category consists of flakes of quartzite-silicate sandstone and light-colored siliceous pebbles; agate also occurs occasionally. These flakes as a rule are larger than the microliths, but their maximum length is still less than 9 centimeters. According to the investigators, direct percussion was the principal technique for making this series of flakes and implements, which include such types as points and scrapers (Fig. 21).

Although more precise dating of the Sha-yüan assemblage is needed, it is one of the most significant discoveries in the prehistoric archaeology of North China in recent years. It is the first evidence in North China proper of a microlithic industry (probably of the early post-glacial period) that shows affinities with the Microlithic horizons in Manchuria, Mongolia, and Soviet Siberia, and thus indicates a widespread cultural substratum in North China on which later cultural developments might have been built.[75] On the other hand, the "Mousterian-like" flakes of this assemblage indicate an unmistakable linkage with the Ordosian industries of the Upper Pleistocene period in the same region.

These Mesolithic sites in North China, Manchuria, and Mongolia indicate a series of closely similar hunter–fisher industries, featuring microblades and pressure-flaking. In view of the ecological characteristics of the areas in which these sites have been found, it is tempting to infer that there might have been at least two regional facies of the Mesolithic cultures in North China, Mongolia, and Manchuria: the Mongolian dune or oasis dwellers, and the North China and Man-

75. Another microlithic assemblage was found in 1965 in Hsü-ch'ang of Honan (see *VP, 10,* 1966, 86), but the site was not excavated and the geological dating is uncertain.

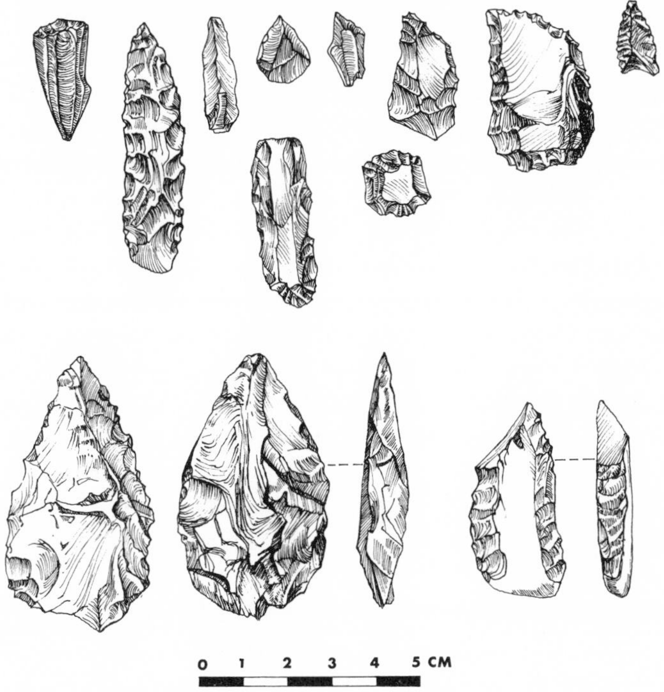

21. Mesolithic implements of the Sha-yüan culture. (After An Chih-min and Wu Ju-tso, *KKHP,* 1957/2, pp. 5, 8.)

churia forest dwellers. The facts that remains of projectile points have been found in the Manchurian sites and the Sha-yüan assemblage of North China, but not in Mongolia, and that the ostrich shell rings occur widely in the Mongolian sites but not elsewhere, give some support to this inference, although much more information is necessary before we can regard this or other subdivisions as probable.

MESOLITHIC CULTURES OF SOUTH CHINA

A different situation prevailed in the early postglacial period south of the Tsinling Shan and the Huaiho Valley. During the Recent period in Southeast Asia, there was widespread expression of the old pebble-tool technological tradition, generally known as the Hoabinhian pebble-tool complex. This can be characterized by chipped pebble tools, reminiscent of the older chopper–chopping tool tradition, including "hand-axes" and scrapers; the absence of blades, "Mousterian" flakes, and the microlithic industry; and the association of "Negroid" skeletons, in contrast to the north where a "Mongoloid" population seems to have prevailed throughout. This general Southeast Asian pattern manifests itself regionally in South China in widespread finds of chipped stone implements in Szechwan,[76] Kwangsi,[77] Yunnan,[78] and in the western part of Kwangtung as far as the Pearl River Delta[79] (Fig. 22). Paucity of reliable data still makes a classification of regional facies extremely difficult, but some significant assemblages from this area offer clues. In the Red basin of Szechwan, the antiquity of the chipped axes is suggested by their geographical distribution[80] but the stratigraphical evidence at Tai-hsi is scanty. Little is known about the cultural associations of these chipped axes in a preceramic context. More is known about Yunnan and Kwangsi, however, where chipped stone tools, shell middens, and charred animal bones have been found in limestone caves and rock shelters. In a cave at Ch'i-lin-shan, in Lai-pin Hsien, Kwangsi Province, cultural debris, charred bones, two quartzite flakes, one chopper made of a quartzite pebble, and parts of a human skull were discovered in 1956 in a yellowish breccia stratum in association with bones of deer, wild boar, and a large number of mollusk shells. The human skull fragments include a large part of the upper jaw, the hard palate, the right zygomatic bone, and the occipital bone; it is reportedly the skull of a male individual of advanced age. Its morphological features are certainly indicative of *Homo sapiens,* but the flat malar bone and a well-marked ridge at the entrance to the nasal floor are said to separate this skull from the Mongoloid pattern.[81] A rock-shelter site at Hei-ching-lung, near Ch'iu-pei in Yunnan, has yielded, in addition to charcoal and ash layers and two pieces of flint flakes, many seeds of *Celtis* and bones of *Canis gray,* Ursidae indet., Felinae indet., *Cervus* sp., Bovidae indet., and *Maca-*

76. Cheng Te-k'un, *Archaeological Studies in Szechwan,* Cambridge Univ. Press, 1957.

77. P'ei Wen-chung, *GSoC Bull., 14* (1935), 393–412. Chia Lan-p'o and Ch'iu Chung-lang, *VP, 4* (1960), 39. Ku Yü-min, *VP, 6* (1962), 193–99.

78. Bien Mei-nien and Chia Lan-p'o, *GSoC Bull., 18* (1938), 327–48.

79. *VP, 4* (1960), 38. W. Schofield, *Hongkong Naturalist,* (1935), 272–75. Mo Chih, *KKHP* (1959/4), 1–15. P'eng Ju-tze and Wang Wei, *WW* (1959/5), 75. R. Maglioni, *Hongkong Naturalist, 8* (1938), 211.

80. Cheng Te-k'un, *Archaeological Studies in Szechwan,* p. 130.

81. Chia Lan-p'o and Woo Ju-kang, *VP, 3* (1959), 37–39.

22. Mesolithic sites in southwest China.

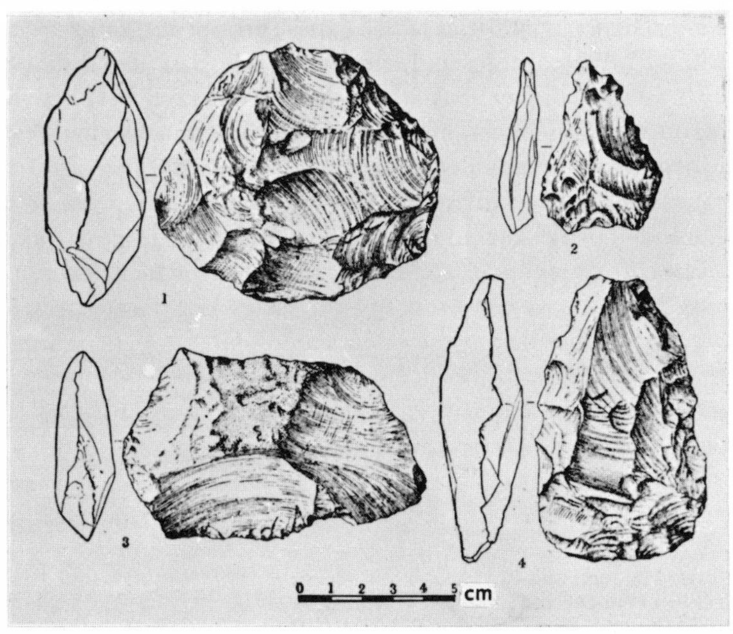

23. Stone implements from Hsi-chiao-shan, Kwangtung. (From *Hsin Chung-kuo ti K'ao-ku Shou-huo,* Peking, Wenwu Press, 1962, Fig. 15.)

cus sp.[82] Similar assemblages were found in 1959 at Ya-p'u-shan near Hsi-chiao Ts'un and Ma-lang-ch'uan-shan near Ma-lang-chi Ts'un, both in Tung-hsing Hsien, western Kwangtung. Four strata are excavated at these two sites: top soil; shell bed with pottery and Neolithic implements; bed with shells and concretions with abundant chipped implements; and red sandstone basement rocks. The cultural remains from the third layer are characterized by core implements including hand axes, choppers, and so forth, most of which retain the original cortex of the pebbles. The associated fauna, all of modern species, is distinguished by such forms as *Rusa, Bubalus,* and various mollusks.[83]

Around the Pearl River Delta area, open sites have been discovered where chipped stone implements were found in a preceramic context. In addition to the somewhat dubious finds in the Hong Kong area,[84] a highly important assemblage has been brought to light since 1955 at Hsi-chiao-shan in Nan-hai County, Kwangtung.[85] An inactive volcano called the Hsi-chiao-shan Hill, approximately 12 square kilometers in area, and surrounded by creeks and dried-up ponds, is about 70 kilometers southwest of Canton. Around the hill have been discovered fourteen prehistoric localities which can be grouped into three classes: preceramic, sub-Neolithic, and Neolithic. The last two will be discussed in a later chapter, but it should be remarked here that these three groups represent a common culture substratum characterized by chipped stone implements. The implements found in a nonceramic context, as well as those in association with pottery and polished stone tools, include both flake and core implements made of flint and sandstone. The core implements apparently resemble the familiar chopper–chopping tool varieties, but some of the flakes bear faceted platforms and many of them fall into the categories of end scrapers, points, and flake blades (Fig. 23).

It is clear that the majority of archaeological finds of the early Recent period in South China indicate a culture confined to the southwestern part of the area,[86] characterized by chipped stone implements of the archaic chopper–chopping tool tradition of the Palaeolithic, by

82. Bien Mei-nien and Chia Lan-p'o, *GSoC Bull., 18* (1938), 345–46.
83. *VP, 4* (1960), 38.
84. W. Schofield, *Hongkong Naturalist, 5* (1935); *PFEPC, 3* (1940), 243.
85. Mo Chih, *KKHP* (1959/4). P'eng Ju-tse and Wang Wei, *WW* (1959/5).
86. For a possible postglacial hunting–fishing culture site in Chekiang, see C. W. Huang and T. C. Meng, *VP, 8* (1964), 91–93.

the hunting of small game animals, and by the collecting of wild plants and mollusks. The single finding of physical remains for this period seems to group the population with the Negroid elements of the rest of Southeast Asia,[87] widely substantiated for this stage, and apart from the contemporary Mongoloid inhabitants to the north.

87. P. V. van Stein Callenfels, *Bull. Raffles Mus.*, ser. B, *1* (1936), 41–51. H. D. Collings, *Bull. Raffles Mus.*, ser. B, *2* (1938), 122–23. I. H. N. Evans, ibid., pp. 141–46. D. A. Hooijer, *Southwestern Jour. Anthropol., 6* (1950), 416–22; *8* (1952), 472–77. G. H. R. von Koenigswald, *Southwestern Jour. Anthropol., 8* (1952), 92–96. M. W. F. Tweedie, *Jour. Malayan Branch, Royal Asiatic Soc., 26* (1953), pt. 2, no. 1. Chang Kwang-chih, *Bull. Ethnol. Soc. China, 2* (1958), 53–133. Joseph B. Birdsell, "The Problem of the Early Peopling of the Americas as Viewed from Asia," in *Papers on the Physical Anthropology of the American Indian,* W. S. Laughlin, ed., New York, Viking Fund, 1951.

CHAPTER THREE

THE EARLIEST FARMERS

More than 99 per cent of the entire history of man, in China and elsewhere, belongs to the Palaeolithic period. During this era progress was slow—measured in terms of millennia and tens of millennia. Throughout the entire Palaeolithic and Mesolithic periods man had been a gatherer, acquiring his food from natural resources: game animals, fish, beetles, and worms; and wild seeds, fruits, nuts, and berries, as these were provided in their natural states. The food gatherer's life is dependent upon nature's bounty, and he must be mobile in order to follow the seasonal and cyclical changes of the natural resources. His culture is necessarily simple, because almost every member of the society must work hard to gain food. The invention of food production—the cultivation of plants and the domestication of animals—was thus a crucial turning point in human history. With resources of food under some degree of human control as to timing, quantity, and quality, man's life began to move toward a more complex and sedentary culture.

The importance of this great transitional process—the late V. Gordon Childe called it the Neolithic Revolution—was not lost on ancient man himself. In early Chinese legends one of the greatest heroes of all was Shen Nung, inventor of agriculture.

> Shen Nung cultivated plants and made pottery [*Chou-shu,* as quoted in *T'ai P'ing Yü Lan*].
>
> Shen Nung invented wooden agricultural implements [*lei* and *ssu*] and taught the whole world his inventions . . . He instituted the market held at noon. He administered all the peoples of the world and gathered their produce in the markets. The people went back to their homes after exchange and rested contented [*Hsi-tz'u,* in *Yi*].
>
> During the Age of Shen Nung, people rested at ease and acted with vigor. They cared for their mothers, but not for their fathers. They lived among deer. They ate what they cultivated and wore

> what they wove. They did not think of harming one another [Chapter "Tao-ch'e," in *Chuang Tzu*].

These passages are sufficient to show that as late as the second half of the first millennium B.C., when they were supposedly written, vivid recollections of the Neolithic life of their ancestors were still in the mind of the Chinese in North China. Concerning the invention of agriculture by Shen Nung, there are some stories of special interest. Some relate that the first plant cultivation was the result of necessity:

> The ancient people ate meat of animals and birds. At the time of Shen Nung, there were so many people that the animals and birds became inadequate for people's wants, and therefore Shen Nung taught the people to cultivate [*Pai Hu T'ung*].

In other stories, the cultivated plants were given by divine forces:

> At the time of Shen Nung, millet rained from Heaven. Shen Nung collected the grains and cultivated them [*Chou Shu,* as quoted by *Yi Shih*].
>
> [At the time of Shen Nung] there was a red bird holding in its mouth a cereal stalk with nine ears. Some of the grains fell onto the ground. Shen Nung picked them up and cultivated them in the field. Those who ate the grains lived long and did not die. [*Shih Yi Chi,* by Wang Chia of the Chin Dynasty].

Whether plant cultivation was independently invented in China and, if so, how the process was first established, we do not know. It is significant, however, that Shen Nung, besides being the inventor of agriculture, was also the first and greatest herbalist. It is said that Shen Nung tasted a "hundred varieties of grasses" and knew the nature of them all. According to one folktale of the people at Szechwan, it was a highly poisonous grass that killed Shen Nung. Even today, Shen Nung, among his numerous other characteristics, is the patron divinity of the Chinese druggist and herbalist. Anthropologists have proposed many theories about the origin of agriculture, but to my knowledge none has suggested that the first cultivation of plants in some parts of the world might have been the work of a (or *the*) herbalist in the hunting-fishing stage of culture. The implications of the tale of Shen Nung the Herbalist seem to open an interesting line of study.

Whatever significance one attaches to the legends about the beginnings of agriculture in China, these passages are not very helpful for understanding the actual process of the Neolithic Revolution. Scientific archaeology has in the last twenty years or so all but established that this revolution took place independently in at least the Near East and Middle America several thousand years before our era and that in both places the process was gradual and cumulative as the result of man's experience over centuries or millennia in experimenting with the domestication of wild plants and animals. In the Near East the experiments centered on wheat; in Middle America maize was the focus of Neolithic life. In the Far East, the prominent crops in historical and ethnographical times are known to have been such cereals as millet and rice and such root crops as taro and yam. What can archaeologists tell us about man's first experiments with these plants? And what can they tell us about the animals that were domesticated at the same time? Unfortunately, they know very little so far about China.[1]

BEGINNINGS OF AGRICULTURE IN SOUTHEAST ASIA

Several ethnobotanists and cultural historians[2] have speculated about an early horticultural revolution in the tropical regions of Southeast Asia, and they agree in characterizing the early garden culture as follows. (1) The area where the first plant domestication and cultivation took place was probably a permanently humid tropical region with a rich flora and an abundance of marine and, to a lesser

1. In his 1936 classic on the phytogeographic differential study of cultivated plants, N. I. Vavilov, the Russian botanist, lists China as one of his eight primary centers of cultivation of the world and assigns 136 cultivated plants (out of 666 for the world) to China (see his "The Origin, Variation, Immunity, and Breeding of Cultivated Plants," *Chronica Botanica, 13,* 1949/51). Vavilov also assigns 172 other plants to his Indo-Malayan area, which should include a large portion of South China. Very few of these plants, however, have been archaeologically discovered as yet in China.

2. J. Barrau, *Ethnology, 4* (1965), 282–94; "The Indo-Pacific Area as a Center of Origin of Plant Cultivation and Domestication," ms., 1966. Carl O. Sauer, *Proc. Amer. Phil. Soc., 92* (1948), 65–77; *Agricultural Origins and Dispersals,* New York, The American Geographical Society, 1952.

extent, freshwater resources. (2) Some "progressive fishermen" dwelling on riverbanks or near estuaries in the Southeast Asian tropics are considered to be the progenitors of the earliest growers of rootcrops. (3) The first gardening in this area was probably done by individual farmers who propagated perennials (such as taro and yam) in fenced gardens. The technique was at most a swidden cultivation with periodic cuttings into the forests from the riverbanks and estuaries. (4) In this early stage of cultivation, when fishing had an important role, fiber was a material of prime importance for making fishlines and nets and as a kind of oakum for calking canoes. In fact, the first uses of plants in this area may have been related to the gathering of fibers. Furthermore, fibrous and edible barks were important items of material culture, and "barking" was probably the first technique of land clearing, perhaps discovered by accident through the gathering of fibrous material from wild plants.

The tropical regions of Asia that scholars have in mind as a nuclear agricultural area include the entire monsoon Asia from southeastern India to mainland and insular Southeast Asia, and solution to the problem must be sought for in the entire region. The archaeological material from South China, a part of the area, has proved to be illuminating and merits consideration in this context.

Not long after the beginning of the postglacial period, at many of the Mesolithic sites in southern coastal China and northern Indochina, what seems to be the earliest pottery of the whole region emerged, pottery of very coarse paste, decorated with marks impressed by cord-wrapped sticks and paddles (Fig. 24). Well-excavated sites of this type have been located throughout the coastal areas in Taiwan,[3] Kiangsi,[4] the entire province of Kwangtung,[5] and as far west as Szechwan.[6] All the sites of this type were near bodies of water from which the inhabitants obtained fish and shellfish. The great variety of cord marks on the pottery demonstrates the existence of highly sophisticated cordage techniques, and fibers for the cord must have been obtained from

3. K. C. Chang, *Discovery, 2* (1967), 2, 3–10.

4. Y. W. Kuo and C. H. Li, *KKHP* (1963/1), 1–16.

5. Y. M. Ku, *VP, 6* (1962), 194–99. C. Mo, *KKHP* (1959/4), 1–15; *KK* (1961/11), 577–84; (1961/12), 666–68. Mo and C. L. Ch'en, *KK* (1961/12), 644–49, 688. Mo and S. W. Li, KKHP (1960/2), 107–19. J. T. P'eng, *KK* (1961/11), 585–88. W. Schofield, *PFEPC*, 3rd, 1938 (1940), 235–305.

6. T. K. Cheng, *Archaeological Studies in Szechwan,* Cambridge Univ. Press, 1957.

24. Cord-impressed and incised sherds from the sites of Ta-p'en-k'eng and Feng-pi-t'ou, Taiwan.

plants among the abundant local flora. The stone sinkers and carpenter's tools (adzes and chisels of various kinds) suggest the construction of canoes and deepwater fishing, for which fibers and cordage were probably needed for calking, fishlines, and nets. Stone barkbeaters are known from Taiwan, and barking was probably one of the means for obtaining fiber from wild plants. All this contextual information at the cord-marked pottery sites in coastal China suggests agreement with the conditions proposed by ethnobotanists for the early horticulturalists. The evidence at the sites shows beyond question that the inhabitants' principal mode of subsistence remained in the hunting-fishing-collecting category, but the probability of some form of gardening among these peoples is very strongly indicated indeed.

Matsuo Tsukada's palynological work in Taiwan[7] shows that as early as 12,000 years before the present the local vegetational record exhibits a disturbance of considerable magnitude (including the

7. *Proc. Nat. Acad. Sci., 55* (1966), 543–48; *Palaeogeography, Palaeoclimatology, Palaeoecology, 3* (1967), 49–64.

growth of secondary forests and shrubs and the marked increase of charcoal fragments in the lake sediments) that can best be accounted for by man's clearance of forests to make fields. Cord-marked pottery assemblages were the only archaeological evidence of human activities on the island at that early date, and this forest disturbance strengthens the view that gardening probably had an early beginning in the cord-marked pottery horizon of coastal China and Southeast Asia. We can anticipate with keen interest the discovery in this area of direct evidence of ancient horticulture—carbonized roots and tubers, identifiable plant protein crystals, pollen grains from the fenced gardens, and perhaps bamboo or wooden dibbles.

THE BEGINNING OF FOOD PRODUCTION IN THE HUANGHO

The Huangho Valley is commonly regarded as another birthplace of agriculture, especially important for the first cultivation of several varieties of millet, and its Neolithic cultures were demonstrably the forerunners of those of historic China. The cultural inventory of the first farmers in the Huangho Valley and the means by which they emerged to a food-producing way of life remain unknown. Theoretically, there are two alternatives: either the Neolithic culture of the Huangho was brought in by immigrants from other regions (e.g. the Near East, where agriculture began about ten thousand years ago, or even perhaps Southeast Asia), or the Neolithic population was a continuation from the Mesolithic substratum which had progressed to food production. Practically all archaeologists would unhesitatingly rule out the first alternative on the basis of the available data. According to physical anthropological studies[8] the earliest known farmers in North China were physically "Mongoloid" beyond any doubt. Since the Mongoloid occupation of the northern part of the Far East can be traced back into the Mesolithic, if not the Palaeolithic, as we have discussed in the previous chapter, a continuity of inhabitants can be assumed as highly probable. These considerations point to the likelihood that the Mesolithic dwellers of the Huangho Valley adopted the cultivation of plants, and that a cultural transformation from forest hunting and fishing groups into full-fledged village farming com-

8. Davidson Black, *PS*, ser. D., *1* (1925); *6* (1928). Yen Yen et al., *VP, 4* (1960), 103–11. Yen Yen, *KKHP* (1962/2), 85–104; *KK* (1965/10), 513–16.

munities took place among them. If we assume this, there is again the question of independent invention versus stimulus diffusion. In other words, questions arise whether the Mesolithic hunter-fishers in this region adopted the food-producing way of life on their own initiative or as a result of the ideas or actual knowledge of food production from the Near East or Southeast Asia. I think it is still too early to ask these questions. To know the cultural contacts between East and West during this early period we must have a valid absolute chronology for the Chinese Neolithic stage; have some evidence in the intervening regions to substantiate the route of diffusion; and/or make an extensive comparison of the Chinese and the Near Eastern Neolithic cultural traditions to demonstrate the cultural affiliations, if any. None of these approaches is feasible at present. It is all well and good to assume that the idea diffused from one region to another, but this assumption is as difficult to prove as it is to disprove when substantial evidence is totally lacking. Some food plants such as wheat, which seem to have been cultivated alongside the millet in North China during the Neolithic period or somewhat later, and domestic animals such as cattle and sheep, apparently had a Near Eastern origin. Moreover, East–West cultural contacts during the Neolithic cannot be denied. But this is far from conclusive evidence that the first idea of plant and animal domestication was carried over with these plants and animals, for we know nothing about the time when these first appeared in China in relation to various other native plants and animals.[9] There has been considerable controversy over this problem, much of which has been charged with bias and emotion. For the present it is best, I think, to concentrate our efforts on learning more about the Neolithic culture in China itself before making any farfetched conclusions. As to the relations between North China and Southeast Asia, diffusion in either direction is possible, but the ecological problems of the various plants involved are highly complex, and absolute chronologies are lacking. The earliest known sites of the Yang-shao culture (pp. 111–12) are in the Tsinling area, and their relationship with the cord-marked pottery assemblages of South China should not be overlooked.

As soon as attention is focused upon the Yellow River valley itself and the earliest evidence of Neolithic culture in this region, several

9. See discussions of the chronological problems in K. C. Chang, in *Chronologies in Old World Archaeology*, Robert Ehrich ed., Univ. of Chicago Press, 1965.

facts become instantly clear and instructive. First, it is highly probable that the Neolithic culture emerged in the central region of the Yellow River valley, which we call the North China Nuclear Area, and subsequently radiated toward both east and west. Second, a distinctive Chinese way of life in cultural terms came into being with the earliest available archaeological record of the Neolithic stage. Third, a distinctive ceramic horizon can probably be assumed to antedate the earliest available Neolithic evidence, continuing into the known Neolithic stage and into the historical period as a persistent and predominant ceramic tradition.

What we have called the Nuclear Area of North China refers to the region around the confluence of the three great rivers in North China: the Huangho, the Fenho, and the Weishui. This area is also about where the three modern provinces of Honan, Shansi, and Shensi come together.[10] It is in fact a small basin encircled in the north, west, and south by the Shansi Plateau, the Shensi–Kansu Loessic Plateau, and the Tsinling Mountains, but open to the eastern plains. The possible role of this region in cradling the food-producing cultures of North China is based on a number of considerations. In the first place, as described in Chapter 1, during the "climatic optimum" the Nuclear Area was on the border between the wooded western highlands and the swampy eastern lowlands, and thus provided both the "hilly flanks" and the habitat for the sedentary waterside fishermen that Braidwood[11] and Sauer,[12] respectively, believe to be the birthplace of farmers and herders. It had enough rain and warmth to be suited to agriculture and enough game and fish to sustain its inhabitants. It was also conveniently located at the intersection of natural avenues of communication. Second, it is in the Nuclear Area—in the Sha-yüan region of Chao-yi and Ta-li counties in eastern Shensi of the lower Weishui Valley—that the only Huangho basin Mesolithic assemblage was found. Third, the only stratigraphically suggested initial Yang-shao Neolithic evidence, which will be mentioned presently, was found in the Weishui Valley within the Nuclear Area. Fourth, the importance of fishing, as shown during the subsequent Yang-shao stage in this same

10. K. C. Chang, *BIHP, 30* (1959), 302.

11. Robert J. Braidwood, *The Near East and the Foundation for Civilization*, Eugene, Oregon State System of Higher Education, 1952, p. 11.

12. Carl O. Sauer, *Proc. Amer. Phil. Soc., 92* (1948), 65–77.

region, is a highly suggestive fact. Fifth, archaeological evidence demonstrates that the Nuclear Area played a leading role in the transition from the Yang-shao to the Lung-shan, the significance of which will be made clear with the description of that crucial event in the next chapter. Finally,[13] during most of the four thousand years of historic China, the Nuclear Area was one of the strategically vital regions that to a considerable extent controlled the destiny of the Empire.

It is thus conceivable that a few millennia B.C. the terminal food gatherers in the Nuclear Area, possibly already settled down with a well-developed culture, switched to food production by inventing or adopting plant cultivation and animal domestication. From what we know of it, Chinese Neolithic culture assumed from the very beginning a distinctive pattern that shows configurational independence and originality. The following traits, singly or totally considered, have been enumerated as characteristic of Chinese Neolithic culture tradition:[14]

1. The cultivation of millet and rice (and possibly kaoliang and the soybean)
2. The domestication of pigs, cattle, sheep, dogs, chickens, and possibly horses
3. The construction of *hang-t'u* and wattle-and-daub structures, and the use of a white limey substance for house floor and wall plaster
4. The domestication of silkworms and the possible weaving of silk and hemp on looms
5. Probable use of tailored garments
6. Pottery with cord-mat-basket designs
7. Pottery tripods (especially *ting* and *li*), steamers (*tseng* and *yen*), and the possible use of chopsticks, perhaps indicating a distinctive cooking style
8. Semilunar and rectangular stone sickles (knives)
9. The extensive development of ceremonial vessels
10. Elaborate complex of jade artifacts; possible wood-carving complex

13. Cf. Owen Lattimore, *Inner Asian Frontiers of China,* New York, American Geographical Society, 1951, pp. 27–33.
14. K. C. Chang, *BIHP, 30* (1959), 266.

11. Scapulimancy
12. A distinctive style of art

In addition, the presumably distinctive Chinese language, which was to be recorded during subsequent stages by the Chinese system of writing, must have had a Neolithic basis. In village planning, the location of the kiln quarter in a separate area within the village also appears to be typical. Other stylistically distinctive socioeconomic and ceremonial features, such as the localization of corporate kinship groups, the preeminence of the ancestor cult, and the mythology, which are known to be characteristic of the immediately following phases, also probably had a Neolithic basis. The items listed above could be seen directly in the archaeological materials. All of them did not emerge from the very beginning, nor are all considered to have been invented in China. These, and others, are the constituents of a cultural tradition distinguished from other comparable cultural centers in the rest of the world. Since the Nuclear Area is traditionally known as the "Chung Yüan," the Central Plain, we may refer to it as the Chung Yüan Tradition.

Cord-marked pottery appears to be among the very first cultural elements that occurred during the initial emergence of the Neolithic stage in North China. Among all the kinds of ceramic wares of a prehistoric nature, cord-marked pottery had the widest distribution and the longest temporal duration in China. Included in cord-marked pottery is a wide variety of colors, pastes, techniques of manufacture, forms, and surface treatments. The predominant colors are red, brown, and gray; the paste may be coarse or fine but usually contains a great deal of temper; the ware is molded or handmade (mostly coiled) and sometimes finished with paddle-and-anvil. The form of the ware ranges from the point-bottomed cooking ware and storage jars to tripods, ring-footed vessels, and flat-bottomed bowls. The surface of the ware was by definition impressed with marks which were applied with cord-marked molds, cord-wrapped sticks, or paddles carved with cord designs, and the marks were either left intact or partially smeared smooth. All these variations can be regarded as the product of a single pottery tradition, since they had an uninterrupted geographical distribution and an uninterrupted temporal duration, were similarly made and probably served for similar purposes, and were associated with similar cultural traits and complexes in the Chinese Neolithic context.

Whether or not this significant pottery tradition constituted a distinctive horizon at one time in North China remains a problem to be explored. There are several basic facts, however, that point to the possibility that this was the case. Stratigraphic evidence at several sites in the Tsinling area of Shensi indicated the possible existence of cord-marked pottery alone in an initial Yang-shao horizon context.[15] The age–area concept gives a great antiquity to this widely distributed pottery tradition.[16] Moreover, in the subsequent horizons the cord-marked pottery tradition is still the predominant component so far as the record goes,[17] which implies, among other things, that this tradition was a kind of main stream, so to speak, of Chinese ceramic history, while other traditions were but successively incorporated tributaries. And, finally, as noted above, it has been stratigraphically established that in South China the cord-marked pottery tradition represents the oldest stylistic horizon in that area. I have proposed, therefore, to set up a more or less hypothetical horizon characterized by cord-marked and other kinds of textile-impressed pottery to antedate and initiate known Chinese Neolithic history, and have given it the name of Sheng-wen horizon, literally the horizon of the cord-marked designs.[18] Evidence is beginning to come to light for the substantiation of this hypothetical ceramic horizon (see pp. 111–12).

LIFE OF YANG-SHAO FARMERS

The earliest well-established cultural stage of the northern Chinese farmers has been named the Yang-shao culture, after the site of Yang-shao-ts'un, in Mien-ch'ih Hsien, western Honan, where in 1921 the Swedish geologist J. G. Andersson excavated the first assemblage characterized by the painted pottery which has been regarded as one of the diagnostic features of this whole culture. Recently, students of early China have begun to realize that the Yang-shao might be much

15. See below, pp. 111–12.
16. Cf. Lauriston Ward, "The Relative Chronology of China Through the Han Period," in *Relative Chronologies in Old World Archaeology,* R. W. Ehrich, ed., Univ. Chicago Press, 1954, p. 133.
17. E.g. Shih Hsing-pang, *KKTH* (1955/3), 12. Li Chi, *Hsiao-t'un T'ao-ch'i,* Taipei, Academia Sinica, 1956, p. 117.
18. K. C. Chang, *BIHP, 30* (1959), 280.

better typified by other sites, and that Yang-shao-ts'un was probably inhabited toward the very end of the Yang-shao stage if not at the beginning of the next—or Lung-shan—stage. For the sake of convenience, the name Yang-shao is retained in this book for this whole cultural period, which may or may not include the site at Yang-shao-ts'un.

The criteria for dating the Neolithic settlement sites to the Yang-shao culture are both stratigraphical and typological. Stratigraphically, the Yang-shao sites or phases of sites lie above the Palaeolithic and Mesolithic strata but beneath the remains of the Lung-shan stage of the Neolithic and of various later historic periods, depending on the area where these several cultural phases were distributed. Typologically, the Yang-shao sites exhibit definite sociocultural and stylistic characteristics, as will be described. The thousand or more prehistoric sites attributable to this cultural stage are found widely in North China but are largely confined to the Nuclear Area and its immediate neighborhood (Fig. 25). Earlier phases of the Yang-shao stage are seen in southern Shansi, western Honan, and central-eastern Shensi, mainly in the valleys of the Huangho, Fenho, and Weishui rivers in that area. Later phases probably expanded into eastern Kansu, central Shansi, and northern Honan. Throughout the entire span of this stage, however, the Yang-shao settlements are largely confined to the river valleys and small basins in the western highlands of North China. It appears likely that the earliest Chinese farmers, after their first emergence in the Nuclear Area, developed only gradually in the vicinity of the natural habitat of the plants and animals they had come to domesticate and slowly came to establish the so-called primary village-efficiency in this region. It was not until the following Lungshanoid stage that these early farmers began to expand, somewhat explosively, outside this area into the humid low country to the east and south.

The principal cultivated crop of the Yang-shao farmers was the fox-tail millet (*Setaria italica* Beauv. var. *germanica* Trin.), actual remains of which have been found at a number of sites.[19] Remains of cultivating implements include hoes, spades, and possibly digging sticks. Perfo-

19. Also reported in the literature were broomcorn millet (*Panicum miliaceum* L.) from Ching-ts'un, southern Shansi (Carl Bishop, *Antiquity, 28,* 1933); grand millet, or *kaoliang* (*Andropogon sorghum* Brot.) also from Ching-ts'un; and wheat, from Wang-chia-wan, in Pao-teh Hsien, Shansi (C. M. An, *Yenching Social Sciences, 2,* 1949, 40). These are all unique occurrences and are, therefore, suspect. If the identification or stratigraphy is reliable in each case, they must have been extremely rare.

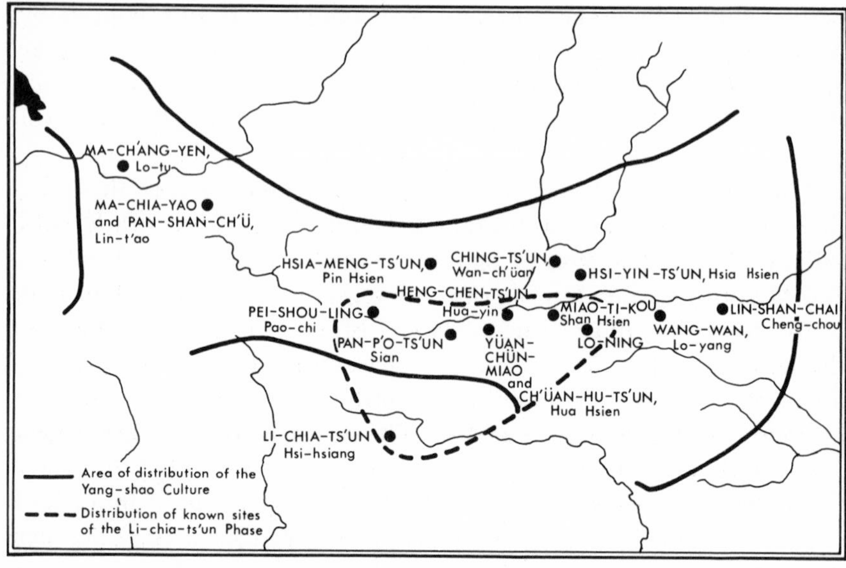

25. Distribution of the Yang-shao culture and its major sites.

rated stone disks, possibly the weights of digging sticks, have been found in considerable quantity. Other relevant implements are polished stone celts, often oval in cross section and presumably effective tools for field clearance, and polished or chipped rectangular and semilunar stone sickles, which were probably fastened to the hand with string or leather ropes through a hole or around two side notches, for cutting, scraping, weeding, and harvesting. Some of the pottery jars found widely in the Yang-shao context were presumably used for storing grains, the remains or impressions of which are sometimes found therein. Some of the harvest must have been prepared and preserved in the form of flour, for grinding stones have also been discovered (Fig. 26).

The most important domesticated animals in this stage were dogs and pigs, whose bones have been unearthed from countless sites. Much less common were cattle (Ching-ts'un and Kao-tui, southern Shansi; and Kwang-wu, northern Honan), and sheep and goats (Ching-ts'un and Lo-han-t'ang).[20] Hemp was probably cultivated,[21] and silk-

20. J. G. Andersson, *BMFEA, 15* (1943), 43. Margit Bylin-Althin, *BMFEA, 18* (1946), 458. T'ung Chu-ch'en, *KKHP* (1957/2), 9.
21. Andersson, *GSuC Bull., 5* (1923), 26; *KK* (1959/2), 73.

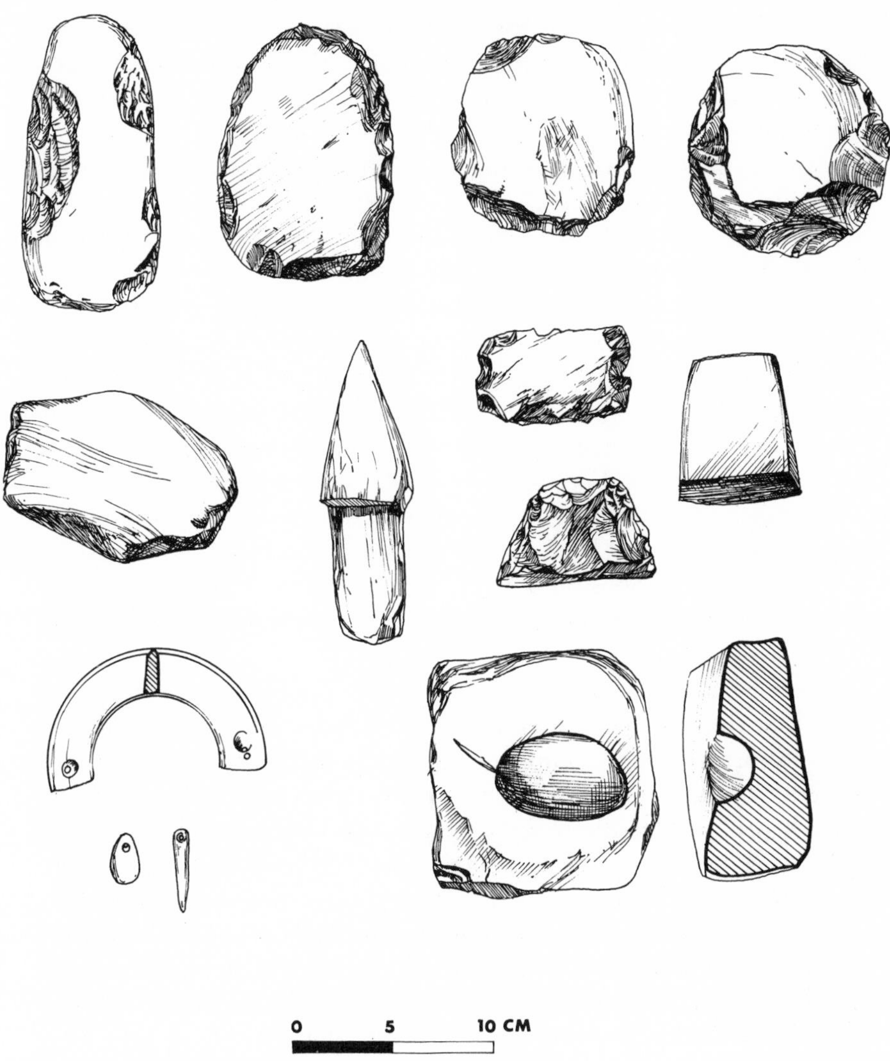

26. Stone implements from the Yang-shao culture site at Pan-p'o-ts'un, Sian. (From *Hsi-an Pan-p'o,* Peking, Wenwu Press, 1963, pp. 61, 64, 65, 70, 71, 74, 90, 96, 192, 195.)

worms (*Bombyx mori*) were raised. A half-cut cocoon of the latter was found at Hsi-yin-ts'un in southern Shansi.[22] The many stone and pottery spindle whorls and eyed bone needles were probably used with hemp, silk, and other fabrics.

Wild-grain collecting, hunting, and fishing supplemented the diet. Remains of a kind of foxtail weed (*Setaria lutescens*) were found at Ching-ts'un, and seeds of vegetables were found in a pottery jar at Pan-p'o.[23] Bones of a variety of wild animals were recovered from the middens of the Yang-shao settlements: horse, leopard, water deer, wild cattle, deer, rhinoceros, bamboo rat, antelope, hare, and marmot. The hunters must have used bow and arrow and spear, for remains of stone and bone points and arrowheads are numerous. Some round-headed arrowheads were probably employed for shooting birds. Stone balls have been found occasionally, perhaps slingstones for the hunt. The importance of fishing is indicated by the abundance of bone fish spears, harpoons, and fishhooks as well as grooved pottery and stone net sinkers, fish designs on pottery, and the bones of fish. The decorative fish motif on pottery is particularly abundant in the Weishui Valley sites[24] (Fig. 27).

These early cultivators lived in villages. There are several indications that their village settlements shifted from one locale to another after a short period of occupancy, that some favorable locales were repeatedly occupied, and that the shifting and repetitive settlement pattern probably resulted from the slash-and-burn technique of cultivation. The deposits of the villages, often very thick, usually consist of multioccupational remains, which seems to indicate that these localities were occupied discontinuously but repetitively. A house at a site near Sian, Shensi, has a succession of three floors, apparently the result of three discontinuous occupations.[25] Furthermore, we find that in the same general neighborhood, the Yang-shao sites were widely distributed over a vast area, and each component consists of remains that show no marked changes in typology through time. In 1952 and 1953 twenty-one Yang-shao sites were located in the vicinity

22. Li Chi, *Hsi-yin-ts'un shih-ch'ien ti yi-ts'un,* Peking, Tsing-hua Research Institute, 1927, pp. 22–23.

23. Bishop, *Antiquity, 28* (1933), 395. H. P. Shih et al., *Hsi-an Pan-p'o,* Peking, Wenwu Press, 1963, p. 223.

24. See e.g. Chao Hsüeh-ch'ien, *KK* (1959/11), 589.

25. Y. H. Chang, *KK* (1961/11), 601–08.

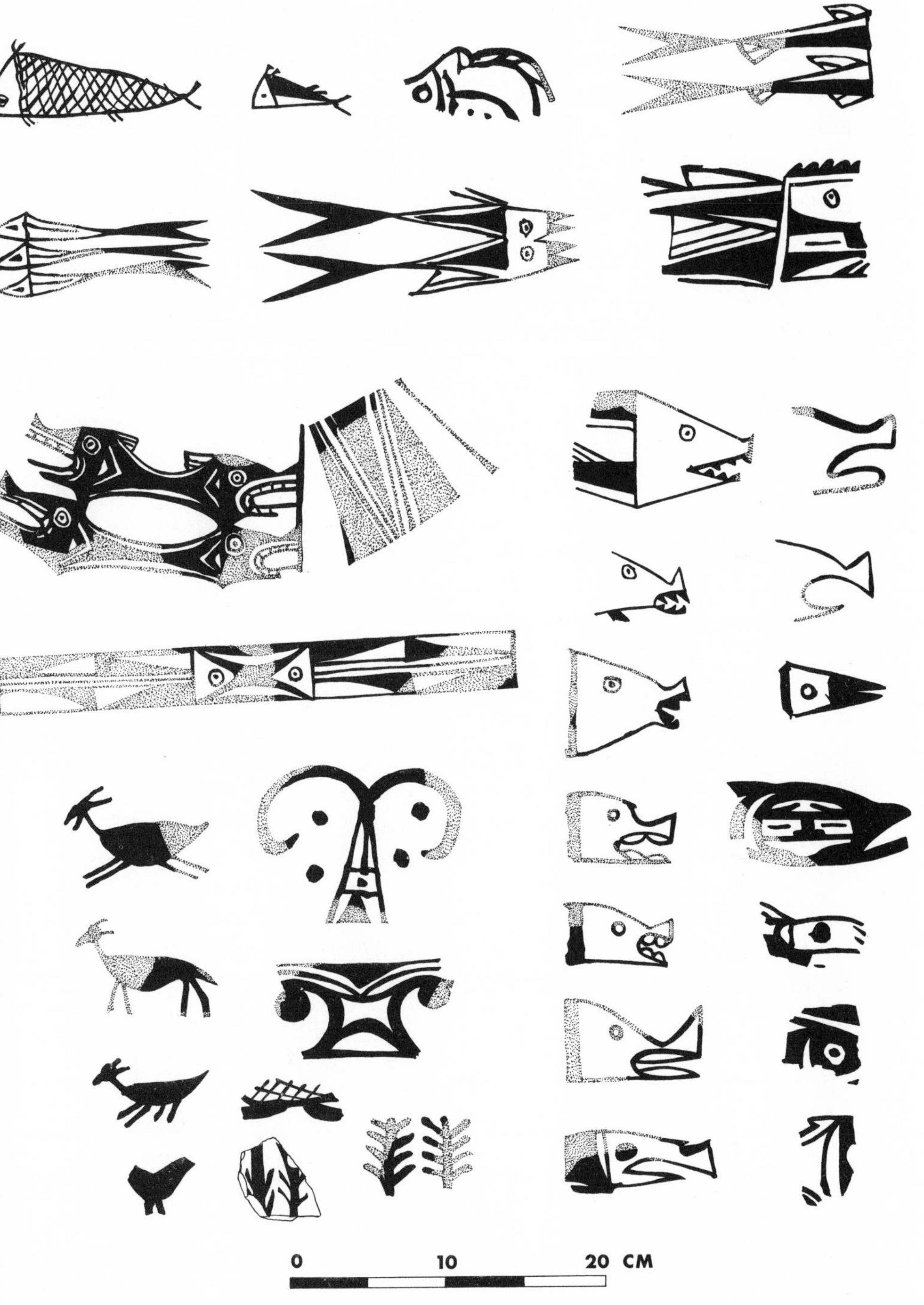

27. Fish, animal, and plant patterns in the pottery decoration of the Yang-shao culture site at Pan-p'o-ts'un, Sian. (From *Hsi-an Pan-p'o,* 1963, Figs. 121–22.)

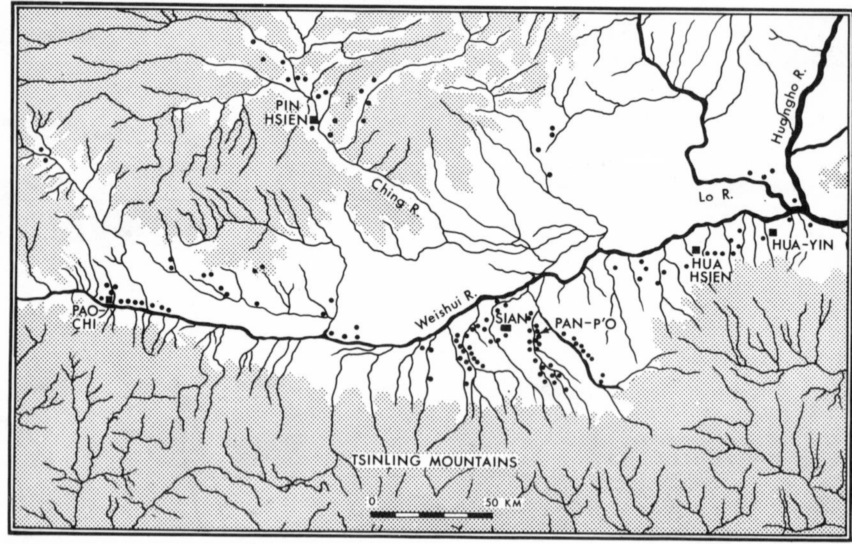

28. Distribution of Yang-shao sites in the Weishui Valley of Shensi. (After *Hsi-an Pan-p'o,* 1963, p. 3.)

of Sian, Shensi (Fig. 28). The investigators of these sites made the following remarks:

> The Yang-shao sites are many and widely distributed. Remains at a single locality are chronologically simple and neighboring localities can easily be given a relative dating on their respective cultural inventories.[26]

At Miao-ti-kou, Shan Hsien, Honan, similar phenomena have also been recorded.[27] And finally, the general cultural configuration gives similar indications which, taken together, point convincingly to the conclusion that the pattern of settlements was characterized by shifting and repetitive occupations. This conclusion is not in agreement with the former impression of most scholars, who considered that "Yang-shao" villages were large, sedentary communities.[28] We are now

26. Su Ping-ch'i and Wu Ju-tso, *KKTH* (1956/2), 37; cf. also Chao Hsüeh-ch'ien *KK* (1959/11), 588–89.
27. *KKTH* (1958/11), 68.
28. E.g. Cheng Te-k'un, *Prehistoric China (Archaeology in China, 1),* Cambridge, Heffer, 1959, pp. 69–72.

able to suggest that this impression is erroneous, and that there are at least two sources of error. First, most of the large Yang-shao sites with apparently deep deposits were measured in a preliminary manner during a survey or survey excavations. Thus it seems likely that the large volume of Yang-shao remains represent discontinuous occupations which the surveyors or the excavators failed to recognize. Second, granted that the measured village site represents one component, that is, a single occupation village, these sites were probably of the very latest Yang-shao stage, which had already begun to show changes toward the next stage, e.g. the Yang-shao-ts'un site itself.

On this basis I presented an argument in 1959 for a repetitive and discontinuous pattern of settlement for the Yang-shao farmers, which was concomitant with a shifting technique of cultivation.[29] This hypothesis was received by a few colleagues with some skepticism. Dr. Cheng Te-k'un, for instance, has cited Pan-p'o-ts'un, near Sian, as a disproof of the view. The site is known to comprise 50,000 square meters, and Cheng seems to think that it was not likely to have been occupied by farmers with such primitive farming techniques.[30] Actually, Pan-p'o-ts'un, certainly the best excavated and described of all Yang-shao sites, offers the best proof yet for the above interpretation of the Yang-shao settlement patterns.

The authors of the report of the Pan-p'o-ts'un site themselves have actually adopted the idea of shifting cultivation for their inhabitants: "Regarding cultivation, the Pan-p'o inhabitants possibly employed a slash-and-burn technique. After burning, the soil in the field becomes more fertile and easy to till. At the time, there was a great amount of land relative to the sparse population, permitting patches of field over wide areas to be fallowed and used in rotation."[31] Although the same authors do not tell us the precise reasons for this inference, the description of the site in the report contains very substantial evidence to support their view. Despite the size of the site and the apparently extensive remains, the debris was deposited during from two to four successive occupations.[32] According to the changes in artifacts, two cultural components are distinguished: The

29. *BIHP, 30* (1959), 268. *Harvard Jour. Asiatic Studies, 20* (1959), 167–68.
30. *Antiquity, 38* (1964), 184–85.
31. H. P. Shih *et al., Hsi-an Pan-p'o,* Wenwu Press, p. 224.
32. Ibid., p. 54.

TABLE 4.

Change of Tree and Grass Pollen During the Yang-shao Occupation at the Pan-p'o-ts'un Site, Sian

	Tree Pollen	*Grass Pollen*
(cm)	(%)	(%)
0– 50	(0)	8 (100)
–50– 60	3 (37.50)	5 (62.50)
–60– 90	(0)	15 (100)
–90–100	20 (27.78)	52 (72.22)
–100–180	2 (1.70)	116 (98.30)
–180–220	15 (31.92)	32 (68.08)

early component includes remains of 22 houses and 43 storage pits; the late contains 24 houses and more than 160 storage pits. According to the writers' estimate, the excavated portion of the site was about one fifth of the total area of settlement. This suggests that perhaps more than a hundred houses were built during each of the two periods of occupation. There is no question that both occupations were by people of the same culture, but minor changes in house construction methods and in artifact style are appreciable. Quite possibly the site was abandoned for a considerable interval between two occupations. An explanation for this phenomenon is provided by a pollen profile taken from a 2.8-meter section of the site that represents both occupations.[33] Table 4, prepared according to the published pollen data, gives an interesting sequence of the change in the relative frequencies of tree and grass pollen.

This shows that at the beginning of settlement the Pan-p'o village was probably still surrounded by a considerable number of trees, whose pollen, transported to the village site from a notable distance, still accounts for 32 per cent of the total. The scanty pollen in the next 80 centimeters suggests extensive clearance and open farming fields. The rise in tree pollen in the next level shows a cessation of agricultural activities at the site, allowing for a considerable regrowth of trees. The soil of this layer is very dark and compact and contains a large amount of organic materials, also indicating a second growth of wild plant life. The next 90 centimeters above again exhibits almost total absence of tall growth; apparently the village once more

33. Ibid., Appendix III.

served as the center of intensive farming activities. Thus this sequence of pollen species, with an interval of forest growth in the middle, agrees with the inference of two discontinuous cultural components, providing an interesting support for our interpretation of the Yang-shao pattern of settlement.

The physical plan of the Yang-shao villages is known only where the sites were extensively excavated and the results given in published accounts. An interesting layout is attributed to the Pei-shouling site of Pao-chi, in central Shensi, where two rows of houses faced each other across a narrow lane, but detailed descriptions are absent.[34] The best-described village plans are available for the Pan-p'o site. It is on a river terrace about 800 meters east of the River Ch'an, a tributary of the Weishui, and about 9 meters above the riverbed. The area of the settlement is estimated at about 50,000 square meters, and its shape is an irregular oval with the long axis north–south. The houses (46 of which were excavated) and most of the storage pits and animal pens are clustered at the center of the site in an area of about 30,000 square meters outlined by a ditch 5 or 6 meters deep and wide. The village cemetery is in the northern part of the village, outside the ditched dwelling area, and pottery kilns are concentrated in the village's eastern portion (Fig. 29). Within the dwelling area, houses of fairly permanent nature were constructed. The most common kinds were 3 to 5 meters in diameter and were square, oblong, or round, with plastered floors. They were semi-subterranean or at ground level, had wattle-and-daub wall foundations, and upper walls and roofs were supported by large and small wooden posts (Fig. 30). During a later occupation, a huge longhouse was constructed (over 20 m long and 12.5 m wide) divided into compartments by partition walls. During this stage the communal house was at the center of the village plaza, with the small houses surrounding the plaza, their doors facing the center. Each house and each compartment of the longhouse was equipped with a hearth (a burned surface in the earlier occupations and a gourd-shaped pit in the later occupations). The pottery-making center east of the dwelling area had no fewer than six kilns (Fig. 31), in one of which were found some unfired pots. North of the dwelling area was the village cemetery, in which were found more than 130 adult burials, single, with the exception

34. *KK* (1959/2), 229–30.

20. A bird's-eye view of the Banpo village (model) (From Hsi-an Pan-p'o 1963, p. 25)

30. Reconstructed house types at the Yang-shao site at Pan-p'o-ts'un. (From *Hsi-an Pan-p'o,* 1963, pp. 15, 19, 24, 27, 31.)

31. Pottery kilns at Pan-p'o-ts'un. (From *Hsi-an Pan-p'o,* 1963, Fig. 118.)

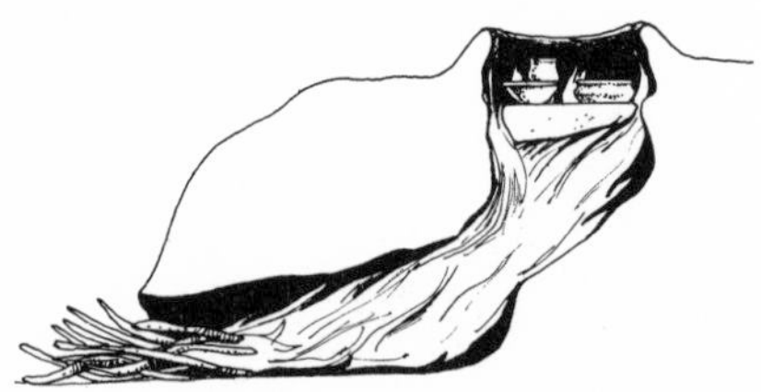

of one double and one quadruple—the skeletons lying face upward and stretched out (Fig. 32). Infants and children were buried in urns between the dwelling houses.[35]

This Pan-p'o-ts'un pattern in subdividing a village into a dwelling area, a kiln center, and a cemetery recurs throughout the Yang-shao settlements that have been extensively excavated, such as those near Pao-chi[36] and Hua Hsien[37] in Shensi, and Lin-shan-chai[38] and Miao-ti-kou[39] in Honan. More detailed information on small houses is known from the Miao-ti-kou site; another huge communal building was found at Liu-tzu-chen, and the cemetery at Pao-chi has yielded more and richer findings. But the general pattern repeats itself throughout, with such exceptions as that at Liu-tzu-chen where the Yang-shao village did not have its own cemetery but seems to have shared a large one some distance away with neighboring villages.

35. *Hsi-an Pan-p'o,* 1963. Shih Hsing-pang, *KKTH* (1955/3), 7–16; (1956/2), 23–30. Hsia Nai, *Archaeology, 10* (1957), 181–87. Shih Hsing-pang, *Rev. archéol., 2* (1959), 1–14.

36. *KK* (1959/2), 229–30, 241

37. *KK* (1959/2), 71–75; (1959/11), 585–87, 591.

38. An Chin-huai, *WWTKTL* (1957/8), 16–20. Chao Ch'ing-yün, *KKTH* (1958/9), 54–57. Mao Pao-liang, *KKTH* (1958/2), 1–5.

39. An Chih-min et al., *Miao-ti-kou yü San-li-ch'iao,* Peking, Science Press, 1959.

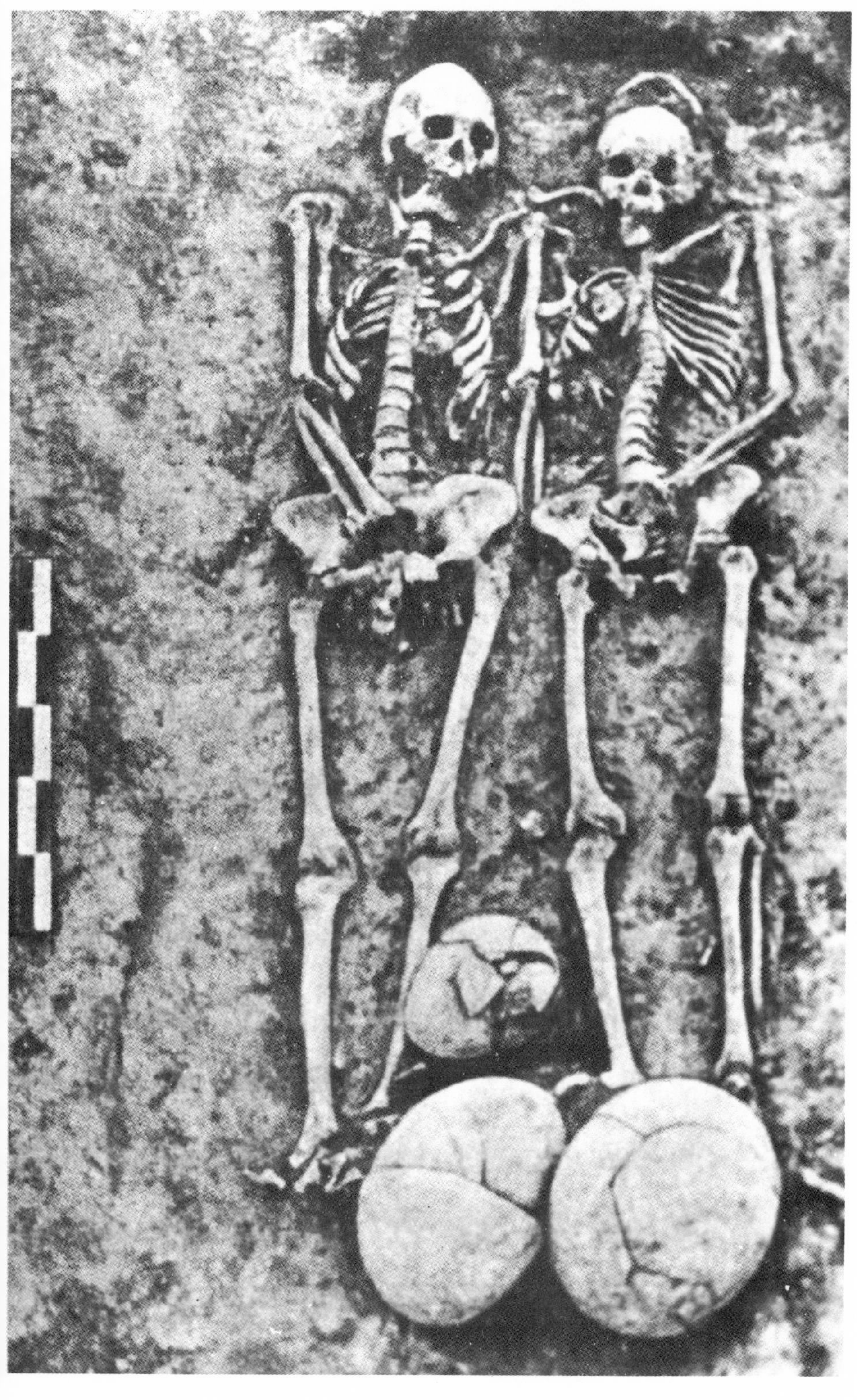

32. A Yang-shao burial at Pan-p'o-ts'un. (From *Hsi-an Pan-p'o,* 1963, Pl. CLXXIII.)

This is a very notable exception nevertheless, since the Liu-tzu-chen site belongs chronologically to a late phase of the Yang-shao stage, for this may indicate a tendency on the part of the farming villages near the end of this stage toward growth and fission. This tendency is made clear by J. G. Andersson's discovery in 1923–24 of a cemetery area on the Pan-shan Hills, in the T'ao River valley in eastern Kansu. The prehistoric cultures in eastern Kansu of the Yang'shao stage, as will be described presently, are generally of a later phase than the Yang-shao sites in the Nuclear Area. The location of the Pan-shan sites is best described in Andersson's own words:

> On both sides of the broad flat river-plain [of the River T'ao] the hill-sides rise in terraces up to 400 m above the river-valley, where we stand upon a dissected peneplane, which, at a level of 2200 m above the sea, extends far to both sides of the T'ao valley. The Pan Shan hills occupy a small area of this elevated plateau.[40]

Five burial areas have been located in the Pan-shan Hills: Pan-shan, Wa-kuan-tsui, Pien-chia-kou, Wang-chia-kou, and another unnamed site. Each is within a short distance (1,000–1,800 m) of the others.

> Each of the five grave sites is situated on one of the highest hills in the district, surrounded by steep and deep ravines, 400 meters above the floor of the neighboring T'ao valley . . . These cemeteries must have belonged to the habitations of the same period down on the valley terraces. It then became clear that the settlers in the T'ao valley of that age carried their dead 10 km or more from the villages up steep paths to hill-tops situated fully 400 meters above the dwellings of the living to resting places from which they could behold in a wide circle the place where they had grown up, worked, grown grey and at last found a grave swept by the winds and bathed in sunshine.[41]

The custom of sharing cemeteries during the later phases of the Yang-shao carries important social implications. It shows that toward the

40. Andersson, *BMFEA, 15* (1943), 116.
41. Ibid., p. 112.

end of this stage the population pressure had caused the fission of residential villages, which probably has important bearings upon the further development of the North China Neolithic culture into the next—Lung-shan—stage. They also show that a strong lineage consciousness must have been behind the custom of sending the dead to rest in the common ancestral ground. This latter inference is substantiated by the community patterns of the Yang-shao farmers. The longhouses at Pan-p'o-ts'un and Liu-tzu-chen, and the planned layout of the Pan-p'o-ts'un, Pao-chi, and Lin-shan-chai villages, as well as the clustered pit houses at Sun-ch'i-t'un, near Lo-yang in Honan,[42] suggest planned and segmented village layouts, and on these grounds and others, lineage and clan types of kinship groupings could be postulated. The graveyards were presumably burial places of kin groups as well as of village residents.

The dead were inhumed in extended or flexed posture, singly or in groups, in rectangular or amorphous pits in the village cemetery. A belief in the afterlife is indicated by the utensils and stored foods buried with the dead. In the Kansu area, pottery painted with red, the color of blood, and decorated with so-called death patterns, was found particularly in funerary association.[43] The probable lineage arrangement in the village cemetery and the regularity of the individual burials within the cemetery in many cases make it highly probable that the cult of ancestors to symbolize lineage solidarity had already been initiated during the Yang-shao stage, although it was not until the Lung-shan stage that the evidence of this cult became remarkable in the archaeological record. There is also some evidence that the Yang-shao farmers may have performed in their villages some kinds of fertility rites for the sake of crop harvests and fishing and hunting gains. This is implied by their burials of deer,[44] the frequent occurrence of female symbols among their ceramic decorative designs, and a painted bowl discovered at Pan-p'o-ts'un, depicting on the inner surface a tattooed face, possibly that of a priest, wearing a fish-shaped headdress (Fig. 33). Some of the beautifully painted bowls and miniature vessels also may have been used in this connection.

42. *WWTKTL* (1955/9), 58–64.

43. Andersson, *Children of the Yellow Earth,* London, Kegan Paul, Trench & Trübner, 1934, p. 315.

44. Andersson, *BMFEA, 15* (1943), 130.

33. A bowl painted with human and fish figures, discovered at the Yang-shao site at Pan-p'o-ts'un. (From *Wu Sheng Ch'u-t'u Chung-yao Wen-wu Chan-lan T'u-lu,* Peking, Wenwu Press, 1958, Pl. I.)

Andersson, on the basis of some incised parallel lines on bone artifacts from Lo-han-t'ang,[45] has also postulated a sort of "cryptic magic."

Turning to the Yang-shao farmers' technological achievements, we have considerable data on their ceramics and on their stone, bone, and antler industries. Stone implements were polished, pecked, and chipped. The most frequently found types are axes and adzes, with cylindrical bodies or an oval or lentoid cross section, used for felling trees and for carpentry; hoes and spades, with flat bodies and often with a hafting portion, for cultivation; chisels for carpentry and possibly woodcarving; rectangular knives, with central holes or two side notches, for weeding, harvesting, skinning, and scraping; and arrowheads. Other stone-made artifacts are net sinkers, mealing, grinding, and polishing stones, spindle whorls, etc. Ornaments such as rings and beads were made often of semiprecious stones, including jade.

Bone and antler were used for implements: needles, awls, fish-

45. Ibid., pp. 252–55.

hooks, arrowheads, spearheads, chisels, hoes, points, polishers, beads, etc. (Fig. 34).

Their pottery was handmade and molded, and indications of coiling techniques were observed at Liang-ts'un, in Ch'i Hsien, Shansi; at Pai-tao-kou-p'ing, near Lanchow in Kansu; at Yang-shao-ts'un in Honan; and at several localities near Sian, Shensi.[46] A turntable may have been used for finishing the rim, in Shansi–Shensi regions.[47] Pottery-making implements recovered include bone scrapers, stone polishers, paint-grinding stones, and paint containers. Kilns were discovered at many settlements. Several classes of pottery were made for various purposes. For cooking there were red or gray-brown thick-walled, pointed-bottomed pots, containing a noticeable amount of sand or mica temper and decorated with thick and thin cord-mat-basket impressions. For storage, coarse or fine red and gray pottery in the form of thin-necked, big-bellied jars were manufactured. Red and gray cups and canteens of a variety of pastes were made for drinking; and beautifully polished red and black bowls and basins, sometimes painted with black or red designs, were made of fine paste for use at meals or for rituals. In addition to these receptacles, spindle whorls, knives, sling balls, and net sinkers were also made of baked clay. The prevalence of cord-, mat-, and basket-impressed decorations on pottery suggests a high level of development of fabric and basket technology, and a variety of basketry techniques is discerned from the remains at Pan-p'o[48] (Fig. 35).

CHRONOLOGICAL AND REGIONAL SUBDIVISIONS

The generalizations about the life of the Yang-shao farmers, despite brevity and unavoidable incompleteness, are sufficient to show that each of the villages was a self-sufficient little community.[49] Such small communities during the earlier stages of the Neolithic dotted the North China landscape in the river valleys and on river terraces, and their ceramic decorative art throughout North China consti-

46. Yang Fu-tou and Chao Ch'i, *KKTH* (1956/2), 42. Ho Lo-fu, *KKHP* (1957/1), 5. Andersson, *BMFEA, 19* (1947), 54. Su Ping-ch'i and Wu Ju-tso, *KKTH* (1956/2), 35. Shih Hsing-pang, *KKTH* (1955/3), 12.
47. An Chih-min, *KKTH* (1956/5), 5.
48. H. P. Shih et al., *Hsi-an Pan-p'o*, pp. 161–62.
49. Robert Redfield, *The Little Community,* Univ. of Chicago Press, 1955.

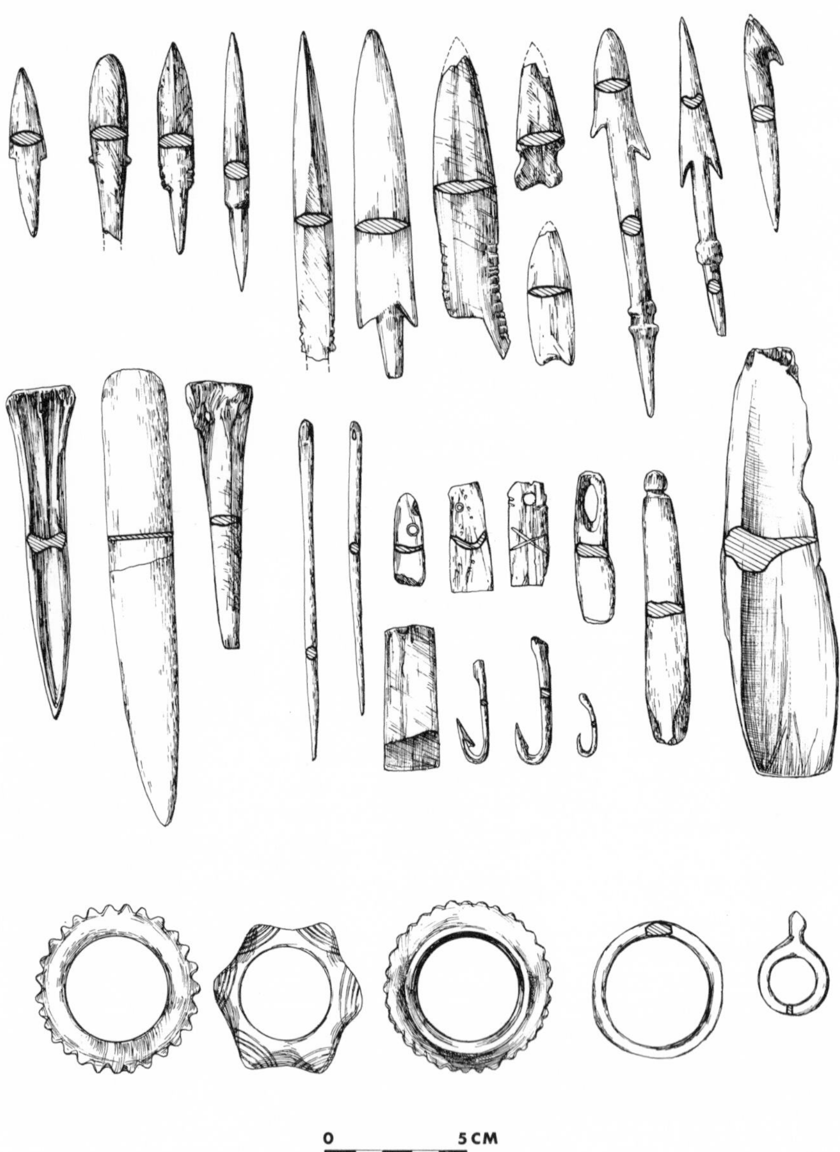

34. Bone artifacts from the Yang-shao site at Pan-p'o-ts'un. (From *Hsi-an Pan-p'o*, 1963, various figures.)

35. Types of basketry at the Yang-shao village at Pan-p'o-ts'un, reconstructed from impressions on pottery. (From *Hsi-an Pan-p'o,* 1963, Fig. 119.)

tutes a well-established horizon style of considerable overall uniformity. This style consists of plastic art and painting. The former is represented by only a handful of human figurines discovered at few and scattered locations (Fig. 36), but ceramic painting is universal and can be given an analytic treatment because of its infinite variety of composition. All the painted pottery of this period in North China has a brick-red or yellowish-brown base, which is then burnished or polished and painted with red or black pigment. Regional variations are to be expected. In some regions, white slips were applied before painting (western and northern Honan and, occasionally, central Shensi); in others (Kansu and Chinghai, southern Shansi and western Hopei), pigment was directly applied on the red or brown surface;

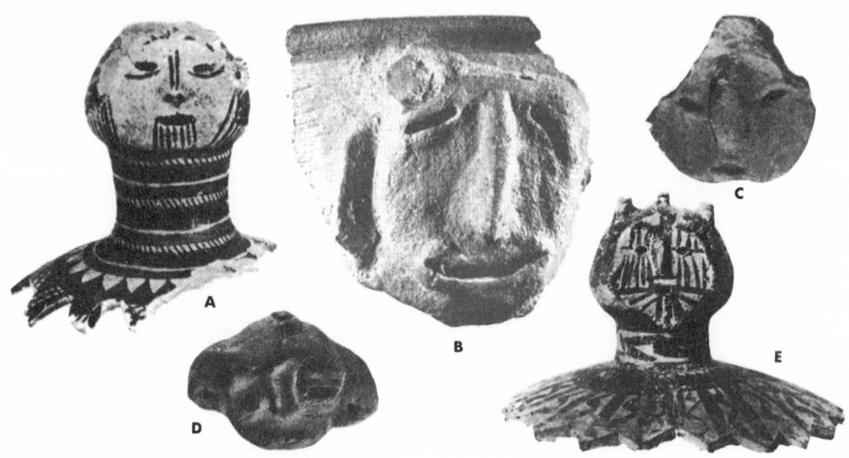

36. Clay heads found at Yang-shao sites. (A, E, Pan-shan, from J. G. Andersson, *BMFEA, 15,* 1943, Pls. 186, 187. B, Chiang-hsi-ts'un, Fu-feng Hsien, Shensi, from *KK,* 1959/11, Pl. VIII, no. 1. C, Liu-tzu-chen, Hua Hsien, Shensi, from *KK,* 1959/2, Pl. II, no. 12. D, Pan-p'o-ts'un, Sian, Shensi, from *Hsi-an Pan-p'o,* 1963, Pl. CLXII. Not to scale.)

black paint was used in all regions, but red was less common; and painted decor was applied on the inner surface of the pottery only in some of the areas (Kansu, Chinghai, and central Shensi).[50] However, a major contrast is seen between the painted pottery of Kansu (including Chinghai for the sake of convenience) and that of the Chung-yüan.

> In a very striking way the painted motifs of the Kansu group are different from those of the other groups. The colours are red and black, but the red is seldom so fresh and bright as it is in western Honan. Except at Hsin-Tien, the painting seems to have been done with the intention of covering the surface as much as possible, and not leaving any blank space, contrary to what is found in the Shansi and Honan groups . . . The painted decoration, unlike that of the other groups, is intended to be viewed from the top, instead of from the side. The motifs are

50. G. D. Wu, *Prehistoric Pottery in China,* London, Kegan Paul, Trench & Trübner, 1938, pp. 145–47. An Chih-min, *WWTKTL* (1956/8), 41–49; *KKTH* (1956/5), 1–11. Shih Hsing-pang, *KKTH* (1955/1), 28–30. T'ung Chu-ch'en, *KKHP* (1957/2), 7–21.

very complicated, though there are a number of stock designs, which frequently occur.[51]

Admitting the differences in decorative motif and form between the painted pottery of Kansu (represented by Ma-chia-yao) and Honan (represented by Yang-shao-ts'un), Andersson nevertheless considers these two phases as "strictly contemporary" regional variations.[52] In other words, according to Andersson the Yang-shao horizon of the North China Neolithic contains no less than two parallel regional pottery traditions.

The excavations and studies of the Yang-shao sites in both the Chung-yüan and Kansu in the past sixteen years have evoked a far more complex picture of their chronology and regional grouping than was realized before. On the basis of the available data we know now that the Yang-shao farmers were distributed in an H-shaped area from eastern Kansu in the west, through the Weishui Valley in the middle, to the Huangho Valley of southern Shansi and northwestern Honan in the east (Fig. 25). Within its area of distribution the Yang-shao culture exhibited differing features in the various regions, and had a considerable time depth susceptible of further subdivisions. For an adequate description of the chronology and subdivisions of the Yang-shao culture it would be necessary to describe and reconstruct a series of regional chronologies and to correlate them into an areal sequence. This cannot be done here, for it would require an inappropriate amount of space, and the results would still be incomplete since new site reports continue to be published. I shall merely summarize the archaeologists' conclusions at this date, but for convenience I will reverse the order of analysis and describe from the top—i.e. from the highest level of cultural contrast—downward.

Within the area of distribution of Yang-shao sites the contrast between the Chung-yüan Yang-shao and the Kansu Yang-shao, as noted by Andersson and G. D. Wu, remains valid. Purely on stylistic grounds Wu had felt that the Kansu group was probably later than the Chung-yüan (= Wu's Honan) group in time, because its decorative designs are more complicated and mature.[53] The sites of these

51. Wu, *Prehistoric Pottery in China,* p. 146.
52. *BMFEA, 15* (1943), 104.
53. Wu, *Prehistoric Pottery in China,* pp. 168–69.

two groups meet and overlap in the upper Weishui Valley of eastern Kansu. Going into the Kansu area from the Chung-yüan along the River Wei, we see a continuation of the Chung-yüan style into the T'ao Valley, especially at the sites in T'ien-shui Hsien, Kan-ku Hsien, Wu-shan Hsien, and Lung-hsi Hsien. However, starting from T'ien-shui Hsien in the upper Wei, remains of painted pottery of the Kansu style begin to occur and become increasingly dominant into the T'ao Valley and farther northwest. In the upper Wei and the T'ao valleys the two styles overlap.[54] A key stratified site was found in 1957 at Ma-chia-yao in Lin-t'ao Hsien, where sherds of the Kansu style were found overlying sherds of the Chung-yüan style:

> On the First Terrace (10–30 m) at the northern bank of the Ma-yü ravine, south of Ma-chia-yao, the cultural deposits are fairly deep. A clear section is seen on an exposed surface. The uppermost layer is a stratum of disturbed modern humus. Beneath the humus, about one meter in thickness, is a layer of prehistoric cultural deposits, about 3.5 meters thick. The upper meter and a half of this layer is composed of loose ashes, from which were derived a great number of potsherds. These are of fine or coarse paste, tempered or not tempered, some with painted designs. The paint was applied in black pigment. The designs are in most cases composed of thick lines, and include many parallel lines and black dots. Sherds painted on the inner surface, and rim sherds with complicated painted patterns are also found. The forms of the painted sherds include bowls, jars, basins, and pots. The unpainted, fine-pasted red or gray sherds are mostly parts of bowls. The sand-tempered sherds are mostly cord-marked, and are in the forms of pots and basins with outcurving, flaring mouths. These types are similar to the Ma-chia-yao types excavated from Yen-erh-wan, near Lanchow. The ashy layers below this stratum consist of compact earth, about two meters thick. Cultural remains from this lower layer include polished stone chisels, bone artifacts, gray rings of baked clay, and potsherds. Some of the sherds are painted in black pigment in the designs of wavy triangles, hooked dots, thin parallel lines,

54. Kuo Te-yüng, *KKTH* (1958/9), 72–73. Chang Hsüeh-cheng, *KKTH* (1958/9), 41. An Chih-min, *KKTH* (1956/6), 13.

thick bands, and net patterns. There are also some rim sherds with simple painted patterns, sherds of basins with inwardly curved mouths, plain fine-pasted red and gray sherds, and a great number of cord-marked pointed-bottomed jars and thick-rimmed basins and pots. In short, this lower cultural stratum is similar to the Yangshao types of the Upper Wei.[55]

According to such distributional and stratigraphic evidence, it appears clear that the Yang-chao culture of the Chung-yüan subdivision expanded westward as far as the T'ao River valley, where it developed into the Kansu subdivision.

Within the Chung-yüan and the Kansu Yang-shao cultures themselves, further subgroupings are recognizable, each apparently localizing in a separate region and overlapping in time with the other subgroups. The following regional complexes of the Yang-shao culture have been proposed.

The Chung-yüan Yang-shao Culture

The most recently recognized, and perhaps the earliest phase of the Yang-shao culture in the Chung-yüan region, is a complex of artifacts first known from the Li-chia-ts'un site[56] of Hsi-hsiang in Shensi, on the southern side of the Tsinling Mountains on the upper Hanshui River, and since identified in a series of sites north of Tsinling in the Weishui Valley and even the Huangho Valley in Honan, including the lower strata at Pei-shou-ling in Pao-chi and Yüan-chün-miao in Hua Hsien, and the sites at Lao-kuan-t'ai in Hua Hsien and on the banks of River Lo near Lo-ning, western Honan.[57] The types of artifacts that characterize this phase of Yang-shao culture include (Fig. 37): "jars and pots of sandy paste with incised, fine-cord-marked, and incised and cord-marked decoration; bowls with quasi-ring-feet or ring feet; light-brown bowls of hard texture with indented rims; plain jars with small mouths and wide, globular bodies; and bowls with three short, solid legs."[58] Stratigraphic evidence at Pei-shou-ling and Yüan-chün-miao shows conclusively that

55. Chang Hsüeh-cheng, *KKTH* (1958/9), 38–39.
56. T. L. Liao, *KK* (1961/7), 352–54.
57. P. C. Su, *KKHP* (1965/1), 55. N. Hsia, *KK* (1964/10), 486.
58. P. C. Su, *KKHP* (1965/1), 55–56.

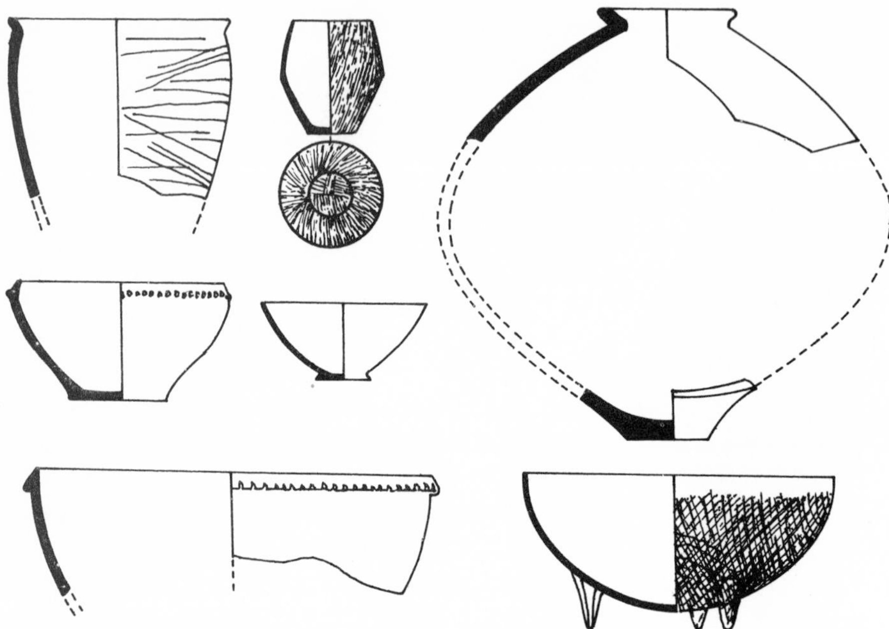

37. Pottery of the Li-chia-ts'un phase of Yang-shao culture. (From Su Ping-ch'i, *KKHP*, 1965/1, p. 55.)

this phase of Yang-shao culture antedates both of the other phases of this culture to be described below, and the absence of painted decoration in the phase and the prevalence of cord marks point to the possibility that this Li-chia-ts'un phase is perhaps the earliest Yang-shao culture now known and is a first substantiation of the hypothetical Sheng-wen horizon. Its proximity to Szechwan, within the area of distribution of the corded-ware cultures of South China, is particularly noteworthy and may provide a link between the North China and the Southeast Asia centers of agricultural beginnings.

A second phase is represented by the site of Pan-p'o-ts'un, and identical assemblages are known from Pei-shou-ling in Pao-chi, Yüan-chün-miao in Hua Hsien, and Heng-chen-ts'un in Hua-yin, all in the Weishui Valley of Shensi.[59] The features that contrast the Pan-p'o phase most sharply with the others are pointed-bottom jars

59. H. P. Shih, *Hsi-an Pan-p'o,* p. 230. P. C. Su, *KKHP* (1965/1), 61–63.

38. Pottery of the Pan-p'o phase excavated from Pan-p'o-ts'un, Sian, Shensi. (From *Hsi-an Pan-p'o,* 1963. Not to scale.)

with so-called gourd-shaped mouths and bowls painted in blackish geometric and fish designs (Fig. 38). The third, or Miao-ti-kou phase —typified by the lower stratum of Miao-ti-kou in Shan Hsien of Honan and the Ch'üan-hu-ts'un site in Hua Hsien, eastern Shensi—is characterized by pointed-bottom jars with double lip and small mouth, and bowls painted with plant-geometric and bird designs (Fig. 39).[60]

The temporal and historical relationship between the Pan-p'o and the Miao-ti-kou phases of the Yang-shao culture is now a focus of archaeological debate.[61] Some believe Pan-p'o is the earlier of the two; others insist it is the later. Shih Hsing-pang[62] and Su Ping-ch'i[63] are both convinced, however, that these phases represent two parallel and contemporaneous "tribal groups." Shih believes the Pan-p'o phase to be the remains of a Yang-shao tribe with fish totems and the Miao-ti-kou phase the remains of a tribe with bird totems. Su has brought attention to the flower designs of the Miao-ti-kou phase pottery and the location of its sites in the neighborhood of Hua (Flower) Mountain in Hua and Hua-yin counties in eastern Shensi, points that may be pertinent to the earliest name of the Chinese people—Hua.

This is very interesting, but more relevant are two items of information that have significant bearing on the temporal relationship of these Yang-shao culture phases. The first is that stratigraphic excavations in 1959–61 at the Yang-shao site near Hsia-meng-ts'un in Pin Hsien, in the Ching River valley of Shensi, have disclosed that the Pan-p'o type of remains was stratigraphically below the Miao-ti-kou type.[64] This would not rule out the possibility that the two cultural phases were contemporaneous, for Pin Hsien is closer to the Pan-p'o sphere of distribution, and the stratigraphy there is what an intrusive situation would be. But the second fact is perhaps even more revealing. Comparing the various types of artifacts found at the Pan-p'o-

60. C. M. An et al., *Miao-ti-kou yü San-li-ch'iao.* P. C. Su, *KKHP* (1965/1), 57–61.

61. *Hsin Chung-kuo ti k'ao-ku shou-huo,* Peking, Wenwu Press, 1962, p. 12. Y. H. Li, *KK* (1964/7), 374–86.

62. H. P. Shih, *KK* (1962/6), 326.

63. P. C. Su, *KKHP* (1965/1), 66.

64. S. K. Li, *KK* (1962/6), 292–94.

39. Pottery of the Miao-ti-kou I phase, Yang-shao culture. (From An Chih-min et al., *Miao-ti-kou yü San-li-ch'iao,* Peking, Science Press, 1959, various plates. Not to scale.)

ts'un and Miao-ti-kou sites,[65] Su Ping-ch'i has concluded that "the Pan-p'o inhabitants put equal emphasis on agriculture, fishing, hunting, and tree-felling, whereas the Miao-ti-kou people engaged principally in agriculture, with only slight fishing and hunting activity. The Pan-p'o people used animal skins for clothing, but the Miao-ti-kou people relied more heavily on plant fabrics."[66] Su intends to show by this that the Pan-p'o and the Miao-ti-kou "tribes" engaged in different types of subsistence activities and were therefore contemporary cultures with different styles. It is apparent, however, that the Pan-p'o phase was at an earlier stage of agricultural development, where fishing and hunting were still important in subsistence, and forest clearance was a major part of its agricultural activity.

In addition to the three phases described above, there are other sites of the Yang-shao culture, less well known and not clearly classifiable. Su Ping-ch'i formulates a fourth phase of Yang-shao culture in the Lo-yang area, and considers the Yang-shao sites in southern Shansi and northern Honan unclassifiable at present,[67] but Yang Chien-fang would not hesitate to expand the areal distribution of the Miao-ti-kou phase and to include under it many sites in southern Shansi and northwestern Honan.[68] It is apparent, in any event, that the classification of the cultural phases of the Yang-shao culture and their chronological placement are only just beginning.

The Kansu Yang-shao Culture

In 1921–23 J. G. Andersson undertook a series of archaeological surveys in eastern Kansu in the Huangho Valley near Lanchow and in the T'ao and Tahsia river valleys.[69] The prehistoric sites he discovered he classified into six groups, three of which are Stone Age and were called Ch'i-chia, Pan-shan/Ma-chia-yao, and Ma-ch'ang. Actually these were four different phases, because the finds at Pan-

65. *Knives:* Pan-p'o 217, Miao-ti-kou 200; *stone axes:* Pan-p'o 313, Miao-ti-kou 27; *stone adzes:* Pan-p'o 71, Miao-ti-kou 5; *stone choppers:* Pao-p'o 59, Miao-ti-kou 0; *fishing spears, harpoons and hooks:* Pan-p'o 36, Miao-ti-kou 0; *net-sinkers:* Pan-p'o 320, Miao-ti-kou 5; *arrowheads:* Pan-p'o 288, Miao-ti-kou 71; *spindle whorls:* Pan-p'o 52, Miao-ti-kou 100; *bone awls and needles:* Pan-p'o 996; Miao-ti-kou 26.

66. P. C. Su, *KKHP* (1965/1), 66.

67. Ibid., pp. 68–69, 74–75.

68. C. F. Yang, *KKHP* (1962/1), 49–80.

69. *Preliminary Report on Archaeological Research in Kansu,* GSuC Memoir, ser. A, no. 5, 1925.

40. Pottery of the Ma-chia-yao phase of Kansu Yang-shao culture. (From *KK*, 1962/6, p. 319.)

41. Pottery of the Pan-shan phase of Kansu Yang-shao culture. (From *KK*, 1962/6, p. 323.)

42. Pottery of the Ma-ch'ang phase of Kansu Yang-shao culture. (From *KK,* 1962/6, p. 324.)

shan were mortuary and those at Ma-chia-yao were habitation remains. Andersson, however, considered these two phases to be entirely contemporary and representative of two different types of assemblage. He thought this stage was strictly contemporary with the Yang-shao culture of Honan.

During the almost half century since Andersson's initial work in Kansu, many more sites have been investigated and several extensively excavated. Andersson's grouping of the four cultural phases remains valid but, aside from the great amount of additional information accruing to each of them, three important modifications must now be made. First, the entire Kansu Yang-shao culture has been shown to be later than and an offshoot of the Chung-yüan Yang-shao culture. Second, the Ch'i-chia phase must now be removed as an early phase of the Yang-shao sequence and placed in a later period (to be described in another chapter). Finally, the Ma-chia-yao and the Pan-shan assemblages are no longer generally regarded as contemporary complexes of different types but are thought by many to be two separate phases of the Yang-shao culture in Kansu. Stratigraphic and stylistic studies now suggest the following sequence of the Kansu Yang-shao phases: Ma-chia-yao, earliest; Pan-shan, following; and Ma-ch'ang, latest and farthest west.[70]

The three phases are best distinguished by their ceramics. The Ma-chia-yao pottery, best known from the site of Ma-chia-yao in Lin-t'ao Hsien,[71] is characterized by a number of distinctively shaped bowls, jars, and small-mouth jars of fine paste, high luster, with black decorations painted on red or yellow. Characteristic designs appear

70. C. F. Yang, *KKHP* (1962/1), 71–77. H. P. Shih, *KK* (1962/6), 318–29.
71. Bo Sommarström, *BMFEA, 28* (1956), 55–138.

on the inside of shallow bowls and beakers. The painted decorations consist of animals (frogs and birds) and geometric patterns, the latter being distinctively curvilinear and gracefully executed (Fig. 40).

The sophisticated artistry of the Pan-shan painted pottery, found in museums around the world and typically from the sites on the Pan-shan Hills in Lin-t'ao Hsien,[72] is characterized by the tall jar with small mouth, wide belly, two loop handles at the largest diameter of the body, and flat bottom. Most of the painted decorations are in red and black and form a wide band covering the upper part of the body; the basic motifs are a large variety of spirals and gourd-shaped units (Fig. 41). The Ma-ch'ang phase, named after the type site at Ma-ch'ang-yen in eastern Chinghai,[73] apparently followed the Pan-shan phase; it had similar pottery forms, but the decorative designs are less elaborate and generally are composed of anthropomorphic patterns (Fig. 42).

72. Nils Palmgren, *PS,* ser. D. (1934). Andersson, *BMFEA, 15* (1943.)

73. Nils Palmgren, *PS,* ser. D., no. 3 (1934); Andersson, *BMFEA, 15* (1943), 107–118.

CHAPTER FOUR

THE LUNGSHANOID EXPANSION AND THE FORMATION OF LOCAL CULTURES

CLASSIFICATION OF NEOLITHIC CULTURES IN NORTH CHINA

The period around 1920 can be called a turning point in the study of ancient China. The history of China before the Three Dynasties had been a legendary account of the Sage Kings; after 1920 it became a true history of China's cultural development from the Stone Age to civilization, based upon archaeological evidence. This change in the basic orientation of historiography occurred in a context of scholarly skepticism of legends that stemmed partly from the May Fourth Movement of 1919 but was directly brought about by a series of significant archaeological discoveries at that time. These included the excavation of Palaeolithic implements in the Ordos in 1920 and of painted pottery sites at Yang-shao-ts'un in Honan and Sha-kuo-t'un in Liaoning in 1921–22—discoveries that helped fill the historiographic void with new empirical data. In view of the fact that Chinese elements plainly occurred in the newly found Painted Pottery Culture and, also, that the human skeletal remains at these sites were quickly pronounced "Proto-Chinese" by physical anthropologists, scholars of ancient China at once undertook to seek in the Painted Pottery Culture the genesis of the ancient civilizations of the land. The two archaeological sites first established in scientific scholarship were Yang-shao-ts'un and Hsiao-t'un (the site of the last Shang Dynasty capital that was not excavated until 1928), and the names Yang-shao and Hsiao-t'un soon became two landmarks of ancient Chinese history and historiography. Andersson, excavator of the Yang-shao-ts'un site, dated the Yang-shao culture to 2200–1700 B.C. in the belief that it immediately preceded the historical civilizations.

It is true that elements of the Shang civilization at Hsiao-t'un can be found at Yang-shao-ts'un, but exactly how far apart were the two? Li Chi, for the first time, undertook to make a detailed comparison between the Yang-shao and the Hsiao-t'un cultures, arriving at the following conclusions:[1] the culture with painted pottery was earlier than the Shang; the Shang culture as represented by the site of Hsiao-t'un was derived from one with which the Yang-shao culture was only indirectly related.

Problems naturally arose about the ethnic identity of the Yang-shao culture in terms of ancient texts—now that it was shown not to be directly ancestral to the Shang—and about the direct antecedents of the Shang in archaeological terms. Hsü suggested that the Yang-shao culture could probably be identified with the Yü Hsia people of the ancient texts and that the Hsiao-t'un culture was probably derived from the eastern coastal portions of North China, the "circum-Pohai Bay area that probably cradled the first Chinese civilization."[2]

It was at this time, when speculations were being ventured that the Shang's antecedents were derived from Shantung and its environs, that a new type of Neolithic culture was discovered in Shantung. In 1928, seven years after the excavation of Yang-shao-ts'un, a so-called Black Pottery site was discovered by Wu Chin-ting (G. D. Wu), a native of Shantung and pupil of Li Chi, at Ch'eng-tzu-yai, near the town of Lung-shan in the heart of this eastern province.[3] The site was not excavated until 1930–31 when the Institute of History and Philology, Academia Sinica, whose excavations at An-yang were forced to a halt in 1930 by outbreaks of civil disturbance in Honan, gave it concentrated attention. Two prehistoric cultural layers were uncovered at Ch'eng-tzu-yai—a Neolithic assemblage in a lower stratum and an upper stratum containing Eastern Chou types.[4] The Neolithic culture exhibited several remarkable characteristics. Its pottery included pieces that were thin, hard, lustrous, and black, drastically different from the painted red sherds at Yang-shao-ts'un. Its stone inventory, though broadly similar to the Yang-shao, contained a number of new types, and its abundant shell artifacts were also distinctive. Thus, in the Neolithic archaeology of North China appeared the concept of a Black Pottery (Lung-shan) Culture to contrast with the Painted Pottery (Yang-shao) Culture. Moreover, in the

1. *An-yang Fa-chüeh Pao-kao, 2* (1930), 337–47.
2. Hsü Chung-shu, ibid., *3* (1931), 523–57.
3. Wu Chin-ting, *BIHP, 1,* fasc. 4 (1930).
4. Li Chi et al., *Ch'eng-tzu-yai,* Nanking, 1934.

new type of culture there were features that indicated close connections with the Shang, especially oracle bones and a village wall constructed by the *hang-t'u* method. Thus it appeared that the prototype of the first civilization of China was located about where scholars speculated it should be. In his preface to the Ch'eng-tzu-yai report, Li Chi made the following observations:[5]

> Because these black-pottery sites are scattered in Shantung and the eastern part of Honan, the central point most likely is in the Shantung region. To what degree they are related to the painted pottery cultures of the northwest and the north, we as yet have no way of knowing. But that there are two independent complexes, and that the development in each area manifested temporal differences is very clear. In the culture of the earliest period of Chinese history as represented at Yin-hsü, according to all our experience, not only was bone divination bound in with all the mental life of that time but also the practice of bone divination probably had a very great motivating influence on the early evolution of Chinese writing. Although the divination bones at Ch'eng-tzu-yai manifested no writing, nevertheless, the pottery sherds of that time period included some which bore symbols, and one could see that the lower-stratum Ch'eng-tzu-yai culture had already freed itself completely from the "Dark Ages." All this gives us a strong hint, namely, that the single most important element composing China's earliest historic culture was evidently one which developed in the east, in the region of the states of Ch'i and Lu, [which flourished] in the Spring and Autumn and in the Warring States periods. If we can take the Ch'eng-tzu-yai black-pottery culture and search out the sequence of its expansion and the exact extent of its sphere, we can then settle the greater part of the history of the dawn period in China.

This new view of culture history quite naturally served to bridge the gap between the historic and the prehistoric. In the Neolithic archaeology of the 1930s the Painted Pottery Culture of western Honan,

5. Ibid., pp. xv–xvi, trans. by Kenneth Starr, Yale University Publications in Anthropology, 52, 1956, pp. 21–22.

Shansi, Shensi, and Kansu, and the Black Pottery Culture of eastern Honan and Shantung, came to be regarded as a pair of opposing, parallel cultures of the "late" Neolithic period that immediately preceded the rise of the Shang civilization. This view was strengthened by discoveries of the Black Pottery Culture sites after Ch'eng-tzu-yai—Hou-kang of An-yang in Honan in 1931;[6] Kao-ching-t'ai-tzu in An-yang[7] and Ta-lai-tien in Chün Hsien[8] in Honan in 1932; Liu-chuang in Chün Hsien in 1933,[9] T'ung-lo-chai in An-yang[10] in 1934, and Liang-ch'eng-chen in Jih-chao in Shantung;[11] and Tsao-lü-t'ai and Hei-ku-tui in Yüng-ch'eng in Honan[12] in 1936, all of them in eastern Honan and Shantung. Furthermore, similar finds were reported from Shou Hsien in northern Anhwei in 1934,[13] Liang-chu near Hang-chow in northern Chekiang in 1936,[14] and Yang-t'ou-wa near Port Arthur on Liaotung Peninsula in 1933,[15] extending the Lung-shan domain to much of the Pacific coast from Pohai Bay to Hangchow Bay. Thus the Two Culture theory became entrenched in the Neolithic archaeology of North China, with the Lung-shan of the east designated as the progenitor of the Shang civilization.[16]

Soon after the discovery of the new Black Pottery Culture, however, archaeologists began to be puzzled by the following phenomena that seemed somewhat at odds with the above view. Remains of both cultures were found at a number of sites in northern Honan and, without exception, Yang-shao culture remains were found from layers lower—and thus earlier—than the Lung-shan remains, a sequence

6. Liang Ssu-yüng, *An-yang Fa-chüeh Pao-kao, 4* (1933), 609–25; *Essays Presented to Mr. Ts'ai Yuan P'ei on His Sixty-fifth Birthday, 2,* Nanking, Academia Sinica, 1933, 555–67.

7. Wu Chin-ting, *An-yang Fa-chüeh Pao-kao, 4* (1933), 627–33; *TYKKPK, 1* (1936).

8. Liu Yao, ibid., pp. 69–89.

9. Ibid., pp. 254–55.

10. Ibid., p. 255.

11. Ibid., p. 255.

12. Li Ching-tan, *Chung-kuo K'ao-ku Hsüeh-pao, 2* (1937), 83–120.

13. Wang Hsiang, ibid., pp. 179–250.

14. Shih Hsin-keng, *Liang-chu,* Hangchow, the West Lake Museum, 1938.

15. Kanaseki Takeo et al., *Yang-t'ou-wa,* Archaeologia Orientalis, ser. B, no. 3, Tokyo, 1943.

16. See e.g. Li Chi, *The Beginnings of Chinese Civilization,* Seattle, The Univ. Washington Press, 1957; Cheng Te-k'un, *Prehistoric China,* Cambridge, Heffer, 1959.

of culture first established by the famous Hou-kang stratigraphy where Yang-shao, Lung-shan, and Shang culture remains were found in temporal succession (Fig. 43). At many sites in western Honan, on the other hand, remains of both cultures were discovered in the same layers without discernible relationship of stratification. Liang Ssu-yüng attempted to explain these by suggesting that the Lung-shan culture intruded into western Honan from the east, thus effecting the appearance of "mixed culture sites" in that area.[17]

If the archaeological data before the Sino-Japanese War of 1937–45 could be explicated within the Two Culture framework and if the puzzling phenomena described above could be explained away by the idea of mixed cultures, new data brought to light during the war could no longer be treated according to this view. These were the discovery of Lungshan-like gray pottery remains in the Weishui Valley of Shensi in 1943.[18] In an article discussing the Neolithic cultures of North China published in 1952,[19] Professor Shih Chang-ju, discoverer of Lungshan-like cultures in Shensi, attempted to solve the dilemma by adding a third—Gray Pottery Culture—to the Neolithic potpourri.

The 1950s, however, witnessed the beginning of a drastic revision of the Neolithic classification, which was attempted from two different but complementary approaches: the synthesizers tried to revise the old framework to accommodate the old and new data that could no longer be adequately encompassed within the older structure; the fieldworkers attempted to analyze the new data and design a new framework on this basis. As late as 1957, when T'ung Chu-ch'en attempted to summarize the Neolithic materials of the Huangho and the lower Yangtze valleys to that date,[20] he still adhered to the Two Culture theory. Two years later, several scholars independently proposed a new scheme of classification under which the Yang-shao and the Lung-shan were considered as two successive stages of development of the same culture rather than two cultures of different origin.

Among the first to plant the seeds of doubt about the Two Culture theory were several foreign scholars who, as relatively impartial observers, were less bound by loyalty to the orthodox views than their

17. *Essays Presented to Ts'ai, 2,* 560–61.
18. Shih Chang-ju, *BIHP, 27* (1956), 205–323.
19. *Ta-lu Tsa-chih, 4* (1952), 3, 65–75.
20. T'ung Chu-ch'en, *KKHP* (1957/2).

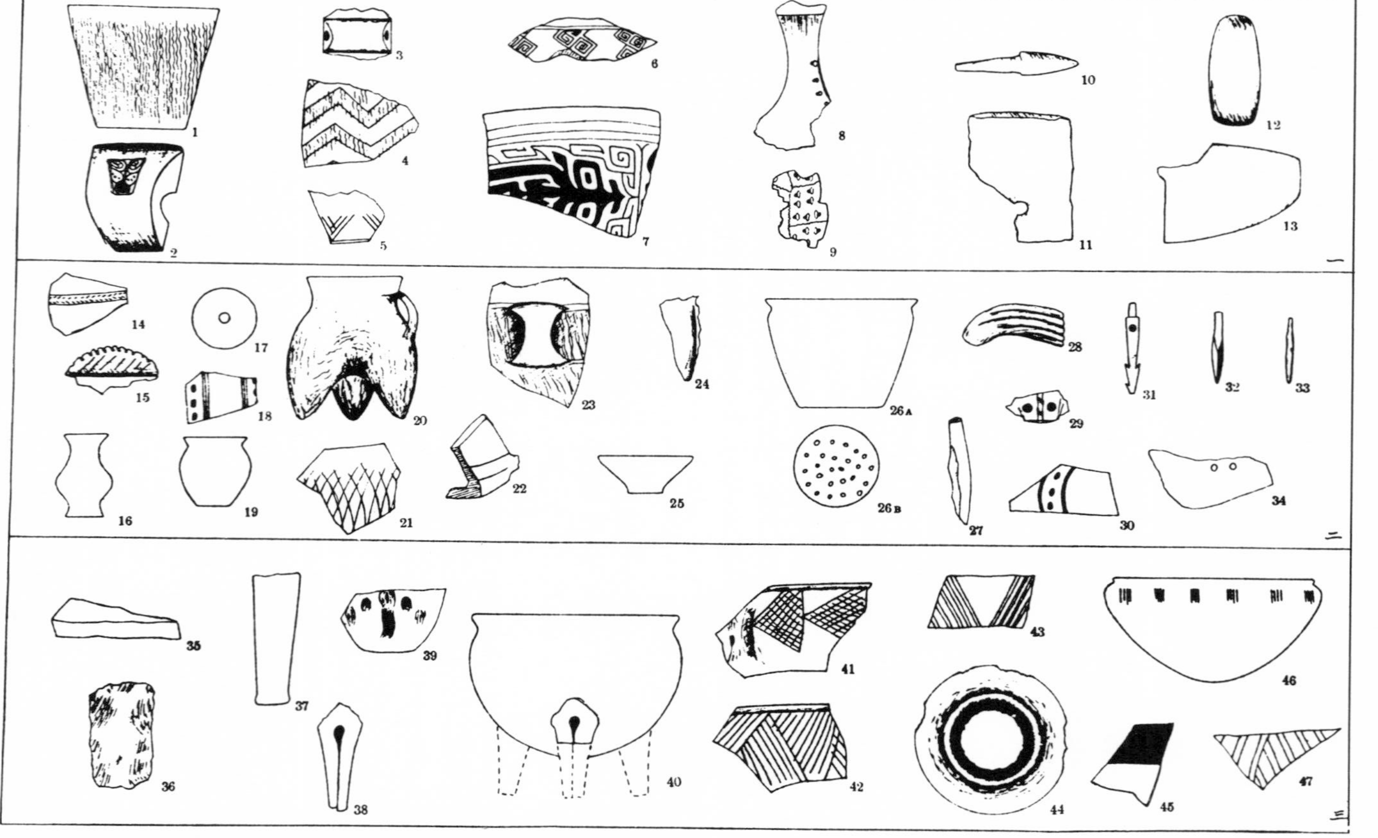

43. Stratigraphy showing the succession of the Yang-shao (*lower*), Lung-shan (*middle*), and Shang (*upper*) cultures at the Hou-kang site, An-yang, northern Honan. (From Liang Ssu-yüng, *Essays Presented to Mr. Ts'ai Yüan P'ei on His 65th Birthday,* Institute of History and Philology, Academia Sinica, 1935, vol. 2, p. 555.)

Chinese colleagues and less hesitant to question and criticize when confronted by new evidence from the field. In reviewing the archaeological developments in China in the early 1950s, the late Lauriston Ward reported, "Excavations of prehistoric sites . . . are stated to show that black pottery is found everywhere in the same levels as painted pottery, thus indicating that earlier views about two separate Neolithic cultures in the North China plain, the Yang-shao or Red Pottery culture and the Lung-shan or Black Pottery culture, may have to be seriously modified."[21] The significance of the divergence between the two ceramic cultures—chronological or cultural—was also questioned by two Japanese scholars, Mizuno Seiichi and Sekino Takeshi, in 1953, at the Fourth Far Eastern Prehistory Congress at Quezon City in the Philippines.[22]

At this time, as Ward pointed out, Lungshan-like remains were discovered at K'o-hsing-chuang in 1951 and A-ti-ts'un in 1953, both near Sian in Shensi, from a layer between a Painted Pottery stratum below and a Western Chou stratum above.[23] Similar findings in an identical stratigraphic situation were made in southern Shansi.[24] These discoveries made untenable the old Two Culture theory and led me, among others, to ponder anew the whole scope of cultural classification in Neolithic North China, seeking answers to the following questions:

1. Could the Gray Pottery Cultures of Shansi and Shensi be contemporary and comparable with the Black Pottery Culture of Shantung?
2. If the answer is affirmative, is it possible that the Lung-shan culture and all Lungshan-like ("Lungshanoid") cultures belong to a developmental level subsequent to the Yang-shao culture of the Chung-yüan?
3. If so, how does one explain the so-called mixed sites of western Honan?

21. L. Ward, in *Current Anthropology,* W. T. Thomas, ed., Univ. Chicago Press, 1956, pp. 89–90.
22. Mizuno, "Prehistoric China: Yang-shao and Pu-chao-chai," and Sekino, "On the Black and Grey Pottery of Ancient China," *PFEFC,* 4th, 1953, vol. 1, fasc. 1, 1956.
23. *KKTH* (1955/1); (1956/2).
24. *WWTKTL* (1956/10).

TABLE 5.

Yang-shao and Lungshanoid Cultural Contrasts

Yangshao	*Lungshanoid*
Shifting settlement; repetitive occupation	Permanent settlement; relatively permanent occupation
Slash-and-burn cultivation	Irrigation? Fertilizer? Fallow fields?
Pigs and dogs as principal domestic animals	Cattle and sheep sharply increased in addition to pigs and dogs
Largely confined to the Nuclear Area; indicative of stable population density?	Far-reaching expansions into eastern plains, Manchuria, Central and South China; indicating population pressure from permanent settlement and great productivity?
Interareal uniformity of style	Emergence of many regional styles
More symmetrical edges than asymmetrical on all edged tools; more circular and oval cross sections; indicates extensive use of the wood-felling complex for field clearance	More asymmetrical edges than symmetrical; more rectangular cross sections; indicates extensive use of carpenters' tools (adzes, chisels, antler wedges)
Rectangular, single-holed or double-notched stone knives characteristic; indicates more game hunting and use of longitudinal cutting tools	Semilunar and double-holed, or sickle-shaped stone knives and shell sickles characteristic; indicates more extensive use of harvesting tools
Pottery handmade	Beginning of wheel-made pottery; indicates intensified crafts specialization
None	Scapulimancy; indicates intensified occupational specialization
No defensive works; few artifacts exclusively for fighting	Appearance of *hang-t'u* village walls and weapons; indicates necessity for fortification and means for offensive action
Burial practice showing age and sex differentiation	Growing number of otherwise differentiated burials; possibly indicates more rigidly constituted classes
Community patterns showing little evidence of major social stratification	Concentration of jade artifacts at isolated spots in one site; indicates more intensive status differentiation

TABLE 5 (*cont.*)

Yangshao	*Lungshanoid*
Art associated with domestic crafts (ceramics)	Art not conspicuously associated with domestic crafts; possible association with theocratic crafts(?)
Utility wares (cord-mat-basket pattern) characteristic	Ceremonial wares (eggshell forms and fine, well-made cups, fruit stands and shallow dishes) characteristic
"Fertility cult" characteristic	Evidence of institutionalized ancestor cult; ceremonials far beyond merely agricultural; possibly associated with specialized groups of people

4. What is the nature of the similarity and difference between the Yang-shao and the Lung-shan cultures both in first principle and in final analysis?

Starting from these premises—or, rather, from a lack of biased premises—we took on the Two Culture theory as hypothesis rather than historic fact and came to call a regional culture precisely a regional culture rather than a standard type with which cultures of other regions had to conform. More specifically, the Lung-shan culture of Shantung was to be regarded as a regional cultural phase in Shantung, but it was not to be used *a priori* as an absolute standard for a "Lungshan culture" for all of North China. In this view, a new frame of reference for the Neolithic archaeology of North China was inevitable. In two papers published in 1959, "Chronology of the Neolithic Cultures in China"[25] and "Chinese Prehistory in Pacific Perspective: Some Hypotheses and Problems,"[26] I have argued that the Lungshanoid cultures throughout North China constituted a horizon for all of North China that must be placed stratigraphically above the whole scope of the Yang-shao culture, and that the differences between the two cultures were developmental (Table 5). From such a perspective the following scheme of levels has been developed.[27]

25. *BIHP, 30* (1959), 259–309.

26. *Harvard Jour. Asiatic Studies, 20* (1959), 100–49.

27. See "China," in *Courses Toward Urban Life,* Robert J. Braidwood and Gordon R. Willey, eds., Viking Fund Publications in Anthropology, *32* (1962).

1. *Incipient agriculture.* The transitional stage from food gathering to food producing in the Nuclear Area; the evidence for this level of culture remains merely circumstantial.

2. *The establishment of village farmers.* The Yangshao culture, described in Chapter 3.

3. *The expansion of advanced village farmers from the Nuclear Area to new frontiers.* The Lungshanoid formative stage during which advanced farmers broke through the natural habitat barriers of the cultigens to expand rapidly toward the fertile plains and river valleys of the east and the southeast. Many Yang-shao elements (especially the painted pottery) remained intact, but innovations emerged. A surprising degree of cultural uniformity could be seen at the sites of this level, to which belonged the so-called mixed culture sites.

4. *The formation of local cultures.* The Lung-shan cultures of various regions assumed distinctive local characters as a result of permanent settlement, isolation, and varying adaptive tendencies. This is the level of the Lung-shan cultures of Shantung, Honan, Shansi, Shensi, and so forth.

This developmental sequence constitutes the backbone of the prehistoric portions of this volume. To be sure, this view is merely a working hypothesis based upon a subjective interpretation of the data. But it is an interpretation that agrees with the new data available and with the classificatory model constructed elsewhere in the world for similar nuclear situations. More important, it in essence agrees with—and, indeed, sinks into relative insignificance in the face of—the new interpretations given the data by several field archaeologists in China. In 1959 An Chih-min[28] proposed to derive the Lung-shan cultures of Honan, Shansi, and Shensi from the Yang-shao culture of the same area, and Shih Hsing-pang[29] sought to explain their differences in terms of economic and societal changes. In 1960 Hsü Shun-ch'en positively stated that "recent discoveries of the sites transitional in nature have demonstrated that the Yang-shao and the Lung-shan were successive cultures of the same sequence rather than a pair of parallel cultural systems."[30] In *The Archaeology of New*

28. *KK* (1959/10).
29. Ibid.
30. *WW* (1960/5), 39.

China, published in 1962 and purporting to sum up results in China during the preceding decade, the authors made the following statement:

> With regard to the interrelationship of the Yang-shao and the Lung-shan, in the past they were generally regarded as cultures of different origins. New discoveries in the last decade gradually forced a change in this view. Particularly as a result of the discovery of the Miao-ti-kou II culture, the hypothesis has been generally accepted by archaeologists that the Lung-shan cultures of the Chung-yüan were developed out of the Yang-shao culture [pp. 20–21].

Despite this, some notable authorities dissent from the new interpretation.[31] Furthermore, the origin of the Lung-shan culture in Shantung has yet to be discussed. The most significant issues here have to do with the nature and distribution of Lung-shan and Lung-shan-like assemblages throughout China, and the following discussion must therefore remain tentative.

FORMATIVE CULTURES OF THE LUNGSHANOID LEVEL: EXPANSION OF THE NUCLEAR CHINESE NEOLITHIC CULTURE AND ITS DYNAMICS

To adequately describe and explain the nature of the interrelationship of the Yang-shao and the Lung-shan cultures, the following evidence must be presented. (1) The Lungshan-like cultures must be shown to be homogeneous throughout the Chung-yüan or even China; they must exhibit cultural identity with the Yang-shao, on the one hand, and developmental contrast, on the other. (2) They must be proven later in time than the Yang-shao culture as a whole, although not necessarily to have preceded the Shang civilization everywhere in China, for the sphere of distribution of the Shang was much smaller than the Lungshan-like cultures. (3) Both in general cultural form and in specific artifact types the steps of change must be traceable from the Yang-shao to the Lungshan-like cultures. (4) Regional chronologies of the Lungshan-like cultures must be established to

31. E.g. Li Chi, *Bulletin of the Department of Archaeology and Anthropology, National Taiwan University, 21/22* (1963), 1–12.

show that those cultures within the sphere of the Yang-shao distribution were earlier in time than (ancestral to) those outside it.

All of this we cannot do. The history of Neolithic archaeology in North China has not been very long, and the new interpretation appeared just a few years ago. I believe that the key to the Lung-shan culture lies in the establishment and further elaboration of the concept of the Lungshanoid, which I proposed in 1959.[32]

Although their first manifestations must be traced to the western Honan "mixed culture sites," the Lungshanoid cultures were not identified until a series of sites with Lung-shan characteristics plus painted pottery was found in eastern and southeastern coastal China. Under Lungshanoid we may group the Miao-ti-kou II culture of Honan (including the mixed culture sites), eastern Shensi, and southern Shansi; the Ta-wen-k'ou culture of Shantung; the Ch'ing-lien-kang culture of the Huaiho and the lower Yangtze; the Ch'ü-chia-ling culture of the lower Hanshui; and the so-called Painted Pottery cultures of Chekiang, Fukien, Taiwan, and Kwangtung. All these cultural phases, each restricted to its own limited area of distribution, shared a number of significant features, as will be discussed later. Largely speaking these phases are all characterized by painted pottery but differ substantially from the Yang-shao, and the features on which they differ from the Yang-shao are similar to those of the Lung-shan. In time they were without exception demonstrably earlier than the Lung-shan cultures wherever they occurred with these cultures, but at the same time they were later than the Yang-shao within the area in which the latter occurred. The only absolute dates of this level of cultures come from Taiwan, where the Lungshanoid cultures are placed within the period 2500 B.C. to the beginning of the Christian era. They must have begun long before 2500 on the mainland, for it must have taken them considerable time to reach Taiwan from the Nuclear Area, and in the Nuclear Area the Lungshanoid level was separated from the Shang civilization—which began around 1750 B.C.—by a Lung-shan interval.

The distribution of the Lungshanoid cultures begins in the west within the sphere of the Yang-shao but extends into the eastern low plains of North China and the coastal valleys and hills of the south-

32. K. C. Chang, *BIE*, 7 (1959). See also Chang, *Current Anthropology* 5 (1964), no. 5.

east. Spread over a vast area characterized by vastly different geographic features, the Lungshanoid cultures nevertheless exhibit strikingly homogeneous characteristics, which would lead one to believe that these cultures represent a rapid, almost explosive, expansion of the Chung-yüan farmers toward the fertile but sparsely populated areas of the east and the southeast. In view of the rarity of antecedent cultures in some of these regions and their total absence in others, we suspect that their cultures were in the main brought from the Chung-yüan area by migrant populations. At least two factors must have been reponsible for the spread of the Lungshanoid farmers eastward and southward: population pressure in the Chung-yüan and the advancement of techniques which enabled a farming subsistence outside the Nuclear Area. If portions of South China were already populated by cultivators of root and fruit crops, which seems likely, this would account for the facility with which the immigrant cultures adapted to the new settings and the rapidity with which they mastered the cultigens native to the south. After the establishment of the Lungshanoid pioneer farmers in the various areas, a series of local cultures began to emerge. One of these, the Honan Lung-shan culture, was probably the progenitor of the Shang civilization.

To support these generalizations one must come back to the empirical archaeology of this level. Space does not allow a detailed description of each of the Lungshanoid cultures, but the following summaries of six of the most important of them will suffice for the purpose of this volume.[33]

The Miao-ti-kou II Culture

Known from the Nuclear Area (western Honan, southern Shansi, and eastern Shensi), the Miao-ti-kou II culture (Fig. 44) is best represented by the upper stratum of Miao-ti-kou, in Shan Hsien, Yang-shao-ts'un, in Mien-ch'ih Hsien, and Wang-wan, in Lo-yang, of Honan; Ch'üan-hu-ts'un, in Hua Hsien, and Heng-chen-ts'un, Hua-yin Hsien, of Shensi; and P'an-nan-ts'un, in P'ing-lu Hsien, Shansi. The Miao-ti-kou stratigraphy shows that this phase of culture was later in time than the Yang-shao, and that the Wang-wan and Heng-

33. Much of the following summary was based on *Hsin Chung-kuo ti K'ao-ku Shou-huo* (*The Archaeology of New China*), Peking, Wenwu Press, 1962, pp. 15, 20, 28, 30–32. New data that appeared after the book have been incorporated.

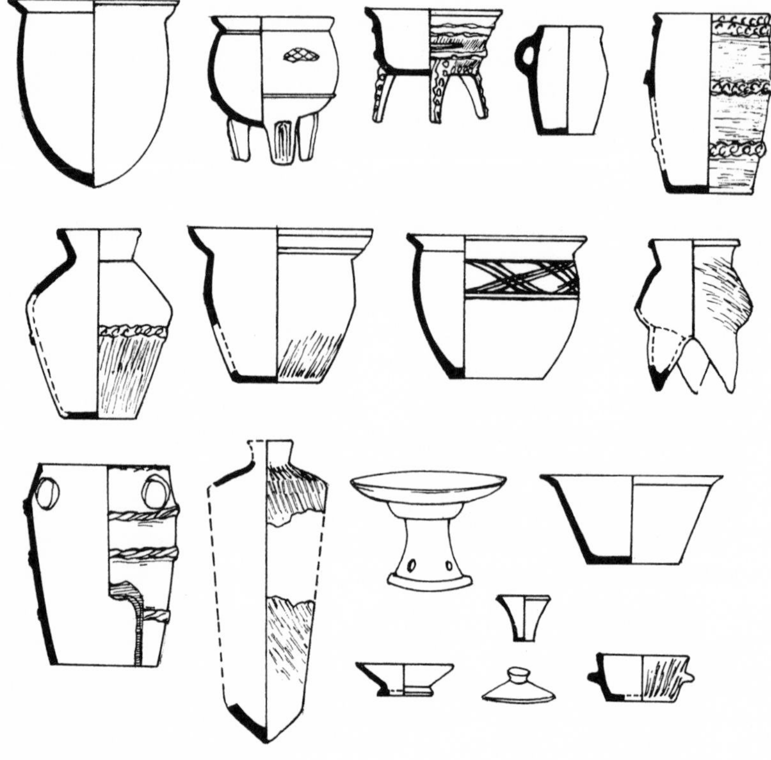

44. Artifacts of the Miao-ti-kou II culture. (From *Hsin Chung-kuo ti K'ao-ku Shou-huo,* 1962, p. 18.)

chen-ts'un stratigraphies indicate that it was earlier than the Honan and Shensi Lung-shan cultures.

In addition to the chipped stone knives with side notches common at Yang-shao sites, there appeared in this phase polished semilunar and sickle-shaped knives and shell knives, indicating a more advanced agriculture. Double-pronged wooden cultivating implements (*lei*) are known from their impressions in the earth. Bones of domestic chicken are found alongside those of dogs and pigs. Stone net sinkers and stone and bone arrowheads are found widely.

Pottery was manufactured mainly by the coiling technique. Occasional wheel-made pieces are reported; the technique of polishing and retouching pottery by rotation was apparently known then, though the true potter's wheel at this time is doubtful. The pottery paste is usually coarse and gray. Decoration was most often done by impression—basket, cord, and check marks occurred—and secondarily by appliqué and incision. Painted pottery still occurred widely, the major type being a large, deep, reddish bowl painted in black in the upper portions. A small amount of thin, hard, lustrous black pottery was found. Aside from bowls, jars, and pots, the shapes of pottery included tripods and some ring-footed vessels. The tripods include *ting* and *chia* but not *li*.

The "transitional" nature of the Miao-ti-kou II pottery is of particular significance; it has caused many scholars to embrace the view that the Honan Lung-shan pottery could have been derived from the Yang-shao:

> Many pottery forms seem to have evolved out of the Yang-shao forms, particularly the cup, pot, pointed-bottomed jar, and the *ting* tripod. The pointed-bottomed jars are typical of the Yang-shao culture; this type of jar, similar to the finds at Miao-ti-kou II, is also found in Yang-shao-ts'un, Mien-ch'ih Hsien, and at Heng-chen-ts'un in Hua-yin Hsien, Shensi, all closely related to but different from the Yang-shao stage forms. The small cups slipped in red pigment are typical of this site, but possibly related to the coarse small cups of the Yang-shao stage. . . . In short, the ceramics of Miao-ti-kou II exhibit features transitional from the Yang-shao to the Lung-shan.[34]

At the Miao-ti-kou site 145 human burials were found; the bodies had been arranged in regular rows, mostly single, stretched, supine, heads to the south. Grave furnishings were minimal.

The Ta-wen-k'ou Culture

Shantung was considered the bastion of the Black Pottery Culture, and one of the older Chinese archaeological axioms was that painted pottery was absent in Shantung. The first painted potsherds were found here in 1952 at Kang-shang-ts'un, in T'eng Hsien in south-

34. An Chih-min et al., *Miao-ti-kou yü San-li-ch'iao,* Peking, Science Press, 1959, pp. 110–11. For other local sequences demonstrating a continuous development of Yang-shao–Miaotikou II and Honan Lung-shan cultures, see the reports on Wang-wan, Loyang (*KK,* 1961/4) and Kao-yai, Yen-shih (*KK,* 1964/11).

45. Painted jars (*left,* 12 cm high; *right* 17 cm) excavated from the site at Pao-t'ou-ts'un, in Ning-yang Hsien, Shantung. (From *WW,* 1960/2, inside cover.)

western Shantung, and the excavation of the Ta-wen-k'ou (or Pao-t'ou) site in Ning-yang in 1959 demonstrated the existence of a Neolithic culture here, significantly different from the classical Lung-shan sites, in which painted pottery was an important element. More than 120 burials were unearthed at Ta-wen-k'ou, most supine, stretched out, heads to the east. Pottery wares are mainly gray in color; red ware was also common, and black pottery accounts for only 12 per cent of the total. In addition, 8 per cent of the pottery was white, and 3 per cent was painted (Fig. 45). Most of the pots were handmade, although some were wheel-made. In shape they were characterized by *ting* and *kui* tripods, high-pedestaled *tou* with cutouts, and water jars with a pair of lugs on the back. Large numbers of finely made bone, horn, and tooth artifacts were also uncovered. Since then, assemblages of the Ta-wen-k'ou type have been widely found in Shantung, including such significant sites as Ching-chih-chen in An-ch'iu, Yü-chia-lin in Tung-a, and a series of sites near Ch'ü-fu (Fig. 46). These sites outline an area of distribution broadly overlapping the sphere of the classical Lung-shan culture sites, and the stratigraphic evidence at two sites in the Ch'ü-fu area (Hsi-hsia-hou and Tung-wei-chuang) shows that the Ta-wen-k'ou culture was earlier in time. Both Yang Tzu-fan and Wang Ssu-li are of the opinion

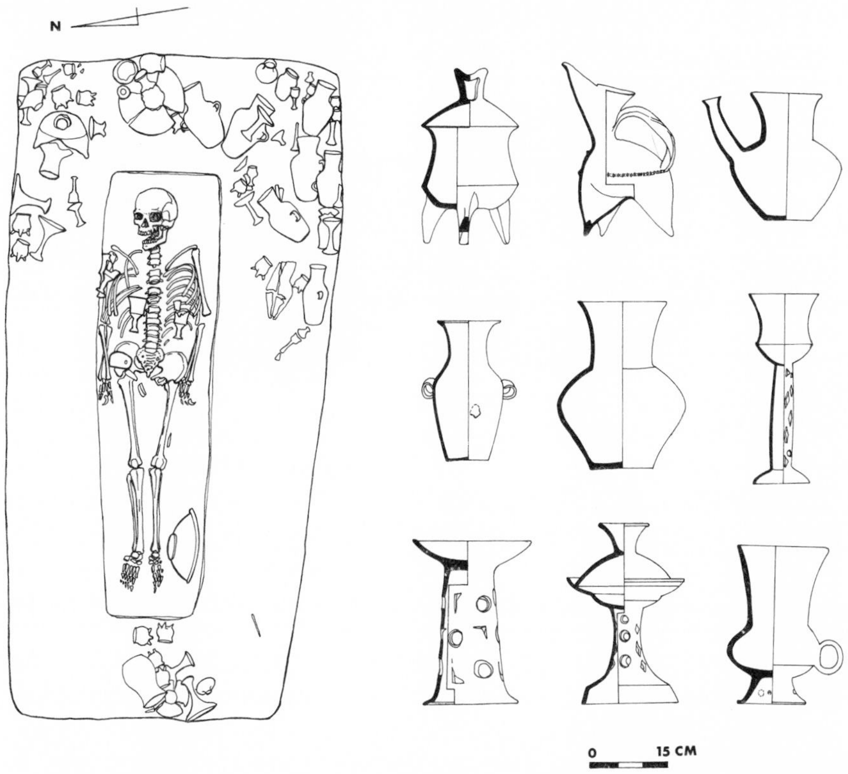

46. A burial and pottery types from the Ta-wen-k'ou culture site at Hsi-hsia-hou, Ch'ü-fu, Shantung. (After *KKHP,* 1964/2.)

that the Shantung Lung-shan culture was derived directly from the Ta-wen-k'ou culture.[35] They also consider that the latter was closely related to the Ch'ing-lien-kang culture of northern Kiangsu (see below) but was probably independent of the Lungshanoid cultures of the Chung-yüan. This will be discussed later.

The Ch'ü-chia-ling Culture

The Lungshanoid Ch'ü-chia-ling culture (Fig. 47), typified by the site of the same name in Ching-shan Hsien of Hupei in the lower Hanshui Valley, is now known from a large series of sites in the

35. *KK* (1963/7), 360, 377–78.

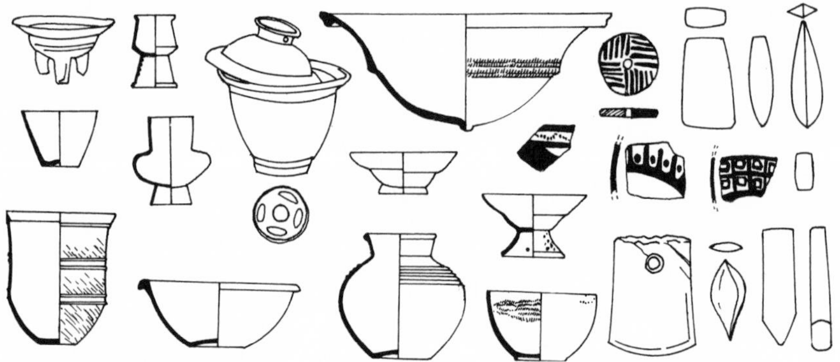

47. Artifacts of the Ch'ü-chia-ling culture. (From *Hsin Chung-kuo ti K'ao-ku Shou-huo,* 1962, p. 29.)

Hupei basin in the valleys of the Hanshui and Yangtze. Stratigraphic evidence from the sites of Ch'ing-lung-ch'üan and Ta-ssu of Yün Hsien on the upper Hanshui shows that the Ch'ü-chia-ling culture was temporally situated between the Yang-shao culture of the upper Hanshui and the Lung-shan culture of the Honan type.

The Ch'ü-chia-ling culture differed from the contemporary Chung-yüan cultures significantly in that rice cultivation was apparently the principal mode of subsistence in this area. Impressions of paddy husks were reported from Yang-shao-ts'un, but rice probably represents an intrusive element (apparently from the south) into the millet area. At the Lungshanoid sites in the south, however, remains of rice husks and straws were found widely.[36] This is of the utmost significance not only in the history of rice cultivation (the rice remains of the Ch'ü-chia-ling and the Ch'ing-lien-kang cultures being the earliest known archaeologically) but also in the nature of the Lungshanoid farming cultures. Stone implements related to agriculture included polished axes and adzes, perforated spades, knives, and sickles. Bones of pigs and dogs were found. Spearheads and arrowheads of stone, bone, and pottery occurred. There were also large numbers and great varieties of pottery spindle whorls, many of which were painted with decorative designs. Pottery included large jars with long narrow necks, *tou* with high stands, and a variety of tripods and ring-footed

36. For Yang-shao-ts'un, see J. G. Andersson, *BMFEA, 19* (1945), 21–22; for the Lungshanoid in the South see *KKHP* (1959/4).

48. Artifacts of the Ch'ing-lien-kang culture. (From *Hsin Chung-kuo ti K'ao-ku Shou-huo,* 1962, p. 29.)

vessels, many having lids. Very thin (1–2 mm) painted pottery bowls and cups are especially distinctive.

The Ch'ing-lien-kang Culture

First identified at the Ch'ing-lien-kang site in Huai-an Hsien, northern Kiangsu, the assemblages of this culture (Fig. 48) have thus far been located at a number of sites throughout the province. Of particular interest are two, recently excavated, at Liu-lin[37] and Ta-tun-tzu[38] at P'i Hsien.

Stone implements of this culure included a variety of polished artifacts such as perforated flat axes, rectangular adzes, square or flat chisels, and long rectangular knives with a number of holes. Perforated hoes, stepped adzes, and shouldered axes are also found. The pottery is characteristically reddish in color, of coarse or fine paste; there was less gray and black pottery. Handmade and polished in general, the pottery vessels are mostly tripods and ring-footed forms (Fig. 49). Among the tripods is a variety of *ting*—three long, solid legs attached to a number of vessel forms. Among the ring-footed vessels the most distinctive are the many *tou,* with high cut-out pedestals. The decoration is by incision, impression, appliqué, and painting.

37. *KKHP* (1962/1).
38. *KKHP* (1964/2).

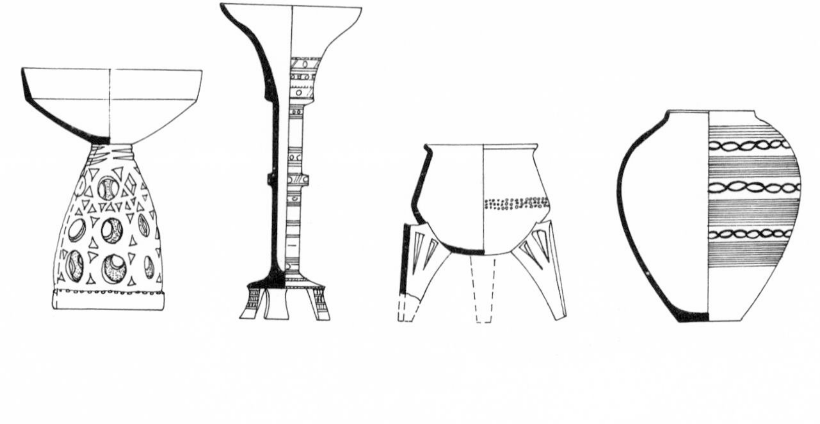

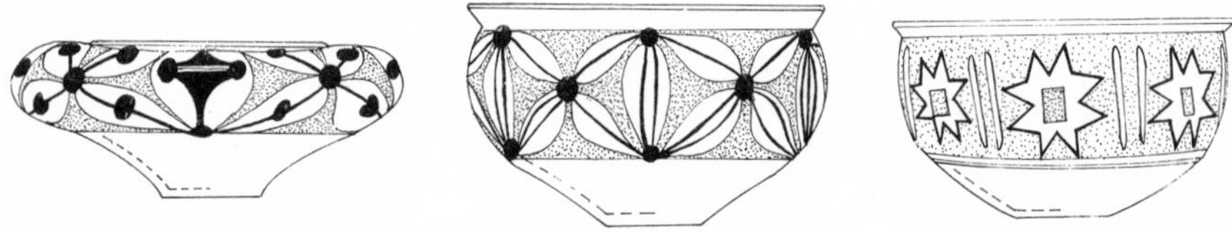

49. Pottery from the Ch'ing-lien-kang Culture site at Ta-tun-tzu, P'i Hsien, Kiangsu. (From *KKHP,* 1964/2.)

The painted pieces are of two kinds: black on red, and red and black on white or black and white on red.[39] At Liu-lin, an elaborate bone assemblage has been found (Fig. 50).

Sites of this phase are usually located on hills and terraces near rivers. Rice husks have been found at several sites. Burials have been excavated at a number of localities; all of them are single, stretched, supine, head to east.

The dating of the Ch'ing-lien-kang culture is still highly problematic. *The Archaeology of New China* (1962) states that it "is situated between the Yang-shao and the Lung-shan cultures or is largely contemporary with the Lung-shan culture of the Huangho Valley." The 1964 report of the site of Ta-tun-tzu, however, raised new issues:[40]

> Ch'ing-lien-kang, Liu-lin, and Hua-t'ing-ts'un . . . are the three principal sites of the Ch'ing-lien-kang Culture that have been

39. Ibid., p. 30.
40. Ibid., pp. 47–48.

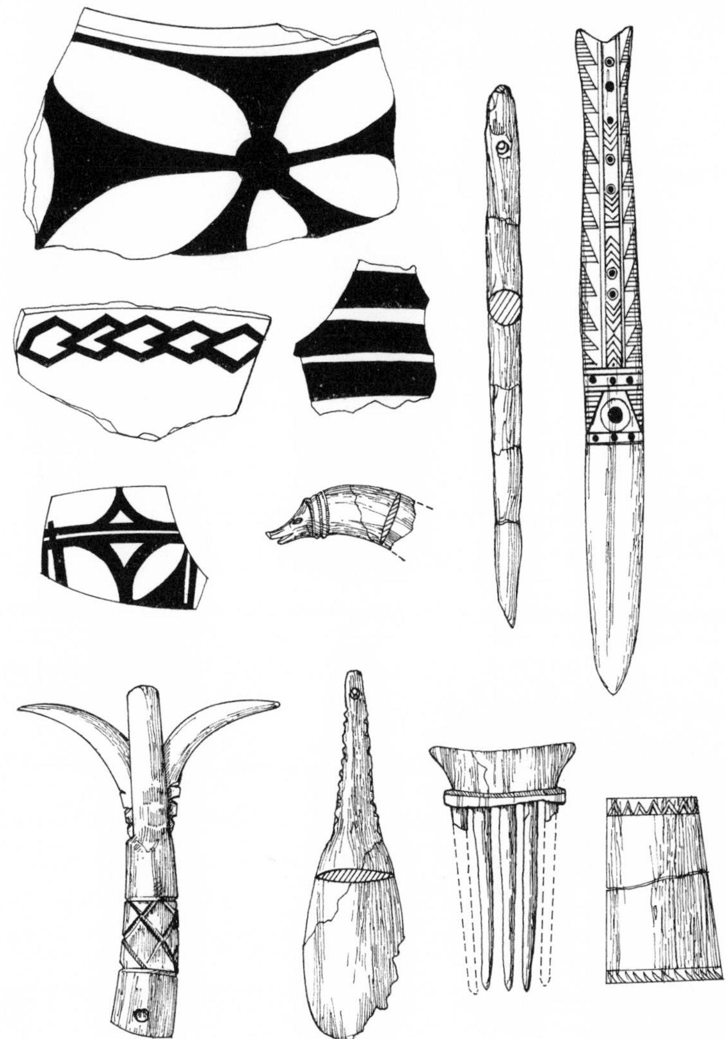

50. Painted sherds and bone implements at the Liu-lin site in P'i Hsien, Kiangsu, Ch'ing-lien-kang culture. (From *KKHP,* 1962/1, p. 89, and 1965/2, p. 30.)

excavated. . . . Their cultures shared a number of characteristics, but each has its own distinctive features.

At the Ta-tun-tzu site, layers of Ch'ing-lien-kang and Liu-lin types have been located, and there are also burial groups of Liu-

> lin and Hua-t'ing-ts'un types. Their stratigraphic interrelationship is: the Ch'ing-lien-kang type is the earliest; the Liu-lin type follows; and the Hua-t'ing-ts'un type is the latest.

This is actually a regional chronological problem of northern Kiangsu. The authors of the above passage, however, have compared the Ta-tun-tzu types with the Chung-yüan and arrived at the following conclusion: "The Liu-lin type remains were somewhat later than the Yang-shao culture of Chungyüan, and the Ch'ing-lien-kang type remains (of northern Kiangsu) were roughly contemporary with the Chung-yüan Yang-shao. The Hua-t'ing type remains are slightly later than the Liu-lin type, and therefore approximately correspond to the early Lung-shan culture of the Chung-yüan." This conclusion, based upon the comparison of a few painted pottery vessels, is highly questionable.

The Early Liang-chu Culture

The Liang-chu culture of Hangchow Bay is the first Lungshan-type culture discovered south of the Yangtze. It has been reported that a layer with painted pottery was excavated from below the Liang-chu black pottery strata, but detailed reports are unavailable.

The Painted Pottery Cultures of the Southeast Coast

Scattered remains of painted pottery and associated artifacts have been collected from Fukien (e.g. the site at T'an-shih-shan) and Kwangtung, but the best known site is Feng-pi-t'ou of southwestern Taiwan.[41]

Prehistoric remains on the Feng-pi-t'ou hills, at the southern end of the Feng-shan tableland southeast of the city of Kao-hsiung in southern Taiwan, about 1 kilometer from the coast, were known toward the end of World War II, but the site was not extensively excavated until early 1965. The earliest culture at the site, characterized by cord-marked pottery, belongs to the early prehistoric horizon of southern coastal China described at the beginning of Chapter 3. From 2500 to 400 B.C. the site was a settlement of considerable magnitude, occupied by people engaging in farming, hunting, fishing,

41. K. C. Chang, *Feng-pi-t'ou, Ta-p'en-k'eng, and the Prehistory of Taiwan*, Yale University Publications in Anthropology, 73 (in press).

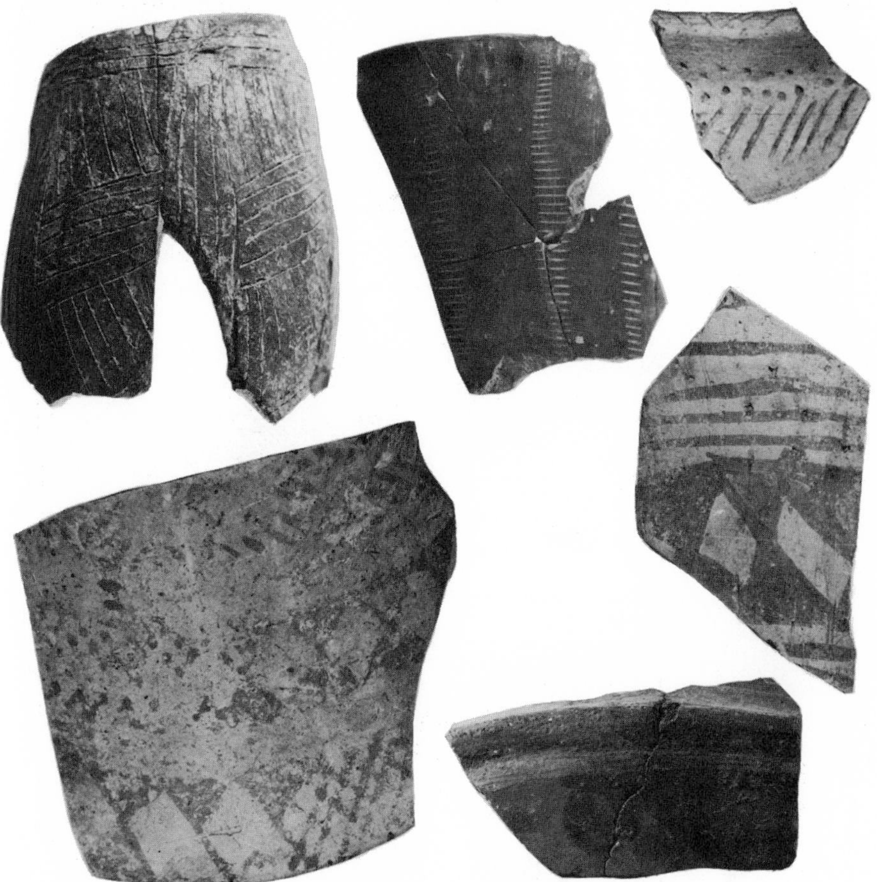

51. Pottery at the Feng-pi-t'ou site, Taiwan.

and shellfish gathering. The pottery at the site has two main phases of development: an earlier phase characterized by red pottery of fine paste with cord impressions in a variety of shapes, including *ting* tripods and *tou* with high cutout pedestals; and a later phase characterized by pottery of coarse paste with impressed, incised, and painted decorative patterns (Fig. 51). The later phase also contained a considerable number of thin, hard, lustrous, wheel-made black potsherds. Shellmounds constitute a large part of the deposits of the later phase; in one of these was found a single burial, stretched, supine, head to south.

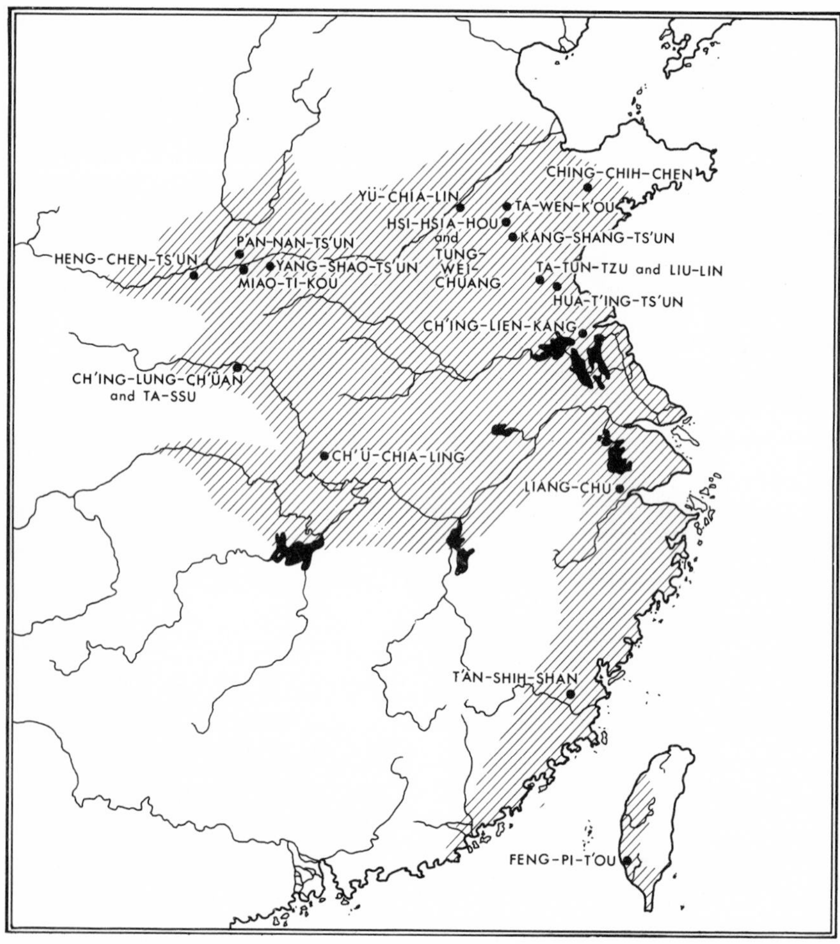

52. Lungshanoid sites and the approximate area of distribution of the Lungshanoid cultures.

The Lungshanoid sites described above under the six regional headings (Fig. 52) are for the most part recent discoveries, still requiring detailed analysis and comparison, and it is apparent that each culture is distinctive. However, we find that the following common denominators unite the various cultural phases in this vast area.

1. All these cultures were based mainly on an agricultural subsistence which was supplemented to various extents by fishing, hunting, and gathering. Remains of rice characterize many sites of these cul-

tures in the Hanshui, Huaiho, and Yangtze valleys and to their south, in significant contrast to the Yang-shao culture of the Chung-yüan with millet as its staple crop. It is notable that the only site in the north where evidence of rice has been reported is in Yang-shao-ts'un itself—a Miao-ti-kou II culture site according to its stone inventory and pottery wares. Probably this indicates an influence from the south, where rice cultivation most likely was first mastered. Whether it was a new invention (and necessarily accomplished with amazing rapidity) by the Lungshanoid cultures, or had a long history of development among the native gardeners of Southeast Asia before its Lungshanoid emergence, is a problem that cannot be solved on the present evidence.

2. All these cultures had polished stone implements that included as major distinctive types rectangular adzes, perforated knives, and sickles. If we assume the primary use of adzes for carpentry rather than for tree-felling and the use of knives and sickles for harvesting stalked plants, this would suggest agriculture of considerably advanced levels.

3. At the sites of these cultures there were greater numbers and varieties of bone, horn, and shell artifacts than at the Yang-shao sites.

4. The most significant common features of the sites are their pottery remains. The pottery at all these sites is a mixture of red, gray, and black wares, and in decoration there is a mixture of impressed, incised, and painted patterns. If one concedes historical relationship of these sites with both the classical Yang-shao and the classical Lung-shan cultures, their pottery must be placed intermediate between the two groups. For instance, if Feng-pi-t'ou site were in Honan instead of Taiwan, one would unhesitatingly place it in the "mixed culture" category. Since it is in Taiwan, Feng-pi-t'ou simply cannot be a mixture of eastern and western cultures of North China and must be regarded as a marginal manifestation of a "transitional" phase. That a transitional culture occurred in Taiwan with characteristic Chung-yüan-type elements is proof that the Chung-yüan culture underwent a rapid expansion southeastward during that transitional period. Feng-pi-t'ou was therefore of particular significance in the formulation of a Lungshanoid concept.

In these Lungshanoid cultures the pottery shapes, though different in detail, shared several basic forms: *ting* tripods with solid legs; *tou* with cut-out ring feet; *kui*-type jars (wide mouth, ring-footed, two loop or strap handles), and the wide occurrence of lids. Pottery of all sites was handmade (mostly from coils), and at all sites there is evidence that the rim and the ring foot were polished on turntables of fast rotation. The homogeneous nature of the black pottery found at all sites indicates a highly sophisticated level of paste preparation and kiln control.

5. All the burials at these sites were single, stretched, supine, head to east or south.

6. All these cultures occupy a comparable chronological position. In terms of relative stratification, the Miao-ti-kou II and the Ch'ü-chia-ling cultures are intermediate between the Yang-shao and the Lung-shan cultures. The other cultures are outside the Yang-shao sphere and cannot have direct stratigraphic relationship with it, but wherever Lung-shan cultures were known the other cultures preceded the Lung-shan. In absolute dates, the culture in Taiwan persisted into the late first millennium B.C., but in the Chung-yüan the same cultures must have begun no later than the fourth millennium.

7. Finally, these cultures not only physically adjoin one another but their distribution follows a pattern determined by the river valleys and seacoasts. The Miao-ti-kou II culture flows down the Huangho to the area of the Ta-wen-k'ou culture and down the Han-shui to the area of the Ch'ü-chia-ling culture. The Ch'ing-lien-kang culture directly adjoins the Ta-wen-k'ou culture to its north and is connected with the Ch'ü-chia-ling culture through the Yangtze. Feng-pi-t'ou of Taiwan is widely separated from the Ch'ing-lien-kang culture of the lower Yangtze, but the early Liang-chu culture of Chekiang helps bridge the gap. In other words, each of the Lungshanoid cultures occupied a natural geographical division of eastern or southeastern China and was interconnected with the areas of the other cultures by a web of waterways that plainly played significant roles in the lives of the inhabitants.

Accordingly, we can say with confidence that the cultures described above constitute a well-defined horizon in the archaeological sense. Each possessing its own distinctive features, these cultures nevertheless shared a number of basic and significant characteristics that contrast them sharply with the Yang-shao culture of the Chung-yüan. As to the genetic relationship of this Lungshanoid horizon with the Yang-shao culture, two possible interpretations present themselves. Either these cultures formed a separate cultural system (in contrast with the Chung-yüan Yang-shao culture), and originated in southeastern China (Huaiho or Yangtze–Hanshui area), moved northwestward to establish contact with the Yang-shao culture, and gave rise to the Lung-shan cultures of eastern North China; or the Lungshanoid cultures were derived from the Yang-shao culture of the Nuclear Area, representing its expansion into the eastern and southeastern areas of China, and were ancestral to the various local Lung-shan cultures. Available archaeological evidence does not yet confirm either of the alternatives. We must know more about the chronology of each of the Lungshanoid cultures and their relations with each other before a final position can be taken. In this connection new data in southeastern Honan and northern Anhwei, the area intermediate between the Chung-yüan and the southeast, may prove decisive in the future.

Insofar as the present evidence is concerned, it leans heavily toward the second of the above alternatives. The data on pottery typology, distributional pattern, and chronological placement all point to the likelihood that the Lungshanoid cultures spread from northwest to southeast. Comparing the Lungshanoid cultures with the Yang-shao, I am inclined to see them as the products of the same cultural tradition but representing different developmental levels and differential adaptations to the various geographical environments. The advanced agricultural technology of the Lungshanoid cultures may contain both of the two principal factors responsible for a rapid expansion of the Chung-yüan culture toward the east and the southeast: the pressure of a growing population and population density in the Chung-yüan as a result of agricultural growth, and the settlers' capability of engaging in an agricultural way of life outside the Nuclear Area. The geographical features of the Huangho–Huaiho plain and the Yangtze Valley and the cultivation of rice provided the dynamics of the spread of the Chung-yüan culture along the major waterways and the seacoasts. In short, it makes more sense, according to presently available evidence, to regard the Lungshanoid culture as that of pioneer farmers expanding into and exploiting the fertile river valleys and plains of the east and the southeast from a Nuclear Area source rather than as a totally independent cultural horizon that arose in the southeast.

At this juncture it may be instructive to take into account the conclusions of physical anthropologists that the Yang-shao farmers' skeletal remains bear a very close morphological resemblance to the modern Oceanic Mongoloid populations (Fig. 53). A study of 99 skeletons found at the cemetery at the Yang-shao settlement of Yüan-chün-miao, in Hua Hsien, Shensi, has led Yen Yen to conclude:[42]

> The physical characteristics of the Neolithic group of the Hua Hsien population are basically Mongoloid. The cranial height (ba-b: 144.30 mm) would place the skulls in the hypsicephal category, and the maximal facial breadth (133.86 mm) indicates a medium breadth category. . . . In general they belonged to the Pacific branch of the Asian Mongoloids. Compared with the Mongoloid populations of the Neolithic period, the Hua Hsien group is basically closest to the Pan-p'o and the Pao-chi groups [of Yang-shao culture], is similar to the Kansu and Honan groups and the Indo-Chinese group in the south, but is relatively distant from the Lake Baikal A group. Compared with the minor branches of the modern Mongoloid populations, it is very close to both the Austroasian group of the Pacific branch and the Far Eastern Mongolian group that is intermediate between the Pacific and the Continental branches. It is closer to the Austroasiatic and the Far Eastern groups than to the Central Asiatic groups of the Continental branch.

This conclusion is certainly of considerable significance, for archaeologically speaking the Lungshanoid cultures are the only known intermediary that could have moved elements of the Yang-shao population to the Pacific areas. The physical anthropologist has long been convinced that the explosive expansion of the Mongoloid populations into the southern part of its present distributional sphere in the Pacific was an event closely related to the spread of agriculture.

42. *KKHP* (1962/2), 89–90. For other recent reports of the physical anthropology of Yang-shao skeletal remains, see Yen Yen's articles in *Hsi-an Pan-p'o*, 1963; *VP, 4* (1960), 103–11; and Woo Ting-liang, *VP, 5* (1961), 49–53.

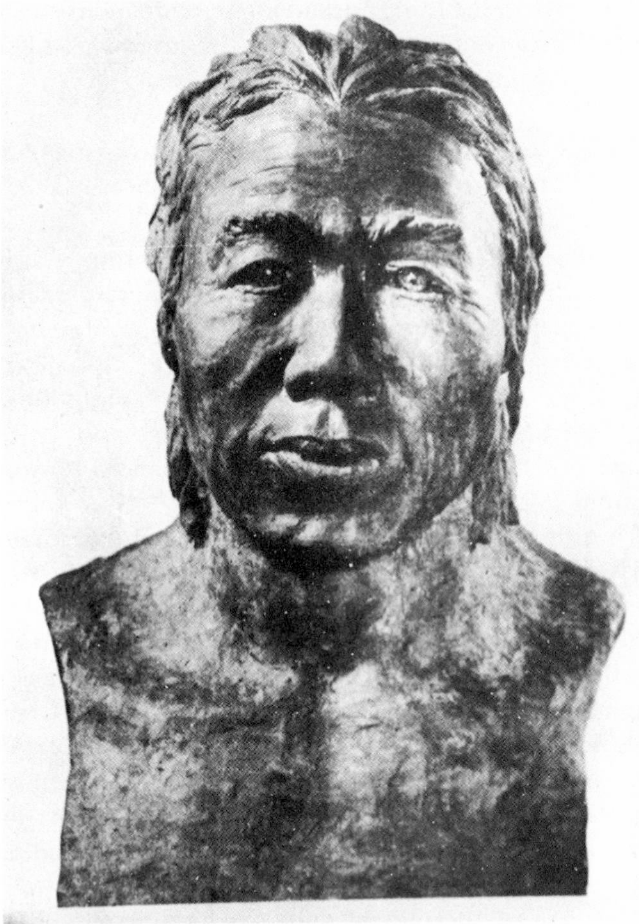

53. Reconstruction of head of a male inhabitant of the Yang-shao culture site at Pan-p'o-ts'un, Sian. (From *Hsi-an Pan-p'o,* 1963, Pl. CXCIII.)

The Lungshanoid horizon, therefore, is not only a crucial concept for the study of much of China's prehistory but more importantly a key concept in the study of the origin of some of the populations of the Pacific Islands and the beginning of cereal agriculture in much of Southeast Asia. Just what roles the native populations of Southeast Asia, who probably included some of the world's earliest farmers, played in the beginning of cereal agriculture in this part of the world (especially the beginning of rice cultivation), and what kind of situation developed when the Lungshanoid immigrants and the native populations came into contact, are topics of the utmost significance for archeologists of the next decade.

FORMATION OF LATE NEOLITHIC LOCAL CULTURES AND THE THRESHOLD OF CHINESE CIVILIZATION

As stated above, the cultural uniformity of the Lungshanoid horizon indicates a rapid process of diffusion and migration. But unless such processes kept repeating themselves—or, rather, despite any repetition of such processes—localization and regionalization of the Lungshanoid cultures were unavoidable. In fact, the following factors must have been at work to cause the Lungshanoid cultures to differentiate as they expanded. (1) The Lungshanoid horizon is distributed from Pohai Bay in the north all the way to the southern coast of China, an area 22 degrees in latitude and including sharply differentiated environmental conditions. (2) In addition to the latitudinal range, there are wide contrasts between interior and coastal environments and those between the valleys and terraces in the plains and the valleys and terraces in the hill regions. (3) As pioneer farmers, the Lungshanoid peoples by definition must have been highly adaptive and susceptible to changing natural conditions. (4) The vastness of the area and the ecological barriers throughout the sphere of the Lungshanoid distribution naturally would tend to discourage continued extensive and close contact among groups and stimulate separate paths of further growth.

The result of the interplay of these and presumably other factors was the formation of local Lung-shan cultures recognizable in the archaeological record. Broadly speaking the local Lung-shan cultures can be grouped into an interior and a coastal group. The interior group of the Chung-yüan exhibited a greater degree of change from the Lungshanoid horizon and was probably the progenitor of the Shang and Chou civilizations. Coastal Lung-shan cultures, on the other hand, were continued and differentiated phases of the Lungshanoid prototypes, and these persisted into the period when historical civilizations had already emerged in the Chung-yüan. The most important contrasts between the two groups are exemplified in Table 6.

TABLE 6.

Contrasts between the Chung-yüan and Coastal Lung-shan Cultures

Chung-yüan	*Coastal*
Pottery mainly characterized by gray ware manufactured by paddle-and-anvil technique; cord and basket marks often impressed on exterior surface by paddles	Pottery characteristically black and lustrous, many made or retouched by wheel; circumferential ridges and incised patterns common, but impressed decorations rare; occasional painted decorations
Major shapes of pottery vessels are *kuan* jars and *li* tripods with short, hollow legs; *ting* tripods extremely rare; *kui* jars and *tou* have low ring feet	Major shapes of pottery vessels are *ting* tripods, *kui* tripods, and *tou* with high and cut-out ring feet; *li* tripods extremely rare
Sites usually on low terraces of river valleys	Sites usually on low terraces in the plains, and often on mounds
Bronzes absent; microliths rare	Persisted into period when bronzes occurred; finely made microlithic implements often seen in northern part

The best known Lung-shan cultures of the Chung-yüan group at the present time are the so-called K'o-hsing-chuang II culture and the Hou-kang II culture. Those of the coastal group are the so-called classical Lung-shan culture and the Liang-chu culture. The major characteristics of these four Lung-shan cultures are given below.[43]

The Shensi Lungshan Culture (K'o-hsing-chuang II Culture)

Confined to Shensi, southern Shansi, and westernmost Honan, this culture is best known from the sites of K'o-hsing-chuang and Mi-chia-yai, near Sian, and at Heng-chen-ts'un in Hua Hsien, Shensi. At Heng-chen-ts'un, remains of this culture were found above the Miao-ti-kou II layer; and at Chang-chia-p'o, also near Sian, the culture is shown to antedate the remains of Western Chou. Largely contemporary with the Lung-shan culture and perhaps the early phases of the Shang civilization of Honan, the Shensi Lung-shan culture's relationship with the Western Chou and its chronological position relative to the Shang are important topics for further study.

43. Mainly based on *Hsin Chung-kuo ti K'ao-ku Shou-huo*, pp. 16–21, 31–32.

Remains of ten semi-subterranean houses were found at K'o-hsing-chuang. The houses have a single room or two adjoining rooms. The double houses, with two rectangular rooms or an interior round room and an exterior square room, are particularly distinctive. The floor inside the house was paved with habitation debris and compacted from use. Pocket-shaped storage pits, with a bottle-neck opening and an enlarged chamber about 4 meters in diameter, are also characteristic.

Of the implements found at the sites, most are for agriculture, but hunting and fishing gear still occurred. These included knives, adzes, axes, spearheads of stone; fishhooks, arrowheads, and spatula-like artifacts of bone; and spindle whorls of clay. Shell objects are absent. Among the animal bones at the site of K'o-hsing-chuang, those of dog, pig, cattle (*Bos* sp.), water buffalo (*Bubalus* sp.), sheep (*Ovis* sp.), rabbit, and water deer were identified. All but the deer and rabbit were domesticated, showing considerable progress from the Yang-shao. Pottery is predominantly gray in color, about 80 per cent of the total. Black sherds like the coastal Lung-shan pieces are no more than 1 per cent. Most of the impressed decorations were cord- or basket-marked, and check-stamped pieces are rare. There are occasional painted sherds (dark red on red slip). In shape, *li* tripods with single handles, cord-marked *kuan* jars, and cord-marked *chia* tripods are most common. *Ting* tripods are extremely rare. Most of the vessels were built by hand from coils, and some of the *li* tripods were apparently modeled. A very few sherds exhibit evidence of the wheel (Figs. 54 and 55).

A double burial, of a man and a woman, was found at Heng-chen-ts'un; it has six pots. At the site of K'o-hsing-chuang bodies were sometimes buried in abandoned storage pits, each pit having from one to five skeletons. Another important trait of the culture is the use of sheep scapulas for divination; burned shoulderblades of sheep were found.

Honan Lungshan Culture (Hou-kang II Culture)

Sites of this culture are known from most of Honan and the southern portions of Shansi and Hopei. The Wang-wan (near Lo-yang) stratigraphy indicates that the Honan Lung-shan culture followed the Miao-ti-kou II culture in time, and the Hou-kang (An-yang) stratig-

54. Pottery of the K'o-hsing-chuang (Shensi Lung-shan) culture: 1, *ting;* 2,3, *chia;* 4, 5, *li;* 6, *kui;* 7–9, *kuan;* 10, lid. (From *KK,* 1959/10, Pl. II.)

raphy places this culture between the Yang-shao Culture, below, and the Shang civilization, above.

The stone inventory of the Honan Lung-shan culture is basically identical with that of the Miao-ti-kou II, but the chipped knives with side notches are absent. In addition to wooden *lei,* bone spades are found in considerable numbers. The most significant difference in tool inventory from the Shensi Lung-shan culture is the wide use of shell artifacts in Honan. Among the bones of domestic animals, those from the pig were most numerous. The discovery of stone and bone arrowheads, shells of mollusks and snails, stone sinkers, and fishhooks indicate the continuing importance of fishing, hunting, and gathering in the Honan Lung-shan subsistence.

A rectangular semi-subterranean house was found at the site of Hui-tsui in Yen-shih, the floor and walls having been hardened by fire. Round houses were excavated at Hou-kang, the floors plastered in white, limey clay. Some pottery remained handmade, but wheel-made pieces increased in number (Fig. 55). (At the site of San-li-ch'iao, Shan Hsien, wheel-made and wheel-touched pieces account for one fifth of the total sherds.) Red ware decreased and black ware increased. The typical eggshell black pottery is also known. Cord impression was the leading decoration and basket-marked pottery followed, but there was also a noticeable increase of check-stamped pieces. In shape there was a greater variety than in Miao-ti-kou II, including *tseng* steamers, *li* and *kui* tripods, handled jars, and cups. There are many corded *li* tripods with single handles, but fewer *chia* and *ting* tripods.

Only scattered remains of human burials have been found; most are similar to the Miao-ti-kou II pattern, with very few grave furnishings. At the site of Chien-kou, near Han-tan in southern Hopei, human bodies were found in abandoned pits and wells. No fewer than ten skeletons were found in a round pit only 1.5 meters in diameter. These include people of all ages who were placed in the pit without any discernible order or pattern but were covered with a layer of burned clay. Five skeletons were found in an abandoned well; some were decapitated and others had died struggling. This seems to indicate an intervillage raid, something yet to be found in the peaceful Yang-shao village settlements.

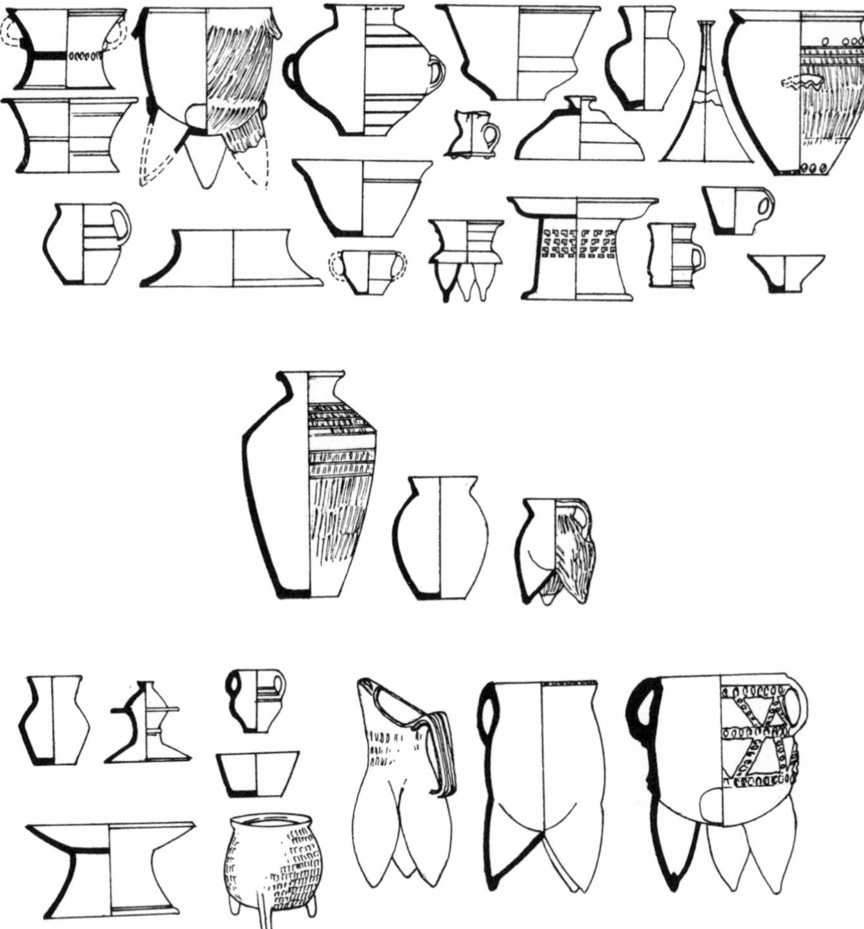

55. Artifacts of the Shensi and Honan Lung-shan cultures: *upper,* Shensi; *lower,* Honan; *middle,* shared. (From *Hsin Chung-kuo ti K'ao-ku Shou-huo,* 1962, p. 18.)

The Classical Lung-shan Culture

The so-called classical or typical Lung-shan culture, typified by the Ch'eng-tzu-yai and Liang-ch'eng-chen sites, is in fact a local Lung-shan-type culture that centered in Shantung and extended north to Liaotung Peninsula and south to northern Kiangsu. In Shantung

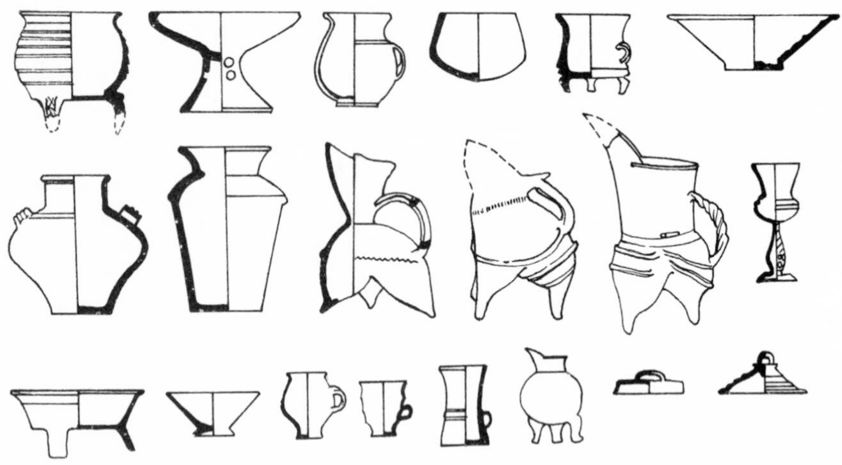

56. Artifacts of the classical Lung-shan culture. (From *Hsin Chung-kuo ti K'ao-ku Shou-huo,* 1962, p. 18.)

alone some hundred sites have been excavated.[44] At one site, the earliest excavated Ch'eng-tzu-yai, the village was surrounded by a wall of *hang-t'u* construction.

The tool inventory includes highly polished stone axes, adzes, knives, sickles, arrowheads, spearheads, and bone harpoons. The square stone adzes and chisels are especially distinctive. At a number of sites very finely chipped microliths (scrapers and arrowheads) were found, apparently related to the microlithic industry of the north.

Pottery was characteristically wheel-made and accounted for over 50 per cent of the sherds at some sites (Fig. 56). The large numbers of jet-black, thin, highly polished pottery and the extremely thin (eggshell) pieces of black pottery are the hallmarks of the Shantung Lung-shan culture. In addition to black and gray sherds, red and white wares also occurred. The most common shapes of vessels are *kui* tripods (tripods with three fat, hollow feet, long body, a spout, and a single handle) and *ting* tripods with the so-called ghost-face legs. Also common are *tou* with high cut-out ring feet, cups, and bowls. Such common Chung-yüan Lung-shan shapes as *li* tripods, *chia* tripods, and *tseng* steamers are totally absent or extremely rare. The pottery is generally plain and highly polished; decorations were

44. *KK* (1963/7), 377.

mostly circumferential ridges and incisions. Impressed patterns of whatever kind were very rare.

Burials are widely found. Those at Ching-chih-chen, placed in rows, are single burials, supine, stretched, head to east. Rich grave furnishings accompanied the dead. Burned shoulderblades of cattle were found, apparently for divination.

The Hangchow Bay Lung-shan Culture (*Liang-chu Culture*)

Previously grouped with the generalized Lung-shan culture, sites of this culture are now known from northern Chekiang in the lower Ch'ient'ang River and Lake T'ai and are sufficiently understood through a series of new excavations (at Liang-chu, Lao-ho-shan, and Shui-t'ien-pan near Hangchow, Ch'ien-shan-yang near Wu-hsing, and Ma-chia-pin near Chia-hsing) to be grouped into a separate local Lung-shan culture phase.

Agriculture of advanced levels was in evidence at many sites. At Ch'ien-shan-yang, remains of rice grains (of both *ting* and *keng* varieties) were found, alongside remains of certain species of peach (*Prunus persica*), melon (*Cucumis melo*), water chestnut (*Trapa natans* or *T. bispinosa*), peanuts (*Arachis hypogaea*), possibly sesame (*Sesamum indicum* or *S. orientale*), and possibly beans (*Vicia faba*).[45] Among these the peanut, a well-known early American species, are of particular interest. Of the agricultural implements, the flat and perforated spades are identical with the Ch'ing-lien-kang type. In addition, there are the so-called winged implements of cultivation, rectangular and semilunar knives with holes, and sickles. A large, coarse-pasted, point-bottomed jar was found together with a wooden pestle, possibly a grain-pounding apparatus. Among the bones of domestic animals, water buffalo, pig, dog, and sheep are recognized. Considerable numbers of water-buffalo bones were identified at Ma-chia-pin.

Remains of net sinkers, wooden floats, and wooden paddles indicate considerable familiarity of the inhabitants with water crafts and fishing. A variety of wild animals (deer, boar, fox) and aquatic species (fish, mollusks, and turtles) has been identified at Ma-chia-pin.

By chance of preservation, the wooden artifacts of this culture are well known; these include remains of house structures, boats, tools,

45. *KKHP* (1960/2), 84–85. Remains of peanuts have also been found at a Neolithic site in Kiangsi. See Ch'in Kuang-chieh et al., *KK* (1962/7), 367.

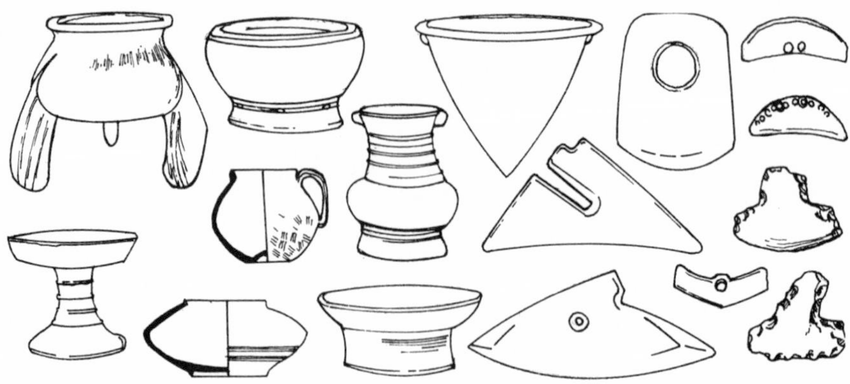

57. Artifacts of the Liang-chu culture. (From *Hsin Chung-kuo ti K'ao-ku Shou-huo,* 1962, p. 29.)

and utensils. Stone and bone artifacts are also highly developed. Black pottery of fine, soft paste is highly characteristic of the Liang-chu culture (Fig. 57); the vessels are constructed by the wheel technique. High luster on the surface was produced by polishing. The shapes include jars with double lugs, *tou,* shallow dishes, *ting* tripods, and *tui* pots, but *li* tripods are again absent. Most of the ring feet found have cut-out designs and are further decorated by circumferential ridges. In addition, red and gray wares of a variety of pastes are also seen here, both handmade and wheel-made. Many of the sandy wares are decorated with cord and basket impressions. Occasional painted pieces occur.

House remains have been found at Ch'ien-shan-yang and Shui-t'ien-pan. These were built on flat ground and are rectangular in shape, ranging in size from 5 to 20 square meters. Walls were built from wattle-and-daub on timber posts. The roof was probably gabled. Ma-chia-pin has thirty burials; most single but prone. A few are supine or flexed.

Other Lung-shan Cultures

The cultures above (two in the Chung-yüan group and two in the coastal group) are obviously from widely separate regions, but they are all referred to as Lung-shan cultures because they were apparently derived from the common Lungshanoid horizon, and they still share a number of characteristic features from their common heritage

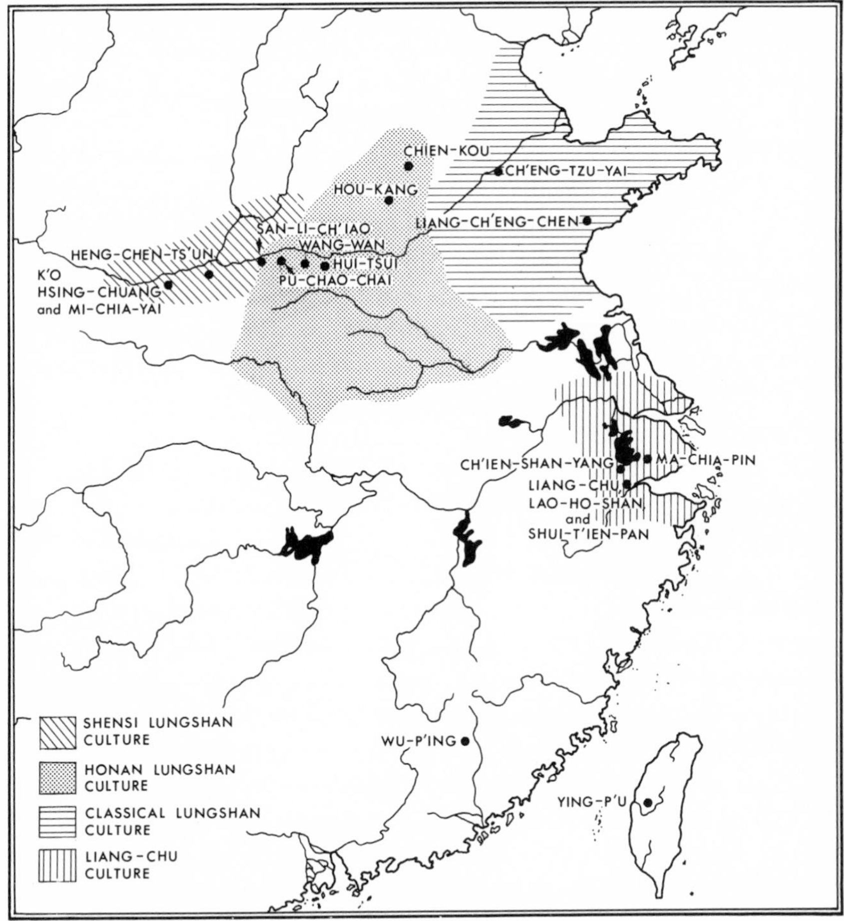

58. The major sites and the approximate areas of distribution of the various local Lung-shan cultures.

and presumably continued intercommunication. They all had advanced agriculture and their general cultural makeup was highly complex. It is very probable that the Honan Lung-shan culture was ancestral to the Shang civilization; that the Shensi Lung-shan culture was related to the antecedents of the Western Chou culture; that the Shantung Lung-shan culture was related to the so-called Eastern Yi peoples in the historical texts; and that the Liang-chu culture was largely ancestral to the subsequent Yüeh culture characterized by geometric-stamped pottery. In other words, the local Lung-shan cultures apparently laid the foundations for the civilizations and ethnic groups in the dawn period of ancient China.

In addition to the above, other Lungshan-type cultural assemblages are known from elsewhere (Fig. 58). The Yang-t'ou-wa site of Liaotung Peninsula,[46] basically a Manchurian Neolithic site, exhibits strong Lung-shan influence from Shantung. The Gray Pottery Culture of the lower Fenho Valley of Shansi, still very inadequately known, appears to resemble the Shensi Lung-shan culture. The Gray and Black Pottery sites in the upper Huaiho, in southeastern Honan and northern Anhwei, are largely similar to the Honan Lung-shan culture but contain elements traceable to southern Shantung and northern Kiangsu.

More problematic is the extent of the Lung-shan distribution in the southern direction. Much of this will be discussed in the next chapter. The pregeometric Gray Pottery Culture of Kiangsi, the Neolithic cultures of Szechwan and western Hupei in the Yangtze Valley, and the Neolithic cultures of the southwest all exhibit strong resemblance to the Lungshanoid horizon and to some Lung-shan phases. The sites of Wu-p'ing in Fukien and of Ying-p'u in Taiwan are unquestionably related to the coastal group of the Lung-shan cultures. Many features of the Ying-p'u pottery—especially the jars with lugs, the ring-footed *tou,* and the sandy pottery *ting* tripods—recall the Liang-chu culture, and the widespread practice of prone burials in central Taiwan in a black pottery context is traceable to the site of Ma-chia-pin. Carbon-14 dates from Ying-p'u place the Lungshan-type culture in Taiwan in the late second millennium B.C., and this may indirectly reflect the time range of the Liang-chu culture on the mainland.[47]

46. Kanaseki et al., *Yang-t'ou-wa,* 1942.

47. For the carbon-14 dates of the Lungshanoid cultures in Taiwan, see Kwang-chih Chang and Minze Stuiver, *Proc. Nat. Acad. Sci., 55* (1966), 539–42; Sung Wen-hsün, *Taiwan Wen-hsien, 16* (1965), no. 4, 144–55.

CHAPTER FIVE

THE SPREAD OF AGRICULTURE AND NEOLITHIC TECHNOLOGY

Efforts have been made in the last two chapters to trace the developments of the Neolithic farmers in North China and their expansion into East and South China. In other areas, a basically hunting-fishing subsistence persisted; during various periods in some regions, the hunter-fishers were exposed to the advanced farming cultures of the Huangho Valley and adopted for local use many Neolithic technological elements such as polished stone tools and pottery, thus giving rise to cultural phases that can be described as sub-Neolithic. In other regions the hunter-fishers adopted the new ways of life and became part-time or full-time farmers. Such cultural transformations took place from the time that Yang-shao farmers first appeared in the Nuclear Area through the subsequent Lungshanoid expansion and early historic periods. The discussion of such transformations is placed here—between the description of the Lungshanoid and the discussion of the emergence of historical civilization in North China—because the cultures in question are classified as "Neolithic." Actually, farming was not introduced into some regions until after historical civilizations had already begun in North China. This will become clear in the following sections, each dealing with a separate historical region (Fig. 59).

NORTHERN SHENSI, SHANSI, AND HOPEI

Since the provincial boundaries have shifted back and forth several times during the present century, a geographical clarification of the title of this section is in order. In general terms, the area referred to is simply the northern part of North China proper and the southern fringes of Inner Mongolia, a region of relatively high altitude, with a steppe vegetation, drained by the northernmost section of the Huangho River, its many small tributaries, and the upper reaches of several rivers in the alluvial plains in the northwestern part of the

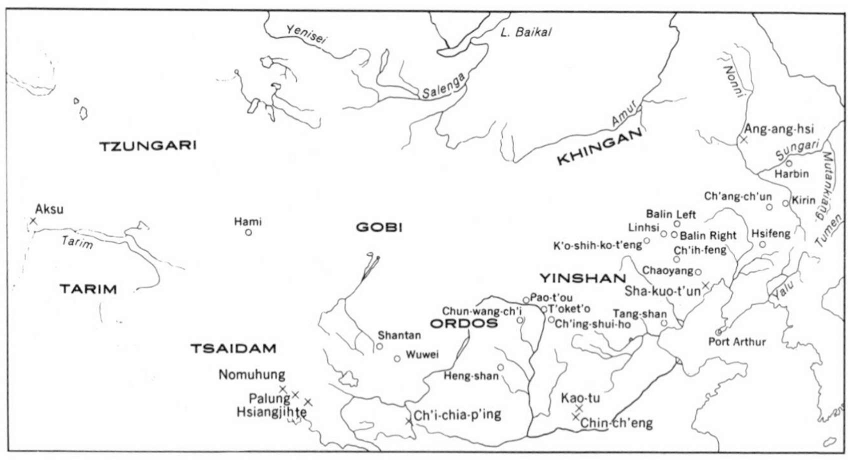

59. Important prehistoric sites (x) and cities near which important prehistoric sites have been found (o) in Inner Mongolia, Sinkiang, and Manchuria.

Pohai Bay area. It is a relatively arid and barren area at present, though oases, parklands, and large and small basins with stable water supplies may have characterized the landscape during the prehistoric period.[1]

The Ordos area in northern Shensi and southern Suiyüan is famous for its Upper Palaeolithic industries, and recent discoveries in the neighborhood of P'ien-kuan Hsien in northwestern Shansi and Ch'ing-shui-ho Hsien in southern Suiyüan appear to indicate Mesolithic assemblages characterized by microblade artifacts and points and scrapers made on "Mousterian" flakes, features resembling the Sha-yüan assemblage of the lower Weishui Valley in central Shensi.[2] Small arrowheads, small elongated scrapers, and microblades have been found in the Heiliut'uho Valley in Heng-shan Hsien, in what may be a nonceramic context.[3] Ceramic assemblages, with and without evidence of agriculture, have been unearthed widely in Ch'ing-

1. For a survey of the Neolithic cultures of this area, see *WW* (1961/9), 5–7; Cheng Shao-tsung, *KK* (1962/12), 658–71; *Nei Meng-ku ch'u-t'u wen-wu hsüan chi,* Peking, Wenwu Press, 1963.

2. Chang Shen-shui, *VP, 3* (1959), 47–56. An Chih-min, *KK* (1959/10), 560.

3. T'ung Chu-ch'en, *KKHP* (1957/2), 11.

shui-ho, Chün-wang-ch'i, and Pao-t'ou.[4] The pottery is red, brown, or gray, of a fine or coarse paste; the red ware is often painted in black pigment, but cord-marking is characteristic of the red pottery. Bowls, jugs, and basins are common forms, but *li* tripods also occur occasionally. The stone industries contain two clear-cut traditions: chipped microliths, in the form of blades, flakes, arrowheads, scrapers, and awls; and polished stone implements, including such agricultural tools as mortars and pestles, hoes, knives, and sickles, in addition to axes and adzes. It is apparent that the Yang-shao technology and subsistence patterns must have been introduced among the Microlithic hunter-fishers of this area, and the Neolithic ways of life may have persisted here well into the historic periods.[5] Subsequent arid conditions apparently did not favor the growth of civilization in the Ordos, and these Neolithic peoples were followed by steppe nomads.

To the east of the Ordos, in northern Shansi and northern Hopei, preceramic assemblages have not been found. Microlithic finds in a ceramic context have been discovered as far south as Chin-ch'eng Hsien and Kao-tu Hsien in southeastern Shansi.[6] But Yang-shao types of sherds have been found in southeastern Shansi[7] and western Hopei,[8] and Microlithic assemblages mixed with the Yang-shao type of red sherds have been uncovered in Shansi and Hopei.[9] Microlithic elements were still very conspicuously present in the Lungshanoid assemblages at Ta-ch'eng-shan in northern Hopei.[10] It seems likely, therefore, that this area had a Microlithic substratum into which Yang-shao and Lungshanoid elements were introduced, with or without agriculture.

4. Egami and Mizuno, *Inner Mongolia and the Region of the Great Wall,* Archaeologia Orientalis, ser. B, *1* (1935). J. Maringer, *Contribution to the Prehistory of Mongolia,* Stockholm, 1950. Wang Yü-p'ing, *KKTH* (1955/5), 9–13. *KKHP* (1957/1), 9–20. Li Yi-yu, *WWTKTL* (1957/4), 26–28; *KKHP* (1959/2), 1–13. *WW* (1961/9), 6, 12, 13. Lü Tsun-eh, *KKHP* (1960/1). Wang Yü-p'ing, *KK* (1963/1), 9–11, 51–52, 55.

5. Wang yü-p'ing, *WW* (1961/9), 10–13. Chou Chieh, *KK* (1962/2), 72–75. Yang Chung-ch'iang et al., *KK* (1965/10), 487–95.

6. Kuo Yüng, *KK* (1959/2), 63.

7. Ibid.

8. Chao Yin-tang and Yang Chien-hao, *KKTH* (1955/1), 45–46. Meng Chao-lin, *WWTKTL* (1955/11), 73–76. Cheng Shao-tsung, *KK* (1962/12), 658–71.

9. *KK* (1959/7), 332–37. Li Chieh-min and Meng Chao-lin, *KKTH* (1958/6), 45–46. Kuo Yüng, *KK* (1959/2), 63. An Chih-min, *WWTKTL* (1953/5/6), 143–52.

10. Ch'en Hui, T'ang Yün-ming, and Sun Te-hai, *KKHP* (1959/3), 21–22.

THE LIAO VALLEY, EASTERN MONGOLIA, AND SOUTHERN MANCHURIA

The Liao drainage is divided into two well-defined sections: the upper Liao Valley in eastern Inner Mongolia and Jehol, with two major tributaries, Hsiliao or Sharamurun and Laoha, which drain the eastern fringes of the Mongolian plateau; and the lower Liaoho Valley of the southern Manchurian erosion plain, immediately north of Pohai Bay. The known cultural history of this region can be summarized as follows: no preceramic industries have been found; there are cultural assemblages characterized by microlithic industries mixed with Yang-shao and non-Yang-shao ceramic features, some of which definitely show, while others conspicuously lack, evidence of agriculture and animal domestication; after these sub-Neolithic and Neolithic phases, in a large part of this area there were occupations of a nomadic kind of culture with assemblages similar to those on the Ordosian steppe.

The best-known prehistoric site in the Laoha River valley is Hung-shan-hou near Ch'ih-feng, discovered by Torii Ryūzō in 1908 and investigated by other scholars in 1924, 1930, and 1935.[11] Two phases of occupation have been distinguished here, the Painted Ware and the Red Ware. The Red Ware phase contains bronze artifacts and other Eastern Chou affinities, and the Painted Ware phase has been synchronized with the Yang-shao stage in North China. This Painted Ware phase undoubtedly has a northern Microlithic and sub-Neolithic cultural base, as indicated by microliths and brownish coarse pottery with loop and lug handles and combed, dentated, and rocker-stamped designs. Yang-shao influence is strongly suggested by remains of thin-walled, handmade orange-red pottery of a fine texture, characterized by bowl and small-necked jar forms, and painted in geometric patterns in dark red and black pigment. Agriculture is indicated by the remains of stone hoes, spades, knives, and pestles and mortars. Cattle, sheep, pig, and horse bones were also found, as well as many spindle whorls of clay and artifacts of shell, bone, antler, and teeth (Fig. 60). In 1943, what was probably a later settlement was found in the nearby village of Tung-pa-chia, also in Ch'ih-feng

11. Hamada Kosaku and Mizuno Seiichi, *Ch'ih-feng: Hung-shan-hou,* Archaeologia Orientalis, ser. A, *6* (1938). Lü Tsun-eh, *KKHP* (1958/3), 25–40.

60. Pottery types at the Neolithic site at Hung-shan-hou, Ch'ih-feng. (From *Ch'ih-feng Hung-shan-hou,* 1938, Pls. 33, 36.)

Hsien.[12] Stone and ceramic remains again indicate a northern Microlithic and sub-Neolithic base, but black pottery and *ting* tripods are found, possibly indicating Lungshanoid or later influences from North China rather than the Yang-shao. The most significant feature of this site is that the whole village was surrounded by a wall of rocks. The village fortification, and the arrangement of houses inside the compound which indicates the existence of a paramount chief in the village, seem to suggest that a tightened social organization also came into being in this part of China after the stage of the first farmers, as was the case in North China proper.

Sites in the Sharamurun River valley have been widely found in Lin-hsi Hsien, K'o-shih-k'o-t'eng Banner, Balin Left Banner, and Balin Right Banner.[13] Microlithic implements were found in most of the cultural assemblages, and the predominant pottery is brownish-gray or red in color, coarse in texture, and characterized by combed and dentated decorative designs. Rocker-stamped pottery, seen at the

12. T'ung Chu-ch'en, *KKTH* (1957/6), 15–22.
13. See n. 4 above.

site of Hung-shan-hou, is especially distinctive in this area.[14] Evidence of contact with North China consists of rare painted sherds and a number of *li* tripods, probably introduced at different times. Remains of polished stone hoes and spades and large pestles and mortars at most of the sites suggest the prevalence of agriculture.

In the lower Liao Valley on the southern Manchurian plains, a cultural sequence similar to that of the upper Liao can be postulated. Cultural assemblages found here show a mixture of microlithic implements; polished stone axes, knives, and sickles; combed ware, painted pottery, black pottery, checker-impressed sherds, and *li* tripods.[15] A northern sub-Neolithic base characterized by microliths and combed pottery can be assumed, and Huangho Neolithic influences seem to have reached this area in successive waves, as indicated by the predominantly Yang-shao elements in the Sha-kuo-t'un site[16] and the predominantly Lungshanoid features at Shao-hu-ying-tzu-shan in Ch'ao-yang Hsien.[17] The Liaotung Peninsula also seems to have had a similar sequence, although it does not appear to have been exposed to the Yang-shao culture but to have been heavily influenced by the Classical Lung-shan, as shown at the site of Yang-t'ou-wa.[18] A series of shellmound sites near Port Arthur and on the islets off the tip of Liaotung Peninsula show clearly the native cultural substratum with microliths and the combed brown pottery of the area.[19]

It is still too early to say whether this Liao Valley was populated during Mesolithic periods, for evidence is completely lacking. It is possible, however, that a significant population of this area was achieved by the Microlithic hunter-fishers of the northern part of China whose culture was enriched by the introduction of North Chinese Neolithic technology and/or agriculture. A Neolithic way

14. Hsü Kwang-chi, *KK* (1964/1), 1–5.

15. Liu Ch'ien, *KKTH* (1955/6), 13–16; (1956/6), 19–25. Wang Tseng-hsin, *KKTH* (1958/1), 1–4.

16. Andersson, *PS*, ser. D, *1* (1923).

17. Liu Ch'ien, *KKTH* (1956/6), 19–25.

18. Burnished red potsherds similar to sherds of the Yang-shao stage in North China were reported from Wen-chia-t'un in the Port Arthur region of the southern Liaotung peninsula, but these were uncovered from a Lungshanoid context; see Kanaseki et al., *Yang-t'ou-wa,* Archaeologia Orientalis, ser. B, *3,* 81, n. 6.

19. Hsü Ming-kang, *KK* (1961/12), 689–90. An Chih-min, *KK* (1962/2), 76–81. Hsü Ming-kang and Yü Lin-hsiang, *KK* (1962/7), 345–52.

of life prevailed here until the Eastern Chou and Han periods, when nomadic tribes roamed on the upper Liaoho steppes, and Han-Chinese settlements began to penetrate this region from North China.

THE SUNGARI VALLEY

The sub-Neolithic and Neolithic cultures of the Sungari Valley in central Manchuria[20] are representative of the entire northern periphery; the native cultural substratum in this region is well established by excavated materials and can be clearly distinguished from the Neolithic influences from the Huangho Valley. This native cultural base is represented by the microlithic and nonceramic assemblages in the Harbin area, apparently a continuation of the Upper Palaeolithic in the north, and by the microlithic and ceramic assemblages at Ang-ang-hsi and other sites in the lower Nonni Valley[21] and a series of sites in the lower Mutanchiang.[22] The ceramic features as well as stone and bone inventories, characterized by flat-bottomed pottery and bone harpoons and needle cases, are definitely linked with the sub-Neolithic cultures on the Pacific coast.

Distinct Huangho Neolithic influences on the native sub-Neolithic substratum are seen in the southwestern part of this area, around the cities of Kirin and Ch'ang-ch'un, where millet agriculture and pig domestication, as well as pottery tripods, polished stone knives, and stone sickles have been found.[23] The same cultural traditions continued in this area even when the Han Dynasty and later civilizations

20. Chang Kwang-chih, *Southwestern Jour. Anthropol., 17* (1961), 56–74. T'ung Chu-ch'en, *KK* (1961/10), 557–67. Tan Hua-sha, *KK* (1961/10), 568–76.

21. For Ang-ang-hsi, see Liang Ssu-yüng, *BIHP, 4* (1932), 1–44; A. S. Loukashkin, *GSoC Bull., 11* (1931), 171–81 and *China Jour., 15* (1931), 198–99; Lü Tsun-lu, *KK* (1960/4), 15–17. For other sites in the Nonni Valley, see Ch'en Hsiang-wei et al., *KK* (1961/8), 398–403, 410; K'uang Yü and Fang Ch'i-tung, *KK* (1961/8), 404–06; Tan Hua-sha, *KK* (1961/10), 534–43.

22. Chao Shan-t'ung, *KK* (1960/4), 20–22. Komai Kazuchika, *Kōkogaku Zasshi, 24* (1934), 11–16. Komai Kazuchika and Mikami Tsuguo, *Kōkogaku Zasshi, 26* (1936), 487–96. Li Wen-hsin, *KKHP, 7* (1954), 61–75. Okuda Naoshige, *JZ, 54* (1939), 459–63. V. V. Ponosov, *Bull. Inst. Sci. Res., Manchukuo, 2* (1938), 23–30. Tan Hua-sha and Sun Hsiu-jen, *KK* (1960/4), 23–30. Lü Tsun-lu, *KK* (1961/10), 546–51. Chang T'ai-hsiang and Wei Kuo-chung, *KK* (1965/1), 4–5, 24.

23. T'ung Chu-ch'en, *KKTH* (1955/2), 5–12; *KKHP* (1957/3), 31–39. Wang Ya-lou, *KK* (1960/4), 31–34.

became firmly established in the Liaoho Valley and Chinese cultural elements appeared in the native artifactual inventories.[24]

THE TUMEN VALLEY

The Tumen Valley of southeastern Manchuria has an early cultural history similar to that of the northern and eastern Sungari in that the native northern sub-Neolithic cultural substratum is strongly marked, and, although the impact of Huangho civilization is shown by occasional import items, hunting-fishing continued to be the principal mode of subsistence during most of its cultural history.[25] The Tumen Valley can best be described as a phase of the Pacific cultural tradition of northeastern Asia.

KANSU AND CHINESE TURKESTAN

Geographically, western Kansu, Chinghai, and Sinkiang are parts of a huge steppe, desert, and oasis belt extending from the Caspian and Black Seas in the west to the upper Huangho Valley in the east. This has proved to be a frequently used corridor for the transmission of cultural ideas and for trade between the East and the West during historical periods. Scholars have therefore had some grounds for speculating that there may have been a similar route of cultural diffusion during an earlier period, whereby the first ideas of agriculture and the first ideas of civilization could have been transmitted from the Near East and Central Asia to the Huangho Valley.[26] This conjecture, however, remains to be borne out by actual archaeological findings in the area.

From a Huangho terrace near Chung-wei in Ninghsia Province, Teilhard de Chardin and C. C. Young in 1930 discovered remains of chipped implements which they regarded as Upper Palaeolithic, and probably of the Ordosian tradition.[27] Nonceramic assemblages which

24. Li Wen-hsin, *KKHP, 7* (1954), 61–75. Wen Ch'ung-yi, *BIE, 5* (1958), 115–210.

25. An Chih-min, *Hsüeh-yüan, 2* (Nanking, 1948), 26–36. T'ung Chu-Ch'en, *KKHP* (1957/3), 31–39. K'ang Chia-hsing, *KKTH* (1956/6), 25–30. Wang Ya-chou, *KK* (1961/8), 411–24. Ch'en Hsiang-wei, *KK* (1965/1), 42–43.

26. E.g. Carl W. Bishop, *Antiquity, 28* (1933), 389–404; *Origin of the Far Eastern Civilization,* Washington, Smithsonian Institution, 1942.

27. *GSoC Bull., 12* (1932), 103–04.

may be of relatively recent periods have been located by the same scholars near Hami in eastern Sinkiang, apparently of the Microlithic horizon.[28] Since these sites remain unexcavated, the Mesolithic stratum has yet to be established. But microlithic implements in association with pottery have been collected widely in southern Ninghsia, Chinghai, and Sinkiang, and even pebble tools predominate in one or two known assemblages in a ceramic context, such as the site of Aksu.[29] The pottery found in some of the sites has no definitely discernible counterpart in the rest of China, but painted sherds have been collected from many parts of the Chinese northwest (Fig. 61), and in the eastern fringes of this region they occur in Neolithic assemblages.[30] As far as the available archaeological record goes, we are sure of the following three facts: archaeological assemblages that can be considered Neolithic are confined to the eastern part of Kansu east of Chiu-ch'üan Hsien and the eastern part of Chinghai in the Huangshui Valley, and these are definitely extensions of the Kansu Yang-shao culture; the ceramic assemblages in Sinkiang and western Chinghai contain elements which indicate that a native microlithic and sub-Neolithic substratum may have persisted in this region into early historical times; and the ceramic assemblages that contain the so-called painted pottery in Sinkiang and western Chinghai are probably late in time, in most cases considerably later than the Neolithic of North China, as indicated by the metal objects sometimes associated with them. Andersson declared in 1943 that "as far as the Yang Shao time is concerned, Sinkiang remains an unknown quantity."[31] Extensive investigations in Sinkiang since 1943 have failed to warrant any significant changes in this view, except by suggesting that during the Yang-shao stage of North China Neolithic, Sinkiang played little if any role in the shaping of cultural history in areas east of it.

But the Yang-shao farmers definitely brought the food-producing

28. Ibid.

29. Folke Bergman, *Archaeological Researches in Sinkiang,* Stockholm, Bokförlags aktiebolaget Thule, 1939, pp. 13–37. Ning Tu-hsüeh, *KK* (1959/7), 329–31. Shih Shu-ch'ing, *WW* (1960/6), 22–31. Li Yü-ch'un, *KK* (1959/3), 153–54. P. Teilhard de Chardin and C. C. Young, *GSoC Bull., 12* (1932), 83–104; Chung K'an, *KK* (1962/4), 170–71; (1964/5), 227–31, 241. Wu Chen, *KK* (1964/7), 333–41. Tung Chü-an, *KK* (1964/9), 475. Li Chün-teh, *KK* (1965/5), 254–55. Li Yü-ch'un, *WW* (1962/7/8), 11–15, 80.

30. See Bergman, Li, Wu, and Teilhard and Young in n. 29 above.

31. *BMFEA, 15,* 280.

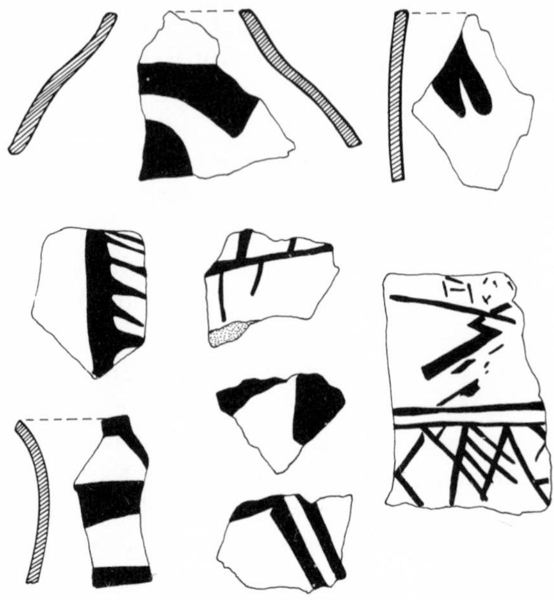

61. Painted sherds from the Astana site in Sinkiang. (From *KK,* 1964/7, p. 341.)

62. Pottery of the Ch'i-chia culture. (From *Sekai Kōkōgakū Taikei,* vol. 5, 1960, Pl. 54).

way of life into eastern Kansu and the Huangshui Valley in eastern Chinghai. After the Lungshanoid farmers evolved in the Nuclear Area to the east, the Yang-shao stage in Kansu and eastern Chinghai seems to have been gradually replaced by several new cultures whose origins remain unclear but which seem to have some sort of connection with the sub-Neolithic and possibly Neolithic peoples to the north and west in the steppe regions. Three such cultures can now be defined—the Ch'i-chia, the Shan-tan (or Ssu-pa), and the Tsaidam (or Nomuhung).

The Ch'i-chia culture, named after its type site at Ch'i-chia-p'ing in Ning-ting Hsien in the T'aoho Valley of eastern Kansu, was discovered in 1923 by Andersson, who regarded it as the earliest Neolithic culture in Kansu, from which the Yang-shao culture in Kansu and Honan was ultimately derived.[32] This thesis, to which a few scholars still subscribe, is—let it be made completely clear once and for all —completely fallacious. Stratigraphical evidence in the entire area of its distribution has shown that the Ch'i-chia culture followed the Kansu Yang-shao culture, but preceded the Chou strata in the upper Weishui and several other contemporary local eneolithic cultures to the west.[33] Its area of distribution is confined to the valleys of the T'ao, the upper Weishui, and the upper Hsi-han-shui, all in the eastern part of Kansu, but remains of Ch'i-chia type are known from Ninghsia and Inner Mongolia.[34] Its pottery is characterized by yellow and buff ware with combed or incised decorative designs and especially by a kind of flat-bottomed jar with a constricted neck, flaring mouth, and two large vertical loop handles on the shoulder (Fig. 62). Painted pots are seen occasionally, and cord marks are another surface feature. Remains of millet were found at the Ta-ho-chuang site in Lin-hsia Hsien; oracle bones of sheep scapula at Ta-ho-chuang and Ch'in-wei-cha in Lin-hsia Hsien; oracle bones of cattle, sheep, and

32. *Preliminary Report on Archaeological Research in Kansau, GSuC,* ser. A, *5; Children of the Yellow Earth,* London, Kegan Paul, Trench & Trubner, 1934; *BMFEA, 15.*

33. The stratigraphical position of the Ch'i-chia culture over the Kansu Yang-shao layers has been observed in a number of sites in the T'ao-ho Valley and the Upper Weishui; see Hsia Nai, *KKHP, 3* (1948), 101–17; An Chih-min, *KKTH* (1956/6), 9–19; Chang Hsüeh-cheng, *KKTH* (1958/5), 1–5 and (1958/9), 36–49; Kuo Te-yüng, *KKTH* (1958/7), 6–16, and *KK* (1959/3), 138–42, 146.

34. Ch'i Yüng-ho, *KK* (1962/1), 22. Chung K'an and Chang Hsin-chih, *KK* (1964/5), 232–33, 244.

pig scapula at Huang-niang-niang-t'ai in Wu-wei Hsien; and copper ornaments and small objects at all three sites.[35] Bones of dogs, pigs, cattle, and sheep and remains of hemp have also been found.[36] All these go to show that the Ch'i-chia was a culture of advanced farmers, among whom domesticated animals were of apparently greater importance than they were in much of the rest of North China.[37]

At the Huang-niang-niang-t'ai site in Wu-wei, rectangular house floors plastered with white limey clay were uncovered; near or within the houses round or square hearths were built. Surrounding the houses were storage pits of various shapes. From the houses and storage pits 23 copper implements and copper slugs were recovered, including knives, awls, chisels, rings, and other forms. An analysis of a knife and an awl discloses that copper accounts for over 99 per cent of the total metal used in their manufacture, with impurities (lead, tin, etc.) less than 0.4 per cent.[38]

Villages of the Ch'i-chia culture incorporate their own burial areas. Two cemeteries have been found at Ch'in-wei-chia, one in the southwestern and one in the northeastern portion of the site. Twenty-nine burials were located in 1960 in the northeastern cemetery in an area about 100 meters square, arranged in three north–south rows, all with heads to the west. Twenty-four of the tombs are single burials, but the other five contained two adults each, a male and a female. The male skeleton lies stretched, and the female, at his left, is flexed (Fig. 63). All tombs contained grave goods of stone and pottery artifacts and the lower jaws of pigs, the last item ranging in number in individual tombs from one to fifteen.[39] The significance of these burial patterns for an understanding of the Ch'i-chia social organization is obvious. At the Ta-ho-chuang site were also discovered rings of small rocks on the ground, possibly a religious construction, near which were the burials of sacrificial animals.

35. Cheng Nai-wu and Hsieh Tuan-chü, *KK* (1960/3), 9–12. Kuo Te-yüng, *KKTH* (1958/7), 6–16. Shih T'ao, *KK* (1961/1), 6. Kuo Te-yüng, *KKHP* (1960/2), 59–60.

36. Margit Bylin-Althin, *BMFEA, 18* (1946), 457–58.

37. For an argument about the relative importance of agriculture and animal husbandry in the Ch'i-chia culture, see Shih T'ao, *KK* (1961/1), 3–11; Yi Ting, *KK* (1961/7), 388–89.

38. Kuo Teh-yüng, *KKHP* (1960/2), 53–70.

39. Hsieh Tuan-chü, *KK* (1964/6), 267–69.

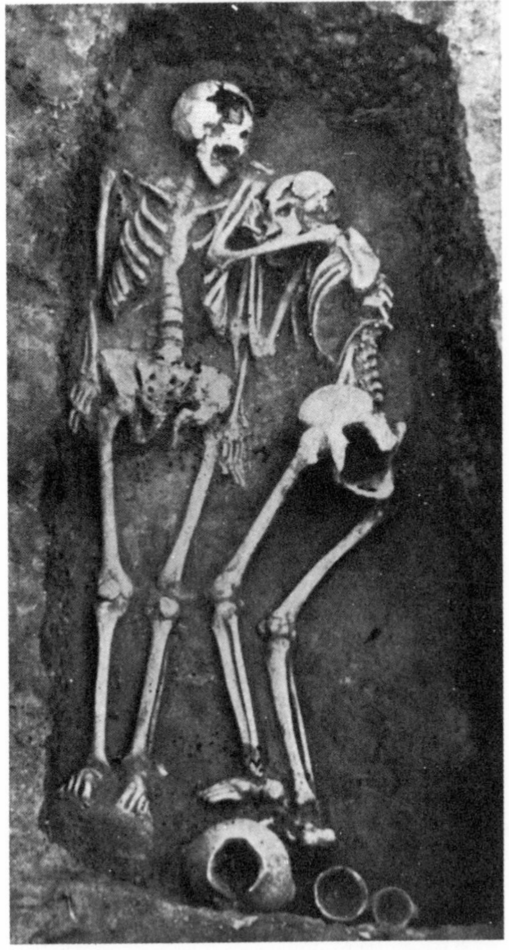

63. A double burial at the Ch'i-chia culture cemetery at Ch'in-wei-chia, Lin-hsia, Kansu. (From *KK,* 1964/5.)

Without question, Ch'i-chia represents the culture of farmers, and their farming tradition was probably introduced from the Yang-shao culture. But there is plenty of room for dispute about its cultural affiliations. Its similarities to the Yang-shao, the Weishui phase of the Lungshanoid, and Western Chou civilizations have been noted,[40] but these could easily be accounted for by cultural contacts during vari-

40. Wang Po-hung, Chung Shao-lin, and Chang Ch'ang-shou, *KK* (1959/10), 517. Jen Pu-yün, *KK* (1959/7), 323–25, 345. Kuo Te-yüng, *KK* (1959/3), 138–42, 146. Shih T'ao, *KK* (1961/1), 10.

ous time periods. It is possible that in this area, which is adjacent to the dry steppes of northwest China and Inner Mongolia, and where the climatic conditions of the present time tend to be on the arid side, the Yang-shao farming culture was not well adapted and was replaced by cultural phases having a native sub-Neolithic base but receiving considerable cultural influence from the Yang-shao farmers. The nature of its contemporary cultural phases and the many local cultural traditions which followed the Ch'i-chia seem to indicate this possibility.

In Shan-tan, Min-lo, Yüng-ch'ang, and Chiu-ch'üan counties of central Kansu, immediately northwest of the Ch'i-chia area, there was probably another cultural phase contemporary with and possibly related to the Ch'i-chia. This could be named the Shan-tan culture, after its type site discovered in 1948 at Ssu-pa-t'an in Shan-tan Hsien. This culture is characterized by agriculture, stone phallus models, and a distinctive kind of pottery of a coarse texture, often painted in very thick pigment which makes the designs stand out in relief. The basic form of pottery is again the double-handled jar. This may very well be a regional branch of the Ch'i-chia, but its distinctive pottery painting and the large number of phallus models seem to warrant its consideration as a separate culture.[41]

The Tsaidam culture is thus far represented by three sites in Nomu-hung, Pa-lung, and Hsiang-jih-te counties of northwestern Chinghai, south of the Tsaidam basin.[42] These were discovered in 1959 and are characterized by houses with mud wall enclosures, urn burials, a large number of bone and horn artifacts, wool fabrics, plain pottery jugs and basins with straight walls, and tent rings of sandbags. Copper objects were found at one of the sites. These remains apparently indicate a food-producing culture leaning toward animal domestication and nomadic life, but the rarity of metal objects seems to provide grounds for synchronizing this cultural phase with the Ch'i-chia to the east. It may very well be one of the cultural phases ancestral to the later Neolithic and metal-age nomads of the steppes, but the culture itself may well have persisted into the early historical period.

41. An Chih-min, *KKHP* (1959/3), 7–15.

42. Chao Sheng-shen and Wu Ju-tso, *WW* (1960/6), 37–40. Wu Ju-tso, *KK* (1961/1), 16; *KKHP* (1963/1), 17–44.

Stratigraphic evidence in eastern Kansu and eastern Chinghai shows that the Ch'i-chia culture was followed by several small local cultural phases possessing metallurgy, with some inclination toward animal domestication, which carried on the painted pottery tradition. These include the well-known phases of Andersson's Hsin-tien, Ssu-wa, and Sha-ching "cultures" and the newly identified "T'ang-wang culture," all of which will be discussed in a later chapter.

THE SOUTHWEST

The greater Chinese southwest includes the Red basin of Szechwan and the hills and plateaus of Kwangsi, Yunnan, Kweichow, and western Kwangtung, on the upper reaches of the Yangtze, the Pearl, the Mekong, the Salween, and the Irrawaddy rivers. When farmers began to appear in North China and while a good deal of "revolutionary" activity was going on there, pottery and polished stone implements also began to appear in the southwest. There is no question that the Neolithic cultures of the southwest continued from the Mesolithic cultural substratum of the area,[43] a condition also prevailing in Indochina,[44] but the life and society of these peoples are little known archaeologically. In the beginning of Chapter 3 I mentioned the probability of a horticultural beginning in the Neolithic period of South China and Southeast Asia characterized by cord-marked pottery, and it appears quite likely that agriculture and a fully Neolithic industry and culture emerged in the southwest long before the full impact of the later Chinese historical civilizations were felt in this region. It is significant to note that the middle Yangtze Valley provided the only major point of contact known in the archaeological record between the North China Nuclear Area and Neolithic South China, and the cultural exchanges between these two regions—in whichever direc-

43. Cheng Te-k'un, *Archaeological Studies in Szechwan,* Cambridge Univ. Press, 1957. Liu Ch'i-yi, *WWTKTL* (1958/3), 69–71. R. Maglioni, *Hongkong Naturalist, 8* (1938), 211. W. Schofield, *PFEPC,* 3d (1940), 259. D. J. Finn, *Hongkong Naturalist, 7* (1936), 258. Chang Kwang-chih, *Ta-lu-tsa-chih, 9* (1954), 4–8. Mo Chih, *KKHP* (1959/4), 1–15.

44. Henri Mansuy, *Stations préhistoriques dans les cavernes du massif calcaire de Bac-Son (Tonkin),* Mémoirs du Service Géologique de l'Indochine, *11, fasc.* 2, 1924; *Nouvelles découvertes dans les cavernes du massif calcaire de Bac-Son (Tonkin),* ibid., *12,* fasc. 1, 1925.

tion—must have been frequent and significant. The fact that the earliest Yang-shao culture phase is known from the Tsinling region (see Chapter 3) and that the Yang-shao sites in southwest Honan exhibit significant "local" characteristics[45] may suggest that the upper Han-shui River valley and the middle Yangtze in western Hupei and eastern Szechwan provided a route of significant contact between the beginning agricultural phases of North China and Southeast Asia. Further information on Neolithic cultures from this area may shed light on the whole range of problems of agricultural origins in the Far East, but at this time excavated sites that are demonstrably earlier than or contemporary with the Yang-shao culture have yet to be reported.

Neolithic sites in the southwest are yet few, but there are many characteristic features that indicate an early separation from Neolithic North China in cultural style. Evidence of agriculture notwithstanding, most of the southwestern Neolithic sites show the great importance of fishing and/or mollusk collecting, but hunting does not appear to be very significant for stone arrowheads and other hunting implements are as a rule rare. The stone inventories include the highly characteristic shouldered axes, remains of which have been unearthed from Ya-an in Sikang in the west, to the island of Hainan in the east.[46] The ceramics are characterized by the long persistence of corded red ware, the abundance of flat-bottomed and concave-bottomed forms, and the wide use of shell and grit temper. Painted pottery, black pottery, stone knives and sickles, and pottery tripods, which may be indicative of North China influences, are all present at various sites but are relatively rare. Geometric ware similar to that of the southeast is seen only along the eastern fringes of this region, while the characteristic southeastern stone implement, the stepped adz, is not present at all. Aside from these generalizations, well-doc-

45. *KK* (1962/1), 23; *KK* (1965/1), 1–3.

46. The shouldered ax has been discovered widely in the Chinese southwest: Szechwan (Cheng Te-k'un, *Archaeological Studies in Szechwan,* p. 60), Yunnan (Huang Chan-yüeh and Chao Hsüeh-ch'ien, *KK,* 1959/4, 175; Wu Chin-ting et al., *Yunnan Ts'ang Erh ching k'ao-ku pao-kao,* Lichuang, National Museum, 1942, p. 37); Kweichou (*KKTH,* 1956/3, 48–50; *WWTKTL,* 1955/9, 67–69); Sikang (Wei Ta-yi, *WWTKTL,* 1958/9, 48–49); Kwangsi (Jung Kuan-hsiung, *WWTKTL,* 1956/6, 58–59; Han K'ang-hsin, *KK,* 1964/1, 591; T'an Chün, *KK,* 1965/6, 313); Kwangtung (Mo Chih, *WWTKTL,* 1956/11, 42; *KKTH,* 1957/6, 9–12; *KKTH,* 1956/4, 5–6); and Hainan (Jung Kuan-hsiung, *KKTH,* 1956/2, 38–41).

umented excavated materials are available at only a few regions in the whole area.

To begin in the Yangtze Valley between Yi-ch'ang (Hupei) and Pa-tung (Szechwan), in the Hsiling Gorge area that was the gateway to the Red basin to the west: fifty-four early sites investigated in 1960 have been grouped into five categories, ranging in date, according to the estimates of the investigators, from Neolithic to Han.[47] At the three sites in the first category (Neolithic), chipped and polished stone implements were found alongside a variety of pottery (Fig. 64). Four wares are recognized: coarse red (30 per cent), coarse brown (30 per cent), fine red (15 per cent), and fine black (15 per cent). The coarse wares were tempered with fibers and shell powders. A few were painted in red or black. Bowl and urn shapes predominated, and a variety of ring feet occurred. The high ring feet were often decorated with cut-out patterns or circumferential ridges. A large number of incised clay pot supporters was found, recalling similar finds in Indochina and the Yüan-shan culture of Taiwan.[48] These characteristic features of the Neolithic sites in the Hsiling Gorge area suggest a culture of considerable distinctiveness, but its ceramics cannot be earlier than the Lungshanoid Ch'ü-chia-ling culture to the east and northeast.

Farther upstream on the Yangtze is the site of Ta-hsi (Huo-pao-hsi) in Wu-shan of easternmost Szechwan, on a terrace at the junction of two rivers.[49] Among the finds excavated here in 1959 are chipped and polished stone axes, hoes, chisels, scrapers, clay spindle whorls, and bone needles; stone arrowheads and bone spear points; a large number of fishbones; and an elaborate assemblage of stone, bone, jade, and shell ornaments. The pottery at the site resembles the Hsiling Gorge wares described above, including sandy red and fine red and black pottery. Some painted sherds of jars, bowls, and urns occurred. In shape, *ting* tripods and ring-footed vessels (including *tou*) again suggest Lungshanoid features of the Ch'ü-chia-ling culture. During a late phase of the occupation, a part of the site served as a cemetery. The burials—all single—were stretched and supine. Grave goods var-

47. Tung Hsi-chen et al., *KK* (1961/5), 231–36. For similar finds in this area, see *WW* (1959/5), 75.
48. W. H. Sung, *Bulletin of the Department of Archaeology and Anthropology,* National Taiwan University, *9–10* (1957), 137–45.
49. Shen Chung-ch'ang and Yüan Ming-shen, *WW* (1961/11), 15–21, 60.

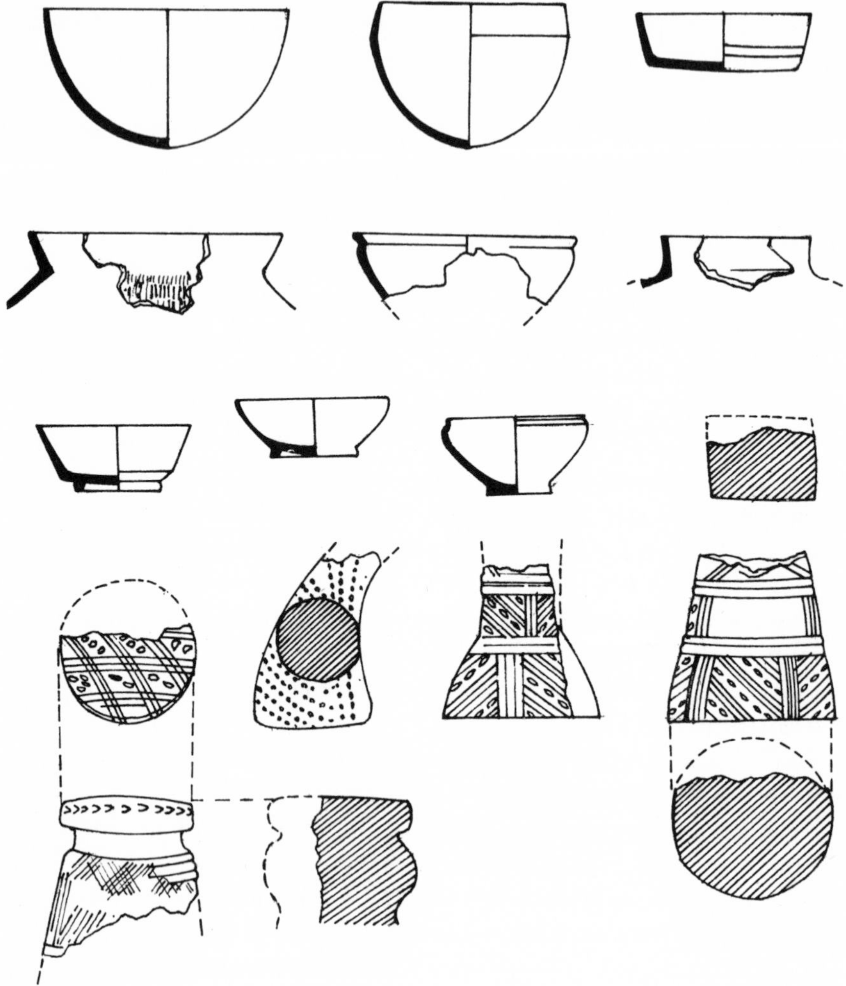

64. Artifacts at the Neolithic site at Yang-chia-wan, in the Hsilinghsia Gorge region of western Hupei. (From *KK,* 1961/5, p. 233.)

ied and a few had peculiar furnishings: two dishes, one on each side of the breast; three painted jars, one on top of the other, lying between the legs; a piece of ivory placed beneath the head; fishbones found in the mouth; a dog.

Not far to the west, along the Yangtze, Neolithic remains have been located in an area approximately 1 kilometer in length on the terraces of both banks of the Hanchingkou River near Chung Hsien.[50] These remains, investigated by the Szechwan Museum in the middle and late 1950s, were concentrated in six clusters on the western bank and one on the eastern. The sites on the western bank, apparently residential settlements, have yielded a large number of sand-tempered, corded ceramics of the *li* tripod and pointed- and round-bottomed jug forms, together with small numbers of gray and black sherds. Basket impression and checker stamping are both seen on some sherds, and some of the rim sherds are painted in black pigment. Stone axes, adzes, chisels, hoes, and pestles, chipped, chipped and polished, and totally ground, have been discovered, together with remains of horses, sheep, pigs, and deer, a human skull, a large number of fishbones, and many mollusk shells. Oracle bones and a bronze arrowhead were found, possibly from a late occupation. The site on the eastern bank, 100 by 50 meters in size, has produced a large number of pebbles, blanks, and finished stone tools from what was possibly a workshop site, near a dwelling house. Seen as a whole, the Chung Hsien sites again show significant similarities to the late Yangshao and early Lungshanoid stages in southwestern Honan and Hupei, but such similarities are fewer here than in the sites farther downstream, described above.

Other than the Szechwan sites,[51] only in Yunnan are significant numbers of Neolithic localities known in the literature. Both in the extreme northeast[52] and the extreme south,[53] distinctively local remains are known, but the best-investigated areas are in the areas of Lake Tien in the east and Lake Erh in the west. No fewer than nine Neolithic sites were located in 1958 on the eastern shore of the Lake Tien in central eastern Yunnan.[54] Most of these can be described as shellmounds or kitchen middens, consisting of compact layers of molluscan shells (most of which had been knocked open) mixed with a

50. Yüan Ming-shen, *KK* (1959/8), 393–97. Yüan Ming-shen and P'ang Yu-lin, *KKTH* (1958/5), 31–32. Yüan Po-shen and Cheng Po-ch'ing, *KK* (1962/8), 416–17.

51. Other than the above sites on the Yangtze in eastern Szechwan, Neolithic sites are also known from the northwestern part of the Red basin where Kansu-style painted pottery has been found. See Ling Hsiang and T'ung En-cheng, *KK* (1965/12), 614–18.

52. *KK* (1962/10), 529–30, 534.

53. Yang Chieh, *KK* (1963/6), 337. Ma Ch'ang-chou, *KK* (1963/10), 573–74. Sung Chao-lin, *KK* (1965/11), 588–89.

54. Huang Chan-yüeh and Chao Hsüeh-ch'ien, *KK* (1959/4), 173–75, 184. Sun T'ai-ch'u, *WWTKTL* (1957/11), 47.

large number of potsherds, some stone implements, and a few shell artifacts. The implements consist of shouldered axes, net sinkers with a constricted waist, perforators, and grinding stones. Potsherds from the middens have been grouped into four classes. (1) Red ware of fine texture, predominantly handmade (coiled), tempered with paddy husks: This pottery is generally of small size, with a plain surface, in the form of cups, small bowls, and shallow dishes with flat or concave bases; it makes up a large percentage of the sherds uncovered from such sites. (2) Gray ware with grit or shell temper, made on wheels and sometimes slipped and then burnished: Pottery of this class, generally larger in size, includes jugs with straight or flaring mouths, basins with two handles, and concave-based cups; its incised or impressed decoration includes feather patterns, lozenges, wavy parallel lines, cross-hatches, basket designs, and rows of dots. (3) Yellow-slipped ware with grit or shell temper, wheel- or mold-made, in the forms of basins, cups, and ring-footed vessels. (4) Orange-yellowish ware with grit or shell temper, sometimes decorated with cord marks and checker impressions. Stone arrowheads were found here, but the remains of rice grains and husks imprinted or embedded in the pottery of the first class suggest the importance of rice farming. Further research on the shores of the lake in 1960 brought to light additional sites of the same culture.[55]

Terraced fields were identified by Wu Chin-ting in the Ta-li region near Lake Erh during the late thirties at the sites of Ma-lung and Fo-ting on the slopes of the Tients'ang Mountains.[56] Natural creeks must have been utilized here for irrigation, and semi-subterranean houses have been excavated. Differing from the Tien-ch'ih region, however, the Ta-li pottery is characterized by spouted jars, *ting* tripods, and stamped designs. Stone sickles and the absence of kitchen middens in the Ta-li area further distinguish it from the Tien-ch'ih phase, and some archaeologists contend that the latter might have been slightly earlier in time.

Satisfactory stratigraphic evidence indicates that such Neolithic farming settlements appeared in the southwest after the Mesolithic and sub-Neolithic cultures but prior to the metal civilizations to be described in a later chapter. The cultural relationship of this area

55. *KK* (1961/1), 46–49.
56. Wu Chin-ting et al., *Yunnan Ts'ang Erh ching k'ao-ku pao-kao.*

with North China was unquestionably very close, as is indicated by the stone inventories and the stylistic similarities in ceramics and by the crops planted in both of these regions. Such Neolithic cultures provided a background for the appearance of the subsequent indigenous civilizations in the middle of the first millennium B.C. under the strong influence of the Eastern Chou civilization in the areas to the north and the east.

GENERAL CONCLUSIONS

The brief descriptions of the emergence of pottery and agriculture in Central and South China demonstrate the pattern of cultural growth in these regions. Clearly, the hunting-fishing Mesolithic populations for the most part continued to occupy their original habitat after the Neolithic ways of life began in the Nuclear Area of North China, but that among them gradually emerged the technology of ceramics and stone polishing. Agriculture and animal domestication emerged or were introduced into some of these regions, and the Neolithic transformation process took place slowly. The whole process and pattern of cultural assimilations can be elaborated and clearly understood when some of the early cultural history of the regions adjacent to China is taken into consideration. While a lengthy discussion of these adjacent regions is not possible in this volume, some general remarks will prove helpful.

The northern Asian regions west and north of the Huangho Valley and immediately adjacent to it can be grouped on the basis of vegetation and topography into three groups: the steppe–desert zone of Central Asia, Sinkiang, Mongolia, and southwestern Siberia; the taiga zone around Lake Baikal and the upper Lena, the Selenga, and the Amur; and the Pacific coast from the Okhotsk down to the coasts of Korea. Sub-Neolithic and Neolithic cultures in these regions more or less follow similar subdivisions.[57] The taiga culture may be omitted from discussion for the present, for the reason that the region directly adjacent to it, northernmost Manchuria, which is separated from Lake Baikal by the Khingan Mountains, is archaeologically unexplored. The available archaeological evidence from central Man-

57. Chester S. Chard, *Anthropologica, 2* (1960), no. 2, pp. 1–9.

churia in the Sungari Valley, as mentioned above, indicates more direct affiliations with the Pacific coast than with the taiga zone to the north.

The northwestern part of China, extending from eastern Mongolia through Sinkiang, is the eastern portion of the steppe–desert belt that consists of Russian Turkestan and eastern European steppes as well as northwest China, and the Microlithic cultural assemblages from the latter region resemble the Kelteminar complex to the west. This complex is characterized by microblade implements which show considerable elaboration but are rarely retouched bifacially and seems to suggest a whole series of local cultures adapted to a similar natural environment. According to A. A. Formozov, the "best witness for the ethnic diversity of this large culture area is the variation of pottery types found within it."[58] On the Chinese periphery, pottery elements in association with microlithic implements can be classified into three groups: those that show connections with the Huangho Valley, such as some of the painted pottery and the *li* and *ting* tripods; those that show connections with the Kelteminar complexes in southwestern Siberia and Kazakhstan, such as the combed and some of the incised pottery; and those that show affiliations with neither, such as the brownish and plain-surfaced wares of eastern Mongolia. This may lead to the conclusion that the microlithic assemblages in the northern frontiers of China, instead of belonging to a single cultural complex (such as the so-called Gobi Culture),[59] may represent a series of local survivals of the Upper Palaeolithic hunting-fishing cultures, which adopted ceramic and other Neolithic technological traits compatible with their local environment and cultural ecology from China and from their northern and western neighbors. Some of these groups in more favorable environments had even adopted agriculture and animal domestication. This process as observed in northern frontiers of China is parallel, for example, to that seen in the eastern Caspian areas where pottery and food production were introduced from the Nuclear Area of Iran, leading to a series of food-producing assemblages such as the Jeitun culture of Jeitun-Tepe and Anau near Ashkhabad.[60] The steppe zone undoubtedly also served as a route of

58. *American Antiquity, 27* (1961), 87.
59. Cheng Te-k'un, *Prehistoric China,* Cambridge, Heffer, 1959, p. 52.
60. M. E. and V. M. Masson, *Cahiers d'histoire mondiale, 5* (1959), 15–40.

cultural movement and diffusion between the high cultural centers in the east and west. In the current archaeological record, we see two radiating centers, one in the Iraq–Iran area and the other in the Huangho, which spread their influence across the intervening steppes from opposite directions and made scattered contacts. We do not yet see, however, that the steppe zone during the sub-Neolithic and the Neolithic stages served as a route of significant cultural transmission from one of the high culture centers to the other.

The influence of the steppe culture phase tapers off toward the east and is only weakly felt in southern and central Manchuria, which may legitimately be classed, during the sub-Neolithic and Neolithic stages, with the Pacific coast traditions. During the several millennia before the Christian era, the regions in northeastern Asia in Manchuria, Korea, and the Maritime Province of the U.S.S.R. can probably be said to belong to a single culture area characterized by flat-bottomed and straight-walled pottery, shell collecting, fishing, and sea-mammal hunting, as well as a distinctive complex of bone artifacts such as barbed and (occasionally) toggle harpoons, bone armors, and needle cases made of bird bones.[61] This phase of culture is of considerable antiquity on the islands off the coast and in scattered areas on the coast. The sub-Neolithic cultures in the Sungari and in the Tumen Valley appear to be the interior phases of this same tradition. It is upon such a tradition that the Neolithic farmers' cultural influences were imposed from the Huangho Valley to the southwest. Farming, however, seems to have been introduced only into the upper Sungari, where the environment permitted it, while elsewhere in central and eastern Manchuria the archaic hunting-fishing cultures persisted into historic periods.

In South China, the early Recent hunter-fishers were apparently part of the widespread population whose cultural remains, discovered throughout all of mainland Southeast Asia, bear striking resemblances from region to region, and which have been named the Hoabinhian after their type region. It has been suggested that in northern Indochina the Hoabinhian horizon, characterized by crude pebble choppers, was followed by a Bacsonian horizon, a continuation of the previous Hoabinhian but with the addition of ceramics

61. A. P. Okladnikov, *Proc. 32nd Internatl. Congress of Americanists,* 1958, pp. 545–56.

and partially polished stone implements. Whether a horticultural beginning was accomplished in this cultural horizon and what its relationship was with the Nuclear Area of North China are important areas of further inquiry.[62] Skeletal remains from Hoabinhian and Bacsonian strata, like those of southwest China, are said to bear Oceanic Negroid features. Lungshanoid farmers coming down into southeast China from the Huangho Valley may very well have been at least partially responsible for the emergence of cereal agriculture in a large part of Southeast Asia, including the Chinese southwest.[63] Furthermore, the Neolithic cultural distributions in Southeast Asia suggest further extensions into the South Seas, following the subdivision of Neolithic cultures of South China. Shouldered axes and corded ware are characteristic of the Indochinese Neolithic as well as the Chinese southwest, whereas rectangular stone axes, stepped adzes, and many other cultural traits are common to both southeastern China and the eastern part of Malaysia and some parts of Oceania.[64]

62. See Kwang-chih Chang, *Discovery, 2,* no. 2 (1967), 3–10.

63. See the special issue on Sa-huynh pottery relationships in Southeast Asia of *AP, 3,* 1959. For possible Lungshanoid influence in Thailand, see Per Sørensen, *East and West,* n.s. *14* (1963), 211–17.

64. Robert von Heine-Geldern, *Anthropos, 27,* 1932. H. O. Beyer, "Philippine and East Asian Archaeology and Its Relation to the Origin of the Pacific Islands Population," *Bull. Natl. Res. Council, 29,* 1948. K. C. Chang, W. G. Solheim, and G. Grace, *Current Anthropol., 5* (1964), 359–406.

CHAPTER SIX

THE EMERGENCE OF CIVILIZATION IN NORTH CHINA

HISTORY AND ARCHAEOLOGY IN THE STUDY OF ANCIENT CHINA

Despite the quality and complexity that distinguish the ancient civilizations from their more barbarous antecedents, these early civilizations continue to be the object of archaeological research, since they are known to us primarily through their material remains: ruins, implements, utensils, and the visual arts. Nevertheless, with the emergence of the Shang in North China, Chinese archaeology advances into a new phase, for in some important aspects the archaeology of the ancient civilizations differs significantly from that of their Palaeolithic and Neolithic predecessors. Civilizations are the outcome of major qualitative developments of culture, as were the other major qualitative transformations before them (e.g. the first use of tools and the invention of agriculture), but in this evolution which produced civilizations, social, political, and economic organizations played especially significant roles. In grasping the essence of ancient civilizations, therefore, the archaeologist must give special emphasis and attention to the articulation of his data as well as to the empirical aspects of the data themselves. Moreover, in most civilizations the first written records emerged. As Christopher Hawkes[1] has pointed out, when texts become available, the scholar must be responsible to them as well as to the archaeological data.

The Shang, the builders of the first verifiable civilization in China, were also the first literate people of Asia east of the Urals. In the royal court of the Shang there were archivists and scribes who recorded important events of the state. With brush and ink, they transcribed characters onto slips of bamboo or wood, and bound them together into book form (the so-called *ts'e*). We know of these books, however, only through reference to them in other contexts, for they

1. *Amer. Anthropologist, 56* (1954), 155–68.

65. Oracle bones of the Shang Dynasty excavated from Hsiao-t'un, Anyang, Honan. (Collection of Academia Sinica; photo courtesy of *Life* magazine.)

have not yet been found. Aside from occasional inscriptions on pottery and other artifacts, the known written records of the Shang that have been preserved intact to this day are primarily of two kinds:

66. Inscriptions cast on a bronze vessel of Shang period excavated in Ch'ang-ch-ing, Shantung. (From *WW,* 1964/4, p. 47.)

records of divination incised on the shoulderblades of animals (mainly oxen) (Fig. 65) and on turtleshells, the two principal media of divination, and signs of possession and offering cast on bronze vessels (Fig. 66). The former are known as the *chia ku wen* (turtleshell and bone scripts), and the latter are known as *chin wen* (bronze scripts). The study of each kind of script is a highly specialized field of learning.[2]

The written records of the Chou, successors to the Shang at the center of the political stage of ancient China, are scarcely more abundant at the beginning. The custom of bone and turtleshell divi-

2. For a comprehensive and authoritative survey of the pre-Ch'in literature see Ch'ien Tsun-hsün, *Written on Bamboo and Silk,* Univ. Chicago Press, 1962. See also Hsün Cho-yün, *Ancient China in Transition,* Stanford Univ. Press, 1965, pp. 183–92.

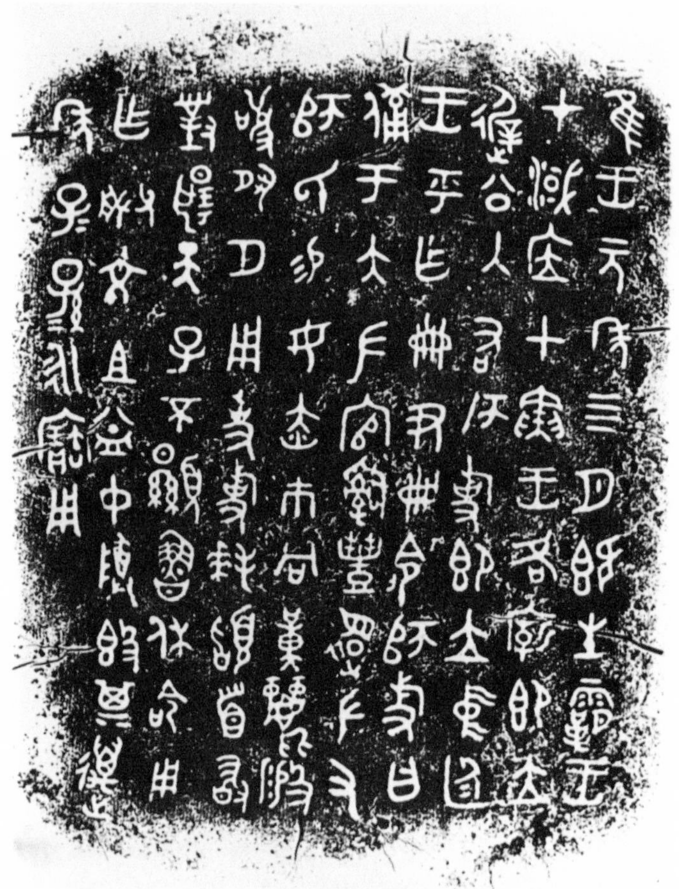

67. A Western Chou inscription cast on a bronze vessel excavated at Chang-chia-p'o. (From *Ch'ang-an Chang-chia-p'o Hsi Chou t'ung-ch'i ch'ün,* Peking, Wenwu Press, 1965, Pl. VIII.)

nation—scapulimancy and plastromancy—was continued by the Chou with much less interest; the practice of inscribing bones and turtleshells was in general discontinued and thus the *chia ku* scripts were no longer a source of textual information for the Chou. On the other hand, the bronze scripts of the Chou have longer texts than the Shang bronzes, often recording the political and ritual contexts in which the vessels were made and offered (Fig. 67). The *chin wen,* therefore, became a major source of the Chou textual information. In addition, there have been rare discoveries of inscribed silk and bamboo and jade tablets (Fig. 68), but the texts are in most cases short and the information they contain inconsequential.

Although archaeologically found Chou texts are scarce, literacy expanded to the local states during the second half of Chou history—the Eastern Chou period—and many more books, archives, and other written materials came into being throughout China. Many of these survived the Chou and were transcribed onto the newly invented paper during the Han Dynasty. Known as the pre-Ch'in texts, these became a part of the traditional literary heritage of China that was handed down through the subsequent two millennia of her historical period. Including such important volumes as the annals of the various states (e.g. *Ch'un Ch'iu* and *Chu Shu Chi Nien*), the *Book of History* (*Shu Ching*), and the *Book of Odes* (*Shih Ching*), the pre-Ch'in texts were the principal source from which Ssu-ma Ch'ien compiled his *Shih Chi,* the first comprehensive and objective history of China, in the beginning of the first century B.C. As sources of information, however, these pre-Ch'in texts are full of problems. Because of the Ch'in upheaval, few of these documents survived into the Han Dynasty intact; most had to be restored by Han scholars, many of whom had their own axes to grind and points to make and have been known to speak their own minds through their ancients. Each book must therefore be authenticated, section by section or even sentence by sentence, in order to be used as a piece of pre-Ch'in textual material. Moreover, few of these texts are accurately dated, and, owing to the scale of cultural change during the periods they represent, the date must be carefully estimated, often on very circumstantial evidence.

Thus, the study of ancient China can be divided into a prehistoric and a historic segment. For the study of prehistory, scholars must rely exclusively on archaeology, but the historical archaeologist has the advantage of the textual information that was available for both the Shang and Chou periods. Since the textual information pertains primarily to political and ritual aspects of the Shang-Chou cultures, aspects that are important concerns of civilizational studies, it is appar-

68. Inscribed bamboo tablets excavated from Ch'u tombs at Chiang-ling, Hupei. (From *WW*, 1966/5.)

ent that research into Shang and Chou culture and society cannot be a purely archaeological task.

It does not, however, necessarily follow that in the study of Shang and Chou China the archaeologist cannot play an independent part. All three main sources of textual information pertaining to the Shang and Chou are highly specialized fields of learning, each containing countless unsolved problems, many of which are perhaps unsolvable. To undertake research in depth in one of these fields one must become a chiakuologist, a chinwenologist, or a pre-Ch'in text specialist. Among the scholars of the last group there are even those who devote their lives to the study of single books. The archaeologist cannot be expected to become master of all these specialized fields, nor should he wait until all the textual information becomes known and all its problems solved before he undertakes his own study. On the other hand, many archaeological problems of ancient China are not only independent of textual study but are capable of contributing solutions to textual problems. The study of Shang and Chou China, therefore, calls for active and close collaboration between the archaeologist and the historian. Each must be aware of the other's results and conclusions and undertake his own research with them in mind, but he cannot be expected to be minutely responsible for the other's data and issues. In dealing with Shang and Chou China in this volume, I adhere strictly to my role as an archaeologist. Textual information and historical conclusions will be used only when and if they contribute to a better archaeological understanding.

A related issue in this connection is the matter of pre-Shang history. There may be two meanings to the phrase. The first refers to written records dated to an earlier period than the Shang. Since such records do not exist at present, and the problem is purely hypothetical, it requires no further discussion. The second meaning refers to the personages and events, recorded in Shang and Chou texts, that were regarded by the Shang and Chou themselves as having existed or taken place before their era.

Such data, collectively referable as the myths and legends of the Shang and Chou, are part of the material for the study of the Shang and Chou themselves, highly useful for an understanding of their views of cosmology and history. Undoubtedly they also included oral traditions that had been handed down from remote antiquity to the

Shang–Chou period and are thus truly reflective of pre-Shang events and conditions. Two such events, the rise of the Huang Ti era and the whole history of the Hsia Dynasty, are illustrative.

The exact nature of Huang Ti, the celebrated Yellow Emperor, and the history of his career, are subjects of numerous studies. His supposed accession took place in 2697 B.C. He was the greatest of the cultural heroes of ancient China, and to him are credited the invention of all the essential elements of the civilization. He was also the greatest war hero of the Flower People, from whom all subsequent dynasties claimed descent. These stories are perhaps more important symbolically than historically: Huang Ti was more a symbol of an era than an actual ancestor.

> During the Age of Shen Nung, men cultivated food and women wove clothing. People were governed without a criminal law and prestige was built without the use of force. After Shen Nung, however, the strong began to rule over the weak and the many over the few. Therefore, Huang Ti administered internally with penalties and externally with armed forces [Chapter "Hua-ts'e," in *Shang Chün Shu*].

Thus is described a major transition of Chinese society from self-contained peaceful villages to warlike states with centralized government. Shen Nung ushered in an era with farming villages, but Huang Ti was responsible for the rise of cities and the state. These tales anticipated the modern archaeologists in giving due recognition to the Neolithic and the urban revolutions as epoch-markers of ancient history. How the ancient Chinese arrived at these notions is unimportant. It is significant that portions of the pre-Shang history in Shang–Chou texts contain grains of historical judgment that would have met the approval of a Gordon Childe.

The records concerning the Hsia Dynasty are of more than symbolic importance. A royal genealogy of the Hsia is known fragmentarily from pre-Ch'in texts and in organized form in *Shih Chi.* Tales about particular kings, events during the reigns of several, and the detailed process in which the Shang overthrew the Hsia are recorded in Ssu-ma Ch'ien's *Shih Chi,* whose credibility in recording some true history of the Three Dynasties is amply demonstrated by the reliability of its Shang and Chou portions. Was there a Hsia Dynasty as well? If so, what was its archaeological equivalent? Several points regarding these problems are self-evident.

In the first place, the archaeological sequence in the northern Honan area is reasonably complete in showing that the Shang civilization in that region was derived from the Lung-shan culture, and that there was no major break in the sequence. Unless this is a strictly local phenomenon (which is not at all impossible, since for other areas the record for this stage is incomplete), it is likely that the legendary history from Huang Ti through the Hsia Dynasty is included in the time span of the Lung-shan. Second, the Lung-shan stage of Chinese Neolithic cannot be considered to have achieved the kind of civilization that has been attributed to Huang Ti through Hsia. This need not, however, worry us particularly, for a strong political organization certainly appeared during the Lung-shan stage, probably along with some other items of civilization such as incipient metallurgy, intensified industrial specialization, and intensified status differentiation. On the other hand, we do not have to believe that the Huang Ti–Hsia interval had achieved a full-fledged civilization, as recorded in the traditional history, for this part of the tradition must have been tempered considerably in accordance with the historical perspectives of these early times. It is possible, therefore, that the Hsia Dynasty was one of the local cultural groups immediately preceding the Shang Dynasty. Finally, this identification may never be certain unless some archaeological finds belonging to the late Lung-shan stage are proved by written records to have been left during the Hsia Dynasty. Since we are still uncertain about the early history of Chinese writing, it is impossible to say now whether this is a likely prospect.[3]

In any event, both archaeological and legendary Chinese prehistory preceded the Shang Dynasty. Earlier chapters have described the former, which ends where the Shang and Chou began. In other words, from two opposite directions Chinese prehistory and history meet at the beginning of the Shang civilization. The legendary pre-

3. Hsü Chung-shu, *An-yang Fa-chüeh Pao-kao, 3* (1931). Hsü Liang-chih, *Chung-kuo Shih-ch'ien-shih Hua,* Hong Kong, Asia Press, 1954, pp. 197–230.

history is certainly contained in the archaeological prehistory, and may enrich and amplify it. A proper study of it, however, must be left to other volumes.[4]

MAJOR SITES OF THE SHANG

At a number of archaeological sites in North China it has been shown that lying above—and temporally subsequent to—strata of the Neolithic Lung-shan culture are remains of a much more advanced civilization that can be identified with the historical Shang civilization. In describing the Shang archaeology we must, at the outset, make a very careful distinction among the following terms. *Shang period* refers to a block of time, approximately from 1850 through 1100 B.C. In ascribing a site to the Shang period we simply date it to that block of time; the site itself may be at the dead center of the Shang civilization, or it may be a barbarous village contemporaneous with but independent of the Shang civilization. By *Shang Dynasty* one refers to a political entity and to the political epoch in Chinese ancient history when, after about 1750 B.C., the Shang royal house ruled the land. A site does not *date* from the Shang Dynasty, but it may have *belonged to* it; that is, it may have been a part of the Shang political sphere during that dynasty's reign. The totality of the Shang culture and society—including its material culture, social and political institutions, and its ideology in organic articulation—constitutes the *Shang civilization.* The archaeological localities where the Shang civilization is significantly manifested are *Shang sites.* Elements of the Shang civilization that are found archaeologically are the *Shang-type remains.* The discovery of Shang remains at a site does not necessarily make it a Shang site; these could have been trade objects in an alien community. It does not ensure that the site belonged to the Shang period; it could have been continuously in use after the twelfth century B.C. These distinctions are necessary at the outset in order to delimit the temporal and spatial expanse of the Shang civilization for

4. For mythology in ancient China, see Marcel Granet, *Danses et légendes de la Chine ancienne,* Paris, Félix Alcan, 1926; Henri Maspero, *Jour. Asiatique, 204* (1924), 1–100; Bernhard Karlgren, *BMFEA, 18* (1946), 199–365; Derk Bodde, "China," in *Mythologies of the Ancient World,* New York, Doubleday, 1961; Yang K'uan, *Ku Shih Pien, 7,* 1941; Hsüan Chu, *Chung-kuo Shen-hua Yen-chiu ABC,* Shanghai, Shih-chieh Book Co., 1929.

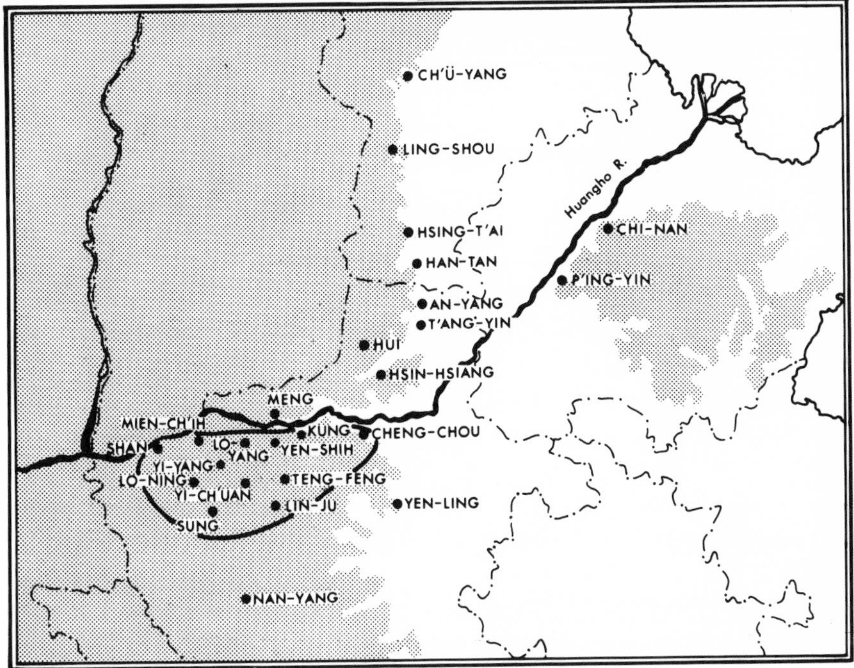

69. Major sites of the Shang civilization and the area of distribution of the Erh-li-t'ou phase (circled area in Western Honan).

my purpose. Shang remains have been found in most of China,[5] but they should not be taken to mean that the Shang culture was similarly distributed. The Shang sites that form the nexus of the Shang civilization in its totality or essence, are much more limited. The center of the Shang is apparently in the northern part of Honan and its immediate surroundings. The best-known archaeological sites are in the following regions (Fig. 69).

1. Yen-shih

The first "king" who founded the Shang Dynasty is known as T'ang or Ta Yi. T'ang overthrew the Hsia Dynasty and made Po the capital of his new state in 1766 B.C. The location of Po is uncertain; according to some scholars it is identified with places in easternmost

5. Cheng Te-k'un, *Shang China (Archaeology in China, 2)*, Cambridge, Heffer, 1961, p. 14.

Honan and adjacent northern Anhwei, but according to others it was near the modern city of Yen-shih in northwestern Honan. Shang sites were not found in the Yen-shih area until 1958,[6] but in the last few years new data have accumulated in this region to indicate the existence here of a Shang settlement of major proportions at an early stage within the Shang period.

Yen-shih and the neighboring Lo-yang are the two major cities in the Loyang basin of western Honan, surrounded on all sides by low mountain ranges and drained by the rivers Yi and Lo, tributaries of the Huangho to the north. In the area of Yen-shih fourteen archaeological localities are known that date from the Shang period,[7] but only at the sites of Erh-li-t'ou,[8] Kao-yai,[9] and Hui-tsui[10] are brief descriptions of the excavated material available (Fig. 70). The site of Kao-yai is of special significance in revealing a Neolithic stratigraphy of Yangshao–Lungshanoid–Lungshan sequence that suggests a continuous cultural development paralleling the sequence brought to light earlier at the Wang-wan site in neighboring Lo-yang.[11] From the Shang stratum at Kao-yai a bronze knife was discovered.

At the Erh-li-t'ou site a developmental sequence continues from Kao-yai and suggests that out of the Honan Lung-shan culture grew an early phase of the Shang culture that can be referred to as the Erh-li-t'ou phase, which was apparently ancestral to the later Shang phases known at Cheng-chou and An-yang. More than 8,000 square meters of the site were excavated between 1960 and 1964, with impressive results leading to the speculation that perhaps the T'ang capital of Po has been uncovered here.

At the center of the site a blunt T-shaped house floor, about 100 meters long and wide, of *hang-t'u* structure, was located (Fig. 71). Along the sides on the floor are large postholes containing stone post-bases. Walls of wattle-and-daub were constructed on foundations of rock-filled ditches. About 50 meters south of the large floor—called a

6. *WW* (1959/12), 41–42.
7. Chao Chih-ch'üan and Kao T'ien-lin, *KK* (1963/12), 649.
8. Hsü Hsün-sheng, *KK* (1959/11), 598–600; *KK* (1961/2), 81–85. Fang Yu-sheng, *KK* (1965/5), 215–24.
9. Li Yang-sung, *KK* (1964/11), 543–47.
10. *WW* (1959/12), 41–42. *KK* (1961/2), 99.
11. Li Yang-sung and Yen Wen-ming, *KK* (1961/4), 175–78.

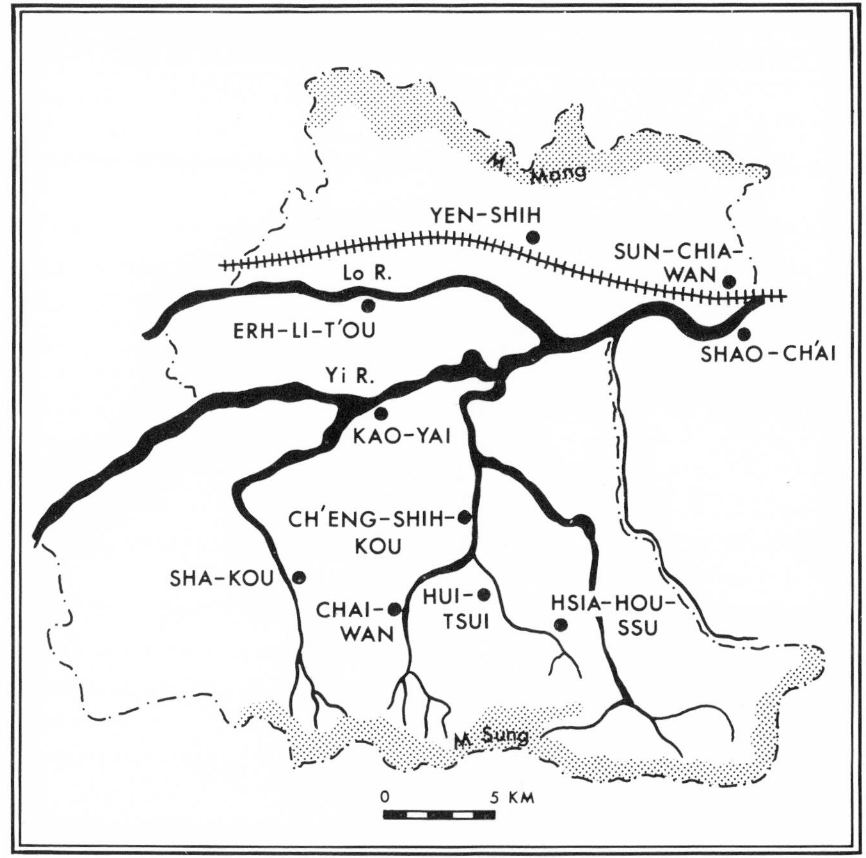

70. Shang sites in Yen-shih, Honan.

palatial foundation by the investigators—are three clusters of smaller house floors. Eleven houses have been excavated, rectangular in ground plan (one over 9 m long E–W), with stamped earth floors and stone post bases. At various parts of the site are 3 pottery kilns, 2 water wells, 48 human burials, and over 260 storage pits. Nineteen of the burials have recognizable grave pits and grave goods, and the bodies in them are all stretched, lying supine or on one side. The grave goods included various kinds of pottery (drinking vessels, cooking wares, containers, and serving vessels and dishes), a bronze bell, and turquoise, jade, and shell ornaments. The burials without grave

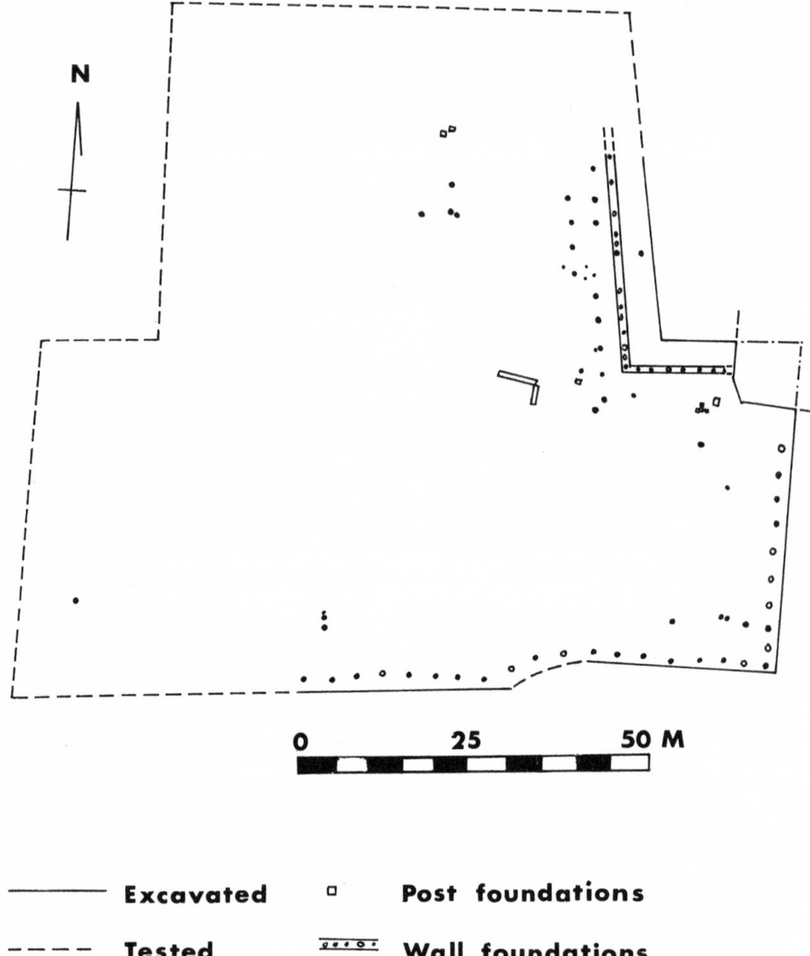

71. A Shang house floor at the site of Erh-li-t'ou, Yen-shih, Honan. (From *KK*, 1965/5, p. 216.)

goods are mostly found in habitation layers and storage pits, and are in various postures such as squatting, flexed, or stretched. Some were apparently victims of some sort, with hands tied and perhaps buried alive; some had heads or parts of the limbs missing. These burials indicate most vividly a stratified society in which members of a lower class were sometimes victims, perhaps of religious ceremonies.

Large numbers of pottery vessels at the site distinguish the Erh-li-t'ou phase as stylistically intermediate between the Honan Lung-shan culture and the later Shang phases. The paste of the pottery varies from very fine to very coarse and ranges in color from white and light yellow to red, gray, and black. Parts of the same vessel were often made in different ways: handmade, modeled, coiled, and wheel-made. Decorations were mostly impressed with cord, basket, and check designs, and appliqued and incised patterns are also found. Among the incised patterns are stylized animals such as dragons, serpents, fishes, and *t'ao-t'ieh*. In shape the vessels include pots, basins, and various kinds of ring-footed forms and tripods (*ting, li, chia, chüeh, ho, kui,* etc.) On the interior of the rims of some *tsun* vessels are incised signs of various shapes that may have been some kind of script. Of special significance is the appearance of specialized wine-serving vessels (*chüeh, chia, ku, ho, kui,* etc.), mostly found in graves with furnishings, indicating a leisurely social class (Fig. 72).

Among the implements found at Erh-li-t'ou are hoes, sickle knives, and flat spades of stone, shell, and bone; arrowheads and spearheads of stone, bone, shell, and bronze; bone harpoons; fishhooks of bone and bronze; and clay sinkers and spindle whorls. Shoulderblades of oxen and sheep with burned marks are found, but no elaborate preparation or inscriptions are in evidence. There are also various art objects and ornaments of clay, stone, jade, turquoise, bronze, and shell. It is significant that bronze artifacts are few and simple (knives, awls, fishhooks, and a bell), but fragments of clay crucibles, bronze slugs, and clay molds indicate a bronze foundry at this site. Many bone fragments and half-finished bone artifacts tell of a developed bone industry.

Stratigraphic evidence at the site and at other sites with remains of the Erh-li-t'ou phase shows that this was earlier than the Erh-li-kang phase (to be described below); in fact, it is the earliest verifiable phase of a full-fledged Shang civilization with bronze metallurgy (of a possibly more primitive state), advanced forms of symbols on pottery, a Shang art, large *hang-t'u* structures, a highly stratified burial pattern, and specialized handicrafts. In pottery, the impressed decorations and such forms of *ku, chia, tou,* and deep pots suggest very

72. Pottery of the Erh-li-t'ou phase of Shang civilization from the Erh-li-t'ou site, Yen-shih. Honan. (From *KK,* 1965/5, Pls. I–IV.)

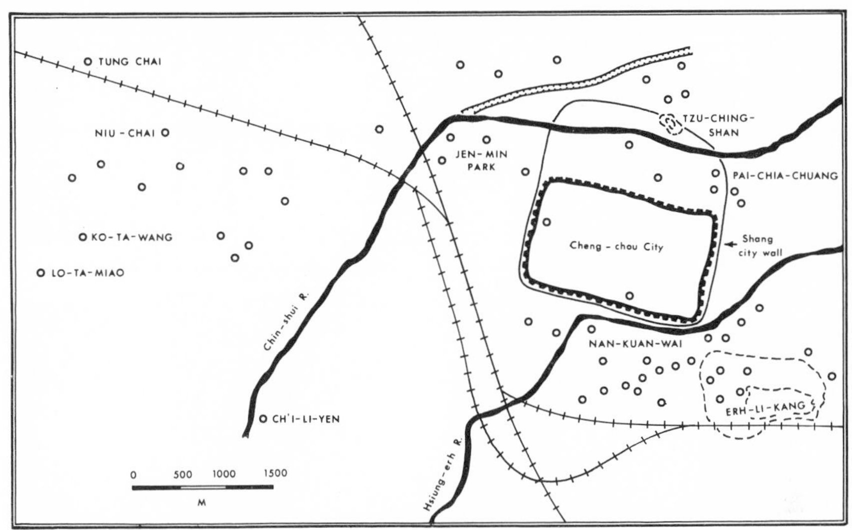

73. Shang sites in Cheng-chou, Honan.

close relationship with and probably direct descent from the Honan Lung-shan culture of the area. The importance of the Yen-shih sites cannot be exaggerated.

Remains of the Erh-li-t'ou phase have been located at the Tung-kan-kou site in neighboring Lo-yang.[12] The distribution of similar remains elsewhere will be described below.

2. *Cheng-chou*

Discovered in 1950, the Shang remains (Fig. 73) in the vicinity of Cheng-chou, northern Honan, are still being excavated and studied. Enough has been discovered, however, for An Chin-huai to conclude that the "Shang Dynasty remains, except for those found in scattered spots in the western suburbs of Cheng-chou, are mostly concentrated within the ancient city site of Cheng-chou and its vicinity. Shang settlements spread continuously in an area of about forty square kilometers east from Feng-huang-t'ai west to Hsi-ch'eng-chuang, and south from Erh-li-kang to the north of Tzu-ching-shan."[13] Before the

12. *KK* (1959/10), 537–40.
13. An Chin-huai, *WWTKTL* (1957/8), 17.

TABLE 7.

Shang Culture Phases at Cheng-chou, Honan

Jen-min Park Phase	Jen-min Park III Ko-ta-wang III
Upper Erh-li-kang Phase	Erh-li-kang II Jen-min Park II Pai-chia-chuang II Nan-kuan-wai III Tung-chai III
Lower Erh-li-kang Phase	Erh-li-kang I Jen-min Park I Pai-chia-chuang I Nan-kuan-wai II Tung-chai II Ko-ta-wang II
Lo-ta-miao Phase	Lo-ta-miao Nan-kuan-wai I Tung-chai I Ko-ta-wang I
Shang-chieh Phase	Shang-chieh

Shang, the area of Cheng-chou was occupied by both Yang-shao and Lung-shan farmers, whose remains have been unearthed at Lin-shan-chai, Niu-chai, Ko-ta-wang, and other sites. Immediately subsequent to, and apparently evolving out of, the Honan Lung-shan culture were strata of the earlier stages of the Shang. The Shang history of settlement seems to be divisible, according to available evidence, into five stratigraphic phases,[14] as shown in Table 7.

The Shang-chieh phase, thus far represented only by the site at Shang-chieh in the westernmost portions of Cheng-chou, is on the very borderline between the Honan Lung-shan culture and the Shang (Fig. 74). At the site several floors were found, all but one rectangular in shape. Over thirty storage pits, most with oval-shaped openings, were excavated. Among the artifacts, the polished stone

14. Cheng Te-k'un, *Shang China,* p. 28. Tsou Heng, *KKHP* (1956/3). Honan Wenhuachü, *Cheng-chou Erh-li-kang,* Peking, Science Press, 1959. Chao Ch'ing-yün, *KKTH* (1958/9), 54–57. *KK* (1960/6), 11–12. An Chin-huai, *WW* (1961/4/5), 79–80.

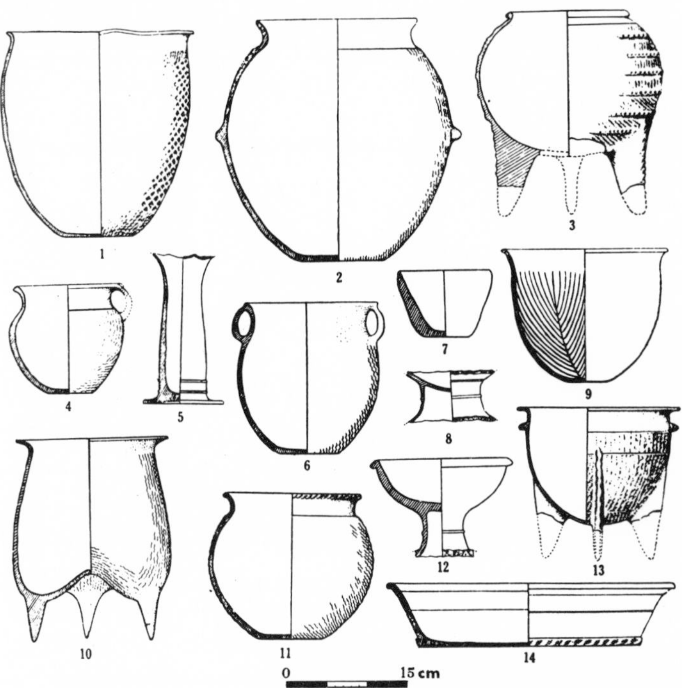

74. Pottery of the Shang-chieh phase, Shang civilization, from the site of Shang-chieh, Cheng-chou, Honan. (From *KK,* 1966/1, p. 5.)

spades and multiperforated knives particularly recall Lung-shan forms. In ceramics, jugs, *tou* fruit stands, bowls, basin, *li* tripods, and wide-mouthed jars are characteristic Shang items, but the flat-bottomed jugs with a high body resemble Lung-shan forms. No metal objects have been unearthed here. Ox and pig bones were found which had been utilized for oracle purposes, but evidence of preparation before heat application is lacking. Five human burials were located. Two of them have clearly outlined rectangular grave pits; one has a "waist-pit" (see p. 320) in which are bony remains of animals, and the other has two pieces of cowrie-shaped bone objects. The other three burials were found in habitation layers, and their unpatterned postures suggest that the bodies were thrown into amorphous pits without ceremony.[15]

Four sites so far can be grouped into the second, or Lo-ta-miao,

15. *KK* (1960/6), 11–12; (1966/1), 1–7.

phase. All seem to have been residential villages, but pottery kilns were also uncovered at Ko-ta-wang. Stratigraphy shows conclusively that this phase was chronologically situated between the Lung-shan and the Lower Erh-li-kang phase, although the relative dating between the Lo-ta-miao and the Shang-chieh phases is still typologically based. Metal objects are lacking in the cultural remains of this phase. In the cultural inventory, typical Shang traits increased, but there were still many Lung-shan features such as the great number of shell artifacts, bone hairpins with awl-shaped heads, pocket-shaped storage pits (which had become rare, however), and the generally unprepared oracle bones. Some diagnostic ceramic features are the round-bottomed and cord-marked jugs with high and nearly vertical bodies, vessels with large mouth openings, small basins and jars, and jugs with checker impressions. This stage is again known only imperfectly, but there is no question of its existence.[16]

Cheng-chou of the Lower Erh-li-kang phase seems to have stepped suddenly into increased activity and expanded the size of its settlement. Sites of this phase contain dwelling houses, burials, workshops, and a city wall.[17] It has been suggested that during this stage dwelling quarters and burials of the aristocrats were inside the city wall, and that the city itself was the center of living and administration, but that the commoners' residences, cemetery, craft shops, and farming fields were outside the wall. According to literary records, the ancient Shang kings changed their capital sites several times before finally settling at Yin, the site of the present city of An-yang. One of these earlier capitals, four capitals before An-yang, is said to have been the city of Ao or Hsiao, probably in the vicinity of the present town of Ying-tse, about 15 kilometers northwest of Cheng-chou. Intensive investigations were undertaken during the 1950s in the neighborhood of Ying-tse, but they failed to turn up any Shang Dynasty remains. In Cheng-chou, however, a full-fledged city site has been located, dating

16. Chao Ch'üan-ku et al., *KKHP* (1957/1), 56–58. Hsia Nai, *China Reconstructs, 6* (1957), 20. An Chin-huai, *KKTH* (1955/3), 18. Chao Hsia-kuang, *KKTH* (1958/2), 6–8. Ch'en Chia-hsiang, *WWTKTL* (1957/10), 48–51. Chao Ch'ing-yün, *KKTH* (1958/9), 54–57. Chao Ch'ing-yün and Liu Tung-ya, *KKHP* (1958/3), 41–62.

17. Honan Wenhuachü, *Cheng-chou Erh-li-kang*. An Chin-huai, *WW* (1961/4/5), 73–80. Chao Ch'üan-ku et al., *KKHP* (1957/1), 53–73.

to the Lower Erh-li-kang phase, which, as will be shown, is considerably earlier than the dynastic phase of An-yang stratigraphy. Some scholars have suggested, therefore, that Cheng-chou may have been the site of the ancient capital of Ao.[18]

The Shang city wall was roughly rectangular in shape, with a total perimeter of 7,195 meters and an enclosed area of 3.2 square kilometers. The maximum height of the surviving wall is 9.1 m, and the maximum width at the base is 36 m. The wall was built in successive compressed layers, each of which has an average thickness of 8 to 10 cm. On the surface of each layer are clear depressions made by the pestles used for compressing, and the soil making up the wall is hard and compact. The inner structure shows that it was built at two different periods, both within the time of the Shang, possibly corresponding to the Lower and the Upper Erh-li-kang phases. The wall was apparently used and mended during subsequent historic periods, but a new wall was built during the Han Dynasty around a smaller enclosure.[19] The Shang wall shows without doubt that the city of Cheng-chou during the Shang Dynasty was of considerable importance and was constructed only with major effort. An Chin-huai[20] estimates the original wall to have been 10 m in average height, with an average width of 20 m, which, multiplied by the total length of 7,195, required 1,439,000 m^3 of compressed soil or (by a ratio of 1:2) 2,878,000 m^3 of loose soil. Experiments carried out by archaeologists show that an average worker produces per hour 0.03 m^3 of earth by means of a bronze pick or 0.02 m^3 by means of a stone hoe. An concludes that to build the whole city wall of Cheng-chou, including earth-digging, transporting, and compressing, required no less than 18 years, with 10,000 workers working 330 days a year. This impressive figure, even though roughly calculated, indicates that Cheng-chou of the Shang Dynasty was no ordinary town.

The enclosure apparently marks the center of administration and ceremony. Since it overlaps the present city site of Cheng-chou and has therefore been only spottily excavated, the layout of this site is

18. An Chin-huai, *WW* (1961/4/5), 73; but see Liu Ch'i-yi, *WW* (1961/10), 39–40; An Chih-min, *KK* (1961/8), 448–50.

19. An Chin-huai, *WW* (1961/4/5), 73–74. Hsia Nai, *China Reconstructs, 6* (1957), 18–19. Chao Ch'üan-ku et al., *KKHP* (1957/1), 58–59.

20. An Chin-huai, *WW* (1961/4/5), 77.

not completely understood. But enough has been found to provide some ground for speculation. A large house floor has been identified at the northwestern corner of the city site, with a compressed, burned-hard, lime-plastered floor, with post holes 14 to 35 cm deep, 19 to 34 cm across. Such large buildings have not been found outside the city area. North of this building was found a platform of compressed earth, with an incomplete length of 25.5 m east to west, and an incomplete width of 8.8 m north to south. This reminds us of the earth altar at the center of Hsiao-t'un in the An-yang area. From a test trench in the northern part of the enclosure, south of the Tzu-ching-shan Hill, archaeologists found (in addition to potsherds) bone artifacts, stone implements, and scores of jade hairpins of excellent workmanship. Only two or three hairpins of this kind have ever been found in the vast area outside the enclosure.[21]

Outside the city enclosure there were many residential sites and handicraft workshops, which can be attributed chronologically to the Lower and Upper Erh-li-kang stages. Two bronze foundry sites have been found thus far; one, north of Tzu-ching-shan Hill, is approximately 100 m north of the city wall, and the other about 500 m south of the wall at the point of the present South Gate (Nan-kuan). The workshop to the south covers an area of 1,050 square meters and has yielded crucibles of pottery, clay molds for both vessels and weapons, bronzes, debris of melted ocher, charcoal, and other stone and pottery remains. They are assigned to the Lower Erh-li-kang phase.[22] The bronze foundry remains to the north are significantly connected with one of four stamped-earth house foundations: on the floor of the house is a layer of fine-grained and hardened light green earth containing copper, on which are some dozen conical depressions, each containing a layer of melted copper; outside the house is another area of verdigris 0.1 to 0.15 m thick; a heap of clay molds and relics of crucibles was placed beside a door connecting two rooms inside the house; a big lump of copper ocher was found 10 m west of the house. This site belonged to the Upper Erh-li-kang phase.[23] The last find is especially interesting, indicating that the bronzesmiths of the Shang

21. An Chin-huai, *WW* (1961/4/5), 78–79.

22. Chao Ch'üan-ku et al., *KKHP* (1957/1), 56. Hsia Nai, *China Reconstructs,* 6 (1957), 20.

23. Liao Yüng-min, *WWTKTL* (1957/6), 73–74.

Dynasty lived in stamped-earth houses and thus seem to have enjoyed a higher privilege than the common folk, who had to be satisfied with semi-subterranean houses.

Approximately 50 m north of the Tzu-ching-shan bronze foundry was a bone workshop. It is a good-sized pit, possibly of the Lower Erh-li-kang phase, containing over a thousand pieces of sawed and polished finished bone artifacts (arrowheads and hairpins), half-finished bone pieces, bone fragments used as raw materials, rejected pieces of bone, and eleven grinding stones. The bones are from human beings (about 50 per cent), cattle, deer, and pigs.[24]

A pottery kiln site of the Erh-li-kang phases has been located on the west side of the Ming-kung Road, about 1200 meters west of the Shang city wall. In an area of 1,250 square meters, archaeologists have located fourteen kilns, near which are storage pits containing unfired and misfired pottery, pottery-making paddles and anvils, and stamps. Among the kilns are stamped-earth house foundations, which may have been the houses of the potters.[25] Since all the pottery found at this site is of fine clay texture, there were presumably other kiln quarters for the manufacture of sand-tempered culinary wares, hard pottery, glazed pottery, and/or white pottery.

At Erh-li-kang, many large, coarse-textured pottery jars were found, on the inner surface of which is a layer of white substance which may indicate that they were containers for a kind of alcoholic beverage. The possibility that this was a wine-making industrial quarter has been suggested.[26]

Besides those listed above, a large quantity of other kinds of remains has been unearthed both inside and outside the city enclosure. House foundations have been located at Pai-chia-chuang.[27] Scattered water ditches have been found at Erh-li-kang, Pai-chia-chuang, Nan-kuan-wai, and the region on the west side of the Ming-kung-lu.[28]

24. Chao Ch'üan-ku et al., *KKHP* (1957/1), 58. Hsia Nai, *China Reconstructs, 6* (1957), 21.

25. Chao Ch'üan-ku et al., *KKHP* (1957/1), 57. Hsia Nai, *China Reconstructs, 6* (1957), 19. Ma Ch'üan, *WWTKTL* (1956/10), 50–51. Chou Chao-lin and Mou Yüng-hang, *WWTKTL* (1955/9), 64–66.

26. An Chin-huai, *WW* (1961/4/5), 78. For a suggested origin of wine-making in the Neolithic period of North China, see Li Yang-sung, *KK* (1962/1), 41–44.

27. Tung Hung, *WWTKTL* (1956/4), 3–5. Chao Ch'üan-ku et al., *KKHP* (1957/1), 57.

28. Chao Ch'üan-ku et al., *KKHP* (1957/1), 58.

These ditches average 1.5 to 2.5 m in width and 1.5 m in depth. Those near Pai-chia-chuang have rows of small round depressions along both sides of the bottom. More than two hundred storage pits have been located throughout the area. Besides cultural debris and occasional pig and human skeletons, some of the pits contain large numbers of dog or cattle burials and apparently had some ceremonial significance.[29] Burials have been located at Erh-li-kang, Tzu-ching-shan, Pai-chia-chuang, and Jen-min Park, and are particularly numerous at the last two sites.[30] Some of the burials at Pai-chia-chuang (Upper Erh-li-kang phase) are described as large graves, with grave furnishings and (in two cases) human sacrifices; the others are small graves, which are numerous at the sites above named, and contain little or no grave furnishing.

These remains indicate that during the Erh-li-kang phases the city at Cheng-chou was a major political and ceremonial center. The population was apparently very large, in view of the extent of cultural distribution, the nature of settlement, and the depth of deposits (1 m average, with a maximum depth of 3 m). The artifacts found here include not only stone, bone, shell, and bronze implements and vessels, as well as pottery, but also bronze ceremonial vessels (Fig. 75), glazed pottery, hard pottery, white pottery, jade and ivory artifacts, and three pieces of inscribed oracle bone. The dating of the inscribed bones is uncertain, but it has been suggested that they were intrusive from later strata and do not antedate the An-yang sequence of oracle records. The city enclosure was apparently occupied by a ruling aristocracy, while the craftsmen and farmers inhabited mainly the suburbs surrounding the city site. It is indeed highly probable that the traditional Shang capital of Ao was located here.

The Shang city life apparently continued into the final, Jen-min Park phase of the Cheng-chou sequence, for large graves of this phase have been located in the park, a short distance west of the Shang city wall.[31] Aside from the findings here, however, Jen-min Park phase

29. An Chin-huai, *WWTKTL* (1957/8), 19. Chao Ch'üan-ku et al., *KKHP* (1957/1), 58.

30. An Chin-huai, *WWTKTL* (1957/8), 19. Chao Ch'üan-ku et al., *KKHP* (1957/1), 70–71.

31. An Chin-huai, *KKTH* (1955/3), 16–19. An Chih-min, *WWTKTL* (1954/6), 32–37. Chao Ch'üan-ku et al., *KKHP* (1957/1), 70–71.

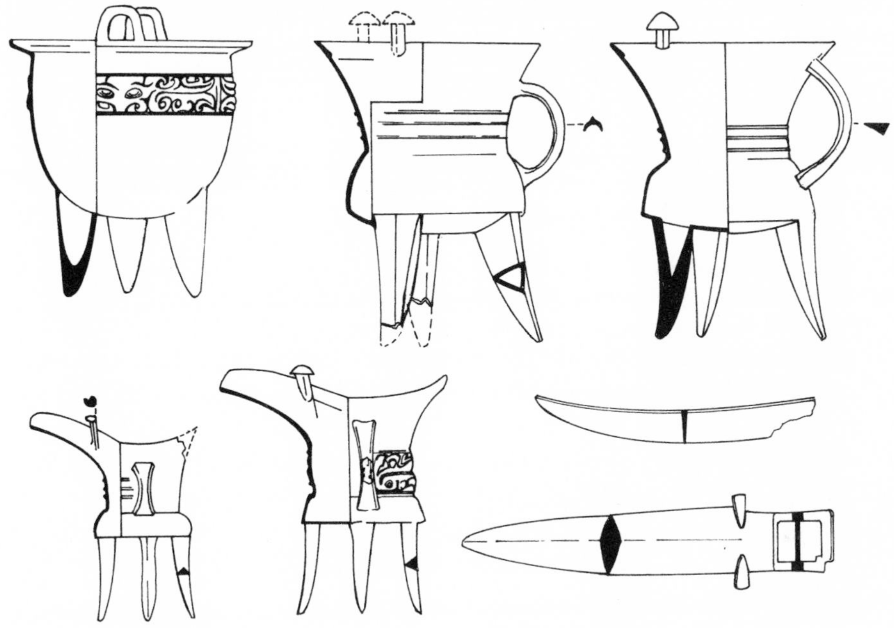

75. Shang bronzes of the Upper Erh-li-kang phase excavated at Ming-kung-lu, Cheng-chou, Honan. (From *KK,* 1965/10, p. 501.)

remains have thus far been found only in the upper stratum of the Ko-ta-wang site and in Ming-kung-lu.[32] Whether this results from incomplete exploration of the area or indicates diminishing activities during this final phase of the Shang Dynasty, when the political center of the aristocracy had shifted away from the city of Ao, is a problem awaiting solution.

Some characteristic features of the Lower and Upper Erh-li-kang and the Jen-min Park phases are listed in Table 8[33] (Fig. 76).

3. An-yang

From King T'ang to King Ti Hsin, seven Shang capitals were recorded in the literature—Po, Hsiao (Ao), Hsiang, Keng (Hsing), P'i,

32. Chao Ch'ing-yün and Liu Tung-ya, *KKHP* (1958/3), 41–62. Yü Hsiao-hsing and Ch'en Li-hsien, *KK* (1965/10), 500–06.

33. Honan Wenhuachü, *Cheng-chou Erh-li-kang*. Chao Ch'üan-ku et al., *KKHP* (1957/1), 53–73. Tsou Heng, *KKHP* (1956/3), 77–103.

TABLE 8.

Characteristic Features of Erh-li-kang and Jen-min Park Phases of the Shang Culture at Cheng-chou

Lower Erh-li-kang Phase: The pottery has relatively thin walls, fine tempering materials, fine cord marks, and is generally well made; the characteristic ceramic forms are *li* tripods with elongated bodies, rounded rims curving outward and downward, high feet with long conical ends; *hsien* tripods with fine tempering materials and breast-shaped feet; *chia* tripods with out-turned rims; *kuan* jugs with fine cord marks and thin bodies; *tsun* jars with squat bodies and short collars; *ting* tripods with basin- or bowl-like bodies; *tou* fruit stands with shallow dishlike bodies. Oracle bones are similar to the Lo-ta-miao forms, and bone hairpins are of the conical-head type.

Upper Erh-li-kang Phase: Pottery of this phase is similar to the previous phase, but the tempering materials are generally coarser, the bodies thicker, and the cord marks made of thicker strands. Many of the Lower Erh-li-kang ceramic forms continued into this phase, but some of the forms that were initiated during the previous phase now became prevalent, such as the *li* tripods with angular and up-turned rims, *hsien* tripods with coarser cord marks and conical feet, *chia* tripods with in-turned rims, *ting* tripods imitating bronze forms, *tou* with bottoms considerably higher than indicated by the external contours (false-bodied *tou*), and *tsun* jars with elongated bodies and long collars. Oracle bones and bone hairpins are similar to the previous phase.

Jen-min Park Phase: The ceramic style has changed markedly, and the pottery is largely of coarse tempering material, thick bodies, large-stranded cord marks, and crude workmanship. Few Erh-li-kang phase forms remain, while squat and short-footed *li* tripods, *tou* with low pedestals, *p'o, yü,* and *yu* vessels appeared. There also appeared bone hairpins with carved heads. Most of the oracle bones are turtleshells, and the preparation was elaborate. The large graves containing human victims and rich furnishings which appeared in the Upper Erh-li-kang phase continued here.

Yen, and Yin.[34] The locations of the first six, although generally assumed to be in northern Honan and its immediate neighborhood, are uncertain; the possibility that Po has been uncovered near Yen-shih and that the Shang settlements near Cheng-chou are the remains

34. For a recent review of the problem relating to the various Shang capitals, see Ch'ü Wan-li, *Bulletin, College of Arts, National Taiwan University, 14* (1965), 105–09.

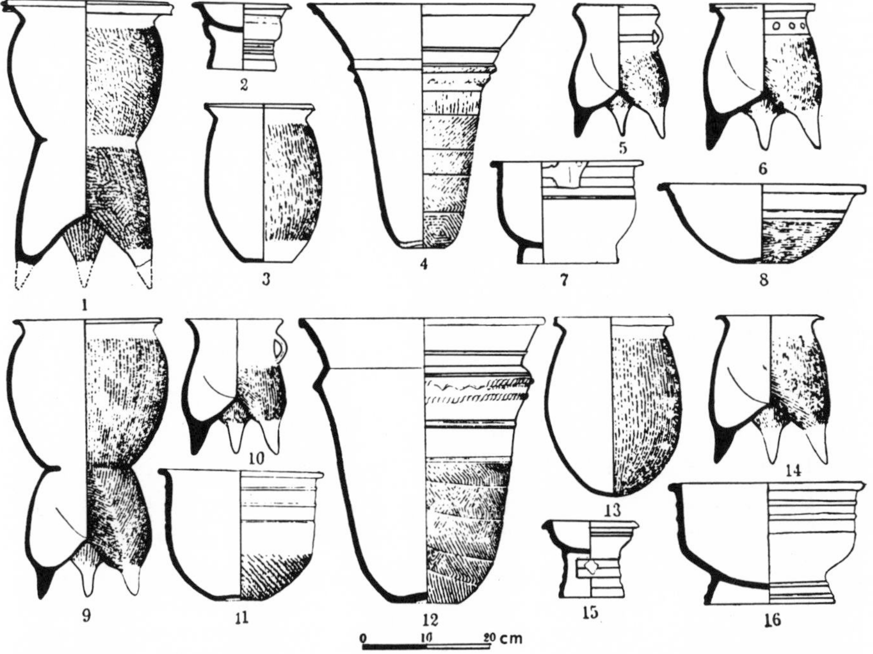

76. Pottery of the Erh-li-kang phase of Shang civilization, Erh-li-kang, Cheng-chou, Honan. (From *Hsin Chung-kuo ti K'ao-ku Shou-huo,* 1962, p. 45.)

of Ao has been discussed above. There is no question that the ruins of the last Shang capital, seat of power for twelve kings from P'an Keng to Ti Hsin for some 273 years until the fall of the dynasty, are situated on both banks of the Huan River northwest of the modern city of An-yang, northern Honan. They have been known to historians for ages past, and were referred to as Yin Hsü, the Ruins of Yin, by Ssu-ma Ch'ien in his *Shih Chi* (Hsiang Yü Biography). But it was not until 1899 when the remains of inscribed oracle bones were known to have been found in this area that the Ruins of Yin were brought to the attention of scholars.[35] From 1928 to 1937, fifteen seasons of scientific excavation were undertaken in this region by the

35. For a history of the archaeology of the area see Tung Tso-pin, *Chia-ku-hsüeh wu-shih nien,* Taipei, Yi-wen, 1955; Kaizuka Shigeki, *Kodai Yin tegaku,* Tokyo, Misuzu Shobo, 1957.

National Research Institute of History and Philology.[36] After 1950, small-scale but intensive diggings have taken place continuously.[37] Shang remains[38] are now known in the An-yang region from no fewer than seventeen sites, covering an area of approximately 24 square kilometers (Fig. 77).

The importance of the An-yang excavations in the history of archaeology in China cannot be exaggerated.[39] The scale of the work, time, money, and manpower devoted to the excavations, and the scientific precision of the digging, are still unsurpassed in China. And it was the An-yang excavation, that settled, once and for all, the controversial problem of the existence of this dynasty, previously accredited only by legends. It was also the first site given a date in the earliest segment of Chinese written history, and thus ties written history to the prehistoric Neolithic cultures. However, work was interrupted by the Sino-Japanese War, leaving many sites in the An-yang group only partially excavated, and results have yet to be completely published. The center of Shang studies has tended to shift from An-yang to Cheng-chou, where a longer sequence has been uncovered and a series of preliminary and final reports has been made available. An-yang's fundamental importance, however, can never be doubted. Among other things, the oracle bone inscriptions from this area furnish much indispensable information concerning Shang culture and society that other Shang sites may never be able to match.

36. It is impossible to provide an exhaustive bibliography for the An-yang material here, but much of the original published material can be found in the following series of publications: *An-yang Fa-chüeh Pao-kao,* four numbers, 1929–33; *T'ien-yieh K'ao-ku Pao-kao,* 1936; *Chung-kuo K'ao-ku Hsüeh-pao,* vols. 2–4 (1938–50); *Archaeologia Sinica,* vol. 2 (Hsiao-t'un) and vol. 3 (Hou-chia-chuang); and the *Bulletin of the Institute of History and Philology, Academia Sinica,* various numbers. Because of national and international events since 1937, much of the An-yang material excavated before the war remains unpublished. See also a recent synthesis of the remains at An-yang by S. Umehara (*Yin Hsü,* Tokyo, Asahi Shinbunsha, 1964).

37. *KKHP, 5* (1951); (1955/1); (1958/3). *WWTKTL* (1958/12). *KK* (1961/2).

38. Following historians, archaeologists often refer to the period of Shang when An-yang (Yin) was the capital as the "Yin period" and the remains found here as Yin remains. For historians, it seems reasonable to make such a subdivision, but the remains at An-yang were deposited during a period that was probably longer than the 273 years when An-yang was the capital site. I shall use the word Shang throughout for the entire period and use archaeological phases to designate chronological segments, of which Yin is one.

39. See Li Chi, "Importance of the An-yang Discoveries in Prefacing Known Chinese History with a New Chapter," *Ann. Acad. Sinica, 2* (1955), 91–102.

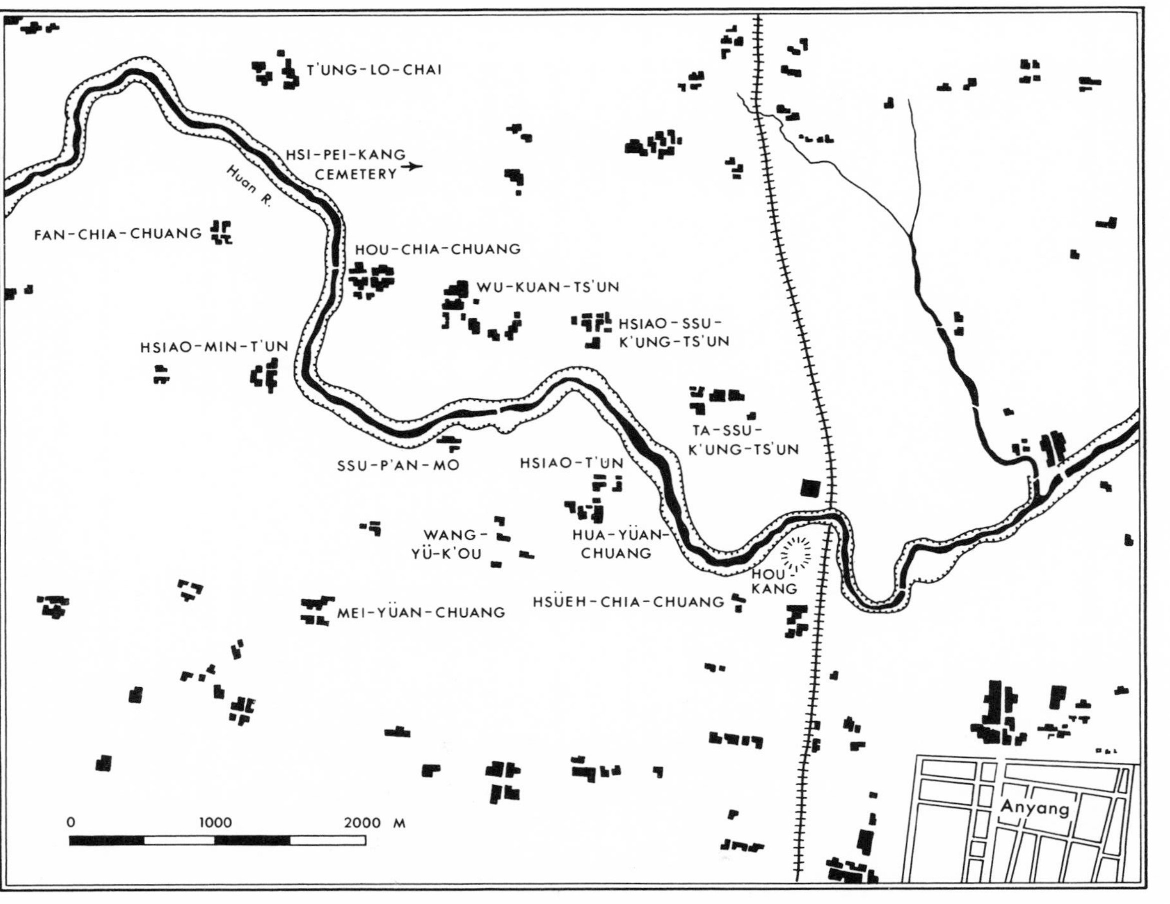

77. Shang sites at An-yang, Honan.

Similar to the settlement pattern of the Shang sites at Cheng-chou, the Shang sites of the An-yang region were apparently articulated into a complex network of specialized parts.

> The Yin palaces south of Huanho (near the modern village of Hsiao-t'un) constituted the center of the Yin Hsü, surrounded on all sides by habitation clusters, workshops, and tombs. North of the Huanho, with Wu-kuan-ts'un and the area north of Hou-chia-chuang [Hsi-pei-kang] as a center, there was the area of the royal cemetery, burials of noblemen, and many thousand sacrificial burials, an area also encircled by Yin settlements and burials. Conditions of cultural deposits indicate that the neighborhood of Hsiao-t'un was the region of the greatest abundance, and on its outskirts were settlements of varying sizes. Remains at these settlements do not occur in a continuous area, but the distribution of the settlements was fairly dense. Distances between settlements became greater as groups moved away from the center. Palaces and the royal cemetery were apparently under the direct control of the ruling class, and the settlements surrounding Hsiao-t'un were probably habitations of [noblemen and the common people]. The latter classes were buried near where they lived, resulting in the intermixture of living and burial remains, although it is possible that [the noblemen] had their own cemeteries also. In the neighborhoods of the settlements were many workshops. For instance, large bronze foundry sites have been found at Miao-p'u-pei-ti and Hsiao-min-t'un, and bone workshops were identified at Pei-hsin-chuang and Ta-ssu-k'ung-ts'un. Even in the area of the palaces, many clay molds and bone materials were found. These may suggest that handicrafts were carried out under the direct control of the [upper classes,] and workshops often occurred in living areas but did not necessarily concentrate in their own quarters.[40]

All this goes to show that the entire An-yang group formed a tightly organized unit, and the presence of the Royal House in this group is

40. An Chih-min et al., *KK* (1961/2), 65.

symbolized by the administrative and ceremonial center near Hsiao-t'un and the "royal cemetery" at Hsi-pei-kang.

The excavated part of the site at Hsiao-t'un (Fig. 78) is divided into three sections, A, B, and C. Section A, the northernmost, consists of fifteen parallel rectangular houses built on stamped-earth foundations. Section B, in the middle, includes twenty-one large houses, rectangular or square, built on stamped-earth foundations, and accompanied by a number of burials. These houses are arranged in three rows on a north–south axis, the central row consisting of three large houses and five gates. Section A and Section B are separated by a square stamped-earth foundation (of pure loess), which is thought to be a ceremonial altar. Section C, at the southwestern corner of the site, consists of seventeen stamped-earth foundations, arranged according to a preconceived plan and again accompanied by burials. Under the foundations in Section B is a complicated system of underground water ditches. The entire area of the Hsiao-t'un settlement includes about 10,000 square meters. According to the interpretation of Shih Chang-ju, Section A was probably the dwelling area of the settlement, Section B the royal temples, and Section C a ceremonial quarter. It is noteworthy, however, that these three sections seem to have been constructed during different time intervals, in the order A, B, and C.[41] In view of the large scale of the construction, the elaborate planning of the houses, the extensive sacrifice of humans in the construction of the temples and the ceremonial altar, the innumerable inscribed oracle bones found at the site, and the mode of construction in stamped earth (Fig. 79) in contrast to the ordinary semi-subterranean dwellings, it appears reasonable to assume that this settlement was the center of the Royal House of the Yin Dynasty. These palaces and temples, as Tung Tso-pin describes them,

> were all above-ground houses with stamped-earth foundations and stone pillar supporters [Fig. 80]. Although they were constructed of wattle-and-daub, these structures looked glorious and solemn enough [Fig. 81]. Near these foundations are often semi-subterranean pit houses, about 4 meters in diameter and

41. Shih Chang-ju, *Yin-hsü chien-chu yi-ts'un,* Taipei, Academia Sinica, 1959.

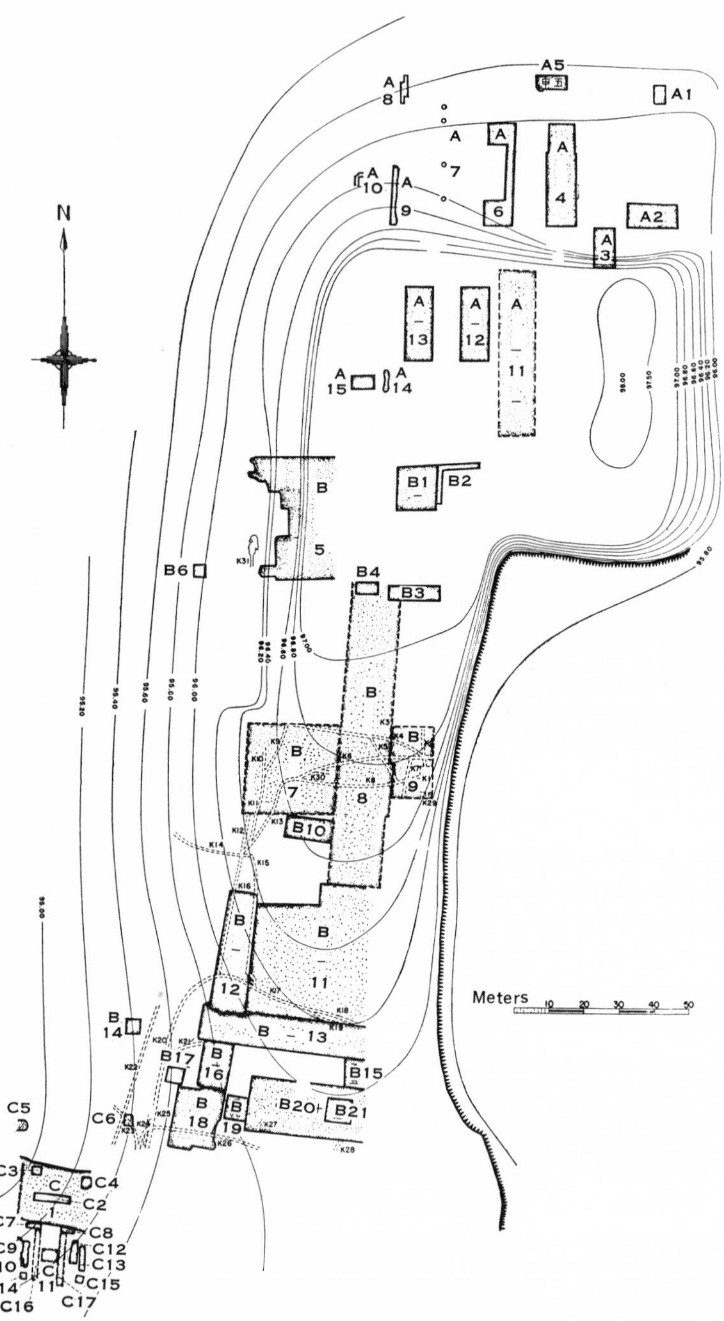

78. Shang house floors at the site of Hsiao-t'un, An-yang. (After Shih Chang-ju, *Yin Hsü Chien-chu Yi-ts'un,* Taipei, 1959, Fig. 4.)

79. Side view of *hang-t'u* layers of a Shang house floor at Hsiao-t'un, Anyang, Honan. (After Shih Chang-ju, *Yin Hsü Chien-chu Yi-ts'un,* Taipei, 1959, Pl. XI.)

> the same in depth. These were presumably the service area of the Royal House subordinates. Inside the pit houses are round or rectangular bins, several meters deep and possibly places of storage.[42]

These service areas included bronze foundries, stone and bone workshops, and pottery kilns. But some of these pit houses must also have served as domiciles. It is apparent that this Hsiao-t'un site served the same function as the city enclosure of Cheng-chou, but remains of a city wall have not been found. Nevertheless, it must be remembered that the Hsiao-t'un site was not completely excavated and that the excavators presumably did not look specifically for a city wall. Since the city walls appeared at Cheng-chou before the Hsiao-t'un phase, and continued into later historical periods, I would not be surprised

42. Tung Tso-pin, *Ta-lu-tsa-chih, 5* (1950), 12.

80. *Hang-t'u* floor with stone post bases of a Shang house at Hsiao-t'un, An-yang. (From Shih Chang-ju, *Yin Hsü Chien-chu Yi-ts'un,* 1959, Pl. IX.)

if more intensive future investigations find that this site also had a walled enclosure.

Hsi-pei-kang, near Hou-chia-chuang, and the contiguous Wu-kuan-ts'un area, is best known for its burial complex that included 11 large graves (the royal cemetery) and 1,222 small graves, although dwellings and workshops have also been found here. The eleven large tombs (Fig. 82) are grouped into a western cluster of seven and an eastern cluster of four, happily coinciding in number with the eleven kings from P'an Keng to Ti Yi who ruled from An-yang. (The last king at An-yang, Ti Hsin, was supposedly burned to death when the capital fell to the Chou invaders.) Although it cannot yet be fully established that these were the kings' graves, we know that they were constructed on a large scale, with elaborate ceremonial procedures, and their furnishings represent the highest achievements of Shang technology and art.[43] According to the estimates of Li Chi,[44] the

43. A full report of the Hsi-pei-kang excavations is being prepared by Kao

earth-digging alone required at least seven thousand working days for each of the large graves of Hsi-pei-kang. All the graves are square or oblong, oriented north–south, with long ramps on two (north and south) or four sides. The best known of the tombs, No. 1001, is shaped like a cross in ground plan and forms a pit about 10 m deep, with slightly sloping walls (Fig. 83). The mouth of the pit is 19 m long north to south, and 14 m wide. A ramp leads from the ground to the bottom of the grave pit on each of the four sides; the southern ramp, the longest, measures about 30 m. Within the pit a wooden chamber was built; the chief coffin of the tomb was probably placed in the center. Many sacrificial burials occurred in various spots within the pit, but were concentrated within the chamber itself and in the southern ramp. Some of the sacrifices were provided with coffins and small grave pits, but most were without either coffin or pit, and many were separate burials of heads and trunks (Fig. 84). The tomb was abundantly furnished with stone, jade, shell, bone, antler, tooth, bronze, and pottery artifacts, including many that are the best examples of Shang art (Fig. 85).[45] Li Chi has listed the following as the most significant contributions of the Hsi-pei-kang excavations to Shang archaeology: (1) importance of pisé construction in Shang architecture; (2) Shang burial institutions and the organization of manpower as indicated by the construction of single tombs; (3) the reality and magnitude of sacrificial burials; (4) the high level of achievement of the Shang material culture and the extent of leisure of the ruling class; (5) the discovery of stone sculptures and the sophistication of the decorative art; and (6) the representative products of bronze industry.[46] To these we must add a point of chronological significance. If these eleven tombs were those of the kings and

Ch'ü-hsün of the Academia Sinica in Taipei, and three of the large tombs have been fully described in *Archaeologia Sinica,* vol. 3 (Hou-chia-chuang), nos. 2, 3, and 4 (1962–67). A large tomb excavated in 1950 is described in Kuo Pao-chün, *KKHP, 5* (1951). Preliminary and general descriptions of the royal cemetery as a whole are available in Kao Ch'ü-hsün, *Bull. Dept. Archaeol. Anthropol., Natl. Taiwan Univ., 13/14* (1959), 1–9; Paul Pelliot, "The Royal Tombs of An-yang," in *Independence, Convergence, and Borrowing in Institutions, Thought, and Art,* Cambridge, Harvard Univ. Press, 1937; Tung Tso-pin, *Ta-lu-tsa-chih, 1* (1950), 15–18.

44. Li Chi's Preface to Shih Chang-ju, *Yin-hsü chien-chu yi-ts'un,* p. iii.

45. Liang Ssu-yung and Kao Ch'ü-hsün, *Archaeologia Sinica,* vol. 3 (Hou-chia-chuang), no. 2 (Tomb 1001), 1962.

46. Li Chi, Preface to ibid.

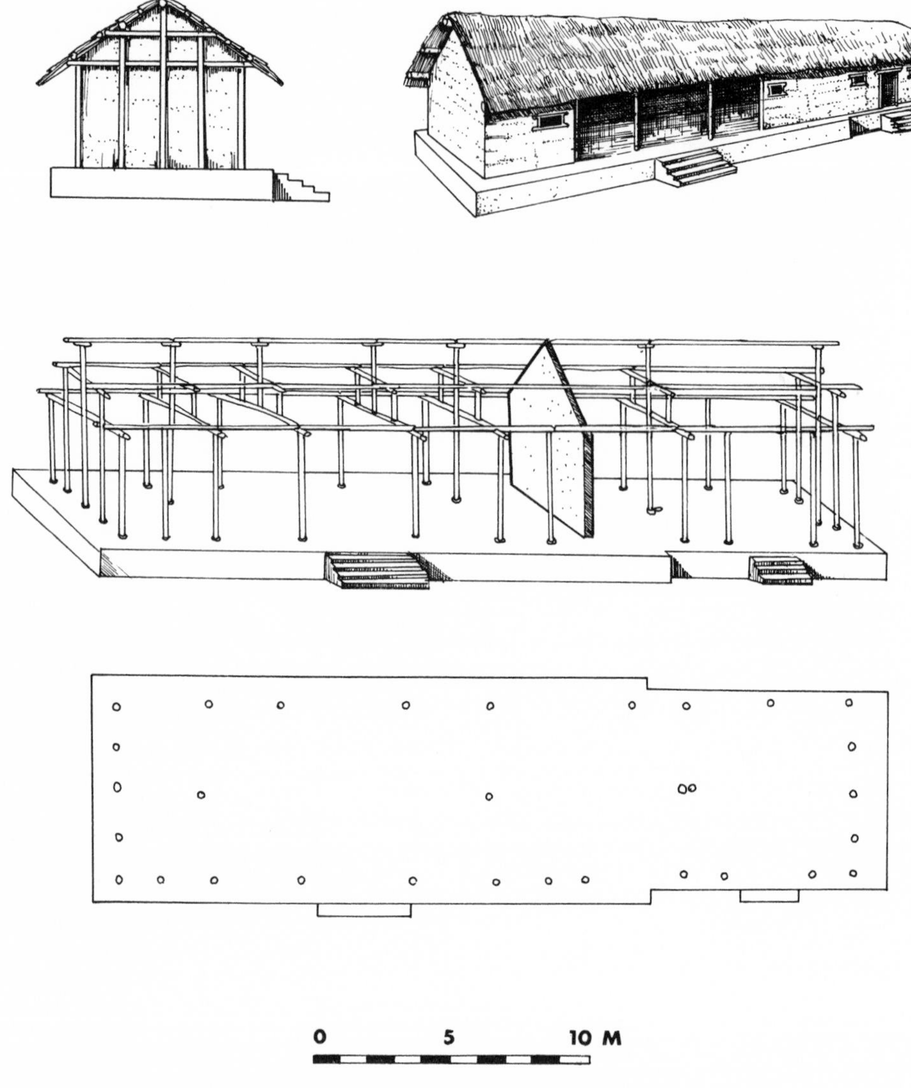

81. Reconstruction of a Shang house at Hsiao-t'un, An-yang. (From Shih Chang-ju, *Annals of Academia Sinica, 1,* 1954, p. 276.)

if these tombs can be chronologically seriated among themselves and together with Hsiao-t'un's habitation remains,[47] then there is a com-

47. Li Chi, *Bull. Inst. Hist. Philol., Acad. Sinica,* no. 29 (1958).

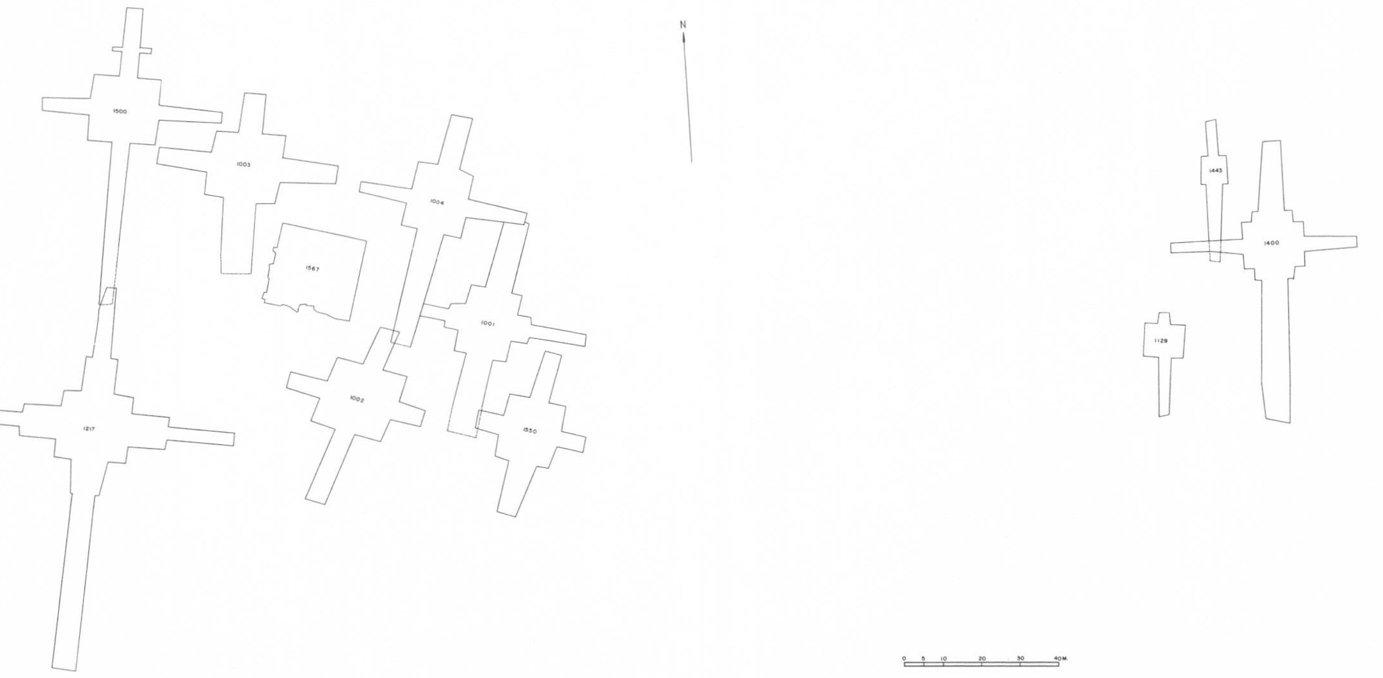

82. The royal tombs in the Hsi-pei-kang cemetery, An-yang. (Courtesy of Academia Sinica and by permission of Dr. Li Chi and Prof. Kao Ch'ü-hsün. The fourth tomb in the eastern sector, excavated in 1950, is not included.)

83. Grave pit of royal tomb no. 1001 at Hsi-pei-kang, An-yang. (From Liang Ssu-yung and Kao Ch'ü-hsün, *HPKM1001,* 1962.)

plete sequence of artifacts and arts available at An-yang that covers the entire range of 273 years when An-yang was the royal capital. Therefore, the Hsi-pei-kang tombs represent a solid chronological segment of the Shang civilization and their sequence provides a basis for the study of cultural change within the segment.

Furthermore, if the Hsi-pei-kang tombs began with P'an Keng, then at the site of Hsiao-t'un the habitation floors and storage pits that are considered on typological grounds to be earlier than HPKM 1001 must belong to an earlier period than P'an Keng, the so-called Pre-Dynastic Period of Hsiao-t'un.[48] In other words, in An-yang there is the segment of 273 years that can be referred to as the Yin or Hsi-pei-kang phase with which Hsiao-t'un II was contemporaneous. Hsiao-t'un I, therefore, must predate the Yin phase. The details of these Hsiao-t'un phases cannot be known until all the excavated materials become available. But excavations at other sites in the An-yang

48. Li Chi, *The Beginnings of Chinese Civilization,* Seattle, Univ. Washington Press, 1957.

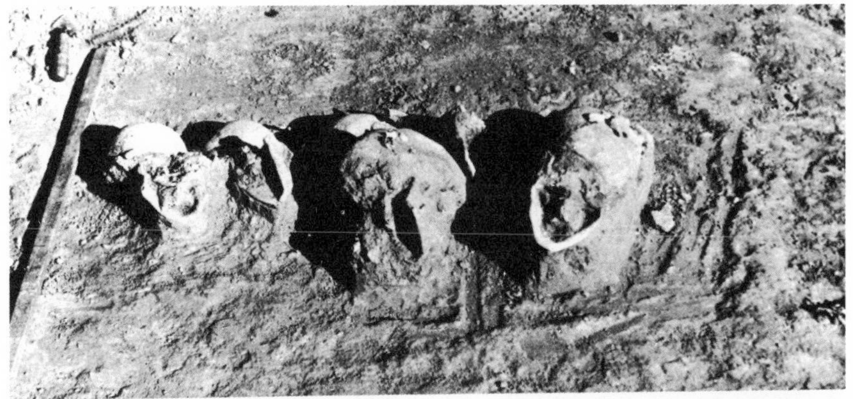

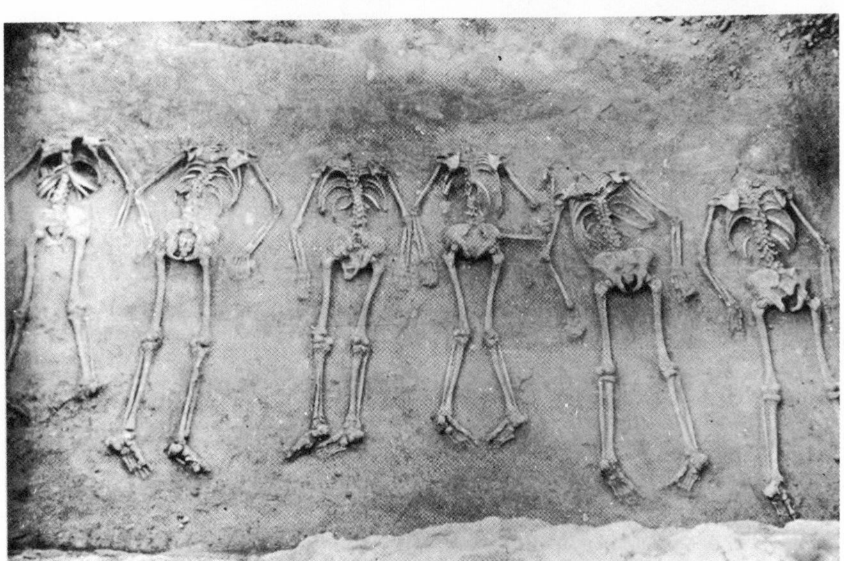

84. Sacrificial burials in royal tomb 1001 at Hsi-pei-kang, An-yang. (From Liang Ssu-yung and Kao Ch'ü-hsün, *HPKM1001*, 1962.)

area are revealing. At Ta-ssu-k'ung-ts'un, remains of habitation floors and burials were found, and four stages of occupation were distinguished.[49] A piece of oracle bone dated to King Wu Ting's reign or thereabouts was discovered from the earliest stratum, suggesting that

49. Ma Teh-chih et al., *KKHP, 9* (1955), 25–90. An Chih-min et al., *KK* (1961/2), 65–66. Cheng Chen-hsiang, *KK* (1964/8), 380–84.

85. Stone sculptures from royal tomb 1001 at Hsi-pei-kang, An-yang. (From Liang Ssu-yung and Kao Ch'ü-hsün, *HPKM1001,* 1962.)

the entire Ta-ssu-k'ung-ts'un sequence can be placed within the Hsi-pei-kang phase. At Mei-yüan-chuang, two cultural strata were recognized, the upper layer similar to the Hsiao-t'un phases but the lower layer similar to Cheng-chou's Lower Erh-li-kang.[50] Thus, at An-yang the following stratigraphical sequence has been suggested: Mei-yüan-chuang I, the earliest; Hsiao-t'un I, possibly of the same phase or slightly later; and Hsi-pei-kang, contemporary with Hsiao-t'un II and Ta-ssu-k'ung-ts'un I–IV, a phase that should be susceptible to finer subdivisions.

Little is known concerning Shang sites in An-yang other than the above. Information is available at the sites of Hou-chia-chuang-nan-ti, Hou-kang, Hsüeh-chia-chuang, and Kao-lou-chuang.[51] Remains of living floors, burials of varying scales and degrees of richness, bronze, pottery, and bone workshops, and storage pits have been reported from these sites, suggestive of the nature of the settlements in the An-yang group other than Hsiao-t'un and Hsi-pei-kang. All these sites are dated within the Hsi-pei-kang range.

The Yin settlement at An-yang may be summarized as follows: prior to the time of P'an Keng (1384 B.C., according to T. P. Tung's chronology), who made An-yang his capital, the Shang had already occupied the An-yang area. At any rate, at Hsiao-t'un,[52] Hsüeh-chia-chuang[53] as well as Mei-yüan-chuang remains were found that are similar to the Erh-li-kang phases of Cheng-chou. These are mostly of a domiciliary nature, but a bronze industry had already been established here.[54] Whether the other settlements had been occupied cannot be established at present because of the lack of stratigraphic evidence. From the time of P'an Keng (so says the traditional history, which is supported by oracle bone records), the An-yang area was the capital of the Royal House of the Shang Dynasty. Most of the settlements of the An-yang group were probably occupied by the people of Yin and by nobility connected with the Royal House. Royal palaces and cere-

50. An chih-min et al., *KK* (1961/2), 65.

51. Tung Tso-pin, *TYKKPK, 1* (1936), 91–166. Shih Chang-ju, *Liu T'ung Pieh Lu, 1* (1945), 1–26. Kuo Mo-jo, *KKHP* (1960/1). Chao P'ei-hsin, *KK* (1960/6). Chao Hsia-kuang, *WWTKTL* (1958/12), 31. Liu Tung-ya, *KKTH* (1958/8), 23–26. Chou Tao and Liu Tung-ya, *KK* (1963/4), 213–16, 220.

52. Li Chi, *The Beginnings of Chinese Civilization,* p. 45. Tsou Heng, *KKHP* (1956/3), 77–103.

53. Liu Tung-ya, *KKTH* (1958/8), 23–26.

54. Shih Chang-ju, *Yin-hsü chien-chu yi-ts'un.*

monial centers were constructed at Hsiao-t'un and Hou-chia-chuang-nan-ti, and the cemeteries of the royal family were constructed at Hsi-pei-kang (and Wu-kuan-ts'un) and Hou-kang. The individual settlements were probably more or less self-sufficient in terms of basic subsistence and handicrafts, but as far as the control of the economy, political administration, and religious and ceremonial affairs is concerned, the entire An-yang settlement group appears to have formed a single unit.

4. Hsing-t'ai

Since 1954, Shang sites have been found widely in the neighborhood of Hsing-t'ai, in southern Hopei, directly north of An-yang. Neither literary tradition nor archaeological evidence itself gives this group of Shang sites a royal capital status, but this site is all the more important in the picture it gives of Shang civilization outside of the settlement groups which were politically prominent. Archaeological work in this area is still going on, and only preliminary reports have been published on the excavated sites. Some socioeconomic characteristics of these sites, however, are of immediate interest.

Over ten Shang sites have thus far been located in the regions north and west of the Hsing-t'ai city, in an area approximately 10 kilometers north to south and 7 kilometers east to west.[55] The cultural deposits at some of the sites attain a maximum depth of 3 meters, testifying to the permanent nature of the settlement and the considerable duration of its habitation. Three cultural phases have been distinguished for the Yin-kuo-ts'un site, which correlate with other stratified sites in this region as follows:[56]

Upper Yin-kuo-ts'un phase: Upper Ts'ao-yen-chuang, Upper Nan-ta-kuo-ts'un
Middle Yin-kuo-ts'un phase: Lower Ts'ao-yen-chuang, Lower Nan-ta-kuo-ts'un
Lower Yin-kuo-ts'un phase

Cultural remains from these Shang phases of Hsing-t'ai include many of the diagnostic Shang traits such as oracle bones, bone hair-

55. *WWTKTL* (1956/9), 70; (1956/12), 53–54; (1957/3), 61–63; (1958/10), 29–31. *KKHP* (1958/4), 43–50. *KK* (1959/2), 108–09. *WW* (1960/4), 42–45, 60.
56. T'ang Yün-ming, *WW* (1960/4), 42–45.

pins, and some characteristic pottery forms and decorative motifs. Pottery kilns were found at some of the sites, but a bone workshop was discovered at only one settlement, indicating that these settlements were tied together in terms of handicraft specialization, as was the case with An-yang and Cheng-chou. *Hang-t'u* house structures, inscriptions, and bronze foundries have not been unearthed, however. Stone was the raw material for all the implements, though bronze arrowheads, awls, adzes, and ornaments appear occasionally in the remains. Further investigations in the Hsing-t'ai area will undoubtedly throw much more light upon this settlement group, but the available data suggest that here in Hsing-t'ai the Shang people had an urban network similar to those at An-yang and Cheng-chou, even though there may not have been an outstanding aristocratic complex.

5. *Other Shang Sites*

Other sites of the Shang period providing sufficient information to warrant their classification as Shang civilizations include Ch'i-li-p'u in Shan Hsien,[57] Lu-ssu in Mien-ch'ih,[58] Chien-hsi in Meng Hsien,[59] a series of sites in the neighborhood of Lo-yang,[60] Lu-wang-fen in Hsin-hsiang,[61] several sites in Hui Hsien,[62] Ch'ao-ko in T'ang-yin,[63] Shih-li-p'u in Nan-yang,[64] and Fu-kou in Yen-ling,[65] all in Honan Province; Chu-chia-ch'iao in P'ing-yin,[66] and Ta-hsin-chuang in Chi-nan,[67] Shantung Province; and Chien-kou-ts'un in Han-tan,[68] Pei-chai-

57. Yang Chi-chang, *KKHP* (1960/1), 25–47.
58. Ch'en Huan-yü, *KK* (1964/9), 435–40.
59. Liu Hsiao-ch'un, *KK* (1961/1), 33–39.
60. Kuo Pao-chün and Lin Shou-chin, *KKHP, 9* (1955), 91–116. Kuo Pao-chün et al., *KKHP* (1956/1), 11–28. An Chih-min and Lin Shou-chin, *KKTH* (1955/5), 26; *KK* (1959/10), 537–40.
61. Wang Ming-jui and Chin Shih-hsin, *KKHP* (1960/1), 51–60.
62. Kuo Pao-chün, Hsia Nai, et al., *Hui Hsien fa-chüeh pao-kao,* Peking, Science Press, 1956. Li Te-pao, *KKTH* (1957/2), 32–35. Ch'i T'ai-ting, *KK* (1965/5), 255.
63. An Chin-huai, *WWTKTL* (1957/5), 86.
64. Yu Ch'ing-ch'üan, *KK* (1959/7), 370.
65. Liu Tung-ya, *KK* (1965/2), 94–96.
66. Chao Lan, *KK* (1961/2), 86–93.
67. F. S. Drake, *China Jour., 31* (1939), 77–80; *33* (1940), 8–10. Yang Tzu-fan, *WW* (1959/11), 8–9. Li Pu-ch'ing, *KK* (1959/4), 185–87.
68. Sun Teh-hai et al., *KK* (1961/4), 197–202.

ts'un in Ling-shou,[69] and Feng-chia-an in Ch'ü-yang,[70] Hopei Province. The sites in Lo-yang and Hui Hsien approach Cheng-chou and An-yang in extent, yielding bronze foundries and large graves with human victims. Bronze foundries have also been found in Nan-yang. The other sites, however, are like the Hsing-t'ai group, yielding networks that were probably economic, yet lacking a clearly defined aristocratic complex. A typological classification of the Shang sites as they are known at present also has a geographical significance: Shang sites with aristocratic complexes are confined to northern Honan, extending as far west as Lo-yang; those showing a similar urbanized structure but without a concentrated aristocratic complex extend to western Honan as far as Shan Hsien, southern Hopei as far as Ch'ü-yang, and Shantung as far as Chi-nan. Shang remains are also found outside of this circle, notably in southern Shansi[71] and especially in the south,[72] but in primarily non-civilizational or non-Shang contexts. These facts are indispensable in delineating the cultural and social boundaries of the Shang civilization.

CHRONOLOGY OF THE SHANG CIVILIZATION AND THE PROBLEM OF ITS ORIGINS

Shang history according to written records can be subdivided into four segments: legendary ancestors, from Ti K'u to Wang Hai; early ancestors, from Shang Chia to Shih Kui, the first six ancestors in the ritual genealogy recorded in the oracle scripts; the dynastic period from T'ang to Yang Chia, when the Shang were rulers of China but before they moved to An-yang; and the dynastic period from P'an Keng to Ti Hsin, when An-yang was the royal capital. Three dates are therefore of crucial significance in the chronology of the Shang: the accession of T'ang, the removal of the Shang capital to An-yang under P'an Keng, and the fall of the Shang dynasty under Ti Hsin. Exact dates for these events are still being debated among historians, but

69. Ch'en Ying-ch'i, *KK* (1966/2), 107–08.
70. An Chih-min, *KKTH* (1955/1), 39–44.
71. Kuo Yüng, *WW* (1962/4/5), 34–35. Chang Yen-huang et al., *KK* (1962/9), 459–64.
72. See Chap. 9.

no conclusions have been reached.[73] However, in this volume I shall adopt some round figures: 1750 for T'ang's accession, 1400 for P'an Keng's move to An-yang, and 1100 for the fall of the Shang Dynasty. For our purposes here, where broad chronological segments are adequate for studies of trends of cultural development and of cultural relationships, it is not necessary to take sides in this technical debate.

Before the Shang sites at Cheng-chou were excavated, the An-yang culture was the sole representative of the Shang civilization, and our understanding of it was accordingly restricted and conditioned.[74] Since those excavations, however, the Cheng-chou sequence, by virtue of its long and seemingly complete stratigraphy, has been used by archaeologists as the yardstick by which other Shang sites are measured. Tsou Heng, for instance, has classified the cultural remains at Hsiao-t'un of the An-yang group into three stages: pre-Hang-t'u, Hang-t'u, and post-Hang-t'u. The Hang-t'u phase of An-yang, according to Tsou, can be synchronized with the Jen-min Park phase of Cheng-chou, whereas the pre-Hang-t'u was earlier than the Jen-min Park phase but later than the Upper Erh-li-kang phase, and the post-Hang-t'u phase later than the Jen-min Park phase of Cheng-chou.[75] The earliest phase at Hsing-t'ai, according to T'ang Yün-ming, was probably earlier than the Erh-li-kang phases, but the later phases correspond to them.[76] For other sites, the terms Erh-li-kang and Hsiao-t'un are used freely for similar chronological and classificatory purposes. Carrying this scheme to the extreme, Cheng Te-k'un boldly attempts to synchronize all of the Shang sites, which he divides into five groups: Proto Shang, Early Shang, Middle Shang, Late Shang, and Post Shang.[77]

It is true that cultural remains similar to this or that phase of the Cheng-chou sequence are found elsewhere, and this may have chronological significance. Until a number of sites other than Cheng-chou

73. For a survey of some pertinent arguments, see Kwang-chih Chang, "Relative Chronologies of China to the End of Chou," in Robert Ehrich (ed.), *Chronologies in Old World Archaeology,* Univ. of Chicago Press, 1965.

74. E.g. H. G. Creel, *The Birth of China,* London and New York, Reynal & Hitchcock, 1937; Li Chi, *The Beginnings of Chinese Civilization.*

75. Tsou Heng, *KKHP* (1956/3), 77–103.

76. E.g. Cheng Te-kün, *Shang China,* p. 27.

77. Ibid., p. 37.

and An-yang are excavated intensively, however, it would be impossible for us to claim that the fivefold subdivision of the Shang sequence at Cheng-chou, as it is known at a certain period in the history of Shang archaeology, is universally valid. The Shang-chieh phase of Cheng-chou, for instance, may possibly be earlier than the Proto Shang phase of Cheng Te-k'un. What, then, should it be called? Cheng's Middle Shang includes both Upper Erh-li-kang of Cheng-chou and Hsiao-t'un I of An-yang, the two phases that are regarded by Tsou Heng as being chronologically successive rather than concurrent. Cheng's grouping them together apparently employs one set of criteria, then, whereas Tsou's setting them apart must use another. In the future, when a number of long sequences will presumably be determined for Shang sites that are not yet extensively excavated, the Cheng-chou sequence may not continue to be serviceable as the basic yardstick. Before we have knowledge of other sequences, any synchronization of all the Shang sites in North China according to the Cheng-chou sequence would seem to be dubious at best. For the time being, I believe that we are better off to confine discussion of the chronological development of the Shang culture to the few sites whose stratigraphy is reasonably well established.

The archaeological remains uncovered at the various Shang sites described above were plainly left during a long period that can be subdivided into a number of segments or phases according to the change of artifacts and styles. Stratigraphic evidence at Yen-shih, Cheng-chou, and An-yang, the three most important Shang sites both in the amount and quality of remains and in terms of the chronological information they provide, appears to warrant the tentative and broad correlation of the various phases indicated in Table 9. In other words, speaking of the total area of distribution of Shang sites in North China, three phases of Shang civilization are definitely indicated: *Erh-li-t'ou,* earliest; *Erh-li-kang;* and *Yin,* the phase of Yin Hsü occupation by the Royal House. Further subdivisions can certainly be made. For instance, several components occurred at the site of Erh-li-t'ou, at least Shang-chieh and Lo-ta-miao phases can be distinguished in Cheng-chou before Erh-li-kang, and the Yin phase contained at least the four minor subphases at Ta-ssu-k'ung-ts'un. These problems, however, require further study on the basis of addi-

TABLE 9.

Tentative Correlation of Shang Culture Phases at Major Sites

<table>
<tr><th>PHASES</th><th>YEN-SHIH
LO-YANG</th><th>CHENG-CHOU</th><th>AN-YANG</th></tr>
<tr><td rowspan="2">ca. 1100
YIN
ca. 1400</td><td rowspan="2">LATE SHANG SITES
LO-YANG</td><td>JEN-MIN PARK</td><td rowspan="2">HSI-PEI-KANG
HSIAO-T'UN II</td></tr>
<tr><td rowspan="2">UPPER
ERH-LI-KANG</td></tr>
<tr><td rowspan="2">ERH-LI-KANG
ca. 1650</td><td rowspan="2">ERH-LI-KANG PHASE
LO-YANG</td><td>HSIAO-T'UN I
MEI-YÜAN-CHUANG I</td></tr>
<tr><td>LOWER
ERH-LI-KANG</td><td rowspan="3"></td></tr>
<tr><td rowspan="2">ERH-LI-T'OU
ca. 1850</td><td rowspan="2">TUNG-KAN-KOU
ERH-LI-T'OU</td><td>LO-TA-MIAO</td></tr>
<tr><td>SHANG-CHIEH</td></tr>
</table>

tional information that is not yet adequate. For the time being, we can only speak of the following broad stages of the development of the Shang civilization.

The Erh-li-t'ou Phase

Up to 1965, Shang sites classified with the Erh-li-t'ou and the Shang-chieh and Lo-ta-miao phases had been known in Shan, Lo-ning, Yi-yang, Lo-yang, Sung, Yi-ch'uan, Yen-shih, Teng-feng, Lin-ju, Kung, and Cheng-chou, all in northwestern Honan south of the Yellow River in an area drained by the Huangho and its tributaries Yi and Lo and the neighboring River Ju, an upper tributary of the Huaiho.[78] *Shih Chi* states that the removal of P'an Keng to An-yang involved the crossing of the Yellow River, and it is likely that prior to P'an Keng all Shang capitals were south of the river, although historians are by no means agreed on this point. If T'ang indeed rose at the present site of Erh-li-t'ou, it appears probable that this earliest Shang phase represents the period immediately before and after the founding of the dynasty, a possibility that suggests a tentative date of 1850–1650 B.C. for the Erh-li-t'ou phase of the Shang civilization.

The important characteristics of the Erh-li-t'ou phase are: large *hang-t'u* floors of palatial buildings; division of human burials into

78. An Chih-min et al., *KK* (1965/5), 223.

those with grave pits and grave goods and those without them, some of the latter seeming to be sacrificial victims; the manufacture of bronze implements (knife, awl, fishhook, and bell); the incision of complex symbols on pottery; divination by the shoulderblades of oxen and sheep; the occurrence in graves of pottery wine utensils; the large numbers of stone, bone, and shell hoes, spades, and sickles; remains of domestic pigs, oxen, sheep, and horses; and bone shops and bronze foundries. Characteristic also is a distinctive group of pottery vessels and decorative patterns that were absent in either the Lung-shan culture before or the Erh-li-kang phase after it (shallow dishes with three legs; flat-bottomed basins; characteristic types of *ting, tou, ho, kui, ku, chüeh, chiao;* "filters"; steamers; deep pots with vertical walls; *ting* with single handles; square *ting* with four legs; *chia* with handles; large check marks; a variety of impressed designs; developed appliqued designs; dotted patterns on the vessel interiors). The forms and modes of some pottery vessels (especially those of wine vessels such as the lids and handles of *ho*) give the impression that metal types were being imitated—the occurrence of bronze vessels in this phase cannot be ruled out. All these features point to a highly stratified, complex society and a culture with advanced agriculture and handicrafts, perhaps some rudimentary form of writing, and definitely a bronze industry at perhaps a lower level of achievement than that of the An-yang bronzes.

Available data of the Erh-li-t'ou phase reveal a stage of cultural development intermediate between the Honan Lung-shan culture and the more advanced Shang civilization of later phases that certainly has great bearing on the problem of origin and process of growth of the Shang culture.

> The Erh-li-t'ou type of culture apparently grew out of the foundation of the Honan Lung-shan culture, having absorbed elements of the Shantung Lung-shan culture. Some pottery types of this phase were common in both the Honan and the Shantung Lung-shan cultures, such as the flat-bottomed basins and the *kui* tripods. Some types find antecedents in the Shantung Lung-shan culture, such as the shallow dishes with three legs and the *kui* tripods. Other types and decorations grew out of Honan

> Lung-shan proto-forms, such as the "filter," *ku,* deep pots with vertical walls, *wung, tou, chia,* and basket, check, and cord marks.[79]

The problem of Shang origins in the light of recent work at the Erh-li-t'ou phase sites is discussed below.

The Erh-li-kang Phase

By the time of the Erh-li-kang phase, Shang sites had already attained their maximal distribution, north as well as south of the Yellow River. If we use the Lower Erh-li-kang phase of Cheng-chou as the type site of this Shang phase and use the beginning of the capital status of An-yang to mark its upper end, then the Erh-li-kang phase of the Shang civilization can be placed between 1650 and 1400 B.C. If the site at Cheng-chou was indeed the capital city of Ao, the supposed date that Ao was made a capital (1557 B.C.) falls within this time span.

Aside from new types and modes of pottery there is little in the Erh-li-kang phase that is significantly different from the previous one. *Hang-t'u* constructions and bronze foundries existed, the latter producing primarily small and simple implements and ornaments but occasionally some ceremonial vessels. No writing has been found, and divination was carried out by means of shoulderblades of oxen and sheep. The pattern of settlement clearly indicates an urban network decisively different from the Neolithic village pattern. Since the Erh-li-t'ou phase is not well known it is difficult to assess how much progress it had achieved, but there is no question that it was still at a more primitive level, compared with the Yin phase, as far as cultural complexity and artistic achievement are concerned.

The Yin Phase

This is the phase represented by the Hsi-pei-kang royal tombs, dated to the period of 1400 to 1100 B.C. The center of the state had shifted to north of the Yellow River and there was a notable decline of cultural intensity at Cheng-chou, but the distribution of remains of this phase appears to be the same as in the previous phase, that is, in the northern half of Honan and adjacent regions in Honan, Hopei, and

79. Ibid., p. 223.

Shantung. This is the phase of the oracle scripts, divination by turtle-shells, advanced bronze metallurgy, and artistic climax.

Before 1950, when the first pre-Yin sites were found in Cheng-chou, the fabulous spectacle of the Shang site at An-yang had no apparent antecedents in China, and the "origin" of the civilization—with its bronzes, stone sculptures, horse chariots, pisé houses, human sacrifices, and writing—was a major enigma in the ancient history of China. As Max Loehr pointed out, "An-yang represents, according to our present knowledge, the oldest Chinese metal age site, taking us back to ca. 1300 B.C. It displays no signs of a primitive stage of metal working but utter refinement. Primitive stages have, in fact, nowhere been discovered in China up to the present moment. Metallurgy seems to have been brought to China from outside."[80] The same held true for other elements of Shang civilization than metallurgy: writing, chariot warfare, bronze types, and so forth. Many scholars, principally because they thought that civilization came to China suddenly and without previous foundation, argued that it came as a result of diffusion from the Near East, where civilization emerged some fifteen hundred years before it came to China.[81] Now, during the last seventeen years, with the revelation of the Erh-li-kang phase and remains even earlier than Erh-li-kang, it appears that the foundation and the primitive stages of Shang civilization elements have been discovered. These have led Cheng Te-k'un to state: "the origin of some of the outstanding elements of the late Shang culture may now be told"; that, "after the recent extensive excavations . . . the problem of the origin of the Shang bronze industry may now be considered solved"; and that "Chinese historic culture of the Shang type stemmed directly from the Grey Pottery Culture."[82]

The "origin" of a civilization or, for that matter, of any of its elements, is a complex and difficult problem that must be tackled with care in regard to data and to concepts. At what point in an archaeological sequence of artifacts can we consider, let us say, that the origin

80. *Amer. Jour. Archaeol., 53* (1949), 129.

81. Ibid., pp. 126–44. Carl Bishop, *Origin of the Far Eastern Civilization*, Smithsonian War Background Series, 1941. Li Chi, in *Ch'ing-chu Ts'ai Yüan-p'ei Hsien-sheng Liu-shih-wu sui lun-wen chi,* Pt. 1, 1933.

82. Cheng Te-k'un, "The Origin and Development of Shang Culture," *Asia Major, 6* (1957), 81, 83. *Shang China,* p. 157.

of bronze metallurgy in China has been established? Is it necessary to have available a sequence of bronze foundry sites and a sequence of bronze artifacts ranging from the most primitive and simple to the most advanced and elaborate before one can make such a claim? With writing, the horse chariot, and so on, the same question should be asked. If there is no complete sequence from the primitive to the advanced, does it then follow that this element came from without? And, finally, when and if the origins of a number of such important cultural elements have been "solved," has this also solved the problem of the origin of the civilization? Civilizations are articulations of cultural elements, each of which occupies a place in the whole but all of which do not occupy positions of equal importance—they are not summations of cultural elements. Knowing the origin of some elements of a civilization is not knowing the origin of the civilization and, conversely, we may know how a civilization began to emerge and form without knowing the history of all of its component elements.

Descriptions of the Lung-shan stage of the Chinese Neolithic in Chapter 4 have shown that the Shang civilization did not evolve out of a vacuum. As I have pointed out, a number of Lung-shan elements foreshadowed the birth of civilization in the Huangho Valley: (1) the permanent settlement and the large area of the farming villages, and the advancement of agriculture; (2) the specialization of industries which had been considerably developed, as shown by the appearance of wheel-made pottery in some of the areas; (3) the village fortifications indicating the need for defense, and hence the frequency of warfare between settlements; (4) the oracle bone, the prone burial, and the concentration of jade objects in certain places within the village, which may imply an intensification of the differentiation of individual status; (5) the regional variation of styles and the possible importance of the residential group at the community-aggregate level which foreshadowed, if it did not indicate, the formation of urban networks and the beginning of regional states, one of which eventually succeeded in expansion and conquest, and was known as the Shang.

The Shang civilization was indeed a new phenomenon in the Huangho Valley, an outcome of a quantum change, which put a full stop to the Neolithic way of life in the area of Shang distribution, and in doing so prefaced a new book which is entitled Chinese history instead of prehistory. But the main stream of this new civilization was evidently handed on from the previous Neolithic substratum. There were, in the Shang culture, new elements and new systems of organization for new and old elements of culture, but this does not necessarily mean that the Shang civilization was not a native growth. Table 10 shows, in a preliminary fashion, the Neolithic heritage of the Shang Bronze Age culture and its innovations. From this enumeration it becomes apparent that the "suddenness" of the emergence of the Shang civilization has been unduly exaggerated by past scholarly

TABLE 10.

North China Neolithic–Bronze Age Continuities and Discontinuities

Continuities	*Discontinuities*
Formation of village-aggregate	Mature urbanism and related institutions (esp. formation of settlement groups)
Raid and warfare	Class differentiation
Industrial specialization	New government and economic patterns (conquest, tribute, redistribution, etc.)
Differentiation of status, and prone burials	Wider trade, currency
Elaborate ceremonial complex (more lineage-ancestral than community-agricultural)	New war patterns (capture of slaves and use of chariots)
Cultivation of millet, rice, kaoliang, wheat, hemp	Chamber burials and human sacrifices
Domestication of dog, pig, cattle, sheep, horse, chicken	Domestication of water buffalo
Stamped-earth structures	Highly developed bronze metallurgy
Semi-subterranean houses and lime-plastered floors	Writing
Scapulimancy	Advanced stone carvings
Some pottery forms (esp. ritual forms with ring feet and lids)	New pottery forms
Some decorative motifs	
Some stone implements and weapons (esp. semilunar knife, sickle, arrowhead, adz, ax, hoe, spade, perforated ax, halberd)	
Shell and bone craft	
Cord-marked pottery tradition	
Silk	
Jade complex	

writing. In fact, few Shang ecosocial and stylistic elements did not have a Neolithic basis. Thus, one thing can be considered settled—that the Chinese civilization, on the whole, was built upon the Chinese Neolithic foundation. With this basic question out of the way, three problems still confront us: (1) the origins of the cultural elements that appeared during the Shang period for the first time, and the extent to which these new elements can be considered responsible for the appearance of the civilization; (2) the new structure and configuration of the Shang civilization which distinguish it from the Neolithic, continuities in cultural elements notwithstanding; and (3) the regional phase of the Lung-shan culture that is directly ancestral to the Shang. The second problem will be discussed at length in subsequent sections of this chapter. Evidence pertaining to the first and the third problems is still meager, but the following remarks may be of some help.

Most of the new features that appeared during the Shang and serve to mark it off from the Neolithic are largely developmental and functional in nature. Urbanism, class distinctions, political systems, and the like are poor indications of historical relationships; the use of currency, patterns of warfare, and many ceremonial practices can probably be said to be concomitant with particular functional contexts. Only bronze metallurgy, the use of writing, and the horse chariot are, therefore, of possible historical significance. Unfortunately, the history of these elements and their occurrence in China have yet to be studied. As mentioned in Chapter 4, horse bones have been found from some of the Lungshanoid sites. It is widely accepted that during the Shang, horses were used only for drawing chariots, and were neither ridden nor used for food.[83] There is no reason to suppose that horses during the Lung-shan stage, if domesticated, were employed for purposes other than warfare. Since the riding of horses during the Lung-shan is highly unlikely, we might even be tempted to conclude that the horse chariot appeared during that period, but the evidence for this conclusion is dangerously thin. In the first place, horse bones have been found only rarely at Lung-shan sites, and the zoological characteristics of those that have been found remain to be specified. Second, chariot warfare does not seem to fit the Lung-shan

83. Shih Chang-ju, *Bulletin, College of Arts, National Taiwan University, 5* (1953), 6–7. Hayashi Minao, *Minzokugaku-Kenkyu, 23* (1959), 39–40.

context satisfactorily. Third, remains of chariots have never been found at Lung-shan sites. A great number of excavations and comparative studies of horse and chariot remains in China and in Mesopotamia must be made before we can be certain about the origin of the horse chariot in the Shang Dynasty.[84]

The history of writing in China is another unknown factor. Palaeographers are agreed that a stage of writing existed in China before An-yang became the capital. The scripts during this pre-Anyang stage were supposedly more representational and elaborate than the An-yang oracle bone inscriptions which were highly simplified and conventionalized. Such archaic characters have been found on Anyang bronzes and oracle bones, along with the simplified and conventionalized form, probably for artistic and ceremonial use.[85] Archaeologically, however, except for the complex symbols on pottery at both Yen-shih and Cheng-chou, this archaic writing has not been found in a stratigraphic context demonstrably earlier than the Anyang period.[86]

The history of bronze metallurgy in China is now better known than previously, although it is not yet a solved problem. Based on recent findings, the following points can be made. An-yang does not represent the oldest Chinese metal age site; the existence of bronze metallurgy during the Shang before the period of An-yang has been established. Even the possibility that metallurgy began to appear in North China toward the end of the Lung-shan stage of the Neolithic cannot be ruled out. At Yen-shih and Cheng-chou, where bronze artifacts have been unearthed from a pre-Anyang stratigraphic context, bronzes are few and less refined than those at An-yang, although metallurgical details are not yet available. It is possible that this marks one of the "primitive stages" that Loehr said was lacking. An intensive investigation into the metallurgical techniques of the Chinese Bronze Age has convinced Noel Barnard[87] that bronze foundry in

84. Cf. Hayashi Minao, *Minzokugaku-zasshi, 23* (1959), 39–40; *24* (1960), 33–57; *Tōhōgakuhō, 29* (Kyoto, 1959), 155–284; M. V. Dewall, *Pferd und Wagen im Frühen China, 1,* Bonn, Saarbrücker Beiträge zur Altertumskunde, 1964.

85. Tung Tso-pin, *Ta-lu-tsa-chih, 9* (1952), 348–58. T'ang Lan, *KKHP* (1957/2), 7–22.

86. In *Paideuma, 4* (1950), 81–99, Robert von Heine-Geldern erroneously stated that writing appeared during the Lung-shan stage.

87. *Bronze Casting and Bronze Alloys in Ancient China,* Tokyo, Australian National University and Monumenta Serica, 1961, p. 108.

China, showing little similarity to Western bronze metallurgy, was invented independently *in situ*. Deposits of copper and tin ores, according to the studies of Amano Motonosuke[88] and Shih Chang-ju,[89] are abundant in North China, and were easily accessible from northern Honan. This indicates that, given appropriate necessity and stimulus, the opportunity for independent metallurgical invention was available to the first Chinese bronze workers. It is generally agreed that the Shang craftsmen used bronze as a new medium for working the traditional artifactual forms; in other words, the Shang bronzes manifested the traditional forms and functions by means of a new kind of raw material and technology. Considering all these points, we can say that much new light has been thrown upon the problem of the origin of bronze metallurgy in China, which renders likely the independent invention of this new technology in China. Much more information, to be sure, is required to transform this possibility into certainty, but the trend of available data is clear, and we are more sure of the various areas in which intelligent questions can be asked.

Furthermore, some new light has also been thrown upon the problem pertaining to the transition from the Lung-shan to the Shang. That the Lung-shan culture was the forerunner of the Shang civilization is certain, but we have yet to pin down the exact region where this transition took place, and—still more difficult—to determine exactly how it took place. The fact that, in the area of Yen-shih and Lo-yang of western Honan, stratified sequences of Honan Lung-shan culture and the Erh-li-t'ou phase of the Shang civilization have indicated a continuous development of culture, is certainly suggestive. One would be tempted to proclaim this area—the Yi and Lo River valleys—the cradle of the Shang civilization if it were not for the very inadequate amount of data available for the Erh-li-t'ou phase.

To conclude, one may find it possible to say that the foundation of the Shang civilization is the Honan Lung-shan culture; that the three phases of Shang civilization provide a preliminary sequence of its gradual development; that the transformation in question is primarily and essentially a societal growth and that its manifestations were rooted in the cultural history of the Yellow River basin itself;

88. *Tōhōgakuhō, 23* (1953), 231–58.
89. *BIHP, 26* (1955).

that the history of development of many of the Shang's essential elements are now clearly demonstrated by archaeological data in North China, but others remain unknown; that some important elements of the Shang civilization that had a role in stimulating its growth were possibly derivative; and, finally, that the actual process of growth of the civilization *in toto* and of its various constituent elements remains a topic for further research, for which future discoveries of Erh-li-t'ou sites will be essential.

CONTENT AND STYLE OF THE SHANG CIVILIZATION

The earliest strata of the Shang civilization known at present in the form of the Erh-li-t'ou phase of western Honan are not adequately known, but it is already clear that by this time (ca. 1850 B.C.) the Neolithic economy had begun to give way to the formation of settlement groups as self-contained units. Bronze metallury was already well started, and at some sites one sees the beginning of a highly intensified and sophisticated aristocratic complex. This stage serves well as a transitional phase between the Neolithic and the climactic Shang civilization.

By the time the city wall was constructed at Cheng-chou, perhaps around 1650 B.C., there can no longer be any doubt that Chinese urbanization was mature and that a Shang style of Chinese art and culture is manifest in the archaeological record. Because the term "urbanization" is somewhat arbitrarily defined in the archaeological literature,[90] we must carefully characterize the nature of city life of the Shang Dynasty in North China. The foremost feature of the Shang sites is that individual villages were organized into intervillage networks in economy, administration, and religion. Each group depended upon others for specialized services, and offered services in return. There was a political and ceremonial center (a walled enclosure in the case of Cheng-chou), where the royal family and the nobles resided. It apparently served as the nucleus of the group and, when the capital of the dynasty was located there, as the center of political and economic control of the whole kingdom. Surrounding and

90. V. Gordon Childe, *Town Planning Review, 21* (Liverpool, 1950), 3–17; but see R. J. Braidwood and G. R. Willey, eds., *Courses Toward Urban Life,* Viking Fund Publications in Anthropology, no. 32, 1962.

centripetal to this nucleus were industrial quarters with high degrees of specialization, and farming villages. Goods apparently circulated among the various villages, with the administrative center serving also as the center for redistribution. The population of the entire settlement group was considerable, as indicated by the spatial dimensions and by the quantity and complexity of the cultural remains, and the social stratification and industrial specialization of the populace were highly intensified. We find in Shang China no physical counterparts to such large population and architectural configurations as Ur of Mesopotamia, Mohenjo-Daro on the Indus, and Teotihuacan of Mexico, yet the Shang capital sites performed all the essential functions of a city, indicating a definite break from the Neolithic community pattern. This basic Shang city pattern continued on into later historic periods. During the Eastern Chou period the capital sites grew into large commercial and political urban centers, as will be described in the next chapter.

Purely from an archaeological perspective, the populace of a Shang city seems to have been divided into three major groups: the aristocracy, the craftsmen, and the farmers.

The aristocracy. Archaeological excavations, oracle bone inscriptions, and historic records have jointly established the fact that the Shang capitals at Cheng-chou and An-yang were seats of a powerful centralized government in control of a number of settlement groups scattered over a part of North China. At one or a few of the sites within the same settlement group, an aristocratic complex of artifacts and architecture can easily be recognized. In architecture, this includes ceremonial altars, rectangular house structures with stamped earth floors, stone pillar foundations, and in some cases, stone sculptures used as pillar bases. Such sites have a complex system of graves, including tombs of gigantic dimensions and sophisticated structure, evidence of human sacrifice and accompanying burials of animal victims and horse chariots. This aristocratic complex is often associated with a sophisticated ritual complex, manifested by human sacrifice, animal sacrifice, scapulimancy, and ceremonial vessels of pottery (e.g. white pottery) and bronze. Horse and chariot fittings and other apparatus for ritual use help to mark the distinction of status, along with such artifacts as prepared and inscribed oracle bones, white, hard, glazed pottery, elaborately carved bone hairpins, jade weapons, and bronze ceremonial and household utensils. Groups of bronze and pottery vessels for use in wine drinking and serving occurred in the Shang burials for the first time. Remains of cowrie shells, probably used as media of exchange, may also be significant. Writing is apparently associated with the aristocracy, as are highly developed decorative arts like the *t'ao-t'ieh* style, mosaic designs, and stone and bone sculptures and engravings. Discovery of such artifacts points to a strongly consolidated aristocracy that was definitely absent prior to the Shang.

From the oracle inscriptions and the historic records, a little is known about the Royal House, the rule of succession to the throne, and the political relationships among the various settlement groups. Mythological sources relate that the Royal House of the Shang Dynasty was a grand lineage by the name of Tzu, attributed to a divine birth in Ssu-ma Ch'ien's *Shih Chi,* volume 3:

> The mother of Ch'i, founder of the Yin Dynasty, was called Chien Ti, a daughter of the tribe Yu Jung and second consort of Emperor K'u. Basking with two companions, Chien Ti saw an egg fall from a black bird [swallow or phoenix] and swallowed it. She then became pregnant and gave birth to Ch'i.

The grand lineage occupied a central position in the state's political, economic, and ceremonial structures, which were expressed and maintained with elaborate and solemn ancestor worship rites. There is little question about the relationship between the ancestor worship rites performed by and for the grand lineages and the origin myths of the descent of these lineages. According to the ancestor cult calendar worked out from the oracle inscriptions, Li Hsüeh-ch'in has been able to generalize that among thirty-five kings of the Shang Dynasty, whose rules of succession are relatively clear, the throne was assumed by sons for eighteen generations, and for seven generations (ten kings) it was taken over by brothers.[91]

The settlement groups that were not under the direct rule of the monarch were administered by lords appointed by the central gov-

91. Li Hsüeh-ch'in, *Wen-shih-che* (1957/2), 31–37. For a new hypothesis on the rules of royal succession in the context of the kinship system, see Chang Kwang-chih, *BIE, 15* (1963), 65–94.

ernment. The lords were relatives of the monarch (sometimes junior sons), high officials who made great contributions to the cause of the Royal House, and the *de facto* rulers of regions that paid tribute to the central government but were out of the reach of the royal forces, and whose administrative status had to be recognized.[92]

The central government and the local governments thus formed a tightly organized hierarchy, with the king at the top, assisted by officials of a royal court and priests who practiced scapulimancy, among other duties. Communications between the various settlement groups and the central administration were possible with the aid of a highly developed system of writing and a standardized currency. Raids and warfare between states were frequent, as judged by the war records in the inscriptions, the abundant remains of weapons, the sacrificial use of what were apparently war captives, and the chariots. The centralized power of government is most clearly indicated by the control of manpower. In addition, public works began to appear to a significant extent. The *hang-t'u* structures at Hsiao-t'un and Cheng-chou, such as the walled enclosure and the temples and altars, were probably built by large groups of people, organized and directed by administrative agencies. The construction of the large royal tombs at Hsi-pei-kang, An-yang, is of particular interest in this connection.

The social institutions that governed the aristocracy and its auxiliary groups, as indicated by the archaeological evidence and the oracle bone inscriptions, were as follows: Marriage in the royal family was as a rule monogamous. The families of the Royal House, the nobility, and some of the craftsmen were of the extended family type, probably patrilineal. Beyond the family, unilinear lineages may have been prevalent among the nobility and some of the craftsmen; these were possibly segmentary lineages based on patrilineality and primogeniture (see below). The lineage system may have been related to a part of the class structure. The kinship terminology of the royal family was possibly of the generation type.

The organization of the royal family is relatively clear. According to the Yin calendar of rituals, as recorded in the oracle bone inscriptions, each king had one particular spouse.

92. Hu Hou-hsüan, *Chia-ku-hsüeh Shang-shih lun ts'ung, 1,* Chinan, Ch'i-lu Univ., 1944.

> *P'i* (grandmothers and female ancestors) was partnered to *tsu* (grandfathers and male ancestors), *mu* (mothers) partnered to *fu* (fathers), and *fu* (daughters-in-law) partnered to *tzu* (sons). Each man usually had only one official spouse. Among all the fathers, one, and one only, had an especially supreme status, and his spouse also had supreme status. The family descent and the calendar of rituals were both based on patrilineality.[93]

The families of the nobility seem to be of the extended type. Their domiciliary house can be represented by the foundation A4 at Hsiao-t'un, which is 28.4 meters long and 8 meters wide, and is divided into two large halls and eleven small rooms, all connected by doors.[94]

There is little question that lineages existed during the Yin Dynasty. But what kind of lineage organization it was is a baffling matter. It is clear that in Yin times the principle of primogeniture played an important role, and that the order of seniority of birth was duly symbolized in the order of rituals and the classification of temples and altars into grand and lesser lines.[95] It is therefore possible that the so-called *tsung-fa* system of kinship, well known to be characteristic of the Chou Dynasty, had already started in the Yin stage, and that the Yin lineages were somewhat like the ramage system characterized by Raymond Firth and Marshall Sahlins, or the stratified lineage named by Morton Fried.[96] This system is characterized above all by the close correlation of political status with kinship descent; i.e. an individual's rank within the clan is determined by his consanguineal proximity to the alleged main line of descent.

The highly organized ceremonial patterns of the Yin Dynasty essentially carried on the Neolithic heritage, as indicated by an institutionalized ancestor worship, the practice of scapulimancy, and the elaboration of ceremonial objects, especially vessels. But by Yin times, the ceremonial structure of society had been very much intensified

93. Li Hsüeh-ch'in, *Wen-shih-che* (1957/2), 36.
94. Shih Chang-ju, *Ann. Acad. Sinica, 1* (1954), 267–80.
95. Hu Hou-hsüan, *Chia-ku-hsüeh Shang-shih lun ts'ung, 1,* 16.
96. Raymond Firth, *We, the Tikopia,* London, Allen & Unwin, 1936. Marshall D. Sahlins, *Social Stratification in Polynesia,* Seattle, American Ethnol. Society, 1958. Morton H. Fried, *Jour. Roy. Anthropol. Inst., 87* (1957), 1–29. Li Hwei, *BIE, 4* (1957), 123–34.

and was unmistakably tied up with the aristocracy. Priests, whose main duty was probably to divine and foretell events, served the royal court; the elaborate and sophisticated ceremonial bronze vessels were apparently used for rituals performed for the Royal House according to an annual calendar, mainly rituals of ancestor worship; the ceremonial center of the An-yang settlement group was spatially identified with the administrative center (Hsiao-t'un); and large-scale human and animal sacrifice was offered for the royal family.

In this manner the ceremonial structure was possibly correlated with the kinship structure on the one hand and with the economic system on the other. Ancestral worship was stressed and the calendar of ancestral worship rituals was carefully scheduled, reminding of and reinforcing the rules of primogeniture, the supremacy of the grand lineages, and the ramification of the lesser lineages, which became more and more degraded with each succeeding generation. The king, at the top of the hierarchal clan, was the supreme ruler of the kingdom and of the clan and also the focus of attention for all rituals. The relationship among the various settlement groups of the Yin Kingdom was thus not only economically based (concentration and redistribution) but also accounted for in terms of kinship, and sanctioned and reinforced by rituals.

The craftsmen. At the Shang cities, craftsmen were physically identified with both farmers and the aristocracy, since the industrial quarters were distributed among the farming villages in the suburbs as well as near the palatial nuclei. Our knowledge about these men is rather limited, but we know that industry was a minutely specialized affair, that each settlement group had a number of industrial centers at the service of the aristocracy to provide for the whole settlement, that the craftsmen probably enjoyed a higher status than the farmers by virtue of their special skill and knowledge, and that various handicrafts may have been tied to kin groups. It is mentioned in the "Chronicle of the Fourth Year of Ting Kung" (of Lu State in the Spring–Atumn Period) in *Tso Chuan* that "after Wu Wang [of the Chou] conquered the Shang, Ch'eng Wang established the regime and selected men of wisdom and virtue and made them feudal lords to protect the Royal Chou." To each of the lords Ch'eng Wang is said to have given a number of *tsu* (= minimal lineage), and the names of the *tsu* mentioned here included words for a drinking utensil, pottery, flag, and pots and pans. This passage shows that during the Shang Dynasty, handicraft was possibly a kin group affair. Some of the lineages specialized in particular branches of handicrafts, either as a supplement to agriculture or full time. The Cheng-chou potters, as mentioned above, seem to have devoted full time to a special kind of pottery, whereas other kinds of ceramics probably were the business of other groups. The skills and special technical knowledge were probably passed down within the kin groups and, because of this, the members of the group may have enjoyed certain privileges that the farmers did not have. At Çheng-chou the bronzesmiths and potters lived in above-ground stamped-earth houses which were usually associated with the nobility. The bronzesmiths' dwellings found in the region north of Tzu-ching-shan in Cheng-chou consist of four houses:

> Each house is partitioned by a wall into two rooms. The two rooms are connected by a door. The two rooms may both have had a door to communicate with the outside, or only one of them may have had. Each room has an earth platform by the door, and a fireplace.[97]

Furthermore, these four houses are arranged according to a definite plan, and each is separated from the next by a distance 10 or 11 meters. These facts may indicate that the bronzesmiths' families were of the extended type, and that their households belonged to the same patrilineage, a conclusion in complete agreement with the historic records concerning the lineage–occupation linkage.

Ground houses have also been uncovered at An-yang in association with the bronze technology. In 1959 and 1960 at the site of Miao-p'u-pei-ti, southeast of Hsiao-t'un, a number of ground-house floors were located, many of which were associated with clay molds. A large floor (more than 8 m long and 4 m wide), partitioned into two rooms, was built on a layer of *hang-t'u,* and the walls were also constructed by the *hang-t'u* technique. Posts were based on rocks here in the same man-

97. Liao Yüng-min, *WWTKTL* (1957/6), 73.

ner as in the Hsiao-t'un palaces and temples. In the house, near the entrance, is a gourd-shaped pit, probably a hearth. Surrounding the floor were found many piece molds of clay and fragments of crucibles, indicating a close connection with bronze work.[98]

From the large number of piece molds as well as the remains of clay models, crucible fragments, and the bronze artifacts themselves, the techniques of bronze-making are well understood. Flat bronze implements such as knives and *ko* halberds were probably manufactured with the aid of a single mold or a two-piece mold into which molten copper and tin were poured. Hollow implements of plain form, such as axes, were also relatively simply made, with an outer mold and an inner core. The complicated vessels, especially large ones and those with cast decorative designs (a square *ting* from An-yang is 137 cm high, 110 cm long, 77 cm wide, and 700 kg in weight), involved a more complex process.

> A bronze casting is simply a replica in bronze of a model created in another medium. In the Western tradition this model has typically been made of wax on a clay core, then sheathed in a solid clay outer mold, melted out and replaced with molten bronze [the so-called lost-wax method]. In ancient China, on the contrary, it appears that the model was made of *clay* (and perhaps of other infusible materials such as wood) around a clay core and that the outer mold was not solid and continuous but segmented. This segmentation (making the outer mold a "piece mold") was necessitated by the fact that the baked clay model, unlike its wax counterpart, could not be melted out but had to be removed bodily. Thus when the mold segments have received the imprint of the model they are detached from it, the model is broken or scraped away from the core, and the mold segments are reassembled around the core ready to receive the molten bronze in the now hollow interstice between the two.[99]

98. An Chih-min et al., *KK* (1961/2), 67.

99. Wilma Fairbank, *Archives of the Chinese Art Society of America, 16* (1962), 9. For detailed analyses of the bronze metallurgy of the Shang, see Noel Barnard, *Bronze Casting and Bronze Alloys in Ancient China,* Tokyo, Monumenta Serica Monograph 16 (1961); Shih Chang-ju, *Bull. Inst. Hist. Philol., Acad. Sinica, 26* (1955), 95–129.

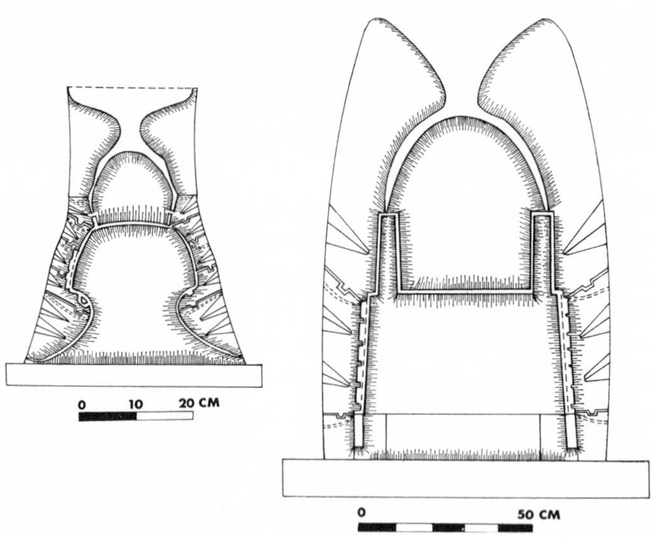

86. Clay molds for casting bronze vessels, Shang period. (From Shih Chang-ju, *BIHP, 26,* 1955, pp. 113, 117.)

This multiple piece-mold process of the Shang (Fig. 86) is what has convinced Noel Barnard[100] that bronze metallurgy independently emerged in China, but Wilma Fairbank[1] goes so far as to see it as a far more complex application of the rudimentary bronze metallurgical principles for processing ores and alloying, heating, and pouring the metal—which may or may not have been diffused into China from the West—made possible by the superior ceramic craftsmanship of the Chinese.

Perhaps the high social status apparently enjoyed by the bronzesmiths resulted from the association of bronze artifacts with the upper class. During the Yin phase of the Shang civilization at least, the bronze artifacts were made for the most part for exclusive purposes like ceremonies, warfare, and hunting. On the other hand, practically all the tools and implements for such basic subsistence purposes as agriculture and domestic utility continued to be made of wood, stone, clay, or bone. In all likelihood the industrial specialization at this time was tightly correlated with status differentiation.

100. Barnard, ibid., pp. 59–62.
1. Fairbank, op. cit., pp. 10–11.

Archaeologically substantiated handicrafts (whose "workshops" have been discovered) include manufacture of bronzes, pottery, and stone and bone artifacts, and possibly wine-making. Other professions that can be inferred from archaeological remains or have been mentioned in the oracle bone inscriptions include carpentry, sculpture, earth construction, masonry, manufacture of drinking utensils, chariots, and weapons, tailoring, fabric-making, and flag-making.[2] Their extent of specialization seems to vary, and they had clienteles of differing social status.

The farmers. The Shang subsistence was based on agriculture and supplemented by hunting and fishing. Remains of crops of the Shang period have been found at Cheng-chou, An-yang, and Hsing-t'ai, but have not been specified. From the oracle bone inscriptions it can be determined that millet (probably both *Setaria* and *Panicum*), rice, and wheat were planted.[3] Little is known about the cultivation techniques except that stone hoes, spades, and sickles were used, as well as a kind of large wooden digging stick which may have been pushed by men or pulled by cattle and dogs, and was possibly a prototype of the plow.[4] Two crops of millet and rice were harvested each year, and irrigation was probably employed,[5] although the connection of the water ditches discovered at An-yang and Cheng-chou with irrigation has not been satisfactorily demonstrated. Those at Hsiao-t'un, at least, are not likely to have been connected with irrigation. Fertilizers may have been used, but this again is by no means certain.[6] An elaborate agricultural calendar was developed.[7] Other archaeological finds connected with farming include pestles and mortars. Among the cultivated materials for fabrics were hemp[8] and silk.[9] In the domesti-

2. Li Chi, *The Beginnings of Chinese Civilization*. Li Ya-nung, *Yin-tai she-hui sheng-huo*, Shanghai, Jenmin Press, 1955. Amano Motonosuke, *Tōhōgakuhō, 23*, 1953. Shih Chang-ju, *BIHP, 26*, 1955. Hsia Nai, *China Reconstructs* (1957/12). Li Chi, *BIHP, 23* (1951), 523–619; *Hsiao-t'un T'ao-ch'i*. Yü Yü, *WWTKTL* (1958/10), 26–28.

3. Hu Hou-hsüan, *Chia-ku-hsüeh Shang-shih lun ts'ung, 2* (1945), 134.

4. Ibid.

5. Ibid.

6. Hu Hou-hsüan, *Li-shih Yen-chiu* (1955/1). *WW* (1963/5), 27–31, 41.

7. Tung Tso-pin, *Yin Li P'u,* Institute of History of Philology, Academia Sinica, Li-chuang, 1945.

8. Li Chi, *An-yang Fa-chüeh Pao-kao, 3* (1931), 466. Iwama, *Manshu Gakuhō, 4* (1936), 1–7.

9. Amano Motonosuke, *Tōhōgakuhō, 1* (1955). Vivi Sylwan, *BMFEA, 9* (1937), 119–26.

cation of animals the Shang carried on the Neolithic heritage (pigs, dogs, cattle, sheep, horses, and chickens), with some additions (water buffalo) and modifications (as the use of dogs, cattle, and sheep for sacrifice and horses for chariot warfare).[10]

Fishing is indicated by fishbones,[11] fishhooks, and the scripts for fishnets and fishhooks. Hunting is indicated by the large quantity of wild animal bone remains (tiger, leopard, bear, rhinoceros, deer, water deer, hare, etc.), by the remains of stone and bronze arrowheads, by the hunting records in the oracle bone inscriptions, and by the animal designs in the decorative art. However, the part played in the basic subsistence by hunting may not have been very significant. According to Li Chi, the "game huntings mentioned in the ancient inscriptions were evidently pursued for pleasure and excitement rather than for economic necessity . . . Such pursuits were the monopolies of a privileged class."[12]

There is no question that agriculture was the basis of Shang subsistence, or that the techniques were highly developed and the yield considerable. In the suburbs of Cheng-chou and An-yang, the many residential hamlets were presumably occupied by farmers who tilled the fields in the neighborhood. One controverisal point among Shang specialists is whether the direct participants in agricultural production were free farmers or slaves. It is known that live slaves suffering from malnutrition, possibly war captives,[13] were sacrificed in the construction of palaces, temples, and royal tombs, were buried dead or alive with the royal body in the royal tomb, and that their bones were used for the manufacture of artifacts. But whether slaves were the sole laborers in the farming fields is not known. Amano suggests that during the Yin Dynasty there were two kinds of fields: the royal field, cultivated by slaves under centralized management, and the clan fields cultivated by the lower classes of clan members.[14] This theory may have some truth in it, but no thorough general conclusion is yet in sight.

10. Shih Chang-ju, *Bull. College of Arts, Natl. Taiwan Univ., 5* (1953), 1–14.
11. Chao Ch'üan-ku et al., *KKHP* (1957/1), 63. Wu Hsien-wen, *KKHP, 4* (1949), 139–43.
12. Li Chi, *Bull. Dept. Archaeol. Anthropol., Natl. Taiwan Univ., 9/10* (1957), 12.
13. Mao Hsieh-chün and Yen Yen, *VP, 3* (1959), 79–80.
14. Amano Motonosuke, *Shigaku Kenkyu, 62* (1956), 11.

Created and sustained by people of all these categories, in concert if not in harmony, the Shang civilization by the Yin period at the latest achieved both distinction and greatness, placing it among the civilized giants of the ancient world. It can best be recognized through its art and religion—those complexes of culture through which the Shang expressed their minds about the world around them and indicated to us how the various aspects of their lives could be articulated.

For much of the Shang religion and ritual we must resort to the information that only written records provide,[15] but archaeology is rich in religious symbols and ritual art. Shang domiciles, palaces, temples, and tombs alike were invariably square or oblong, governed in orientation by the four cardinal directions and dominated in design by a persistent attempt at symmetry. The ancestral temples in Section B at Hsiao-t'un were constructed in two north–south rows facing each other east and west, with an earthen altar at the northern end to provide focus; the Hsi-pei-kang royal tombs, neatly square and angular themselves, formed an eastern and a western half. In the decorative art of the bronzes "there is never any asymmetry,"[16] and in inscribing the plastral shells of turtles after a divination the messages were repeated on the left and the right sides.[17] As shown in the *chia ku* scripts, the world is square, and each of the four directions probably had its own symbolic color and certainly its own deity with its own name; winds blown from the four directions were the deities' agents, and countries beyond the kingdom were grouped into four directional classes.

Above the four directional deities—and also deities of sun, moon, earth, mountains, clouds, rivers, and other natural beings—was a Shang Ti, Supreme God on High, who presided over a court consisting usually of five ministers. He was all-powerful, controlling human affairs large and small, but he was never directly sacrificed to or specifically located. With all deities and, especially with Shang Ti, ancestors of the royal lineages were in constant and easy communication, and plastromancy and scapulimancy were the means by which living man achieved communication with the ancestors in the other

15. Ch'en Meng-chia, *Yin Hsü p'u-tz'u tsung-shu,* Peking, Science Press, 1957, pp. 551–603.
16. B. Karlgren, *BMFEA, 34* (1962), 16.
17. Ch'en Meng-chia, op. cit., p. 13.

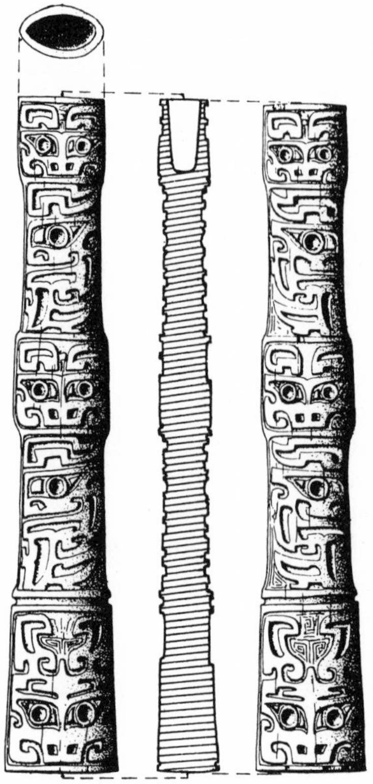

87. Shang bone carving excavated from Hsiao-t'un, An-yang. (From Li Chi, *The Beginnings of Chinese Civilization*, Seattle, Univ. Washington Press, 1957, p. 30.)

world. Probably carrying on an ancient shamanistic tradition, the Shang had access to the other world through animal agents. In death, the nobleman's living possessions were buried with him in his chamber of eternal rest; in life, he burned animal bones to reach the ears of his ancestors and performed ancestral worship rites, using utensils covered with animal images.

Shang art, in other media as well as in bronze, was "an art that exclusively worked with animal motifs."[18] Images and forms of animals —serpent, dragon, phoenix, owl, falcon, tiger, sheep, oxen, buffalo, cicada, elephant, rhinoceros, among others—and their bodily parts, in realistic or stylistic motifs, permeated Shang ritual art on bronze vessels, stone sculptures, bone, jade, and ivory carvings, white pottery, plastic clay, and wood carvings with stone and bone inlays (Fig. 87). Human images constituted another significant category of artis-

18. B. Karlgren, *BMFEA, 34* (1962), 16.

tic work (Fig. 88). The interrelationship of animal and human images in Shang art is an interesting topic whose significance, however, will not become explicit until after we have observed, in the next chapter, how it changed during the subsequent Chou period.

Bernard Karlgren[19] has isolated a number of bronze decorative motifs and analyzed the distribution patterns of these motifs in the total decor of complete vessels of Shang types. Finding that some motifs tend to be associated with one another but to be excluded from other motifs, Karlgren has constructed two contrasting styles that he calls A and B, each consisting of a number of motifs. Both A and B styles were components of the same Shang art, for "the intimate connection between all the classes of both styles is emphasized by a series of 'neutral' elements which constitute constantly recurring paraphernalia of the bronze decor and which appear in various classes of both A style and B style vessels."[20] But Karlgren also believes that they were perhaps chronologically distinct (A being earlier than B in the beginning) or that they were perhaps the art styles of two contending social groups of the ruling class, each claiming a style exclusive to its own families of artisans. An analysis of the bronze motifs of vessel assemblages discovered in Shang graves has convinced me that the A and B styles were indeed not only favored by different artisans in making the bronze vessels but were also favored by different social groups who selected these ceremonial paraphernalia for burial with their dead members, because all bronze vessels found in each grave tend to exhibit either A or B style preferences.[21]

These studies may have revealed a significant key to the meaning of a number of apparently interrelated phenomena of Shang art, archaeology, and history. The late Tung Tso-pin[22] was the first scholar to discover the significant internal criteria that enabled the oracle texts, fragmentary and disjoint, to be placed in a chronological sequence within the 273 years of their history at An-yang and, in so doing, was the first to bring into focus the cyclical changes of the Shang institu-

19. *BMFEA, 9* (1937), 1–117; *34* (1962), 1–28.

20. *BMFEA, 34* (1962), 18. See Max Loehr, *Archives of the Chinese Art Society of America,* 7 (1953), for a different classification of bronze styles in An-yang.

21. Kwang-chih Chang, *Jour. Asian Studies 24* (1964), 45–61. *Symposium in Honor of Dr. Li Chi on his Seventieth Birthday* (Taipei, *The Ch'inghua Journal*), Pt. 1, 1965, 353–70.

22. *Yin Li P'u,* Li-chuang, 1945.

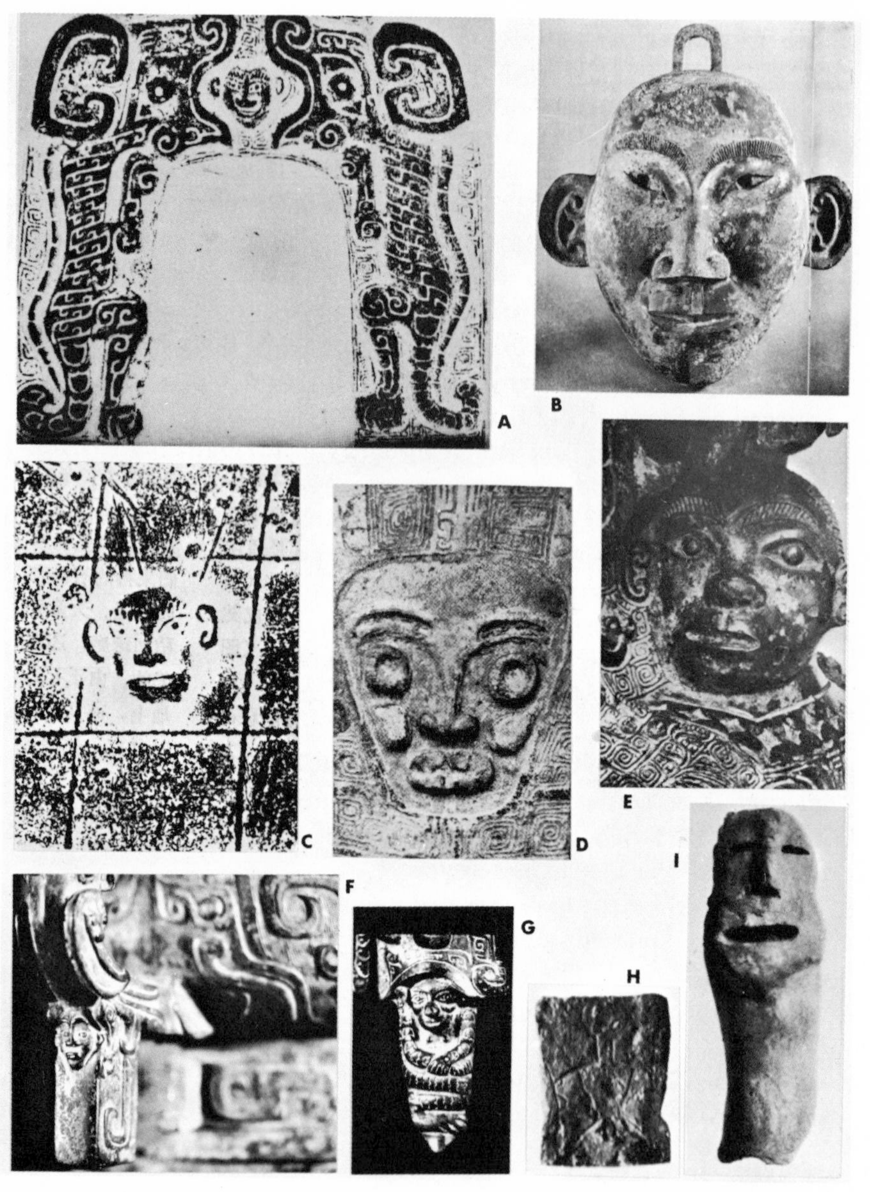

88. Human faces in Shang art. (A, An-yang, from Li Chi, *Beginnings of Chinese Civilization,* Pl. I. B, An-yang, from *Life,* vol. 51, 1961, no. 13. C, Presumably An-yang, from *KK,* 1964/11, p. 592. D, E, Presumably An-yang, from *Sekai Bunka-shi Taikei,* vol. 15, 1958, p. 26. F, G, Collection of the Freer Art Gallery, Washington, D.C. H, Erh-li-t'ou, Yen-shih, Honan, from *KK,* 1965/5, Pl. III. I, Shang-chieh, Cheng-Chou, from *KK,* 1966/1, Pl. I. H and I are of clay; the rest are bronze.)

tions—ritual calendar for one, and court etiquette for another—which he characterized as two contending traditions. I have come to notice the cyclical pattern of distribution of the temple designations of the Shang kings and their spouses in their genealogical sequence, and from this I have worked out a dualistic scheme of royal succession whereby two parallel but different groups within the Royal House alternated in ascent to the throne.[23] This would provide a basis not only for an interpretation of the A and B styles of Shang bronzes and the two institutional traditions in the *chia ku* scripts but also explain why Hsiao-t'un had two parallel rows of temples and Hsi-pei-kang had two clusters of royal tombs. The genalogical duality of the Shang kings would dictate a division of the eleven Shang kings at An-yang (again excluding the last king, who presumably was not buried in the same manner as his eleven predecessors) into a left (eastern) cluster of four and a right (western) cluster of seven, which is exactly what we find at Hsi-pei-kang. Many of these dualistic phenomena are identical with the essential features of the so-called *chao mu* institution of the Chou, a point worthy of attention in discussing the Shang–Chou cultural identity in the next chapter.

23. Kwang-chih Chang, *BIE, 15* (1963), 65–94. See also the many articles, pro and con, discussing the problem raised therein, in *BIE, 19* (1965) and *21* (1966).

CHAPTER SEVEN

FURTHER DEVELOPMENTS OF CIVILIZATION IN NORTH CHINA TO 221 B.C.

The nucleus of the Shang civilization, as outlined above, was probably confined to the northern third of Honan and some of its immediate surrounding areas. While the Shang civilization flourished there Neolithic and sub-Neolithic cultures apparently continued in most of the rest of China. The Shang, however, was such a consolidated and vigorous power that its influence was widely felt, and there is archaeological evidence that Shang traits had probably penetrated into such distant places as the Liaotung Peninsula in the northeast, Chinese Turkestan in the west, and the South China coast. Whether the Shang civilization elements played consequential roles among these Neolithic and sub-Neolithic peoples is a question for discussion in subsequent chapters; at this juncture it can be said that in areas immediately adjacent to the Shang territory the Shang influence was significant enough to have stimulated societal changes in the native cultures. These areas will be discussed in Chapter 9, but one of them must be described here, for a civilization that emerged in the Wei-shui Valley, later known as the Chou, replaced the Shang after it was weakened by long and exhausting military involvement with some Huai Valley powers. Until the unification of China under Shih Huang Ti of the Ch'in Dynasty in 221 B.C., North China was dominated by the Chou.

The nine hundred years of the Chou period constituted an exciting epoch for the student of early China, because during it all aspects of Chinese civilization throughout the country underwent some elemental changes that brought about the end of formative Chinese antiquity and the beginning of Imperial China and its "traditional" pattern that was to last for the next two thousand years. A comprehensive description and discussion of Chou China is impossible in a brief chapter. Moreover, it would require much greater use of the written records—of which there are many—than the nature and scope of this volume would justify. But there are compelling reasons for some discussion of this period. First, the literary records of the period are still fragmentary and incomplete, and many aspects of the Chou civilization must depend upon the archaeological data, as will become self-evident below. Furthermore, the next two chapters will discuss the emergence of civilizations and states in other parts of China which took place in most cases as a result of the expansion of the northern Chinese civilizations. Without a brief description of events in the north during the Shang and Chou periods, contemporary events elsewhere in China become difficult to understand; nor could we even engage in a chronological study of these peripheral, but highly important, civilizations, most of which during the initial phases were illiterate.

A few historical dates are important for this chapter. According to the traditional Chinese chronology, the conquest, which caused the fall of the Shang and raised the Chou to the center of North China's historical stage, took place about 1122 B.C. Historians are not in agreement on this date, however, and no fewer than ten other dates have been suggested for this important historical event: 1116, 1111, 1070, 1067, 1066, 1050, 1047, 1030, 1027, and 1018.[1] Since the ancient Chinese calendrical system is still imperfectly known, the selection among these eleven different dates is more or less a matter of convenience—depending upon which date suits each author best for any particular historical problem. For the purpose of discussing civilizational and societal trends on a macroscopic scale, a precise dating of the conquest is of secondary importance; I shall, as stated before, use 1100 as an approximation.

The Chou period is ordinarily divided into the Western and Eastern Chou. The former designates the period during which the royal capitals of the Chou were located in the Weishui Valley of Shensi, of which Hao, near Sian, was the best known and probably the most important. Eastern Chou refers to the period following the removal in 771 B.C. of the royal capital to Lo-yang in western Honan, under the reign of P'ing Wang. Eastern Chou is divisible into two minor periods, Ch'un-ch'iu, or Spring and Autumn, and Chan-kuo, or Warring States. The dividing date between these two stages is vari-

1. Tung Tso-pin, *Bull. College of Arts, Natl. Taiwan Univ., 3* (1951), 178. Chou Fa-kao, *Harvard Jour. Asiatic Studies, 23* (1960–61), 108–12.

ously set at 481, 478, 468, 453, and 403. For our purpose, round figures are again sufficient: 770 for the beginning of the Eastern Chou and 450 for the beginning of the Warring States period. These are all political events, and for cultural historical studies other subdivisions are often made, as will be made clear below.

CHOU BEFORE THE CONQUEST

In the study of early China few topics are more difficult to define than the interrelationship of the Shang and the Chou. In his famous essay, *Yin Chou Chih-tu Lun* (*On the Institutions of the Yin and the Chou*), Wang Kuo-wei, one of the most brilliant and literate scholars of modern China, argued that "the change and revolution in Chinese politics and culture have never been greater than those that took place between Yin and Chou." The capitals of the ancient rulers from the Five Emperors to the Shang had been in the east, according to Wang; only the Chou arose in the west. But the shift from Shang to Chou was more than a change in ruling clans or capitals; "in essence, it signifies the fall of old institutions and the rise of new ones; the fall of old cultures and the rise of new ones."[2] Wang enumerated the following new institutions and cultures of the Chou that distinguish them from their Shang predecessors: the system of political succession by the primary son of the primary wife, which gave rise to the *tsung fa* lineage and the mortuary system that, in turn, were at the root of the *feng chien* ("feudal") system; the plan of the ancestral temples; and the marriage taboo within the clans. In the same vein, the late Fu Ssu-nien divided the ancient ethnic groups of China into the western Hsia and the contrastive eastern Yi, thus making the conquest an outcome of a perennial ethnic conflict—a triumph of the Chou, a Hsia tribe, over the Shang, a Yi tribe.[3]

There is no question that the conquest was a political upheaval of the first magnitude that affected the total alignment of the political map of ancient China. Nor is there any doubt that the ruling families of the Shang (Tzu) and of the Chou (Chi) came from different parts of

2. Wang Kuo-wei, *Kuan T'ang Chi Lin,* new printing, Taipei, Yi-wen Press, 1956, p. 116 (original publication 1923).

3. Fu Ssu-nien, *Ch'ing-chu Ts'ai Yüan-p'ei Hsien-sheng Liu-shih-wu Sui Lunwen Chi,* Peiping, Institute of History and Philology, Academia Sinica, 1933, pt. 2.

North China with somewhat different subcultural heritages. To what extent the conquest was an event of "cultural" significance in the total picture of ancient Chinese history, however, is a highly debatable point. Did the Chou have a separate civilization of their own that was comparable to the Shang in magnitude and intensity but was different in style and replaced the Shang civilization after the conquest? Or was the Chou civilization primarily a local manifestation of the Shang so that the conquest resulted merely in its propagation? To answer these questions we must take a look at the Chou culture before the conquest to see how far it had developed and how different it was from the Shang. What happened after the conquest and what contributions the Chou brought to Chinese civilization will be described in the following sections of this chapter.

The legendary ancestor of the Chou rulers, known as Hou Chi or Ch'i, had his own myth of birth. According to Ssu-ma Ch'ien,

> Hou Chi's mother, a daughter of the tribe Yu-yi, was known as Chiang Yüan. Chiang Yüan was the first consort of Ti K'u. Once Chiang Yüan was out in the field and saw a giant's footprint. She was delighted and desired to fit her own foot into it. She did so and she became pregnant. After the usual interval of time, she gave birth to a child, Ch'i [*Shih Chi,* vol. 4].

The *Book of Odes* locates the birthplace of Hou Chi at Yu-yi, which has been identified with several places in the middle Weishui Valley of Shensi and the lower Fenho Valley of Shansi. It has been well established, in any case, that the Chou had settled in the Weishui Valley since the reign of T'ai Wang at the latest, who is said to have moved to Ch'i, near the modern city of Pao-chi in the middle Weishui. T'ai Wang was the great-grandfather of Wu Wang, under whom the conquest was accomplished. There is no question that for at least four generations the seat of the state of Chou was the Weishui Valley of Shensi, during a later part of the Shang Dynasty.

Archaeological excavations of the lower Fenho and the Wenshui valleys have established the fact that the ancient cultural sequence in these regions is a succession of Yang-shao Neolithic, Lung-shan Neolithic, and Western Chou. Western Chou remains in the Weishui Valley were identified and excavated by Hsü Ping-ch'ang, Su Ping-ch'i, and Shih Chang-ju during the 1930s and 1940s,[4] but it was not until the early fifties that the Neolithic–Chou sequence began to be clearly defined and formulated. At K'o-hsing-chuang, near Sian, Su Ping-ch'i and Wu Ju-tso grouped the early cultural remains according to stratigraphic evidence into three classes: Yang-shao, Lung-shan, and Chou, and characterized the Chou stratum as follows:[5]

> Gray pottery with relatively homogeneous color, wheel marks, angular rims, and clearly defined decorative cord marks confined to the body parts of vessels; *li* tripods with low feet, low collars, and nearly flat bottoms; basins, *tou,* and plain jugs with undecorated surfaces.

Nine localities in the neighborhood of Sian are assigned by Su and Wu to the Chou stratum; these are characterized by deep cultural deposits, rectangular pits, graves containing human sacrifices, and relatively concentrated habitations.

The important question at the moment is not whether Chou civilization was later than the Neolithic stage in time, which is certainly the case, but whether in archaeological remains we can identify the period of the Western Chou before their conquest of the Shang. We know from *chia ku* scripts that during the Yin phase of the Shang period the Chou were referred to as a powerful subordinate state to be reckoned with. Archaeological remains of Shang types have been located in the Weishui Valley in a Neolithic context,[6] but archaeological remains of the Chou demonstrably contemporary with the Shang have been wanting. Ritual bronzes and large tombs of the Chou period have long been known in the Weishui Valley, but all that have been found thus far seem to date within the latter part of the Western Chou Dynasty.[7]

If there was a Chou civilization comparable in magnitude and in-

4. Shih Chang-ju, *BIHP, 27* (1956), 205–323. Su Ping-ch'i, *Tou-chi-t'ai Kou-tung-ch'ü mu-tsang,* Peiping, National Academy of Peiping, 1948. Hsü Ping-ch'ang and Ch'ang Hui, *Bull. Peiping Acad. Sci.,* vol. 4, no. 6.

5. *KKTH* (1956/2), 36.

6. Shih Chang-ju, *BIHP, 27* (1956), 315. Hsü Yi, *WWTKTL* (1956/3), 65.

7. The only existing inscribed bronze vessel that *could* date from the pre-conquest period of Western Chou history is the so-called *T'ien-wang Kui;* see Sun Tso-yün, *WWTKTL* (1958/1), 29–31; Ch'ien Po-ch'üan, *WWTKTL* (1958/12), 56–57; Sun Tso-yün, *WW* (1960/5), 50–52; Yin Ti-fei, *WW* (1960/5), 53–54.

tensity with the Shang civilization in Honan, its ruins and relics should at least exist around the capitals of Wen Wang and Wu Wang, probably in an area southwest of the modern city of Sian on the banks of the Feng River. Archaeological explorations in this area will be described below. The modern village of Chang-chia-p'o and its environs have yielded the largest amount of relics dating to the Western Chou period. Between 1955 and 1957 a habitation area and a number of human burials were excavated; two occupational components were distinguished at the habitation area, and the tombs have been grouped into five stages. The early occupational stratum of the habitation area antedates the earliest burials which have been dated to Ch'eng and K'ang, the two kings who reigned immediately after Wu Wang, according to the typology of the bronze vessels found in the tombs, which are comparable with bronze vessels of known date. The site therefore must have been inhabited before King Ch'eng. Since the region was not a major Chou area until Wen Wang, it is possible that the early habitation component of the Chang-chia-p'o site can be dated to Kings Wen Wang and Wu Wang, that is, to the Chou immediately before and after the conquest.[8] The cultural remains at the site thus have a direct bearing on the level of culture of the Chou at that time.

Archaeological remains uncovered from this early habitation stratum indicate very strongly that during its occupation—which probably contained the period of Chou before the conquest—the Chou was already a bronze-making culture with a sophisticated social organization. Many bronze implements were found at the site, including a socketed ax, 15 knives, 62 arrowheads, and several horse and chariot fittings. The knives are characteristically bent, with a concave back and equipped with a square loop at the end (Fig 89), distinct from the common Shang types at Hsiao-t'un, and the arrowheads also differ from the Hsiao-t'un types in minor features.[9] It is not clear from the report of the site whether these bronze implements came from the early stratum or from a later occupation (also Western Chou but near the end), but from the early occupation four pieces of clay molds (for casting horse and chariot fittings) were excavated, indicating that dur-

8. Wang Po-hung et al., *Feng Hsi Fa-chüeh Pao-kao,* Peking, Wenwu Press, 1962.

9. Compared with Hsiao-t'un types described in Li Chi, *Bull. College of Arts, Natl. Taiwan Univ., 4* (1952), 179–240.

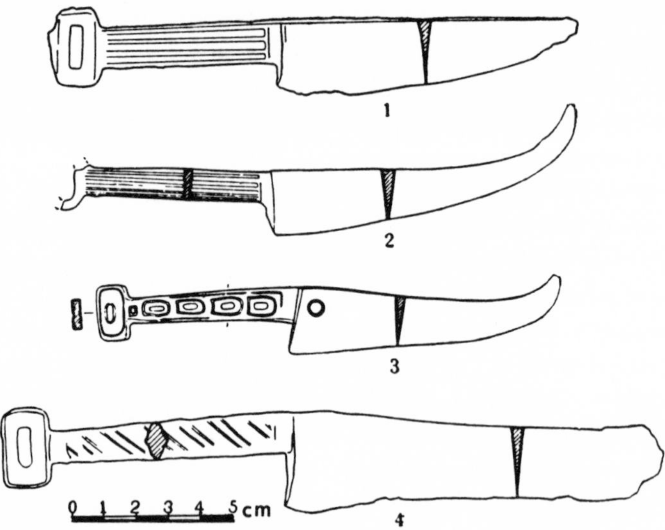

89. Bronze knives of early Western Chou from the Chang-chia-p'o site, Sian, Shensi. (From *Feng Hsi Fa-chüeh Pao-kao,* Peking, Wenwu Press, 1962, p. 83.)

ing the early period the Chou were not only bronze-casters in the Shang tradition but also horse-chariot warriors. Also from the early period was a workshop that manufactured only hairpins and arrowheads of bone and antler. The bone hairpins are of several types, but all find counterparts in the specimens from Hsiao-t'un and Hsi-pei-kang.[10]

Apparently the Chang-chia-p'o village of the early Western Chou period provided some essential services to the men of the upper classes whose center of activity was in the cities (Feng and/or Hao) nearby that remain to be identified. Presumably a great deal more will be known about the level of achievement of Chou civilization when these city sites have been identified, but the new data from Chang-chia-p'o suffice to show that the Chou before the conquest had already achieved a level much higher than the Neolithic K'o-hsing-chuang culture (Shensi Lung-shan culture) of the same area, from which, or from a

10. Li Chi, *BIHP, 30* (1959), 1–69.

culture similar to which, the Chou were apparently derived. It would indeed be strange if the Chou, who were able to overthrow the powerful government of the Shang Dynasty at An-yang, were still at a barbarous Neolithic level of culture and came empty-handed into the Shang legacy.[11]

MAJOR SITES OF THE CHOU

For a civilization like the Chou, whose temporal duration was close to a millennium and whose areal expanse covered most of China, it is no longer possible to enumerate all the important archaeological sites or necessary to describe even the most characteristic. But the nucleus of the Western Chou civilization, located in the neighborhood of Sian, Shensi, must be discussed. By the time the royal capital had shifted to Lo-yang in western Honan, a series of local states had risen to eminence, each achieving its own subcivilization within a Chou Chinese common framework. The archaeological data from the Lo-yang area must of course be described, and some local subcivilizations whose archaeological data are abundant will be included. Then, using data from these areas and from other sites throughout China, I shall discuss the developmental trends of the Chou civilization in several archaeologically most important aspects.

The Sian Area

From Hou Chi to Wu Wang, five or six capitals of the Western Chou Dynasty were recorded in historical literature. Of these, the last one, Hao, was the most important, not only because it provided the center of stage for Wu Wang's conquest but also because it served as the seat of power for twelve kings from Wu Wang to Yu Wang for a period of 352 years (1122–771 B.C.). The exact location of Hao has been described in historical records, and there is little question that it was in an area southwest of the modern city of Sian, in Shensi Province, on the east bank of the River Feng, a

11. See Magdalene von Dewall, *Symposium in Honor of Dr. Li Chi on His Seventieth Birthday* (Taipei, *The Ch'ing-hua Journal*), pt. 2, 1966, 1–68, for a discussion of the "creative" aspects of the Chou as against the Shang according to the Hsin Ts'un finds.

small tributary of the Weishui River in the north. On the west bank of the same river is said to be the site of Feng, Wen Wang's capital for only fifteen years. Although the capital was moved across the river to Hao, Feng remained the site of the royal temples. The well-drained plain west of Sian, located between the Tsinling Mountains in the south and the Wei River in the north, was thus the center of the Royal Chou until they came to an end in 771 B.C.[12] The Han historian Pan Ku, writing toward the end of the first century of the present era, praised this region thus,[13]

> In abundance of flowering plants and fruits it is the most fertile of the Nine Provinces
>
> In natural barriers for protection and defense it is the most impregnable refuge in heaven and earth
>
> This is why its influence has extended in six directions
> This is why it has thrice become the seat of imperial power

The last line "refers to the successful use of the area as a center of power by the Chou who launched from this plain their conquest of the Shang, by the Ch'in, the creators of unified empire, and by the great Han during the first two centuries of their rule."[14]

The archaeological investigations of the Chou settlements in the Feng Hao area began in the 1930s, but not until the last decade was this region given the concentrated effort it deserves. Sites containing Western Chou remains appear to cluster in two loci on both banks of the Feng (Fig. 90). One is on the west bank from K'o-hsing-chuang in the northeast to Feng-ts'un in the southwest, in an area about 5 kilometers east–west and 2.5 kilometers north–south, a site approximating the location of the old capital Feng in the literature. The other, coinciding with the location of Hao, is on the east bank from Lo-shui-ts'un in the north to south of Tou-men-chen, covering an area about 4 kilometers north–south and 1.5 east–west. Outside these two clusters, isolated remains and ruins have been found throughout the neighbor-

12. Shih Chang-ju, *Ta-lu Tsa-chih T'eh-k'an, 1,* Taipei, Ta-lu Tsa-chih She, 1953. Hu Ch'ien-ying, *KK* (1963/4), 188–97.
13. Translated and quoted by Arthur F. Wright, *Jour. Asian Studies, 24* (1965), 668–69.
14. Ibid., p. 669.

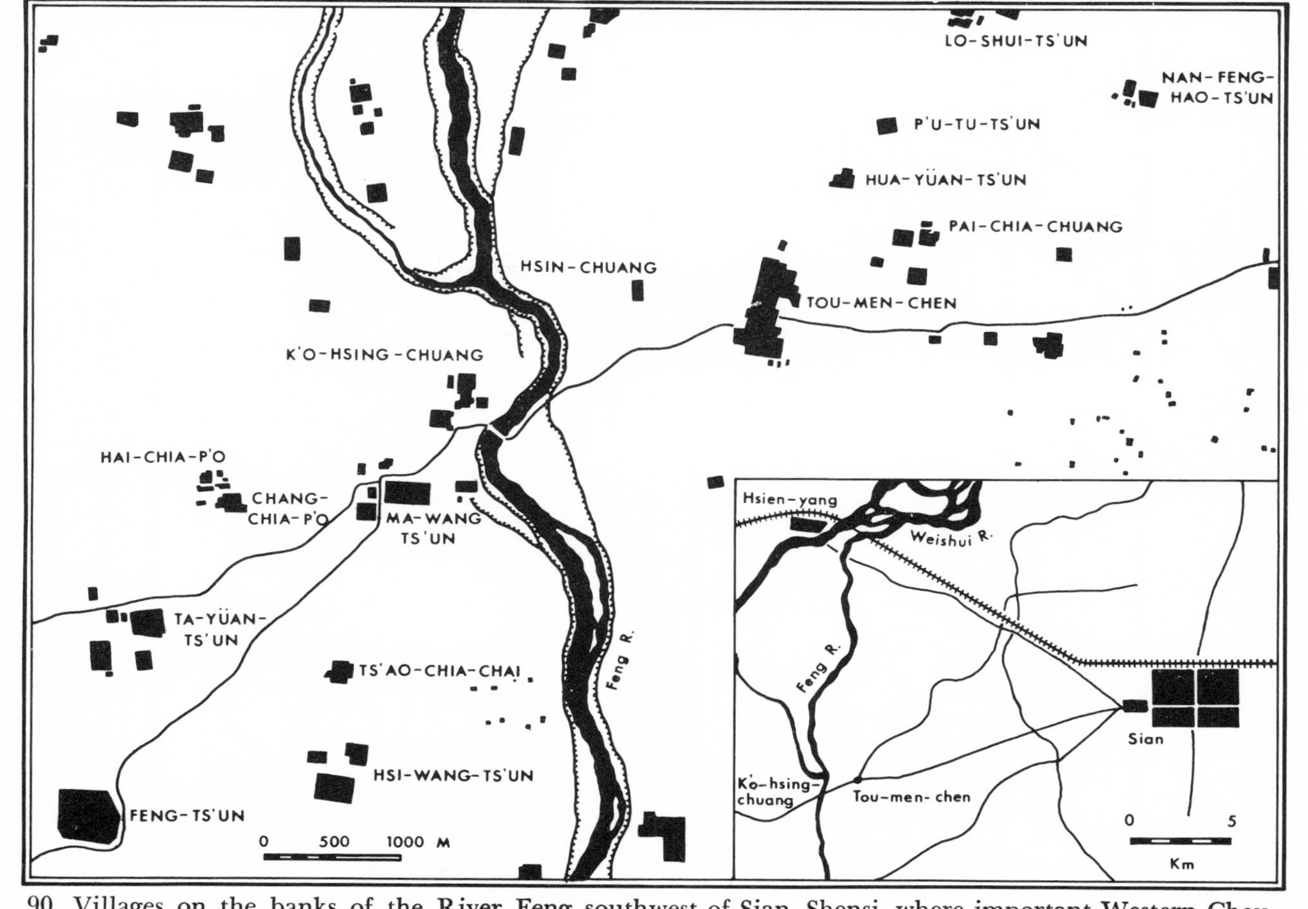

90. Villages on the banks of the River Feng southwest of Sian, Shensi, where important Western Chou sites have been discovered.

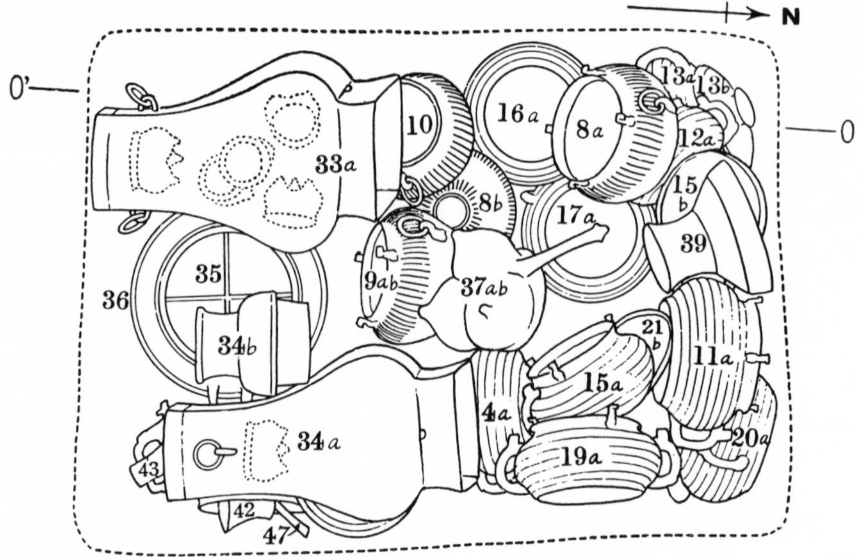

91. A hoard of Western Chou bronze vessels found at Ma-wang-ts'un, Sian. (From *Ch'ang-an Chang-chia-p'o T'ung-ch'i Ch'ün,* 1965, p. 12.)

hood.[15] For the sake of convenience, I refer to the cluster of sites on the west and east banks as the Feng and Hao areas respectively.

The Feng area has yielded a large number of Western Chou remains as a result of intensive excavations since 1955. The area west of the village of Chang-chia-p'o is the best known: dwelling remains, 136 tombs, and 4 horse-and-chariot burials excavated in 1955–57;[16] dwelling remains, 4 burials, and 1 horse-and-chariot burial in 1960;[17] and a large tomb with ceremonial bronzes in 1964.[18] East of Chang-chia-p'o in the vicinity of the village of Ma-wang-ts'un, dwelling remains were brought to light during 1959–60;[19] a hoard of 53 bronze vessels (11 of which were inscribed) was uncovered in 1961 (Fig. 91);[20] and

15. Hsü Hsi-t'ai, *KK* (1962/6), 306–07.

16. Wang Po-hung et al., *Feng-hsi Fa-chüeh Pao-kao; KK* (1959/10), 516–30. Ho Han-nan and T'ang Chin-yü, *KK* (1964/9), 441–47, 474.

17. Yang Kuo-chung and Chang Ch'ang-yüan, *KK* (1962/1), 20–22.

18. Chao Yüng-fu, *KK* (1965/9), 447–50.

19. Hsü Hsi-t'ai, *KK* (1962/6), 307–09.

20. *Ch'ang-an Chang-chia-p'o Hsi Chou t'ung-chi ch'ün,* Peking, Wenwu Press, 1965.

a large tomb with 28 bronze vessels was investigated in 1963.[21] North of Ma-wang-ts'un, in the K'o-hsing-chuang area, habitation remains and 51 tombs of the Western Chou period were excavated during 1955–57.[22] Southwest of Chang-chia-p'o, near the village of Ta-yüan-ts'un, habitation remains, wells, and burials were excavated during 1959–60.[23] We know that habitation debris is scattered throughout the area; that "workshops" for bone, pottery, bronze, and tile have been found at various localities; that tombs of various kinds with furnishings of varying degrees of luxuriousness (including a few with up to four human sacrificial victims for a single tomb) are scattered; and that horse-chariot burials were constructed presumably to accommodate some departed noblemen. The remains in the whole area range in date from possibly the Wen Wang reign through the end of the Western Chou. Apparently this Feng area was a major center of cultural activity during the entire Western Chou period, and the royal capital of Feng is perhaps still buried, to be brought to light in the future. Until that happens, however, the pattern and history of settlement west of the Feng River remains unknown.

It is significant, however, that the 182 tombs in the Chang-chia-p'o and K'o-hsiang-chuang area excavated during 1955–57 by the Institute of Archaeology (Academia Sinica, Peking) were apparently constructed throughout the span of the Western Chou's some 330 years, and the typology of artifacts and tomb construction here constitutes a complete sequence of development that can well serve as a standard scale for other Western Chou sites in the vicinity and beyond. Five major typological phases have been distinguished, primarily on the basis of ceramic types (Fig. 92), and habitation remains throughout the Feng area have been cross-dated with the tombs accordingly.

Compared with the Feng area, there are fewer archaeological remains in the Hao area. Historical records relate that during the T'ang Dynasty the construction of a K'un-ming Lake in the royal gardens destroyed a good part of the ancient ruins of Hao, which could account for the relative scarcity of remains of Western Chou date, but exploration is only just beginning. Large tombs with a ritual bronze vessel dating to the reign of Mu Wang in the early part of Western Chou,

21. Liang Hsing-ping and Feng Hsiao-t'ang, *KK* (1963/8), 413–15.
22. Wang Po-hung et al., *Feng-hsi Fa-chüeh Pao-kao; KK* (1959/10), 516–30.
23. Hsü Hsi-t'ai, *KK* (1962/6), 309.

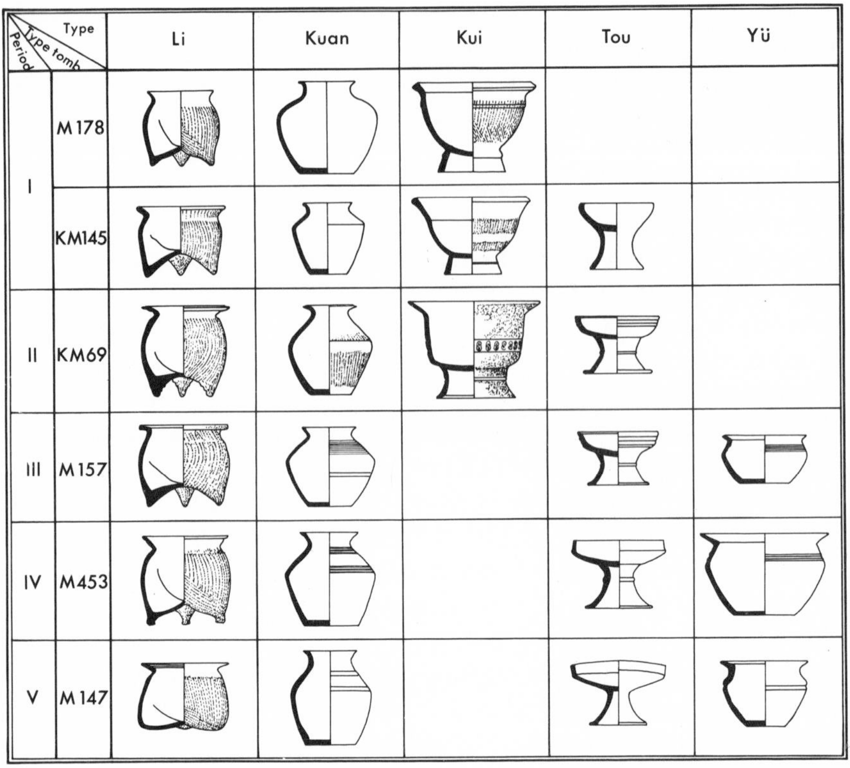

Period / Type tomb / Type		Li	Kuan	Kui	Tou	Yü
I	M178					
	KM145					
II	KM69					
III	M157					
IV	M453					
V	M147					

92. Characteristic pottery types of the five stages of Western Chou tombs in the area of Sian, Shensi. (From *Feng-hsi Fa-chüeh Pao-kao,* 1962.)

were uncovered in 1954 and 1955,[24] and large areas of habitation and burial remains have been located from Pai-chia-chuang in the south to Lo-shui-ts'un in the north.[25] If this was indeed the old site of Hao, further investigations in the area and in the interrelationship of the Hao government center and the Feng temple area of the Royal Chou will be extremely revealing and important for Western Chou archaeology.

Other Western Chou Sites

Prior to the establishment of the Chou in the Sian area the Chou ancestors are said to have emerged either in the upper Weishui in

24. Shih Hsing-pang, *KKHP, 8* (1954). Ho Han-nan, *KKHP* (1957/1), 75–85.
25. Hu Ch'ien-ying, *KK* (1963/8), 403–12.

western Shensi[26] or in the Huangho Valley in southern Shansi.[27] In either area the available archaeological data cannot push back the Western Chou civilization (as known in its earliest manifestation at Chang-chia-p'o, Sian) in time, and the Neolithic sites characterized by the gray corded pottery (of the K'o-hsing-chuang culture) everywhere preceded the known Western Chou remains. The initial base of the Western Chou in the Weishui Valley and in southern Shansi and the Shang territory in western and northern Honan constituted the area of effective control of the new Western Chou Dynasty (immediately or some time) after the conquest about 1100 B.C.

Events that took place during the decade after the conquest were highly important in shaping the subsequent developments. Wu Wang captured Wu Keng, Crown Prince of the Shang Dynasty, but let him continue to head the fallen dynasty at Yin under the tutelage of Princes Kuan, Ts'ai, and Huo, three of Wu Wang's many brothers. The Shang, however, continued to claim the loyalty of the people in the old Shang territory in eastern Honan, Shantung, and northern Anhwei. Seven years after the conquest, Wu Wang died. His successor, Ch'eng Wang, was young, and he ascended the throne under the regency of his uncle Chou Kung, another younger brother of Wu Wang. Taking advantage of the unstable situation, Prince Kuan and Wu Keng, with the support of the former Shang vassal states in the east, rebelled against the new regime. Thereupon Chou Kung embarked on a series of moves that resulted in the thorough subjugation of all the Shang territory. First, having recaptured Yin and executed Prince Kuan and Wu Keng, he appointed another brother, Prince K'ang, the Duke of Wei, to rule the old Shang royal territory; second, he moved farther east and conquered the state of Yen in western Shantung, where he created the state of Lu and appointed his son, Po Ch'in, its duke; third, he built an eastern capital at Lo-yang in western Honan to facilitate total control of the eastern parts of North China. Thus, Wu Wang merely conquered the Shang Dynasty, but Chou Kung unified the Shang and Chou territories into a Chou China. The regimes immediately after Chou Kung, those of Ch'eng (Chou Kung stepped down when the boy was old enough to rule) and K'ang, were the peaks of Western Chou royal power, reaching beyond the civilized

26. Shih Chang-ju, *Ta-lu Tsa-chih T'eh-k'an, 1.*
27. Ch'ien Mu, *Yenching Jour. Chinese Studies, 10* (1926), 1,955–2,008.

areas of the Shang and the Chou into the north (as far as Inner Mongolia) and the south (as far as beyond the Yangtze Valley).

Archaeological assemblages of bronzes, the surest indications of the political and ritual aspects of the Royal Chou regime, that are dated by inscriptions, typology, and context between shortly after the conquest to the reigns of the last Western Chou kings, have been unearthed in the old Chou domain of Shensi and Shansi, in the old Shang territory of Honan and Shantung, and also in areas farther north and south in the newly civilized areas of China (Fig. 93). In most cases they came from tombs, but in a few instances hoards of bronze vessels were found, probably indicating the burial of ritual treasures at times of upheaval. In the Shensi and Shansi region they included such significant finds as those in Pao-chi,[28] Mi Hsien,[29] Fu-feng,[30] and Lan-t'ien[31] in Shensi;[32] and Hung-chao[33] and Yi-ch'eng[34] in Shansi. In the old Shang domain Western Chou finds occurred in Lo-yang,[35] Chün Hsien,[36] and Huai-yang[37] in Honan; and Tsou Hsien[38] in Shantung. Farther north, a Western Chou bronze assemblage was found in Ling-yüan in Jehol.[39] It is even said that the masked horses at Chang-chia-p'o were probably the prototype of those at Pazyryk.[40] In the south, whole bronze assemblages of Western Chou types are known from Tan-t'u in

28. Su Ping-ch'i, *Tou-chi-t'ai Kou-tung-ch'ü mu-tsang*. Chao Hsüeh-ch'ien, *KK* (1963/10), 574–76. Umehara Sueji, *Research Report, no. 2, Kyoto Tōhō Bunka Kenkyū so,* 1933.

29. Li Ch'ang-ch'ing and T'ien Yieh, *WWTKTL* (1957/4), 5–9.

30. *Fu-feng Ch'i-chia-ts'un Ch'ing-t'ung-ch'i ch'ün,* Peking, Wenwu Press, 1963. Ch'en Kung-jou, *KK* (1962/2), 88–91. *WW* (1961/7), 59–60; (1963/9), 65–66. Chao Hsüeh-ch'ien, *KK* (1963/10), 574–76.

31. *WW* (1960/2), 5–10; (1960/8/9), 78–79. *KK* (1960/5), 33–36.

32. Other important Shensi bronzes of Western Chou date include *Ch'ing-t'ung-ch'i T'u Shih,* Peking, Wenwu Press, 1960; Tuan Shao-chia, *WW* (1963/3), 43–45; Ho Han-nan, *WW* (1964/7), 20–27; Tai Chung-hsien, *KK* (1965/3), 152; Chu Chieh-yüan and Hei Kuang, *WW* (1965/7), 17–19; Chu P'ei-chang et al., *WW* (1966/1), 1–6.

33. Wang Chi-sheng, *WWTKTL* (1955/4), 46–52; (1955/8), 42–44.

34. Li Fa-wang, *WW* (1963/4), 51–52; *KK* (1963/4), 225.

35. *KKTH* (1955/5), 30. *KK* (1959/4), 187. *WWTKTL* (1955/5), 116–17; (1955/6), 124. *Lo-yang Chung-chou-lu,* Peking, Science Press, 1959.

36. Kuo Pao-chün, *Chün Hsien Hsin-ts'un,* Peking, Science Press, 1964.

37. Liu Tung-ya, *KK* (1964/3), 163–64.

38. Wang Hsüan, *KK* (1965/11), 541–47.

39. *WWTKTL* (1955/8), 16–27.

40. John F. Haskins, *Arch. Chinese Art Soc. America, 16* (1962), 92–96.

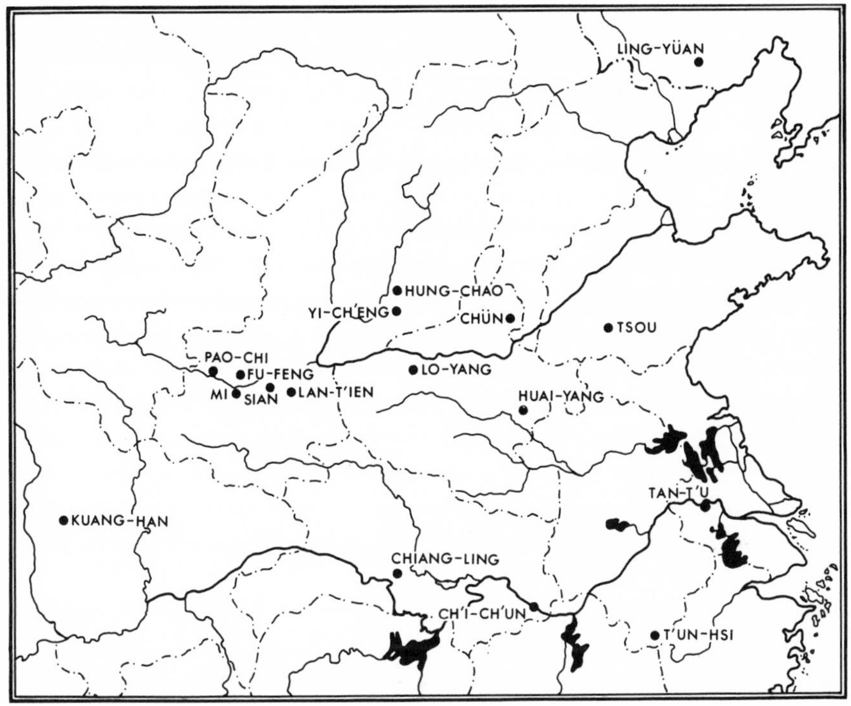

93. Major sites of the Western Chou

Kiangsu,[41] T'un-hsi in Anhwei,[42] Ch'i-ch'un[43] and Chiang-ling[44] in Hupei, and Kuang-han in Szechwan;[45] that is, throughout the Yangtze Valley. The glazed pottery from T'un-hsi is so similar to that at Chang-chia-p'o in technique of manufacture and mineral composition that scholars are convinced the Chang-chia-p'o pottery was imported from the south.[46] If this is true it is a significant indication of the extent of Western Chou contact and communication in the southern direction. Further discussion of the south will be undertaken in the final chapter.

41. *WWTKTL* (1955/5), 58–63; (1956/1), 45–46. T'ang Lan, *KKHP* (1959/2), 79–84.
42. Yin Ti-fei, *KKHP* (1959/4), 59–90.
43. Chang Yün-p'eng, *KK* (1962/1), 1–9.
44. Li Chien, *KK* (1963/4), 224–25. Wang Yü-t'ang, *WW* (1963/2), 53–55.
45. Cheng Te-k'un, *Hsieh-ta Jour. Chinese Studies, 1* (1949), 67–81.
46. Chou Jen et al., *KK* (1961/8), 444–45.

Other than indicating the extent of the Western Chou civilization, these sites and their various remains are of varying importance in the study of ancient China. Many bronzes are inscribed: one more inscribed bronze vessel means one more piece of textual material for the study of Western Chou society and history. The bronzes found in archaeological sites provide a body of data that not only helps to identify the thousands of unauthenticated ritual bronze vessels of the same period in public and private collections but provides a contextual background for the study of cultural associations and chronology. With these data, old and new, that furnish a series of bronze assemblages from the beginning to the end of Western Chou, historians and historians of art, as well as archaeologists, have a source of information far exceeding that provided by the pre-Ch'in texts. In addition to the bronzes and their inscriptions, these sites also tell scholars about the developments of technology, art, and burial customs, aspects that will be dealt with at some detail in the following sections.

The Lo-yang Area

Lo-yang in western Honan, like Sian, has been a city of great significance throughout Chinese history and served as the capital of the Empire repeatedly. The sites of the Lo-yang city (Fig. 94) during the various dynastic periods were not identical but were all situated in an area south of Mang Mountain where two small rivers, Chien in the west and Ch'an in the east, flow southward into the River Lo, a tributary of the Huangho. The present walled city of Lo-yang is on the west bank of the Ch'an, but most of the early ruins of Lo-yang occur in the suburban areas to its east and west. The city was built by Chou Kung at the site of an existing Shang settlement after his eastern military campaign and apparently consisted of two separate sites, Wang Ch'eng and Ch'eng Chou. Wang Ch'eng was in the western suburb of modern Lo-yang on the eastern bank of the River Chien, and Ch'eng Chou was east of Lo-yang, east of the River Ch'an. During the Han Dynasty, a new and smaller enclosure was built in the Wang Ch'eng area and was known as Ho-nan; the Han capital of Lo-yang was probably built at the site of Ch'eng Chou in the east.

Although the twin cities of Lo-yang were constructed at the beginning of Western Chou, archaeological remains in the Lo-yang area dating from Western Chou are relatively few, largely known at three

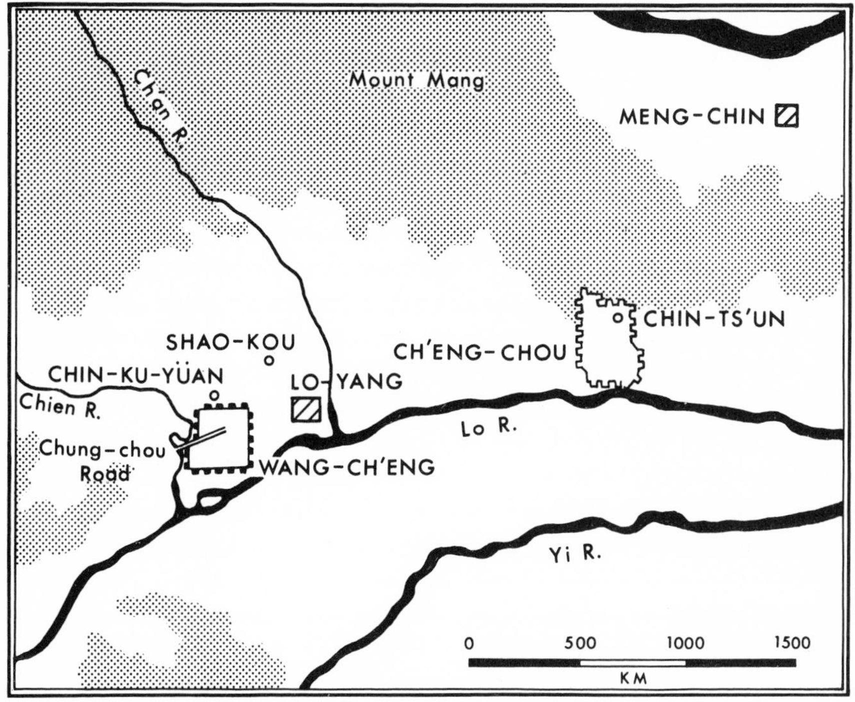

94. Eastern Chou sites in the Lo-yang area, Honan.

or four localities in the western,[47] northern,[48] and eastern[49] suburbs of modern Lo-yang. All of these are tombs. Remains of the Eastern Chou period increase noticeably in the Lo-yang area, which after 771 B.C. became the seat of the Royal Chou. When additional data from the Western Chou period become known, especially data concerning Wang Ch'eng and Ch'eng Chou, a comparison between the Western Chou and the Eastern Chou cities of Lo-yang will be interesting.

Major Eastern Chou remains at Lo-yang are known from four archaeological loci: the Wang Ch'eng walls, the Chung-chou Road, and Shao-kou on the Wang Ch'eng side, and Chin Ts'un on the Ch'eng Chou side. The walls of Wang Ch'eng were outlined during 1954–58;[50]

47. *Lo-yang Chung-chou-lu,* pp. 139–40. Li Yang-sung and Yen Wen-ming, *KK* (1961/4), 178.

48. *KKTH* (1955/5), 30. *KK* (1959/4), 187. *WWTKTL* (1955/5), 116–17; (1955/6), 124. Ho Kuan-pao, *WW* (1964/9), 54–55.

49. Kuo Pao-chün and Lin Shou-chin, *KKHP, 9* (1955), 104–08.

50. Ch'en Kung-jou, *KKHP* (1959/2), 15–36.

a study of the Eastern Chou relics in relation to the city wall will bring to light some aspects of the pattern of urbanism in a Chou royal capital for the first time and will be described below. The tombs at both Shao-kou[51] and Chin-ts'un[52] are dated to the Warring States period. The Chin-ts'un tombs were particularly prolific in fine specimens of art and vessels with inscriptions pertaining to affairs of various states, attesting to the continuing role of the Royal Chou as the center of some ritual and social transactions throughout North China.

Eastern Chou sites along the Chung-chou Road[53] are of special significance in yielding remains dating from the Eastern Chou period of more than half a millennium and providing a master sequence against which other Eastern Chou sites can be measured for chronological placement. In the last decade a new urban expansion project took place in the western suburbs of Lo-yang, and a main road, Chung-chou-lu, was constructed between the old walled city of modern Lo-yang and the new housing area, from the western bank of the Ch'an River to the eastern bank of the Chien River; it cuts across the middle of the Wang Ch'eng city site. In 1954 and 1955, archaeologists investigated the Chung-chou Road for a 2,100-meter distance to the east from the eastern bank of the Chien, bringing to light an east–west cross section of the Eastern Chou city. Yang-shao, Shang, and Chou (both Western and Eastern) storage pits were found, but the largest group of remains consisted of 260 burials of the Eastern Chou. On the basis of stratigraphy and the association patterns of some characteristic pottery vessel types, Su Ping-ch'i, An Chih-min, and Lin Shou-chin have grouped the 260 tombs into seven periods (dates are approximate and furnished by the present author): (1) Early Spring Autumn (770–670 B.C.); (2) Middle Spring Autumn (670–570); (3) Late Spring Autumn (570–470); (4) Early Warring States (470–400); (5, 6) Middle Warring States (400–300); (7) Late Warring States (300–220) (Fig. 95). This is the longest single typological sequence of Eastern Chou archaeological remains to date, and many other Eastern Chou sites in North China can be placed according to this sevenfold scheme on the basis of their bronze and ceramic types.

51. Wang Chung-shu, *KKHP, 8* (1954), 127–62.

52. William C. White, *Tombs of Old Lo-yang,* Shanghai, Kelly & Walsh, 1934. S. Umehara, *Rakuyō Kinson Kobo shūei,* Kyoto, Hayashi Press, 1936.

53. *Lo-yang Chung-chou-lu.*

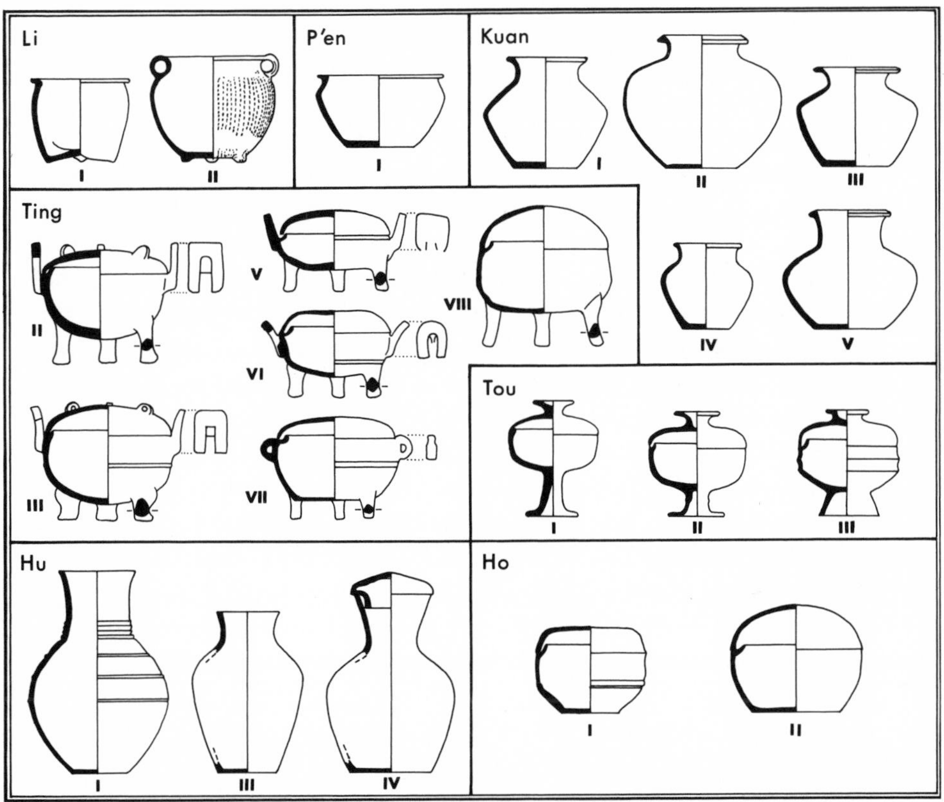

Associations / Periods	Li – P'en – Kuan	Ting – Tou – Kuan	Ting – Tou – Hu	Ting – Ho – Hu
I	I – I – I I – I – II			
II	II – I – II			
III	II – I – III II – I – IV	II – I – III II – I – IV		
IV		II – I – V	II – I – I II – II – I III – II – I	
V		V – II – V	V – II – I V – II – III	
VI		VI – III – V	VI – III – III	
VII		VII – III – V	VII – III – III	VII – I – III VIII – II – IV

95. Characteristic pottery types of the seven stages of Eastern Chou tombs of Chung-chou-lu, Lo-yang. (Based on *Lo-yang Chung-chou-lu*, 1959.)

Other Eastern Chou Sites

The eighth and seventh centuries B.C. were a great turning point in the ancient history of China—a turning point that was probably of even greater consequence than the Wu Wang and Chou Kung conquests of the eleventh century in long-term developmental trends of the Chinese civilization. The Royal Chou's power had weakened toward the beginning of the eighth century to such an extent that the growing pressure of the warlike mounted nomads in the northwest became unbearable, and the capital had to be moved, in 771 B.C., to Lo-yang. In inverse proportion to the dwindling status of the Royal Chou, the local lords of the feudal states, appointed in the beginning of the Western Chou Dynasty mainly from among the royal brothers and relatives, grew more prosperous, mighty, and independent. The archaeological remains of the Eastern Chou period (Fig. 96) show this new trend of development in several ways. Rich assemblages of bronzes and other artifacts found at large habitation sites and lavishly furnished tombs are now commonplace throughout China. Many inscribed pieces show they were made for the stately courts and local lords, in contrast to the Western Chou pieces which concerned either the Royal Chou themselves or the Chou relatives. It is now no longer practical to describe or enumerate the sites of the period under a simple heading of "Eastern Chou"; rather, important finds must be referred to the states to which they belonged (Fig. 97). The number of walled city sites, now scattered over the country, drastically increased, testifying to the growing localization of political and military affairs. Data for the following discussion of cultural developments must be selected, for my purpose here is not to compile a complete catalogue of archaeological finds. A number of classical or extremely important sites, however, must not be left unmentioned.

In the *area of Chin*—the biggest of the Eastern Chou states, which includes the modern southern Shansi, southern Hopei, and northern Honan and broke up around 450 B.C. into three smaller states, Chao, Wei, and Han—large and well-known sites of Eastern Chou are the most numerous. In the region of Chao[54] are two well-known sites

54. Region of Chao and of Wei and Han below, is used only to identify the location of sites and does not necessarily indicate that the sites were within these states, which were not formed before 453 B.C.

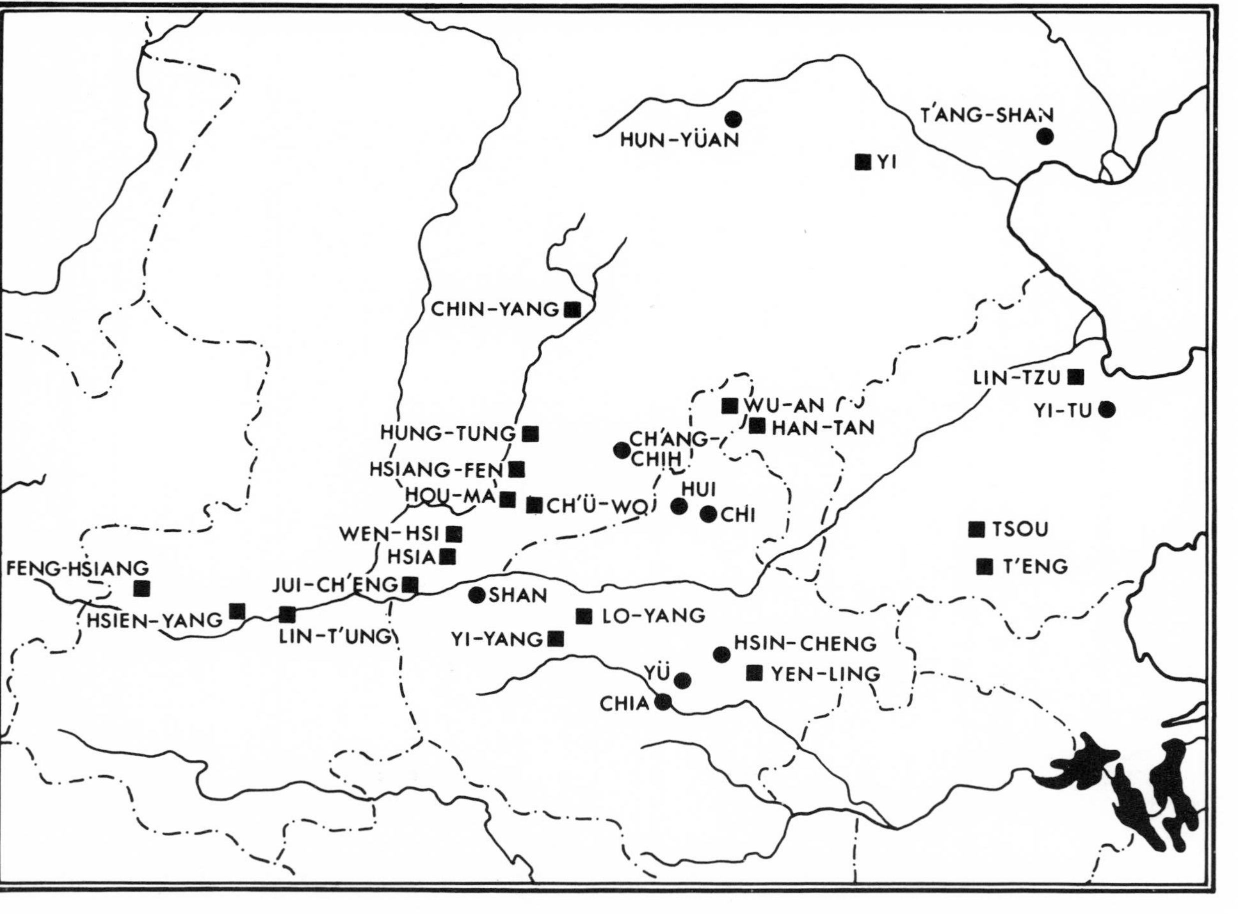

96. Major sites of the Eastern Chou civilization. (*Circles,* tombs only; *squares,* city ruins.)

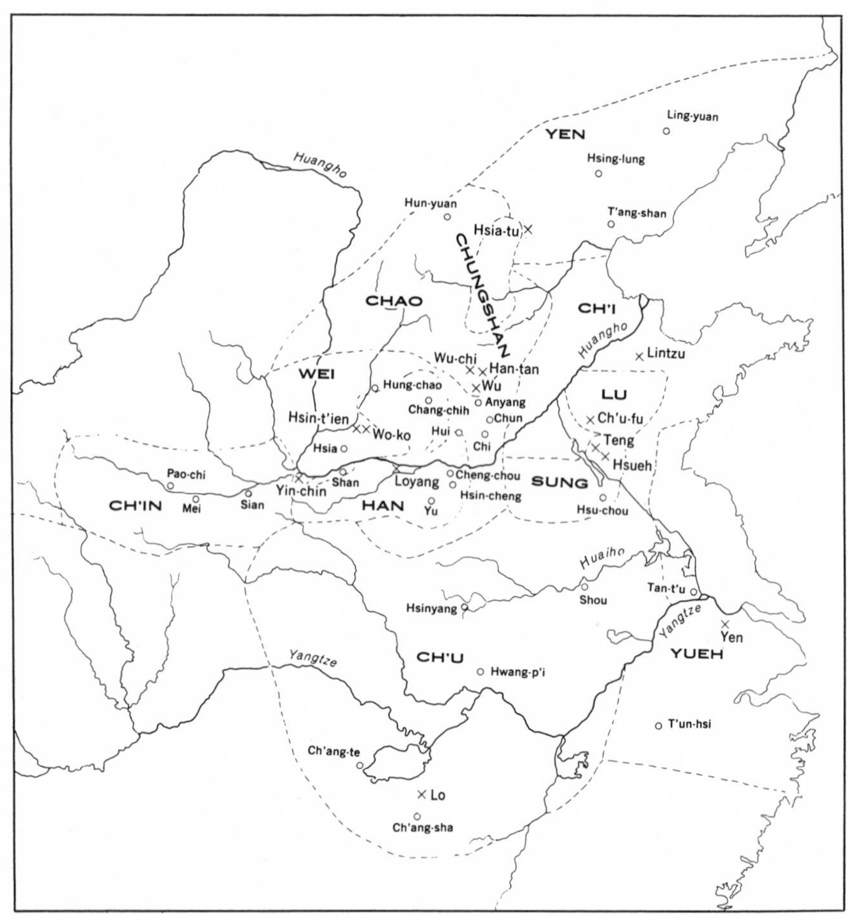

97. Important Bronze Age sites in China in relation to the boundaries in the Warring States period, at approximately 350 B.C. (State boundaries drawn after Yang K'uan, *Chan Kuo Shih,* Shanghai, Jenmin Press, 1957.)

found before World War II, Li-yü-ts'un in Hun-yüan, northern Shansi,[55] and Han-tan, in southern Hopei.[56] Li-yü-ts'un, a tomb of the Warring States period discovered by accident in 1923, was one of the earliest sites found in modern Chinese archaeology and is often used to illustrate the Warring States types of bronzes. The Han-tan

55. Shang Ch'eng-tso, *Hun-yüan Yi-ch'i,* Shanghai, 1936.
56. Komai Kazuchika and Sekino Takeshi, *Han-tan,* Archaeologia Orientalis, ser. B, 7, 1954.

city site, Chao's capital during 386–228 B.C., was investigated in a preliminary manner before the war, and recent work around it has uncovered many contemporary remains of various kinds.

The region of Wei in southern Shansi and northern Honan includes the remains of an important urban complex near the town of Hou-ma (Shansi)[57] and a series of tombs at Fen-shui-ling, in Ch'ang-chih (Shansi),[58] and at Liu-li-ko and Ku-wei-ts'un in Hui Hsien[59] and Shan-piao-chen in Chi Hsien,[60] northern Honan. The tombs here provide some of the best samples of Warring States artifacts, and the bronze vessels and iron implements are used as type specimens of the period. The city site of Hou-ma consists of a complex of earthen enclosures, a ceremonial locus, farming villages, and workshops, and is perhaps one of the three or four best-known city sites in the archaeology of ancient China.

Farther south in the region of Han, at the heart of Honan, three well-known bronze assemblages were found in tombs in Hsin-cheng,[61] at Pai-sha in Yü Hsien,[62] and at T'ai-p'u-hsiang in Chia Hsien.[63] Of these, the Hsin-cheng bronzes were among the earliest found of the Chou period (1923), and their dating problem has engaged the attention of scholars for many years.

Important sites in the area of Chin must include the burials at Shang-ts'un-ling in Shan Hsien, westernmost Honan.[64] Inscribed bronzes found here ascribe the burials to the state of Kuo, a small state annexed by Chin in 655 B.C., thus providing a rare find that dates during the crucial period from late Western Chou through the early Spring Autumn period.

In the *area of Yen* northeast of Chin, the city site of Hsia-tu in Yi

57. See below, pp. 283–87.

58. Ch'ang Wen-chai, *KKHP* (1957/1), 103–18. *WW* (1957/12), 77. Pien Ch'eng-hsiu et al., *KK* (1964/3), 111–37.

59. Hsia Nai et al., *Hui Hsien Fa-chüeh Pao-kao,* Peking, Science Press, 1956. Kuo Pao-chün, *Shan-piao-chen yü Liu-li-ko,* Peking, Science Press, 1959.

60. Kuo Pao-chün, *ibid;* 1959.

61. Carl W. Bishop, *Chinese Jour. Science and Arts, 3* (1925), 72–74. Sun Hai-p'o, *Hsin-cheng yi ch'i,* K'ai-feng, 1937. Kuan Po-yi, *Cheng chung ku-ch'i t'u-k'ao,* Shanghai, Chung-hua Book Co., 1940. Meng Chao-t'ung, *KK* (1964/7), 368.

62. Ch'en Kung-jou, *KKHP, 7* (1954), 87–101.

63. *WWTKTL* (1954/3), 60–62. T'ang Lan, *WWTKTL* (1954/5), 38–40.

64. Lin Shou-chin et al., *Shang-ts'un-ling Kuo kuo mu-ti,* Peking, Science Press, 1959.

Hsien, central Hopei,[65] furnishes information of city life in the state, and the burials at Chia-ko-chuang, near T'ang-shan in northern Hopei,[66] contained bronze vessels that well attest to the occurrence of some of the finest art of the Eastern Chou in the northernmost area of China proper. In the *area of Ch'i* in Shantung, east of Chin, the city site of Lin-tzu[67] and the burials at Su-fu-t'un in Yi-tu[68] provided the initial impetus of Eastern Chou archaeology in that part of China. In the *area of Ch'in* in Shensi, west of Chin, perhaps the recent discovery and excavations at several city sites, including the principal state capital at Hsien-yang, are most noteworthy.[69] In the *area of Ch'u* in Hupei, Anhwei, and Hunan, tombs in Shou Hsien and Ch'ang-sha are the most outstanding. These, and other Eastern Chou sites of South China, will be described in Chapter 9.[70]

The archaeological data unearthed at the Chou sites characterized above and at many other sites that cannot be mentioned here[71] are a treasure trove that will probably engage many archaeologists and historians in lifetimes of study. Drawing on some of the pertinent material, I shall discuss only a small number of the most important aspects of the development of the Chou civilization that are of general significance for the purpose of this book. A full treatment of Chou archaeology is not intended, nor is any attempt made here to use the written materials for a comprehensive history of the Chou society and culture.

DEVELOPMENT OF CITIES

In the last chapter the characteristics of the first cities in North China have been described; the Shang cities are shown to have consisted physically of an aristocratic center, in the shape of a walled enclosure of pounded earth, in which the aristocratic and ceremonial buildings and structures were located, and the area around this en-

65. See below, pp. 295–99.
66. An Chih-min, *KKHP, 6* (1953), 57–116.
67. See below, pp. 299–301.
68. Ch'i Yen-p'ei, *Chung-kuo K'ao-ku Hsüeh-pao, 2* (1947), 167–71.
69. See below, pp. 303–05.
70. Including the earlier tomb of the Marquis of Ts'ai, dating to a period before the Ch'u annexation of the Shou Hsien area. See *Shou Hsien Ts'ai-hou mu ch'u-t'u yi-wu,* Peking, Science Press, 1956.
71. Cheng Te-k'un, *Chou China* (*Archaeology in China, 3*), Cambridge, Heffer, 1963, includes very useful summaries of other Chou sites throughout China.

closure, where specialized industrial quarters and farming villages are dispersed. When we trace these constituents of Shang cities in time, a number of persistent traditions can be shown to have continued throughout the span of the Chou Dynasty, such as the wall of stamped earth, the ceremonial and palatial platform, and the aristocratic center. The basic pattern of urban organization, however, underwent some important changes with time.

In the history of city development, unfortunately, archaeological materials are totally lacking for the entire Western Chou period. This hiatus is not fatal, however, for the culture during this interval of approximately four hundred years is known from other kinds of remains, to be discussed later in this chapter. Moreover, as we shall see, the basic change in the pattern of urbanization seems to have come after the beginning of the Eastern Chou period.

There is no question that the Western Chou aristocracy were city builders. The poem Wen Wang Yu Sheng in the section Ta Ya of the *Book of Odes* describes how Wen Wang built the city of Feng, and Wu Wang built the city of Hao. Lo-yang was, according to Tso Lo Chieh in *Yi Chou Shu,* situated between the River Lo in the south and Chia Mountain in the north, and consisted of two enclosures of considerable dimensions. The city enclosure was apparently again built of layers of stamped earth, the construction of which was described vividly in the poems of Hung Yen Chih Shih and Mien P'ien in the Ya sections of the *Book of Odes,* which are generally regarded as containing reliable data from the Western Chou period. As described above, the Chou cities at Sian and Lo-yang consisted of two neighboring enclosures, one in the west, the other in the east, separated by a river. The significance of this is not clear.

During the Eastern Chou period, when a series of local states came of age, the number of cities certainly increased greatly and they expanded throughout North China. Oshima Riichi has been able, according to *Tso Chuan* and *Kung Yang Chuan,* to list 78 cities that were built during the Ch'un-ch'iu period from 722 to 480 B.C. These include 27 cities in the state of Lu, 20 in Ch'u, 10 in Chin, 4 in Cheng, 3 in Ch'i, 2 in Sung, and 1 each in Chu, Ch'en, Wu, and Yüeh, extending in area throughout North China and the lower and middle Yangtze valley.[72] There were presumably other cities in these and

72: Oshima Riichi, *Tōhōgakuhō, 30* (1959), 53.

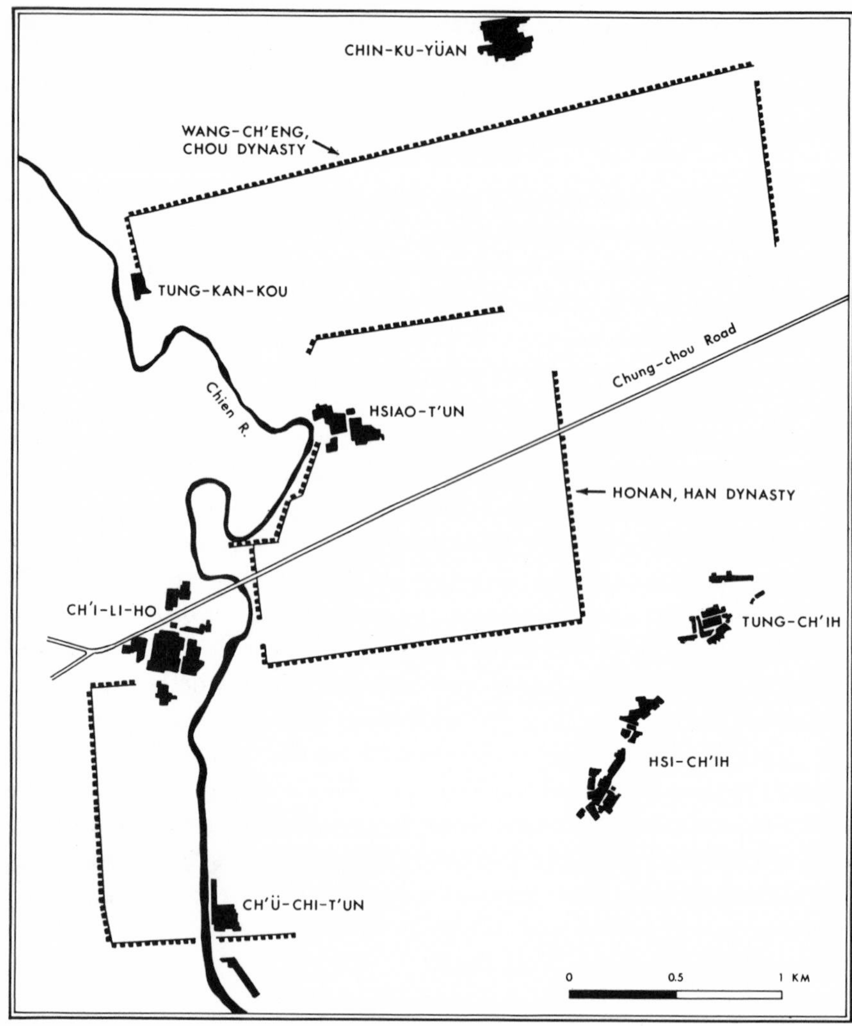

98. The Eastern Chou city of Wang Ch'eng, near Lo-yang, Honan. (Based on *KKHP,* 1959/2, figure facing p. 16.)

other states that were not recorded in the two sources Oshima has consulted. Archaeological surveys and excavations have thus far located and explored the remains of the following cities of the Eastern Chou period (see Fig. 96).

Lo-yang, Honan (probable site of Wang Ch'eng, Royal Chou).

The royal city of Lo-yang during the Eastern Chou Dynasty has only begun to be explored; the results published thus far are preliminary.[73] The city wall of the Eastern Chou period has been outlined, although only the northern wall, the northern sections of the western and eastern walls, a southern section of the western wall, and a western section of the southern wall have been located (Fig. 98). These walls made an enclosure approximately square in shape, 2,890 m long on the northern side. The walls were built in stamped-earth layers, averaging about 5 m wide at the base, with a surviving height of 1.5 to 4 m. Excavations carried out within the enclosure tend to show that important buildings were located in the southern or central part of the enclosure, as indicated by many stamped-earth house floors and a large amount of tiles (both flat and semicylindrical types) and eave tiles with *t'ao-t'ieh* and *yün* patterns. A pottery kiln area and one adjacent house foundation were located in the northwestern section of the enclosure; southeast of the kiln area there was a bone factory, and, farther south a factory for making stone ornaments. Water ditches have been identified at scattered spots within the city. Associated cultural remains show that the city was built before the middle of the Ch'un-ch'iu period and was continuously in use until the later phases of the Western Han Dynasty, when a smaller enclosure within the former Lo-yang site was constructed. This Han Dynasty town is known as the seat of Honan county.[74]

Hou-ma, Shansi (*probable site of Hsin-t'ien, state of Chin*). The ruins of two old cities northwest of Hou-ma in southern Shansi were brought to light in 1957. Fieldwork is still actively going on there and walls of additional city sites are being discovered within the same complex, but a general idea about the setup of the first two cities can be obtained from a series of preliminary reports.[75] These ruins have been dated to a late phase of the Ch'un-ch'iu period, with one of the two probably succeeding the other, and are identified with the city of Hsin-t'ien, one of the capitals of the prince of Chin (Fig. 99).

73. Ch'en Kung-jou, *KKHP* (1959/2), 15–34. *KK* (1961/4), 216.
74. Kuo Pao-chün, *KKTH* (1955/1), 9–21.
75. Yang Fu-tou, *WWTKTL* (1957/10), 55–56. Ch'ang Wen-chai, *WWTKTL* (1958/12), 32–33. Ch'ang Wen-chai et al., *WW* (1959/6), 42–44; (1959/6), 43, 44–45. Chang Shou-chung, *WW* (1960/8/9), 11–14. Chang Han, *WW* (1961/10), 25, 31–34. Chang Wan-chung, *WW* (1962/4/5), 37–42. Yeh Hsüeh-ming, *WW* (1962/4/5), 43–54. Chang Han, *WW* (1966/2), 1–3. *KK* (1959/5), 222–28; (1962/2), 55–62. Wang K'o-lin, *KK* (1963/5), 229–45.

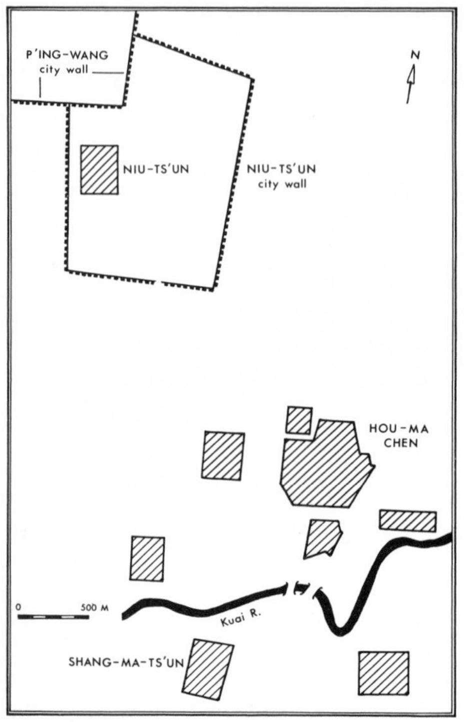

99. City of Hsin-t'ien, state of Chin, near Hou-ma, Shansi. (Based on *KK*, 1963/5, p. 229.)

The two cities adjoined each other diagonally. The one in the northwest has been called the Old City of P'ing-wang, named after a village nearby, and the one in the southeast, the Old City of Niu-ts'un, after a village of that name. Most of the walls of Niu-ts'un have been located in an enclosure 1,340–1,740 m N–S and 1,100–1,400 m W–E, forming a rough rectangle with an oblique northern wall. Only the southeastern corner of P'ing-wang has been found, which intruded into the northwestern corner of Niu-ts'un, and its general outline is still unknown. Both cities were built in stamped-earth layers by means of the pisé technique, but the surviving walls, completely covered under the ground, are only about 1 m high. The earth making up the wall is fairly pure, and each stamped layer is about 6 cm thick. The cities seem to have been built on top of a cemetery area of early Ch'un-ch'iu period, but were both intruded into by tombs of the Warring States period and by vehicle roads constructed during the Warring States and Western Han. It seems probable, therefore, that the two cities were built successively during a later period of the Ch'un-ch'iu.

The only remains within the enclosures are a road section in Niu-ts'un and two platforms, one in each city, on which relics of buildings were found. The platform of P'ing-wang is in the southern part of the enclosure, but since the northern wall of this city has not been found the precise location is not clear. It was built on three levels. The bottom level is a square of 75 m to a side, oriented according to the four cardinal directions. Only the top of this level, which is of stamped-earth construction, has been excavated. A stamped-earth rectangle, 30 m wide and over 20 m long, adjoins the center of the southern side of the bottom level, and is attached to a sloping ramp, about 6 m wide and over 20 m long, extending toward the south. The second level is about 4 m above the ground; the central portion of its southern side is sloping. The third level is situated atop the northern portion of the second level, making a rectangle 35 m N–S and 45 m E–W. Fragments of tiles and a stone block, possibly a pillar foundation, were found on the top level of the platform. The whole platform is 8.5 m high, consisting entirely of compactly stamped pure earth. The Niu-ts'un platform, in the northern part of the center within the city enclosure, is a rectangle 52.5 by 52.5 m and 6.5 m high, composed of compactly stamped earth. Remains of buildings, such as fragments of tiles, are found on top of the platform, which has a depth of over 1 m. The northern side of the platform is vertical, and the southern side forms a slope. Investigators of the site call both of these platforms palace foundations. Apparently the buildings atop the platforms were of considerable dimensions, facing south, and accessible by long ramps extending from the top of the platforms toward the bottom and the south.

A section of ditch 6 m wide and 3–4 m deep, possibly the remains of a defensive watercourse surrounding the city, was found outside the south wall of Niu-ts'un.

Outside of the Hsin-t'ien cities, but in the immediate neighborhood, a variety of other remains of approximately the same age has been found. Three foundries were located south of Niu-ts'un, over 200 m apart. Tens of thousands of fragments of clay molds and remains of crucibles were found. At one of the foundries the molds were used exclusively for the manufacture of such implements as spades and chisels and *pu* coins; at another foundry only molds for the making of belt hooks and carriage fittings were uncovered. The third one, the largest, has seventeen semi-subterranean houses, and clay piece molds for making bronze vessels, implements, and weapons. Remains here were left during two occupations, the earlier dating from late Spring Autumn and the later from early Warring States. Three bone manufactories have been located in the Hou-ma group, two in the neighborhood of the foundries, the other one over 1,000 m to the southeast. Wastes and raw materials, mostly deer bones, constitute the bulk of recovered remains at these three spots. A pottery kiln area has been located 1,000 m southeast of Niu-ts'un; kilns are concentrated within an area of about half a square kilometer, some of them adjoining. The pots found in and near the kilns are of the same types as those found in the Niu-ts'un city area.

A residential village, also of the same age, was approximately 5 km east of Niu-ts'un. The dwellings were all semi-subterranean, 1.4–1.5 m deep into the ground and 3 by 2.4 or 4 by 3 m in dimensions. The doors always face south and have stairways to the ground. Each house has a small niche on the wall, some divided into two levels. The upper part of the house was apparently built with wooden beams and covered with tiles. These houses are always in clusters and are accompanied by storage pits and sometimes by wells. Potsherds, shell saws, shell knives, bone hairpins, and bronze awls were found in and near the houses. Storage pits have been found at most of the sites in the Hsin-t'ien area; some were apparently for grains and soybeans, remains of which have been found.

Three groups of animal burials have been located: 0.5 km south, 2.5 km southeast, and 3 km east of Niu-ts'un. These were oval pits, arranged regularly in groups, in which skeletons of horses (many), sheep (relatively few), and cattle (rare) were excavated. The animals seem to have been tied and placed upside down alive in the pits. Associated with the skeletons were bronze ornaments and jade artifacts. From the southeastern complex of sacrificial pits, discovered at the end of 1965, large numbers of brush-and-ink inscribed stone and jade tablets were brought to light.

About 2 km south of the Niu-ts'un city an Eastern Chou cemetery was excavated in 1961. Bronzes and pottery found in the tombs (fourteen were opened) are of types ranging from late Western Chou through the middle Warring States. This cemetery was possibly related to the city ruins to its north, and its earlier date may suggest existence in this area of previous city structures that are yet to be located.

The Hsin-t'ien cities near Hou-ma, as described above, strongly recall the cities of the Shang Dynasty in their basic constitution. The enclosures were probably the seats of aristocracy and state religion, and the farming and handicraft hamlets were located in the surrounding suburbs. The investigators have concluded, rightly I think, that these were no ordinary cities but the capitals of princes. They have attempted to identify these ruins as the Hsin-t'ien city of Chin, capital of thirteen Chin princes, on the basis that their geographic location matches the description given to this city in the historic records.

Chin-yüan, Shansi (probable site of Chin-yang, state of Chin). Besides Hsin-t'ien, four other walled towns dating from the Spring Autumn period in the area of Chin have been located in Shansi in the Fenho Valley. These are, from north to south, the city ruins in Chin-yüan, Hsiang-fen, Ch'ü-wo, and Wen-hsi. All of them are known only through preliminary work, and none approaches Hsin-t'ien's magnitude.

Near the modern town of Chin-yüan, southeast of T'ai-yüan, remnants of an Eastern Chou city wall found in 1961 indicate an enclosure of *hang-t'u* construction, probably square and oriented north-northeast to south-southwest, about 2,700 m long N–S. The investigators identify it with the city of Chin-yang of the state of Chin.[76]

Chao-k'ang Chen, Hsiang-fen, Shansi (probable site of Chiang, state of Chin). Beginning in 1960, investigations undertaken east of Chao-k'ang Chen, in the southwestern corner of Hsiang-fen, have disclosed a rectangular *hang-t'u* enclosure, 2,600–2,700 m long north-south, 1,530 m wide on the north and 1,650 m wide on the south. A moat closely encircled the entire city wall. A smaller enclosure, approximately 800 m square, is inside at the north-central part, its northern wall identical with the northern wall of the larger enclosure (Fig. 100). The location of the site suggests the Chin city of Chü or Chiang, sometime capital of the state.[77]

Ch'ü-wo, Shansi (probable site of Wo-kuo, state of Chin). A city site of the Eastern Chou period with a double enclosure was found in 1956 about 1 km southwest of Ch'ü-wo in southern Shansi, 8,700–11,200 m east of the city of Hsin-t'ien, described above. The inner en-

76. Hsieh Yüan-lu and Chang Han, *WW* (1962/4/5), 55–58.
77. Ch'ang Wen-chai, *KK* (1963/10), 544–46.

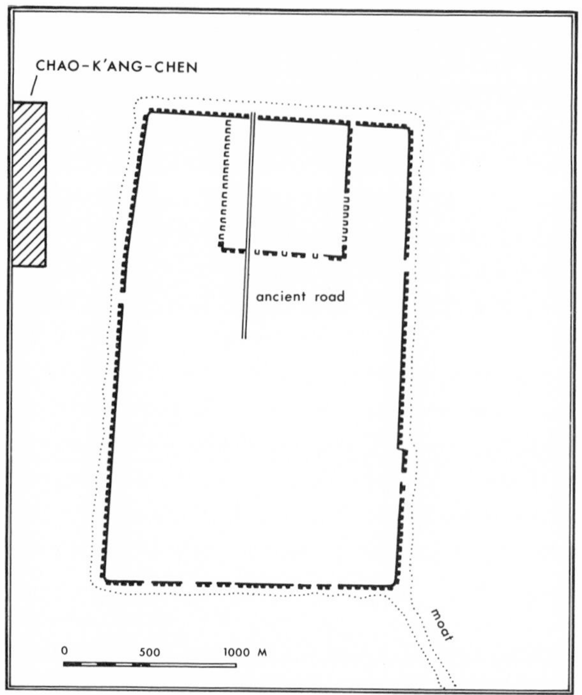

100. City of Chiang, state of Chin, near Hsiang-fen, Shansi. (Based on *KK,* 1963/10, 544.)

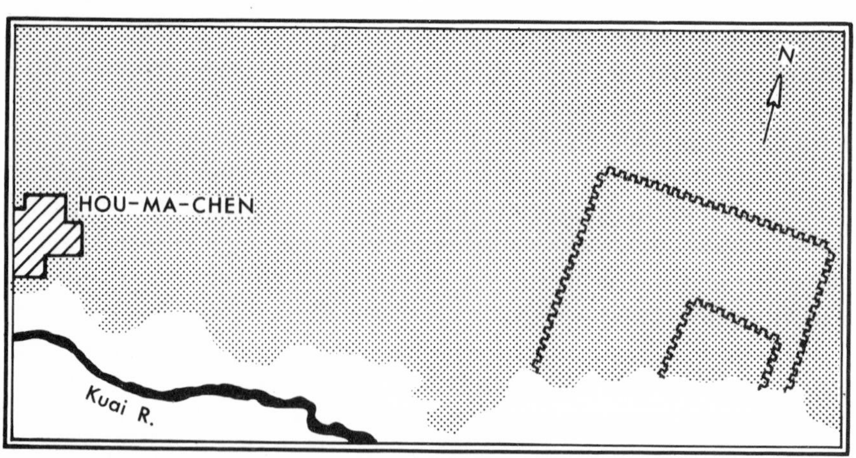

101. City of Wo-kuo, state of Chin, near Ch'ü-wo, Shansi. (Based on *WW,* 1960/8/9, p. 15.)

closure is a square of about 1,100 m to a side, but the southern wall has been eroded by the River Kuai and only 600 to 1,000 m of the east and west walls are left (Fig. 101). The walls have a remaining height of 1–3 m, are about 12 m wide at the base, and are composed of stamped earth in layers 6 cm thick. The outer enclosure now has only the northern and western walls left, the former over 3,100 m long and the latter 2,600 m. The distance between the northern walls of these two enclosures is about 1,400 m. Preliminary surveys at this site show that cultural remains are abundant within the inner enclosure, including some tiles and pottery of the Hsin-t'ien type, and also a large number of tiles which are probably Warring States and Han Dynasty in date. The location of this site coincides with the description given in historic records for the Wo-kuo city, capital of the state of Chin before it was moved to Hsin-t'ien, although the ruins that have been found here seem to date from later periods.[78] West of the city site a Warring States tomb containing human sacrificial victims has been found.[79]

Wen-hsi, Shansi (probable site of Ch'ing-yüan, state of Chin). A square *hang-t'u* enclosure, around 980 m to a side, was located about 17.5 km northeast of Wen-hsi, southwestern Shansi. Remnants of the city wall exhibit clear signs of pisé construction: a ditch was dug, filled with layers of compact clay to make the base, and then the wall, about 10 m wide, was built up in layers of clay rammed between two planks tied together by ropes. Around the wall were remains of an ancient moat (Fig. 102). Within the wall Lung-shan Neolithic, Eastern Chou, and Han relics were found.[80] The Eastern Chou city may correspond to Ch'ing-yüan, a fort town of importance in the Chin defense against the nomads from the west.

Hsia Hsien, Shansi (probable site of An-yi, state of Wei). Around 450 B.C. Chin was split into three separate states, Chao in the north, Wei in the middle, and Han in the south. The cities described above probably began under the Chin regime, but they continued to be in use during the Warring States period and even later. Other than Chin-yang, which fell within Chao's boundaries, all the others became cities of the state of Wei. In addition, ruins of three or four other cities have been located in the Wei area, which can be dated no earlier than

78. *KK* (1959/5), 222–23.
79. Ch'ang Wen-chai, *WW* (1960/8/9), 15–18.
80. T'ao Cheng-kang, *KK* (1963/5), 246–49.

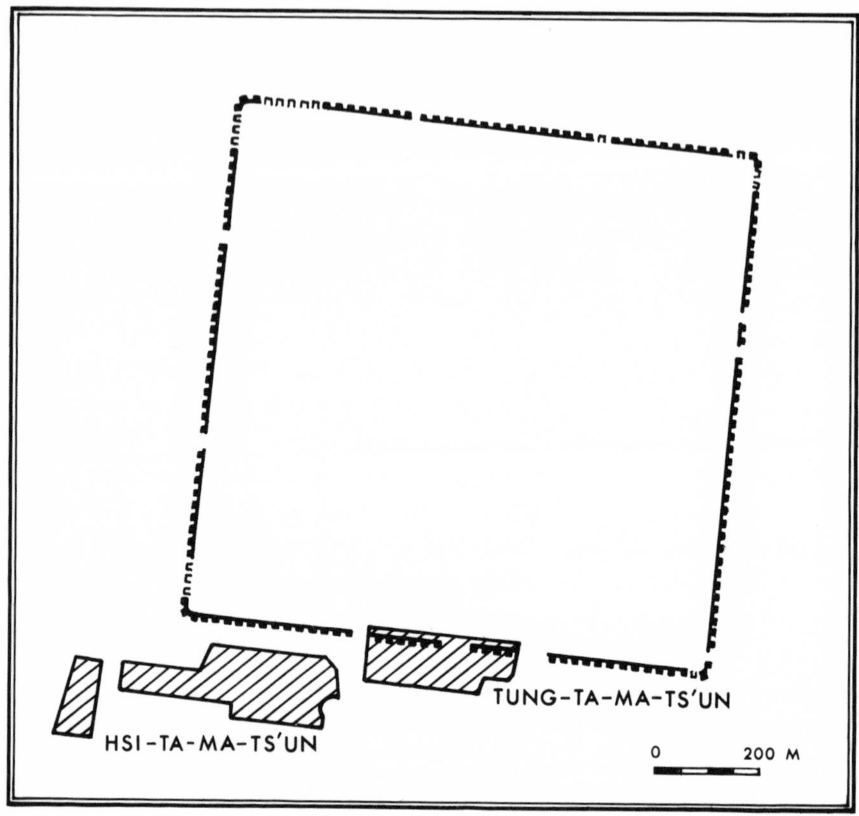

102. City of Ch'ing-yüan, State of Chin, near Wen-hsi, Shansi. (Based on *KK*, 1963/5, p. 246.)

the Warring States,[81] including the probable site of the state capital at one time, An-yi. This is the site of Yü-wang-ch'eng, about 7 km northwest of Hsia Hsien, southwestern Shansi, investigated in 1959, 1961, and 1962. It consists of three enclosures. The largest is oriented north-northeast and south-southwest, is trapezoidal, and is about 4,500 m long (N–S) and 2,100 m wide on the south side. Remnants of a moat were found nearby. Its southwestern quarter forms a second enclosure, and the third—smallest—enclosure is at the center of the site (Fig. 103). The investigators believe that the largest and smallest enclosures

81. See Li Yü-ch'un, *KK* (1959/11), 604–05, for the probable site of Yin-chin, state of Wei, near Hua-yin, Shensi, in addition to the three sites described below.

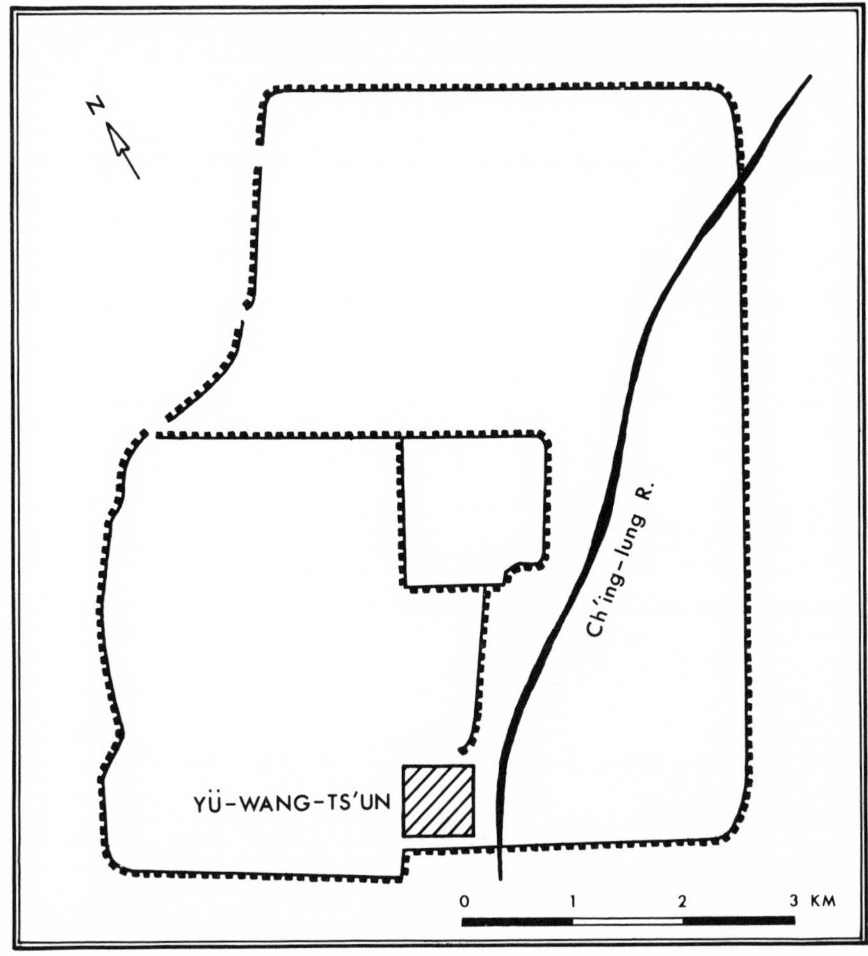

103. City of An-yi, state of Wei, near Hsia Hsien, Shansi. (Based on *WW*, 1962/4/5, p. 61.)

were the original Warring States city and that the smallest enclosure was probably the site of palatial structures.[82]

Jui-ch'eng, Shansi (*probable site of Wei-ch'eng, state of Wei*). A square (about 1,000 m to a side) *hang-t'u* enclosure of an Eastern Chou town site was located north of Jui-ch'eng, southwestern Shansi (Fig.

82. T'ao Cheng-kang and Yeh Hsüeh-ming, *WW* (1962/4/5), 61–64. Chang Yen-huang and Hsü Tien-k'uei, *KK* (1963/9), 474–79.

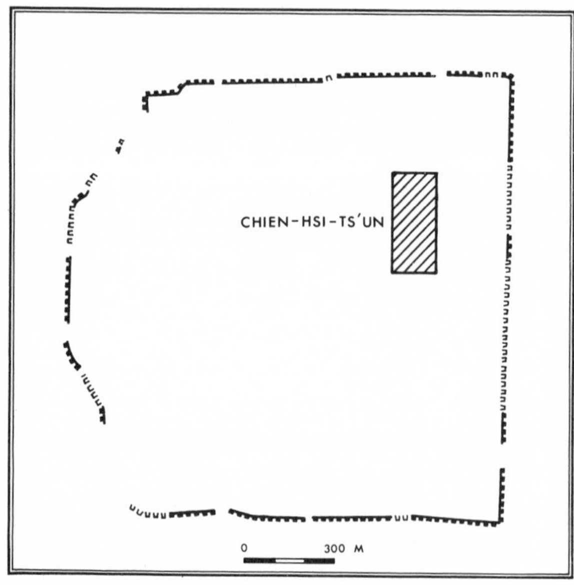

104. City of Wei-ch'eng, state of Wei, near Jui-ch'eng, Shansi. (Based on *WW*, 1962/4/5, p. 60.)

104). Tiles, pottery, and tombs of Warring States types were found inside. It is suggested that this was the ruins of Wei-ch'eng, another Wei capital city.[83]

Hung-tung, Shansi (probable site of Yang, state of Wei). An early town site was investigated in 1962 southeast of Hung-tung in southern Shansi. Rectangular, it is 1,300 m long (E–W) and 580 m wide (N–S). Remains of pottery and tiles were found inside, concentrated in the western and central parts, and burials were located northwest of the city. It is possibly the ruins of Yang, a small town ruled by a Wei minister.[84]

Yi-yang, Honan (probable site of Yi-yang, state of Han). A square *hang-t'u* enclosure, about 1,400 m to a side, was found in 1959 northwest of Yi-yang, western Honan. Tiles and potsherds of Warring States types occurred on the surface inside.[85]

83. T'ao and Yeh, ibid., 59–61.
84. Chang Te-kuang, *KK* (1963/10), 547–49, 552.
85. *KK* (1961/1), 32.

Han-tan, Hopei (probable site of Han-tan, state of Chao). Three city sites are probably attributable to the state of Chao, namely, Han-tan, Wu-ch'eng, and Wu-chi, all in the southern part of Hopei.

The name of Han-tan was first mentioned in *Tso Chuan,* the Tenth Year of Ting Kung (500 B.C.), and was the capital city of Chao from 386 (the first year of Ching Hou) to 228 B.C., when Ch'in conquered the city and terminated the state. This old city of Han-tan, known throughout Chinese history to be about 4 km southwest of the present city of Han-tan in southern Hopei, was investigated by a group of Japanese and Chinese archaeologists in 1939.[86]

The ruins of Han-tan consist of two adjoining enclosures, with a possible third to the north. The city proper is roughly square, about 1,400 m to a side. An eastern annex, using the eastern wall of the city proper as its western wall, is about half the size. A section of a wall over 520 m long, possibly the remains of a second annex, has been found, which extends from the northern wall of the city proper northward. The wall, of *hang-t'u* construction, is given a reconstructed height of over 15 m and a base width of over 20 m. Each of the walls of the city proper has one to three openings, near which are scattered tiles and bricks. These were probably the gates of the city. Within and near the enclosures are remains of sixteen earth platforms, ten of which are of considerable dimensions. At the middle of the city proper, four platforms are located along the north–south axis. The first one from the south, known among the natives as Lung T'ai, is the largest; it is 13.5 m high, 210 m (E–W) by 288 m (N–S) at the base, and 105 (E–W) by 130–140 m (N–S) at the top. On its flat surface no cultural remains of any significant amount have been found. The second platform, north of Lung-t'ai, is 4.5 m high and 49 by 51 m in size. On top of it were found two parallel rows of stone pillar foundations, lying N–S, and, outside of these, two more rows of bricks. These are considered to be the remains of two corridors, on top of which was probably a second floor. The platform to its north, 3 m high and 60 by 70 m in size, has no stone foundations. On it were fragments of tiles, pottery, knife coins, and a small number of other bronze and iron implements. The northernmost platform of this row is round, with a diameter of 62 m and a height of 7.5 m. Two square platforms are located in the eastern

86. Komai Kazuchika and Sekino Takeshi, *Han-tan,* Archaeologia Orientalis, ser. B, 7, 1954.

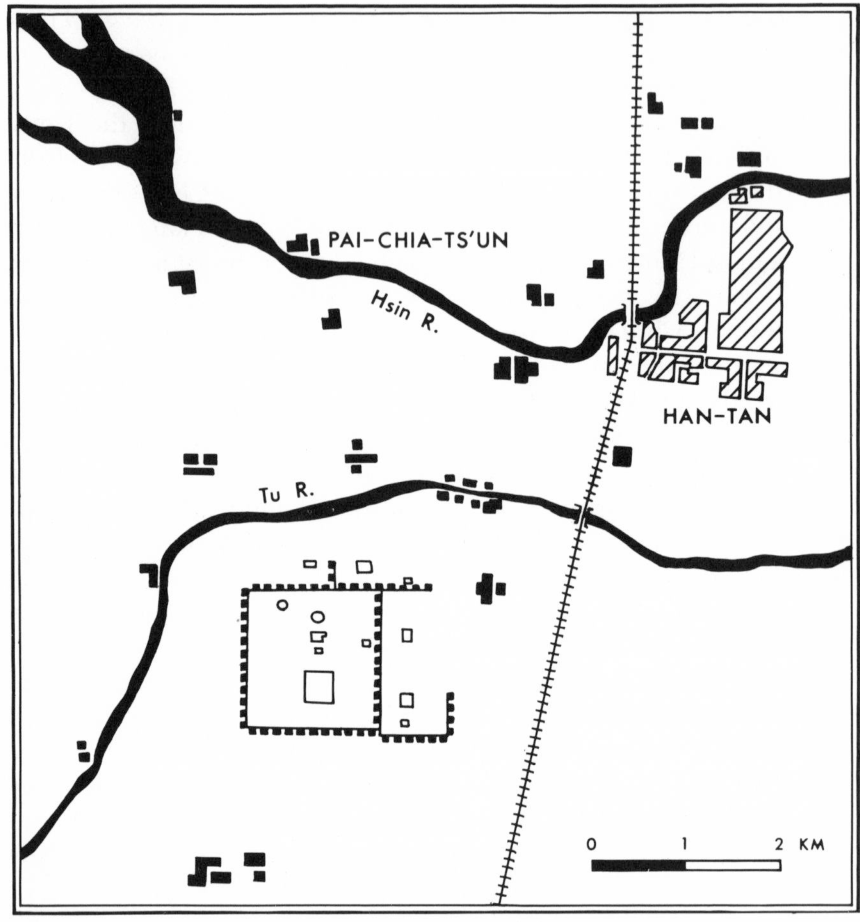

105. City of Han-tan, state of Chao, near Han-tan, Hopei. (From *Han-tan,* Tokyo and Kyoto, 1954, Fig. 2.)

annex, again along the north–south axis, slightly to the west of the middle. The other platforms, all rectangular or square except for one which is round, are scattered in and around the city (Fig. 105). Bricks and tiles are found atop all the platforms; the eave tiles and pottery types date the city site to the Warring States period.

A cemetery of this period was excavated in 1957 and 1959 in the Pai-chia-ts'un area north of the Chao city. Forty-nine tombs and six horse-chariot burials were excavated. Of the twelve lavishly furnished tombs, five have yielded sacrificed humans. One tomb had an earthen mound above the ground.[87]

Wu-ch'eng, Hopei (probable site of Wu-ch'eng, state of Chao). The ruins of Wu-ch'eng, found recently, form a rough square enclosure, about 1.1 km to a side. The wall, with a remaining height of 6 m and a base width of 12 m, is constructed of stamped-earth layers, each 8–11 cm thick. Five or six openings are located in the western and northern walls, which are intact. A water ditch, 20–30 m in length, was found along the northern wall. Cultural remains within the city, consisting of tiles, eave tiles, potsherds, *pu* coins, spindle whorls, and bronze arrowheads, are mostly of the Warring States type, with some Han Dynasty forms. Urn burials of infants have been excavated in an eastern part of the city.[88]

Wu-an, Hopei (probable site of Wu-chi, state of Chao). Two ancient city ruins are known southwest of Wu-an Hsien, southern Hopei. The one in the west, near the town of Wu-chi, was investigated in 1956. The earthen walls, again of stamped earth, 8–13 m wide and with a remaining height of 3–6 m, form a roughly rectangular enclosure, 889 m E–W and 768 m N–S. A paved road led through one gate in each wall. Residential remains, wells, pottery kilns, and burials were found in the western part of the enclosure and indicate a dating of Eastern Chou through Western Han.[89]

Yi Hsien, Hopei (probable site of Hsia-tu, state of Yen). Hsia-tu, near Yi Hsien in central Hopei, was an important city of the state of Yen, possibly occupied between 697 and 226 B.C. It was investigated and excavated in 1930,[90] 1957,[91] 1958,[92] 1961–62,[93] and 1964–65,[94] turning out to be perhaps the best excavated and described of all the Chou cities (Fig. 106).

The city was a rectangular *hang-t'u* enclosure, about 8 km long

87. *KK* (1959/10), 531–36; (1962/12), 613–34.
88. Ao Ch'eng-lung, *KK* (1959/7), 354–57.
89. Meng Hao et al., *KKTH* (1957/4), 43–47. Meng Hao, *KK* (1959/7), 338–42. Ch'en Hui, *KK* (1959/7), 343–45.
90. Fu Chen-lun, *Kuo-hsüeh Chi-k'an, 3,* Peking University, 1932, pp. 175–82. Fu Chen-lun, *KKTH* (1955/4), 18–26.
91. Hsieh Hsi-yi, *WWTKTL* (1957/9), 61–63.
92. Huang Ching-lüeh, *KK* (1962/1), 10–19, 54.
93. Li Hsiao-tung, *KKHP* (1965/1), 83–106. Sun Teh-hai, *KKHP* (1965/2), 79–102.
94. Ch'en Hui, *KK* (1965/11), 548–61, 598. Ch'en Ying-ch'i, *KK* (1965/11), 562–70. *WW* (1965/9), 60.

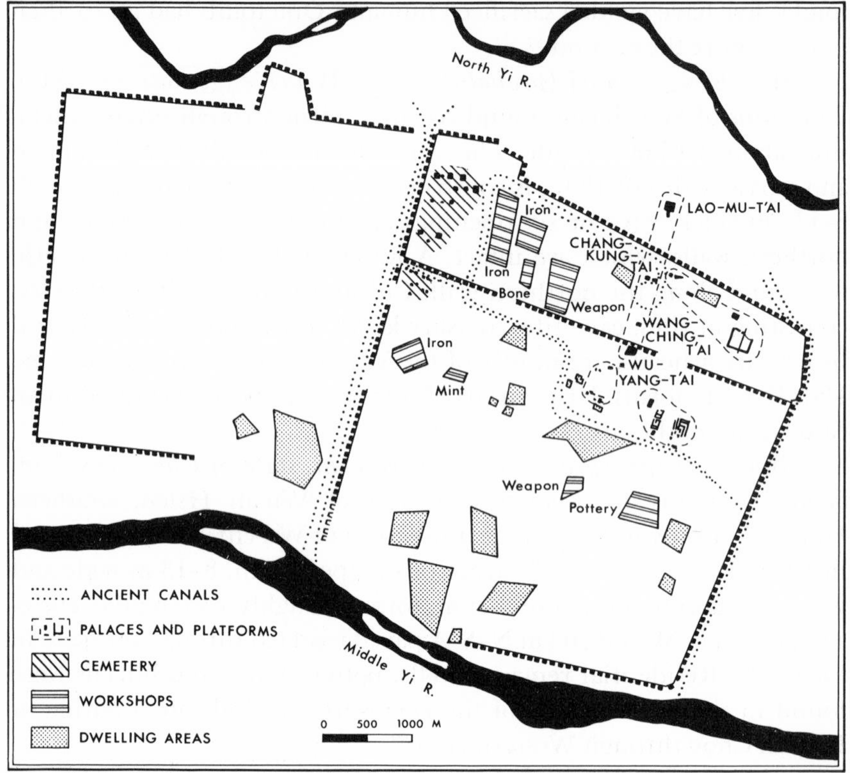

106. City of Hsia-tu, state of Yen, near Yi Hsien, Hopei. (Based on *KKHP*, 1965/1, Fig. 1. following p. 84.)

E–W and 4 km wide N–S, separated in the middle by a north–south wall and a water ditch ("canal") on its west into an eastern and a western half. Another partition wall further separated the eastern city into a northern section of about a third and a southern section of two thirds. Gates and garrison barracks were associated with the walls. A section of the western wall, almost 40 m thick, excavated in 1957, exhibits its *hang-t'u* structure clearly: the core of the wall was constructed first and then the exterior and interior faces added. Two planks were placed on edge a little distance apart and loose earth filled in between, the boards were tightened with ropes, mats were placed on top of the earth which was pounded to compact it, and then the ropes were cut and the boards removed. When the core of the wall was done, the same procedure was repeated for the outside and inside layers. Sections of walls were thus built successively one on top of the other until the desired height was reached.

The western city, although dating from the Warring States period, was apparently built later than the eastern city. Only two dwelling houses, some tombs, and a number of weapons were found in it; possibly it was a defensive adjunct to an existing city. The major activities of the Hsia-tu life took place in the eastern city, which was clearly divided into four functional regions: palatial, industrial, dwelling, and burial.

The palatial area is in the northern part of the eastern city and has yielded remains of large structures on *hang-t'u* platforms, ground structures, bricks, and elaborately decorated tiles and eave tiles. There are remains of four large platforms, forming a north–south line. These, referred to by the local inhabitants as Wu-yang-t'ai (southernmost), Wang-ching-t'ai, Chang-kung-t'ai, and Lao-mu-t'ai (northernmost), were all rectangular, built in *hang-t'u* layers, and of various sizes and heights. The largest, Wu-yang-t'ai, has a remaining height of 11 m, divided into two levels, the base about 140 m E–W and 110 m N–S. On top of these platforms are remains of tiles, burned clay, and fragments of wattle-and-daub. Clay water-pipe sections were found on Wu-yang-t'ai, presumably used for drainage, and a bronze human statuette (Fig. 107) was found in the vicinity. Archaeologists who excavated the site believe that these four platforms and the old structures on top of them were the dominating features of the city. Three clusters of rectangular house floors (*hang-t'u* built, with large post holes with chicken and animal bones inside) surrounded Wu-yang-t'ai on its northeastern, southeastern, and southwestern sides. These houses were built at ground level, but each cluster had a large house constructed on a platform several meters high.

The industrial region forms a belt west and south of the palatial region in the eastern city. Three iron workshops, two weapon manufactories, a coin mint, a pottery kiln area, and a bone workshop were identified within the belt. Slugs, wastes, molds, kilns, tools, and other handicraft artifacts were found alongside storage pits, dwelling floors, wells, and remains of buildings and utensils.

Surrounding the palatial complex and the industrial belt were remains of dwelling houses and domiciliary artifacts, especially abun-

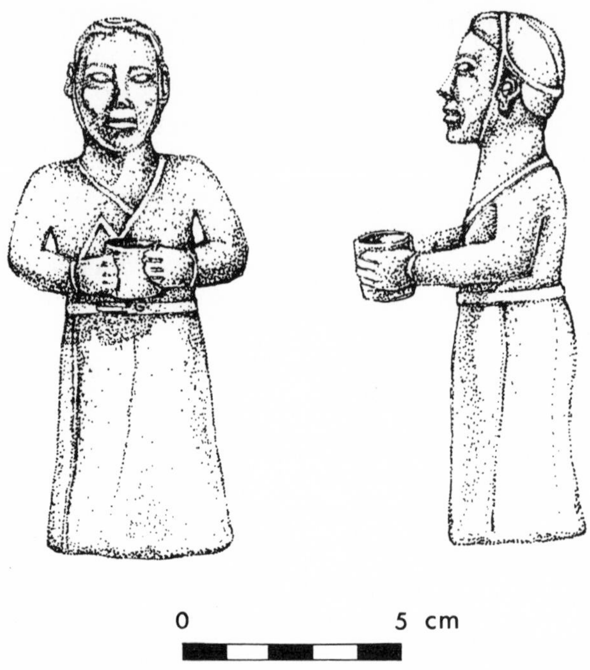

107. Bronze statuette discovered in the Yen city of Hsia-tu, in Yi Hsien, Hopei. (Based on *WW,* 1965/2, p. 43.)

108. Yen pottery *chien* with bronze vessel-style decorative patterns, excavated from a burial mound in the city of Hsia-tu, near Yi Hsien, Hopei. (From *KKHP,* 1965/2, p. 89.)

dant in the southwestern, central, eastern, and northeastern parts of the eastern city.

At the northwestern corner of the eastern city was the burial area. Twenty-three burial mounds were identified, divided into two groups by the partition wall. North of the wall are 13 mounds, arranged in four rows, 4, 3, 3, and 3. South of the partition are 10 mounds, arranged in two rows, 5 and 5. These are all pit graves, richly furnished with pottery (some very elaborately decorated in imitation of bronze vessels; Fig. 108), a few bronzes, and stone and shell artifacts; they are equipped with ramps and are capped with *hang-t'u* mounds. South of the city, a cemetery of Warring States date was located in 1964; its relation with Hsia-tu remains to be determined.

A network of water ditches completes the layout. In addition to the long ditch separating the two cities, a section of a moat was located outside the east wall, and two ditches continue from the central "canal" into the eastern city. One in the north separated the cemetery from the palatial and industrial regions; the other in the south kept the palatial and the industrial regions apart. The excavators believe that these ditches were constructed to isolate (and facilitate the defense of) the central part of the city, to provide water for the households and industries, for communication, and for drainage.

A city of this magnitude was certainly no ordinary town; its well-planned total layout, the palatial complex, the interrelationship of the different quarters, and the pattern of arrangement of tombs are rare features among the known ruins of the contemporary cities and are indicative of the level of cultural and societal achievement of Yen.[95]

Lin-tzu, Shantung (probable site of Lin-tzu, state of Ch'i). The ruins of a Warring States city, identified as the Ch'i capital of Lin-tzu, were investigated by Sekino in 1940 and 1941 and by the Shantung Bureau of Culture in 1958.[96] The city consists of two enclosures of stamped-earth walls. The larger one, rectangular in shape, is approximately 4 km E–W and over 4 km N–S. At the southwestern corner of the large enclosure was built a smaller one, about 1,350 m square. An oval-shaped earthen platform was located west of the center of the smaller enclosure, approximately 65 by 73 m in size, atop which were

95. For the remains of another possibly Yen town, in Hsü-shui, Hopei, see Ao Ch'eng-lung, *KK* (1965/10), 540.

96. Sekino Takeshi, *Chugaku Kōkōgaku Kenkyū,* University of Tokyo, Institute for Oriental Culture, 1956, pp. 241–94. *KK* (1961/6), 289–97.

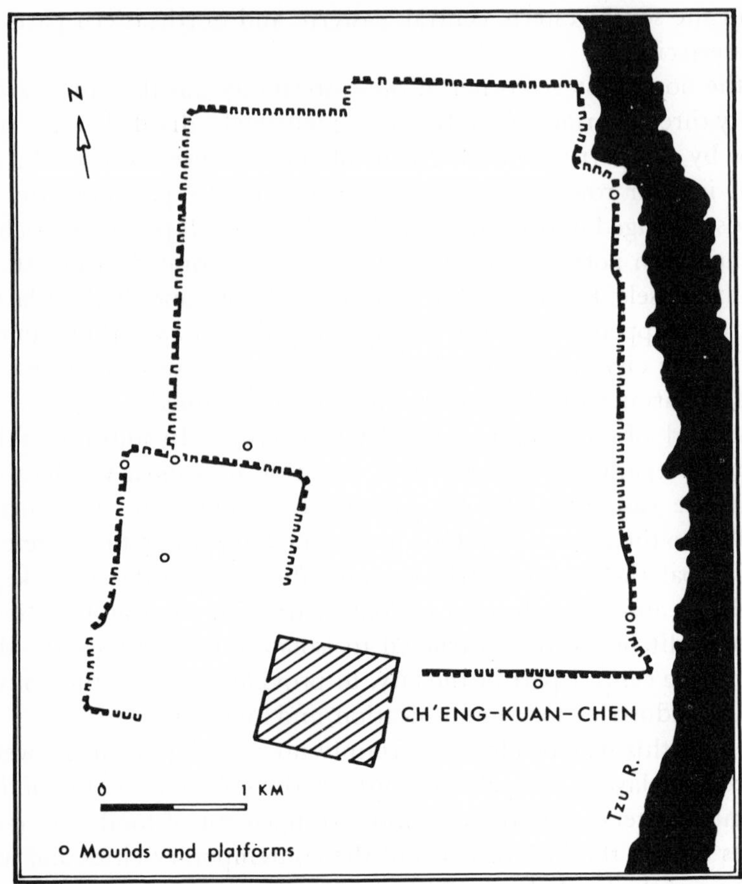

109. City of Lin-tzu, state of Ch'i, near Lin-tzu, Shantung. (Based on *KK*, 1961/6, p. 289.)

found remains of tiles (Fig. 109). Several other platforms were also found, one at the northeastern corner of the larger enclosure, and the others outside the city area. Cultural remains have been brought to light from all over the city, including tiles, eave tiles, bricks, potsherds, knife coins, coin molds, and bronze arrowheads. Cowrie shells, a clay mold for mirror manufacture, and a clay seal were purchased from the natives and were reportedly found at various localities within the larger enclosure. According to Sekino,[97] the small enclosure

97. Sekino, ibid.

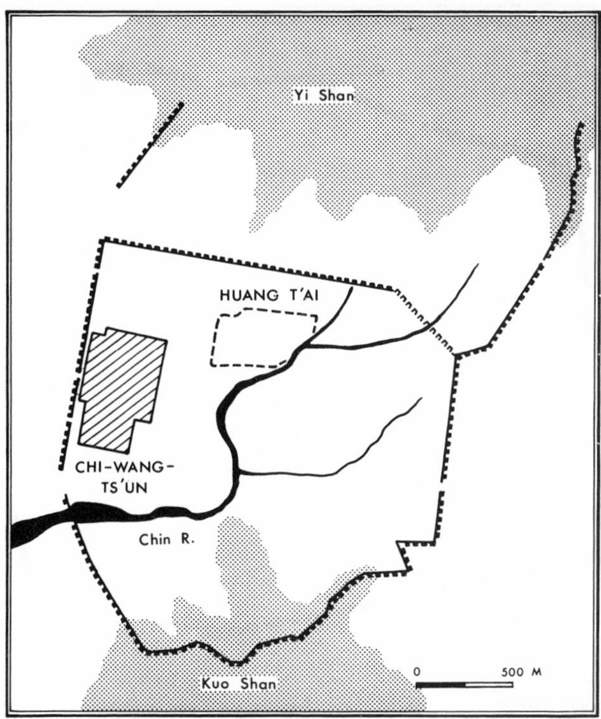

110. City of Chu-ch'eng, near Tsou Hsien, Shantung. (Based on *KK,* 1965/12, p. 623.)

was probably the seat of the Ch'i prince, where palaces and administrative offices were located, and the larger enclosure housed the markets and the residential area. According to Sekino's estimates, the dimensions of the city and the amount of cultural remains indicate a population of scores of thousands of households.

Tsou Hsien, Shantung (probable site of Chu-ch'eng, state of Chu). Investigated in 1964, a *hang-t'u* enclosure of a Chou and Han occupation was located about 10 km south of Tsou Hsien in Shantung, in a small valley about 1,200 m wide between the Yi Shan and the K'uo Shan hills. Roughly rectangular, the northern and the southern sections of the east and west city walls were built on the low foothills. At the center of the enclosure is an earthen platform 500 by 250 m, referred to by local inhabitants as Huang-t'ai (Fig. 110). Remains of pottery, tiles, and pottery-making implements have been collected

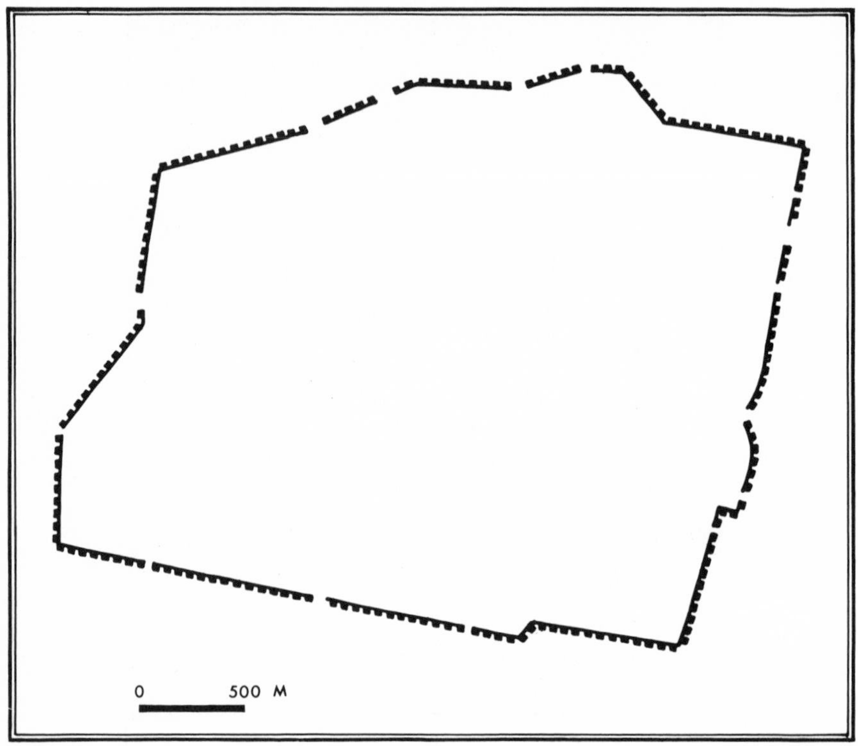

111. City of Hsüeh, near T'eng Hsien, Shantung. (Based on *KK,* 1965/12, p. 628.)

inside the enclosure. This was possibly the Chu-ch'eng site, capital of the small state of Chu from 615 to 281 B.C.[98]

T'eng Hsien, Shantung (*probable sites of Hsüeh-ch'eng and T'eng-ch'eng, states of Hsüeh and T'eng*). Two *hang-t'u* city enclosures of Eastern Chou date, one south and the other southwest of T'eng Hsien in southern Shantung, were investigated by Sekino Takeshi during the World War II[99] and by the Institute of Archaeology in 1964.[100] The former site was probably the ruins of the ancient city of Hsüeh (Fig. 111); and the latter was possibly the ruins of T'eng (Fig. 112), both small states of Eastern Chou. Both were *hang-t'u* structures,

98. Jen Shih-nan and Hu Ping-hua, *KK* (1965/12), 622–27.
99. Sekino, op. cit.
100. Jen Shih-nan and Hu Ping-hua, *KK* (1965/12), 627–33.

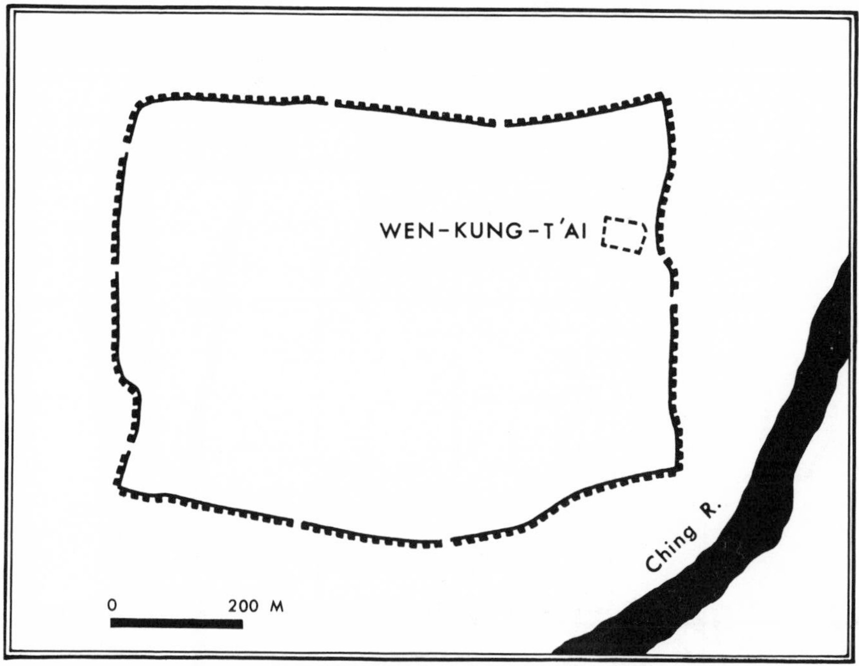

112. City of T'eng, near T'eng Hsien, Shantung. (Based on *KK,* 1965/12, p. 632.)

roughly rectangular. An earthen platform was found at the northeastern corner of T'eng, seemingly a focal spot of intensive cultural activities.

Yen-ling, Honan (probable site of Yen-ch'eng, state of Cheng). A rectangular *hang-t'u* enclosure, about 1,600 m long (N–S) and 800 to 1,000 m wide (E–W), was found in 1961 northwest of Yen-ling, central Honan. A smaller enclosure (148 by 184 m) was located in the northeastern part of the city, and a habitation area occurred in the southeastern part. Remains of corded tiles and *li* tripods found on the surface of the site indicate a Spring Autumn dating, and it has been identified with the Yen-ch'eng city of the state of Cheng of the early Eastern Chou period.[1]

Lin-t'ung, Shensi (probable site of Li-yang, state of Ch'in). Inves-

1. Liu Tung-ya, *KK* (1963/4), 225–26.

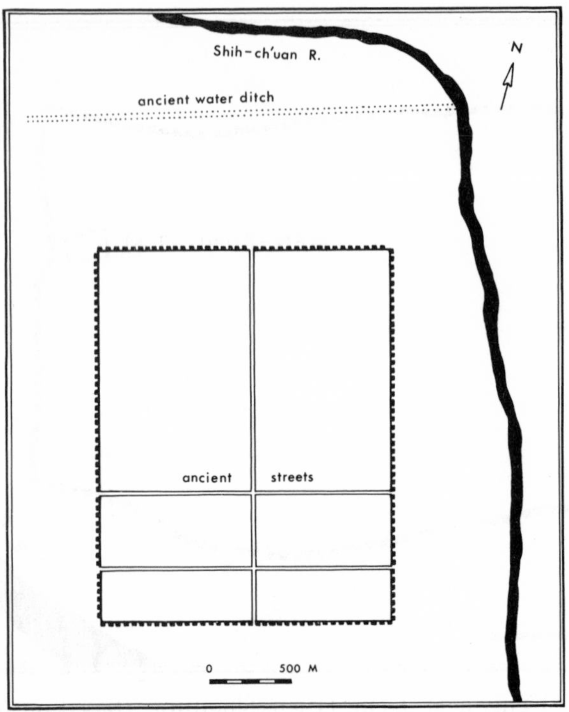

113. City of Li-yang, state of Ch'in, near Lin-t'ung, Shensi. (Based on *WW*, 1966/1, p. 12.)

tigated in 1963 and 1964, the ancient city site 12.5 km northeast of the present town of Li-yang, in Lin-t'ung Prefecture, eastern Shensi, consists of ruins forming a rectangular enclosure about 2,200 m long N–S and 1,800 m wide E–W. Segments of *hang-t'u* walls were identified, and one north–south main street across the entire length of the city and two parallel east–west streets across the width were traced. Remains collected and excavated in the city included architectural relics, pottery, tiles, well rings, sewers, and kilns of Eastern Chou types. North of the city area a segment of an ancient irrigation ditch was found, and two mounds were located south of the city (Fig. 113). The investigators of the site believe this was probably the ruins of Li-yang of Ch'in State, capital from 383 to 350 B.C.[2]

2. T'ien Hsing-nung and Lo Chung-ju, *WW* (1966/1), 10–16.

Hsien-yang, Shensi (probable site of Hsien-yang, state of Ch'in). From 1959 to 1963, archaeological investigations were carried out in an area east-northeast of the modern city of Hsien-yang, eastern Shensi, on the northern bank of the River Wei, an area believed to be the site of the ancient city of Hsien-yang, important capital of the Eastern Chou state of Ch'in from which the conquest of China, completed in 221 B.C., originated. Two segments of *hang-t'u* walls were located, but the outline of the entire city remains to be worked out. In the northern part of the ruins twelve house floors were excavated, some built on *hang-t'u* platforms. A house has the base parts of the walls left, which were plastered and painted with polychromic murals. Bronze vessels, iron nails, and bone artifacts were found in some of the houses. In the same area are many remains of clay pipes, probably the relics of an ancient network of underground drainage. In addition, wells, pottery kilns, and storage pits were found throughout the ruined area, yielding pottery, bronze and iron artifacts, and tiles, and urn burials of children occurred at a spot in the eastern part.[3]

Feng-hsiang, Shensi (probable site of Yüng-ch'eng, state of Ch'in). South of Feng-hsiang, central Shensi, in an area 4.5 km long E–W and 2 km wide N–S, was a ruined city of Eastern Chou period, identified with the Yüng-ch'eng city, an early capital of the state of Ch'in. Pottery, tiles, and clay sewage pipes were found; some of the eave tiles have inscriptions indicating their use on palatial structures.[4]

Summary. In Chinese archaeological studies of the Chou period attention is often focused upon tombs and their yields of works of art, whereas habitation sites—cities and villages—are sometimes neglected. For the study of cultural and societal change during the Chou period, however, the cities provide a focus for the studies of the various aspects of the Chou civilization. For this reason I have undertaken a rather detailed summary of all the printed information concerning the Chou cities that is known to me.[5] In assessing its signifi-

3. Wu Tzu-lin and Kuo Ch'ang-chiang, *KK* (1962/6), 281–89. Wu Tzu-lin, *WW* (1964/7), 59.

4. Hsü Hsi-t'ai and Sun Teh-jun, *KK* (1963/8), 419–22.

5. Except for brief references in publications to possible Eastern Chou sites, so brief that the data cannot be relied upon, and for sites whose dating from the Eastern Chou is doubtful. Examples are the Ch'ü-fu site of Shantung (see Komai Kazuchika, *Archaeological Research Reports, 2,* 1951, Tokyo University, Faculty of Letters) and the Ku-ch'eng site in Yen-shih, Honan (see *KK,* 1964/1, 30–32).

114. *Hang-t'u* layers of a section of the Eastern Chou city near Lo-yang, Honan. (From *KKHP,* 1956/2, Pl. II.)

cance in the development of city life in North China, however, the nature of the data must be constantly borne in mind. Among the scores of Eastern Chou cities we know from history, the above twenty or so represent a mere fraction. Of those that have been described, only the ruins at Hou-ma and Yi Hsien have been intensively excavated, so that the available information is sketchy and uneven. Their chronological positions are not all certain, and these cities belonged to different states which must have had distinctive cultural characteristics within the general framework of the North China civilization of the Chou period. Some of these cities were probably royal or princely capitals, while others were presumably provincial towns or even fortified villages. Undoubtedly their natures were not universally the same, and their basic constitutions not always comparable.

Even so, some broad general trends of city growth can be ascertained from the data, which include some major cities of not only the Royal Chou but also all the important states such as Chin, Chao, Wei, Han, Yen, Ch'i, Cheng, and Ch'in. Many were probably the state capitals at

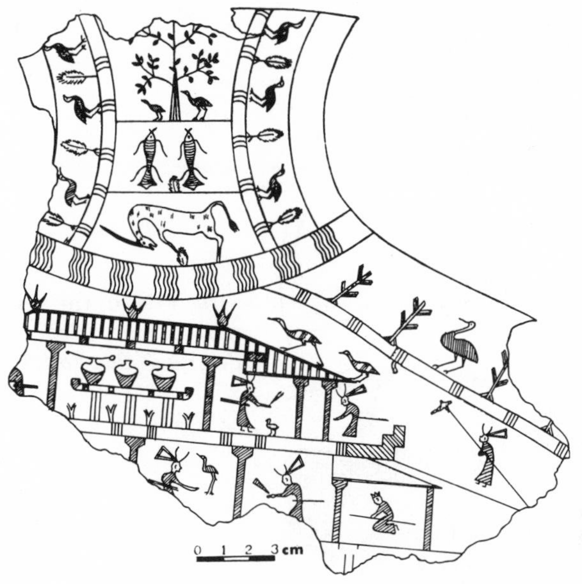

115. Decorative patterns with scenes of platforms and rituals on a bronze vessel excavated from a Warring States period tomb at Fen-shui-ling, Ch'ang-chih, Shansi. (*KKHP,* 1957/1, 109.)

one time or another. The data should be adequate for a contrastive analysis between the earlier cities of the Shang Dynasty and the general patterns of the Eastern Chou city ruins.

There are some observable constants in the city history from the Shang through the beginning of the Han Dynasty. (1) The cities were always located on level plains near waterways. (2) They tended to be walled. (3) The city wall was in all cases constructed of stamped earth (Fig. 114), and the technique of *hang-t'u* or pisé construction remains identical throughout the period. (4) The majority of the cities were oblong or square, though in rare cases they were rather irregular. (5) The orientation of the city enclosure and the ceremonial and palace structure was constantly guided by the four cardinal directions, with an emphasis upon the north–south axis. (6) Earthen platforms or mounds always served as the foundations of structures which were politically and/or ceremonially important and prominent (Fig. 115). (7) The basic constitution of specialized quarters is constant to all the cities where excavated data are sufficient for an understanding of its

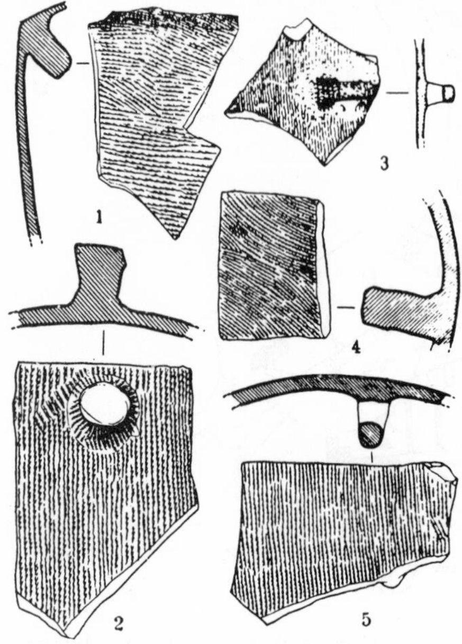

116. Tiles of the Western Chou period, Sian. (From *Feng-hsi Fa-chüeh Pao-kao,* 1962, p. 26.)

functional layout: a city always consisted of a number of parts, no one of which could be considered totally independent in terms of economy, political organization, or religion.

There are obviously also some profound differences and changes. Some of these are in the area of architecture, such as the beginning of the use of tiles (Fig. 116) during the Western Chou period and of bricks during the Warring States period. Others, however, reflect socioeconomic changes, one of the most important of which has to do with the general layout of the city and its interior subdivisions.[6]

The Shang city of Cheng-chou had a walled enclosure as its administrative and ceremonial nucleus; the nature of the remains inside is not altogether clear, but outside the enclosure industrial quarters and residential and farming villages were dispersed in a wide area without apparent planning. The city of An-yang had the same arrangement: settlements of various kinds were spread in a wide area along the

6. Cf. Li Ya-nung, *Chung-kuo ti nu-li-chih yü feng-chien-chih,* Shanghai, Hua-tung Jen-min Press, 1954, pp. 138–46. Oshima Riichi, *Tōhōgakuhō, 30* (1959). Miyazaki Ichisada, *Asiatica, Studies in Oriental History, 1* (1957), 50–65; *Essays in Oriental Studies, Jubilee Volume on the Fifteenth Anniversary of the Tōhōgakukai,* Tokyu, The Tōhō Gakkai, 1962, pp. 342–57.

banks of the River Huan, and the royal temples of Hsiao-t'un and the royal tombs at Hsi-pei-kang provided the focus of the ruined area. The essential contrasts within the city area, then, are those between the aristocratic nucleus and the rest of the community. This basic pattern seems to be retained by the Chin State capital at Hsin-t'ien as late as the second half of the Ch'un-ch'iu period. In ancient literature pertaining to the Chou, this contrast appears to be reflected in several terms which are not, however, always clearly definable. The city as a whole seems to have been referred to as *yi,* a general term for settlements of all sizes and kinds that began to appear in the oracle bone inscriptions. The *yi* physically has two divisions, *tu* or *kuo,* where *chün-tzu* (gentlemen) lived, and *pi,* occupied by *min* (folk) or *yieh-jen* (people of the field).

A new layout of the city began to appear, in the case of Lin-tzu for example, toward the end of the Ch'un-ch'iu period. In addition to a walled enclosure which housed the aristocratic center, a larger area was enclosed within another wall which included the industrial quarters along with residences and commercial streets, in layouts that show careful and total planning. In Lo-yang, as far as the available archaeological record goes, this change involves simply an enlargement of the enclosure to include some residential and industrial quarters that were formerly outside the city. But in most cases, an inner enclosure was built. In most of the Eastern Chou cities there now were three contrasting spatial units within the city: aristocracy in a small enclosure or a special area; industrial and commercial quarters in a larger enclosure; and the farming fields outside the city wall. In *Mencius,* this triple division is made clear in the following quotation:

> [If so, then] the gentlemen scholars would be anxious to serve in Your Excellency's court, the farmers would be anxious to till Your Excellency's land, and the merchants would be anxious to store their goods in Your Excellency's market.

In the Ch'i Yü section of *Kuo Yü,* the same divisions are given as administration (*kuan-fu*), market (*shih-ching*), and fields (*t'ien-yieh*). In some of the lesser cities which were not capital seats of the princes, such as the Wu-chi city described above, the aristocratic center may not have been a major center within the city; but the same principle, that of the walled enclosure including industries and residences as well as the aristocracy, still held. When there was a double enclosure, the outer wall was referred to as *kuo,* and the inner as *ch'eng.* Both terms can be applied to the wall when there is only a single enclosure.

This change in the city layout during the Eastern Chou period, which archaeological materials have amply substantiated, is surely significant. In the first place, it is apparent that the more people there are enclosed within a walled area, engaging in specialized activities, the fewer there are to participate directly in farming the fields outside the enclosure. Such large Warring States cities as Lo-yang (ca. 3,000 m square), Liu-tzu (ca. 4,000 m square), and Hsia-tu (ca. 8,000 by 4,000 m) presumably housed a considerable population of remarkable density. This indicates, among other things, the existence of a highly developed technology, advanced cultivating techniques, and sophisticated administration.

Secondly, the new layout symbolizes the growing importance and increasing specialization of the handicrafts. Cheng-chou and Hou-ma cities have produced evidence that minute subdivisions within the manufacture of bronze artifacts alone were already developed. The new city layout further intensified this specialization by enclosing the industrial quarters within the control and protection of the walled city itself. Inscriptions on pottery often indicate the names or groups of the manufacturers, perhaps suggesting a more private kind of ownership of manufactured goods and a more commercial nature of the industrial undertakings. In the third place, commercial streets, which had not been seen before, now form an important part of the city structure. Historic records show that jewelry, curios, furs and leathers, fabrics and clothing, salt, drugs, food, and wine were all purchased at stores in the Warring States cities, where inns, restaurants, gambling houses, and brothels were also found. The widespread appearance of state currency and the construction of roads shown in the archaeological data further testify to the important role played by commerce in the cities. And finally, the enlarged enclosure and the moats surrounding the city indicate a growing need for defense against invasions. In Tsa-shou-p'ien of *Mo Tzu,* Mo Tzu listed five conditions under which a city could not defend itself: when a large city had a small population; when a small city had a large population; when a large population had insufficient food supply; when the market area was too far from the administrative center; and when the wealth and the wealthy were outside the city wall. Thus a prevailing principle of urban planning during the latter part of the Eastern Chou was apparently to enclose the market, the industries, and the wealth within the city wall for defensive purposes.

Other aspects of Chou cultural history, important to the history of city development in North China, will be discussed below.

TECHNOLOGY

Throughout the Shang and Chou periods stone, bone, antler, and shell remained among the principal materials for implements in the villages, and bronze-making was an essential industry. The Chou bronzes continued to be manufactured by the piece-mold method, but new techniques appeared during the Eastern Chou period. Remains of four furnaces were found in 1959 at Hou-ma; the base of the furnaces was round, about 70 centimeters in diameter. Beginning in the late Spring Autumn and early Warring States periods, techniques were developed to cast the body and the appendages of the vessels separately, as is shown by bronzes in the Chung-chou Road sequence. Appendages (handles, lugs, legs, etc.) were cast first and then attached to the clay body mold before the molten bronze was poured into the mold; or the body was manufactured first, and clay molds for appendages were applied to the body before casting; or they were made separately and then welded together. Another development was the very fine casting of decorative patterns by means of copper, gold, and silver pieces attached to the bronze surface.[7] The clay piece molds at the Hou-ma site also show that the negative decorative patterns on the piece molds were often impressed on the clay with stamps,[8] resulting in decorated bronzes of identical design, something that has not been found among the Shang and Western Chou assemblages. This, plus the intensified specialization (different kinds of artifacts being made at different foundries and the separate casting of bodies and appendages of vessels), indicates that handicrafts in general and bronze-making in particular were becoming increasingly sophisticated and commercial.

7. *Hsin Chung-kuo ti k'ao-ku shou-huo,* Peking, Wenwu Press, 1962, p. 65.
8. *KK* (1962/2), p. 59.

In addition to the advances in bronze-making during the Eastern Chou period, there were other considerable or even revolutionary advances in other technologies during the latter half of the Eastern Chou period: highly developed iron metallurgy and extensive use of iron for implements; the use of iron plows, possibly drawn by cattle; and sophisticated, intensive irrigation systems.[9]

Umehara[10] suggested that the bronzesmiths of the Shang Dynasty probably already had some chemical knowledge of iron and had a practical mastery of its use, as is shown by the chemical analysis of some An-yang bronze artifacts. There is little question, however, that bronze was the only significant material for making metal artifacts throughout the Shang, Western Chou, and early part of the Eastern Chou periods. It is significant that during this long interval (1750 to 500 B.C.) bronze was used primarily for ceremonial vessels and weapons and thus was in the service, so to speak, of the aristocracy. Huang Chan-yüeh stated in 1957:[11]

> Bronze agricultural implements of Shang and Chou that have been excavated by archaeologists up to this date consist of only three Shang Dynasty spades (found from An-yang, Cheng-chou, and Lo-yang, respectively), and no more than ten adzes and axes . . . Extensive excavations undertaken by the Institute of Archaeology, Academia Sinica, in recent years in such regions as Feng, Hao, and Lo-yang, where there was intensive activity during the Western Chou Dynasty, have so far failed to turn out either a single piece of iron or agricultural implement made of bronze. On the other hand, the agricultural implements and handicrafts tools that have been found there consist of stone adzes, stone axes, stone knives, shell knives, shell sickles, bone needles, and bone chisels. Weapons, however, except for some bone and shell arrowheads, were all cast in bronze . . . We have, thus, reason to believe that the principal agricultural implements during the Western

9. For general discussions on some aspects of these problems, see Sekino Takeshi, *Chugaku Kōkōgaku Kenkyū;* Joseph Needham, *The Development of Iron and Steel Technology in China,* London, Newcomen Society, 1958; Wang Chung-shu, *KKTH* (1956/1), 57–76.

10. Umehara Sueji, *Shina Kōkōgakū Runkō,* Tokyo, Kōbundō, 1929, pp. 179–80.

11. *KKHP* (1957/3), 106.

> Chou Dynasty were basically wooden and stone; there were some that were made of bronze, but these are rare and of secondary importance and supplementary nature.

To my knowledge, this statement has thus far not been invalidated by more recent discoveries. Starting with the Warring States period, however, the wide use of iron implements is amply substantiated by archaeological discoveries of remains of this period from all over China.

> Recent archaeological discoveries indicate a highly noteworthy phenomenon. Namely, tombs dated before the Warring States, whenever and wherever the dating is certain, do not contain iron artifacts. Every cemetery of the Warring States period and the Han Dynasty, on the other hand, yields some amount of iron artifacts, with almost no exceptions; in some cases the amount is even considerable. This is certainly not accidental . . . It is, therefore, our studied opinion that as a new and significant raw material of implement manufacture, the use of iron began toward the end of the Ch'un-ch'iu period and the beginning of the Chan-kuo period.[12]

This is confirmed by the first occurrence of iron objects in Period IV (early Warring States) of the Chung-chou Road sequence at Loyang.[13] It would be strange, however, if iron technology suddenly began in the Warring States period without antecedent, and archaeological evidence in the area of Ch'u (see Chapter 9) shows that iron implements began to appear in the earliest Ch'ang-sha tombs, many of which date from the late Spring Autumn period. It seems very likely that the emergence of iron metallurgy as a major industry for toolmaking should be placed in the sixth century B.C. at the latest, although the techniques probably were not perfected and widely used until the fifth century, so far as archaeological evidence is concerned.

Moreover, as soon as iron implements began to appear in significant quantity in archaeological assemblages, both cast iron (pig iron) and wrought iron appeared at the same time. Sekino pointed out some

12. Hua Chüeh-ming et al., *KKHP* (1960/1), 82–83.
13. *Lo-yang Chung-chou-lu,* p. 146.

time ago that many iron implements excavated before World War II in southern Manchuria and Korea which had been dated to the Warring States period had been cast, according to laboratory analysis. He speculated that the same technique must have been developed in North China.[14] A recent metallographical study of four iron implements from the Warring States period (excavated from Hopei, Jehol, and Hunan) shows that they were all cast, and confirms Sekino's speculation.[15] The significance of this fact in Old World iron prehistory has been discussed by Sekino,[16] Joseph Needham,[17] and Nikolaas van der Merwe.[18] The discussions by the last author are the most up-to-date and concise; with his kind permission passages from his work are quoted below:[19]

> Cast iron is a brittle alloy of iron with a carbon content ranging between 1.5% and 5%, which occurs in two forms: white iron and grey iron. . . . The best known attribute of cast iron is its melting point (ca. 1150°C), which is lower than that of steel (ca. 1400°C) or wrought iron (1535°C) and allows it to be cast in the molten state. While the discovery of iron which could be cast added a significant new dimension to the existing techniques of iron metallurgy, the real significance of cast iron involves the economics of iron production. A larger proportion of the ore is reduced when cast iron is manufactured, while steel can be mass-produced through oxidation of the carbon in cast iron—a procedure which is considerably less laborious than cementation. Wrought iron can be manufactured in the same way; the production of wrought iron and steel from cast iron is known as the *indirect process*.
>
> Although cast iron may have a melting point as low as 1130°C, depending on its carbon content, this temperature must not be

14. Sekino Takeshi, *Chugaku Kōkōgaku Kenkyū,* pp. 187–88.
15. Hua Chüeh-ming et al., *KKHP* (1960/1).
16. Ibid., pp. 189–91.
17. See n. 9 above.
18. *The Metallurgical History and Carbon-14 Dating of Iron.* Unpublished Ph.D. dissertation, Yale University, 1966.
19. Ibid., pp. 29–31, 57–59. This work also reports a C-14 date of an iron object excavated from Chin-ts'un, Lo-yang, in the Royal Ontario Museum collection.

confused with the much higher temperature at which it is produced. A number of variables combine to make a temperature as high as 1400°C one of the requirements for the production of cast iron. . . .

The solution of the problems described here requires a sophistication in furnace construction and operation which took the Europeans more than 3000 years to develop; only in China was the appropriate furnace in use before the Christian era. . . . The early development of this [indirect] process can be said to have taken place almost exclusively within the borders of China, where the history of iron metallurgy followed a radically different course from that of the countries to the west. . . .

It is possible that the early Chinese iron smelters may have known how to produce wrought iron in a bloom furnace; however, the evidence for it is entirely lacking. The blast furnace seems to have been the mainstay of Chinese iron metallurgy from the very beginning. It is significant that there seem to be no Chinese words for the reduction of iron ore in a solid form; the words for smelting, *chu* and *yeh,* refer to the production of iron in its liquid form. It can therefore be assumed that the early occurrences of wrought iron were probably the result of the fining of cast iron; the fact that the Chinese words for cast iron (*sheng t'ieh*) and wrought iron (*shu t'ieh*) mean "raw iron" and "ripe iron," respectively, supports this view of the indirect process as the basic tradition of Chinese metallurgy. The technological and economic factors which made possible this early production of cast iron have been explored by Sekino and Needham. The most important of these are probably to be found in an early sophistication in the control of heat: Chinese artisans of the 7th century B.C. possessed great skill in the casting of intricate bronze objects and were able to fire pottery at high temperatures. . . . The initial production of cast iron was reinforced by the invention of double-cylinder bellows with reciprocating motion (4th century B.C.), the double-acting (push–pull) cylinder bellows (2nd century B.C.), and the application of water power to these bellows in the 1st century A.D. A reinforcing result . . . is the fact that the rendering of cast iron from ore allows for the mass production of the full

> range of alloys at a highly efficient rate. Thus iron became the metal of the Chinese peasantry and found its early and large-scale use in the fashioning of agricultural implements.

The use of cast iron for agricultural implements is undoubtedly a highly significant event in Chinese economic history. The common types of implements during the latter part of the Eastern Chou period included axes, adzes, chisels, spades, sickles, and hoes (Fig. 117); the plow was manufactured, but was relatively rare and does not seem to have been effective enough to replace the spade and hoe as a cultivating tool. The earliest iron plows that are well documented archaeologically come from the Warring States tombs at Ku-wei-ts'un, in Hui Hsien, northern Honan.[20] These are flat, V-shaped iron pieces which probably were mounted on wooden blades and handles to serve as working edges (Fig. 118). The width of each arm, measured from two complete specimens, averages 18 centimeters. In view of its relatively small size and its mounting device, which could not have been too secure, this primitive plow was probably not capable of turning over the soil to any considerable depth.[21] There is no archaeological evidence that cattle were used to draw the plows. Cattle-drawn plows of considerable size, capable of deep plowing, did not appear in the archaeological record until the middle of the Western Han Dynasty (Fig. 119).

However, with the advent of new iron cultivation implements, revolutionary changes must have occurred. There is no question that they are more effective and efficient than stone and bone implements, and their development must have been related to the growth of population in the cities. Another of the most significant and consequential of the changes, which may or may not be related to the use of iron implements, is that irrigation techniques became highly elaborated and intensified during the latter part of the Eastern Chou period. Literary sources indicate that both Shang and Western Chou practiced irrigation to some extent, but the earliest reference to irrigation on a large scale appeared in 563 B.C. in the state of Cheng of central Honan.[22]

20. Kuo Pao-chün et al., *Hui Hsien Fa-chüeh Pao-kao,* p. 91.
21. Huang Chan-yüeh, *KKHP* (1957/3), 105. Fang Chuang-yu, *KK* (1964/7), 355–61.
22. Hsü Chung-shu, *BIHP, 5* (1935), 255–69.

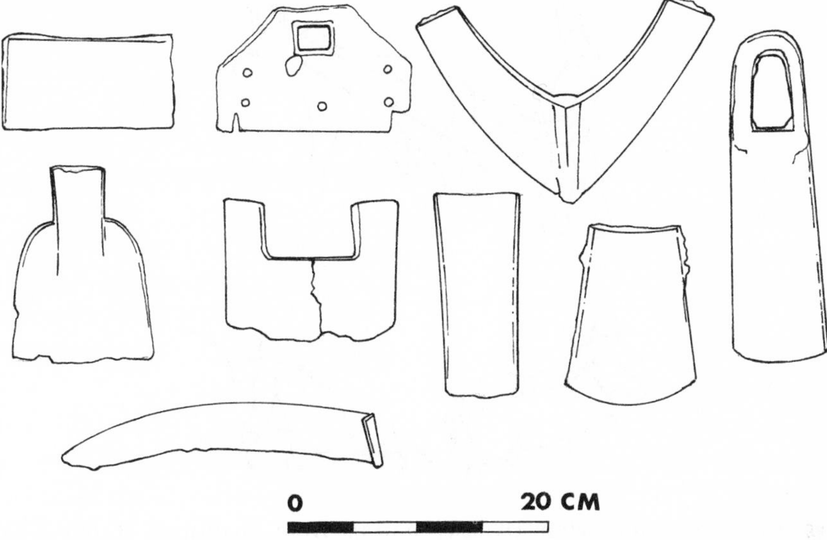

117. Iron implements of the Warring States period. (From *Hsin Chung-kuo ti K'ao-ku Shou-huo,* 1962, p. 61.)

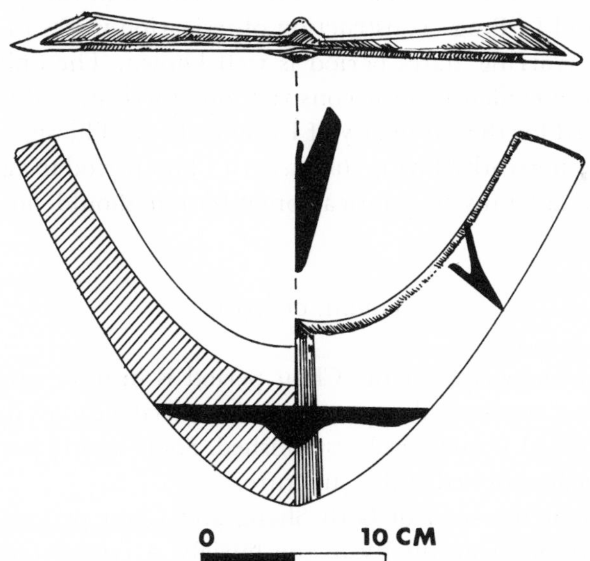

118. Iron plow blade excavated from a Warring States tomb in Hui Hsien, Honan. (From Hsia Nai et al., *Hui Hsien Fa-chüeh Pao-kao,* Peking, 1956, p. 92.)

119. Cattle plowing; Han Dynasty murals from Shantung. (From *KK*, 1964/7, p. 356.)

Hsün Tzu recorded state officials who specialized in this phase of agriculture, and Li Ping's construction of irrigation works in Szechwan during the Warring States period is well known. The only piece of archaeological evidence of the construction of irrigation ditches is the one described for the Ch'in city of Li-yang above. The significance of large-scale waterworks during the Eastern Chou period to agricultural production and thus to political organization should not be overlooked.[23]

BURIAL CUSTOMS

Since our knowledge of the Chou period is in most cases derived from tombs, a typological sequence of the burial customs during this dynastic interval is fairly well established. Some highly pertinent aspects may be mentioned at this juncture.

Throughout the span of both Shang and Chou periods, cultural constants are met continually in the burials. A typical tomb can be described as follows (Fig. 120). The deceased was interred in a rec-

23. See e.g. K. A. Wittfogel, "The Theory of Oriental Society," in: M. H. Fried, ed., *Readings in Anthropology, 2,* New York, Crowell, 1959.

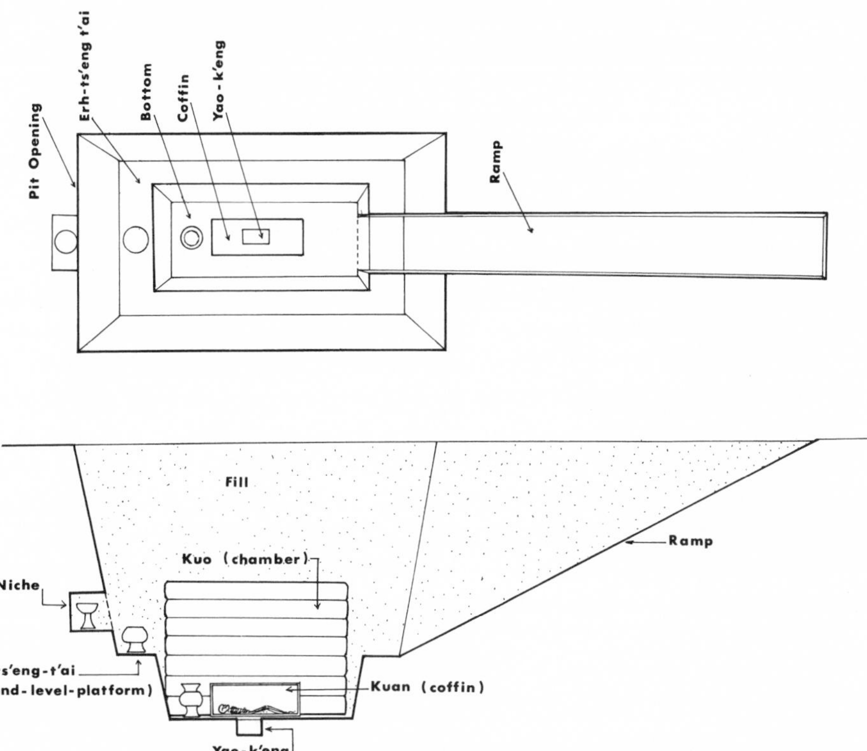

120. A typical Chinese Bronze Age pit-grave tomb.

tangular pit (*shu hsüeh,* or vertical pit), slightly or much larger than the size of the body, excavated to a considerable depth. The walls of the pit were vertical or sloped slightly inward or outward. Frequently, about half a meter before the desired depth was reached, a smaller pit was continued to the bottom, which left a ledge around the lower pit for the placement of grave goods (*sheng-t'u erh-ts'eng-t'ai,* or raw earth second level platform). In some cases, the pit was dug clear to the bottom on all four sides, but a ledge of fresh earth was built around the lower part of the pit (*shu-t'u erh-ts'eng-t'ai,* or ripe earth second level platform). Sometimes niches were dug into the walls for the placement of goods. The floor and the walls were often plastered, and the walls were sometimes painted, occasionally with drapery designs like the inside of a bed or room. At the center of the bottom in many pits was a small square pit (*yao-k'eng*, or waist pit, since it was located below the waist of the body) in which an animal, usually a dog, was buried. Then, the bottom and the lower walls of the pit (above the level of the *erh-ts'eng-t'ai* if there was one) were lined with wooden planks to form a chamber (*kuo*), in which the body was placed in a wooden coffin (*kuan*). Grave goods, consisting of utensils, ornaments, weapons, food in containers, and so on, were placed in the coffin, outside the coffin in the wooden chamber, or outside the chamber on the ledge or in the wall niches. The pit was then filled with earth, often pounded in layer by layer. Many larger graves had, in addition to these elemental components, one, two, or four ramps that ran from the ground to the floor level of the pit. Bodies of sacrificed humans and animals, and sometimes horse chariots, were buried in various spots in the tomb (in the wooden chamber, outside in the pit, on the ledge, under the floor of a ramp, or in the fill) or outside the pit in separate graves nearby, depending on the size and elaboration of the burial.

Many of these features of a typical Shang or Chou burial (of the upper class) were apparently manifestations of a prevailing ancestor worship and a deep belief in life in the afterworld. Details and features of the tomb construction, the posture and orientation of the dead, and the nature and amount of grave goods, were presumably more significant of cultural traditions and styles or of the societal status of the dead.

In tomb construction, the basic vertical pit pattern prevailed throughout, although variations were plentiful. This basic pattern is exemplified by the graves of Shang,[24] Western Chou,[25] and the early part of Eastern Chou.[26] At Pai-sha in Yü Hsien and Pi-sha-kang in Cheng-chou, both in Honan, the tombs dated to the end of the Ch'un-ch'iu and the beginning of the Chan-kuo were still exclusively of this vertical pit pattern.[27] Later in the Chan-kuo period, however, another style of tomb construction began to appear, the so-called *tung-shih-mu*, or cave-chamber graves. For such graves a vertical pit was dug as usual,

24. Kao Ch'ü-hsün, *Bull. Dept. Archaeol. Anthropol., Natl. Taiwan Univ., 13/14* (1959). Shih Chang-ju, *BIHP, 23* (1953), 447–87.

25. Shih Hsing-pang, *KKHP, 8* (1954), 110–13. Ho Han-nan, *KKHP* (1957/1), 75–77. Wang Chi-sheng, *WWTKTL* (1955/4), 49. Kuo Pao-chün, *TYKKPK, 1* (1936), 167–200.

26. E.g. Lin Shou-chin et al., *Shang-ts'un-ling Kuo-kuo mu ti*, pp. 3–4.

27. Ch'en Kung-jou, *KKHP, 7* (1954), 89.

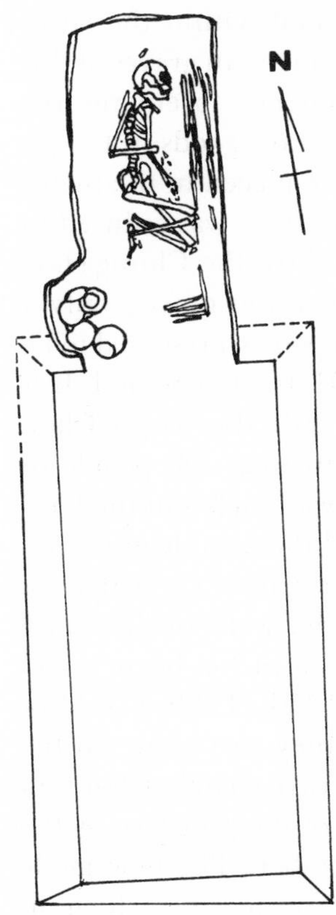

121. A Warring States cave-chamber tomb, at T'ai-shan-miao, Lo-yang. (From *KKHP, 9,* 1954, p. 110.)

but a cave was excavated into one of the pit walls and the coffin placed in this chamber instead of at the bottom of the pit (Fig. 121). At the Warring States cemetery near Shao-kou in Lo-yang, there were 16 cave-chamber graves as against 43 vertical pit graves.[28] Of the 112 Warring States graves at the Pan-p'o cemetery near Sian, only 11 retained the old vertical pit pattern; the rest were of the cave-chamber variety.[29] According to Kuo Pao-chün and Lin Shou-chin,[30] an evolutionary sequence of change from the traditional pit grave to the new cave-

28. Wang Chung-shu, *KKHP, 8* (1954), 130.
29. Chin Hsüeh-shan, *KKHP* (1957/3), 67–70.
30. *KKHP, 9* (1955), 109–10.

chamber tombs took place during a short interval within the latter part of the Warring States. Although many wall niches in graves of this period contained grave goods, there was a tendency to enlarge the niche and place the body in it and to place the grave goods in the pit itself. When both grave goods and the body were placed in the niche, it had to be enlarged into a chamber, and the pit itself was reduced in size and importance to the role of shaft or ramp. In the Chung-chou Road sequence of Lo-yang, of the 260 Eastern Chou graves, only 4 are of the cave-chamber type. One of these is too poorly preserved to be dated, but all the others are dated to Period VII, the last period. It is conceivable that the inhabitants of Lo-yang, still the Royal Chou stronghold, were more resistant to change than were the people of other areas of North China, but the number of wall niches in the Eastern Chou graves tells an interesting story. Of all the datable graves on the Chung-chou Road, ten were of the Western Chou; six had waist pits, but none had a wall niche. There are neither waist pits nor wall niches in graves of Period I of Eastern Chou; wall niches begin to appear in Period II and continue through Period VII (Table 11). Most of the niches are in the north wall, although they also occur on the other three sides. These facts indicate that the cave-chamber tomb of the late Eastern Chou probably did evolve out of the pit grave by the conversion of the wall niche into a burial chamber. The new mode of construction may merely represent a fashion of the time, which, in combination with bricks, completely replaced the vertical pit graves during the following Han Dynasty as the principal mode of tomb con-

TABLE 11.

The Increase of Wall Niches in Tombs of the Pit-Grave Type During the Chou

	Period	*Total Graves*	*Graves with Wall Niches*	(%)
Western Chou		10	0	0
Eastern Chou	I	6	0	0
	II	30	3	10.0
	III	37	2	5.40
	IV	26	5	19.23
	V	15	3	33.33
	VI	22	7	31.81
	VII	26	10	38.46

122. A burial mound in the city of Hsia-tu, Yen. (From *KKHP,* 1965/2, p. 102.)

struction. Use of bricks of a hollow variety for the construction of the tomb chamber was also a late Warring States innovation.[31]

A related item has to do with the earthen mound built on top of the grave after the pit was filled. Historical records and many local traditions relate to burial mounds of the Eastern Chou period, but those in the city of Yen Hsia-tu are the only known graves with earthen mounds that have been excavated (Fig. 122). Confucius, of the Spring Autumn period, was quoted as saying, "I hear that in ancient times the dead was interred but no mounds were built." Ancient times to Confucius were apparently the Shang and Western Chou periods. The Hsi-pei-kang royal tombs of the Shang Dynasty probably had no mounds, and Kuo Pao-chün, who specifically looked for evidence of mounds at the Western Chou cemetery at Hsin-ts'un in Chün Hsien, Honan, found none for that period.[32] Until there is definitive evidence to the contrary, it appears that the custom of building mounds atop a burial was another innovation of the Eastern Chou period.

The posture and orientation of the corpse pose special and difficult problems. Throughout most of Shang and Chou, the stretched-out posture predominated. The Shang and Western Chou burials, however, are differentiable into supine and prone groups. Among the

31. *Lo-yang Chung-chou-lu,* Tables 3–11; and Honan Bureau of Culture, *Cheng-chou Erh-li-kang,* 1959, pp. 80–81.
32. *TYKKPK, 1* (1936), 174.

Shang burials at Ta-ssu-k'ung-ts'un excavated in 1953, 89 have enough bony remains to determine that 67 were supine and 22 prone.[33] Of the 109 Western Chou tombs at Chang-chia-p'o and K'o-hsing-chuang, near Sian, 70 bodies were supine, 39 prone.[34] All the bodies in these two groups are stretched out; the prone burials, though in the minority, account for a considerable percentage (25 per cent for Ta-ssu-k'ung-ts'un and 36 per cent for the Sian group) and cannot be dismissed as mere exceptions. Obviously, during the Shang and Western Chou periods, these two postures had a significant contrast that must have had to do with the social and ritual status of the dead.

This contrast, however, was replaced by another pair of contrasts in burial posture at the beginning of the Eastern Chou—between the stretched and the flexed posture (Fig. 123). Burials with a flexed or contracted posture were not absent in Western Chou burials. The late Western Chou tomb at P'u-tu-ts'un, near Sian, contains three bodies, two of which were flexed.[35] Among the 18 early Western Chou tombs at Fang-tui-ts'un in Hung-chao, Shansi, four flexed burials are found.[36] At the late Western Chou and early Eastern Chou cemetery at Shang-ts'un-ling, 221 graves contain recognizable skeletons, 44 of which are flexed.[37] However, there is no question that the flexed posture was relatively rare during this period. Among the 109 burials in the Sian group at Chang-chia-p'o and K'o-hsing-chuang and the 10 burials at Chung-chou Road of Lo-yang of the Western Chou period, not a single flexed burial occurred. Along the Chung-chou Road in 256 Eastern Chou tombs, in contrast, 215 are contracted, and the stretched bodies are a distinct minority. Moreover, the flexed posture became a predominant manner of burial with the beginning of the Chung-chou road sequence (the beginning of the Spring Autumn period). Of 6 Period I tombs, 5 are flexed; of 30 Period II tombs, 20 are flexed; after this time stretched burials are exceptions. It is evident that the flexed posture and burial in wall niches and cave chambers were related: it was easier to place a flexed body in a small niche or cavity. Since flexed burials preceded the cave-chamber burials, the former may be said to have influenced the latter development but they

33. Ma Teh-chih et al., *KKHP, 9* (1955), 27–71.
34. Wang Po-hung et al., *Feng Hsi Fa-chüeh Pao-kao,* p. 116.
35. Ho Han-nan, *KKHP* (1957/1), 76.
36. Wang Chi-sheng, *WWTKTL* (1955/4), 49.
37. Lin Shou-chin, *Shang-ts'un-ling Kuo-kuo mu-li,* p. 4.

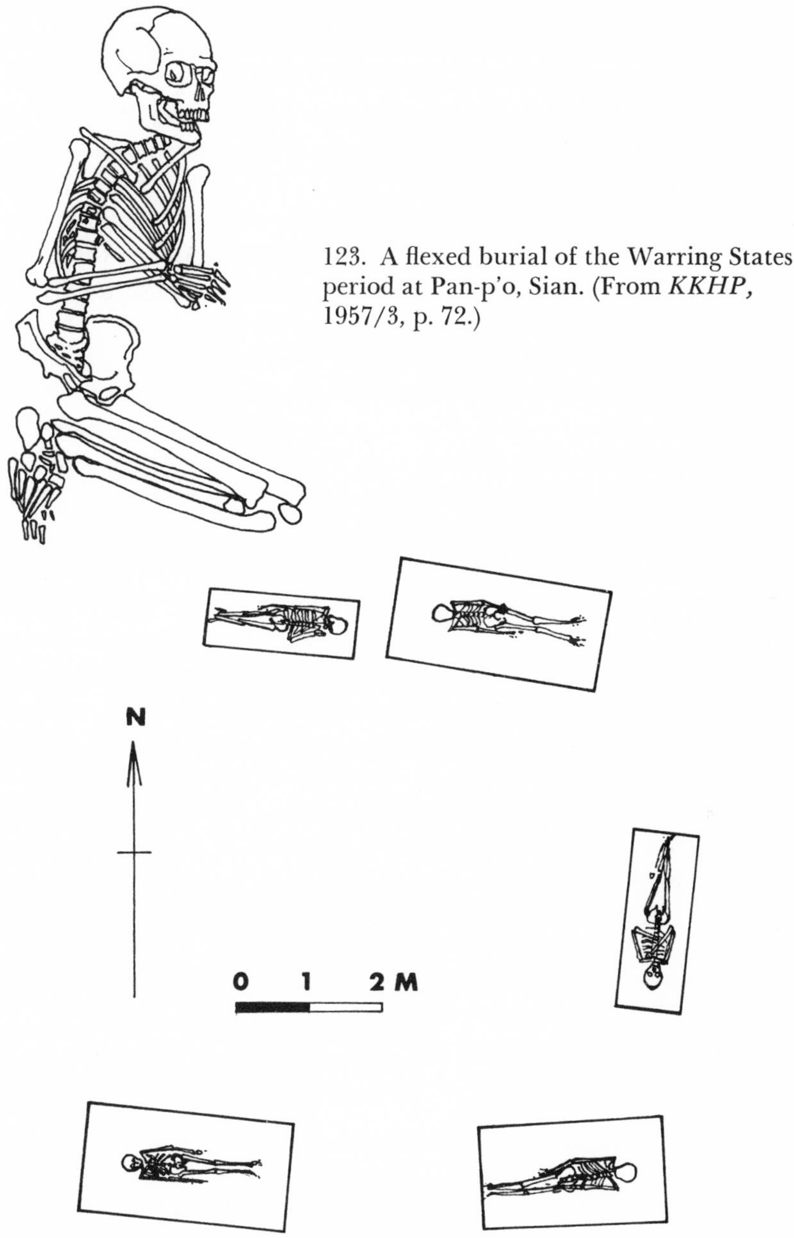

123. A flexed burial of the Warring States period at Pan-p'o, Sian. (From *KKHP,* 1957/3, p. 72.)

124. Five Western Chou burials near Sian. (From *Feng-hsi Fa-chüeh Pao-kao,* 1962, p. 116.)

cannot be explained by it. Burial in Han Dynasty tombs again favored a stretched posture, which must be related to the enlargement of the cave chambers in Han tombs.

The problem of the orientation of the tomb and of the corpse is even more perplexing; one finds all sorts of variations but no clear-cut regularities which change with time. All the Yin tombs of the Hsi-pei-kang group were south–north oriented, but since all of them had been robbed during early historic times and no skeletons of the tomb masters were left at the time of excavations, the orientation of the corpses is a matter for speculation. During the Chou Dynasty, in all its various subphases, both north–south and east–west orientations are found, and in the former case the head is sometimes oriented toward the north and sometimes toward the south. It is tempting to make a case here for a correlation of the orientation with the posture of the corpse or with the status of the dead, but generalizations should not yet be made.

It is evident, however, that in the interpretation of burial remains from both Shang and Chou periods the scholar must bear in mind that the burial ritual was to transport the deceased from the world of the living to the world of the dead, a transportation that involved his social and ritual status as well as his worldly possessions. The meaning of the postures and the orientations of the dead must be sought in terms of the varying ritual and social importance of the dead. An indication of this is the spatial position of his tomb in relation to the tombs of his contemporaries. The possible meaning of the arrangement of the royal tombs in An-yang in two east-west clusters has been mentioned before. Among the Western Chou tombs at Chang-chia-p'o and K'o-hsing-chuang, a particular layout is especially interesting. Five tombs, containing artifacts of apparently a single period, were placed as shown in Figure 124. Between neighboring pairs the heads were placed one against the other or the feet pointed to each other. Similar clusters are not rare among the early Western Chou tombs.[38] The large burial mounds of Hsia-tu, it may be recalled, were also placed in regular rows.

Also to be accounted for by the social and ritual status of the dead person as well as by the fashion of the times are the amount and nature of the grave goods. The contrast in social levels cannot be more vividly

38. Wang Po-hung et al., *Feng Hsi Fa-chüeh Pao-kao,* pp. 115–16.

demonstrated in archaeology than by burials. Among the Chung-chou Road burials of the Eastern Chou, for instance, the very few rich graves have large pits, double wooden chambers, many bronzes, and much pottery; the very poor ones have no shaped pits, no coffins, and no grave goods. The roles played by the various burials in each of the royal tombs in An-yang are well known. But changes can be observed between tombs of different periods. The typology of the grave goods of course goes with the burial chronology, and the changes in this respect during the Chou period will be discussed below. Another important shift concerns the human retainers. Of 182 Western Chou tombs in the Chang-chia-p'o and K'o-hsing-chuang group, 9 contained sacrificed humans. Of more than 3,000 tombs of the Warring States period from various parts of China known up to 1962, only about a dozen have sacrificed retainers (Fig. 125).[39] On the other hand, in tombs of the late Eastern Chou period large numbers of figurines were substituted for human beings. In the north these images were made of clay and, occasionally, of lead; wooden ones prevailed in the south. The implications of this change from humans to figurines in terms of social and economic history of the Shang and Chou periods are self-evident.

ARTIFACTS

The study of artifacts (of stone, bone, jade, pottery, bronze, and iron) of the Shang and Chou periods is the hallmark of Chinese archaeology. Sites and tombs were not excavated and examined in their totality until less than fifty years ago, but individual works of art have been the object of scholarly research in China for the past two thousand years, and as material for study there are as many artifacts in artistic collections as there are in archaeological assemblages brought to light under scientific supervision. There are many studies of Shang and Chou artifacts, and they are admirably treated in many textbooks of Chinese archaeology and art history.[40] For the present pur-

39. *Hsin Chung-kuo ti K'ao-ku Shou-huo,* p. 70.

40. See e.g. Chu Chien-hsin, *Chin Shih Hsüeh,* Shanghai, Commercial Press, 1940; Jung Keng, *Shang Chou Yi-ch'i T'ung-k'ao,* Peiping, Yenching University, 1947; William Watson, *Ancient Chinese Bronzes,* Rutland, Vt., Tuttle, 1962; Cheng Te-k'un, *Chou China,* Cambridge, Heffer & Sons, 1963; Max Loehr, *Relics of Ancient China,* New York, Asia Society, 1965.

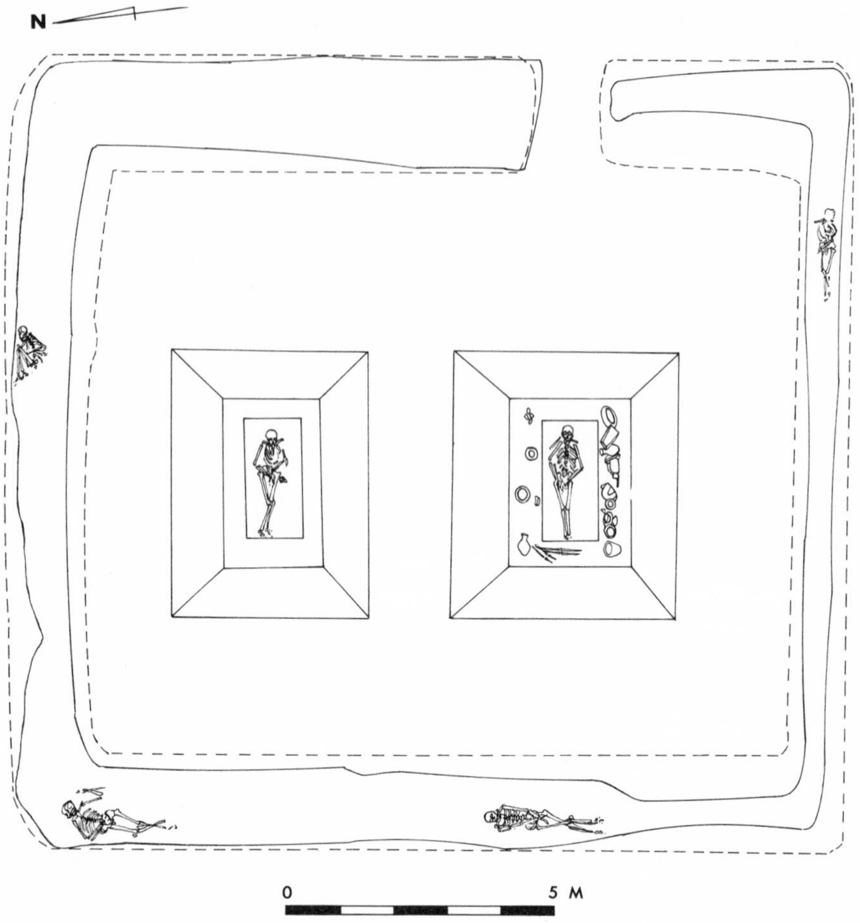

125. An Eastern Chou tomb with sacrificed humans, excavated near Hou-ma, Shansi. (From *Hsin Chung-kuo ti K'ao-ku Shou-huo,* 1962, p. 71.)

pose, our discussion must be highly selective, and it is concerned largely with bronzes. Stone and bone implements of the Shang and Chou do not materially differ from their Neolithic prototypes except in a few special cases, and iron artifacts began only toward the end of the period. Ceramics is highly important, to be sure, and its chronological uses have been demonstrated by the Sian and Lo-yang sequences of Western and Eastern Chou tombs. But research in ceramics has been much less extensive, and in many ways it must be based on a thorough understanding of the bronze vessels, for many forms and decorations of the pottery in the Chinese Bronze Age were manifest imitations of their bronze counterparts.

The central problem for the study of bronzes is the formulation of types.[41] The abundant data on the chronology of Shang and Chou archaeological sites provide a solid basis for a chronological arrangement of the occurrences and changes of individual types of bronzes throughout the period in question. Furthermore, it is possible to examine the history of change of individual modes that compose the types, as well as the history of change of whole assemblages of artifacts consisting of types in association. Since my purpose here is not the history of bronze types, modes, and assemblages per se, but is the examination of aspects of the history of Shang and Chou civilizations as revealed by these studies, I shall confine the discussion to the general problem of type formulation and some significant developmental trends in the history of bronze artifacts.

The formulation of types of Chinese bronzes has its own conventions. In Chou and Han texts there are numerous references to bronze utensils, and some bronze vessels name themselves in their inscriptions. The identification of their "native lexicons" with the actual bronze types would be an important terminological problem of general anthropological interest. But scholars can hardly choose to use or not use the native terms for the types, for ever since the Sung Dynasty there has been a standard terminology in the Chinese antiquarian and archaeological literature, consisting of lexicons taken from the Chou and Han texts. A tripod with three solid legs, for instance, is a *ting,* and one with hollow legs a *li.* Moreover, since these terms in their textual contexts refer to artifact types in regard to use but not to form, these terms carry implicit meanings of use. A *ting,* for instance, refers to a container for food (mostly meat) used for ritual purposes, and a *chüeh,* also a tripod with three solid legs, immediately calls to mind a ritual wine cup. Therefore, the standard Chinese terminology for the bronzes of Shang and Chou is by definition "functional," presumably ideal and useful for the purpose of archaeological reconstruction

41. For "type" and "mode," the definitions of Irving Rouse are adopted in this section. See his *Prehistory in Haiti: A Study in Method,* Yale University Publications in Anthropology, *21;* 1939.

of the ancient culture and society. The question, however, is whether the identification of the Chou and Han terms with actual artifact types is correct (except for cases where the vessels are named in their inscriptions). Another complicating factor is the problem of hierarchy of taxa. A *tsun,* for instance, often refers to a bronze vessel of a specific form, but on other occasions it includes all classes of ceremonial vessels. With these considerations, Li Chi, in his studies of the bronze vessels of An-yang, has sought to establish a separate system of terminology based exclusively on the shape of the lower part of the vessel, a system that he used first to classify the pottery of Hsiao-t'un.[42] Thus the Shang bronzes at Hsiao-t'un were first grouped into the following five "orders": *round-bottomed,* 1 vessel; *flat-bottomed,* 2 vessels; *ring-footed,* 34 vessels; *tripod,* 36 vessels; *Quatripod,* 3 vessels; and *lid-shaped,* 6 pieces. Under each order, the traditional terms are adopted for finer characterizations—*ting*-shaped, *chüeh*-shaped, and so forth. This new system based on shape is used entirely for description and has proved useful. The traditional terminology, however, continues to be used. In the current Chinese archaeological literature, the ancient terms are used freely when the artifacts can be typed with certainty or near certainty; when they cannot, descriptive terms such as those coined by Li Chi are used. Although there is a considerable confusion of terms in Chinese archaeology, especially in the classification of bronze and ceramic vessels, the following categories of some of the most common bronze artifacts are more or less in general use (Fig. 126):

1. Cooking and dining vessels: ting, li, yen, fu, kui, hsü, tui, tou
2. Drinking vessels: chüeh, chiao, chia, ho, tsun, ku, chih, yu, kuang, yi, niao shou tsun, hu, lei, shuo
3. Water utensils: p'an, yi, chien, yü, p'en, cheng, chu, wan
4. Musical instruments: cheng, jao, chung, to, ling (varieties of bell), ku (drum)
5. Weapons: ko (halberd), chi (halberd), mao (spear), shih (tsu) (arrow), chien (sword), fu (ax), tao (knife)
6. Horse and chariot fittings
7. Mirrors and belt hooks

42. Li Chi, *Chung-kuo K'ao-ku Hsüeh-pao, 3* (1948), 1–99; *Hsiao-t'un T'ao-ch'i,* Taipei, Institute of History and Philology, Academia Sinica, 1956.

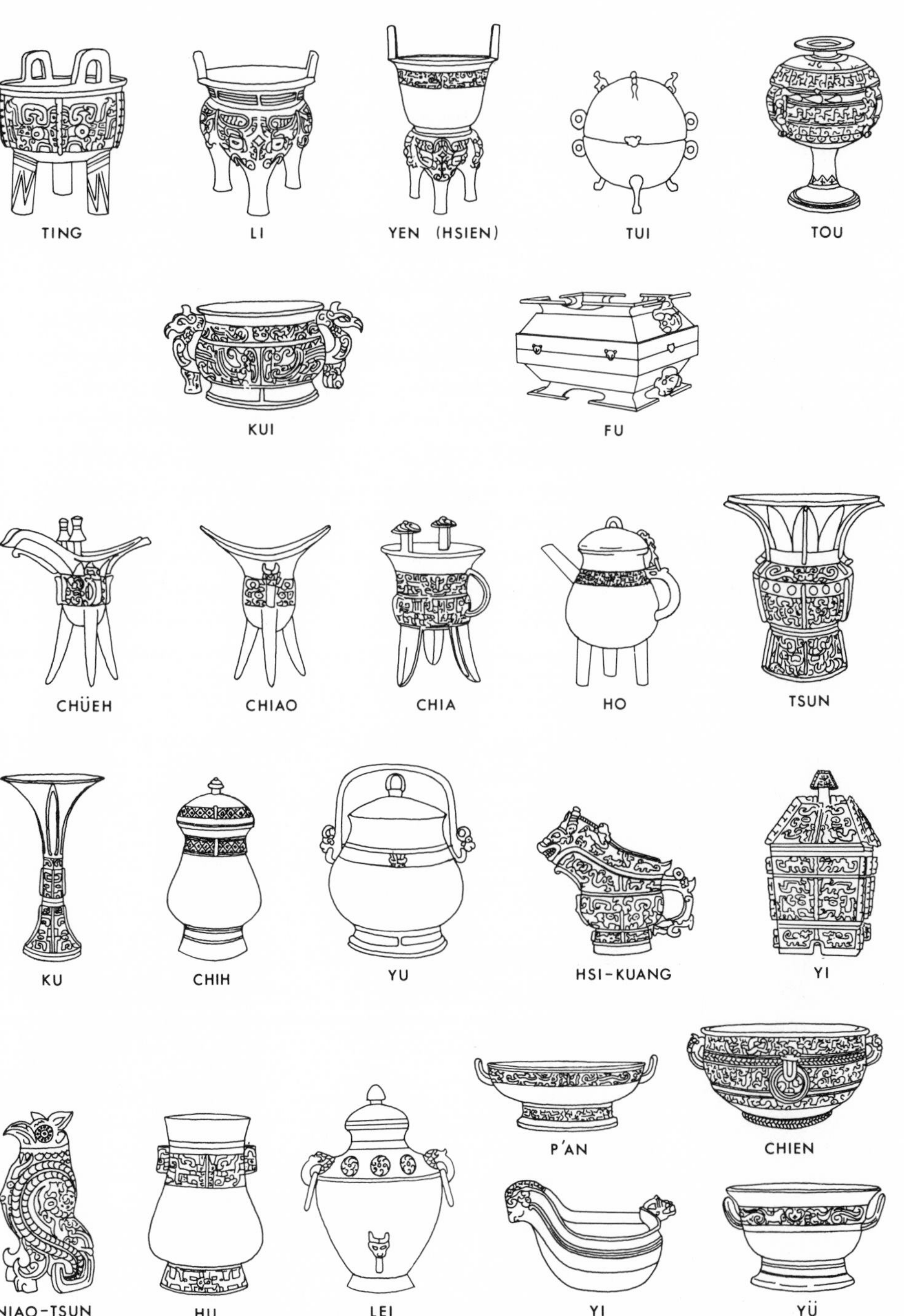

126. Major types of Shang and Chou bronze vessels.

Some of these types occurred throughout the Shang and Chou periods, but in some intervals they exhibited variations in mode. Others occurred only during certain intervals. The occurrence and variation of these types, either singly or in association, during the different periods of Shang and Chou are, therefore, significant. For example, *ting* and *ko* are two types that are almost universal at Shang and Chou sites, but the changes in mode are chronologically significant. All *ting* consist of three components: body, two handles, and three legs. In Shang and early Western Chou periods, the two handles were placed on the rim, and the three legs were straight. Later, the handles were sometimes lowered to the body and had to be bent, and the legs were made thicker and bent to resemble the legs of animals (Fig. 127). The earlier *ko* halberd consisted of merely a cutting blade and a flat hafting tongue, but as time went on the lower edge at the end of the blade extended downward to accommodate an increasing number of holes for greater security of hafting, the tongue became increasingly pointed to change from a purely hafting device to an auxiliary part of the weapon (Fig. 128).

Other types of bronze artifacts occurred only at a certain time in the

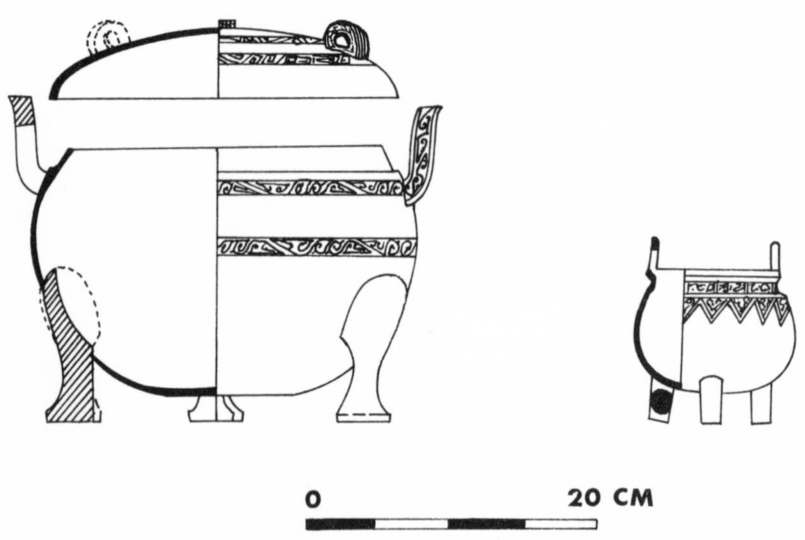

127. *Ting* tripods of the Shang (*right*) and Warring States (*left*) periods. (Right, from Li Chi, *KKHP, 3,* 1948; left, from Kuo Pao-chün, *Shan-piao-chen yü Liu-li-ko,* 1959, p. 11.)

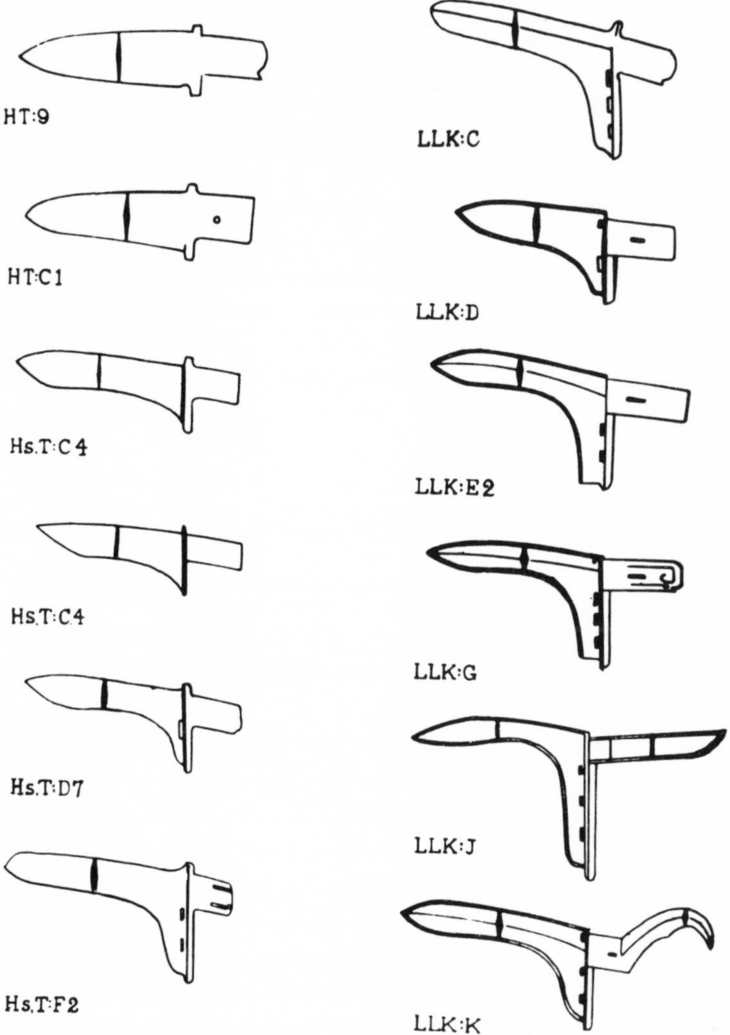

128. Changes in *ko* halberd forms from Shang to Warring States period. (From Li Chi, *Beginnings of the Chinese Civilization*, 1957, p. 57.)

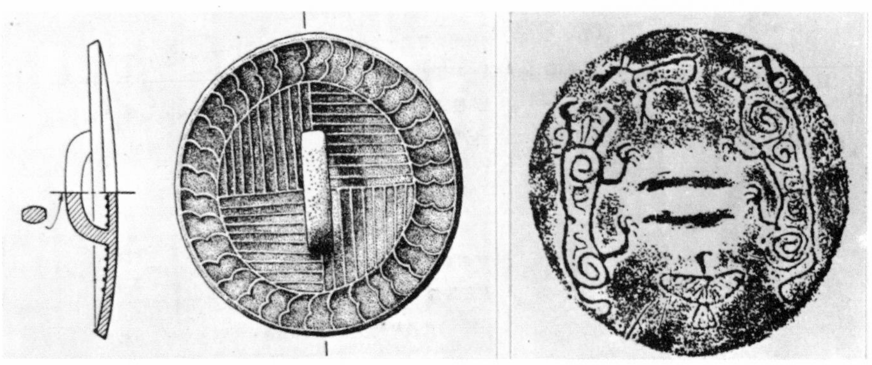

129. Bronze mirrors of Shang (*left*) and Western Chou (*right*) types. (Left, from Kao Ch'ü-hsün, *BIHP, 24,* 1958, p. 689; right, from *Shang-ts'un-ling Kuo kuo Mu-ti,* 1959, p. 27.)

Shang and Chou periods, and their occurrence alone is chronologically significant. Bronze swords, mirrors, and belt hooks, for instance, were most commonly found in tombs of the Warring States period, and it used to be thought that they were innovations at that time. Recent reports and discoveries have pushed the first occurrence of swords to the late Western Chou or initial Eastern Chou period;[43] that of the mirror to the Shang period (Fig. 129);[44] and that of belt hooks to the early Spring Autumn period.[45] The earlier finds, however, are not the same as the later varieties, and there is no question that these types did not become prevalent until the middle of Eastern Chou.

The decorative art of the bronzes is another area of research in which a great deal of data has been accumulated. Most of the decorative motifs of Shang and Chou bronzes are derived from the animal world; floral patterns did not significantly occur until late Eastern Chou.[46] Again, individual motifs occurred in different periods or underwent changes throughout the era. The most characteristic single motif of Shang and early Western Chou bronzes is the *t'ao-t'ieh* face (without the lower jaw) of a mythical creature. During the latter half

43. Lin Shou-chin et al., *Shang-ts'un-ling Kuo kuo mu-ti. Lo-yang Chung chou-lu.* Lin Shou-chin, *KKHP* (1962/2), 75–84.
44. Kao Ch'ü-hsün, *BIHP, 29* (1958), 658–719.
45. *Lo-yang Chung-chou-lu,* pp. 145–46.
46. Bo Gyllensvärd, *BMFEA, 34* (1962), 29–47.

130. Principal decorative motifs in Shang and Chou bronze art: A, T'ao-t'ieh; B, Ch'ieh-ch'ü; C, P'an-ch'ih.

of the Western Chou and the early part of Eastern Chou, the most characteristic motif is the *ch'ieh-ch'ü* pattern, a pair of interlocked serpents. After this, the latter part of the Eastern Chou is most distinguished by the *p'an-ch'ih* design, an area of many interlocking small serpents. Also characteristic of this last period are scenes of rituals on bronze vessels, that provide material for the study of the architecture, garments, ceremonial paraphernalia, and other aspects of life of the Warring States period (Fig. 130).

In the early 1930s Kuo Mo-jo and Bernhard Karlgren, probably independently studying the bronze vessels of the Shang and Chou dynasties, arrived at very similar methodologies and conclusions.[47] Their aims were to arrange the Shang and Chou bronzes into a chronological order and, from this, to study the problems of stylistic evolution. "We shall try first," Karlgren states, "to classify the inscriptions in their chronological order, without any side glances at the types of the vessels; and once this literary chronology has been established we shall use it as a means for classifying the vessels, their types and decoration, in chronological groups."[48] In similar fashion, Kuo Mo-jo attempted to subdivide the Chinese Bronze Age into five stages:[49]

1. *Stage of Beginnings:* a hypothetical stage in which bronzes first appeared in China. The time was possibly "late Hsia" Dynasty and early Shang Dynasty. The place was possibly the lower courses of the Yangtze and Huaiho, where copper mines were known in early historic periods. The bronze metallury in the Huangho Valley, according to Kuo, may have been introduced from this area.

2. *Stage of Florescence:* late Shang-Yin and early Chou Dynasty, including the reigns of kings Ch'eng, K'ang, Chao, and Mu. The characteristic artifacts were *ting,* square *yi,* lidless *kui, tsun, yu, chüeh, chia,* and *tuo. Li* and *chung* were present but rare. *Fu, hu, p'an,* and *yi* were absent. The artifacts were either completely decorated or not at all. The characteristic designs included *k'ui-lung, k'ui-feng, t'ao-t'ieh,* elephant, and *lei-wen,* the *t'ao-t'ieh* and the *lei-wen* being predominant. In general, the decorative patterns were "primitive" in character. In inscriptions, the composition was simple and succinct, and the calligraphy solemn and grave. The form of the vessels tended to be "heavy and solid," without any exhibition of "frivolity."

3. *Stage of Decadence:* from the middle of the Western Chou Dynasty, including the reigns of kings Kung, Yi, Hsiao, and Yi, through the middle of the Ch'un-ch'iu period. In bronze artifacts, *ting, li, kui, fu, chung* (bell), *fu* and the like grew in quantity; the square *yi, yu, chüeh, chia, ku,* and the like became extinct; and *p'an, yi, hsü,* and *hu* began to appear. The decorations were thin-line geometric patterns made by shallow incisions and engravings. The *lei-wen* became rare,

47. Kuo Mo-jo, *Liang Chou chin-wen-tz'u ta-hsi,* Tokyo, Bunkyūdō, 1932; *Ku-tai ming-k'e ts'ung-k'ao,* 1933; *Liang Chou chin-wen-tz'u ta-hsi t'u-lu,* Tokyo, Bunkyūdō, 1934. Bernhard Karlgren, *BMFEA, 6* (1934); *8* (1936).

48. *BMFEA, 8* (1936), 10.

49. *Liang Chou chin-wen-tz'u ta-hsi t'u-lu; Ch'ing-t'ung shih-tai,* Chungking, Wen-chih Press, 1945.

and the elephant pattern disappeared. The *ch'ieh-ch'ü* pattern replaced the *t'ao-t'ieh* as the leading decorative motif, and the *t'ao-t'ieh* was demoted to the feet of *ting* and *kui* vessels. *K'ui-lung, k'ui-feng,* and *p'an-k'ui-wen* became deformed. In inscriptions, the characters became "relaxed" and random, including some cursory forms. The form of vessels was simple and crude, but was emancipated from the primitive style and mythological tradition to a feeling of freedom.

4. *Stage of Renaissance:* from the middle of Ch'un-ch'iu through the end of Chan-kuo. In artifact types, *tui* and *cheng* appeared, *pien-chung* became popular, *li* and *yen* became rare, and *hsü* was extinct. In decoration, the incisions and engravings became shallower and thinner. Repetitive motifs were widely applied with molds. The patterns included a great variety of motifs. Most accessory ornaments were realistic animals. In inscriptions the composition tended to rhyme, and the characters, a part of the total decor, were refined, regularly arranged, and placed in conspicuous places. In form the artifacts were light, convenient, and style-conscious, indicating, according to Kuo, the commercialization of the bronzes during this period.

5. *Stage of Decline:* after the end of the Chan-kuo period. Bronze vessels became simple and coarse but practical and convenient. Decorative patterns became a rarity. Most of the inscriptions were incised rather than cast, and pertained to weight, volume, or names of the manufacturers rather than to history or morality. Bronze mirrors and coins prevailed, but otherwise iron served as the raw material for artifacts.

Karlgren's classification closely parallels this scheme of Kuo Mo-jo's. Omitting Kuo's Stage of Beginnings and Stage of Decline, which are beyond the temporal scope of the Yin and Chou anyway, Karlgren subdivides the Yin and Chou bronzes into three classes:[50]

1. *Archaic,* further divisible into Yin, prior to 1122 B.C.; and Yin-Chou, 1122 to ca. 950 B.C.
2. *Middle Chou,* ca. 950 to 650 B.C.
3. *Huai,* ca. 650 to 200 B.C.

Thus, both in time and in definition, Karlgren's Archaic is identical with Kuo's Florescence, Middle Chou with Decadence, and Huai with

50. *BMFEA, 9* (1937), 5.

Renaissance. In addition, Karlgren has painstakingly worked out a list of stylistic criteria which characterize each of his classes.

Kuo and Karlgren have thus demonstrated that the political subdivisions of Chou into such categories as Western Chou, Ch'un-ch'iu, and Chan-kuo are not necessarily meaningful in the evolution of artifacts and art. Instead, three well-marked artistic and typological stages are discernible. The first is the early part of the Western Chou, up to the reign of King Kung, or roughly the year 950 B.C. The bronze art of this stage, called Yin-Chou by Karlgren, "in all essentials an epigonous art,"[51] "was still essentially the same as that of the Yin, with but small innovations."[52]

The second stage, starting from the middle of Western Chou (ca. 950), through the middle of the Ch'un-ch'iu period (ca. 650), Kuo's stage of decadence or Karlgren's *Middle Chou style,* witnessed a

> sudden, complete and fundamental change in the art tradition in China. It is characterized on the one hand by a ruthless abolition of the whole array of Yin elements . . . on the other hand by the introduction of a series of new elements, most of which were entirely unknown in China before that time, and some of which had cropped up but sporadically, in exceptional cases, anterior to 947.[53]

Kuo characterizes the art of this stage as "degenerate," and Karlgren describes it as "poor and mediocre."[54] The latter has further attempted to explain the sudden appearance of a whole series of new stylistic motifs as the "result of the widening of the sphere of Chinese civilization from the Shensi and Honan centers to large districts of China north of the Yangtze"[55] where contacts with alien peoples were made and new artistic inspirations were received.

On the basis of the Middle Chou style, an artistic renaissance occurred in the middle of the Ch'un-ch'iu period (ca. 650 B.C.) which gave rise to a new style, the Huai.[56] Karlgren characterizes this style as

51. *BMFEA, 8* (1936), 139.
52. Ibid., p. 89.
53. Ibid., p. 116.
54. Karlgren, *BMFEA, 13* (1941), 4.
55. *BMFEA, 8* (1936), 146.
56. Ibid., p. 90.

a self-conscious art, a "highly sophisticated one working with all the paraphernalia and tricks of a pompous baroque," and "keen on a brilliant impression of richness and variety." He states that "during the 7th–3d centuries B.C. the Chinese world was already sufficiently advanced in culture to allow a conscious artistic renaissance movement, which incorporated elements now already ancient and venerated in the new pompous baroque art,"[57] and fresh artistic inspirations resulting from the expanding sphere of the North China civilization and increased contacts with the Ordos area in the north gave impetus to the development of the Huai style. The warfare scene, for instance, is common to the Huai (Fig. 131) and the Ordos; both of these styles, furthermore, contained such curious and specific elements as pear-shaped cells or figures, comma-shaped figures, circles on the body of animals, and so forth, indicating an exchange of artistic ideas during this period (Fig. 132).[58]

These studies of Kuo Mo-jo and Bernhard Karlgren are of great importance to an understanding of cultural growth during the Chou period in North China. For the entire time span of the Western Chou Dynasty, archaeological discoveries are few and most frequently confined to tombs. We must therefore depend largely upon such studies of bronze vessels for an insight into the problems of cultural change during this period. However, as more than two decades have elapsed since these studies were published, we might ask what, if any, major strides have been made to bring the Kuo and Karlgren material up to date. The answer is that potentially useful data have been found in great quantities, but that studies utilizing these new data are unfortunately lacking. Many details can now be added, however, to the Kuo and Karlgren schemes and many others should be modified, sometimes quite drastically. I will give a few examples.

First, several graves have been excavated in recent years, such as P'u-tu-ts'un (Sian) and Li-ts'un (Mi) in Shensi, and Fang-tui-ts'un and Tung-pao (Hung-chao) in Shansi, that are attributed to the early part of the Western Chou period.[59] Bronze vessels found in these tombs are indistinguishable from Yin pieces both in form and in decoration;

57. *BMFEA, 13* (1941), 4.

58. Karlgren, *BMFEA, 9* (1937), 102–11.

59. Shih Hsing-pang, *KKHP, 8* (1954), 109–26. Li Ch'ang-ch'ing and T'ien Yieh *WWTKTL* (1957/4), 5–9. Wang Chi-sheng, *WWTKTL* (1955/4), 46–52. Hsieh Hsi-kung, *WWTKTL* (1957/8), 42.

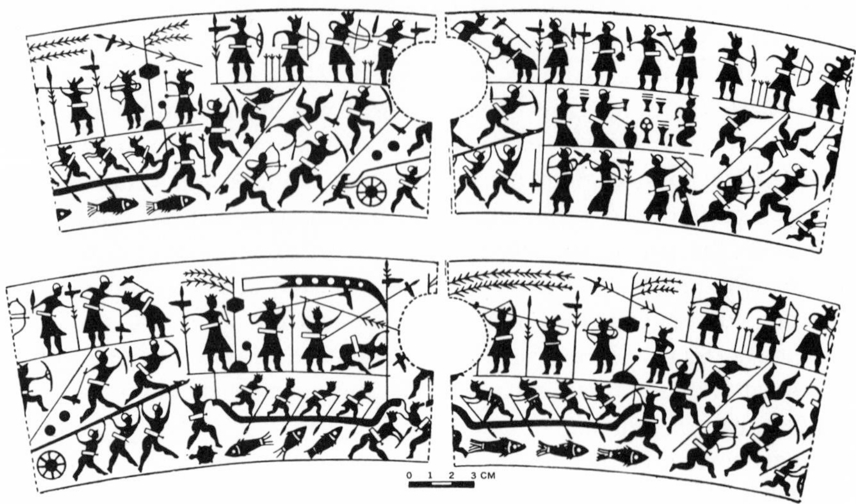

131. Decorative patterns on a Warring States-period vessel excavated from the site at Shan-piao-chen, Chi Hsien, Honan. (From Kuo Pao-chün, *Shan-piao-chen yü Liu-li-ko,* 1959, Fig. 11.)

132. A bronze plaque of the Eastern Chou period from an Eastern Chou tomb at K'o-hsing-chuang, Sian. (From *Feng-hsi Fa-chüeh Pao-kao,* 1962, p. 139.)

in fact, in most cases these are dated to the Western Chou by inscriptions. On the other hand, two out of the four Yin-Chou style innovations claimed by Karlgren, namely, bent ear and *p'an,* were found, as pointed out by Karlgren himself, at An-yang; their Yin Dynasty dating, which was doubted by Karlgren, is no longer doubtful since the Anyang finds at Hsi-pei-kang are now well dated stratigraphically. Thus only two of Karlgren's Yin-Chou innovations are left—hook projections and tail-raising birds. To these, Ch'en Meng-chia would add the following as exclusively Western Chou but not Yin traits: *kui* with four ears; *kui* with square supports; independent square or rectangular vessel supports (the so-called *chin*); bent handle of *tou* (or *shuo*); projecting flanges; some combinations of vessels that differ from the Yin pattern; and the absence of some Yin decorative patterns.[60] These traits, whether valid or not, do not occur universally among Western Chou vessels; among the early Western Chou tombs enumerated above we find evidence of only one of these new elements, the bent handle of *tou,* which was found at an early Western Chou tomb at P'u-tu-ts'un.[61] I think we can positively say that the bronze art of early Western Chou was a continuation of the Yin bronze art. Karlgren justifies his separation of the Yin-Chou art from the Yin on the basis of the innovations.[62] But, as he himself points out, there were greater and more significant innovations within the Yin style. Karlgren attacks T'ang Lan for making divisions of art history on the basis of political considerations only. What then are his own grounds (except for political considerations) for not subdividing his Archaic style into more stages than Yin and Yin-Chou? The present evidence shows that the Archaic style of bronzes of the Florescence Stage (Yin and early Western Chou) is a continuous development; it can certainly be further subdivided, but the segment that is described as Yin-Chou by Karlgren is not stylistically significant enough to indicate either that the Chou art was different from the Shang art, or that the Chou people made any real contributions to their Shang heritage after the conquest.

Another important fact concerning the Western Chou bronzes is their widespread geographic distribution. Not only have they been

60. Ch'en Meng-chia, *KKHP, 9* (1955), 138. Ch'en Meng-chia, *WWTKTL* (1955/5), 65.
61. Shih Hsing-pang, *KKHP, 8* (1954), 120.
62. *BMFEA, 9* (1937), 96.

found in an area ranging from Jehol in the north to Anhwei and Kiangsu in the south[63] but we also find that funeral assemblages of typically early Western Chou types found at Yen-tun-shan in Tan-t'u, Kiangsu, can be dated to the reign of King Ch'eng or King K'ang at the latest.[64] The fact that during the early period of Western Chou the Chou sphere of cultural influence had already become so wide seems to be in strong support of Karlgren's contention that the emergence of the Middle Chou style was the result of this widening of territory and consequently the greater extent of cultural contacts and exchange of new artistic ideas. This is, however, more apparent than real. Unless and until it can be demonstrated that the new Middle Chou elements pre-existed (either in bronzes or in some other media) in other regions in China, which archaeological data from regions outside the Nuclear Area of the Chou do not yet indicate, the basic dynamics of the emergence of this new style in North China must be sought elsewhere. Cultures and civilizations in regions both north and south of North China contemporary with the Western Chou will be described in the following chapters. Both the Western Chou assemblages and the native cultural contexts show that the Middle Chou style, in elements and in total, was not apparent anywhere in these areas before the cultural impact of the Chou civilization.

As far as North China is concerned, two of the most important discoveries of bronzes of the Middle Chou style are tombs at P'u-tu-ts'un, Sian, near those mentioned above of the early Western Chou stage,[65] and a large cemetery at Shang-ts'un-ling in Shan Hsien, western Honan, possibly of the state of Kuo.[66] The former assemblage is dated to shortly after the reign of King Mu, whose name was mentioned in the inscriptions, and the latter is placed at the end of Western Chou and the beginning of the Ch'un-ch'iu period. Thus, these two discoveries chronologically mark both the beginning and the end of the Middle Chou style and the Stage of Decadence as defined by Karlgren and Kuo respectively. Typologically, they do the same. The P'u-tu-ts'un find includes such Archaic elements as *ku, chüeh, yu,* and *ting* with vertical ears and cylindrical legs. But bells, *ting* with curved legs, and

63. Higuchi, *Tōyōshi-Kenkyu, 16* (1957), 40–61.
64. Ch'en Meng-chia, *WWTKTL* (1955/5), 65.
65. Ho Han-nan, *KKHP* (1957/1), 75–85.
66. Lin Shou-chin et al., *Shang-ts'un-ling Kuo kuo mu-ti.*

the *ch'ieh-ch'ü* pattern (a variety of Karlgren's "broad band"), which are all diagnostic of Karlgren's Middle Chou style, had already appeared. It is indeed possible that some of the Archaic elements of this group may have been relics or antiquities at the time of the burial, and vessels that happened to be placed in one grave are not necessarily "contemporary" in the usual archaeological sense. However, this cannot explain both Archaic and Middle Chou elements combined in one vessel. A *lei* and a *ho,* for instance, have both the hanging blade of Karlgren's Archaic style and the *ch'ieh-ch'ü* of his Middle Chou style. Such combinations lead us to conclude that the Middle Chou did not replace the Archaic style suddenly and completely, as Karlgren has suggested. A transitional period, around the time of kings Kung and Mu, perhaps, may have existed before the Middle Chou style became mature and well established. The Shang-ts'un-ling cemetery, on the other hand, shows a well-defined Middle Chou style of bronzes which had already foreshadowed the succeeding Huai style with such typical elements as the *t'ao-t'ieh* and the mirror. In many other aspects also, such as the type of weapons and modes of burial, the Shang-ts'un-ling find pushes back many of the Huai elements in time.

Our knowledge of the stylistic evolution of the Chou bronze vessels can be supplemented considerably by a study of the evolution of bronze weapons in North China,[67] but for a full understanding of the meaning and significance of the stylistic changes, formal analysis alone will hardly suffice. Chinese bronzes as a source of information in Shang and Chou society are only beginning to be tapped. In discussing the stylistic differentiations of Shang bronzes we have already mentioned the sociological significance of the A and B styles of Karlgren revealed by the association of artifact and stylistic types.[68] In the Chung-chou Road sequence of Lo-yang, the chronological importance of the association of vessel types during different periods has already been described. Such association studies should also be undertaken from a sociological perspective.

> In Period I [of the Eastern Chou sequence at Chung-chou Road] *ting* occurred only in large graves with bronzes, but *ting* appeared

67. Chou Wei, *Chung-kuo ping-ch'i shih kao,* Peking, San-lien, 1957. Kuo Pao-chün, *KK* (1961/2), 111–18.
68. See p. 253.

> in graves of middle size with only pottery goods in Period II and in graves of small size with only pottery goods in Period III. Pottery *ting* appeared in Period II only in graves of middle size with only pottery goods, but they appeared in large graves during Period IV.[69]

The *ting* was central in the ritual vessel complex of Shang and Chou periods, and the ritual vessel complex was an unequivocal marker of the upper class. This ancient ritual tradition was maintained in Period I (the beginning of Eastern Chou), but soon afterward it broke down entirely, and the vessel-type alignment within a grave changed completely. This may indicate a major change of social status alignment from the Western Chou to the Eastern Chou.[70] Another example of the functional study of stylistic shift during the Shang and Chou is that of the changing relationship between man and animal in both mythology and decorative art (Fig. 133) of this period.[71] It provides an insight into basic attitudes of the Shang and Chou peoples toward their world and thus furnishes a clue to the interrelationships of the various aspects of that world, aspects whose changes throughout the period have been described above (Table 12).

GENERAL CONCLUSIONS

In the foregoing passages, information about the development of cities, technology, burial customs, and artifacts has been presented to fill in the pattern of cultural growth during the Chou period. The question now is: What is the summation of all these data?

In speaking of the cultural growth during the Chou period in North China, literary records must be consulted to provide a complete picture. For the purposes of this volume, however, the archaeological data are sufficient to outline the high points and to relate the cultures of North China and the rest of the country.

The trends of cultural growth can be described in two ways. First, there was a constant territorial expansion of Chinese civilization. Second, there was an accelerated growth of the internal society, econ-

69. *Lo-yang Chung-chou-lu,* p. 145.
70. *Hsin Chung-kuo ti k'ao-ku shou-kuo,* p. 69.
71. Kwang-chih Chang, *BIE, 16* (1963), 115–46.

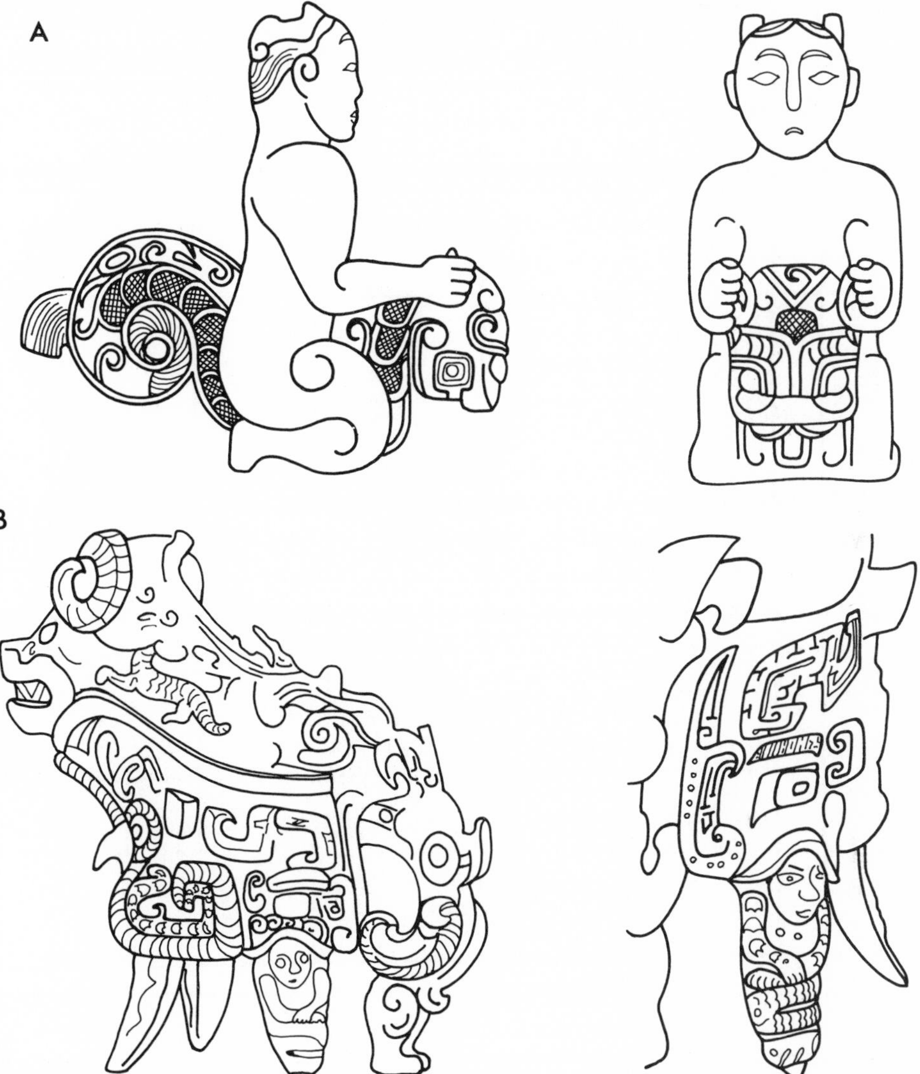

133. Changing relationship of man and animal in Shang and Chou bronze art. A, A carved jade figurine from a Warring States tomb in Lo-yang. (After *KK*, 1959/11, p. 657.) B, Leg of a *kuang* of the Shang type. (From *Sekai Bijutsu Zenshū*, Tokyo, Kado Kawa, 1962, vol. 12, p. 167.)

TABLE 12.

Some Aspects of Interrelated Changes of Chinese Civilization in Its Formative Stages

Dates (B.C.)	Dynastic & Predynastic periods	Technology	Settlement patterns	Political forms	Mythological types	Some religious concepts	Art styles	Animals
206	Han	stone, bronze, iron		Empire				
221	Ch'in	stone, bronze, iron		Empire				
	Eastern Chou: Warring-States	stone, bronze, iron	Political-ritual-commercial-industrial cities plus farming hamlets	States: competition of local powers	Clan origins Heaven-Earth separation Cosmogonic origins Heroes as saviors	Total separation of world of gods from world of ancestors God's supreme authority challenged Individual virtues and merits stressed	Late Chou	"Hunting scenes" Animals being subdued Conventionalized animal motifs
450	Eastern Chou: Spring-Autumn	stone, bronze, iron						
770	Western Chou	stone, bronze	Administrative-ceremonial centers plus farming and industrial satellites (urbanization)	States: total royal power (Chi)	Clan origins	World of gods ≠ world of ancestors God goes to Heaven King rules Earth as God's agent by virtue of <u>te</u>	Middle Chou	Conventionalized animal motifs
1100	Shang: Yin	stone, bronze		States: total royal power (Tzu)		Supreme Being (Shang Ti) Identification of Shang Ti with ancestors of Tzu World of Gods ≑ world of ancestors	Archaic: Yin-Chou, Yin	Potency in art Scapulimancy Scripts with animal compounds
1400	Shang	stone, bronze					Archaic	Potency in art Scapulimancy Scripts with animal compounds
1700	Lungshan	stone	Permanent farming villages	Villages	?	Institutionalized ancestor cult	Lungshanoid	Scapulimancy
	Yangshao	stone	Shifting farming villages	Villages		Fertility cult	Yangshao	
	Mesolithic	stone	Camps					

omy, and political organization. Moreover, these two phenomena are probably interrelated and mutually conditioning.

In speaking of the territorial expansion of the Chou civilization, we again face the problem of cultural definitions. When archaeological assemblages of a certain type—of Western Chou, for example—are found distributed in a certain area, they may or may not indicate the complete geographical distribution of that civilization. Undoubtedly there was a nuclear region of this civilization, whereas the other regions into which it radiated may be regarded as marginal or peripheral. A variety of situations may be encountered in the marginal areas. Some may have been occupied by native cultures which received some cultural imports from the Western Chou civilization while maintaining their own ways of life and political autonomy. In such cases, in recovering artifacts of Western Chou types, archaeologists probably can speak only of the cultural influences of the Western Chou but not the geographical distribution of the dynasty. In other regions, the Western Chou had accomplished military conquests and established political control, while allowing the native cultures to continue. We may certainly include these regions in the political sphere of influence and/or control of the Western Chou government, but we must not generalize to include these territories in the Western Chou economy and society. Still other regions, although occupied by native, probably Neolithic, cultures during the Shang Dynasty, may have been assimilated into the Western Chou civilization to the extent that in cultural style and socioeconomic situations alike the native cultures had become indistinguishable from the heartland of the Western Chou Dynasty. These may legitimately be called part of the expanded Western Chou territory of civilizational distribution. These distinctions, however, while easy to make on paper, are in most cases impossible to recognize in the archaeological material.

In the first section of this chapter it was suggested that the "Western Chou people" during the Shang Dynasty may have been no more than a group of local inhabitants under Shang rule who were within the expanse of the Shang civilization. To be sure, the Western Chou had their subcultural characteristics, but the "conquest" in 1122 B.C., whereby the Chou replaced the Shang as China's masters, cannot be called a conquest by an alien people having an alien culture. It was, in fact, from all evidence, no more than an internal struggle for power. The notion that the conquest of the Shang by the Chou represents the triumph of the Western Hsia over the Eastern Yi, as has been suggested by Fu Ssu-nien, is correct only if the Hsia and the Yi are considered no more than geographical variants of the same Chinese people.

There is no archaeological evidence for significant change in the basic pattern of Chinese civilization in North China immediately after the conquest. The Western Chou took over the Shang culture in bronze metallurgy, burial rites, and decorative art in virtually unaltered forms. Karlgren's Yin-Chou elements plus Ch'en Meng-chia's Western Chou innovation in the style of bronze vessels involved no basic changes in cultural beliefs and artistic styles. Changes inevitably occurred but are such that would take place over any period of time under normal incentives during the development of the same culture.

Nor, in the sense defined a few paragraphs back, did the Western Chou gain any new territory during the first years of the dynasty. The sphere of cultural influence may have been expanded, compared to the Shang, as shown by the finding of Western Chou types of bronze vessels in a wider area. But the Western Chou territory was wider than the Shang mainly because the Western Chou had as a base Shensi and Shansi, where the Shang civilization has not been significantly in evidence archaeologically. Chou assemblages have been found as far north as Jehol, but we know, as will be shown in the next chapter, that native cultures persisted in the northern frontiers in essentially unaltered forms until the Han Dynasty. A few Chou imports and isolated settlements in the north do not necessarily make the north a part of the Western Chou territory. In the south, we know from history that Huaiho Valley natives considered themselves akin to the Shang rulers and were continuously disaffected under the Chou rule. A widespread rebellion shortly after the conquest was soon subdued by the military expeditions of Chou Kung. Western Chou bronze assemblages found in Anhwei and Kiangsu, in the Huai region, bear out the historical records and indicate that Western Chou powers became established in this region. But as will be shown in a later chapter, the Huai River valley cultures during both the Shang and the early Western Chou dynasties were in the main Neolithic and maintained their own cultural identity. A significant breakdown of the native cultural traditions and the establishment of typical North China kingdoms did not take place in the Huaiho Valley and the Yangtze Valley until after the beginning of the Western Chou period. Contacts with alien peoples surrounding the Royal Chou and a resulting fresh impetus in artistic inspiration may only partially account for the emergence of the Middle Chou style. A more compelling explanation must be sought for in the development of Chou civilization. The later parts of the Western Chou and the beginning of the Eastern Chou, the period covered by the Middle Chou style, was between the classical "Archaic" Yin and Chou civilization and the youthful and spirited Eastern Chou renaissance in style and revolution in technology and economy. The Middle Chou period thus represents a transitional stage wherein the classic systems began to give way to the innovations in all Chinese territory.

A new era in the history of North China began with the Eastern Chou. In political history, ancient China had the Shang and Chou dynasties; but in cultural history, the subdivision may be placed at the middle of the Chou Dynasty, dividing the Shang–Chou periods into two stages, Shang and Early Chou, and Late Chou. Iron metallurgy was developed in the Eastern Chou, and industrial specialization was very much intensified. The old Yin and Western Chou pattern of urban constitution lingered on for a while but, from the late Ch'un-ch'iu period on, new cities emerged in all of North China, which indicated the importance of industry and commerce by incorporating their quarters physically into the walled city. The new technology and economy undoubtedly intensified and consolidated the Chinese way of life and enabled it to expand, explosively, toward the rest of China. States of the Chou type which were established in the Huaiho Valley and in much of the Yangtze will be described in the following chapters. Cultural contacts with foreign lands became very much more frequent, particularly in the north. During the Eastern Chou period, common cultural traits, including important elements of daily life, were shared more and more by North China and the steppe nomads. In art, too, we have seen that the Huai style shared a number of characteristic traits with the Ordos and its adjacent cultures. The horse became a mount as well as a draught animal, and swords came into wide use. Burial mounds were fashionable, belt hooks were used for a new style of dress, and flexed burials became important. These new cultural elements, and the old traits that had gained in popularity at this time, are certainly indicative of the wider circle of cultural contact and communication between North China and the northern nomads, although the direction of flow of these exchanges cannot always be ascertained.[72]

This chapter shows what took place in North China, as a background for understanding the emergence of civilizations in other parts of China. It shows, moreover, that in most of China a single center of radiation conditioned the patterns of the local cultural growth, and that the road to the unification of Chinese territory under the Emperor Shih Huang of Ch'in in 221 B.C. was paved during the Eastern Chou period.

72. Kao Ch'ü-hsün, *KKHP, 2* (1947), 121–66. Karlgren, *BMFEA, 13* (1941), 1–125. Kao Ch'ü-hsün, *BIHP, 23* (1951), 489–510.

CHAPTER EIGHT

FARMERS AND NOMADS OF THE NORTHERN FRONTIER

During the late second and most of the first millennium B.C., various cultural transformations took place among the Neolithic farmers and sub-Neolithic hunter-fishers on the northern frontiers of the Shang and Chou civilizations, apparently as a result of native cultural growth. But their processes and patterns were greatly conditioned by events in the adjacent regions, mainly North China and the steppe regions to the west. Literary records of the Eastern Chou and Han periods refer to the peoples in these various regions by various names: the Wei-Mo people in southern Manchuria and the Pohai Bay coasts; the Northern Ti, Hu, or later, Hsiung-nu in the Yin Shan Mountain area between and including the upper Liaoho and the Ordos; and the western Jung to the northwest.[1] To what extent this ethnic classification of the Eastern Chou and Early Han periods for the northern frontier peoples was true and can be traced back in time is an ethnohistoric problem. The archaeological material, however, tends to bear out this subdivision, in that three regional cultural complexes can be distinguished for the Shang–Chou period in this area: the cist-grave builders of the Pohai Bay area and southern Manchuria; the mounted nomads and farmers north of the Great Wall; and the "eneolithic" painted pottery cultures in Kansu and Chinghai. The geographical distribution of these various cultures, their different ecological situations, and the diverse historical influences to which these groups were exposed are problems of great theoretical interest.

THE POHAI CIST-GRAVE BUILDERS

This cultural complex was centered in the area of the northern coasts of the Pohai, the lower Liao Valley, and the upper Sungari River. It was essentially a continuation of the old Neolithic cultures

1. E.g. Lin Hui-hsiang, *Chung-kuo Min-tzu Shih,* 2 vols. Shanghai, Commercial Press, 1936.

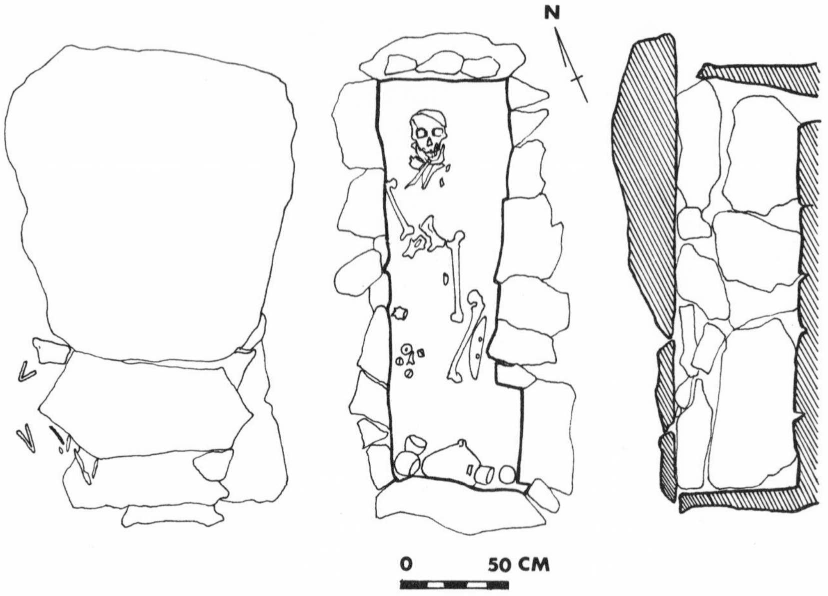

134. A cist grave at the site of Hsi-t'uan-shan-tzu, near Kirin. (From *KKHP,* 1964/1, p. 33.)

described in Chapter 5, but numerous cultural elements of North China origin or affinity have also been found from archaeological assemblages dated to this period. The people represented were farmers and pig-raisers, who made flat-bottomed pottery and polished slate and other stone implements, and buried their dead in cist graves (Fig. 134). Hunting was apparently still extremely important, as shown by the large number of arrowheads, mostly chipped in the old Microlithic tradition.[2]

Archaeologically speaking, definite Yin-Shang influences in this area are rare. Several "white sherds" of Shang type have been reported at the Lao-t'ieh-shan site in the Port Arthur region at the tip of Liaotung Peninsula,[3] and the historic records indicate that the people in this area were among the so-called Eastern Yi groups whose cultures were considered very close to the North Chinese. Chi Tzu, a brother of the

2. Chang Kwang-chih, *Southwest. Jour. Anthropol., 17* (1961), 70–71.

3. Hamada Kosaku, *JZ, 44* (1929), 319–26. Umehara Sueji, *Tōa Kōkōgakū Kaikan,* Kyoto, Hoshino, 1947, p. 63.

last Yin monarch, is said to have led a group of Yin refugees into exile in northern Korea, where they established a civilization and taught the local inhabitants to raise silkworms and to farm. In the archaeological record, however, decisive evidence of significant North Chinese historical cultural penetration into the Pohai Bay area and southern Manchuria began to show up only during the Eastern Chou period. Metal objects such as axes, arrowheads, spearheads, and ornaments of Eastern Chou type were found east from Liaotung peninsula (at such sites as Kao-li-chai and Mu-yang-ch'eng),[4] and west to the upper Liao Valley (at such sites as the Red Ware cemetery at Hung-shan-hou near Ch'ih-feng).[5] To the north, metal objects reached as far as the upper Sungari around the city of Kirin. Sites have been found here at which burials in pits lined with granite slabs (cist graves) are characteristic. Bronze knives and fishhooks occurred at the site of Ch'ang-she-shan,[6] and stone arrowheads and spearheads apparently imitating bronze prototypes have been found at the site of Liang-pan-shan, in the eastern suburb of Kirin.[7] Skeletal remains from the cist tombs at the Hsi-t'uan-shan site, southwest of Kirin, indicate that the inhabitants at this time were physically classifiable as "Tungusic."[8] Stone imitations of metal swords and spearheads have been reported farther east, in the Tumen Valley, on the Pacific coast around Vladivostok, and in Korea and Japan.[9]

Settlements of Eastern Chou style in which cultural influences ranging from stylistic imports to the socioeconomic sphere are found at least as far away as northern Hopei. Stone molds, for instance, for making metal axes, knives, and spearheads (which were found at the Pao-shen-miao site near T'ang-shan), are dated to an earlier period than the Warring States.[10] These molds undoubtedly indicate a local metallurgy and point to a much more intensified acculturation of the natives by the oncoming North Chinese civilization than occurred among the peoples to the north who apparently continued the Neo-

4. *Mu-yang-ch'eng, Archaeologia Orientalis, 2,* 1931; *Pi-tzu-wuo,* ibid., *1,* 1929.
5. See below, p. 356.
6. Chang Chung-p'ei, *KK* (1964/1), 11.
7. Ibid., pp. 6–12.
8. T'ung Chu-ch'en, *KKHP* (1964/1), 29–49. Chia Lan-p'o and Yen Yen, *KKHP* (1963/2), 101–09.
9. Chang Kwang-chih, *SJA, 17* (1961), 70. G. O. Andreev, *KKHP* (1958/4), 36. J. E. Kidder, *Japan,* New York, Praeger, 1959, p. 93.
10. An Chih-min, *KKHP, 7* (1954), 85.

lithic way of life while adopting some cultural imports. However, by the end of the Han Dynasty at the latest, highly sophisticated civilizations were recorded in Chinese annals in a large part of southern Manchuria.[11]

During the Eastern Chou and the following Han period, the southern Manchurian farmers apparently were also intruded upon by alien peoples and cultures from the steppes to the west. Whereas the Chinese influences from the Huangho during the Eastern Chou took the form of cultural infiltration and assimilation, the steppe nomads apparently took possession physically of territories in the lower Liao Valley, as shown by the cultural remains of steppe origin in whole assemblages discovered in isolated regions in Liaoning Province. By the middle of the Western Han Dynasty, however, Wu Ti's military expeditions were successful enough to have incorporated the entire area of southern Manchuria and northern Korea into the vast empire of Han, though even the Han forces at times could not withstand the fierce inroads of the steppe nomads.[12]

FARMERS AND MOUNTED NOMADS NORTH OF THE GREAT WALL

The Great Wall of China, which begins at Shan Hai Gate between Hopei and Liaoning in the east and ends at Chia Yü Gate in eastern Kansu in the west, was built during various periods of early Chinese history, but sections of it were begun during the Eastern Chou. It may be said to symbolize two ways of life—the agrarian of the Huangho Valley to the south, and the nomadic of the steppes and deserts to the north—but the demarcation between the two was never as sharp and clear as the Great Wall itself, and the early history of the area north of it during the Shang and the Chou periods is complex and not at all well understood from the archaeological evidence.

The northern frontiers of the Shang and Chou civilizations of North China, embracing the area known at the present time as Inner Mongolia, and the northern portions of Hopei, Shansi, and Shensi, were typically grasslands and plateaus. During early postglacial times, as shown in Chapter 1, the region was drained by a great number of small

11. Wen Ch'ung-yi, *BIE, 5* (1958), 115–214.
12. T'ung Chu-ch'en, *KKHP* (1956/1), 29–42. Ch'en Ta-wei, *KKTH* (1956/2), 54–59. Li Wen-hsin, *KKHP* (1957/1), 119–26.

rivers and large and small inland lakes and ponds. Today, many of these rivers and lakes are diminished in size or have dried up. It is, however, still not known when the desiccation process began in this part of China. In the Huangho Valley, we know that desiccation was not widespread until after the Shang, and then only as a result of intensive deforestation combined with climatic deterioration. In the steppe zone of the north, large sedentary farming settlements seem to have existed at some spots as late as the Eastern Chou period, or even later, near water sources that are now dry. It appears, therefore, that during the Shang–Chou period the northern frontier experienced no catastrophic desiccation, which may have had a decisive effect upon the pattern of human settlement at that time.

Nevertheless, in many regions of the north where farming villages appeared during the Lungshanoid stages, a new way of life emerged during the period when the Shang and Chou civilizations thrived in the Huangho Valley, a way of life in which the domestication of animals and the mobility of settlements became increasingly important. There were still farming settlements in the northeastern part of North China and in the Ordos, but animal herders had also appeared on the scene. We are not clear about the relationship between the farmers and herders. It is possible that farmers engaged in herding as a supplement or during some part of the year; it is also possible that farmers and herders were symbiotic occupants of the steppes and the oases. The possibility also exists that the northern farmers and herders were hostile toward each other and may have been of different cultural origins and traditions. Soon after the Shang–Chou period, nomads began to dominate the northern steppes. Farming lands shrank and in many places disappeared altogether. This process, however, took a whole millennium to complete.

The eastern and western parts of the Great Wall must be distinguished in order to study the prehistory of the area north of it during the Shang and Chou periods, for their histories and their archaeological cultures appear to differ. The eastern part refers to the upper courses of the Liao River, in the provinces of Liaoning, northern Hopei, and eastern Inner Mongolia; the western part refers to the area of Ordos, namely, the western part of Inner Mongolia in the Huangho Valley in the former province of Suiyüan.

In the east, significant excavations took place in 1960 at the sites of

Yao-wang-miao and Hsia-chia-tien, near the city of Ch'ih-feng.[13] Two cultural phases are distinguishable: *Lower Hsia-chia-tien,* including the site of Yao-wang-miao and the lower stratum of the site of Hsia-chia-tien, and *Upper Hsia-chia-tien,* typified by the upper stratum of the site of that name. The Lower Hsia-chia-tien phase, which has a wide distribution throughout the upper Liao Valley, is characterized by a distinctive stone inventory (polished cylindrical axes, flat hoes, shouldered hoes, flat perforated axes, knives, and microliths) and ceramic ware (sand-tempered gray pottery, in the forms of *li* and *yen*), and copper and bronze artifacts and foundry remains have been uncovered at its sites. Layers of this phase are known to have been intruded into by a Western Chou bronze assemblage at Ling-yüan in Jehol, which indicates that the Lower Hsia-chia-tien culture was probably contemporary with the Shang civilization of North China.[14]

The Upper Hsia-chia-tien culture, typified by red and brown wares and a larger number of bronze artifacts and characterized by burial sites with slab cists, has a slightly larger area of distribution and has been dated to the Chou period.[15] The Western Chou civilization apparently had a deeper penetration than the Shang into this region, as shown by a group of typically Western Chou bronze vessels discovered in Ling-yüan,[16] but it was not until the Eastern Chou period that the Huangho River civilization pushed extensively into the northern frontier, as shown by widespread intensive settlements where objects of Eastern Chou style remained, such as the so-called Red Ware Settlement at Ch'ih-feng, the best known of the Upper Hsia-chia-tien sites.[17] The intensity of Chou acculturation of this region is shown by an iron workshop discovered at Hsing-lung in Jehol. At this site 87 pieces of molds for casting iron or bronze hoes, sickles, axes, chisels, and cart fittings were excavated, indicating that during the Warring States period, to which the site has been dated, iron foundries as well as Chinese stylistic imports were brought into eastern Inner Mongolia.[18] However, the frontier position of the Inner Mongolia province of the East-

13. *KK* (1961/2), 77–81.
14. Cheng Shao-tsung, *KK* (1962/12), 658–71.
15. Ibid.
16. Li Ting-chien, *WWTKTL* (1955/8), 16–27.
17. Hamada Kosaku and Mizuno Seichi, *Ch'ih-feng Hung-shan-hou,* Archaeologia Orientalis, ser. A, *6,* 1938.
18. Cheng Shao-tsung, *KKTH* (1956/1), 29–35.

ern Chou civilization is clearly demonstrated by the presence of many cultural traits that point to either the microlithic substratum or to the contemporary northern cultures. Such traits include, for instance, slab graves, the red-brownish, flat-bottomed pottery prevalent during the Neolithic period of the same area, stone battleaxes, and microlithic implements which persisted even into Han Dynasty sites.

At some of the Eastern Chou period settlements of the Upper Hsia-chia-tien culture in eastern Inner Mongolia there is already emphasis upon the domestication of animals. At Hung-shan-hou, Ch'ih-feng, for instance, considerable numbers of cattle bones were found at the site, though the predominant mode of subsistence may still have been farming.[19] By the latter half of the Eastern Chou, however, a nomadic life better adapted to the steppe environment appears to have prevailed in a large part of eastern Inner Mongolia, as shown by the recent discovery of a series of so-called Bronze Dagger tombs. The tombs probably represent a regional and temporal phase of the Upper Hsia-chia-tien culture and are typified by the site of Nan-shan-ken, in Ning-ch'eng Hsien, Inner Mongolia.[20] These tombs, in which remains of a T-shaped bronze dagger are characteristic, have been located primarily in the lower Liao Valley in southern Manchuria;[21] they yield, besides the daggers, bronze weapons (halberds, helmets, and arrowheads), horse fittings, implements, mirrors, and ornaments (animal-style pendants, buttons, and beads) (Fig. 135), together with stone artifacts (including microliths and rare agricultural implements) and pottery. These remains apparently indicate a mounted culture, based for subsistence upon herding and hunting-fishing, with little farming. It must have had a closer cultural affiliation with the western part of the steppe belt than with the Huangho Valley, even though many Eastern Chou types of artifacts, such as halberds, spearheads, and knives, have been found, by which these finds are dated.

A recent discovery of sixty-three graves dated to Western Han, but apparently a continuation of the basic cultural tradition of the Eastern Chou nomads, is abundant in cultural remains and particularly revealing as to the inhabitants' mode of subsistence.

19. Lü Tsun-eh, *KKHP* (1958/3), 25–40.
20. *KK* (1962/5), 272.
21. Chu Kui, *KKHP* (1960/1), 63–70. *KK* (1964/1), 44–45. Sun Shou-tao and Hsü Ping-k'un, *KK* (1964/6), 277–85.

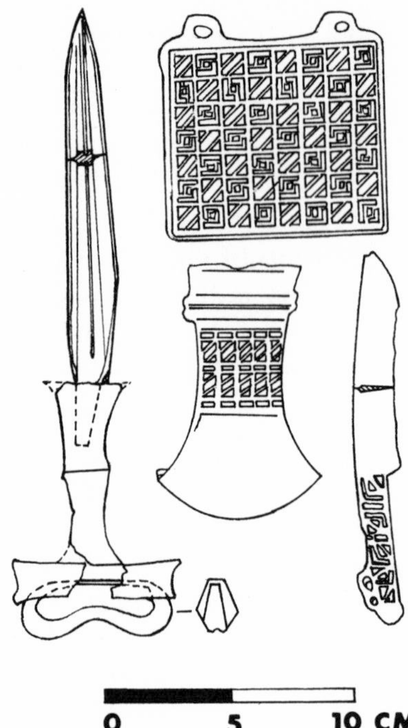

135. Artifacts from the Bronze Dagger tombs in the Liao Valley. (From *Hsin Chung-kuo ti K'ao-ku Shou-kuo,* 1962, p. 72.)

This cemetery was found in 1956 at Hsi-ch'a-kou in Hsi-feng Hsien, in northeastern Liaoning. All the graves in the group were single burials, and each was accompanied by weapons, horse fittings, pottery, and ornaments. Horse teeth were collected from many of the graves, and three horse skulls were found buried on top of a hill within the cemetery area. The human bones were entirely decomposed, but some remaining teeth show that aged people were rare among the dead. Many of the bronze ornaments depicted cattle, horses, sheep, dogs, and camels. These and other bits of evidence have led to the conclusion that

> This tribe [whose members were buried in this cemetery] belonged to a nomadic people, and pastoral nomadism occupied a principal position in the social economy. The bronze ornamental plates found from the graves indicate that horse, cattle, sheep, and camel were the major domestic animals in this society. The horse, particularly, was highly important both economically and militarily and was the basic means for transportation and warfare,

> as shown by the horse teeth and skulls. The large amount of handmade, sand-tempered pottery, the persisting use of a small quantity of microliths, the hunting dogs and hunting falcons portrayed on the bronze ornamental plates, some microlithic arrowheads, a great variety of bronze and iron arrowheads, and remains of fur clothing, all indicate that these northern peoples engaged in hunting and pastoral nomadism. It is noteworthy that not a single agricultural implement has been recovered from the cemetery.[22]

A similar culture, also among a militant people, emerged in the western Ordos area in the eastern part of Inner Mongolia. Among the so-called Ordos bronzes, most of which can best be described as "stray finds," pieces occur that bear close similarities to the Shang bronzes.[23] In the Altai and the Minusinsk basin of the upper Yenisie Valley, the Karasuk culture is usually considered a direct product of Shang stimulation,[24] but in the Ordos the process of introduction of Shang and Western Chou civilizations is not known.[25] By the Warring States[26] and Han[27] periods, however, the complex of the Ordos bronzes became recognizable in the archaeological record, characterized by bronze weapons and ornamental horse fittings that unmistakably indicate a mounted nomadic culture and by an ornamental art in which animals (sheep, deer, horse, wolf, and a variety of birds) are prominent (Fig. 136). The culture of the Ordos bronzes differs from the Bronze Dagger Tomb Culture of eastern Inner Mongolia in the style of artifacts, but it represents the same kind of militant nomadic life of the steppes.

For the gradual replacement of farmers by herders in the northern frontiers, several probable causes can be discerned. First, the high grassland of the northern frontier had never been as favorable to agriculture as the fertile plains and river valleys of the Huangho or the lower Liao drainage systems. In the present day it has an extremely continental climate, cold and arid, with long winters. During and after the climatic optimum of early post-Pleistocene times, the continental-

22. Sun Shou-tao, *WW* (1960/8/9), 20.
23. Max Loehr, *Artibus Asiae, 14* (1951), 1/2.
24. K. V. Jettmar, *BMFEA, 22* (1950). B. Karlgren, *BMFEA 17* (1945).
25. For possible Western Chou influence in the area, see *WW* (1961/9), 6.
26. Li Yi-yu, *WW* (1959/6); (1959/6), 276–77. Cheng Shao-tsun, *KK* (1962/12), 644–45. Cheng Lung, *WW* (1965/2), 50–51.
27. Li Yi-yu, *WWTKTL* (1957/4), 29–32; *KKTH* (1956/2), 60–61. Kai Shan-lin *WW* (1965/2), 44–45.

136. Animal art on Ordos bronzes excavated from Zungar, Inner Mongolia. (From *WW*, 1965/2, Pl. VI.)

ity of climate in this area may have been less severe, but the difference is probably one of degree. Second, and this may be the principal factor, during the first millennium B.C. a mobile and militant culture known as the Scythian appeared in the steppe zone of the heartland of Asia. By the end of the eighth century B.C., the Scythians and related complexes had replaced the Late Timber Culture in South Russia, the Late Andronovo Culture in Kazakhstan, and the Karasuk Culture in the Altai and Minusinsk basin.[28] Karl Jettmar has pointed out that by the time the Maiemiric period appeared in the Altai to replace the Karasuk Culture, the whole steppe zone of Asia, from Pannonic steppes to China, had been unified into a pattern characterized by mounted warfare.[29] This common Eurasian steppe culture, characterized by a mobile settlement pattern, a subsistence mode based principally upon the herding of sheep, cattle, and horses, mounted militancy, and an animal style of art, was apparently built upon an ecological adjustment to the steppe environment, and a number and a variety of ethnic

28. See Karl Jettmar, *Art of the Steppes,* New York, Crown, 1967, for an up-to-date summary of the pertinent data and an extensive bibliography.
29. Jettmar, *BMFEA, 23* (1951), 148.

and cultural elements must have participated in this pattern.[30] However, the wide similarities must have resulted primarily from historical contacts among peoples, and the rapid and expansive cultural flow was greatly facilitated by the steppe environment and the mobile way of life.

Seven hundred years B.C., the time when the so-called steppe nomads appeared in numbers in the vast steppe belt of Eurasia, was coincident with the wide expansion of the Eastern Chou civilization toward the north and the south. Cultural exchange between the Huangho and the steppes and taigas in the north had been a constant phenomenon since the Palaeolithic, but now such contacts took the form of conflicts between the agrarian Huangho-type of farmers and the nomads. These conflicts often resulted in warfare and were amply recorded in the historical sources dated to the Eastern Chou and Han periods. The Great Wall symbolizes these conflicts and demarcates the two basically different ways of life. Under such circumstances it is small wonder that herders' remains have been documented archaeologically on the northern frontier of Eastern Chou China and the Han Empire. Farmers, who found the new colonies not highly favorable for their settled way of life in the first place, were no match for the militant nomads, and gradually gave way to the new masters of the steppe. As far as the Chinese steppes are concerned, physical anthropological evidence is lacking to indicate whether the nomads, whose cultural remains have been widely found and clearly bear cultural affinities to the steppe cultures toward the west, were "intrusive" ethnic elements. We can therefore regard the hostility as one between two ways of life, although it is not unlikely that foreign ethnic elements were responsible for some of the cultural groups whose archaeological remains have been found.

Militant nomads are known to have appeared on the northern frontier at least as early as the Eastern Chou period of North China, marking the eastern extension of a Eurasian steppe culture pattern, and apparently making the life of farmers in these regions increasingly difficult. The Great Wall marks the resistance of the agrarian residents to these intruders, but in spite of it, mounted warfare, certain

30. Ralph M. Rowlette, *Early Phases of Horse Nomad Cultures of the Eastern Terminus of the Eurasiatic Steppe*, Report for Anthropology 111, Cambridge, Harvard University, 1960.

burial customs, and many stylistic motifs in the decorative art were introduced into North China to enrich and provide variety to the Eastern Chou cultural life and artistic style. We need much more archaeological evidence to enable definite cultural delineations and to understand the process of these cultural contacts.

THE "ENEOLITHIC" PAINTED POTTERY CULTURES OF KANSU

The site of Yang-shao-ts'un in western Honan was discovered in 1920 by Liu Ch'ang-shan, a field assistant of J. G. Andersson. In 1921 Andersson investigated the site himself, finding, among other things, some painted pottery which he considers to be related to the painted pottery cultures of Anau and Tripolye. In 1923–24 Andersson made an extensive survey in the area of eastern Kansu, presumed to be the area linking the east with the west. In the Huangho Valley in eastern Kansu around the city of Lanchow and in the river valleys of T'ao and Huangshui (Hsi-ning-ho), Andersson found a considerable number of early culture sites. Grouping these into six stages, he considers them to be the linear succession of a "Painted Pottery Culture" tradition and gives a series of consecutive dates B.C. to each of the six stages.[31] Andersson's Kansu chronology, in its final modified version, is as follows:[32]

Late Stone Age:

Ch'i Chia (2500–2200)
Yang Shao (Pan-shan) (2200–1700)
Ma Ch'ang (1700–1300)

Bronze Age:

Hsin Tien (1300–1000)
Ssu Wa–Ch'ia Yao (1000–700)
Sha Ching (700–500)

The Introduction to this volume might have been a more appropriate place for this chronological table, for such a succession of stages in Kansu is of little more than historical interest. I have cited it here, however, because this scheme is still adopted by some writers of books and articles dealing with prehistory. Archaeological materials collected since Andersson offered his Six Stage theory have proved it to be er-

31. Andersson, *GSuC, Mem.*, ser. A, *5* (1925).
32. *BMFEA, 15* (1943), 295.

roneous except for the fact that the Late Stone Age was earlier than the Bronze Age, and that, within the Late Stone Age, Ma-ch'ang was probably later than Pan-shan. Otherwise there is no reason whatever to adhere to Andersson's scheme. The Ch'i-chia stage, as shown in a previous chapter, followed the Yang-shao instead of preceding it. The chronologically linear succession of his three Bronze Age stages is not proven; rather, it has been demonstrated that after the Ch'i-chia stage there were probably several contemporary cultural assemblages such as Hsin-tien, Ssu-wa, and Sha-ching in the eastern Kansu area. Some of these may be slightly earlier or later than the others, but all of them overlapped in time and cannot be considered successive "stages" of a single culture. With these two major shifts of classification, Andersson's absolute dates become obsolete; he sees the whole sequence as ending around 500 B.C., which, according to Andersson's authority, Bernhard Karlgren, is when iron came into use in North China. However, iron was not found in any of these sites, so that this evidence cannot be considered conclusive.

Archaeological materials that have accumulated since the early twenties in eastern Kansu show that the first farmers who occupied eastern Kansu were the Yang-shao of the Kansu subdivision, a derivative of the Yang-shao peoples in the Nuclear Area. These were followed by peoples of the Ch'i-chia culture, corresponding in time to the Lungshanoid cultures to the east but possibly of a different ethnic strain and probably of a distinctive cultural tradition. Between the Ch'i-chia and the Ch'in civilization, which swept into this region and made it a part of the Ch'in Empire, and contemporaneous with the Shang and the Chou civilizations in the middle and lower Huangho Valley, the area in eastern Kansu was occupied by several contemporary or overlapping cultures: Hsin-tien, Ssu-wa, and Sha-ching (Fig. 137).

The Hsin-tien Culture. Archaeological assemblages of the Hsin-tien culture have been recognized in the lower T'aoho Valley north of the town of Lin-t'ao, the Huangho Valley around the city of Yüng-ching, and the lower Huangshui Valley east of the town of Lo-tu.[33] They consisted of some stone implements, copper and bronze objects, and, above all, a distinctive ceramic style characterized by coarse

33. *KK* (1958/9), 47; *KK* (1959/7), 379.

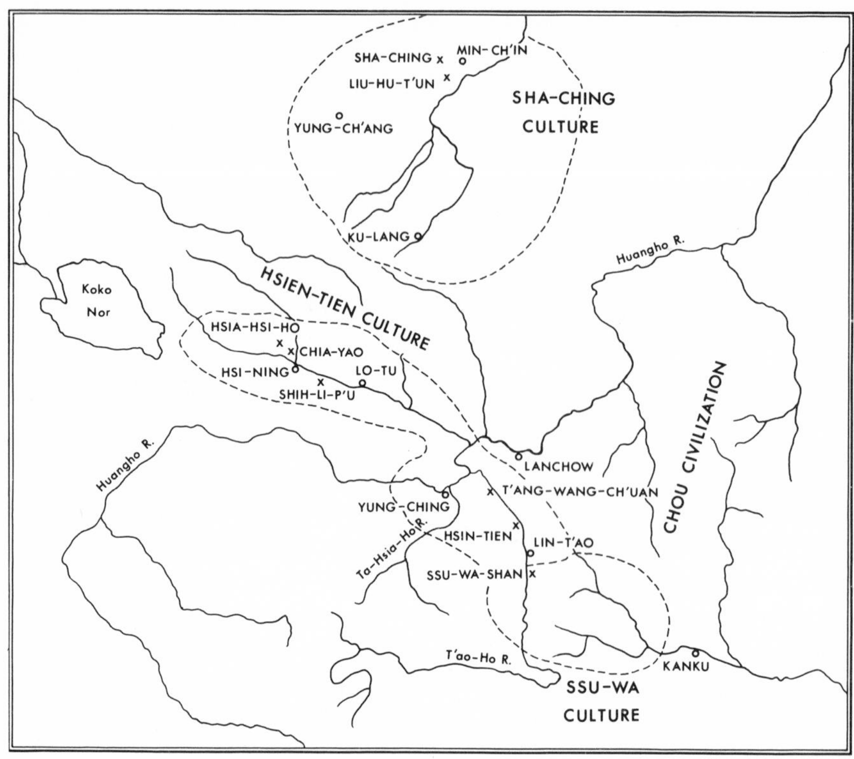

137. Eneolithic cultures in Kansu.

red and gray fabrics, white and red slip, and geometric patterns painted in black pigment. The pottery was handmade by means of the coiling technique and a beater. Both the coiled surface and the cord impressions produced by the beater were then smoothed over with wet fingers. The black paintings were simple and robust, executed freehand in bands around the shoulder and the middle circumference of the pot; the designs were mostly curvilinear and round. The pottery is characterized by a distinctive demarcation between the body and the collar, a large mouth, and one or two large vertical handles attached to the middle part of the pot or with one end connected to the body and the other attached to the rim or below the rim.[34] Within this

34. Wu Chin-ting, *Prehistoric Pottery in China,* pp. 105–06.

culture, at least two phases are distinguishable: Hsin-tien Phase A, centering in the T'aoho Valley; and Hsin-tien Phase B, concentrated in the Huangho Valley near the city of Yüng-ching. Two other ceramic phases, T'ang-wang, near Yüng-ching, and Chia-yao (classified by Andersson with the Ssu-wa Culture), both in the lower Huangshui, may also be related to the Hsin-tien culture.

Hsin-tien Phase A, the classical Hsin-tien phase recognized by Andersson, is represented by dwelling sites at Hui-tsui, T'ao-sha Hsien, and Chi-chia-ch'uan, Lin-hsia Hsien; and the cemetery at Hsin-tien (Hsin-tien Locality A), T'ao-sha Hsien. Burial sites of this phase have also been found in Lin-t'ao, Lin-hsia, and other localities in T'ao-sha.[35] The Hui-tsui dwelling site was on a high terrace surrounded by deep ravines and was probably highly advantageous for defense purposes. Andersson believes that the natural topography of this site was essentially the same as it is today.[36] From this locality, pottery, stone and bone implements, beads, half a cowrie shell, a bronze knife, and a bronze button were discovered by Andersson. The bronze knife has very similar counterparts among the Yin knives, and Wu Chin-ting finds some of the meander designs on the pottery reminiscent of North China bronze patterns.[37] A *wu-shu* coin of the Han Dynasty was found, but Andersson considers it intrusive. The pottery is coarse and highly porous, mostly of a gray or red color. The vessels were coiled, beaten, and then smoothed over with wet fingers. Two forms predominate—round-bottomed bowls and big-mouthed, high-collared jars with two handles. The handles are all vertical, either placed at the belly at the maximum diameter of the piece or below the rim with one end attached to the rim or the upper part of the collar and the other end to the shoulder. The bottoms are predominantly concave. On the whole, the pots are relatively small, with an average height and diameter of 15 centimeters. The surface designs consist of the beaten cord marks that were not obliterated, incisions, scratched short parallel lines, and paintings in black pigment. The painting is largely confined to the shoulder and collar parts, consisting of simple geometric designs of forcefully but freely executed thick lines, such as horizontal black

35. Andersson, *BMFEA, 15* (1943), 167–79; Hsieh Tuan-chü, *KK* (1962/2), 69–71.
36. *BMFEA, 15* (1943), 168.
37. *Prehistoric Pottery,* London, Kegan Paul, Trench & Trübner, 1938, p. 106.

bands, narrow wavy lines, triangles, meanders, and N-shaped patterns. Some conventionalized anthropomorphic and zoomorphic patterns are also present. The Chi-chia-ch'uan site has yielded a similar ceramic ware, as well as a semi-subterranean rectangular house, a number of storage pits, and a flexed burial.[38]

Hsin-tien Phase B is represented by three localities in Yüng-ching Hsien: Chang-chia-tsui, Han-chia-tsui, and Wa-cha-tsui.[39] In the same area, assemblages of Hsin-tien Phase A were also found. It is probable that these two phases were chronologically successive, with B the earlier of the two, although no stratigraphic evidence has been uncovered to confirm this view.[40] At the Chang-chia-tsui site, eighty-six round and rectangular pits were excavated, packed within a small area and yielding deep cultural debris. Chipped stone axes with ground edges, stone spades, knives (rectangular or notched), spindle whorls, perforated disks, and mortars and pestles were collected, along with bone spades, needles, awls, combs, ornaments, and two fragments of bronze or copper. Among the pottery remains, some red and gray pieces with a fine texture were noted, but most are of a kind of brick-red ware tempered with sand or powdered pottery. They were also coiled and smoothed over and burnished, like the pottery of Phase A, but on the whole they have a finer paste and there is a greater proportion of white slipped specimens. For surface decoration, cord marks, applied ridges, beaten checkers, and paintings are reported. The painting is again done in black pigment, but a few red patterns are found. The designs consist of parallel lines, deformed S-shapes, double spirals, N-shaped patterns, chevrons filled with parallel lines, sun patterns, crosses, and X-shaped patterns; most are common to both Phase A and Phase B, but others bear strong resemblance to the T'ang-wang phase. The vessels are more elongated, with larger handles than their Phase A counterparts, and the bottoms are uniformly flat rather than concave. In addition to jugs and bowls, pans, mugs, and *ting* and *li* tripods are also common[41] (Fig. 138).

Closely related, if not practically identical, to the Hsin-tien Phase B

38. Hsieh Tuan-chü, *KK* (1962/2), 69–71.
39. An Chih-min, *KKHP* (1957/2). *KK* (1959/4).
40. An Chih-min, *KKHP* (1957/2), 30.
41. Ibid. Hsieh Tuan-chü, *KK* (1959/4), 182–83.

138. Pottery of the Hsi-tien Phase B, Kansu. (From *KKHP,* 1957/2, plate facing p. 33.)

is a ceramic phase that has been termed the T'ang-wang style.[42] The type site of this style is Shan-shen, near T'ang-wang-ch'uan, in Tung-hsiang Hsien, Kansu, in the lower T'aoho Valley, but pots and sherds of the same style have been collected at other sites near Yüng-ching, in Lin-t'ao Hsien in the Lower T'aoho, and along the lower Huangshui east of Lo-tu.[43] The site of Shih-li-p'u near Hsi-ning in Chinghai, found by Andersson, who classified it with the Ma-ch'ang phase of the Kansu Yang-shao horizon, yielded pottery which shows no relation whatsoever to the Ma-ch'ang,[44] but unmistakable resemblance to the T'ang-wang style. The pottery is characterized by red ware of coarse paste, tempered with powdered pottery and occasionally with sand. Most of the sherds and pots are plain or corded cooking ware, but some of them were burnished and painted in black pigment. The surface was first smoothed over (thus obliterating the coil marks) and then, very often, slipped in red. Black patterns were executed on the slipped surface, most confined between two parallel lines around the belly, and consisting of spirals and whorls. Additional geometric patterns, such as S-shaped designs, parallel oblique lines, N-shaped designs, meanders, and chevrons filled with parallel lines, adorn parts of the rest of the pot on the collar, shoulder, or handle. The forms include jars with two or four vertical handles, basins with two handles, single-handled mugs, *tou,* and *li* tripods. The most conspicuous feature in vessel forms is the very large loop handle, often higher than the mouth (Fig. 139). Both in form and in decoration, the T'ang-wang style is closely similar to the Hsin-tien phases, particularly Phase B, to which some investigators would assign this style altogether.[45]

In the same area of distribution is another ceramic phase typified by the site of Chia-yao, which was grouped by Andersson with the Ssu-wa culture but is considered by many other fieldworkers as an independent culture.[46] I believe that it is neither, but that it should be regarded as a ceramic phase related to that of Hsin-tien, which we may call the Chia-yao phase. The type sites, Chia-yao and Hsia-hsi-ho, were first

42. An Chih-min, *KKHP* (1957/2), 23–27.
43. Ibid. An Chih-min, *KK* (1959/7), 379. Andersson, *BMFEA, 15* (1943), 160–61.
44. Chang Kwang-chih, *BIHP, 30* (1959), 298.
45. Hsieh Tuan-chü, *KK* (1959/4), 184.
46. Andersson, *BMFEA, 15* (1943), 222; but see An Chih-min, *KKTH* (1956/6); Chao Sheng-shen and Wu Ju-tso, *WW* (1960/6), 36.

139. Pottery of the T'ang-wang style, Kansu. (From *KKHP,* 1957/2, Pls. I–III, following p. 32.)

discovered during 1923–24 by Andersson in the valley of a tributary of the Huangshui in Hsi-ning Hsien, Chinghai.[47] The Chia-yao (Ch'ia-

47. Andersson, *BMFEA, 15* (1943), 185–97.

yao, K'a-yao) site, a cemetery, yielded thirteen skeletons which lie stretched on their backs, most with the head west. Some of the corpses had been sprinkled with red ocher. Eight burials were found at Hsia-hsi-ho, another burial site across the river. The vessels found in the graves have flat or (more rarely) concave bases, big bellies, and collars of varying length. The saddle-shaped mouth occurs on some of the pots. Most of the jars are equipped with two vertical handles, of the shoulder or collar type. Four-handled jars, with two large collar handles and two small shouldered loops, are also present. The surface of the pottery is brick-red or grayish, mostly plain, but corded specimens are also reported. Andersson recorded no painted specimens.

In addition to pottery, in the Chia-yao and Hsia-hsi-ho graves were found perforated stone disks, bone awls, plates, arrowheads, turquoise beads, clay spindle whorls, bronze buttons, folded buttons, links, openwork funnels, a knife, and some "rectangular objects." Andersson classifies these assemblages as Ssu-wa solely on the basis of some jars with saddle-shaped mouths, which are characteristic of the Ssu-wa culture. This classification is dubious. It appears to me that the Chia-yao assemblages resemble the Hsin-tien phases more closely than the Ssu-wa culture for the following reasons: (1) the saddle-shaped mouth is not common and is also found in the Hsin-tien phases, which may indicate cultural contacts with the Ssu-wa; (2) large collar handles, some of which are higher than the rim, are present; (3) four-handled jars are found; (4) concave bases are represented; and (5) geographically the Chia-yao phase is separated from the Ssu-wa region by a considerable area occupied by the Hsin-tien. This classification—with Hsin-tien instead of Ssu-wa—is strengthened by the result of new investigations since 1959 in Huang-chung Hsien and near the Hsi-ning city, which brought to light thirty-one localities of the Chia-yao phase.[48] Among the pottery remains were coarse red sherds tempered with powdered pottery and occasionally with sand or mica. These were coiled, some slipped (in red or, rarely, grayish-white), and painted, corded, applied, incised, or combed. The painting was done in black pigment, in designs of zigzags, triangles, and spirals. In form, the pottery is characterized by a wide mouth and large and small vertical handles, mostly on the collar part of the jar. A few *li* tripods are

48. Chao Sheng-shen and Wu Ju-tso, *WW* (1960/6), 35–36. *KK* (1964/9), 475–76.

found. Concave bottoms occurred quite frequently. In addition, some stone, horn, and bronze artifacts were also found. Among the bronzes, the *ko* halberds, buttons, and two-winged arrowheads are said to resemble Chou types.[49] The close similarity of this Chia-yao assemblage to the T'ang-wang phase of the same region has been noted,[50] and there is some speculation that the T'ang-wang phase was probably the proto-Chia-yao, so to speak. At any rate, the Chia-yao phase is shown to be related to the Hsin-tien phases by the new finds in the following aspects: temper of powdered pottery, coiling, red slip, black pigment in painting, and spiral designs. It is thus possible that the Hsin-tien B phase and the T'ang-wang style represent an earlier stage of the Hsin-tien culture, evolving into the Hsin-tien A in the T'aoho Valley and into the Chia-yao phase in the Huangshui Valley.

The Ssu-wa culture. This culture is now represented by over a dozen archaeological sites in the upper T'aoho Valley, south of Lin-t'ao Hsien, and in the upper Weishui tributaries in eastern Kansu.[51] The type locality of this culture is the Ssu-wa-shan cemetery in Lin-t'ao Hsien, discovered by Andersson in 1924.[52] The pottery remains in the eight burials here were plain, rather large, and brick-red or red in color. The shape of the vessels is characterized by jars with saddle-shaped mouths; some *li* tripods were found, and these also had saddle-shaped mouths. The body of the vessels is essentially oval, which has led Wu Chin-ting to conclude that the pots are designed to be easily portable.[53] Two vertical handles are attached to the upper part of the vessel. On the collar between the two handles there is in some cases an indented applied ridge. The average height of the vessels is 24 centimeters. They are coarse, sand-tempered, and handmade and smoothed out while still wet. Wu also observes that "every characteristic of the pottery seems to testify that the Ssu-wa culture is not Chinese, though it might have been influenced by that culture."[54] In addition to pottery, Andersson found an armlet of bronze, a perforated ax, and two

49. An Chih-min, *KK* (1959/7), 380.
50. Ibid., p. 379.
51. An Chih-min, *KKTH* (1956/6), 15. Chang Hsüeh-cheng, *KKTH* (1958/9), 47. An Chih-min, *KK* (1959/7), 327, 380. Yüan An-chih, *KK* (1963/1), 48.
52. Andersson, *BMFEA, 15* (1943), 179–85.
53. *Prehistoric Pottery,* p. 107.
54. Ibid.

goat horns. According to Andersson the goats were probably domesticated.[55]

The Ssu-wa-shan site was again investigated in 1945 by Hsia Nai, who excavated six additional burials. Three ways to dispose of the dead were distinguished by Hsia in his data: cremation and ash urns; interment of the dorsal and stretched type; and probably secondary burials. These burial customs, Hsia contends, indicate that the Ssu-wa-shan people were not Chinese but were possibly the Ch'iang recorded in Chinese annals.[56] Pottery similar to Andersson's finds was uncovered by Hsia, who also recognized the use of the coiling technique and of powdered-pottery tempers. A stone and a clay ball were collected, possibly slingstones. On the surface of a potsherd, impressions of grains were noted.[57]

More sites of the Ssu-wa tradition were investigated in the T'aoho and upper Weishui valleys in 1956,[58] 1957,[59] and 1958.[60] In 1957, some painted sherds were discovered in the Ssu-wa assemblages, with such patterns as concentric semicircles, meanders, and other geometric designs executed in black. Stone implements associated with the Ssu-wa pottery were mostly chipped, including edge-ground axes, knives with side notches, and shouldered axes.

The Sha-ching culture. Approximately 200 kilometers north of Lanchow, in the arid land between the Huangho and the Ch'ilien Mountains, lies the eastern segment of the so-called Hohsi Corridor, drained by the Pait'ing River. Ecologically, this region is on the border between the Huangho Valley and the steppe, but is still on the south side of the Great Wall. During the final Neolithic period, the area contained the Shan-tan (or Ssu-pa) culture, described in Chapter 5. When the Ch'i-chia culture in the Huangho and T'aoho valleys to the south gave way to the eneolithic Hsin-tien and Ssu-wa phases described above, the arid land in the north was occupied by a different cultural tradition, the Sha-ching. Archaeological remains of this culture have been located in Min-ch'in, Yüng-ch'ang, and Ku-lang coun-

55. *BMFEA, 15* (1943), 185.
56. *KKHP, 4* (1949), 96.
57. Ibid., pp. 106–07.
58. An Chih-min, *KKTH* (1956/6), 15.
59. Chang Hsüeh-cheng, *KKTH* (1958/9), 45.
60. An Chih-min, *KK* (1959/7), 327.

ties.[61] It is typified by the archaeological sites at Sha-ching-ts'un, in Min-ch'in (Chen-fan) Hsien, which were discovered in 1923–24 by Andersson.[62] These consist of a fortified dwelling site, Liu-hu-t'un, and a cemetery. The former was a mud-walled fortress, 50 meters in diameter. Found inside were a *li* tripod, some handled high bowls, a steatite pan, some bone artifacts (needles, arrowheads, etc.), a bronze knife, a bronze prismatic arrowhead, and a piece of golden string. The cemetery is 260 meters to the west, and in it over forty burials were excavated. The skeletons lay on their backs, stretched or slightly flexed. The pottery was reddish, containing sand or mica for temper, beaten and red-slipped. Some of the pots were painted in red pigment, and the favorite designs were horizontal lines, triangles, and bird figures. In form, two shapes are characteristic, handled mugs with vertical walls and small jars with two small shoulder loops. The bodies and the collars of the jars are not distinctively demarcated. In addition to pottery, Andersson found in the burials stone and turquoise beads, marble rings, perforated stone objects (similar in shape to the banner stones of the eastern United States), cowrie shells (all ground flat and open at the back), and copper and bronze artifacts including a spearhead, an arrowhead (with square cross section), a ring, a knife tip, a flat three-lobed piece with spiral design on the front and a bridge on each of the end lobes on the back (similar to an object found in a Warring States grave in Luan-p'ing, Jehol), tubes which were annulated at the ends and widened and smooth in the center (identical with objects found in the Ordos), and a button.

The chronological position of the above three cultures is stratigraphically clear insofar as they can be shown to be earlier than the Han Dynasty but later than the Ch'i-chia culture in the same area. Stratigraphical evidence at Chang-chia-tsui and Wu-chia in Yüng-ching Hsien shows that the Hsin-tien culture was definitely later than the Ch'i-chia,[63] and that at Ssu-wa-shan the Ssu-wa culture was subsequent to the Ma-chia-yao phase of the Kansu Yang-shao culture.[64] Furthermore, the saddle-mouthed jars sometimes found in the Hsin-tien

61. An Chih-min, *KKTH* (1956/6), 16.
62. Andersson, *BMFEA, 15* (1943), 197–215.
63. An Chih-min, *KKTH* (1956/6), 15.
64. Hsia Nai, *KKHP, 4* (1949), 74.

assemblages indicate that the Hsin-tien and the Ssu-wa at least overlapped in time.[65] Some idea of the absolute dating of these approximately contemporary cultures can be derived from the typology of the *li* tripods found in these assemblages (most of which are said to be of the Yin-Chou types), from the metal objects of Yin, Chou, and Ordosian affinities, and from the fact that within the Ssu-wa, which adjoined the Western Chou civilization of the Weishui Valley, cultural elements such as specific types of shouldered axes and side-notched stone knives have been found which indicate contacts with the Chou. It seems reasonable to place the Kansu eneolithic cultures at the end of the second millennium and during the first half of the first millennium B.C., an interval long enough for subdivisions to be made, such as the development of the Hsin-tien phases (Hsin-tien B and T'ang-wang to Hsin-tien A and Chia-yao).

If, as is shown, the Hsin-tien, Sha-ching, and Ssu-wa were approximately contemporary cultures, what are they exactly in terms of archaeological nomenclature? Archaeologically all three cultures are known primarily by their ceramics. The following characteristics are common to all of them: in shape, jars with vertical handles predominate, and the handles include both the small-belly and large-collar varieties, seeming, in these aspects, to carry on the basic ceramic forms of both the Pan-shan stage and the Ch'i-chia culture *in the same area;* pottery of all three cultures was coiled and beaten, with the roughened surface mostly smoothed out; ceramic painting is seen in all three, although it occurs only rarely (as recorded thus far) in the Ssu-wa; the painted designs are geometric and conventionally realistic in all three, and the lines are robust and the patterns simplistic. In shape and in decorative painting, the minimum denominators common to all three cultures, still sufficiently specific in terms of style to make cultural historic connections, are of such a basic nature as to lead us to suspect that they may have been three different regional phases of the same culture, one that carries on the basic ceramic features of both the Kansu Yang-shao and the Ch'i-chia culture in the area of eastern Kansu. It must also be noted that it is not at all impossible that some of the late Kansu Yang-shao phases and the Ch'i-chia culture over-

65. An Chih-min, *KKTH* (1956/6), 15. Chang Hsüeh-cheng, *KKTH* (1958/9), 47.

lapped in time in the marginal regions of this area, which may have resulted in a mutual influence or even a merging of styles.

On the other hand, many ceramic stylistic features set the Hsin-tien, the Ssu-wa, and the Sha-ching cultures apart from one another and from their local predecessors, a fact that also finds support from the little information available on their respective cultural contexts. In subsistence patterns, all three cultures appear to have been based on agriculture, but animal domestication may also have played an important role in the Ssu-wa, as indicated by remains of goat horns and the shape of pottery that may well have been designed for a mobile life, as Wu suggested. In burial customs, the Hsin-tien and Chia-yao used red ochers, the Ssu-wa had cremation, and the Sha-ching placed some of the dead in a somewhat flexed posture. In ceramics, the red pigment for painting and the flat-bottomed mugs are distinctive of the Sha-ching culture, whereas both the Ssu-wa and the Hsin-tien stressed large-handled jars with well-defined bodies and collars, and used powdered pottery for tempering material. To what extent these differences in culture and technology indicate ethnic differences or diverse "origins" is an open question.

CHAPTER NINE

EARLY CIVILIZATIONS IN SOUTH CHINA

During the late second and the first millennium B.C., cultural elements and complexes of the Shang and Chou civilizations penetrated deep into the northern part of eastern Asia, causing widespread cultural changes, but the Great Wall to a large extent marks the northern limits of the civilized states built on the foundation of agriculture. No such limits in ecology were imposed upon the spread of civilization into subtropical South China, where the Shang and the Chou helped stimulate the formation of a number of early kingdoms. The introduction of North China civilizations into South China followed closely the paths used by the early Lungshanoid pioneer farmers: agricultural kingdoms emerged first in the Huaiho and the Yün-meng basin in the middle Yangtze, and from there expanded to the lower Yangtze and the southeastern coast, and to the Red basin and the Yunnan Plateau in the southwest.

The Tsinling Mountains and the Huaiho River did not form a barrier to an agrarian way of life, as the Great Wall did, but they do mark off the southern from the northern ecological zone, and the ancient civilizations divided by these formations had to adapt to very different climatic conditions. At present, most of South China receives more than fifty inches of rainfall annually, but north of the Tsinling there is a drop to twenty inches or less. In the Yangtze Valley the growing season continues for 250 days of the year, but in the delta of the Huangho the season is 225 days and even less west of the delta.[1] Two or three thousand years ago these figures may have been different, but the north–south difference must have been there, and the climatic contrast would account for many of the cultural distinctions between North and South China. The early civilizations in South China were largely based upon rice cultivation, whereas millet was the staple food in the north. Moreover, the emergence of civilizations in South China took place on the foundation of its own advanced Neolithic farming practices, although cultural stimulations from other civilizations—pri-

1. George B. Cressey, *Land of the 500 Million,* New York, McGraw-Hill, 1955, pp. 66, 69.

marily those of the Shang and Chou of North China—must have provided an initial or crucial impetus. For these reasons, as well as for convenience, the civilizations in South China are described in a separate chapter, even though in many cases the southern civilizations may be regarded as regional variants of the Shang and Chou civilizations described in Chapters 6 and 7.

THE HUAIHO VALLEY

Centered in northern and western Honan, Shang Dynasty influences are discernible in the archaeological materials excavated from Kiangsu, Anhwei, Hupei, and Hunan. In the Huaiho Valley of northern Kiangsu and Anhwei, an area whose ancient inhabitants, the Huai Yi, are known to be among the staunchest allies of the Shang at the time of their rebellion against the Chou after Wu Wang's death, the Shang impact was so pronounced that archaeologists have often been tempted to speak of Shang sites in these regions, wherever Shang-type remains are encountered, as though the Huaiho Valley was as much a part of the Shang state as, let us say, northern Honan. In the neighborhood of Hsü-chou, for instance, some sites have been listed in current publications as "Yin Shang sites."[2] Remains of stone, bone, and ceramic artifacts do occur at some of these sites, indicating cultural contacts with the Shang; in addition, small numbers of bronze knives, arrowheads, and spearheads, as well as oracle turtleshells, were unearthed at Kao-huang-miao, and corded *li* tripods with nipple-shaped feet at some of the other sites. On the other hand, fieldworkers have not reported evidence of local metallurgy or urban settlement patterns from this area, and we cannot fail to take note of the fact that practically all the implements and tools of these archaeological assemblages were made of stone, shell, or bone. Some archaeologists who have reported on these sites may have been too liberal in using such terms as "Shang culture" and "Shang period." Positive identifications have sometimes been made upon very general and meager data. Take, for instance, the following reports:

> The Middle Stratum [of Kao-huang-miao] has relatively thick deposits, and represents a fairly long time duration. Among the

2. Hsieh Ch'un-chu, *KKHP* (1958/4), 7–17. Yin Huan-chang and Chang Cheng-hsiang, *KK* (1960/3), 28.

> remains that have been unearthed, stone, bone, and shell tools and implements predominate in quantity. Some of these implements, such as stone sickles and shell knives, are more advanced than the Lower Stratum specimens . . . In addition, bronzes have been found, and oracle bones and turtle shells discovered. All such circumstances indicate that the cultural remains of the Middle Stratum belonged to the Yin-Shang period.[3]
>
> The lower stratum [of the Liang-wang-ch'eng site] has yielded *li* tripods and urns of gray ware with corded surface, black pottery *tou* with string patterns, and, in addition, deer antlers, mollusc shells, and perforated flat axes, evidently showing characteristic features of Shang Dynasty remains.[4] . . .
>
> The Shang Dynasty sites [in the Hsü-chou area investigated in 1959] include Ch'iu-wan. . . . In the remains, such items as bronze arrowheads, bone hairpins, bone awls, bone arrowheads, corded *lei,* corded *li,* corded urns, pottery with *t'ao-t'ieh* patterns, and helmet-shaped pots, indicate Shang Dynasty characteristics.[5]

Some of these Shang characteristics, to be sure, are of such specific and significant nature as to warrant the connection, but others are too general and widespread to do so. In either event, the designation Shang sites is unwarranted unless its meaning is made completely clear. It is probably safe to say that the Shang cultural influences were felt by the Lung-shan farmers of the Hsü-chou area of Kiangsu. The same can also be said for northern Anhwei in the Huaiho Valley. Cultural elements similar to those of the Shang have been found in Shou Hsien, Fu-nan, and Chia-shan. Wang Hsiang reported under the term "Hsiao-t'un stage" many early cultural sites in Shou Hsien, including those where the following traits were present: short-footed *li* tripods; urns with cord marks and corded appliqued ridges; *tou* with thick rims; and deep dishes.[6] Li Chi[7] added what he calls the "Hsiao-t'un stone knife" from Yang-lin-chi to this list. In the district of Fu-nan, in the area of Anhwei closest to Honan, twenty-six bronze vessels have

3. Hsieh Ch'un-chu, *KKHP* (1958/4), 17.
4. Yin Huan-chang and Chang Cheng-hsiang, *KK* (1960/3,) 26.
5. Ibid., p. 28.
6. *Chung-kuo K'ao-ku Hsüeh Pao, 2* (1947), 250.
7. *BIHP, 23* (1951), 612.

been found since the 1940s, but their provenance and cultural contexts are not known.[8] Farther east, in the area of Chia-shan, four Shang-type bronze vessels (*chüeh, chia, ku, lei*) were discovered in 1953.[9] These vessels have been described as Shang bronzes, but they could equally well date from the early Western Chou period. Western Chou bronzes have been found in well-documented circumstances as far south as the lower Yangtze, as will be described below, and typology alone could not distinguish between Shang and early Western Chou.

Although the extension of the Shang and the Western Chou civilizations into the Huaiho Valley, presumable according to literary history, can be only meagerly substantiated by the available archaeological data, there is no longer any ambiguity about the Eastern Chou period. An assemblage of bronze vessels found in Shu Hsien, central Anhwei, could be the relics of the ancient state of Shu (657–615 B.C.).[10] But the most important discoveries in the Huaiho Valley of Eastern Chou sites are those of the state of Ts'ai.

According to *Shih Chi,* Ch'u invaded Ts'ai and forced the Marquis Chao to move his capital to Chou-lai in 493 B.C. Chou-lai is generally agreed to have been in the neighborhood of Shou Hsien. Ssu-ma Ch'ien also reported that in 447 Ts'ai was finally overthrown by the Ch'u, who, in 241, in the reign of King K'ao-lieh, moved their capital to Shou-ch'un, southwest of the present town of Shou Hsien. An Eastern Chou tomb discovered in 1955 at Shou Hsien, in which over five hundred artifacts have been found, including bronze vessels with inscriptions mentioning the Marquis of Ts'ai, can thus be dated to the narrow temporal interval between 493 and 447 B.C., although exactly who this Marquis of Ts'ai might have been (five marquises had Chou-lai for their capital before the fall of the marquisdom under the Ch'u) is a controversial subject.[11]

The tomb is a rectangular earthen pit, oriented north–south, 8.45 m long N–S, and 7.1 m wide E–W. Remains of a lacquered wooden coffin were found at the center of the tomb; the skeleton is completely gone but, according to the position of the jade ornaments and a

8. Ko Chieh-p'ing, *WW* (1959/1).
9. Ibid. (1965/7), 23–25.
10. Yin Ti-fei, *KK* (1964/10), 498–503.
11. *Shou Hsien Ts'ai-hou mu ch'u-t'u yi-wu,* Peking, Science Press, 1956.

bronze sword presumably worn at the side, the body was probably buried with its head to the north. A skeleton was found at the southeastern corner of the grave, probably a sacrificed victim. Pottery, lacquer, and bronze vessels, musical instruments, weapons, and horse and chariot fittings were buried in various places within the grave. Some of the vessels were inscribed, indicating that the master of the tomb was a Ts'ai marquis. Typologically, the decoration and the shape of the bronze artifacts present another example of the Huai style and, since they are precisely dated, they can also be taken as a type assemblage for the bronzes of the late Ch'un-ch'iu and early Chan-kuo periods.

Two other large tombs, also in the area of Shou Hsien, were excavated in 1958–59, yielding a total of 112 bronze artifacts. Inscriptions on the bronze weapons found in one of the tombs (approximately 5 by 4 m at the opening and 3 by 2 at the bottom, with *erh-ts'eng-t'ai* and a northern ramp) suggest that this was the tomb of Marquis Sheng of Ts'ai (enthroned 471; died 457 B.C.)[12]

These finds show that by the Eastern Chou period at the latest, typical North China art, writing, and crafts had been implanted in the Huaiho Valley. The political system of this area as indicated by the artifacts is probably comparable with the states in North China described in Chapter 7.

THE LOWER YANGTZE AND THE SOUTHEASTERN COAST

In Chapter 4 it was shown that the Lungshanoid farmers brought agriculture and a Lungshanoid cultural style with them into the eastern part of South China—the part that is drained by the middle and lower Yangtze, the Huaiho, and many small rivers along the southeastern coast, and consists of the present provinces of Anhwei, Kiangsu, Hupei, Kiangsi, Chekiang, Fukien, Taiwan, and the eastern part of Kwangtung. The Lungshanoid in South China is an authentic horizon in the sense used by American archaeologists—a highly homogeneous style of artifacts brought into a large area by a rapid, or even explosive, expansion out of a center which was, in this case, the North China Nuclear Area. In eastern South China, the Lungshanoid and the

12. Ma Tao-k'uo, *KK* (1963/4), 204–12.

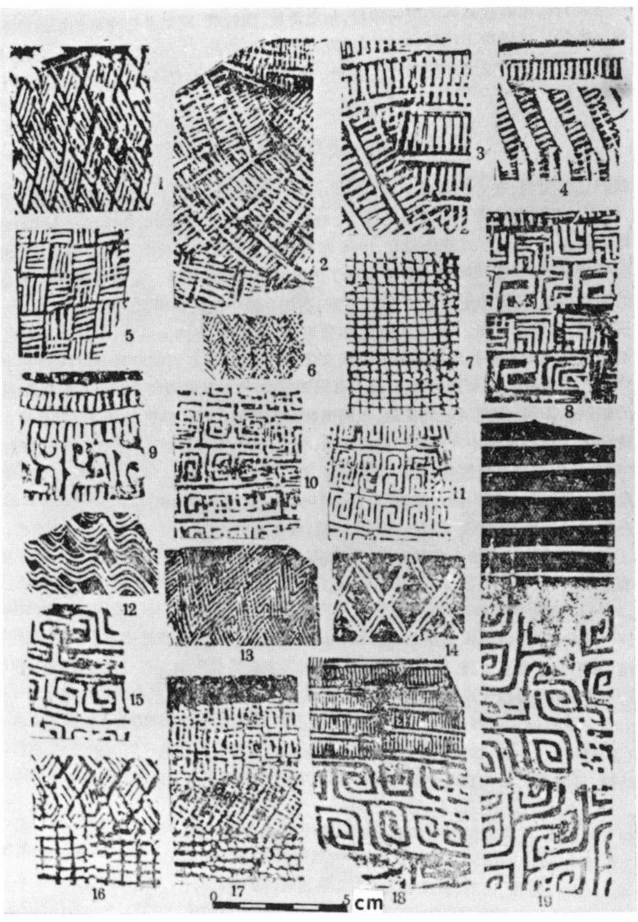

140. Rubbings of geometric patterns on pottery in the Hu-shu culture, southeast China. (From *KKHP,* 1958/1, p. 79.)

Lung-shan cultures were followed by another highly homogeneous and even more widespread horizon, the Geometric.

The name Geometric, used in archaeological literature to refer to the impressed designs on pottery in this area of this horizon, is used here to designate the horizon style primarily characterized by the geometric stamping manifested in the pottery remains. Both pottery stamps and the geometric patterns (such as checkers, parallel lines, and wavy lines) appear in the Lungshanoid horizon, but in the Geometric

141. Pottery urns with stamped geometric decorative patterns in the Hu-shu culture. (From *KKHP,* 1958/1, Pl. III.)

horizon, geometric stamping dominated the ceramic decoration, was used far more extensively than before, and had greatly diversified design motifs. The color of the Geometric wares is predominantly red or grayish; the ware is handmade, beaten, and hard-fired. The beater also served as a stamp for decorative designs, which include a long list of such geometric basic patterns as checkers, chevrons, cross-hatches, meanders, spirals, triangles, quadrangles, and circles (Fig. 140). In shape, small-mouthed and flat- or round-bottomed urns (Fig. 141) predominate, though to some extent all Lungshanoid forms are continued. This new ceramic style of South China can certainly be linked with the "hard ware" of the Yin-Shang pottery, and the Geometric horizon in eastern South China was apparently a development of the local Lung-shan substratum, under the continuous stimulation of the Shang and Chou cultural impacts.

In addition to the new ceramic style, the geometric horizon carries over from the Lungshanoid Neolithic essentially the same cultural traditions of the area, such as the stone inventories (among which the stepped adz is the most characteristic) (Fig. 142),[13] agricultural crops (primarily rice), habitation patterns (dwellings on mounds or on wooden piles, apparently a feature which is environmentally oriented in the main), and other aspects of the material culture. However, at least one other significant addition was made to the Lungshanoid foundation during the Geometric period, namely, bronze metallurgy. Small pieces of bronze objects have been found at many Geometric

13. Lin Hui-hsiang, *KKHP* (1958/3), 1.

142. Shouldered (*left*) and stepped (*right*) axes and adzes in the Neolithic period of the southeast. Excavated from Ta-p'en-k'eng, Taiwan.

sites dated to a pre-Han Dynasty period, and evidence of local bronze foundry has been discovered at many sites in southern Kiangsu.

The Geometric horizon spread over a wide area, largely the same as the Lungshanoid, but including Hunan and more of Kwangtung and excluding most of Hupei. This horizon, however, occupied each of these regions far more intensively and lasted for a long time. For the entire area, the Geometric horizon started with the first influence of the Shang civilization from the north, probably during the second half of the second millennium B.C., and ended toward the end of the first millennium B.C., although the Geometric Stamped Pottery as a stylistic tradition of the area persisted throughout South China into the Han Dynasty.[14] The Geometric horizon evolved in a number of different ways. At the beginning, the local communities in this area probably carried on the Lung-shan Neolithic ways of life, even though the new ceramic styling and some bronze metallurgy were introduced. In some regions, however, continuous Shang and Chou influences helped the local cultures develop into states modeled on those of North China. To describe the contextual variations within the Geometric horizon during the different periods in the regions of eastern South China, we must try to trace the southern limits and extent of the historical cultural influences step by step.

The late prehistoric culture in the lower Yangtze Valley in southern Kiangsu and central Anhwei during the interval approximating the Shang and Chou periods has been referred to as the Hu-shu culture, a term coined in 1959 by Tseng Chao-yüeh and Yin Huan-chang after the site at Hu-shu in Chiang-ning Hsien, Kiangsu.[15] The sites of this culture are on mounds or low hills and hillslopes, and the archaeological inventories are characterized by many distinctive common features in stone implements, ceramics, bone and antler artifacts, bronze metallurgy, house construction, scapulimancy, and burial customs. Among the ceramic remains, red and black pottery of a Lungshanoid heritage still constitute the majority, but geometric wares are important elements also.

Although the continuity from its Lung-shan antecedents is evident in the Hu-shu culture, important new elements appeared in addition to the Geometric pottery. Bronze knives, arrowheads, axes, fishhooks, and handles and legs of bronze *ting* tripods have been found at a number of sites near Nanking (Fig. 143) and Tan-t'u.[16] Pottery crucibles and fragments of bronze have been found from a lower stratum of this culture at Pei-yin-yang-ying, near Nanking, indicating the prac-

14. Yin Huan-chang, *KKHP* (1958/1), 84.

15. *KKHP* (1959/4), 47. For subsequent discussions of this culture see Chang Yüng-nien, *KK* (1962/1), 32–37; Wu Ju-tso, *KK* (1962/1), 38–40; Yin Huan-Chang and Yüan Ying, *KK* (1962/3), 125–28, 133.

16. Chang Yüng-nien, *KK* (1962/1), 32–33.

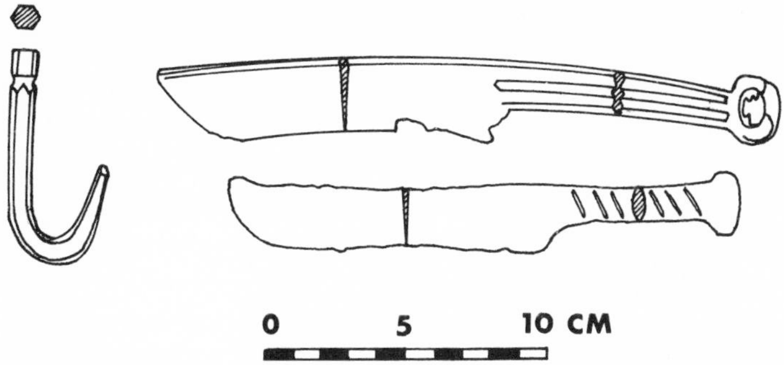

143. Bronze artifacts from the site of So-chin-ts'un, near Nanking. (From *KKHP,* 1957/2, p. 29.)

tice of bronze metallurgy in the local village communities. Not only Shang and Chou type bronze arrowheads and knives but also copper ores and pottery spoons (probably for bronze smelting) have been found at a number of sites in the Yi-cheng and Liu-ho area.[17] At the site of T'ai-kang-ssu near Hsi-shan-ch'iao, in Nanking, excavated in 1960, twenty-nine bronze artifacts, three pieces of oracle turtleshells, and stone, bone, and shell implements and pottery were discovered, together with ten burials. Some were headless bodies, some were heads only, and others had legs as though they had been tied.[18] The culture at these sites was apparently more advanced than the Neolithic Lungshan culture from which they were derived. Most archaeologists would impute the impetus of the new cultural growth in this area to Shang and Chou China, and the thesis has been advanced that the Hu-shu culture sites were habitations of very advanced bronze cultures whose cemeteries, with large assemblages of Western Chou bronzes, provide unmistakable links with the north.[19]

It is difficult to specify the cultural traits of the Hu-shu culture that came about from the Shang influence. Yin Huan-chang[20] has singled out the following traits of the Geometric horizon in southern Kiangsu which he considers to be derived from Yin or early Western Chou influences: (1) in ceramics, such forms as *p'o, lei, li, yen, kui, yu, min,* and *tou,* such accessory parts as lugs, and such decorative designs as

17. Yin Huan-chang and Yüan Ying, *KK* (1962/3), 128.
18. Lo Tsung-chen, *KK* (1962/3), 117–24.
19. Chang Yüng-nien, *KK* (1962/1), 35.
20. Tseng Chao-yüeh and Yin Huan-Chang, *KKHP* (1959/4), 54.

yün and *lei* patterns, cowrie, bands of triangles, and strings, all similar to the bronzes of the late Yin and early Chou; (2) in stone typology, stone halberds and stone arrowheads similar in form to the bronze halberds of the Yin and Chou dynasties and the bronze arrowheads excavated from Yin-hsü; and (3) bronze knives, arrowheads, and handles and feet of the *ting* tripods of the late Yin and early Chou styles. According to Jao Tsung-yi,[21] potsherds found in such regions to the far south as the Hanchiang River valley in eastern Kwangtung resemble the "white pottery" of the Shang Dynasty to such an extent in color and decorative designs as to suggest cultural influence.

Although conclusions regarding the extension of the Yin–Shang influence to the Yangtze Valley or even farther south might be regarded as farfetched on the basis of the available archaeological evidence, there is no question that the Western Chou civilization extended to the lower Yangtze. Groups of bronze vessels of probable Western Chou types have been discovered not only in the lower Yangtze Valley in Tan-t'u, Yi-cheng, and Nanking in southern Kiangsu but also from such southern localities as Ch'ang-hsing, on the western shore of T'ai-hu Lake in northern Chekiang, and T'un-hsi in southern Anhwei (Fig. 144), in the upper reaches of the Ch'ien-t'ang-chiang, or Chekiang River.[22] These bronzes exhibit either characteristic features that have been attributed to the Yin–Chou substage of the Archaic style according to North China criteria, or typical diagnostics of the Middle Chou style as defined by Bernhard Karlgren. Accordingly, these five sites can be grouped into two classes:

1. Early Western Chou: Tan-t'u and Yi-cheng finds, characterized by an Archaic style with features assumed to be Western Chou instead of Yin—four-eared *kui, p'an* with bent ears. These two sites are in the lower Yangtze in southern Kiangsu.
2. Late Western Chou or early Eastern Chou: Nanking, T'un-hsi, and Ch'ang-hsing finds, characterized by a typical Middle Chou style with local characteristics. The Nanking site is in

21. *Ta-lu-tsa-chih, 8* (1954), 65–67.

22. *WWTKTL* (1955/5), 58–62. Wang Chih-min and Han Yi-chih, *WWTKTL* (1956/12), 31; *WW* (1960/7), 48. Li Wei-jan, *KK* (1960/6), 41. Yin Ti-fei, *KKHP* (1959/4), 59–87. Yu Chen-yao and Ch'en K'o-yu, *KK* (1961/6), 321–23. Hu Wen, *WW* (1965/6), 52.

144. Bronze vessels of Western Chou types found at T'un-hsi, southern Anhwei. (From *KKHP,* 1959/4, Pl. I.)

the Yangtze Valley of southern Kiangsu, but the other two sites are farther south, in the Chekiang Valley in southern Anhwei and northern Chekiang.

These findings are of considerable importance for the study of Western Chou bronzes, and in connection with the present discussions their composition and geographical distribution are highly significant for the following reasons. The distribution of the bronzes of different ages indicates that the southbound expansion of the North Chinese cultural influences extended toward the south from the lower Yangtze to the Chekiang Valley during the span of the Western Chou Dynasty. In addition to some bronze types that are so similar to their North China counterparts as to suggest importation from the north, a suggestion strengthened by the inscriptions of Western Chou characters on a *kui* vessel from the Yen-tun-shan site of Tan-t'u, there are other forms of bronze and other decorative designs on the vessels that find no counterparts in North China but must be considered as having been manufactured *in situ* and influenced stylistically by the local cultural tradition.

> Some of the vessels [from the Tan-t'u group] are not identical with North China bronzes stylistically. For instance, the lid-knob and *ting* ears in the shape of standing animals . . . are rarely seen on North China bronzes. The body shape and the foot form of two small *ting* tripods resemble the pottery *ting* tripods of the [local Geometric horizon] cultures. The textile pattern on a pair of horn-shaped vessels and on several horse fittings is identical with the textile patterns on the local Geometric Stamped Pottery. One can positively say that these bronzes were manufactured *in situ,* thus exhibiting some characteristic features of the local culture.[23]

At the T'un-hsi site, many ceramic remains found in association with the Western Chou type of bronzes are indistinguishable from the Geometric pottery discovered elsewhere in the same area in less glamorous contexts,[24] and the bronzes differ from North Chinese bronzes in decorative patterns, shapes, and sometimes even in type, as, for example, a special local kind of musical instrument. These distinctive features, if they mean the local manufacture of some bronzes, are significant indicators of the nature of the communities which were responsible for the making, use, and burial of these bronzes.

Another highly suggestive fact about these Western Chou bronzes is that, as they appear in the present archaeological record, they are isolated islands of high civilization surrounded by the sea of less advanced communities of the local Geometric horizon. In these communities, cultural elements indicative of Western Chou contacts, such as ceramic shapes, decorative designs, and the remains of bronze artifacts, are few and insignificant in comparison with the overwhelming majority of other remains found at the same sites, which consist of

23. Tseng Chao-yüeh and Yin Huan-chang, *KKHP* (1959/4), 54.
24. Ibid., p. 78.

stone, bone, and shell implements of a local Neolithic tradition and ceramics of the Geometric Stamped style.

These facts suggest that the introduction of the Western Chou civilization into the lower Yangtze Valley may have been brought about by an elite class, of Western Chou extraction, who ruled the natives of the region, established a local technological and societal pattern after the North China model, and gradually acculturated the local Neolithic inhabitants in the farming villages. The region of southern Kiangsu was known in Western Chou as the state of Wu, and, according to local traditions, was the location of the burial place of two Western Chou princes, T'ai Po and Chung Yüng. These princes, according to Ssu-ma Ch'ien's *Shih Chi* "escaped to the habitations of the Ching Man barbarians, tattooed themselves and cut off their hair [according to the local customs] to indicate their decision of not returning . . . They called themselves Kou Wu. The Ching Man people considered them as righteous men, and more than a thousand families followed their leadership." To what extent the details of this story are valid is debatable, but the story in its broad outline and the archaeological facts have jointly established the process of acculturation in this region by the Western Chou civilization.

Such events were not confined to the lower Yangtze and the Chekiang valleys. Eastern Chou historical documents have recorded that many civilized kingdoms in southeast China had communications, transactions, and warfare with the Royal Chou and other northern Chinese states. Of these kingdoms, Wu of southern Kiangsu, Yüeh of Chekiang, Fukien, Kwangtung, and Yen of southern Kiangsu are the best known. It is evident that such kingdoms emerged during the Western Chou Dynasty, and the process described above may very well represent the initial phase of such an emergence. But in the archaeological record it was not until the Eastern Chou period that the remains of these early kingdoms in South China became widely found and substantially represented. In terms of society and cultural changes, Eastern Chou may be considered to be the period when these kingdoms, archaeologically speaking, were formed.

In the area of the Wu, a cemetery in the uppermost stratum of the Pei-yin-yang-ying site, probably dating from the Eastern Chou period, yielded finely polished stone artifacts and jade and opal objects in numbers varying widely from grave to grave—from over forty items to a single piece—which suggests sharply differentiated social status.[25] Such indications undoubtedly support the historical records of the Wu and Yüeh states in this and neighboring regions, although such states are yet to be identified precisely in the archaeological remains. Remains of stone plows, triangular in shape and closely similar to the iron plows of North China, have been unearthed in a Geometric horizon context at Yü-yao Hsien, Chekiang,[26] suggesting that the iron plow technology of the contemporary civilizations elsewhere had local imitations in the Hu-shu culture and its related phases. The cultural and social implications of such influences cannot be overemphasized.

Yen-ch'eng, the town of Yen, is a walled site south of Wu-chin (Ch'ang-chou), south of the Yangtze Valley in southern Kiangsu Province. It has three concentric walls called the outer wall, the inner wall, and the Tzu-lo or royal wall. The outer wall is an irregular circle, about 1500 meters across, surrounded by a defensive moat. Both the inner wall and the royal wall make approximately square enclosures within the northeastern part of the outer enclosure, with another protective moat surrounding the inner wall. Between the outer and the inner walls, in the western part of the outer enclosure, is a row of three earthen mounds. The arrangement of this town is similar to some of the Eastern Chou cities in North China, as described above. Local traditions regard this town site as the remains of the capital of Yen, a Yüeh-related state in southern Kiangsu. Archaeological investigations were made at the site in 1935 and again in 1958, bringing to light a small amount of pottery, stone implements, bronze vessels, and wooden boats, but full-scale scientific excavations have yet to be carried out.

Pottery remains at the Yen site belonged to the Geometric variety, including nearly twenty whole urns covered with impressed geometric designs, some of which apparently were imitations of bronze patterns.[27] The bronzes, discovered in 1958, consist of three *tsun* vessels, a *p'an* with a handle, a spout, and three *ting*-like feet, a bronze *p'an* with two wheel-feet and two animal-head handles, a set of seven

25. Chao Ch'ing-fang, *KKHP* (1958/1), 7–18.

26. Hsieh Ch'un-chu, *WW* (1958/11), 80.

27. Wei Chü-hsien, *Chung-kuo k'ao-ku-hsüeh shih,* Shanghai, Commercial Press, 1937, p. 255. Tseng Chao-yüeh and Yin Huan-chang, *KKHP* (1959/4), 54; *WW* (1959/4), 54; *WW* (1959/4), 5.

portable bells, and an animal-shaped *yi* vessel.[28] One hundred and fifty meters south of the spot where the bronzes were found, in the moat surrounding the inner wall, three dugout canoes were uncovered, one of which is 11 meters long and 90 centimeters wide at the top.[29]

The shape and decor of the bronze vessels find counterparts in the Huai style of North China, but many local characteristics are still highly conspicuous, such as the three-wheeled *p'an,* the *yi* vessel with an animal-head spout, and the needle-shaped decorative designs on the *tsun* vessels. The associated Geometric pottery clearly indicates the basic cultural affiliation of this town site. In any case, this find gives an interesting example of the Yüeh civilization in the Eastern Chou period.

By the time of Eastern Chou when civilizations flowered in the Wu and Yüeh strongholds of Kiangsu and Chekiang, evidence is widespread that bronze (and iron) metallurgy was established in the Geometric Ware sites of Kiangsi[30] and bronze objects are found in Fukien[31] and Taiwan.[32] Habitation sites and tombs of the Warring States period have recently come to light in central Kwangsi in Tseng-ch'eng and Shih-hsing in the north,[33] and near Canton in the region of Ch'ing-yüan in the south.[34] In all these southeastern coastal areas bronzes of the Warring States types were still found in association with stone implements of Neolithic type and with vessels of Geometric Ware. At the habitation sites in Tseng-ch'eng and Shih-hsing, iron axes and hoe blades were found, indicating that by this time the use of iron for agricultural implements was widespread throughout the eastern part of South China. The construction of the tombs in Ch'ing-yüan and the general types of bronze vessels are in the Warring States pattern of the Chou civilization of the north, but the decorative patterns of the bronzes, the shapes of some bronze tools (such as the fan-shaped ax), and a dagger handle in the form of a human figure are

28. Ni Chen-k'ui, *WW* (1959/4), 5.

29. Hsieh Ch'un-chu, *WW* (1958/11), 80.

30. Yang Hou-li et al., *KK* (1962/4), 172–81. Hsüeh Yao and Ch'eng Ying-lin, *KK* (1965/6), 265–67.

31. Ch'en Chung-kuang, *KK* (1961/4), 179–84.

32. Liu Pin-hsiung, *AP,* 7 (1964), 217.

33. Mo Chih and Li Shih-wen, *KK* (1964/3), 143–51, 160. Mo Chih, *KK* (1963/4), 217–20.

34. Mo Chih, *KK* (1963/2), 59–61; Mo Chih et al., *KK* (1964/3), 138–42.

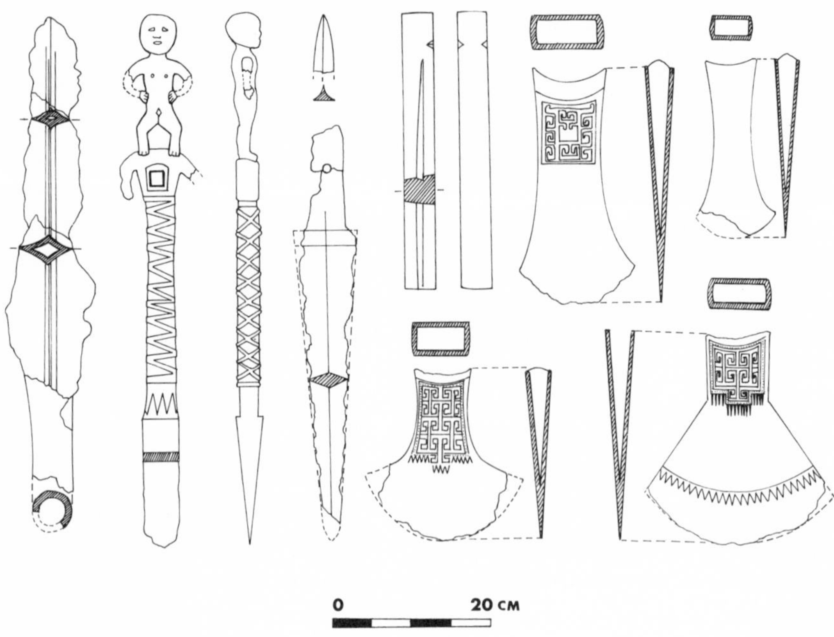

145. Bronze artifacts from the Warring States tombs in Ch'ing-yüan, Kwangtung. (From *KK,* 1964/3, p. 141.)

distinctive local features (Fig. 145). The hard, geometric-stamped urns at all these sites also indicate a local Neolithic background. According to Mo Chih and Li Shih-wen,[35] the geometric stamped pottery was a long stylistic tradition in the area of Canton. Those with *k'ui*-shaped designs probably date from late Western Chou and the Spring and Autumn period, and those with "Union Jack" designs were associated with iron implements and came from sites of the Warring States.

THE HANSHUI VALLEY AND THE YÜN-MENG BASIN

Originating in southern Shensi, the Hanshui River connects the northern province of Honan with the middle Yangtze River in eastern Hupei and throughout Chinese history has been an important avenue of communication between the north and the south. At its mouth it opens into the central Chinese lacustrine basin, now drained by the

35. *KK* (1964/3), 151.

middle Yangtze and the two largest lakes of China, Tung-t'ing in the west and Po-yang in the east; in ancient times most of this region was covered by the Great Lake Yün-meng. Prehistoric and early historic cultures around the shores of the Great Lake, in the modern provinces of eastern and central Hupei and northern Hunan and northwestern Kiangsi, formed well-defined entities. The Lungshanoid Ch'ü-chia-ling culture of the Neolithic period, discussed in Chapter 4, was one such.

Bronze vessels and weapons of Shang types were unearthed in at least three localities in Huang-p'i, near the confluence of the Hanshui and the Yangtze in central Hupei; the most important of these were five tombs and two storage pits opened in 1963 at P'an-lung-ch'eng.[36] The tombs were rectangular pit graves with *erh-ts'eng-t'ai* and *yao-k'eng,* and the bronze artifacts include ceremonial vessels (*ting, li, chia, chüeh, ku*) and weapons (spearheads, *ko* halberds, knives, axes, and arrowheads), decorated with *t'ao-t'ieh, k'ui,* and *hsüan* patterns. Many of these vessels, as well as a bronze *chüeh* tripod from the Yang-chia-wan site and three bronze *ko* halberds, are not only of the ordinary Shang type but are closer to varieties of the *Erh-li-kang* phase at Pai-chia-chuang, Cheng-chou, and at Hui Hsien. Associated with the bronzes at the P'an-lung-ch'eng site are potsherds of Ch'ü-chia-ling and Lung-shan types, and those at the other sites include sherds of Geometric Ware.

Farther south, on the eastern and southern shores of the Great Lake, pottery with Shang forms and decorative patterns has been reported from a prehistoric site at Tsao-shih, in Shih-men, northern Hunan,[37] and two Shang-type bronze vessels (*yü* and *ting*) were investigated in 1963 near Huang-ts'ai, in Ning-hsiang, Hunan, near the mouth of the River Hsiang on the southern shore of the Great Lake.[38] Both vessels were decorated with *t'ao-t'ieh* patterns of the A-style of An-yang and marked with names in the Ten-Stem System of the Shang style. In the *yü* were over a thousand stone and jade beads. These Hunan bronzes are indeed very similar to the Shang types of

36. Kuo Ping-lien, *KKTH* (1958/1), 56–58; (1958/9), 72–73. Kuo Teh-wei and Ch'en Hsien-yi, *KK* (1964/8), 420–21.

37. Chou Shih-jung, *KK* (1962/3), 144–46.

38. Kao Chih-hsi, *KK* (1963/12), 646–48; see also Ts'ai Chi-hsiang, *WW* (1960/3), 75.

the north, but certain decorative motifs and vessel shapes have local characteristics.

Distinctively Western Chou assemblages have also been found on the northern shores of the Great Lake, such as an assemblage of seventeen bronze vessels with inscriptions in a tomb near Wan-ch'eng in Chiang-ling, central Hupei,[39] and a village of timber structures excavated in 1958 at the site of Wang-chia-tsui, northeast of Ch'i-ch'un, in eastern Hupei.[40] The Wang-chia-tsui site is of particular interest and import. Remains of an ancient habitation were found in an area about 30,000 square meters in size, where relics of timber structures were found in clusters in two small ponds. In the western cluster 109 wooden posts (0.2 m in diameter) and remains of timber walls were brought to light, and three adjoining rooms (8 by 5 m) were restored, apparently three separate parts of a large, continuous structure. Remains of stairs were found. In the eastern cluster 171 posts were counted, but only two rooms were restorable. Other than pottery, which is Lungshan-like, and stone and clay artifacts, there were bronze arrowheads of the Shang and early Chou type, a bronze *chüeh* tripod, wooden containers, a lacquered cup (with bronze-vessel type decorative patterns) (Fig. 146), pieces of oracle bones and turtleshells, and remains of rice husks. The local character of this site is pronounced—witness the black pottery, paddy husks, and apparently a pile-type of house construction—but the bronze vessel forms, bronze and ceramic decorative patterns, and the oracle bones indicate very clearly northern Chinese influences.

It is apparent from the few but notable remains of the Shang and Western Chou period that the shores of the Great Lake during these times were inhabited by peoples with a culture based upon the native Neolithic cultures but with advanced Shang and Chou civilization elements. Probably the Ch'u civilization of the Eastern Chou period was a further development from such a foundation.

During the Chou period, particularly the Eastern Chou, the state of Ch'u was the most powerful country in South China, and probably also the most civilized. Furthermore, this state was not only a political but also a cultural and ethnic entity. In the poem Pi-kung, in the Lu Sung section of the *Book of Odes,* literature dating possibly from

39. *KK* (1963/4), 224–25.
40. Chang Yün-p'eng, *KK* (1962/1), 1–9.

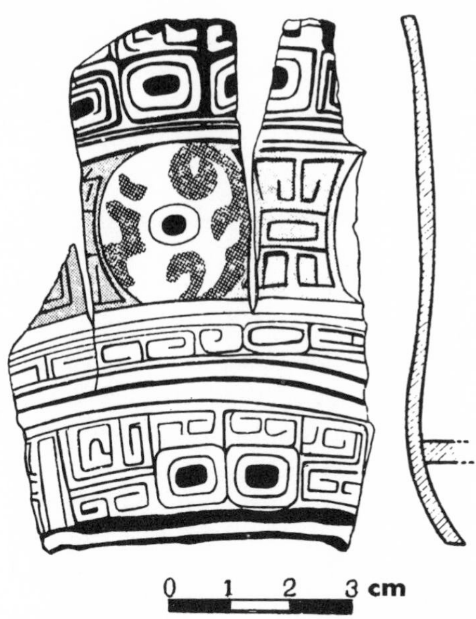

146. A fragment of a lacquered cup from the Western Chou site in Ch'i-ch'un, Hupei. (From *KK,* 1962/1, p. 7.)

an early period of the Chou Dynasty, the peoples to the south are referred to as Ching and Shu. The inhabitants of the lower Hanshui Valley in northern Hupei are known as Shu; Ching, originally the name of a plant which was also known as Ch'u, refers to the people living around Ching Mountain, thought to be in the present Nan-chang Hsien, near Hsiang-yang, Hupei Province. The names of Ch'u and Ching, therefore, were used interchangeably during the Chou period to designate the people in the lower Hanshui and the middle Yangtze valleys. The name of Ching seems to have appeared earlier than Ch'u, although Ch'u has since become widely used.[41]

The legendary beginnings of the Ch'u rulers were recorded in various literary records, but only around the time of Wen Wang of Western Chou did the genealogical record become historically established. Ssu-ma Ch'ien's *Shih Chi* says that Ch'eng Wang of Western Chou made Hsiung Yi, the contemporary ruler of Ch'u, an earl to govern the people of Ch'u, and made Tan-yang his capital. The exact geo-

41. Oyanagi Shigeta, *Tōhōgakuhō, 1* (1931), 196–228, Kyoto.

graphical location of Tan-yang is disputed. Four hypotheses have been advanced to identify it as one of the following present-day locations: Tang-t'u, in central-eastern Anhwei on the Yangtze; Chih-chiang or Tzu-kui in western Hupei in the Yangtze Valley; the area between Shang Hsien in southeastern Shensi and Hsi-ch'uan in southwestern Honan, in the upper middle Hanshui Valley.[42] Thus the majority of scholars believe that Tan-yang was somewhere in the Hanshui and middle Yangtze valleys, but the Tang-t'u theory, advanced by the authoritative *Han Shu Ti Li Chih,* also deserves serious consideration. No matter where the original center of the political Ch'u may have been, by the beginning of the Eastern Chou period, under the reign of Earl Hsiung T'ung, the Ch'u state had already become a major power in Central China. Hsiung T'ung went so far as to defy the Royal Chou authority and to call himself a king. From then on, throughout the Eastern Chou period, Ch'u was a major power to be reckoned with, not only in Central China but in North China as well. At the peak of their power, the territory of the Ch'u extended from eastern Shensi east to the lower Yangtze Valley, as far north as the heart of Honan, and as far south as the Tung-t'ing Lake area in southern Hupei and northern Hunan. This powerful state was overthrown by the Ch'in Dynasty in 223 B.C., but the people and the culture maintained their distinct identity into the Han Dynasty.

Cultural remains of the Ch'u dated to the Eastern Chou period have been found in a very wide area of the central part of South China, covering the Huaiho Valley in southeastern Honan and northern Anhwei and the Great Lake area of Hupei and Hunan (Fig. 147). Ch'u remains over such a wide area bear out the literary tradition that the state of Ch'u expanded territorially around the beginning of the Eastern Chou, which is also suggested by the relative homogeneity of the cultural style represented by the relics from this region.

Under the state of Ch'u, town and city settlements were built that compare in urbanization with the northern Chinese cities described earlier, but habitation sites are few, and none has been thoroughly excavated. A Ch'u site of great promise is the walled ruins of Chi-nan-

42. Hsü Hsün-sheng, *Chung-kuo Ku-shih ti Ch'uan-shuo Shih-tai,* enlarged ed., Peking, Science Press, 1960, pp. 167–70. Ch'en P'an, *Proceedings of the International Conference of Historians of Asia, Hong Kong, 3* (1964), Prepublication reprint.

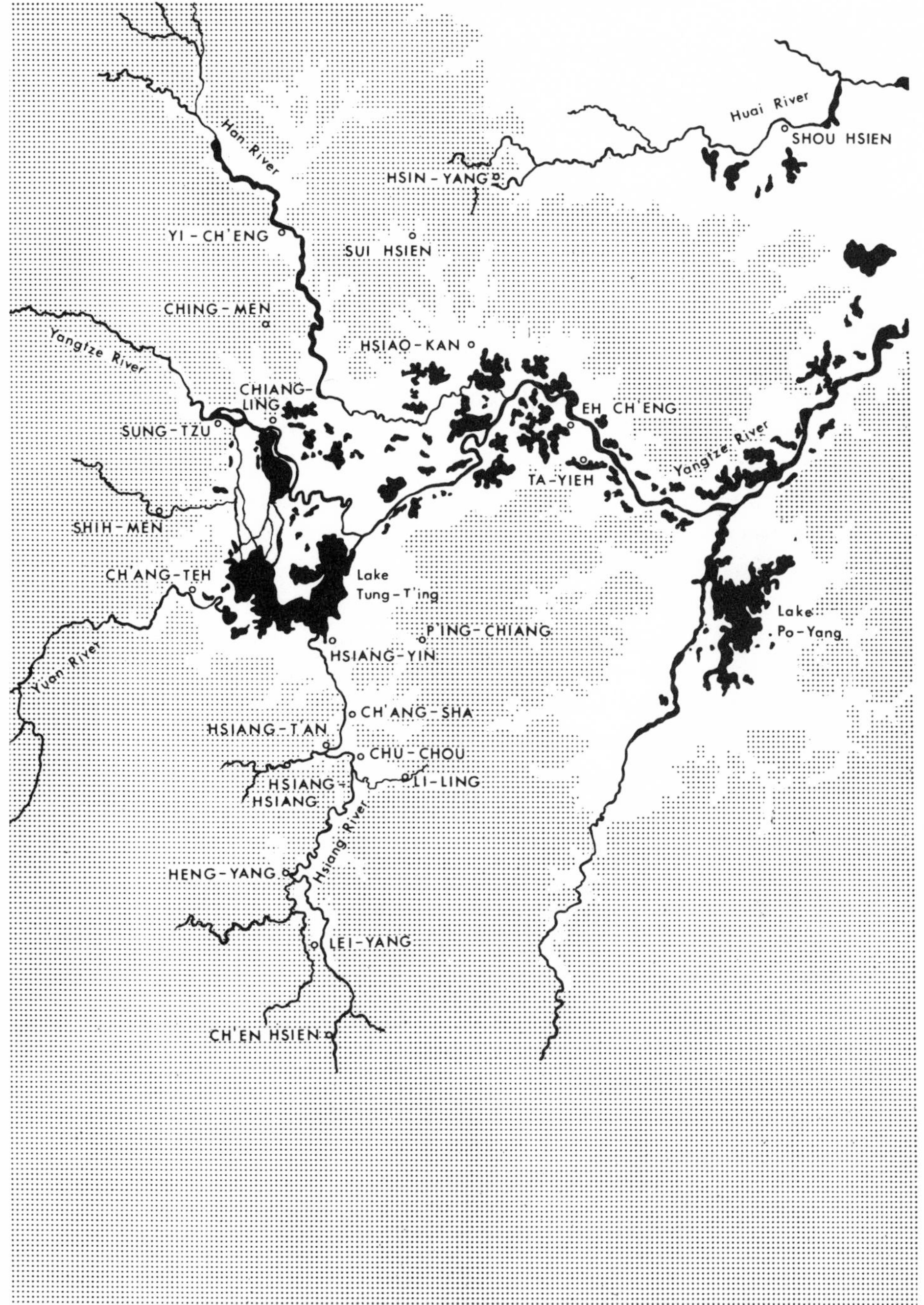

147. Principal cities in which Ch'u sites have been found. Dotted areas are over 100 m in elevation. Solid areas are bodies of water, probably remnants of the ancient Lake Yün-meng in the middle Yangtze area.

ch'eng, near the modern city of Chiang-ling on the Yangtze in central Hupei, traditionally held to be the site of Ying, Ch'u capital from 689 until 278 B.C. Clusters of burial mounds are found around the site, some of which have been excavated in recent years, but the walled town itself has yet to be investigated.[43] So far, only three walled sites have been explored by archaeologists: Yi-ch'eng in Hupei in the Han-shui Valley, and Shih-men and Hsiang-yin in northern Hunan. The Yi-ch'eng site, 2 by 1.5 kilometers, is the largest; remains of *li* tripods, *tou,* and *yi-pi* coins were collected inside.[44] All that is known of the ruins at Shih-men is that the walled enclosure was rectangular and only 300 by 600 meters in size.[45] The Hsiang-yin site, 490 by 400 meters, was enclosed by *hang-t'u* walls, 14 meters wide and 3 high, traditionally believed to be the site of Lo, a small vassal state of the Ch'u. Cultural remains in association with the town site probably belonged to an early phase within the Eastern Chou period.[46] A dwelling site of a comparable period was found at T'ai-tzu-ch'ung near Ch'ang-sha, Hunan Province, where storage pits, pottery, and stone knives were collected.[47] Near the town of Wung-chiang in P'ing-chiang, northern Hunan, storage pits, pottery, and iron axes, and bronze vessels, weapons, and implements and evidence of a bronze foundry, have been found, indicating a local workshop.[48] In Hupei, village remains with characteristic *li* tripod sherds have been reported in Sui Hsien.[49] Needless to say, these discoveries are insufficient evidence of the kind of urbanism and civic and public structures that we can surely assume existed in the state of Ch'u. Painted scenes on lacquerware may give a notion about what some of their houses looked like (Fig. 148).

The Ch'u sites so far discovered consist mainly of tombs. Within the province of Hunan alone, large numbers of Ch'u graves have been located in Ch'ang-sha, Hsiang-t'an, Hsiang-hsiang, Chu-chou, Li-ling, Heng-yang, Lei-yang, and Ch'en Hsien of the Hsiang River valley and Ch'ang-teh at the mouth of the River Yüan.[50] Of these sites Ch'ang-sha is the most prolific, having up to 1960 yielded twelve hun-

43. *WW* (1966/5), 33–55.
44. Wang Shan-ts'ai, *KK* (1965/8), 377–82.
45. Chou Shih-jung, *KK* (1964/2), 104–05.
46. Chou Shih-jung, *KKTH* (1958/2), 10–14.
47. *WW* (1960/3), 66.
48. Chou Shih-jung, *WWTKTL* (1958/1), 39–41.
49. Mao Tsai-shan and Li Yüan-k'ui, *KK* (1959/11), 635–36.
50. Kao Chih-hsi, *WW* (1960/3), 33.

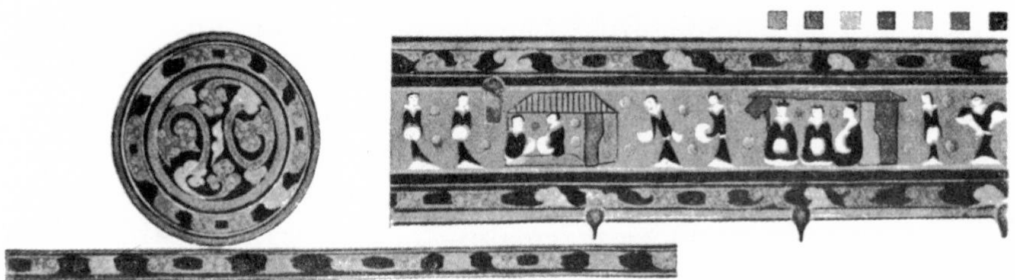

148. Decorative scenes on Ch'u lacquerwares, spread out, showing aspects of Ch'u life, Ch'ang-sha. (From *Ch'ang-sha ch'u-t'u ku-tai ch'i-ch'i t'u-an hsüan chi,* Peking, Historical Museum, 1954.)

dred individual graves dated to the Eastern Chou period.[51] Ch'ang-teh[52] and Heng-yang follow in number of graves produced, with approximately a hundred each. In Hupei, the area where most of the capital sites of the Ch'u were located, the archaeology of this early civilization is only beginning, but important Ch'u tombs have already

51. Hsia Nai et al., *Ch'ang-sha fa-chüeh pao-kao,* Peking, Science Press, 1957. Wen Tao-yi, *KKHP* (1959/1), 41–58. Chang Chung-yi, *KKTH* (1958/9), 57–61. Chang Hsin-ju, *KKTH* (1958/12), 28–34. Kao Chih-hsi and Liu Lien-yin, *KK* (1959/12), 649–52. Chou Shih-jung and Wen Tao-yi, *WW* (1960/1), 63–64. Lo Chang, *WW* (1960/3), 38–49; (1960/3), 51–56. Chou Shih-jung, *WW* (1960/3), 64–66. Jao Tsung-yi, *Ch'ang-sha ch'u-t'u Chan-kuo tseng-shu hsin-shih,* Hong Kong, privately printed, 1958. Chiang Hsüan-yi, *Ch'ang-sha Ch'u min-tsu chi ch'i yi-shu,* Shanghai, Kunstarchäologie Society, 1949. Shang Ch'eng-tso, *Ch'ang-sha ku-wu wen-chien-chi,* Chengtu, Chinling University, 1939. Shih Shu-ch'ing, *Ch'ang sha Yang-t'ien-hu ch'u-t'u Ch'u chien yen-chiu,* Shanghai, Ch'ün-lien Press, 1955.

52. Wen Tao-yi, *KK* (1959/12), 658. Yang Hua, *KK* (1959/4), 207–08; (1963/9), 461–73, 479.

been reported from Sung-tzu,[53] Chiang-ling,[54] and the Eh-ch'eng and Ta-yieh area of eastern Hupei.[55] Other than these two provinces, highly important Ch'u remains are known in Hsin-yang[56] in Honan, and Shou Hsien[57] in Anhwei, both in the Huaiho Valley. These centers of Ch'u finds outline the geographical extent of the Ch'u territory represented by archaeological remains—the four shores of the Great Lake Yün-meng, valleys of the three major rivers that flow through or into the area (the Yangtze, Hsiang, and Hanshui), and the upper Huaiho Valley that is separated from the Yün-meng basin by the Ta-pieh Mountains. The cultural influence of the Ch'u civilization surely went beyond its territories, and evidence of such influence is seen clearly in northern Kiangsu in the east[58] and Szechwan and Yunnan in the west.

These finds show that the Ch'u built elaborate graves for their dead. All the tombs in the area were earthen pit graves, rectangular, with or without entrance ramps. Some pits were narrower than others and may have been earlier in date. The orientation of the tombs was somewhat irregular, but heads to north or east were relatively more common.

The bottom of the pit was often plastered with a layer of limey white clay, and around the pit walls a platform was sometimes built, corresponding to the *erh-ts'eng-t'ai* of northern Chinese tombs. Niches or cavities in the wall were excavated for the storage of grave goods. At the center of the tomb, a wooden chamber was built, inside which a wooden coffin was placed. The coffin was often wrapped with cloths, probably a measure against moisture. Grave goods were placed inside the coffin or in the pit, and the whole pit was then filled with earth, sometimes compacted by stamping. Both the Shou Hsien and the

53. Ch'eng Hsin-jen and Wang Fu-kuo, *KK* (1966/3), 122–32.

54. Kuo Teh-wei, *WW* (1962/2), 56. Kuo Teh-wei and Liu Pen-hui, *WW* (1964/9), 27–32. Hupei Bureau of Culture, *WW* (1966/5), 53–55.

55. Hsiung Ya-yün, *KKTH* (1958/8), 50–51. Kuo Chia, *KK* (1959/11), 622.

56. P'ei Ming-hsiang et al., *WWTKTL* (1957/9), 21–22. Kuo Mo-jo, *WWTKTL* (1958/1), 5. Ku T'ieh-fu, *WWTKTL* (1958/1), 6–8. Wang Shih-hsiang, *WWTKTL* (1958/1), 15–23. Ho Kuan-pao and Huang Shih-pin, *KKTH* (1958/11), 79–80. *Honan Hsin-yang Ch'u mu ch'u-t'u wen-wu t'u-lu,* Honan, Jenmin Press, 1959.

57. Li Ching-tan, *TYKKPK, 1* (1936). Liu Chieh, *Ch'u Ch'i T'u Shih,* Peiping, National Library of Peiping, 1935. O. Karlbeck, *BMFEA, 27* (1955). Yin Ti-fei, *WW* (1959/4), 12. Pai Hsia, *KK* (1959/7), 371–72.

58. Yin Huan-chang and Chang Cheng-hsiang, *KK* (1960/3), 29.

Hsin-yang tombs were built in a similar manner, but the latter (two of which have so far been discovered) had a far more complicated wooden chamber structure and were divided into several sections.

Such elaborate burials indicate a highly stratified society and an advanced technology and economy, but direct evidence of farming techniques is limited to the occasional discovery of farming implements, including hoes and spades of iron.[59] There is no evidence of the use of the plow, which had begun both in contemporary North China and in the territory of Yüeh to the east. According to historical records, however, it is fairly certain that in the state of Ch'u as well as Yüeh, rice was cultivated and irrigated by both artificial and natural means. To the northerners of the Eastern Chou period as well as to those of subsequent historical periods, the rich natural resources in and south of the Yangtze Valley were objects of constant envy. Ssu-ma Ch'ien says in Ho-chih Lieh-chuan, *Shih Chi,* that the "territory of the Ch'u and the Yüeh is vast but the population sparse. Rice is the staple food, and fish the main dish. The people *keng* with fire, and *ju* with water." There are various interpretations of the last sentence,[60] but, whatever the interpretation, the use of water for the cultivation of rice can be inferred. *Shih Chi* also mentions the collection of mollusks for food, a practice substantiated by the shell-tempered pottery at one of the Sui Hsien sites in Hupei. In a tomb in Chiang-ling were found remains of chestnuts, fresh ginger, and sweet fennel; cherry, apple, and plum pits; melon seeds; and bones of fish, chickens, and animals.

In addition to agricultural implements, iron was employed to make axes, knives, adzes, weapons (swords, *chi* halberds, and arrowheads), and even ornaments (rings and belt hooks).[61] Lead was another metal melted by the Ch'u smiths, who fashioned it into mortuary money and covers for wooden handles. But as far as the archaeological data show, bronze was still the basic raw material for artifacts. In the tombs, bronze vessels (*ting* tripods, *tui* tripods, *hu,* and dippers), weapsons (swords, *ko* halberds, and spears), horse and chariot fittings, belt hooks, mirrors, musical instruments (such as *pien* bells, portable bells, and

59. Wen Tao-yi, *KKHP* (1959/1), 43.

60. Nishijima Sadao, "The System of Rice Cultivation in Ancient China," in *Oriental Studies Presented to Sei (Kiyoshi) Wada,* Tokyo, Dainippon Yūbenkai Kōdansha, 1951, pp. 469–87. Amano Motonosuke, *Shigaku-Zasshi, 61* (1952), 58–61. Yoneda, *Shirin, 38* (1955), 1–18.

61. Huang Chan-yüeh, *KKHP* (1957/3), 97–98.

kettledrums), and even seals have been found in great numbers. A chemical analysis of some specimens of bronze[62] shows that the ratio of copper, tin, and various impurities was completely controlled. A large *ting* tripod unearthed from the Shou Hsien tomb is said to weigh nearly 400 kilograms,[63] indicating an advanced level of bronze metallurgy. The large number of bronze artifacts and their distinctive local features (such as the numerous stylistic motifs in the decoration and the inscriptions) rule out the possibility that these bronze artifacts were imports from North China, and the bronze foundry site in P'ing-chiang Hsien, Hunan, mentioned above, bears this out.

In addition to metallurgy of both bronze and iron, the Ch'u civilization was apparently highly developed in handicrafts, including ceramics, wood carving, carpentry, bamboo crafts, leatherwork, lacquerwork, silk and hemp weaving, and stone and jade crafts. The pottery is predominantly grayish or brownish in color, either of fine texture or tempered with sand, depending upon the kind of vessel and its purpose. Glaze was applied in some cases. The basic technique of manufacture was by wheel, although handmade and molded pieces occur not infrequently. Most of the pots are plain, but there is also decorated pottery, which is corded, stringed, incised, or painted in red, yellow, blue, white, or black, in spirals and geometric designs. *Ting* and *li* tripods, *hu, tou,* bowls, cups, stoves, urns, and so forth are all represented, and the occurrence of particular shapes seems to have some chronological significance (Fig. 149). Bamboo mats, bows, suitcases, wooden combs, spears, and leather remains are among the extraordinary discoveries made in recent years. Bamboo was also cut into elongated slips for writing; dozens of these inscribed slips have been found in tombs in Ch'ang-sha, Chiang-ling, and Hsin-yang (Fig. 68), along with remains of a writing brush and its container. Wood carving is another noted craft of the Ch'u, and wooden human and animal figurines, drums, animal tomb-guardians with antler horns (Fig. 150), and carved boards have been found. Remains of wooden bases for the musical instrument, *se,* have been collected from the tombs at Hsin-yang and Chiang-ling (Fig. 151). These relics vividly testify to the fact that industrial specialization had developed to a very considerable extent in this part of China during the Eastern Chou

62. Wen Tao-yi, *KKHP* (1959/1), 48.
63. Liu Chieh, *Ch'u Ch'i T'u Shih,* p. 3.

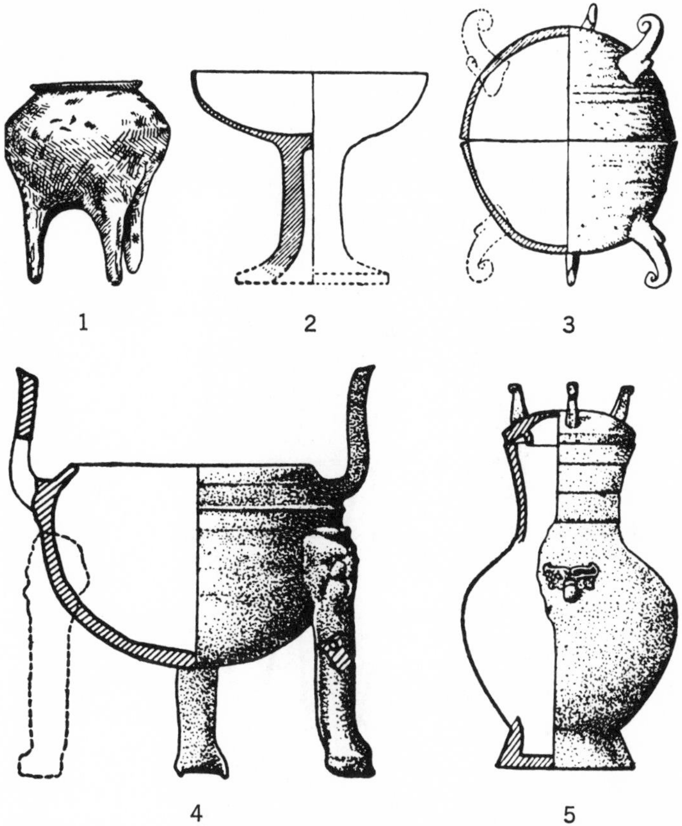

149. Principal types of Ch'u pottery of chronological significance, found in the tombs in Ch'ang-sha: 1, *li;* 2, *tou;* 3, *tui;* 4, *ting;* 5, *hu.* (From *Ch'ang-sha Fa-chüeh Pao-kao,* various figures.)

period, which is confirmed by the many names of handicraft products written on the bamboo tablets—probably lists of grave goods, many of which have since perished.

Supported by agriculture and industry of such high levels of complexity, the political and social organizations of the Chou were presumably also complex. No doubt Ch'u deserves the designation of "state," and the titles of king and earl must have been accompanied by corresponding political institutions. Archaeological evidence is lacking, but the remains of bronze coins (*yi-pi-ch'ien,* or "ant-nose" coins) and bronze scales and weights show a good deal of social and economic

150. Wooden sculpture of a monster, excavated from a Ch'u tomb in Hsin-yang, Honan. (From *WW*, 1957/9, frontispiece.)

sophistication. Moreover, the Ch'u was certainly a literary civilization, with writing still to be seen on bamboo tablets, weapons (Fig. 152), bronze vessels, and silk clothing (Fig. 153). As in North China, the writing is composed of characters, many of which are identical with those used elsewhere in China. But unique characters, a distinctive calligraphy, and another distinctive system of character composition, mostly inscribed on weapons, indicate local characteristics. Kuo Mo-jo believes that during the Eastern Chou period, efforts were made

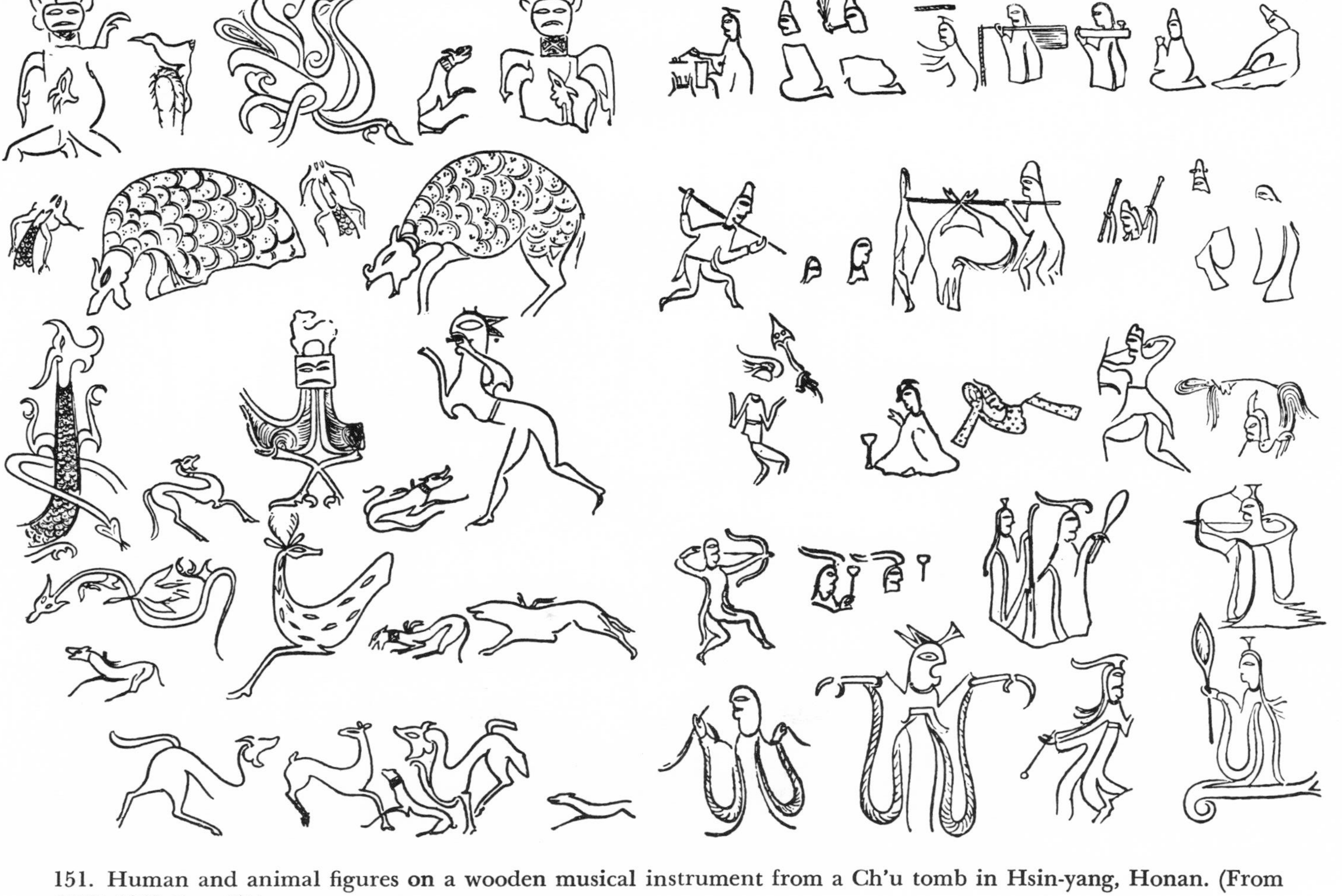

151. Human and animal figures on a wooden musical instrument from a Ch'u tomb in Hsin-yang, Honan. (From *WW*, 1958/1, p. 27.)

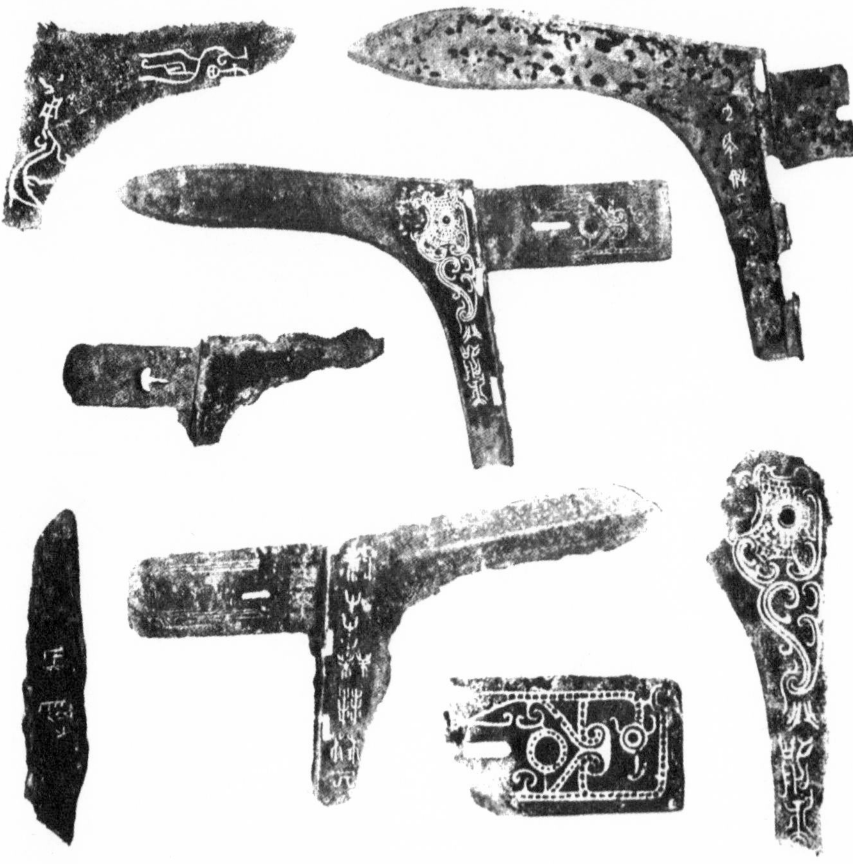

152. Decorated *ko* halberds excavated from Ch'u tombs in Ch'ang-sha. (From *KKHP,* 1959/1, Pl. XI, following p. 60.)

to unify writing in the whole of China under the sovereignty of the Royal Chou, although various regional writing systems were still being used for certain specific purposes.[64]

Compared with contemporary North China, the Ch'u are also distinctive in being an especially religious-minded people. The Eastern Chou and Han saying, that the "Ch'u people are particularly superstitious," testifies to this fact. The elaborate burial customs indicate a highly complex system of ancestor worship. In *Ch'u Tz'u,* a piece of

64. *WWTKTL* (1958/1), 5.

153. Silk with paintings and inscriptions from a Ch'u tomb in Ch'ang-sha. (From *The Ch'u Silk in the Sackler Collections*, New York, International Arts Press. Reprinted by permission of the Sackler Foundation.)

genuine Ch'u literature handed down through subsequent historical periods, there is a long poem entitled T'ien Wen, in which Ch'ü Yüan, the alleged author and an officer of the King's Court, asks a series of questions concerning the creation of the cosmos, of man, the various deities, and the legendary history of the Ch'u kings. It has been suggested that this poem was composed in the ancestral temple of the Ch'u ruler, on the internal walls of which pictures depicting the various myths and legends were painted, and that Ch'ü Yüan asked questions on various topics as he looked at these pictures. Ancestral temples of this nature have yet to be found. But among the Ch'u people there must have been beliefs concerning various spirits and deities, as indicated by the text of a silk writing,[65] by the remains of wooden animal tomb-guardians, wooden human figurines, and wooden human statues with protruding tongues and antler horns. Snakes, phoenix, and dragons were favorite decorative motifs, and musical instruments (wooden and bronze drums, bells, various kinds of wooden and bamboo wind and string instruments, and pottery whistles) must have had some ceremonial use.

These descriptions of the Ch'u civilization suffice to show that it was basically derived from the Chou civilization of North China, but that distinctive characteristics are at the same time plentiful. Legends of the Ch'u, as recorded by North Chinese historians, say that the founders of the Ch'u were descended from Tuan Hsü, a grandson of the Yellow Emperor. One may be tempted to regard the Ch'u rulers as North Chinese and the ruled people as indigenous natives. This, however, was not necessarily so. Hsiung Ch'ü, an Earl of Ch'u and a near descendant of the First Earl, was quoted in *Shih Chi* as saying: "We are barbarians." The Ch'u system of government closely followed that of the Chou Dynasty, but according to the accounts in *Tso Chuan* (first year of Wen Kung and thirteenth year of Chao Kung), the succession to the monarch of the earldom or, later, the kingdom, seems to have favored a junior son rather than the primary son as in the Chou Dynasty. The Ch'u language was somewhat different from the contemporary northern Chinese, as is shown by a few lexical elements recorded in North Chinese literature. In the archaeological remains,

65. An Chih-min and Ch'en Kung-jou, *WW* (1963/9), 48–60. Shang Ch'eng-tso, *WW* (1964/9), 8–20. Jao Tsung-yi, *Ch'ang-sha ch'u-t'u Chan-kuo tseng-shu hsin-shih,* Hong Kong, 1958.

154. Wooden sculptures of tigers and birds, probably used as drum supports in the manner shown in the dancing scene at bottom, found in Ch'u tombs. (A and B, Chiang-ling, from *WW,* 1964/9. C, Hsin-yang, after *KKTH,* 1958/11, and *WW,* 1964/9. D, Enlarged from a segment of a scene in Ma Ch'eng-yüan, *WW,* 1961/10.)

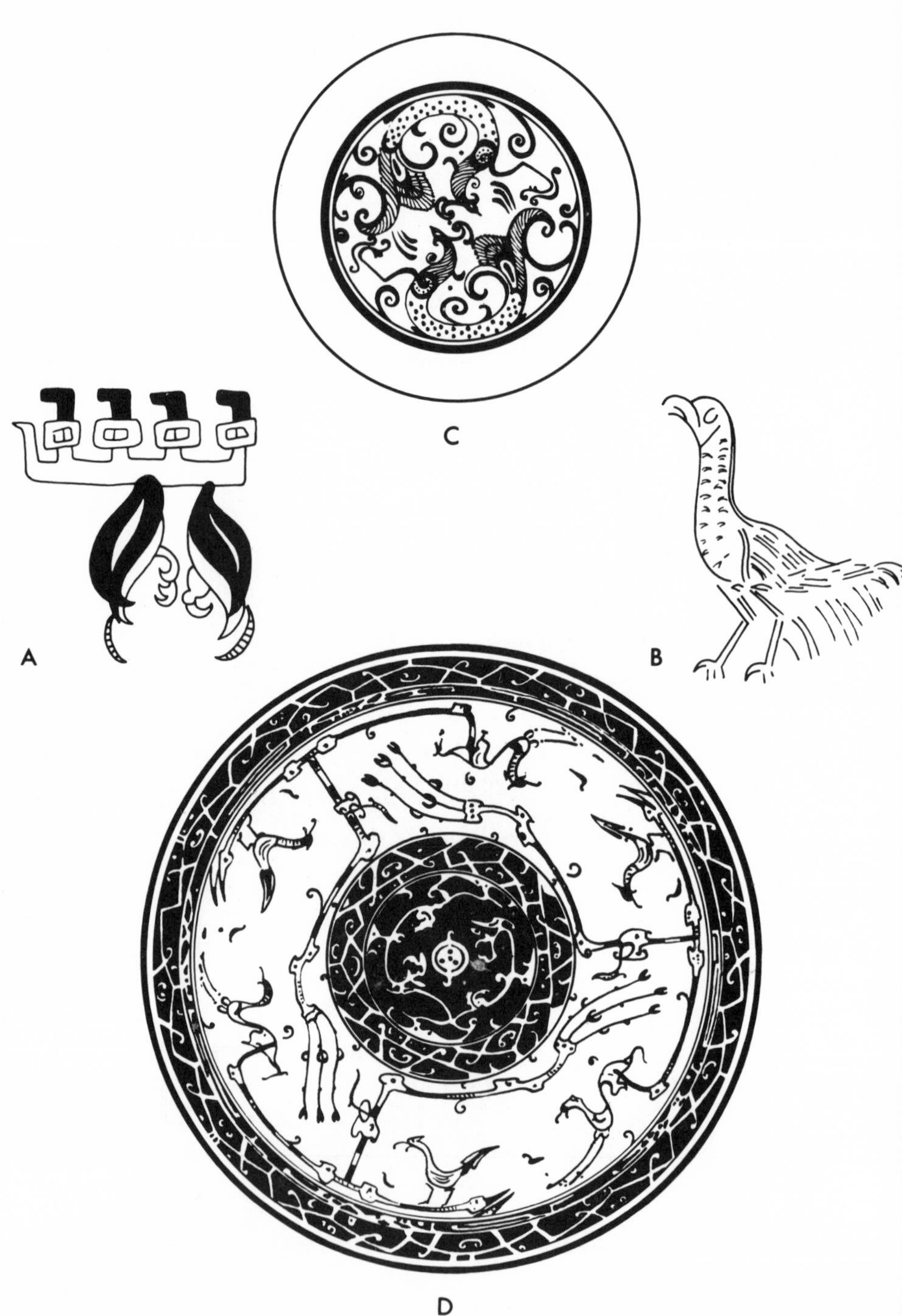

155. Various bird forms in Ch'u art. (A, Ch'ang-sha, silk manuscript, after Shang Ch'eng-tso, *WW,* 1964/9. B, Interior decoration of a winged cup, Singer Collection, after Max Loehr, *Relics of Ancient China,* 1965. C, D, Ch'ang-sha, painted lacquered dishes, after *Ch'ang-sha ch'u-t'u ku-tai ch'i-ch'i t'u-an hsüan chi,* 1954.)

156. Wooden figurines found in Ch'ang-sha. (A, From *Ch'ang-sha Fa-chüeh Pao-kao,* 1957. B–E, From Chiang Hsüan-yi, *Ch'ang-sha Ch'u min-tsu chi ch'i yi-shu,* 1950.)

although the culture is shown to be basically the same as the Eastern Chou of North China, many distinctive local features are discernible, such as the characteristic writing styles, the special deities and ceremonies, the highly developed wood carving and bamboo crafts, the wooden drum frame consisting of a pair of birds and a pair of tigers (Fig. 154), the bird motif in a distinctive style of decorative art (Fig. 155), the great abundance of lacquerware, silk fabrics, mirrors, and swords, the tattooing of faces (Fig. 156), and the different systems of currency (*ying yüan* and *yi-pi-ch'ien*). Many of these, as well as rice cultivation, can be attributed to the riverine and lacustrine environment, but others must indicate a distinctive Ch'u cultural style.

The widely distributed Ch'u remains show remarkable homogeneity in style, although regional phases are discernible within this vast territory.[66] Ch'u remains began to appear at the beginning of the Ch'un-ch'iu period and, as far as we know from the available material, underwent a similar sequence of change and development throughout

66. Shang Ch'eng-tso, *Ch'ang-sha ku-wu wen-chien-chi,* Ch'en Meng-chia's "Preface," p. 10.

the area. In the region of Ch'ang-sha, three well-defined stages can be distinguished both stratigraphically and typologically.[67]

1. *Early:* Ch'un-ch'iu and the beginning of Chan-kuo. Approximately one hundred tombs (among the more than twelve hundred in the area) belong to this stage, and are characterized by smaller and narrower tombs than the later ones; wall niches mostly at the head end; a scarcity of ramps; in ceramics, three combinations: *li*-bowl-*hu-tou*-jug, *lei*-bowl-*tou,* or *hu*-bowl-*tou*-urn; *li* tripods of pottery; certain types of bronze weapons and vessels; some iron implements.

2. *Middle:* early Chan-kuo period. Over six hundred graves belong to this stage, characterized by a growing number of wider grave pits, side niches, and ramps; pottery *ting* tripods taking the place of *li* tripods; the appearance of pottery *tui* tripods; bronze vessels and weapons of later types; more iron implements.

3. *Late:* late Chan-kuo and the beginning of Western Han. Characterized by predominance of rectangular grave pits of great width; a growing number of side niches; the appearance of cave chambers and multiple burials; the use of clay to seal off the wooden chamber; complex wooden chamber structures; much painted pottery; more complex bronze artifacts; more iron implements and even iron weapons; the occurrence of stone *pi* rings; decorative inscriptions on bronze weapons.

A similar sequence can also be found in the burials of the Ch'ang-teh area.[68] Ch'u graves in Hupei and in the Huaiho Valley are not yet susceptible to such chronological treatment. However, it is noteworthy that the Hsin-yang tombs, while probably dated to an early period comparable to Ch'ang-sha's Early Stage,[69] contain many features that did not appear in Ch'ang-sha until later. This may very well indicate that the cultural flow from North China to the Ch'u region was continuous throughout the Eastern Chou period and reached such regions as Hsin-yang earlier than the more distant Hunan area south of the Great Lake.

67. Li Cheng-kuang and P'eng Ch'ing-yieh, *KKHP* (1957/4), 47–48. Wen Tao-yi, *KKHP* (1959/1), 55–56. Chang Chung-yi, *KKTH* (1958/9), 60–61. Chang Hsin-ju, *KKTH* (1958/12), 34. Kao Chih-hsi, *WW* (1960/3), 33–34; Hsia et al., *Ch'ang-sha fa-chüeh pao-kao,* p. 37.

68. Wen Tao-yi, *KK* (1959/12), 662.

69. Kuo Mo-jo, *WWTKTL* (1958/1), 5.

EARLY CIVILIZATIONS IN SZECHWAN

In the upper Yangtze Valley in the Red basin (Fig. 157), less is known about the beginning of civilization than in eastern and central South China, but the development must have been quite different. The native cultural substratum in Szechwan differs from that of the southeast in that neither the Lungshanoid nor the Geometric existed as a well-defined cultural horizon. Although agriculture and the domestication of animals were apparently introduced here after stone polishing and ceramics, these innovations were made in an already established Mesolithic and sub-Neolithic population. The Neolithic culture, which in contrast to the Lungshanoid to the east must have retained a considerable number of native elements, continued in Szechwan during the Bronze Age of North and Central China but received increasing influence from these civilizations, as the archaeological remains of this period show.[70]

The late Shang and early Western Chou civilizations appear to have had some contact with the Szechwan Neolithic, as indicated by the remains of *li* tripods of gray and cord-marked ware, and sherds of *tou* of the Bronze Age style[71] found in the Yangtze Valley in the extreme eastern end of Szechwan Province, where it adjoins Hupei. The contacts probably resulted in no more than the introduction of these and perhaps a few other stylistic elements, whereas the native cultural context remains Neolithic, and even the few indications of influence are limited geographically. "The cord-marked *li* tripods extended westward no further than Wan Hsien, and the gray *li* tripods did not even reach Feng-chieh."[72] Some authors maintain that the Yin culture reached as far as the Min River valley, as shown by such sites as Shui-kuan-yin in Hsin-fan Hsien.[73] This view is perhaps given support by

70. Recent carbon-14 dates from northeastern Thailand reported by Wilhelm G. Solheim (MS, 1967) suggest that bronze artifacts appeared here during the third millennium B.C. If these dates are confirmed in the future by a larger series of carbon-14 samples, they would suggest an additional inspiration or even direct source of the bronze metallurgy in the Chinese southwest.

71. Yang Yu-jun, *KK* (1959/8), 399–400.

72. Ibid., p. 401.

73. Ibid. Cheng Te-k'un, *Shang China* (*Archaeology in China, 2*), Cambridge, Heffer, 1961, p. 16.

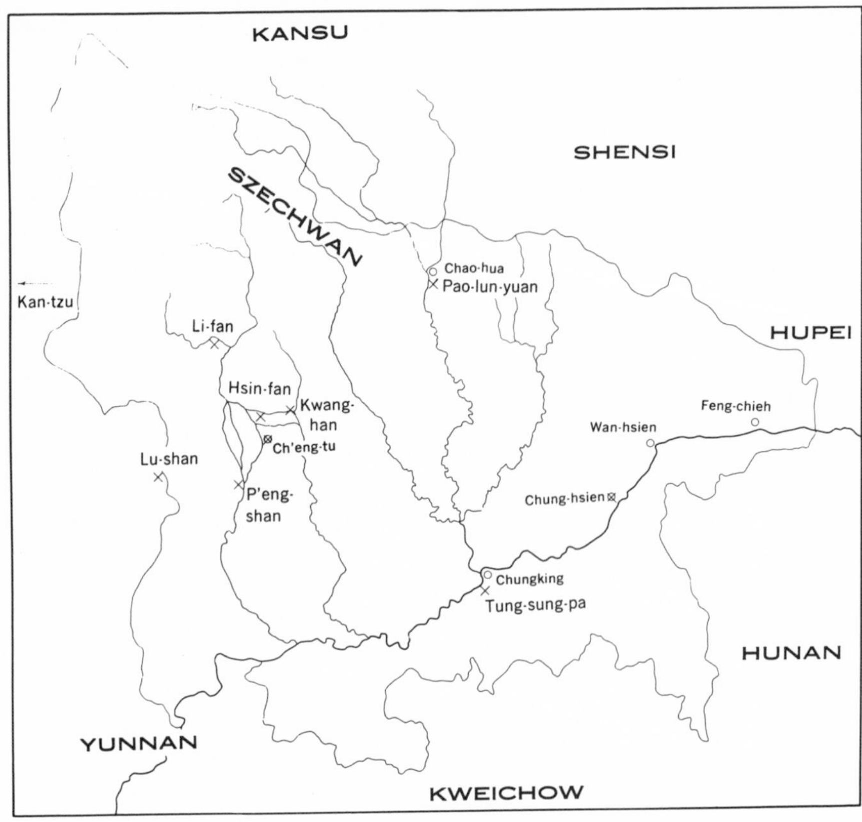

157. Early historical sites in Szechwan.

the bronze *ko* halberds and ceremonial vessels with *t'ao-t'seh* decorative patterns discovered at Chu-wa-chieh in P'eng Hsien.[74] The nature of the Shang influence in this area remains, however, to be clarified by additional excavated evidence.

The western part of Szechwan, nevertheless, was definitely reached by the influence of Western Chou civilization. Archaeological remains that can probably be dated to late Western Chou or early Eastern Chou have been discovered thus far in four counties: Han-chow (Kwang-han), Hsin-fan, Ch'eng-tu, and Mien-yang, in the P'ei, T'o, and Min River valleys. The T'ai-p'ing-ch'ang site in Kwang-han was

74. *WW* (1961/11), 30.

discovered in 1931 and investigated in 1933 by David C. Graham of the University Museum of West China Union University.[75] At this site, a habitation area was located, and a ceremonial pit was uncovered which contained over twenty stone disks of various sizes and a number of jade and stone ceremonial objects (circular *yüan,* square *tsung* tubes, *wuan-kui,* etc.). Some stone implements and a large number of potsherds were brought to light from the habitation layer. The pottery was red or grayish, with corded or plain surface, and in such forms as high-stem *tou,* urns, and tripods. No metal artifacts have been found, but a red iron nugget, a fragment of iron ore, and a small lump of copper ore were collected from the cultural debris. Cheng Te-k'un thinks that the ceremonial pit and the cultural debris were of different ages, the former probably dating from the Eastern Chou and representing the remains of a mountain-worship ceremony (possibly the worship of Min Mountain, as recorded in *Shan Hai Ching*) belonging to the so-called "eneolithic," dating from 1200 to 700 B.C.[76] Cheng's chronology is open to doubt. The stratigraphical relationship of the ceremonial pit and the habitation layers is not altogether clear, but they could very possibly be contemporary since jade and stone rings and plates similar to those found in the ceremonial pit have been unearthed in the cultural layer, and perhaps they should not be dismissed as "intrusive," as Cheng has called them. Recent findings of cultural remains probably dating from a comparable stage seem to confirm this, since stone and jade ceremonial objects and pottery, that resemble the objects found at T'ai-p'ing-ch'ang from both the pit and the cultural layer, have been shown to come from the same cultural stratum.

North of the city of Ch'eng-tu in the Min River valley is a low hill, known as Yang-tzu-shan. An earthen ceremonial platform was excavated on top of the hill in 1956. Since Warring States tombs were built into it, the platform must have been constructed some time earlier than the Chan-kuo period.[77] The platform is square and oriented northwest–southeast. It is constructed in three levels, measuring 31.6, 67.6, and 103.6 meters across, respectively, and has a total height exceeding 10 meters (Fig. 158). Within the platform, stone disks and pot-

75. David C. Graham, *Jour. West Border Research Soc. 6* (Cheng-tu, 1933/34), 114–31.

76. *Hsieh-ta Jour. Chinese Studies, 1* (Foochow, 1949), 67–81.

77. Yang Yu-jun, *KKHP* (1957/4), 17–31.

158. A ceremonial platform of possibly Western Chou period found at Yang-tzu-shan, Ch'eng-tu, Szechwan. (From *KKHP,* 1957/4, p. 20.)

tery remains similar to those of T'ài-p'ing-ch'ang were found. Similar pottery sherds have also been unearthed at the Pien-tui-shan site in Mien-yang Hsien, on the upper P'ei River.[78] High-stemmed *tou* vessels similar to those found in Kwang-han have been unearthed from the cultural strata at the site of Shui-kuan-yin in Hsin-fan Hsien, mentioned previously. At this site both habitation remains and burials have been found, but more than a single cultural stage is probably represented. Bronze arrowheads of the two-winged type, *ko* halberds of the Yin type, spearheads, axes, *yüeh* axes, and knives have been unearthed, but the overwhelming majority of the associated remains indicates a persisting Neolithic context.[79] This site has been given a Yin Dynasty date mainly on the basis of the Yin type of *ko* halberds; but the same type of weapon has been found in association with typical Warring States inventories from the tomb at Yang-tzu-shan (intruded into the ceremonial platform described above), and this particular evidence is therefore of doubtful dating value.[80] Since the arrowheads and some of the pottery and other bronze weapons do not show characteristic Chan-kuo features, the Shui-kuan-yin site can probably be dated to either late Western Chou or early Eastern Chou, broadly contemporary with the T'ai-p'ing-ch'ang and Yang-tzu-shan ceremonial assemblages.

These archaeological discoveries in the western part of Szechwan indicate a cultural tradition, essentially a continuation of the local

78. Ibid., p. 30.
79. Yang Yu-jun, *KK* (1959/8), 401.
80. *KKHP* (1956/4), 6.

Neolithic, which was heavily influenced by the Western or early Eastern Chou civilizations of North China, and in which ceremonial structures and stone and jade ceremonial objects played significant roles, though metallurgy may not have developed locally to any considerable extent. In this part of Szechwan, megalithic structures have been noted in the historical literature and investigated by archaeologists; their correlation with archaeological remains is still not clear. Cheng Te-k'un[81] is inclined to correlate the megalithic monuments with the ceremonial pit at T'ai-p'ing-ch'ang, and this seems to be supported by the ceremonial platform at Ch'eng-tu. Such structures and objects certainly invite inferences regarding the religion and political authority of the people who left such remains, but further characterizations in cultural and social terms are impossible to make at the present time.

Whatever the nature of the civilizations in Szechwan during the Western Chou and early Eastern Chou periods of North China, by the beginning of the Warring States period intensified civilizations appeared in many parts of the province, as indicated by archaeological remains abundant in bronze and iron artifacts, evidence of tightened political control, and writing. Three groups of metal culture sites in Szechwan in the Warring States period can be discerned in the archaeological material: one represented by burials in the Chialingchiang Valley of eastern and central Szechwan; one centering in the valley of Min near the plains of Ch'eng-tu; and one confined to the extreme northwestern portion of the province, in the foothills and river valleys of the eastern Tibetan plateau. The former two groups, while exhibiting certain distinctive features, seem to have formed a single cultural tradition; whereas the third constitutes a separate culture of its own.

Two sites of the Chialingchiang burials have been discovered so far: the Pao-lun-yüan cemetery in Chao-hua in north central Szechwan, and the Tung-sun-pa cemetery in Pa Hsien, near the confluence of the Chialingchiang and the Yangtze, close to the city of Chungking.[82] At least thirteen individual burials, four of which are intact, have been brought to light at the Pao-lun-yüan site, and eighteen, with one com-

81. Cheng Te-k'un, *Archaeological Studies in Szechwan,* Cambridge Univ. Press, 1957, p. xiv.

82. Feng Han-chi et al., *KKHP* (1958/2), 77–95. Szechwan Museum, *Szechwan Ch'uan-kuan Tsang Fa-chüeh Pao-kao,* Peking, Wenwu Press, 1960.

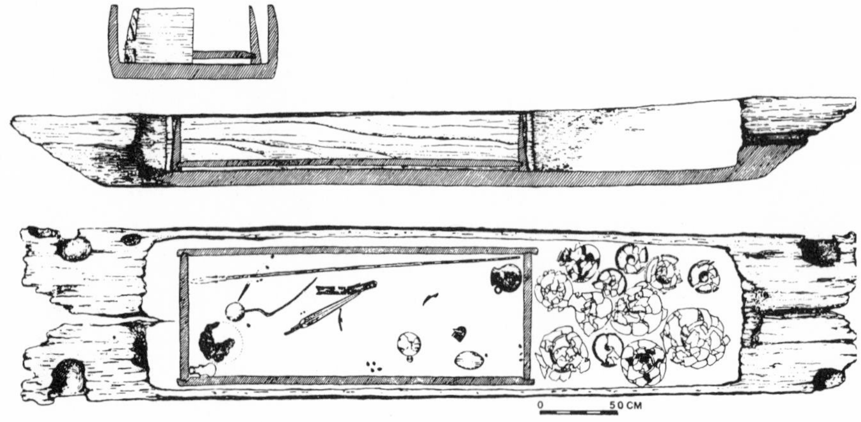

159. A boat coffin excavated at the Bronze Age site at Pao-lun-yüan, Chao-hua, Szechwan. (From *KKHP,* 1958/2, p. 81.)

pletely preserved, at Tung-sun-pa. Both of these cemeteries were situated on river terraces. The individual graves, arranged in regular rows crowded into small areas, were rectangular earthen pits, perpendicular to the riverbank. The pits were only just large enough to contain individual dugout canoes which served as coffins. Each canoe was about 5 meters long and 1 meter wide, with a flattened bottom, two beveled ends, each with a big hole, and a dugout cavity at the top, which contained the body as well as grave goods (Fig. 159). In several cases the canoe was so large that the cavity served as a chamber into which a smaller coffin containing the body was placed, together with grave goods, but these are believed to be of a later type. Bronze, iron, stone, bamboo, and wooden artifacts, pottery, lacquer, silk and hemp clothes, and clay and glass beads were uncovered from the graves. Among the bronze artifacts are axes, spears, *ko* halberds, arrowheads, vessels, mirrors, belt hooks, knives, seals, and scale weights, mostly of the Warring States variety, but the most typical bronzes are a willow-leaf-shaped sword and a socketed axe with a circular blade. The blade of the sword tapered toward the end to become a handle, which was then lengthened with the addition of wooden splints and decorated with many kinds of unusual designs such as tiger heads, tiger-skin patterns, "hand-and-heart" patterns, and writings (Fig. 160). The hand-and-heart pattern is seen only on the bronze swords, not only in these boat

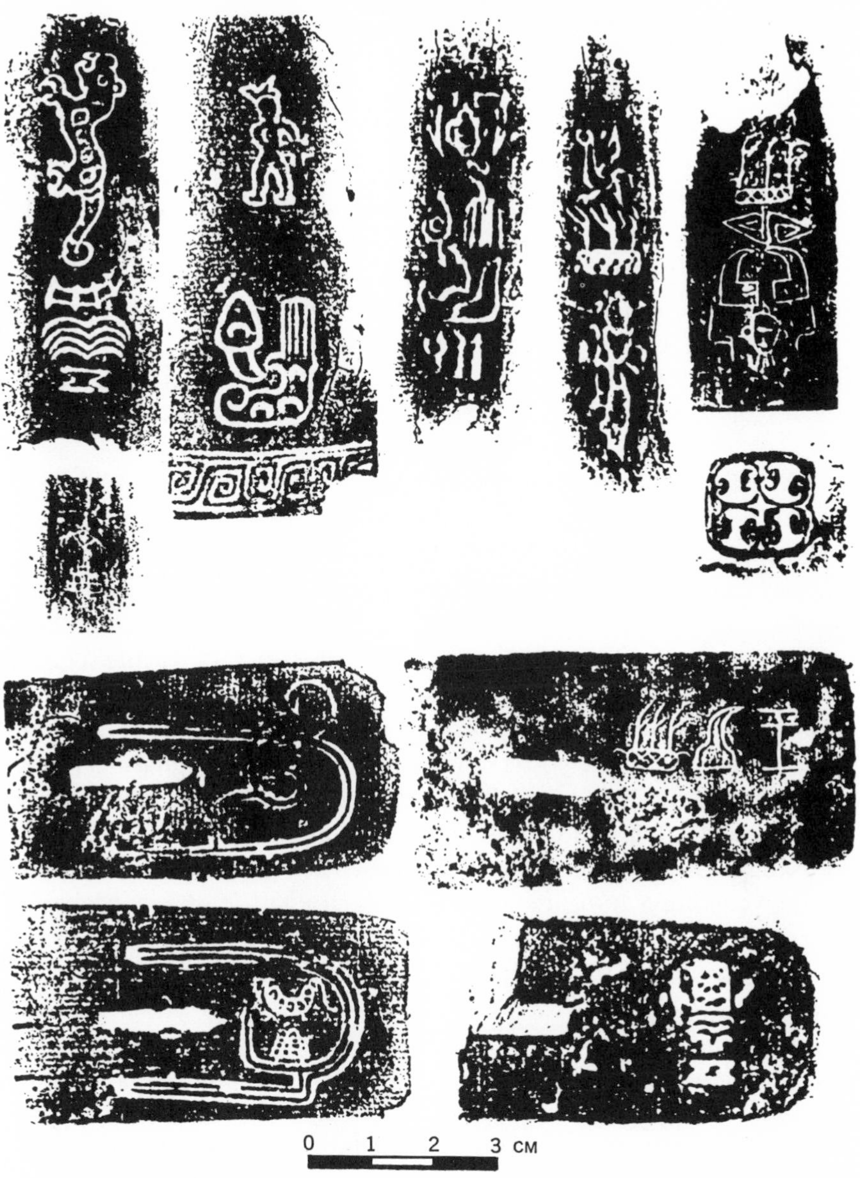

160. Designs on spearheads (*above*) and halberds (*below*) from the Eastern Chou and Han burials in the Chialingchiang region of Szechwan. (From *KKHP,* 1958/2, p. 89.)

burials but throughout the Szechwan area,[83] and is never used for other kinds of weapons or vessels with the single exception of one spearhead. The other decorative patterns are found on other kinds of implements and weapons. Metallurgical analysis has shown that the bronzes in the boat burials contain a lower quantity of tin than is usually found in Chinese bronzes, and that the artifacts are therefore relatively soft. In several burials, bronze *pan-liang* coins of the Ch'in Dynasty were found, but these burials are thought to be of a later phase than the rest. Iron artifacts are few, and consist only of knives and axes. The pottery is predominantly brownish in color and sand-tempered; in form it is characterized by flat or round bottoms and the use of ring feet. It is mainly wheel made, and painted decorations are rare.

The Warring States period sites in the Ch'eng-tu area include a cemetery in P'eng-shan, a group of bronzes from Lu-shan,[84] and several groups of burials and habitation remains in the neighborhood of the city of Ch'eng-tu, such as Ch'ing-yang-kung, Yang-tzu-shan, Pai-ma-ssu, and one outside the southern city gate. Of these, P'eng-shan and the site at Pai-ma-ssu were discovered before and during World War II, and it has been reported that the heart-and-hand patterned bronze sword is characteristic of the Pai-ma-ssu burials[85] (Fig. 161). Sand-tempered brown pottery similar to that of the Chialingchiang sites is found at Ch'ing-yang-kung site in Ch'eng-tu, where a bronze knife, oracle bones, and turtleshells were also reported.[86] Generally speaking, however, the Warring States period cultural remains at Ch'ing-yang-kung indicate certain similarities to—or more probably continuities from—the period represented by the Shui-kuan-yin locality. The site outside the southern city gate of Ch'eng-tu was a secondary burial, in association with which were pottery, some bronze vessels, weapons, and implements. Among the weapons is a type of *ko,* triangular in shape and having a tiger-head decoration, which is one of the most characteristic types of artifacts in the Ch'eng-tu area.[87] The Warring States burials at Yang-tzu-shan, north of the Ch'eng-tu city, were

83. Seen as far east as the Ch'ü-t'ang Gorge area of the Yangtze River in Szechwan; see T'ung En-cheng, *KK* (1962/5), 253.
84. Lu Te-liang, *KK* (1959/8), 439.
85. Wei Chü-hsien, *Shou-wen Yüeh-k'an, 3* (1941), 1–29.
86. Chiang Hsüeh-li and Lu Te-liang, *KK* (1959/8), 411–14.
87. Lai Yu-te, *KK* (1959/8), 449–50.

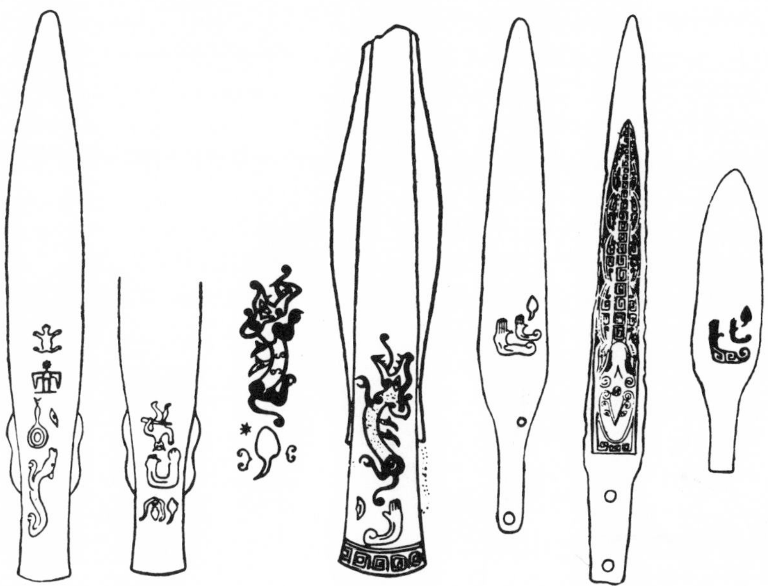

161. Decorated bronze swords and spearheads from the Pai-ma-ssu site, near Ch'eng-tu, Szechwan. (From *Shuo Wen, 3,* 1941, Shanghai.)

intrusive into, and hence subsequent in time to, the ceremonial square platform described above. A tomb, No. 172, that has been described in published reports, is of the usual Warring States type, with rectangular pit, wooden chamber, and a wooden coffin. The burial goods include gray pottery, bronze vessels, weapons, implements, mirrors, belt hooks, seals, horse and chariot fittings, lacquers, jades, precious ornaments, glass beads, and an iron tripod. Most of these are of the typical Warring States types seen in North China. It is, nevertheless, of particular interest that among the findings many characteristic features recall the Ch'u civilization to the east, such as the "bronze sword with jade-decorated handle, the *t'ao-t'ieh* pattern of the feet of the big *ting* tripods, the *yen* steamers divided into two parts, the shape and decor of the bronze *lei,* the decorative patterns of bronze spearheads and lacquer boxes, and the gold- and silver-inlaid decorative designs."[88] Furthermore, some features of this assemblage are said to have local characteristics: the shape of the pottery urns, the bronze

88. *KKHP* (1956/4), 19.

vessel handles with stranded-cord designs, the white cement used to attach the gold and silver pieces of the inlay designs, the lack of any attempt to achieve symmetry in the decor, the bas relief animals on the belt hooks, and the distinctive writing system. On the other hand, some decorative motifs, such as the moth-brow pattern, find close relatives in the Dongson culture to the south. On the whole, the Yang-tzu-shan burial exhibits its Szechwan characteristics, but an increasingly strong influence of North China traditions upon the native civilization is indcated toward the end of the Warring States period.

To the west of both of these two groups—Chialingchiang and Ch'eng-tu—there was another cultural tradition, beginning no later than the final phases of the Chan-kuo period. This is represented by the finds at Li-fan (or Fan) and Kan-tzu in westernmost Szechwan, the region that begins to climb uphill toward the Tibetan plateau. At Li-fan, a large group of slab tombs (cists of slates) was excavated during World War II, and from the burials pottery, bronzes, iron, glass beads, and a wooden container were brought to light. The interesting and instructive point concerning the Li-fan slab tombs is that among the grave goods cultural influences from more than a single direction are discernible. Contacts with the Chinese civilization of late Eastern Chou and Ch'in and Han dynasties are indicated by Chinese inscriptions (of the styles of the various stages) and many types of pottery and bronze artifacts, including *pan-liang* and *wu-shu* coins.[89] On the other hand, cultural contacts with Kansu, directly north, are shown by some ceramic features, particularly the flat-bottomed jars with two large vertical loop handles and the concave bottom of several jars "which [were hollowed out] with a sharp implement, probably of bamboo, when the paste was still wet,"[90] both of which recall the Hsin-tien ceramics described in the previous chapter. Moreover, the so-called Ordos bronze features are very strongly represented in (1) the large numbers of weapons and armor which indicate the prevalence of close combat; (2) the small artifacts such as bells, buttons, tubes, rings, and plates; (3) the bronze kettles; (4) the dotted designs; and (5) the animal

89. An iron object collected from a Li-fan slab tomb by Ling Shun-sheng of the Academia Sinica was sent to the Yale Radiocarbon Laboratory for age determination; it yielded a date of 2130 ± 100 B.P. (180 ± 100 B.C.). See Nicholaas van der Merwe, *The Metallurgical History and the Carbon-14 Dating of Iron* (Ph.D. dissertation, Yale University, 1966), pp. 113–14.

90. Cheng Te-k'un, *Harvard Jour. Asiatic Studies, 9* (1946), 67.

style represented by a bronze ring with three birds in relief. Glass beads, according to Cheng, suggest indirect contacts with western Asia via the steppe nomads. A group of similar bronze artifacts, among which the horse fittings are outstanding, has been found farther west, in the area of Kan-tzu.[91] This area of Li-fan and Kan-tzu is now inhabited by the Ch'iang people whose legends relate that a slate-tomb building people, called the Ko, occupied the region before the Ch'iang came.[92] These Ko may have been farmers, as Cheng suggests, but apparently their settlements were mobile and mounted warfare prevailed. This region is separated from the steppe nomads by a great expanse of land which was occupied by the farming peoples of Kansu during its "eneolithic" stage. Whether there were direct connections between the Li-fan region and the steppe, or whether any such connections were by way of the Chinese civilization, cannot be certainly determined until the intervening regions are better known archaeologically.

It is evident that these three groups of Warring States period cultures in Szechwan represent two principal cultural traditions. With the Li-fan and Kan-tzu finds being placed in a separate category, the Warring States period civilizations of both the Chialingchiang and the Ch'eng-tu groups were probably the development of a single local culture, with intensive influences from North China and from the Ch'u of the middle Yangtze. Cheng Te-k'un points out that "Szechwan is fundamentally a marginal area, and the culture of this province had never been a result of independent development. It has always been under the influence of some neighboring culture."[93] Applied to the Warring States period, this statement must not be taken literally, for the many distinctively local stylistic characteristics make it hard to believe that all the Szechwan civilizations were nothing but imports from North and Central China. Although the bronze and iron implements and weapons in this region closely follow North Chinese prototypes, they were apparently modified to conform to local beliefs, usages, and traditions. The hand-and-heart design, the characteristic writing and other decorative symbols on weapons, the tiger as a favorite decorative motif, the distinctive types of willow-leaf-shaped bronze swords and

91. An Chih-min, *KKTH* (1958/1), 62–63.
92. Cheng Te-k'un, *Harvard Jour. Asiatic Studies, 9* (1946), 77.
93. *Archaeological Studies in Szechwan,* p. xix.

the circular-socketed *yüeh* axes, the triangular *ko* halberds, the bridge-shaped bronze "coins," the bronze seals with undeciphered signs,[94] and the boat burials and cliff burials (which have been found dating to the Han Dynasty, but must have had a pre-Han background), all testify to the fact that the civilization of Szechwan had a distinctive and original spirit that is more than a pure imitation of North China prototypes, let alone a full-scale importation. Eastern Chou and Han literature refers to the ancient peoples dwelling in the Red basin as the Pa and the Shu peoples; according to *Hua-yang-kuo Chih,* compiled during the Chin Dynasty, the Pa territory was in the eastern part of Szechwan, and the Shu territory in the western, coinciding with the division made above into the Chialingchiang and the Ch'eng-tu subareas, although a positive identification must await further findings and more precisely dated discoveries. To be sure, the Chialingchiang and the Ch'eng-tu groups were probably only slightly different phases of the same cultural tradition, but nevertheless some differences can be enumerated between these two subareas. For instance, the circular-socket *yüeh* ax is relatively rare in the Ch'eng-tu area, but the same area is abundant in the triangular shaped *ko* halberds and in bird designs as decorative motifs, which are scarcely represented at all in the Chialingchiang boat burials.[95] Feng Han-chi has convincingly shown that the Chialing and the Ch'eng-tu *ko* and swords can be distinguished by some minute and distinctive differences.[96] As a cultural complex, boat burials have so far not been found west of the Chialing Valley. Moreover, the eastern division of the Szechwan civilization appears to continue into the area of Hupei, and its relations with the Ch'u must have been highly intimate. Boat burials, for instance, have been recorded widely in the historical documents of South China, particularly the Ch'u and the Yüeh areas.[97] On the other hand, the western division of the Szechwan civilization shares with the contemporary civilization of Yunnan (Tien and the Dongsonian) many decorative motifs and implement types, as well as the kettledrum. This does not mean that the east–west subdivision of the Szechwan civilizations of the Chan-kuo period was clearly demarcated. Szechwan civilization as a whole

94. Lu Te-liang, *KK* (1959/8), 439.
95. Feng Han-chi et al., *KKHP* (1958/2), 94.
96. *WW* (1961/11), 33.
97. Ling Shun-sheng, *BIHP, 23* (1951), 639–64.

shared with both the Ch'u and the Tien many stylistic characteristics. This civilization, furthermore, must have had a complex political organization and a sophisticated social stratification approaching the levels of a state structure. Throughout this civilization, the tiger played a prominent ritualistic role. In *Hou Han Shu,* in the "Biography of the Southern Man," a story relates that when the paramount chief of the Pa died, his soul was reincarnated as a white tiger, and that the people made offerings of human victims to him, believing that tigers ate human blood. If this story was indeed that of the Szechwan people of that time, which is likely in view of the prevalence of tiger motifs in their civilization, it gives us an idea of many political and religious institutions existing among them at that time. Historical books say that the Pa–Shu civilization came under the control of the state of Ch'in in 329 B.C., over a century before the Emperor of Ch'in conquered the whole of China, but the distinctive civilization of Szechwan apparently persisted, in quite undisturbed form, into the Ch'in and early Han dynasties until the time when the Han style of brick tombs appeared widely in the province.

EARLY CIVILIZATIONS IN YUNNAN

Farther upstream along the Yangtze from the Red basin is the high hilly plateau country of the Chinshachiang Valley, drained by the upper reaches of the Yangtze, the Red, and the Mekong rivers, where the modern provinces of Szechwan, Sikang, and Yunnan meet (Fig. 162). This country, inhabited by Neolithic peoples as late as the first millennium B.C., was open to cultural influences from at least three sources besides the south: the Yüeh and the Ch'u civilizations to the east, which could gain access to this area via the Pearl River; the Pa-Shu civilization of Szechwan, a little way down the Yangtze; and the Li-fan and Kan-tzu hilly country to the north, which connects this area with the steppe zone in the far north. Since these last regions had no highly developed civilizations themselves until the Eastern Chou period, Yunnan was not exposed to the influence of the Shang and early Chou cultures. Archaeological evidence of any such influences, direct or indirect, is completely lacking.

The available archaeological record shows that civilization apparently came to Yunnan during the latter part of the Eastern Chou pe-

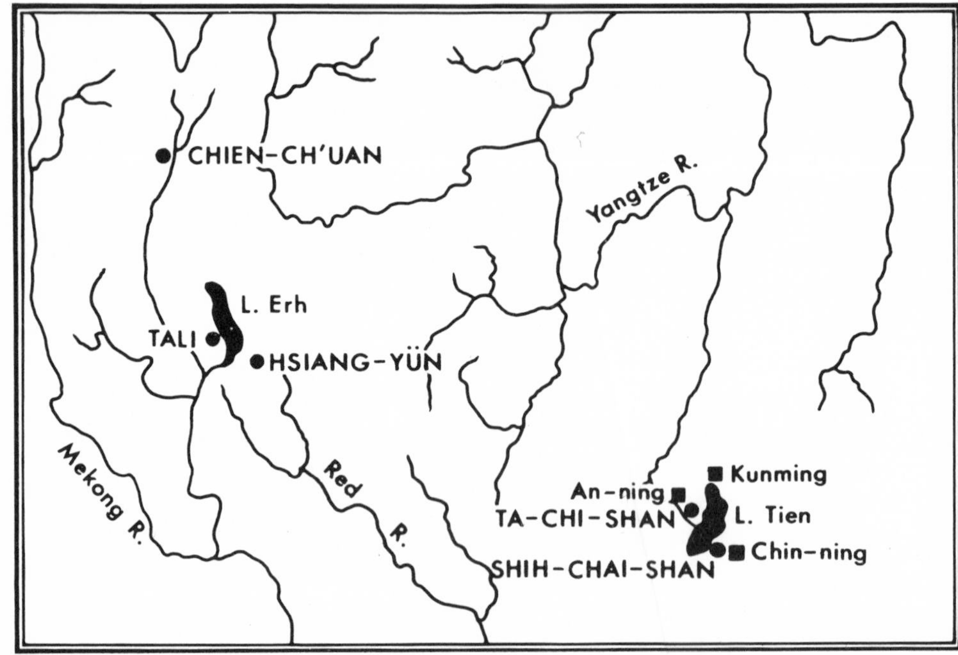

162. Bronze Age sites in Yunnan.

riod, simultaneously with irrigated farming and the use of iron implements. In this connection, Wu Chin-ting's investigations during 1938–40 in Ta-li Hsien, in the Lake Erh and Tients'ang Mountain area of western Yunnan a little way below the Chinshachiang, are highly important.[98] At the site of Ma-lung, a protracted occupation by prehistoric inhabitants has been brought to light. During the period when the site was continuously inhabited by people of the same cultural tradition, a major change occurred which divides the culture of this site into two stages: the first is the Neolithic culture described in Chapter 5; the second, although a continuation of the same cultural tradition, is marked by the simultaneous appearance of terraced fields, construction of water ditches probably for irrigation purposes, construction of mud village walls, growing use of potters' wheels, and use of both bronze and iron as shown by remains of bronze objects, an iron fragment, and an iron sickle. This discovery, which has never re-

98. Wu Chin-ting et al., *Yünnan Ts'ang Erh ching k'ao-ku pao-kao,* Lichuang, National Museum, 1942.

ceived the recognition it deserves, is important in giving a basis for dating the appearance of metallurgy and irrigation in the area of Yunnan, and it suggests that societal changes (such as the beginning of fortification and the intensification of industrial specialization) were concurrent with the appearance of metallurgy and irrigation. The full implication of the latter innovations can be realized in two recently discovered sites, one in Chien-ch'uan, north of Ta-li, and the other in Hsiang-yün, south of Ta-li, both in the general area of Lake Erh.

A habitation site at Chien-ch'uan, between the Chinshachiang Valley and Lake Erh in northwestern Yunnan, discovered in 1957, is a pile village, built along the Haiwei River, half on the bank, the other half submerged. Remains of agricultural implements and grains of rice, wheat, and millet were found, together with a large number of mollusk shells, animal bones, and fishhooks. Implements were mainly made of stone, including axes, adzes, sickles, chisels, scrapers, arrowheads, awls, spindle whorls, and grinding stones. Pottery is of the local Neolithic tradition, but the percentage of striking Lungshanoid types, such as lustrous black pottery, ring-footed vessels, high-stemmed *tou,* and perforated ring feet, is remarkably large for this area. Fourteen copper artifacts were found at the site, including axes, knives, chisels, rings, fishhooks, and ornaments, all hammered except for the axes, which were cast.[99] This site can be classified as essentially Neolithic in character, but it represents the first step taken by the early Yunnan civilization to achieve a full-fledged metal culture.

At Ta-p'o-na Commune in Hsiang-yün, southeast of Ta-li, a burial area was discovered in 1961. A tomb, excavated in 1964, proved to be a rectangular pit grave, 4 m deep, 7.5 by 2.5 m at the mouth and 7 by 2.2 m at the bottom. A wooden chamber, about 3.75 by 1.85 m in size, was built at the bottom of the pit from large timber posts and was plastered on the outside with a layer of very sticky white limey clay. Inside the chamber was a bronze coffin, assembled from seven pieces, in the shape of a house with a gabled roof, standing on twelve short legs. The entire exterior of the coffin was cast with decorative patterns, those on the roof and the side walls were composed of geometric elements and those on the two walls at the ends consisted of various animal forms such as falcons, swallows, tigers, leopards, wild boars, deer,

99. *KKTH* (1958/6), 5–12.

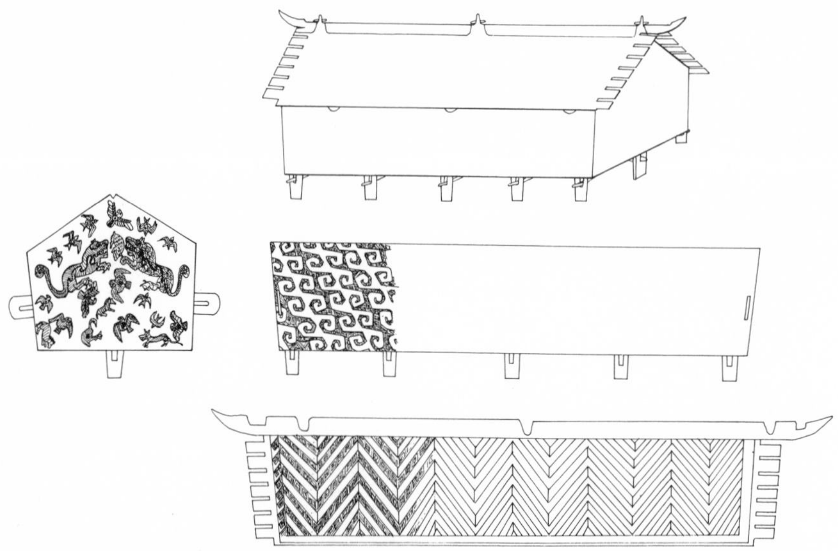

163. A bronze coffin at Ta-p'o-na, in Hsiang-yün, Yunnan. (From *KK,* 1964/12, pp. 608–09.)

horses, and waterbirds (Fig. 163). The coffin contained only a bronze stick and several pieces of limb bones; in the chamber and in the fill were found more than a hundred pieces of bronze artifacts and a few gray and orange-sandy sherds. The bronze included implements (hoes and plow blades, axes, knives); weapons (spearheads, swords, picks, fan-shaped axes, spear ends); vessels (*tsun* goblets, cups, dibbles, fruit stands, a cooking pot); spoons and two pairs of chopsticks; musical instruments (a kettledrum, two gourd-shaped *sheng,* a bell); models of houses, cattle, horses, sheep, pigs, dogs, and chickens; ornaments; and other miscellaneous items.[100]

Compared with the Chien-ch'uan site, the Ta-p'o-na bronze coffin indicates a far more advanced bronze-making culture; the casting of the coffin itself must have involved a complex metallurgical process. On the other hand, iron artifacts have not been found here, and the composition of the bronze artifacts appears to be uneven, uncontrolled, and less than effective (Table 13), suggesting a more primitive stage of metal civilization than the Shih-chai-shan finds to be described be-

100. Hsiung Ying and Sun T'ai-ch'u, *KK* (1964/12), 607–14.

TABLE 13.

Percentage of Metals in Selected Ta-p'o-na Bronze Coffin Artifacts

	Copper	*Tin*	*Lead*	*Iron*
Coffin	89.60	5.02	2.25	
Hoe	92.77	0.19		
Adz	94.20	3.71		0.20
Spearhead	93.79	2.35	0.62	
Cooking pot	93.25			
Spoon	84.13	13.69		
Bell	79.96	16.34	trace	
Kettledrum	87.96	6.87	3.46	0.64
Gourd *sheng*	97.63	1.32	0.52	
Ring	79.60	14.75	2.89	
Horse figurine	93.80	1.92	1.12	

low. The culture must have been one with advanced agriculture and domesticated animals. The tomb construction (pit grave with a wooden chamber), some of the bronze vessel types (*tou* and bell), and the use of chopsticks are within the Chinese tradition of the Shang and Chou periods, but the form of the house, bronze kettledrum, the fan-shaped axes, and the decorative art characterize an essentially indigenous civilization, possibly antecedent to the Shih-chai-shan culture of eastern Yunnan. It is regarded as the culture of the K'un-ming people[1] or one of the Mi-mo tribes[2] described by *Shih Chi* for the area of the southwest, and it has been placed within the middle Eastern Chou period.[3]

The sites in the area of Lake Erh of northwestern Yunnan have already shown a sequence of development of the Bronze Age civilization in Yunnan from the most primitive to more advanced, but the climax of this civilization occurred in the southeastern part of the province in the area of Lake Tien, not far from North Vietnam, the country of the classical Bronze Age site at Dong-son. Bronze remains suggestive of Dong-son types have been known from various localities in Yunnan for a long time,[4] but few scholars were prepared for the truly spectacu-

1. Ibid., p. 614.
2. T'ung En-cheng, *KK* (1966/1), 45, 46–48.
3. Li Chia-jui, *KK* (1965/9), 478–79.
4. Komai Kazuchika, "On Stone Implements and Bronze Artifacts of South China," in *Lectures on Anthropological and Prehistoric Topics, 19* (1940), Tokyo.

lar finds in the cemetery at Shih-chai-shan, in Chin-ning, and a burial site of the same culture in An-ning, on the southern and eastern shores of Lake Tien. Shih-chai-shan, a small, low hill (about 20 m high), is between Lake Tien to the west and the city of Chin-ning to the east. A Bronze Age cemetery was found on the eastern part of the hilltop, and four seasons of excavation were carried out between 1955 and 1960 by the Yunnan Provincial Museum. Thirty-four individual tombs were opened, and over four thousand pieces of artifacts have been brought to light.[5] A summary of the findings and their culture and society are given in Table 14.

A detailed account of the Shih-chai-shan culture is possible because the finds of representative art are abundant, and archaeologists can *read* rather than *interpret* the life of a people depicted in the bronze art. This pictorial account represents a lengthy period of occupation during which cultural changes occurred. The excavators have been able to distinguish four classes of tombs, which can be grouped into three stages. The first stage, probably dated to the late Chan-kuo period and the beginning of the Western Han, has relatively few iron implements, and no Chinese coins or other imported artifacts such as the mirrors, belt hooks, and bronze utensils which came later. The second stage, which can probably be dated by the Chinese coins to between 175 and 118 B.C., witnessed a growing incidence of mirrors, iron axes, and swords, and bronze implements made in China. The third stage is dated by Chinese coins to late Western Han and early Eastern Han.[6]

Across the lake from Shih-chai-shan is another burial site of the same culture—Ta-chi-shan, located between Lake Tien in the east and the town of An-ning in the west.[7] Seventeen tombs, all of the rectangular pit-grave type, were found. Most of the grave goods are pottery, but thirty-two bronze and iron implements of the Shih-chai-shan type

5. *Yün-nan Chin-ning Shih-chai-shan ku mu ch'ün fa-chüeh pao-kao,* Peking, Wenwu Press, 1959. *WW* (1959/5), 59–61. *KK* (1959/9), 459–561, 490; (1963/9), 480–85. For a perceptive analysis of the Shih-chai-shan art in terms of the ethnic components of the culture and the various ritual observances, see Feng Han-chi, *KK* (1961/9), 469–87, 490; Feng Han-chi, *KK* (1963/6), 319–29. English summaries of the remains of the site are available in Richard C. Rudolph, *AP, 4* (1960), 41–9; Magdalene von Dewall, *Antiquity, 41* (1967), 8–21.

6. *Yün-nan Chin-ning Shih-chai-shan ku mu ch'ün fa-chüeh pao-kao,* p. 133.

7. Chang Tseng-ch'i and Yang T'ien-nan, *KK* (1965/9), 451–58. See M. von Dewall, op. cit., for a description and analysis of the site.

TABLE 14.

Summary of the Tien Culture at Shih-chai-shan, Yunnan

Tombs: Mostly oriented E–W, with the head pointing to the east; simple earthen pits, without a regular plane, sometimes outlined by naturally placed rocks. When the body and grave goods were in place, the pit was filled with the dug-out earth or sandy earth mixed with pebbles. One tomb has fire-hardened walls, a wooden chamber, and an *erh-ts'eng-t'ai.* Remains of wooden coffins covered with lacquer and wrapped with cloths have been found in some graves.

Implements: Of the 706 implements reported in May 1959, 558 are bronzes, 92 iron, 43 stone, and 13 clay (spindle whorls). The bronze implements include 21 plows, 23 spades, 1 saw, 108 axes, 11 adzes, 23 chisels, 5 sickles, 26 knives, and a cylindrical object probably used for collecting mollusks. According to some depictions of the plow on the bronzes (Fig. 164), it was probably hafted onto a bent wooden handle with a small cross-

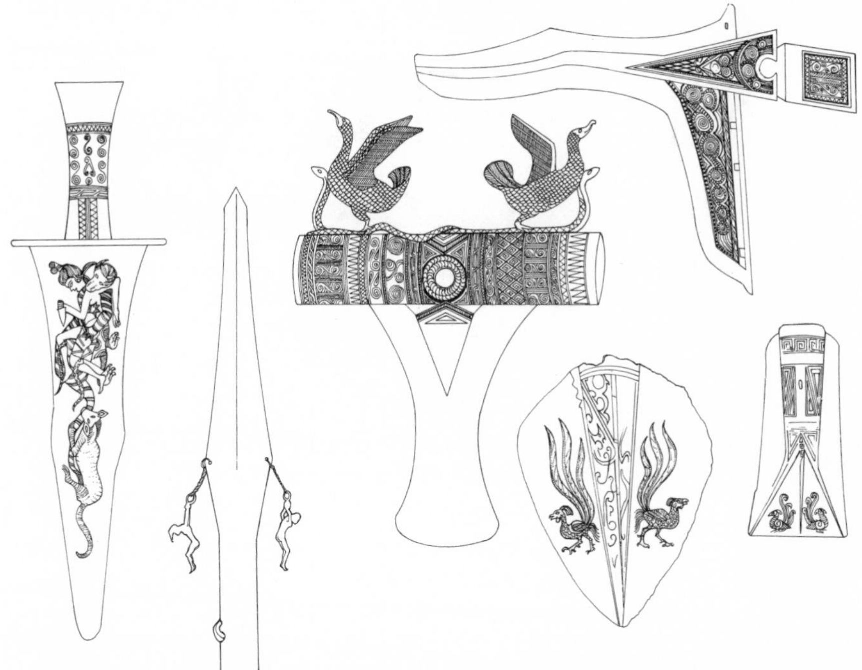

164. Bronze implements and weapons at the Tien site at Shih-chai-shan, Chin-ning, Yunnan. (From *Hsing Chung-kuo ti K'ao-ku Shou-huo,* 1962, p. 90.)

165. Market scenes cast in the round on the top of a bronze vessel from a Tien tomb at Shih-chai-shan. (From *Yün-nan Chin-ning Shih-chai-shan ku mu ch'ün fa-chüeh pao-kao,* Peking, Wenwu Press, 1959.)

bar at the end. One or two men pulled the plow with a rope, and another pushed from behind. The biggest plow found weighs 750 grams and is 29 cm long by 20 cm wide. Iron implements include adzes, axes (iron-edged), and knives.

Subsistence and Handicrafts: Agriculture was apparently practiced. Cattle, sheep, dogs, horses, chickens, and pigs are depicted in the decorative and plastic art; horses were used for riding and warfare, and cattle probably only for meat and ceremonial use. Hunting with dogs was carried on. Handicrafts were highly developed, as shown by the wine ware, finely made bronzes, iron metallurgy, opal work, and leatherwork.

Trade and Currency: Hundreds of thousands of cowrie shells were found in drum-shaped containers. Plastic market scenes depicted the exchange of cattle and food (Fig. 165). Some of the coins, mirrors, lacquers, crossbows,

166. A ritual scene cast in the round on the top of a bronze vessel from a Tien tomb at Shih-chai-shan (From ibid.)

167. Battle scene cast in the round on the top of a bronze vessel from a Tien tomb at Shih-chai-shan. (From ibid.)

ko halberds, arrowheads, and *chi* halberds were identical with North China types of Eastern Chou and Han periods, and were probably imports.

Weaving: A plastic bronze model shows a type of horizontal loom now widely seen in Southeast Asia. Hemp was probably cultivated.

Utensils: Sophisticated sets of daily utensils, of pottery or bronze.

Habitation: Pile dwellings, shown in plastic bronze models, have two stories (upper level for inhabitants and lower level for domestic animals) and thatched roofs (Fig. 166).

Social Stratification: Three social classes are distinguished by the excavators according to the hair styles and dresses of the human figurines in the plastic bronze models:

1. Aristocracy and the rich, the "owners of the cowrie shells." One of the tomb masters was particularly wealthy; he was accompanied by a *pien* bell set, jade objects, bronze *ting* tripod, four cowrie-shell containers, and a gold seal with four Chinese characters inscribed: *Tien Wang Chih Yin* (the Seal of the King of Tien). Women apparently enjoyed higher status

than men, or at least had special deference shown them, such as being carried sitting on stools, as is seen in the plastic bronze models.

2. Freemen, the commoners of the same group, serving as managers.
3. Slaves.

Warfare: A large number of weapons (Fig. 164) is found, including some iron types. Most were of bronze, including 214 swords, 299 spearheads, 14 crossbows, and 266 arrowheads. Iron was used only to make swords, and these were protected by gold sheaths. Warfare is also depicted in plastic models, which show mounted horsemen and headhunters (Fig. 167). Horse-and-chariot fittings of bronze are also abundantly represented.

Luxuries: Ornaments and objects of gold, silver, jade, opal, turquoise, and lacquerware.

Rituals: Many ritual scenes are depicted in bronze plastic models; e.g. one in which a pillar, with a snake coiling around it and a tiger at the top, is surrounded by people killing human victims. Several others show the ceremonial killing of cattle. Bronze kettledrums, many of which were found, figured importantly in rituals, as shown in Figure 166. Some ritual participants wore feathered plumes, such as the cattle killer and the dancers. Priests and/or shamans played musical instruments, made gestures, and danced. The wooden boat (Fig. 168) was another important element of the rituals. Cattle and peacocks apparently had some special ritualistic significance.

Art: The bronzes display extremely sophisticated decorative art, in plane or plastic forms. Dancing was probably part of the rituals. Musical instruments included bronze kettledrums, *sheng*-pan-pipes, flutes, and *pien* bells.

168. Boats in the decorative scenes of the Shih-chai-shan bronzes. (From *WW,* 1964/12, p. 44.)

also came to light. Much less lavishly furnished, the Ta-chi-shan cemetery may have been the resting place of lesser noblemen or even commoners, in contrast to the kingly tombs of Shih-chai-shan, and it is therefore significant for its more balanced and complete depiction of the Tien civilization.

The importance of the Shih-chai-shan and Ta-chi-shan discoveries can hardly be exaggerated. The proximity to the classical site of Dong-son in the Gulf of Tonkin[8] and the many stylistic similarities which these two sites share indicate without question that they represent the same culture, characterized by the following stylistic elements: bronze kettledrums; fan-shaped and boot-shaped bronze axes; plastic bronze art as a decorative adjunct to ceremonial objects, artifacts of high prestige value (e.g. heads for sticks and tops of cowrie-shell containers), and similar weapon forms; cattle and peacocks as favorite decorative motifs, with ceremonial implications; and certain other distinctive decorative motifs such as connected concentric circles, whorls, moth-brow designs, and S-shaped patterns.[9] In terms of society and economy, there is no question that the Dong-son culture had a highly sophisticated and stratified society and intensive industrial specialization. On the other hand, it seems to have had no writing, and the dwelling sites that have been found show no evidence of mature urbanization. Typologically, the civilization represented by the sites of Dong-son and Shih-chai-shan appears to be comparable with the Yayoi culture of Japan and the Circum-Caribbean culture of South America, in both of which socially stratified villages were the prevalent unit of social interaction and economic self-sufficiency, but in none of which is shown an urban–rural interdependence such as that achieved by the Shang and probably by the Ch'u and Yüeh civilizations.[10]

This highly developed civilization apparently centered in Yunnan and the northern part of Indochina, but its influence was widely felt. Bronze drums have been found or recorded in most of South China,[11] including the regions of the Ch'u and the Pa–Shu civilizations, and

8. O. R. T. Janse, *Archaeological Research in Indo China III: The Ancient Dwelling-site of Dong-Son (Thanh-Hoa, Annam)*, Bruges, Institut Belge des Hautes Etudes Chinoises, 1958.

9. Chang Kwang-chih, *BIE, 7* (1959), 56. Kobayashi Tomowo, *Kōkōgakū-Zasshi, 26* (1936), 701–18.

10. Chang Kwang-chih, *BIE, 13* (1962), 1–26.

11. Ling Shun-sheng, *Bull. College of Arts, Natl. Taiwan Univ., 1,* 1950. Ho Chi-sheng, *KK* (1965/1), 31–39.

Dongsonian elements have been enumerated from a large part of Southeast Asia.[12] The discovery at Shih-chai-shan, furthermore, shows that the initial stimulation which brought about the emergence of this civilization in Yunnan was introduced mainly from the areas of Ch'u and Szechwan toward the end of the Eastern Chou period, approximately the fourth and the fifth centuries B.C. Many bronze elements in the Shih-chai-shan cemetery also indicate direct influence from the Li-fan and Kan-tzu group of Eastern Chou and early Han bronzes, such as the vivid animal style of art depicted in small, single-motif art objects. Heine-Geldern believes that the Dong-son owed its impetus directly to the western Asian and European Bronze Age and Iron Age cultures.[13] The Li-fan and Kan-tzu group of Szechwan civilizations, however, certainly provided the immediate sources for any western Asian elements in the Dong-son culture.

GENERAL CONCLUSIONS

South China's prehistory and early history are full of intriguing problems; with the cultural framework outlined in Chapter 5 and in the present chapter, many specific questions remain to be answered and a good many details of tremendous historical significance deserve more extensive treatment than the space here can afford. In concluding the discussion of the emergence of civilizations in South China, a few paragraphs should now be devoted to this area as a whole, pulling together the fragmentary information given above to show the general tendency of its cultural development during the Shang and Chou periods of North China and the patterns involved in the process.

Attention must once more be directed to the native cultures of South China, which in the main played recipient roles under the tremendous impact of the ever-expanding Bronze Age and Early Iron Age civilizations of the Huangho Valley. Two main cultural traditions played important parts in South China—the Lungshanoid farmers in eastern South China, and the southwestern Neolithic in Szech-

12. H. R. van Heekeren, *The Bronze-Iron Age of Indonesia,* The Hague, Martinus Nijhoff, 1958. R. J. Pearson, *BIE, 13* (1962), 27ff.

13. Robert von Heine-Geldern, *Saeculum, 2* (1951), 225–55; and *Paideuma, 5* (1954), 347–423; see also his "Some Tribal Art Styles of Southeast Asia: An Experiment in Art History," in Douglas Fraser (ed.), *The Many Faces of Primitive Art,* Englewood Cliffs, Prentice-Hall, 1966, pp. 161–221.

wan and Yunnan. The Lungshanoid was essentially an extension of the Lungshanoid in North China and was composed of immigrant farmers who brought along a North China heritage, although many adjustments were necessary in coping with the new problems that arose from change of habitat. The southwestern Neolithic probably developed on the southwestern Mesolithic and sub-Neolithic base, under the Lungshanoid influences that above all included the introduction of cereal agriculture and the domestication of certain animals.

The civilizations of the Shang Dynasty and of the Western Chou apparently had continuous contacts with the aboriginal peoples of South China, but archaeological data indicate that their cultural influences were largely confined to the middle and lower Yangtze Valley and the Huaiho Valley. State organizations came into being toward the end of this stage in the Huaiho Valley and probably in the lower Yangtze, and late Western Chou and early Eastern Chou impacts probably reached as far south as the Chekiang Valley. Elsewhere in eastern South China the introduction of metallurgy and the bronze and pottery arts of the Shang and Chou styles brought about the formation of the Geometric horizon. It can be clearly seen, however, that the native Lungshanoid tradition persisted into this period, and even in the Huaiho states where sinicization was most extensive, native pottery styles continued.

Archaeological evidence indicates two major waves of North Chinese civilizations into South China, the first dated to the Eastern Chou period, probably closer to the Warring States period than to the Ch'un-ch'iu, and the second, the political and military expansion of the Ch'in and the Han empires. Various southern states emerged, probably as a result of the Eastern Chou expansion, but they were subsequently incorporated, one after another, into the Ch'in and Han.

The Eastern Chou expansion into South China was closely linked to the internal changes taking place in North China itself. Archaeological materials from the Eastern Chou states of South China indicate that iron implements were found from the beginning of their civilizations along with bronze implements, although the latter were far more abundant in most regions. The evidence from Ch'u and from Ta-li in Yunnan further suggests that the Eastern Chou expansion was probably also linked with the increased use of irrigation. It is thus apparent that the Eastern Chou civilization of North China not only changed its structure in its homeland but expanded geographically toward the north and the south.

The South China Neolithic cultures, already infiltrated by Shang and Early Chou cultural elements, and presumably already stimulated toward an intensive internal growth in some regions, swiftly grew into a metal age culture under the suddenly accelerated impacts of the Eastern Chou North China. In some regions where previous contacts with Shang and Western Chou were frequent and considerable, such as the Ch'u and the Yüeh, there were probably transitional stages between village and state, and upon this basis state organizations and a literate civilization came into being during the Eastern Chou period. In other regions, such as Yunnan, the Eastern Chou civilization found a primarily Neolithic base. With the sudden burst of metal culture and sophisticated art, these cultures were apparently boosted onto a level approaching that of the great civilizations, but at a societal level these civilizations lacked urbanism and writing. The precise form of the Pa–Shu civilizations in terms of such typological classifications is not clear at the moment.

In addition to typological differences among the southern civilizations in the Eastern Chou period, there are also stylistic differences which may serve among other things in making cultural groupings. Many common characteristics are found throughout South China as a cultural sphere, in contrast to the North, which may indicate that the southern civilizations contained some unifying factors, many of which were apparently the result of similar ecological adjustments to a similar natural environment, but some of which probably indicate a certain degree of historical connection. Common features in South China include, for instance, pile dwellings, rice cultivation, the tubular borer, burial in boats and on cliffs, and bronze kettledrums. Distribution of these and other traits, however, suggests that there were actually parallel cultural traditions rather than a single cultural area in South China during this time interval, and that the widespread occurrence of certain characteristic features was the result of cultural contacts or similar ecological conditions. At least the following different cultural traditions can be distinguished among the Eastern Chou civilizations in South China:

1. Wu and Yüeh: in the eastern and southern coastal areas
2. Ch'u: in the middle Yangtze and the western Huaiho Valley
3. Pa–Shu: in the Red basin of Szechwan
4. The Li-fan and Kan-tzu assemblages of westernmost Szechwan
5. The Tien and related civilizations of Yunnan

The stylistic characteristics of these traditions have been enumerated above, and repetition is not necessary. The powerful expansion of the Ch'in and Han Empires brought all these cultural traditions under the same political system and civilization, but in different areas the actual process of assimilation, as well as its rate and tempo, apparently differed. These different traditions also had dissimilar relations with cultures and civilizations in areas outside of China. Historical and modern non-Han Chinese ethnic groups have claimed descent from the various cultural traditions of the Eastern Chou period. Discussions of these problems must be left out of the present volume, but there is material here for many future studies which could make significant contributions to our knowledge of the culture history of Southeast Asia.

CONCLUSIONS AND PROSPECT

The year 221 B.C. has been chosen as a terminal date for the present study of ancient Chinese archaeology for two reasons. First, the year marked the unification of China under Shih Huang Ti, the first emperor of the Ch'in Dynasty, and the consolidation of the Chinese as a single people with a single culture and a sense of common nationality. The various local cultures which flourished in different parts of China up to this time were from the formative stage of Chinese civilization. Second, we find that for the various cultures before the Ch'in and the Han dynasties, either no historical record was kept at all or the historical documents that survive are fragmentary and far from complete. The basic data for a study of the culture, society, and history of prehistoric and early historic China are provided by archaeology. It is true that for a complete history of the Shang and Chou dynasties, literary records would have to be utilized to a far greater extent than has been done in this book, which includes them only when they render archaeological data more meaningful. But these historical documents have been neglected for other considered reasons. The data for the same periods from literary sources is readily available in many good books already in existence. The writing of a book which uses both historical and archaeological materials to the full may be highly desirable, but it cannot be undertaken at a time when the archaeological data, much of which has only been made available in very recent years, still need processing and interpretation. Moreover, archaeology and history, by virtue of their different source materials, tend to stress different aspects of the same culture history. In historical studies, political events are often given paramount attention at the expense of cultural and social changes and information about the origins and development of cultural traditions. Archaeological data happily fill such vacuums, and the present book supplements rather than overlaps the works on ancient Chinese history which have made use of literary sources.

A cultural historical framework has thus been presented in this book, within which most of the available archaeological data from the area of China can be interpreted. We have seen that this region has been occupied since the beginning of the Middle Pleistocene period at the latest, and that industrial diversification and innovation and the evolution of man himself occurred within China during the Pleistocene. In the early postglacial period, Mesolithic cultures of two major types were distributed in the northern and the southern parts of China, respectively. Subsequently the food-producing way of life developed in the north, which ignited an explosive cultural growth leading to the formation of a Chinese civilization which has been carried down uninterruptedly to the present time and has helped to shape the course of civilizational development in the entire Far East.

Agriculture and the domestication of animals in North China probably emerged in what I have called the Nuclear Area. The exact time at which this important event took place, gradually or abruptly, is unknown, and its relation to the Neolithic revolution in the distant Near East is not clear. But however the inception of the new subsistence and technological patterns came about, the Neolithic culture of the Huangho Valley possessed a distinctive and highly original character which characterizes a Chung Yüan cultural tradition and was carried over into the historical civilizations of this area. The early farmers underwent at least two major stages of cultural and social development—the Yang-shao stage of primary village efficiency and the Lungshanoid stages of expanding village farmers—before the first civilization, the Shang, appeared in the plains of the lower Huangho. The Shang civilization was taken over by the Western Chou Dynasty, but by the middle of the Eastern Chou period a series of interrelated events and factors appeared, among which the highly developed iron metallurgy and intensified communications throughout the country were paramount. These made the Huangho tradition expand toward the north and the south, thus paving the way for the unification of China under the Ch'in and Han empires (Table 15).

In the northern parts of China, primarily because of ecological limitations, the Mesolithic hunting–fishing cultures lingered on for a considerable time during the same period in which farming and, subsequently, civilization developed in the Huangho Valley to the south. Agriculture and the domestication of animals were introduced to the southern fringes of this area, and Neolithic technology penetrated even deeper. But on the whole, the northern frontiers remained a

TABLE 15.

Ancient Culture Chronologies of North China

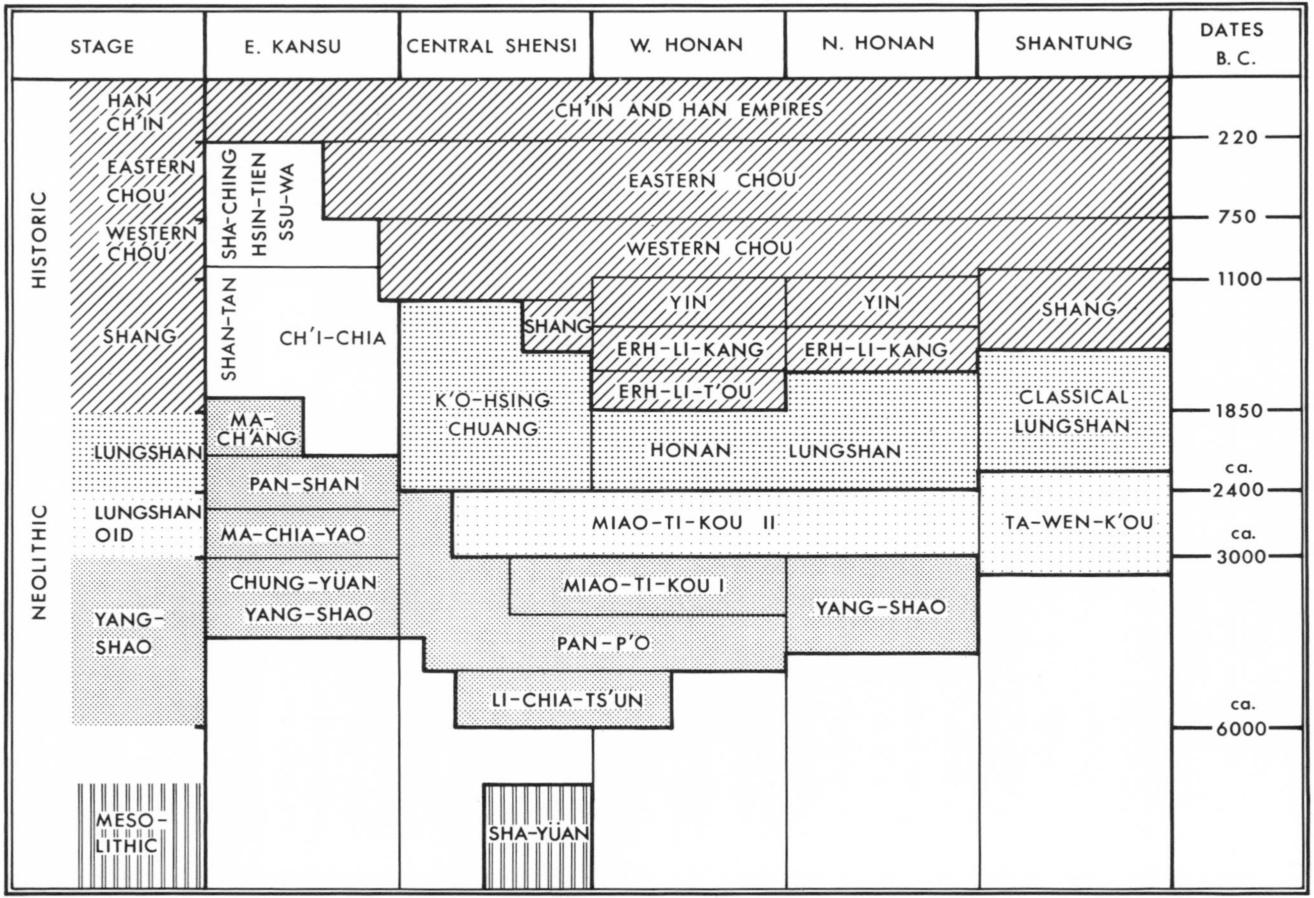

STAGE		E. KANSU	CENTRAL SHENSI	W. HONAN	N. HONAN	SHANTUNG	DATES B. C.
HISTORIC	HAN CH'IN	CH'IN AND HAN EMPIRES					220
	EASTERN CHOU	SHA-CHING HSIN-TIEN SSU-WA	EASTERN CHOU				750
	WESTERN CHOU		WESTERN CHOU				1100
	SHANG	SHAN-TAN CH'I-CHIA	SHANG	YIN ERH-LI-KANG ERH-LI-T'OU	YIN ERH-LI-KANG	SHANG	
NEOLITHIC	LUNGSHAN	MA-CH'ANG	K'O-HSING CHUANG	HONAN	LUNGSHAN	CLASSICAL LUNGSHAN	1850
	LUNGSHAN OID	PAN-SHAN MA-CHIA-YAO	MIAO-TI-KOU II			TA-WEN-K'OU	ca. 2400
	YANG-SHAO	CHUNG-YÜAN YANG-SHAO	MIAO-TI-KOU I PAN-P'O LI-CHIA-TS'UN		YANG-SHAO		ca. 3000
							ca. 6000
	MESO-LITHIC		SHA-YÜAN				

province of the Northeast Asia culture area throughout the Neolithic, sub-Neolithic, and early metal age periods. By the middle of the first millennium B.C., there were two major expansions into this area, one from the Eastern Chou, the other from the central Asian steppes which were dominated by mounted nomads of a variety of cultural extractions and affiliations. The Great Wall symbolizes the conflicts of these two ways of life—agricultural and pastoral nomadic. The zigzag boundary between China and the nomad territory results from the frequent changes of sovereignty over the small strip of arable land along the borders of the Eastern Chou territories.

In the early postglacial period Southeast Asia—including South China—may have been another separate and independent center of a horticultural revolution, but this process remains to be elucidated by further archaeological work. The widely found cord-marked pottery assemblages in South China and Southeast Asia still represent a hunting-fishing-gathering way of life, but I am increasingly convinced that these remains were left by people with at least an incipient form of plant cultivation. The interrelationship of the North China and Southeast Asia centers of plant cultivation commands the closest attention of archaeologists in the future. Presently available material, however, indicates that as far as cereal agriculture in most of South China is concerned, it was probably brought into this area by the Lungshanoid pioneer farmers coming down from the north. The Neolithic cultures in South China continued into the Shang and Early Chou periods, although the North China Bronze Age civilizations incorporated the Huaiho and the lower Yangtze into their sphere of influence and made significant and even consequential changes in some of the other areas where certain elements of civilization were adopted as a result of increased contact. By the middle of the Eastern Chou, incentives for expansion once more increased enough to cause another explosive expansion of the Huangho civilization into South China, resulting in the formation of a number of contemporary states and regional cultural traditions. These states and cultural traditions were incorporated into the succeeding Ch'in and Han empires (Table 16).

This brief outline of South China prehistory and early history shows that three major waves of cultural influence reached South China from the north: the Lungshanoid, the Eastern Chou, and the

TABLE 16.

Ancient Culture Chronologies of South China

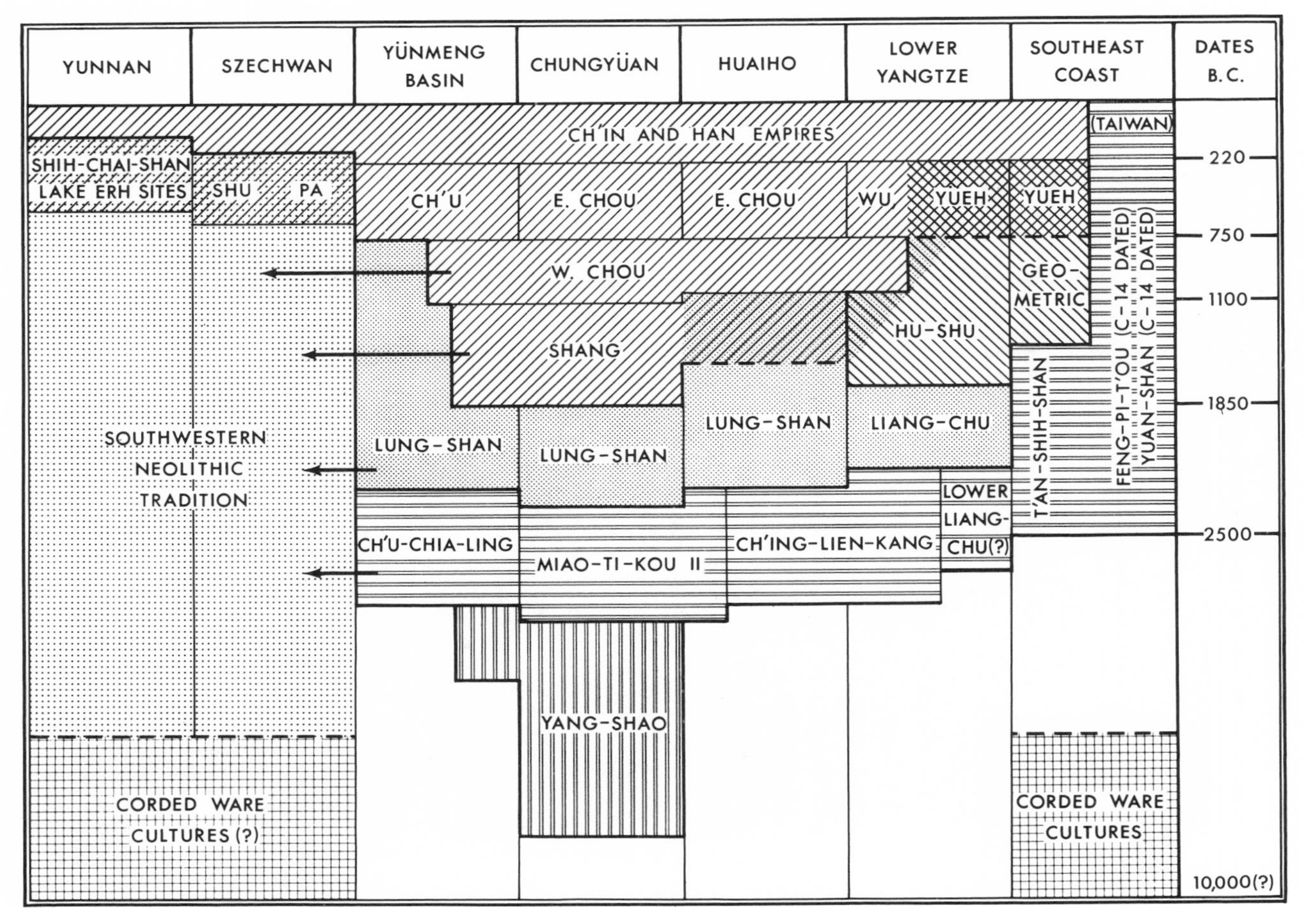

Ch'in and Han, before South China became an integral part of cultural China. In speaking of "Chinese influences" in South China and Southeast Asia, it is thus necessary to specify which of these major waves of influence is referred to.

These events finally led to the unification of China, the history of which concludes this volume. It can clearly be seen that by the end of the Warring States period much of China was already unified culturally, as indicated by the tradition and style which are encountered in almost all of China, from southern Manchuria to the coasts of Kwangtung. We encounter variations of the same civilizational form and spirit, exemplified in the tomb construction patterns, in the remains of a bronze mirror and an iron sword, in the decorative patterns of pottery and bronzes, and in the forms of writing. The unification of China by the Ch'in and the Han empires was not a conquest accomplished by a single powerful state and culture over a miscellaneous assortment of political groups and cultural traditions. Essentially this unification was a political follow-up of the cultural unification and the emergence of the Chinese national spirit which were already in force toward the end of the Eastern Chou, and which probably not only stimulated but also enabled—or at least facilitated—the political conquest which marked the year 221 B.C.

In that year the state of Ch'i, in Shantung, the last remaining power of the Warring States, was officially dissolved by General Wang P'en of the Ch'in. But the actual political unification of China was more or less continuous, for several centuries. The state of Ch'in claimed the status of kingdom in 325 B.C. Four years before, it had already taken over Szechwan. Many historians believe that the rich resources and the high civilization of Szechwan which came under Ch'in control were largely responsible for the phenomenal rise of the Ch'in state and its overwhelming power. In 256 B.C., the Ch'in overthrew the Royal Chou. By 221 B.C., all the major states in North and Central China, including Ch'u, Yen, Chao, Wei, Han, and Ch'i, bowed to the military might of the Ch'in. However, the incorporation of southern Manchuria[1] and southern Yüeh[2] came later. By the time of Han, what is now southern Manchuria, Inner Mongolia, and all of China proper

1. T'ung Chu-ch'en, *KKHP* (1956/1), 29–43.

2. L. Aurouseau, *Bulletin de l'Ecole Française d'Extrême-Orient, 23* (1923), 127–265.

were completely and directly dominated by the Han civilization. Sugimoto and Kano[3] have listed the Han Dynasty remains brought to light within recent years in China. Three things are made clear by that list: (1) Han remains have been found in every province of China proper and many regions in southern Manchuria, indicating the extent of the Han civilization within China; (2) in each province the number of Han Dynasty sites is considerable, suggesting the intensity of the Han acculturation in some of the marginal provinces; (3) it is clear that the Han remains from all China represent a single major cultural tradition.

I have mentioned that the Ch'in and Han political unification was essentially a political follow-up of a cultural unification which had been developing for some centuries before 221 B.C. I did not mean to say, however, that the total cultural unification of China was completed in every region of the area by that date. Native civilizational elements persisted into the Han and subsequent historical periods in many regions, particularly in the southwest.[4] But the political control of these regions under the Han Empire certainly accelerated and intensified their cultural assimilation into the Han civilization.

My interpretation of the formative process of the Chinese civilization, summarized above, can be regarded as only a working hypothesis, for there are still many gaps in our knowledge. Much of the archaeological data has been made available so recently, and the amount of painstaking research demanded is so vast, that this hypothesis is at best a tentative arrangement of the material according to my perspectives and judgments at this time. There are already large numbers of topics and problems emerging from the existing data, which demand close attention, and intensive, well-planned, and well-executed research is needed to formulate and clarify objectives for future field projects.

The first on my list of items for urgent research in prehistoric and early historical archaeology of China is chronology. The production of fresh data from the field increases the number of archaeological cultures to be correlated within a temporal and spatial framework and compounds the enormous chronological problem involved. For the

3. *Tōyōshi-Kenkyu, 16,* 1957.

4. Chang Kwang-chih, *COWA Survey,* Area 17, No. 1, 1959, p. 6; *Current Anthropol., 5* (1964), 359, 368–75, 399–400.

Pleistocene period, it is true, only broad geological segmentations suffice to synchronize industrial assemblages discovered in widely separated localities, but for many problems of great significance in Palaeolithic archaeology, a minute subdivision is necessary. The emergence of *Homo sapiens* and the blade industry, for instance, were major events in the history of man, but only with a fine chronology of the Ta-li Glacial stage can we hope to compare and contrast their occurrence in North China and in South China, and in China and other regions. For events of a more recent date, when a difference of a century or even a decade is significant in tackling the problems of origin and diffusion, the Chinese chronologies are sometimes so uncertain that problems worldwide in magnitude are left unsolved. In the Near East, the Neolithic Revolution is known to have taken place during an interval of several millennia before the time of Christ, and the earliest known occurrence of pottery in Japan is now placed at least another thousand years or two before that, but the lack of *any* absolute chronology for all the Neolithic cultures in the area of China makes it impossible to reassess the chronological issues and the developmental process of much of the Old World. Within China itself, archaeological cultures are placed in relation to one another primarily by means of typology and, on rare occasions when it is possible, by stratigraphy. These placements are reliable when they are worked out with care, but they have natural limitations. Such questions, for instance, as the survival of the Yang-shao culture in marginal areas after the emergence of the Lung-shan, the interrelationship of the Lungshanoid cultures in the southeast and the Chung-yüan Neolithic, and the condition of the Chou civilization before the conquest cannot be easily settled without some very tight absolute dates. For all its stress on archaeology, China, whose technology is capable of producing the hydrogen bomb, has yet to establish a radiocarbon dating laboratory. It is almost certain that the chronological assessments made here of various archaeological cultures are due for some drastic revision when several dozen well-placed carbon-14 dates become available. I am no radiocarbon-date worshipper, but I know what it has done for archaeological chronology in other parts of the world.

A second area in which I look forward to seeing more enthusiastic and intensified research is in interdisciplinary study. The Lan-t'ien Conference of 1964 is an excellent example of what can be accomplished with such an approach, but there cannot be too many such projects, and the scholars with whom the archaeologist should collaborate need not always be natural scientists. To be sure, the importance of Pleistocene and postglacial palynological work in environmental studies for ancient man has been amply demonstrated by new pollen profiles from many localities throughout China, and the assistance of biologists in identifying animal bones and plant remains at many kitchen middens and tombs has been extremely useful. No doubt such efforts should continue and improve. But there is much in ancient Chinese studies that requires the collaboration of historians, palaeographers, linguists, and ethnologists. I need merely mention the following topics as examples of the kind of research in which the unaided archaeologist is handicapped: the relationship between the Neolithic cultures of North China and the modern minority groups in South China and the South Seas; the sociological interpretation of the Shang and Chou cities, temples, and graves; the problem of currency during the Eastern Chou; the interpretation of Eastern Chou mythology, art, and society; the ethnic identity and subdivisions of the ancient social classes; the linguistic prehistory of the Chinese; and the use of ethnological and folklore data in archaeological interpretation. Many studies along these lines have already been undertaken, such as the use of the burial customs of the Mo-so groups in the southwest for interpreting the grave finds of the Yang-shao culture,[5] the many studies of Kuo Mo-jo in employing the information contained in *chin wen* scripts for discussions of archaeological cultures,[6] the lexicostatistical studies of the Formosan aboriginal languages which have contributed to a fresh appraisal of southeastern Chinese prehistory,[7] and an analysis of Shang bronzes using information provided by the *chia ku* scripts,[8] to mention only a few recent examples. These isolated incidents have demonstrated the fruitfulness—or even necessity—of the team approach in which the archaeologist can take a part.

Another area of urgent research is the comparative study. By this I do not mean—but I would not exclude—the comparison of Chinese data with distant (Mesopotamian or Mesoamerican, for instance) par-

5. Sung Chao-lin, *KK* (1964/4), 200–04.
6. E.g. *WWTKTL* (1958/1), 5.
7. I. Dyen, *AP, 7* (1964), 261–71.
8. Kwang-chih Chang, *Jour. Asian Studies, 24* (1964), 45–61.

allels to demonstrate early connections and contacts of cultures across whole continents and oceans. I refer to the study of ancient areas of culture of which archaeological localities within China were only a part. It is superfluous to stress that ancient cultures were not limited by current national boundaries, but I am perplexed to note that, with a few notable exceptions,[9] archaeologists, in reporting and interpreting the sites in border areas of China, have yet to demonstrate knowledge of what their colleagues in neighboring countries have been doing. In the publications on the prehistoric cultures of Manchuria, for example, no discussion has been made of the abundant and directly relevant data in Siberia, the Soviet Far East, Korea, or Japan, and the data of the "Dong-son" culture have yet to be utilized in any of the Chinese reports and writings about the Bronze Age civilizations in Yunnan.

Such a practice—if not policy—of self-containment not only hampers a fuller understanding of the data in China itself but makes it difficult for all archaeologists working in the Far East to apprehend that the archaeological materials reported in different countries in different languages with few reciprocal references are in fact the relics of identical peoples and cultures. Indeed, the early development of Chinese civilization and the contemporary cultural traditions in the area of China are topics essential for students of prehistory and early history of the whole continent of Asia.

Other potential contributions from China to the general prehistories of the world are manifold. For example, the archaeological data from China afford a good deal of raw material for studies in the classification of culture. Taking the Eastern Chou civilizations in the area of China as an example, it is clear that a number of regional traditions can be distinguished, which pose different problems pertaining to the cultural development. One in particular is the distinction between nuclear and marginal areas, such as can be made between the Huangho Valley and the areas north of the Great Wall. Cultural sequences, the progression in which various cultural elements appeared, and the incentives behind the development and the appearance of new elements must be dealt with quite separately in the nuclear and the marginal areas. In making a "developmental classification," therefore,

9. Such as Hsia Nai's study of ancient Persian coins found in China; see *KKHP* (1957/2), (1958/1), (1959/3); *KK* (1961/3).

it is often necessary to distinguish between the different roles played by the cultures of the nuclear areas and those of the marginal phases. For the Nuclear Area in North China, the formative sequence from the terminal Mesolithic to the emergence of the Empire is both interesting and instructive; reference might be made to this sequence in formulating "stages" of cultural growth of universal validity and applicability.[10] The technological models of the Stone Age, Bronze Age, and Iron Age must also be differently applied to North China and the middle Yangtze, for example.

Finally, the problems concerning the dynamics and processes of cultural growth in this part of the world are certainly of wide interest. It is evident that many factors are known to have played a part in bringing about cultural and social change and growth in China, and that a monolithic deterministic cause cannot account for them. Ecology is certainly highly significant in shaping the courses of development, as shown by the cultural and natural groupings made in this volume, and the importance of technology is most clearly revealed by the development of cities and the expansion of North China civilization during the Eastern Chou period when iron metallurgy made significant strides. Irrigation, which to some authors is the single factor in bringing about the emergence of civilization,[11] played a considerable role in the development of North China Bronze Age civilizations and in the expansion of the Eastern Chou, but archaeological data have failed to prove that irrigation was the leading and decisive factor. The evolution of the Neolithic culture in North China from the Yang-shao to the Lung-shan and the emergence of the Shang civilization cannot be accounted for entirely in terms of technological advances, for, as has been shown, the agricultural techniques did not undergo decisive and major changes until the Eastern Chou. These advances must additionally be explained in terms of a tightened social organization and an intensified political control, phenomena which are amply demonstrated by the archaeological data in such spheres as industrial specialization and social stratification. Moreover, cultural contacts are shown to have played decisive roles in some regions of

10. E.g. Robert J. Braidwood, "Levels in Prehistory," in Sol Tax, ed., *Evolution after Darwin, 2,* Univ. Chicago Press, 1960. Julian H. Steward, *Theory of Culture Change,* Urbana, Univ. Illinois Press, 1955.

11. E.g. J. H. Steward, ed., *Irrigation Civilizations: A Comparative Study,* Washington, D.C., Pan American Union, 1955.

China, as with the emergence of the sub-Neolithic cultures in the northern frontiers and the southwest, the advent of cereal agriculture in South China, and the appearance of civilizations in the Yangtze Valley. Patterns of diffusion and acculturation are not only revealed by such events as the expansion of the Huangho civilizations but are also exemplified by the internal development of the Huangho cultural tradition itself in such significant phenomena as the formation of the different horizon styles and the various local traditions. Unless and until the mechanisms and patterns involved in the formation of the horizons and traditions of, for example, the Lungshanoid stage in northern and eastern China are made demonstrably clear, the cultural growth of the Huangho civilization itself cannot be said to be sufficiently understood.

So much for the possibilities. After all, Chinese archaeology is still young, and I look forward to the day when new data and research will compel me once again to rewrite this volume completely anew.

RECOMMENDATIONS FOR FURTHER READING

The references cited in this volume are given in full in the footnotes, which constitute an intensive bibliography for the field on ancient Chinese archaeology up to mid-1966. The following list is in two parts. The first gives titles of periodicals and serial publications, wherein the overwhelming majority of the original data is reported. The second part consists of a highly selected minimum of titles that are recommended for their wide coverage and general significance and can also be used as a reading list for a graduate course in the archaeology of ancient China.

Major Periodicals and Serial Publications

Archaeologia Orientalis, series A and B, Tokyo and Kyoto, The Toa-Koko-Gakukwai.

Archaeologia Sinica, Nanking and Taipei, Institute of History and Philology, Academia Sinica.

Archaeologia Sinica, new series, Taipei, Institute of History and Philology, Academia Sinica.

Chung-kuo K'ao-ku Hsüeh Pao, No. 2–4, 1937–49, Nanking, Institute of History and Philology, Academia Sinica.

Chung-kuo Ku Chi-chui Tun-wu yü Ku Jen-lei Yen-chiu Suo Chuan-k'an, Peking, Science Press.

K'ao-ku, 1959– , Peking, K'ao-ku Tsa-chih She.

K'ao-ku Hsüeh Chuan-k'an, series A, B, C, and D, Peking, Science Press.

K'ao-ku Hsüeh Pao, no. 5– , 1951– . Peking, Science Press.

K'ao-ku T'ung-hsün, 1955–58, Peking, Science Press.

Vertebrata Palasiatica, vol. 1 (1957)– , Peking, Science Press.

Wen-wu, 1959– , Peking, Wenwu Press.

Wen-wu Ts'an-k'ao Tzu-liao, 1950–58, Peking, Wenwu Press.

Other Important Titles

Amano Motonosuke, "Yintai no nōgyo to shakai kozo," *Shigaku Kenkyū, 62* (1956), 1–16.

———, "Chugaku Kodai nōgyo no tenkai–Kahoku nōgyu no keiseikatei," *Tōhōgakuhō,* Kyoto, *39* (1959).

An Chih-min, "Chung-kuo shih-ch'ien shih-ch'i chih nung-yieh," *Yenching Social Studies, 2* (1949), 37–58.

———, comp., *Chung-kuo shih-ch'ien k'ao-ku-hsüeh shu-mu,* Peking, 1951.

Andersson, J. G., "Preliminary Report on Archaeological Research in Kansu," *GSuC, Memoirs,* ser. A, *5* (1925).

———, "Selected Ordos Bronzes," *BMFEA, 5* (1933), 143–54.

———, "Researches into the Prehistory of the Chinese," *BMFEA, 15* (1943).

An-yang Fa-chüeh Pao-kao, Peiping, Institute of History and Philology, Academia Sinica, 1929–33.

Barnard, Noel, "Bronze Casting and Bronze Alloys in Ancient China," *Monumenta Serica Monograph, 14* (1961), Australian National University and Monumenta Serica.

Black, Davidson, P. Teilhard de Chardin, C. C. Young, and W. C. P'ei, "Fossil Man in China," *GSuC, Memoirs,* ser. A, *11* (1933).

Boule, M., H. Breuil, E. Licent, and P. Teilhard de Chardin, "Le Paléolithique de la Chine," *Archives de l'Institut de Paléontologie Humaine, Mémoire, 4* (1928).

Chang Kwang-chih, co-editor, *COWA Survey and Bibliography, Area 17 Far East* (*China and Formosa*), no. 1 (1959), no. 2 (1961), no. 3 (1963).

———, "Neolithic Cultures of the Sungari Valley, Manchuria," *Southwestern Jour. Anthropol., 17* (1961), 56–74.

———, "New Evidence on Fossil Man in China," *Science, 136* (1962), 749–60.

———, "Prehistoric and Early Historic Culture Horizons and Traditions in South China," *Current Anthropol., 5* (1964), 359, 368–75.

———, "Prehistoric Archaeology in China: 1920–60," *Arctic Anthropol., 1,* no. 2, 29–61.

Cheng Te-k'un, *Archaeological Studies in Szechwan,* Cambridge Univ. Press, 1957.

———, *Archaeology in China;* Vol. 1, *Prehistoric China,* 1959; Supplement to Vol. 1, *New Light on Prehistoric China,* 1966; Vol. 2, *Shang China,* 1961; Vol. 3, *Chou China,* 1963; Cambridge, Heffer.

Chung-kuo Ko-hsüeh-yüan K'ao-ku Yen-chiu-suo, *Hsin Chung-kuo ti K'ao-ku Shou-huo,* Peking, Wenwu Press, 1962.

Chung-kuo K'o-hsüeh-yüan, Ku Chi-chui Tung-wu yü Ku Jen-lei Yen-chiu Suo, *Shensi Lan-t'ien Hsin-sheng-chieh Hsien-ch'ang Hui-yi Lun-wen Chi,* Peking, Science Press, 1966.

Creel, H. G., *The Birth of China,* New York, Ungar, 1937.

Finn, D. J., *Archaeological Finds on Lamma Island near Hong Kong,* University of Hong Kong, 1958.

Hu Hou-hsüan, *Chia-ku-hsüeh Shang-shih lun ts'ung,* 2 vols. Chinan, Ch'i-lu Univ., 1944, 1945.

———, *Yin-hsü fa-chüeh,* Shanghai, Hsüeh-hsi-sheng-huo Press, 1955.

Jung Keng, *Shang Chou Yi-ch'i T'ung-k'ao,* Peiping, Yenching University, 1941.

Karlgren, Bernhard, "Yin and Chou in Chinese Bronzes," *BMFEA, 8* (1936).

———, "New Studies on Chinese Bronzes," *BMFEA, 9* (1937).

———, "Huai and Han," *BMFEA, 13* (1941).

Kuo Mo-jo, Young Chung-chien, P'ei Wen-chung, Chou Ming-chen, Woo Ju-k'ang, and Chia Lan-p'o, *Chung-kuo jen-lei hua-shih ti fa-hsien yü yen-chiu,* Peking, Science Press, 1955.

Kuo Pao-chün, *Chung-kuo Ch'ing-t'ung Ch'i Shih-tai,* Peking, Sanlien Books, 1963.

Li Chi, *The Beginnings of Chinese Civilization,* Seattle, Univ. Washington Press, 1957.

Liang Ssu-yüng, "The Lungshan Culture," *Proc. 6th Pacific Science Congress, 4* (1939), 69–79.

Loehr, Max, "Ordos Daggers and Knives," *Artibus Asiae, 14* (1951), 77–162.

———, *Chinese Bronze Age Weapons,* Ann Arbor, Univ. Michigan Press, 1956.

———, *Relics of Ancient China,* New York, Asia Society, 1965.

Maringer, John, *Contribution to the Prehistory of Mongolia,* Stockholm, 1950.

Mizuno, Seiichi, *Yinshū Seidoki to Gyoku,* Tokyo, Nihon Keizaishinbun Sha, 1959.

Movius, Hallam L., Jr., *Early Man and Pleistocene Stratigraphy in Southern and Eastern Asia,* Papers of the Peabody Museum, *19,* Cambridge, Harvard University, 1944.

———, "The Lower Paleolithic Cultures of Southern and Eastern Asia," *Transactions of the American Philosophical Society,* n.s. *38* (1949), Pt. 4.

———, "Palaeolithic Archaeology in Southern and Eastern Asia, Exclusive of India," *Cahiers d'Histoire Mondiale, 2* (1955), 257–82, 520–53.

Needham, Joseph, *Science and Civilization in China, vol. 1,* Cambridge Univ. Press, 1954.

———, *The Development of Iron and Steel Technology in China,* London, Newcomen Society, 1958.

Ōshima Riichi, "Chugaku kodai no shiro no tsuite," *Tōhōgakuhō, 30* (1959), 39–66.

P'ei, Wen-chung, *Chung-kuo Shih-ch'ien Shih-ch'i chih Yen-chiu,* Shanghai, Commercial Press, 1948.

Sekai Kōkōgakū Taikei; vol. 5, Eastern Asia: Prehistoric Period; vol. 6, Eastern Asia; Shang and Chou Periods; Tokyo, Heibonshya, 1958, 1960.

Sekino Takeshi, *Chugaku Kōkōgakū Kenkyū,* Univ. Tokyo, Institute for Oriental Culture, 1956.

Shih, Chang-ju, *K'ao-ku Nien Piao,* Yangmei, Institute of History and Philology, Academia Sinica, 1952.

Szechwan Museum, *Szechwan Ch'uan-kuan Tsang Fa-chüeh Pao-kao,* Peking, Wenwu Press, 1960.

Teilhard de Chardin, P., *Early Man in China,* Peking, Institut de Géo-Biologie, 1941.

Tseng Chao-yüeh et al., *Chiang-su Sheng Ch'u-t'u Wen-wu Hsüan Chi,* Peking, Wenwu Press, 1963.

Umehara, Sueji, *Yin Hsü, Ancient Capital of the Shang Dynasty at Anyang,* Tokyo, Asahi Shinbunsha, 1964.

Von Dewall, Magdalene, "The Tien Culture of South-west China," *Antiquity, 40* (1967), 8–21.

Watson, William, *Archaeology in China,* London, Parrish, 1960.

———, *China Before the Han Dynasty,* New York, Praeger, 1961.

———, *Ancient Chinese Bronzes,* Rutland, Vt., Tuttle, 1962.

———, *Early Civilization in China,* London, Thames & Hudson, 1966.

Wei Chü-hsien, *Chung-kuo K'ao-ku-hsüeh Shih,* Shanghai, Commercial Press, 1937.

White, W. C., *Bronze Culture of Ancient China,* Toronto, Royal Ontario Museum, 1956.

Wu, G. D., *Prehistoric Pottery in China,* London, Kegan Paul, Trench & Trübner, 1938.

Wu, C. T., C. Y. Tseng, and C. C. Wang, *Yünnan Ts'ang Erh Ching K'ao-ku Pao-kao,* Lichuang, National Museum, 1942.

Yunnan Museum, *Yün-nan Chin-ning Shih-chai-shan Ku mu ch'ün Fa-chüeh Pao-kao,* Peking, Wenwu Press, 1959.

APPENDIX

CHINESE CHARACTERS FOR PROPER NAMES AND TECHNICAL TERMS

This appendix lists the Chinese characters, transliterations of which appear in the text. Characters for materials used in the footnotes and for such common geographical and historical names as Huangho, Yangtze, the provincial names, and the dynastic names and subdivisions (e.g. Shang, Chou, Chan Kuo, etc.), are not included.

A-ti-ts'un 阿底村
Aksu 阿克蘇
Amano Motonosuke 天野元之助
An Chih-min 安志敏
An Chin-huai 安金槐
An-ch'iu 安丘
An-ning 安寧
An-yang 安陽
An-yang Fa-chüeh Pao-kao 安陽發掘報告
An-yi 安邑
Ang-ang-hsi 昂昂溪
Ao 隞
Astana 阿斯塔那

Balin 巴林

Chang Shen-shui 張森水
Chang-chia-p'o 張家坡
Chang-chia-tsui 張家嘴
Chang-kung-t'ai 張公台
Chao 趙
Chao Hou (Ts'ai) 昭侯
Chao Kung (Lu) 昭公
Chao Wang (Chou) 昭王
Chao-hua 昭化
Chao-k'ang-chen 趙康鎮
Chen-fan 鎮番
Cheng 鄭
cheng 鉦、[illegible]
Cheng Te-k'un 鄭德坤
Cheng-chou 鄭州
Chi 姬
chi 戟
Chi Hsien (Honan) 汲縣
Chi Hsien (Hopei) 薊縣
Chi Tzu 箕子
Chi-chia-ch'uan 姬家川
Chi-nan 濟南
Chi-nan-ch'eng 紀南城
chia 斝
Chia Hsien 郟縣
chia ku wen 甲骨文
Chia Lan-p'o 賈蘭坡
Chia-hsing 嘉興
Chia-ko-chuang 賈各莊
Chia-ling-chiang (R.) 嘉陵江

Chia-shan 嘉山
Chia-yü-kuan 嘉峪關
Chiang 絳
Chiang Yüan 姜原
Chiang-hsi-ts'un 姜西村
Chiang-ling 江陵
Chiang-ning 江寧
chiao 角
Chien (R.) 澗
chien 鑑、劍
Chien Ti 簡狄
Chien-ch'uan 劍川
Chien-hsi 澗溪
Chien-kou 澗溝
chih 觶
Chih-chiang 枝江
Chin 晉
chin 禁
chin shih hsüeh 金石學
chin wen 金文
Chin-ch'eng 晉城
Chin-ning 晉寧
Chin-sha-chiang (R.) 金沙江
Chin-ts'un 金村
Chin-yang 晉陽
Chin-yüan 晉源
Ching 荊
Ching Hou (Chao) 敬侯
Ching Man 荊蠻
Ching-chih-chen 景芝鎮
Ching-shan 京山
Ching-ts'un 荊村
Chiu-ch'üan 酒泉
Chou Kung 周公
Chou K'un-shu 周昆叔
Chou Shu 周書
Chou-k'ou-tien 周口店
Chou-lai 州來
Chu 邾
chu 枓、鑄
Chu Shu Chi Nien 竹書紀年
Chu-chia-ch'iao 朱家橋
Chu-chou 株州
Chu-wa-chieh 竹瓦街
Chuang Tzu 莊子
chung 鐘
Chung Hsien 忠縣
Chung Yüng 仲雍
Chung-chou-lu 中州路
Chung-kuo K'ao-ku Hsüeh Pao
中國考古學報
Chung-kuo K'o-hsüeh Yüan
中國科學院
Chung-wei 中衛
Chung-yüan 中原
Chü 聚
chüeh 爵
Chün Hsien 濬縣
chün tzu 君子
Chün-wang-ch'i 郡王旗

Ch'an (R.) 滻、瀍
Ch'ang-chih 長治
Ch'ang-chou 常州
Ch'ang-ch'ing 長清
Ch'ang-ch'un 長春
Ch'ang-hsing 長興
Ch'ang-sha 長沙
Ch'ang-she-shan 長蛇山
Ch'ang-teh 常德
Ch'ang-yang 長陽

Ch'ao-ko 朝歌
Ch'ao-yang 朝陽
Ch'ao-yi 朝邑
Ch'en 陳
Ch'en Hsien 郴縣
Ch'en Meng-chia 陳夢家
Ch'en-chia-wo 陳家窩
ch'eng 城
Ch'eng Wang 成王
Ch'eng-chou 成周
Ch'eng-tu 成都
Ch'eng-tzu-yai 城子崖
Ch'i 齊、岐、契、棄
Ch'i Hsien 祁縣
Ch'i Lien Shan (Mt.) 祁連山
Ch'i Yen-p'ei 祁延霈
Ch'i Yü 齊語
Ch'i-chia 齊家
Ch'i-chia-p'ing 齊家坪
Ch'i-ch'un 蘄春
Ch'i-li-p'u 七里鋪
Ch'i-lin-shan 麒麟山
Ch'ia-yao 卡約 (甲窰)
Ch'iang 羌
ch'ieh-ch'ü 竊曲
Ch'ien-hsi 黔西
Ch'ien-shan-yang 錢山漾
Ch'ien-t'ang (R.) 錢塘
Ch'ih-feng 赤峯
Ch'in Shih Huang Ti 秦始皇帝
Ch'in-huang-tao 秦皇島
Ch'in-wei-chia 秦魏家
Ch'ing-lien-kang 青蓮崗
Ch'ing-lung-ch'üan 青龍泉
Ch'ing-shui 清水
Ch'ing-shui-ho 清水河
Ch'ing-yang 慶陽
Ch'ing-yang-kung 青羊宮
Ch'ing-yüan 清遠、清源
Ch'iu K'ai-ming 裘開明
Ch'iu-pei 邱北
Ch'iu-wan 丘灣
Ch'u 楚
Ch'u Tz'u 楚辭
Ch'un Ch'iu 春秋
Ch'ü Yüan 屈原
Ch'ü-chia-ling 屈家嶺
Ch'ü-fu 曲阜
Ch'ü-wo 曲沃
Ch'ü-yang 曲陽
Ch'üan-hu-ts'un 泉護村

Djalai-nor 札賚諾爾

Eh-ch'eng 鄂城
Erh (L.) 洱 (海)
Erh-li-kang 二里崗
Erh-li-t'ou 二里頭

Fang-tui-ts'un 枋堆村
Fen (R.) 汾
Fen-shui-ling 分水嶺
Feng 豐
Feng (R.) 灃
Feng Han-chi 馮漢驥
Feng Hu Tzu 風胡子
Feng-chia-an 馮家岸
Feng-chieh 奉節
feng-chien 封建
Feng-huang-t'ai 鳳凰臺

Feng-hsiang 鳳翔
Feng-pi-t'ou 鳳鼻頭
Feng-shan 鳳山
Feng-ts'un 馮村
Fo-ting 佛頂
fu 父、婦、斧、簠、鎛
Fu Ssu-nien 傅斯年
Fu-feng 扶風
Fu-kou 扶溝
Fu-nan 阜南

Ha-mi 哈密
Hai-wei (R.) 海尾
Han 韓
Han Fei Tzu 韓非子
Han Shu Ti-li Chih 漢書地理志
Han-chia-tsui 韓家嘴
Han-ching-kou 淪井溝
Han-chou 漢州
Han-shui (R.) 漢水
Han-tan 邯鄲
Han-yüan 漢源
hang-t'u 夯土
Hao 鎬
Hei-ching-lung 黑景隆
Hei-ku-tui 黑孤堆
Hei-liu-t'u-ho 黑流兔河
Heng-chen-ts'un 橫陣村
Heng-shan 橫山
Heng-yang 衡陽
ho 盉
Ho Hsi 河西
Ho Hsü 赫胥
Ho-nan 河南
Hou Chi 后稷
Hou Han Shu 後漢書
Hou-chia-chuang 侯家莊
Hou-chia-chuang-nan-ti
侯家莊南地
Hou-kang 後岡
Hou-ma 侯馬
Hu 胡
hu 壺
Hu-shu 湖熟
Hua 華
Hua Hsien 華縣
Hua Ts'e 畫策
Hua Yang Kuo Chih 華陽國志
Hua-t'ing-ts'un 花廳村
Hua-yin 華陰
Huai (R.) 淮
Huai Yi 淮夷
Huai-an 淮安
Huai-yang 淮陽
Huan (R.) 洹
Huang Chan-yüeh 黃展岳
Huang Ti 黃帝
Huang-niang-niang-t'ai 皇娘娘台
Huang-p'i 黃陂
Huang-shui (R.) 湟水
Huang-ts'ai 黃材
Hui Hsien 輝縣
Hui-hsing-kou 會興溝
Hui-tsui (T'ao-sha) 灰嘴
Hui-tsui (Yen-shih) 灰嘴
Hun-yüan 渾源
Hung Yen Chih Shih 鴻雁之什
Hung-chao 洪趙
Hung-shan-hou 紅山後
Hung-tse (L.) 洪澤

Hung-tung 洪洞
Huo Chih Lieh Chuan 貨殖列傳
Huo Shu 霍叔
Huo-pao-hsi 火爆溪

Hsi Tz'u 繫辭
Hsi-chiao-shan 西樵山
Hsi-chiao-ts'un 西樵村
Hsi-ch'a-kou 西岔溝
Hsi-ch'eng-chuang 西成莊
Hsi-ch'uan 淅川
Hsi-han-shui (R.) 西漢水
Hsi-hou-tu 西侯度
Hsi-hsia-hou 西夏侯
Hsi-hsiang 西鄉
Hsi-liao (R.) 西遼
Hsi-ling-hsia 西陵峽
Hsi-ning 西寧
Hsi-pei-kang 西北岡
Hsi-shan-ch'iao 西善橋
Hsi-t'uan-shan 西團山
Hsi-yin-ts'un 西陰村
Hsia 夏
Hsia Hsien 夏縣
Hsia Nai 夏鼐
Hsia-chia-tien 夏家店
Hsia-hsi-ho 下西河
Hsia-meng-ts'un 下孟村
Hsia-tu 下都
Hsiang 相
Hsiang (R.) 湘
Hsiang Yü 項羽
Hsiang-fen 襄汾
Hsiang-hsiang 湘鄉
Hsiang-jih-te 香日德
Hsiang-t'an 湘潭
Hsiang-yang 襄陽
Hsiang-yin 湘陰
Hsiang-yün 祥雲
Hsiao 囂
Hsiao Wang 孝王
Hsiao-ch'iao-pan 小橋畔
Hsiao-min-t'un 孝民屯
Hsiao-nan-hai 小南海
Hsiao-t'un 小屯
hsien 縣
Hsien-yang 咸陽
Hsin-cheng 新鄭
Hsin-fan 新繁
Hsin-hsiang 新鄉
Hsin-min 新民
Hsin-tien 辛店
Hsin-t'ien 新田
Hsin-ts'un 辛村
Hsin-yang 信陽
Hsing 邢
Hsing-t'ai 邢台
Hsiung Ch'ü 熊渠
Hsiung Nu 匈奴
Hsiung T'ung 熊通
Hsiung Yi 熊繹
hsü 盨
Hsü Chung-shu 徐中舒
Hsü Ping-ch'ang 徐炳昶
Hsü Shun-ch'en 許順湛
Hsü-chou 徐州
Hsüan Yüan 軒轅
hsüan-wen 弦紋
Hsüeh-chia-chuang 薛家莊
Hsüeh-ch'eng 薛城

Hsüeh-fu-t'un 薛埠屯
Hsün Tzu 荀子

jao 鐃
Jao Tsung-yi 饒宗頤
Jen-min 人民
Jih-yüeh-t'an (L.) 日月潭
Ju (R.) 汝
ju 耨
Jui Yi-fu (Ruey Yih-fu) 芮逸夫
Jui-ch'eng 芮城
Jung 戎

Kan-ku 甘谷
Kan-tzu 甘孜
Kang-shang-ts'un 崗上村
Kao Ch'ü-hsün 高去尋
Kao-ching-t'ai-tzu 高井台子
Kao-huang-miao 高皇廟
Kao-hsiung 高雄
Kao-li-chai 高麗寨
Kao-lou-chuang 高樓莊
Kao-tu 高都
Kao-tui 高堆
Kao-yai 高崖
Keng 耿
keng 耕
Kirin 吉林
Ko 戈
ko 戈
Ko-ta-wang 圪峪王
Ko-tzu-t'ang 鴿子堂
Kou Wu 句吳
ku 觚、鼓

Ku Chi-chui Tung-wu yü Ku Jen-lei Yen-chiu Suo 古脊椎動物與古人類研究所
Ku Chieh-kang 顧頡剛
Ku Shih Pien 古史辨
Ku-hsiang-t'un 顧鄉屯
Ku-lang 古浪
Ku-wei-ts'un 固圍村
Kuai (R.) 澮
kuan 鑵、棺
Kuan Shu 管叔
kuan-fu 官府
kuang 觥
Kuang-han 廣漢
Kuang-wu 廣武
kui 鬹、毀
Kung 鞏
Kung Ho 共和
Kung Wang 恭王
Kung Yang Chuan 公羊傳
Kung-wang-ling 公王嶺
Kuo 虢
kuo 國、郭、槨
Kuo Mo-jo 郭沫若
Kuo Pao-chün 郭寶鈞
Kuo Yü 國語

K'ang Shu 康叔
K'ang Wang 康王
K'ao Lieh Wang 考烈王
K'ao-ku 考古
K'ao-ku Hsüeh Chuan-k'an 考古學專刊
K'ao-ku Hsüeh Pao 考古學報
K'ao-ku T'u 考古圖

K'ao-ku T'ung-hsün 考古通訊
K'ao-ku Yen-chiu Suo 考古研究所
K'o-ho 㕡河
K'o-hsing-chuang 客省莊
K'o-shih-k'o-t'eng 克什克騰
k'ui 夔
k'ui-feng 夔鳳
k'ui-lung 夔龍
K'un-ming 昆明
K'un-ming (L.) 昆明
K'uo Shan 廓山

Lai-pin 來賓
Lan-t'ien 藍田
Lao-ha (R.) 老哈
Lao-ho-shan 老和山
Lao-kuan-t'ai 老官台
Lao-mu-t'ai 老姆台
Lao-t'ieh-shan 老鐵山
Lee J. S. 李四光
lei 耒、罍
lei-wen 雷文
Lei-yang 耒陽
li 鬲
Li Chi 李濟
Li Ching-tan 李景聃
Li Hsüeh-ch'in 李學勤
Li Ping 李冰
Li Shih-wen 李始文
Li Yu-heng 李有恒
Li-chia-ts'un 李家村
Li-ch'eng Hsien 歷城縣
Li-fan 理番
Li-ling 醴陵
Li-shih 離石
Li-ts'un 李村
Li-yang 溧陽
Li-yü-ts'un 李峪村
Liang Ssu-yüng 梁思永
Liang-chu 良渚
Liang-ch'eng-chen 兩城鎮
Liang-pan-shan 兩半山
Liang-ts'un 梁村
Liang-wang-ch'eng 梁王城
Liao (R.) 遼
Lin Shou-chin 林壽晋
Lin-hsi 林西
Lin-hsia 臨夏
Lin-ju 臨汝
Lin-shan-chai 林山砦
Lin-t'ao 臨洮
Lin-t'ung 臨潼
Lin-tzu 臨淄
ling 鈴
Ling Shun-sheng 凌純聲
Ling-shou 靈壽
Ling-yüan 凌源
Liu Ch'ang-shan 劉長山
Liu-chiang 柳江
Liu-chuang 劉莊
Liu-ch'eng 柳城
Liu-ho 六合
Liu-hu-t'un 留胡屯
Liu-li-ko 琉璃閣
Liu-lin 劉林
Liu-tzu-chen 柳子鎮
Lo 羅
Lo (R.) 洛

Lo-han-t'ang 羅漢堂
Lo-ning 洛寧
Lo-shui-ts'un 洛水村
Lo-ta-miao 洛達廟
Lo-tu 樂都
Lo-yang 洛陽
Lu 魯
Lu Sung 魯頌
Lu-ssu 鹿寺
Lu-shan (Kiangsi) 廬山
Lu-shan (Szechwan) 蘆山
Lu-wang-fen 璐王墳
Luan-p'ing 灤平
Lung-hsi 隴西
Lung-shan 龍山
Lung-t'ai 龍台
Lü Ta-lin 呂大臨

Ma-chia-pin 馬家濱
Ma-chia-yao 馬家窰
Ma-ch'ang 馬廠
Ma-ch'ang-yen 馬廠沿
Ma-lan 馬蘭
Ma-lang-chi-ts'un 馬郎磯村
Ma-lang-ch'uan-shan 馬郎船山
Ma-lung 馬龍
Ma-pa 馬壩
Ma-wang-ts'un 馬王村
Ma-yü-kou 麻峪溝
mao 矛
Mei-yüan-chuang 梅園莊
Meng Hsien 孟縣
Mi Hsien 湄縣
Mi-chia-yai 米家崖
Mi-mo 靡莫

Miao-p'u-pei-ti 苗圃北地
Miao-ti-kou 廟底溝
Mien P'ien 緜篇
Mien-ch'ih 澠池
Mien-yang 緜陽
Min (R.) 泯
min 民、皿
Min-ch'in 民勤
Min-lo 民樂
Ming-kung-lu 銘功路
Mizuno Seiichi 水野清一
Mo Chih 莫稚
Mo Tzu 墨子
Mo-ling 秣陵
mu 母
Mu Wang 穆王
Mu-tan-chiang (R.) 牡丹江
Mu-yang-ch'eng 牧羊城

Nan-chang 南漳
Nan-hai 南海
Nan-kuan-wai 南關外
Nan-shan-ken 南山根
Nan-ta-kuo-ts'un 南大郭村
Nan-yang 南陽
Ni-ho-wan 泥河灣
niao shou tsun 鳥獸尊
Ning-ch'eng 寧城
Ning-hsiang 寧鄉
Ning-ting 寧定
Ning-yang 寧陽
Niu-chai 牛砦
Niu-ts'un 牛村
No-mu-hung 諾木洪
Nonni (R.) 嫩江

Nü Wa 女媧

Ordos 河套
Oshima Riichi 大島利一

Pa 巴
Pa (R.) 灞
Pa Hsien 巴縣
Pa-lung 巴隆
Pa-tung 巴東
Pai Hu T'ung 白虎通
Pai-chia-chuang 白家莊
Pai-chia-ts'un 百家村
Pai-ma-ssu 白馬寺
Pai-sha 白沙
Pai-tao-kou-p'ing 白道溝坪
Pai-t'ing (R.) 白亭
Pan Ku 班固
Pan-ch'iao 板橋
pan-liang 半兩
Pan-p'o-ts'un 半坡村
Pan-shan 半山
Pao-chi 寶雞
Pao-lun-yüan 寶輪院
Pao-shen-miao 雹神廟
Pao-teh 保德
Pao-t'ou (Inner Mongolia) 包頭
Pao-t'ou (Shantung) 堡頭
Pei-chai-ts'un 北宅村
Pei-hsin-chuang 北辛莊
Pei-shou-ling 北首嶺
Pei-yang 北洋
Pei-yin-yang-ying 北陰陽營
pi 鄙
Pi Kung 閟宮
Pi-sha-kang 碧沙崗
Pi-tzu-wo 貔子窩
pien chung 編鐘
Pien-chia-kou 邊家溝
Pien-tui-shan 邊堆山
Pin Hsien 邠縣
Po 亳
Po Ch'in 伯禽
Po-yang (L.) 鄱陽
pu 布

p'an 盤
P'an Keng 盤庚
P'an Ku 盤古
p'an-ch'ih 蟠螭
p'an-k'ui-wen 蟠夔文
P'an-lung-ch'eng 盤龍城
P'an-nan-ts'un 盤南村
P'ei (R.) 涪
P'ei Wen-chung 裴文中
p'en 盆
P'eng Hsien 彭縣
P'eng-shan 彭山
P'i 庇
p'i 妣
P'i Hsien 邳縣
P'ien-kuan 偏關
P'ing Wang 平王
P'ing-chiang 平江
P'ing-lu 平陸
P'ing-wang 平望
P'ing-yin 平陰
p'o 瓿
P'u-tu-ts'un 普渡村

San Huang 三皇

San-ho 三河
San-li-ch'iao 三里橋
San-men-hsia 三門峽
Sang-kan-ho (R.) 桑乾河
se 瑟
Sekino Takeshi 關野雄
Sian 西安
Sjara-osso-gol 薩拉烏蘇河
ssu 耜
Ssu-ma Ch'ien 司馬遷
Ssu-pa-t'an 四壩灘
Ssu-wa 寺窪
Ssu-wa-shan 寺窪山
Su Ping-ch'i 蘇秉琦
Sui Hsien 隨縣
Sun-ch'i-t'un 孫旗屯
Sung 宋、嵩
Sung-tzu 松滋
Sungari (R.) 松花江
Suo-chin-ts'un 鎖金村

Sha-ching 沙井
Sha-kang 沙崗
Sha-kuo-t'un 砂鍋屯
Sha-yüan 沙苑
Shan Hai Ching 山海經
Shan Hai Kuan 山海關
Shan Hsien 陝縣
Shan-piao-chen 山彪鎮
Shan-shen 山神
Shan-tan 山丹
Shang Chia 上甲
Shang Chün Shu 商君書
Shang Hsien 商縣
Shang Ti 上帝

Shang-chieh 上街
Shang-ts'un-ling 上村嶺
Shao-hu-ying-tzu-shan 燒户營子山
Shao-kou 燒溝
Shen Nung 神農
sheng 笙
Sheng Hou (Ts'ai) 聲侯
sheng-t'ieh 生鐵
sheng-t'u erh ts'eng t'ai 生土二層台
sheng-wen 繩紋
shih 矢
Shih Chang-ju 石璋如
Shih Chi 史記
Shih Ching 詩經
Shih Hsing-pang 石興邦
Shih Kui 示癸
Shih Kuo 十過
Shih Yi Chi 拾遺記
Shih-chai-shan 石寨山
shih-ching 市井
Shih-hsing 始興
Shih-li-p'u 十里鋪
Shih-men 石門
Shou Hsien 壽縣
Shou-ch'un 壽春
Shu 蜀、舒
Shu Ching 書經
shu-hsüeh 豎穴
shu-t'ieh 熟鐵
shu-t'u erh ts'eng t'ai 熟土二層台
Shui-kuan-yin 水觀音
Shui-mo-kou 水磨溝
Shui-tung-kou 水洞溝
Shui-t'ien-pan 水田畈
Shun 舜

shuo 杓

Ta Ya 大雅
Ta Yi 大乙
Ta-chi-shan 大極山
Ta-ch'eng-shan 大城山
Ta-ho-chuang 大何莊
Ta-hsi 大溪
Ta-hsia-ho (R.) 大夏河
Ta-hsin-chuang 大辛莊
Ta-kou 大溝
Ta-ku 大姑
Ta-lai-tien 大賚店
Ta-li (Shensi) 大荔
Ta-li (Yunnan) 大理
Ta-pieh-shan (Mt.) 大別山
Ta-p'en-k'eng 大坌坑
Ta-p'o-na 大波那
Ta-ssu 大寺
Ta-ssu-k'ung-ts'un 大司空村
Ta-tun-tzu 大墩子
Ta-wen-k'ou 大汶口
Ta-yieh 大冶
Ta-yüan-ts'un 大原村
Tai-hsi 代溪
Tan-t'u 丹徒
Tan-yang 丹陽
Tang-t'u 當塗
tao 刀
Tao Ch'e 盜跖
Teng-feng 登封
Ti 狄
Ti Hsin 帝辛
Ti K'u 帝嚳
Ti Yi 帝乙

Tien 滇
Tien (L.) 滇
Tien Wang Chih Yin 滇王之印
Tien-ts'ang-shan (Mt.) 點蒼山
ting 鼎
Ting Kung 定公
Ting-ts'un 丁村
Torii Ryozō 鳥居龍藏
tou 豆
Tou-men-chen 斗門鎮
tu 都
Tuan Hsü 顓頊
tui 敦
Tung Tso-pin 董作賓
Tung-a 東阿
Tung-chai 董砦
Tung-hsiang 東鄉
Tung-hsing 東興
Tung-kan-kou 東乾溝
Tung-pa-chia 東八家
Tung-pao 東堡
Tung-sun-pa 冬笋壩
tung-shih-mu 洞室墓
Tung-t'ing (L.) 洞庭
Tung-wei-chia 東魏家
tuo 鐸

T'ai (L.) 太(湖)
T'ai Po 太伯
T'ai P'ing Yü Lan 太平御覽
T'ai Wang 太王
T'ai-kang-shan 太岡山
T'ai-p'ing-ch'ang 太平場
T'ai-p'u-hsiang 太僕鄉
T'ai-shan-miao 泰山廟

T'ai-tzu-ch'ung 太子冲
T'ai-yüan 太原
T'an-shih-shan 曇石山
T'ang 湯
T'ang Lan 唐蘭
T'ang Yün-ming 唐雲明
T'ang-shan 唐山
T'ang-wang 唐汪
T'ang-yin 湯陰
T'ao-ho (R.) 洮河
T'ao-sha 洮沙
t'ao-t'ieh 饕餮
T'eng Hsien 滕縣
T'eng-ch'eng 滕城
T'ien Wang Kui 天亡毀
T'ien Wen 天問
T'ien-shui 天水
t'ien-yieh 田野
T'ien-yieh K'ao-ku Pao-kao 田野考古報告
T'o (R.) 沱
T'u-men (R.) 圖們
T'un-hsi 屯溪
T'ung Chu-ch'en 佟柱臣
T'ung-lo-chai 同樂寨

Tsa Shou P'ien 雜守篇
Tsao-lü-t'ai 造律台
Tsao-shih 皂市
tseng 甑
Tseng Chao-yüeh 曾昭燏
Tseng-ch'eng 增城
Tsinling (Mts.) 秦嶺
Tso Chuan 左傳
Tso Lo Chieh 作洛解

Tsou Heng 鄒衡
Tsou Hsien 鄒縣
tsu 族、祖、鏃
Tsukada Matsuo 塚田松雄
tsun 尊
tsung 琮
tsung-fa 宗法

Ts'ai 蔡
Ts'ai Shu 蔡叔
Ts'ao-yen-chuang 曹演莊
ts'e 冊

Tzu 子
tzu 子
Tzu-ching-shan 紫荆山
Tzu-kui 秭歸
Tzu-lo-ch'eng 子羅城
Tzu-yang 資陽

Umehara Sueji 梅原末治

Wa-cha-tsui 瓦碴嘴
Wa-kuan-tsui 瓦罐嘴
wan 盌
Wan Hsien 萬縣
Wan Wei-ying 萬維英
Wan-ch'eng 萬城
wan-kui 琬圭
Wang Chia 王嘉
Wang Hai 王亥
Wang Hsiang 王湘
Wang Kuo-wei 王國維
Wang P'en 王賁
Wang Ssu-li 王思禮

Wang-chia-kou 王家溝
Wang-chia-tsui 王家嘴
Wang-chia-wan 王家灣
Wang-ching-t'ai 望景台
Wang-ch'eng 王城
Wang-wan 王灣
Wei 衛、魏
Wei (R.) 渭
Wei Chü-hsien 衛聚賢
Wei-ch'eng 魏城
Wei-mo 濊貊
Wen Hua Chü 文化局
Wen Kung 文公
Wen Wang 文王
Wen Wang Yu Sheng 文王有聲
Wen-chia-t'un 文家屯
Wen-hsi 聞喜
Wen-wu 文物
Wen-wu Kuan-li Wei-yüan-hui 文物管理委員會
Wen-wu Ts'an-k'ao Tzu-liao 文物參考資料
Woo Ju-k'ang 吳汝康
Wu 吳
Wu Chin-ting 吳金鼎
Wu Hsin-chih 吳新智
Wu Ju-tso 吳汝祚
Wu Keng 武庚
Wu Ti 武帝、五帝
Wu Ting 武丁
Wu Wang 武王
Wu-an 武安
Wu-chi 午汲
Wu-chia 吳家
Wu-ch'eng 午城
Wu-hsing 吳興
Wu-kuan-ts'un 武官村
Wu-p'ing 武平
Wu-shan 武山、巫山
wu-shu 五銖
Wu-wei 武威
Wu-yang-t'ai 武陽台
wung 甕
Wung-chiang 甕江
Wuo-kuo 沃國

Ya-an 雅安
Ya-lu (R.) 鴨綠
Ya-p'u-shan 鴨蹼山
Yang 楊
Yang Chia 陽甲
Yang Chien-fang 楊建芳
Yang Chung-chien 楊鍾健
Yang Lien-sheng 楊聯陞
Yang Tzu-fan 楊子範
Yang-chia-wan 楊家灣
Yang-lin-chi 楊林集
Yang-shao-ts'un 仰韶村
Yang-t'ou-wa 羊頭窪
Yang-tzu-shan 羊子山
Yao 堯
yao-k'eng 腰坑
Yao-wang-miao 藥王廟
Yen 燕、奄
yen 甗
Yen Yen 嚴闇
Yen-ch'eng 奄城、郾城
Yen-erh-wan 雁兒灣
Yen-ling 鄢陵
Yen-shih 偃師

Yen-tun-shan 煙墩山
Yi 夷
Yi (R.) 易、伊
yi 彝、匜
Yi Chou Shu 逸周書
yi pi ch'ien 蟻鼻錢
Yi Shan 嶧山
Yi Shih 逸史
Yi Wang 夷王、懿王
Yi-cheng 儀徵
Yi-ch'ang 宜昌
Yi-ch'eng 宜城、翼城
Yi-ch'uan 伊川
Yi-liang 宜良
Yi-tu 宜都
Yi-yang 伊陽、宜陽
yieh 冶
yieh-jen 野人
Yin 殷
Yin Chou Chih-tu Lun 殷周制度論
Yin Huan-chang 尹煥章
Yin Hsü 殷墟
Yin Shan (Mts.) 陰山
Yin Ta 尹達
Yin-chin 陰晋
Yin-kuo-ts'un 尹郭村
Ying 郢
Ying-p'u 營埔
Ying-tse 滎澤
ying-yüan 郢爰
yu 卣
Yu Jung 有娀
Yu Wang 幽王
Yu Yi 有駘、有侁
Yü 虞、禹
yü 盂
Yü Hsien 禹縣
Yü-chia-lin 于家林
Yü-wang-ch'eng 禹王城
Yü-yao 餘姚
Yüan (R.) 沅
yüan 瑗
Yüan K'ang 袁康
Yüan-chün-miao 元君廟
Yüan-shan 圓山
Yüeh 越
yüeh 鉞
Yüeh Chüeh Shu 越絶書
Yün Hsien 鄖縣
Yün-meng 雲夢
yün-wen 雲文
Yüng-ching 永靖
Yüng-ch'ang 永昌
Yüng-ch'eng 永城、雍城

Zungar 準噶爾

INDEX